W9-AUN-810

Annette Friskopp
Sharon Silverstein

STRAIGHT JOBS Gay Lives

Gay and Lesbian Professionals, the Harvard Business School, and the American Workplace

A TOUCHSTONE BOOK
Published by Simon & Schuster

TOUCHSTONE
Rockefeller Center
1230 Avenue of the Americas
New York, NY 10020

First Touchstone Edition 1996

TOUCHSTONE and colophon are registered trademarks
of Simon & Schuster Inc.

Designed by Levavi & Levavi

Manufactured in the United States of America

10 9 8 7 6 5 4 3 2 1

Library of Congress Cataloging-in-Publication Data
Friskopp, Annette.
Straight jobs, gay lives: gay and lesbian professionals, the Harvard Business School, and the American workplace / Annette Friskopp, Sharon Silverstein.
p. cm.
Includes bibliographical references.
1. Gays—Employment—United States. 2. Business students—Employment—United States. 3. Harvard University. Graduate School of Business Administration—Students—Employment—Case studies. 4. Gays—United States—Interviews. 5. Business students—United States—Interviews. 6. Professional employees—United States—Interviews. 7. Gays—Employment—United States—Handbooks, manuals, etc. 8. Harvard University. Graduate School of Business Administration. I. Silverstein, Sharon. II. Title.
HD6285.5.U6F75 1995
331.5—dc20 95-12714
CIP

ISBN: 0-684-80424-7
ISBN: 0-684-82413-2 (Pbk.)

Contents

We dedicate this book to our parents,
Betty Mae and Karl Friskopp and
Klara and Larry Silverstein

Acknowledgments

This book would not have been possible without the support and assistance we received from all those we interviewed, our professors at the Harvard Business School, all of our reviewers, editors, critics, and our mentors and role models.

Initially we had to find support within Harvard Business School for our research to be accredited. Annette's professor and personal friend Willis Emmons made this possible. He suggested we approach Mary Gentile, who agreed with great enthusiasm, along with Anne Donnellon, to supervise our research. We greatly appreciate the direction and guidance they gave us.

When we began we knew only a handful of gay HBS alumni. Our greatest thanks goes out to Jon Zimman, a founder and, at the time, president of the Harvard Business School Gay and Lesbian Alumni group, who personally mailed our survey, so members' names were kept in the strictest of confidence.

We'd also like to reiterate a big thank-you to all of the people who allowed us to interview them. They invited us into their homes and lives as if we'd known one another for years, often introducing us to their partners and friends, which allowed us to get a fuller picture of their lives.

Each had a story to tell, which they shared with great generosity and openness; in this book we have tried to portray their opinions and experiences to the fullest extent possible. In addition to providing material, many have become role models we admire deeply.

Also, with much feeling of loss, we wish to extend a special thank-you to those who have passed on. We were told by some that their interview with us was one way they hoped to leave something behind—so others could learn from them. Sadly, we weren't able to interview everyone in time.

We would also like to thank all of the pioneers who have gone before us. The gay men and lesbians who have openly lived their lives while working at their jobs have done much to make this book possible.

We also wish to express our thanks to everyone who helped in the nitty-gritty process of writing and editing the proposal, including Jean Stine, Stever Robbins, Lisa Spinalli, C. H. and Ann Marie Wells. As for this book itself, thanks to our parents and Annette's Aunt Maxine for their encouragement. Thanks also to Eva Shaw, who came to our rescue when most needed. For his endless hours and edits, many thanks and hugs go to Joe Columbo.

Of course no book makes it to the shelves without untold hours of hard work by the editor. We thank Nan Graham, editor in chief at Scribner, and Carlo Devito, editor at Simon & Schuster, for his enthusiasm for the book and insightful edits. Also we thank Bert Holtje, our agent, for his excellent contacts and work in selling this book. Special thanks also goes to Mark Chimsky, who originally acquired this book for Macmillan before that firm became part of Simon & Schuster.

Introduction

The important figures in this book are not its authors. All we did was analyze data and draw conclusions. The book's real heroes and heroines are the gay men and lesbians who courageously and generously —sometimes in the face of great fear—shared their personal experiences with us.

Their voices fill this book. Most gay people in business will recognize themselves in these voices. The stories our interviewees tell are inspiring, touching, funny, and sometimes heartbreaking. Although the stories are most typical of people in business, they relate experiences that almost every lesbian and gay man has had, whether they have tried to remain closeted or to come out, to "play the game" or to "color outside the lines," at work or in school.

In this book, readers will meet lesbians and gay men of all ages, races, ethnic and class backgrounds. The names of some of these people are pseudonyms. Although most are out to some or most of the people they work with, many preferred to disguise their names and the names of their companies.

You will also hear the stories of many individuals who courageously allowed us to use their real names and places of business. These men and women, working in a variety of industries and locations, are role models and inspirations to us all. While all have different approaches to letting people know who they are, their stories share a common thread of trust in themselves, of character, and of persistence. The stories of individuals who have recently been lost to AIDS are also included in this work.

Perhaps surprisingly, most of the stories in this book are success stories. But although stories of negative experiences are infrequent, and though most had positive outcomes eventually, we do not turn a blind eye to the difficulties some experienced. Their stories are here too.

The Resource Section is intended as a reference tool for networking and information about gay issues in the workplace; it contains comprehensive information about gay professional organizations, gay employee groups, statutes, and company policies on nondiscrimination and domestic partner benefits.

A note on terminology: when we say "gay" or "gay professionals," we mean to include both gay men and lesbians. When we want to refer to one group or the other, but not both, we say so.

Chapter 1

Overview

Several years ago, while we were still attending the Harvard Business School, Annette decided it was time to discuss her sexual orientation with her parents. Very quickly they moved from guilt and dismay, typical of many parents with gay sons and daughters, to questions that were right on target with our own concerns: "Will being a homosexual have a negative impact on your career? What of all the time and expense of going to the Harvard Business School? Won't that have been wasted?"

Like other parents and the majority of gay people, Annette's parents believed that the simple fact of being gay would carry an irrefutable stigma in the workplace. As proud parents who avidly anticipated her next career move, they feared that her sexual orientation would seriously hinder her future in business. Needless to say, Annette didn't see it that way, nor had Sharon when she came out to her parents many years before.

We wouldn't have wanted to change our sexual orientation, even if we thought we could. Like a growing number of gay people our age, we were also sure that any attempt to conceal important and natural parts of our lives would limit our ability to experience life fully. Our love for each other and our desire to build a home and family together is too important to us to deny on a day-to-day basis. It would have been just as impossible to ignore our professional ambitions. Failing to recognize and accept ourselves as people with strong professional aspirations would also have led to a self-destructive struggle.

It was with this conviction that we seriously contemplated: Just how does being gay affect one's employability, earning capacity, and professional career? Does it have the negative consequences so many feared? Or was the business world, like much of mainstream society, becoming more open to diversity?

We sought answers but came up with more questions: What would happen if we wanted to be openly gay at work? Would we be limited to certain industries or job functions? Would we be as successful as if we attempted to remain closeted?

Bottom-line, we wondered: What sort of career and home life would we find most satisfying? Knowing only a few gay people who were also business professionals, we wondered: How are others handling their careers? Is anyone open and successful in a mainstream career?

We knew that some of our gay classmates were also experiencing this dilemma regarding being open about themselves at work. In fact, it was one of the most important questions they faced in their lives. We and they knew some openly gay professionals, such as doctors or lawyers. But few of us knew anyone who was openly gay in business. We and our peers also knew that people suspected of being homosexual or known to be gay often encounter homophobia, discrimination, harassment, and even violence in various aspects of their lives.

Were these experiences widespread in the white-collar business world? If so, could they be avoided or managed? To what degree did they impact the lives and careers of lesbians and gay men who sought to succeed in business?

When we sought answers in the academic literature just a few short years ago, we found there was almost no information to be had specifically or even tangentially on these subjects. At the time there were also no books on the subject, whether from gay or mainstream publishing houses. There were almost no articles in mass-market or specialized business journals. We found a few doctoral theses; most focused on a very small interview sample.

We wondered about the paucity of information. Trouble getting funding for studies or articles focusing on gay people was doubtlessly one factor. Another was probably the difficulty in finding closeted gay people to cooperate. Additionally, there seemed to be little academic or popular-press interest in this area, whether by heterosexual or gay researchers. And we found that even the most broadly constructed studies on gay life fell short on this issue. Most included only one or two questions on work. Yet this is the place where most of us spend the largest portion of our adult lives!

As a result, there was little information to further our quest for answers about how gay men and lesbians fared in the business world. In the last few years, the situation has improved exponentially. Yet even today very few books or full-length studies are available on this subject.

The books that have been published recently tend to be limited in one of two ways. Some books attempt to focus broadly on certain companies or industries, but fail to interview many gay senior managers. Other books employ the "snowball" technique, finding interviewees through personal contacts; thus their subjects were found by happenstance and tend to be quite similar to one another. One book, for example, almost exclusively covers closeted white gay men of Christian background. Another describes white lesbians in lower middle management. The few short articles that have appeared profile just a few openly gay exceptional cases.

Because we were about to undertake an independent research report for the Harvard MBA program, we realized we had a unique opportunity. Not only could we answer our own questions, but we might be the first to profile a group of gay professionals who were demographically similar to a heterosexual group, i.e., their business-school classmates.

Recognizing the potential magnitude of this project, we decided to proceed by systematically identifying as many of the gay graduates of the Harvard Business School as we possibly could. We also decided to get to know gay alumni of other prestigious business schools and to meet members of gay professional organizations across the United States. While we were not able to study the members of these groups exhaustively, their anecdotal experiences served as a kind of control for our own work.

We knew that we had an enormous goal ahead of us. Our ultimate intention was threefold. We wanted to inform gay people about the experiences of gay professionals. We also hoped to assist heterosexual managers and corporate employees in understanding the changes that we believed were coming their way. Lastly, we intended to satisfy our own intellectual curiosity and, hopefully, allay some of our own concerns about our future careers.

Early on, doubts plagued us. Could we find enough people to interview? Would their stories be encouraging, or just one more nail in the coffin of the closet?

Immediately, as we began our work, our zeal for the project increased. From the beginning we found a highly diverse and truly interesting group of gay business professionals. As one line of questions led to the next, we knew we were hearing things no one had ever written about. When we talked about our interviews, whether with acquaintances or with total strangers, the response was genuinely enthusiastic. Both gay and heterosexual friends who heard about our research demanded to know our findings, even before we had formulated them ourselves.

As we spent the next several years finding and interviewing an increasingly large group of gay professionals, we continued to eagerly await the day when we could share the results, which we believe are quite hopeful.

Are Harvard Business School Graduates Unique?

When we began, we assumed almost reflexively that Harvard MBA graduates were an ideal microcosm for such a study. The Harvard Business School is known as the West Point of capitalism, and its 750 or so yearly graduates have the reputation of being brighter, more diverse, and more highly motivated than those of other business schools (although Stanford, Wharton, and several other schools dispute this!). These people are said to have the Golden Passport—they are seen as individuals who could go anywhere and do anything in their business careers.

Most *Fortune* 500 and *Fortune* Service 500 companies, Wall Street, and top international consulting firms have scores of Harvard MBAs throughout their management teams, and Harvard MBAs are disproportionate among the top ranks of many companies. Many eventually run their own highly successful businesses. A number of comprehensive studies have been done on Harvard MBAs, but none included any findings about gay ones.

We wondered: How did gay professionals with the Golden Passport handle their home and work lives? Were there inevitable trade-offs between career success and personal happiness?

If gay HBS alumni were as successful as their heterosexual counterparts, then there was hope that if other gay men and women worked hard enough and handled their business relationships correctly, they could be successful too. If in spite of all these advantages, these gay professionals lagged in promotions or earning capacity, then gay people in general would have evidence that even the best work record or earnings report would not be enough to protect them from discrimination, whether they tried to be closeted or sought to be open about being gay.

We initially hypothesized that Harvard MBAs might see themselves as having the most to lose by being open at work, so we expected to find many who were highly closeted. But we also figured that if any group of senior-level lesbians and gay men were likely to have the track record and confidence to come out at work, it would surely be Harvard MBAs.

When we began sharing our findings with those outside the Harvard community, some questioned whether our discoveries would be truly comparable to the experiences of other gay professionals. One argued, "Those with Harvard MBAs are a breed apart. They are accorded special treatment and perceived as far more indispensable than other employees. If they come out at work they will have an easier time." Another offered a contrasting view: "Harvard MBAs have a harder time coming out to themselves, because they've spent so many years trying to be Mr. or Ms.

Perfect. Even after they come out to themselves, they won't want to make waves by being open at work. They'll leave that hard work to others."

We agree that it is conceivable that having a Harvard MBA might protect certain select gay employees in certain companies. However, many we interviewed disputed the notion that a Harvard MBA automatically confers prestige and success. A number found their credential was sometimes more a burden than an asset. Reported one interviewee, "Employers often believe Harvard MBAs are superwomen and -men. It is expected and demanded that we carry an incredible workload and produce miracles that no one could accomplish." Some said their Harvard MBA also made them the target of workplace tests designed to prove that their privileged background was less important than experience in the real world of business. Adding to these extra hurdles, many asserted that it is actually easier to be gay in middle, rather than upper management, citing examples from their own lives and their observations of people they have worked with.

The strongest argument that the experiences of our Harvard sample are largely similar to those of other gay professionals is that both the positive and negative sides of our findings are supported by first-person accounts in on-line discussion forums as well as in recent magazine articles.

We also found commonalities with other groups of gay people in business to whom we presented our preliminary findings. These attendees of gay workplace conferences include graduates of other top business schools and members of gay professional organizations in major cities throughout the United States. Since these groups were largely male, we also presented our findings to lesbians at a women's music festival in the South and on a lesbian cruise ship. We found that these gay men and lesbians largely shared the experiences we recounted.

Additionally, in reaching the conclusions offered here, we've drawn not only on our own surveys and interviews but also on our reading of the recent flurry of books, articles, reports, and theses on lesbians and gay men in the workplace. We have also drawn on the personal observations of leaders in national gay advocacy organizations like the Lambda Legal Defense and Education Fund, the Gay and Lesbian Alliance Against Defamation, the National Center for Lesbian Rights, the National Gay and Lesbian Task Force, the Human Rights Campaign Fund, and Hollywood Supports. Invaluable as all these sources have been, the conclusions presented in this book are our own.

Finding a Hidden Population

As members of the Gay and Lesbian Student Association of Harvard Business School (HBS GLSA), we had personal access to alumni in their twenties and thirties. This is a diverse group of people in a variety of career fields that includes members of all the major demographic groups found at HBS today: men and women, Protestants, Catholics, Jews, whites, Blacks, Hispanics, Asian Americans, and non-U.S. citizens. Studying this group of people is exceptional in and of itself because of our ability to compare these gay people with a known sample of their (and our) heterosexual peers. But we always believed that it would also be meaningful to include older gay graduates, those who have been in the business world most of their adult lives.

HBS GLSA was in touch with scores of gay alumni who had graduated since the group was founded in 1979. It also had strong ties to the New York–based HBS Gay and Lesbian Alumni Association (HBS GALA). Some of the members of HBS GALA, which formed in the 1980s, provided us an entrée to a range of gay business-school alumni who had entered the workforce since the 1940s. With the assistance of these individuals, we had credible referrals to gay professionals in their forties, fifties, sixties, and seventies—individuals in a position to evaluate the long-term impact of their homosexuality on their careers.

We decided to conduct a two-part study. The first part would be a questionnaire disseminated by GALA; the second part would be interview based. We intended to use our own contacts, GLSA ties, and our acquaintances in GALA to refer us to potential interview subjects. Almost as an afterthought, we asked survey participants whether some of them would be willing to be interviewed.

The Survey

In the afternoons after class, we developed a highly detailed multipart questionnaire. With our faculty advisor's approval, we focused on every aspect of an individual's personal and professional life that we thought might prove relevant. These included (1) demographics, (2) family of origin, (3) educational history, (4) work history, (5) mentor-protégé relationships, (6) success, (7) interpersonal relations at work, (8) experience of and response to discrimination, (9) degree of disclosure of sexual orientation, (10) couple relationships, and (11) AIDS.

We knew we'd be asking a lot from our respondents. We've been told that the ninety-six multiple-choice responses took two to three hours to complete. At this time our goal was to shed light on the main questions we had about gay people in business:

- Were they out (and how far) in the workplace?
- What was the degree of success relative to heterosexual peers when they were out?
- To what degree did their sexual orientation affect their choice of location, industry, and job function?
- What obstacles and discrimination had they faced in their careers?
- Was being gay ever an advantage in business?
- How did their heterosexual colleagues respond to the knowledge of their sexual orientation?
- What were their sources of support? Were they part of a network of gay professionals?
- How did the issues differ for men, women, WASPs, and ethnic minorities?
- What effect did their personal life have on their business life and vice versa?
- What was the impact of AIDS on their lives and careers?

The questions were formatted to reveal how other choices affected these gay professionals. We wanted to ascertain how decisions regarding industry, geographic location, partner selection, and degree of being out positively or negatively affected their careers—in a monetary as well as emotional way. In our follow-up interviews we hoped to discover how gay people identified one another in management jobs and how they identified potential allies among heterosexual coworkers.

The president of the HBS GALA maintained the database of names, addresses, and phone numbers of Harvard Business School gay alumni. Some had heard about the group from friends. Other people were added to the master list as they came out to classmates who were already members, for a total of well over a hundred names. In other cases, the president added their names to the master list after chance encounters at gay bars, summer resorts, or community events such as Gay Pride.

To orchestrate our survey and to protect the confidentiality of GALA members and friends, we provided the organization's president with sealed envelopes containing our survey, and he mailed them out to over one hundred people.

On each survey was a place for an individual to give us his or her name and phone number for a follow-up interview. We received sixty-seven completed survey responses to our questionnaire, more than half the number we mailed out. In addition, we were surprised to find, over half of those who returned the survey were willing to be interviewed.

As the responses began to roll in, we were thrilled to see that our respondents included gay businesspeople from all walks of life throughout the United States and from abroad. Not only did we achieve a fairly representational set of survey respondents as compared to the demographic profile of the HBS GALA master list; we had one of the highest response rates in any research done at Harvard. And we had just begun.

Tabulating answers to the questionnaires, we began to see that there is a range of closeted and open behavior. Almost no one was completely open at work, yet few were completely closeted. Most were somewhere in the middle.

Nonetheless, it was illustrative to compare those who were primarily open and those who were primarily closeted. Perhaps most important, those who were more open felt more personal fulfillment in their careers and more loyalty to their company than those who were more closeted. And it seemed that women and people of color were less likely to be open at work.

We also unearthed common factors among those who viewed themselves as primarily closeted and those who viewed themselves as somewhat open at work. To our surprise, these commonalities, which included encounters with homophobia, the presence of a number of other gay people at their company, and much more, seemed to cut across all age, gender, and racial lines.

As we began to develop theories about our initial findings, we decided to test them in a series of follow-up interviews. We interviewed a number of our own contacts as well as survey respondents, thus broadening our initial pool. While we were still at the Harvard Business School, we interviewed over twenty HBS gay alumni. An additional fifteen or so gave us their names, but due to time and travel constraints we were not able to include them all in our first round of interviews. In the process of interviewing we collected another fifteen names. In addition, Sharon went to the annual HBS GALA party in the spring of 1990 and found another fifteen gay professionals who were willing to be interviewed.

The Interviews

Late in our Harvard careers, with student ID cards in hand, we became frequent fliers from Boston to New York to conduct interviews. After graduation we moved to the gay male summertime community of Fire Island Pines to continue our research and interviews there. After the summer we drove from the East Coast to San Diego to begin our careers, interviewing along the way. A task that began as an independent research project and a personal information search had become an endeavor with a life of its own.

We continued to interview gay HBS alumni whenever and wherever possible from 1991 through 1994. Over a hundred thousand miles later, we have interviewed over one hundred people in Seattle, Maine, Miami, San Diego, and numerous points in between. (Although we also contacted gay professionals working outside of the United States, we ultimately decided to save their experiences for future publication.)

The vast majority of the interviews you'll read were taped and transcribed. These are the voices we heard and the authentic stories of the people we spoke to. Complete interviews sometimes lasted hours, and our findings could easily have filled more than one book. While we focused primarily on workplace issues and experiences, this was not the only subject that our interviewees ended up talking about. They spoke generally—about their personal lives, community involvements, political opinions, and dreams for the future.

Many said that their friends had previously raised the questions we asked. They were happy to answer us but were also anxious to hear what we had found out from others. Yet other interviewees had never been asked about these issues, and some had never before felt comfortable discussing these potentially threatening subjects. A few had been profiled in short newspaper or magazine articles as openly gay business professionals, but none had previously discussed their experiences in depth.

Now, in their living rooms, in noisy bistros, favorite bars, upscale restaurants, and airport lounges, these gay professionals had the opportunity to tell their life stories and reflect on their business careers. For some the interview was a laboratory to examine the way they handled the issues in their lives. One interviewee's comments mirrored many; she said, "Even though I don't want my name used in this book, a lot of people at work know I'm gay. And I want to contribute something to the advancement of gay people in the business world beyond my own workplace."

When we began, we knew some of those we wanted to interview were successfully out at work and would have little hesitation about cooperating. Others, we realized, had been in the closet at work for their entire lives. This was often the case with older gay professionals. They had entered the business world when it was still highly homophobic or were employed in companies or industries with a reputation for discriminating against gay people. While it made our job more challenging, we needed the opinions of those who would be reluctant to participate. We enlisted them with the agreement that their names would not be used. It is impossible to express the depth of our gratitude to everyone who participated in our survey and interviews, as even anonymous participation in our study meant some risk of exposure and required great courage.

Although we always collected referrals, we were initially reluctant to call people who had not volunteered. We feared that they would be more highly closeted than those who had volunteered to be interviewed, and averse to talking with us. This assumption proved to be unfounded. Some who initially volunteered to be interviewed were highly closeted at work.

And some whom we found later were far more out at work than those who had originally volunteered.

Today our own master list contains over 275 gay graduates of the Harvard Business School. It includes gay men and women who are white, Black, Hispanic, Asian American, Jews, Protestants, and Catholics, roughly in proportion to their admission to HBS for every decade since the 1940s. As this was a major objective of ours, we are particularly happy to have met it. Our ability to locate gay people who fit the general demographics of the business school and who work in a wide spectrum of industries and locations gave us a breadth and a point of reference not available in other studies of gay people, particularly in regard to their workplace experiences.

The HBS GALA master list, under new copresidents, has also continued to grow to over two hundred names. Although promises of confidentiality keep us from exchanging lists, we have reason to believe that each list has many unique names. For example, many of those we interviewed, whether highly closeted or very open, told us that they didn't even know how to get in touch with HBS GALA or weren't interested in belonging to a group that met only once a year in New York.

As one might expect, it was not possible to be certain that we could find all the most hidden gay or bisexual graduates of the Harvard Business School. However, we were able to establish contact with gay professionals from every class since the late 1960s, as well as a number from the 1940s, 1950s, and early 1960s.

Because of the long-lasting ties between Harvard Business School graduates, virtually everyone we spoke with knew at least a few other gay classmates, whether or not any of them had come out to themselves at HBS. Many older alumni we interviewed especially delighted in telling us stories about running into classmates years out of business school in one gay context or another.

Over and over we were told that virtually no one is so tightly closeted that they have no gay friends or never go to a gay bar sometime in their lives. Thus we believe that at some point most gay graduates of HBS become known to others who are also gay, including those who are the most discrete and powerful. While the total number of gay graduates known to us and HBS GALA may seem small, we have independent confirmation that the true number may not be much higher. An anonymous survey of the HBS student population conducted by the *Harbus* in the early 1990s showed that well under 2 percent identified as gay or bisexual. While other portions of the survey were released, this finding was held back because the editors felt the numbers were too low. While we found that another 25 percent come out to themselves after business school, this does not dramatically raise the numbers per class.

Even though we did not have the time or resources to continue to interview everyone we were referred to, we are confident we achieved a fairly representative sampling of our target group, at least for those who attended HBS in the last twenty-five years. In addition, almost everyone we personally approached participated in our research process in some way, either by survey, interview, or mini-interview (background information only, in writing or in a shortened format).

Our Sample Population

By the conclusion of our study we had conducted well over one hundred interviews. In addition to interviewing gay alumni of the Harvard Business School, we spoke with some of their significant others, children, bosses, and work colleagues.

One reason we were so interested in studying Harvard MBAs is that they have experience in so many different fields of business, both before and after business school. And their partners have even more diverse careers, providing yet another comparative group for us.

Participants in our study are multigenerational, multiracial, and multicultural, from every geographic area of the United States, in a wide variety of industries. The only thing they have in common is that they are gay or bisexual graduates of the Harvard Business School MBA program or partners of gay alumni.

Their views on how to manage their personal and professional lives contrasted sharply. Some have felt it imperative to mask their homosexuality throughout their business careers and continue to be closeted to this day. Others feel safe in living and working openly as gay people. A fairly significant group of interviewees are so driven to be role models that they granted us permission to use their names and identify the positions they held. But they were not the only ones who are brave.

To make the project as informative as possible, we purposely elected to oversample lesbians, Jews, Blacks, Hispanics, and Asian Americans. HBS did not admit women until the 1960s and has admitted ethnic minorities in more than token numbers only since the 1970s.

Even today the number of women in any class is less than 30 percent, and the number of U.S. nonwhite students is less than 20 percent. Oversampling has allowed us to distinguish between shared and unique aspects of these gay businesspeople.

We didn't pause one day and say, "The interviews are getting redundant." Every new person we interviewed had unique and interesting personal circumstances. In addition, we knew that many of those we did not interview were quite out at work and that their stories would be fascinating. Nonetheless, we reached a turning point in early 1994 when we realized that we didn't need to interview everyone we could find. It was far more important to get our findings out to the public.

Our Findings

Cause for Hope

In the course of our lengthy research, we found much good news; there is strong cause for optimism about the eventual acceptance and integration of gay people in the American workforce. Contrary to many people's expectations, the vast majority of the gay professionals in our study who have revealed their sexual orientation to some or all of the people in their workplace said they had never experienced discrimination on the job. Because many gay professionals still remain in the closet from fear of discrimination, these findings may change the way many people think about the risks associated with coming out. Perhaps not surprising, those who had the easiest time being out were in cities or at companies with codes barring discrimination based on sexual orientation. In addition, we found something we believe to be highly significant: Those who chose to come out had a much easier time than those who were suspected of being gay, were outed, or were found out.

We also found that many shared the common misconception that one is either in or out of the closet. But in our interviews we always found shades of gray. Most who consider themselves closeted come out selectively to someone at work at some point in their career.

We hope the discovery that so many gay professionals are at least partially out at work without negative repercussions provides inspiration and encouragement to those considering taking the next coming-out step.

Our study may also help to dispel another myth. Many gay people who are more out than closeted and many of those who are attempting to gain equal benefits for gay people in their places of employment hold a common misperception: "You can't work with closet cases," or "It's best to go around closeted people in power." They see closeted people as threats or nonentities rather than potential sources of support. We believe this is an unfortunate misconception. For one thing, their perception of someone else's closet may be inaccurate. They falsely assume, "If I don't know that someone is gay, they are not open." We found many people who were in very high positions who were out to colleagues at their level but not to the lower ranks. They had made significant contributions to the betterment of conditions for gay people in their companies and communities.

Thus, many higher-level people who do not attend the meetings of their company's gay and lesbian employee organization or are not out widely among their management tier have been instrumental behind the scenes. Some promoted the welfare of other gay people within their company; others helped secure tangible benefits such as a corporate nondiscrimination policy, domestic partner benefits, or funding for a gay employee organization.

In general, the gay businesspeople we spoke with seem to be successful at work, happy at home, and less closeted at work than most might expect. Whether closeted or open, they generally believe they have achieved the same promotions and income levels as heterosexuals in their industries. We were also interested to find that while almost half the gay professionals felt they were as prosperous as their heterosexual HBS classmates, over 10 percent felt they had flourished even more.

Just like their heterosexual peers, many are part of stable long-term committed relationships. Their partners are often the motivation and support for their coming-out process. Most of the gay businesspeople we interviewed do not have children, but a number intend to. This trend will also have far-reaching implications for the workplace.

In addition, we found that parents and other family members have a great impact on the lives of gay professionals. Parental approval and support gives many the inner fortitude to tackle the challenges they encounter and the drive to seek their goals. For many, building close relationships with their families has taken much time and energy, but those who have done so have reaped enormous benefits.

As more and more gay individuals fully accept themselves and obtain support from those who love them, they will continue to challenge obstacles to their career aspirations.

The Specter of Fear

There's a darker side to this picture. As positive as all these signs are, they should not be misinterpreted. Almost one out of three gay professionals we surveyed had experienced on-the-job discrimination because they were known as or suspected of being gay. This ranged from the most sinister incidents of homophobia to the merely farcical. But even the mildest discrimination left the gay professional with deep feelings of humiliation and resentment. It would be a major error for anyone, heterosexual or gay, to overlook these incidents or to minimize their significance.

We heard reports of gay professionals who were demoted, sidetracked, transferred to a remote branch, passed over for promotion, given poor performance ratings, denied annual raises, or even terminated from employment. These individuals also faced homophobia and harassment from unsympathetic heterosexual colleagues in the form of threats, insults, jokes, harassing phone calls, ostracism, sexual harassment, and various other acts of disrespect.

It is important to note two things, however. One, the gay professionals in our study reported far fewer and far less serious incidents of workplace homophobia over time. Many have pointed to a changing business environment, in which corporate nondiscrimination policies and diversity-training seminars are being implemented and taken more seriously than they have before.

Two, most of these horror stories involved people who were trying to stay closeted. Obviously, those who attempted to conceal their sexual orientation were the most susceptible to blackmail threats, but we found that the entire litany of atrocities was far more likely to befall those who were largely closeted. The more open gay people were about their sexual orientation, the less discrimination they encountered.

This indicates that in some situations it may be safer to be out of the closet than in it. Those who came out selectively usually found that work colleagues treated them respectfully. Those who were completely open found that bosses, peers, and subordinates completely stopped their most overt homophobic jokes and comments, and none felt they have suffered any identifiable discrimination.

While openly gay professionals agreed that they do not always know what goes on behind the scenes, and some were told by friends of malicious comments, few felt their career performance was significantly impaired. All were glad that they had come out. For many, being out resulted in increased closeness to and support from key coworkers, bosses, or mentors; for most there were meaningful improvements in the way they felt about themselves, their relationships, their careers, their companies, and their colleagues.

Whichever choice gay professionals make, whether silence or openness, may have trade-offs. Almost all who have come out agreed that on balance, openness is preferable with regard to their own personal happiness. In our open-ended questions about advice to gay people starting out in business, many spontaneously recommended that being out at work should be a goal. "Young people entering the workforce shortly must give some thought about how they are going to achieve that," advised one interviewee.

Over and over we were told that by overcoming fear and by maintaining a positive outlook and an acceptance of oneself, one person's efforts to curtail discrimination can exponentially enhance the work environments for many other gay people. Those we interviewed felt they could overcome any negative repercussions by transferring departments, changing jobs, or becoming self-employed.

They recognized that they had a unique set of abilities and credentials to implement this strategy. But they also pointed out that there is such a thing as becoming too specialized to change and that this risk increases as one moves up the income scale. While it's good advice for all businesspeople, they recommended that gay people especially keep their options open by acquiring skills and making contacts that will allow them to survive being fired or to leave any situation they find unbearable.

Finding a Gay-Friendly Workplace

Where people live and work plays a very influential role in their lives. Although gay people hold jobs in every city and state in the country, those who choose to come out generally gravitate to larger, more cosmopolitan cities. They are most attracted to cities where there is already a strong and visible gay community, with laws protecting gay people from discrimination, and our interviewees are no different. Also, not surprising, the most frequent and recent encounters with homophobia and discrimination were described by those from less cosmopolitan cities, primarily in the Midwest, Texas, or the South.

Most gay people believe that there are companies and fields of business that are more tolerant of gay people or even gay friendly. Yet they don't always know which ones these are or how to find them. These companies and industries are not just rumors; they exist. But our interviews also debunked some popular myths about them.

For example, certain companies had a gay-positive reputation, but we found that this didn't always hold across every location or department. XYZ Company may have a positive reputation in New Orleans, but its Houston branch may be playing a different tune. Other industries were described as homophobic, yet certain companies in these industries had a large number of gay people in top executive positions who described a comfortable work environment.

We also found that while the existence of a company policy of nondiscrimination on the basis of sexual orientation was a good sign, it was not a panacea. But if a company had a policy of giving significant domestic partner benefits like health insurance, it was more likely to stand behind its policy of nondiscrimination.

Perhaps most important, our interviewees suggested that those who want to work for gay-friendly companies should try to find out how much a company or department truly values diversity. "See how they treat women, Blacks, Hispanics, Asians, Jews: Do they have any? Are such people getting promoted?" many said. Our interviewees told us that companies that value diversity are more likely to accept gay people, whether they choose to be "discreet" or to come out. We found ample evidence to support this belief.

And what of the so-called double whammy? Did those from minority ethnic and racial backgrounds face a double dose of discrimination? Was it true that lesbians encountered a double threat? Our findings are mixed. A number of lesbians reported that being gay provided a common ground with gay men that led to career opportunities. A number of nonwhite gay professionals found a similar common ground with white gay people. White lesbians and gay professionals of color also cited certain advantages they felt they had over white gay men. However, a number in both groups said that they faced so much discrimination based on their gender or race that they were almost completely unwilling to seek out support from other gay people.

Those who were Jewish often handled being Jewish and being gay in a very similar way. Some tried to pass as both heterosexual and Christian. Others were up-front about the ways they are different from the majority of those they work with.

The experiences of gay Jews with a strong ethnic or religious identity was a good counterpoint for our study. Many were all too painfully aware of the price they paid as Jews for having a so-called concealable difference. If they concealed their Jewish identity, they were not fully able to integrate all the parts of their lives. Many said their experience of being Jewish was very similar in this respect to being gay.

Equal Pay for Equal Work?

Although the salaries of a gay person and a heterosexual might be the same, the gay person typically receives significantly less compensation overall. Our study verified how a heterocentric workplace offers benefits and privileges to married employees that are not available to gay employees with significant others: health insurance for spouses and children, life insurance and pension plans that support spouses, family use of company health clubs and recreational facilities, and other family perks are taken for granted by most married managers, but not available to most gay professionals.

When we began this research in 1990, the gay people we interviewed took this for granted as the way the world is, and very few companies offered these benefits; by 1994, most interviewees felt angry if their company did not. Some had been active in achieving or seeking such benefits. A list of companies as well as academic and public employers that offer these perks is included in the Resource Section. We believe this trend is likely to continue.

MANAGING A GAY IDENTITY AT WORK

How to manage one's gay identity day to day is one of the ongoing career issues for almost everyone we interviewed. Whether one attempts to remain 100 percent closeted, 100 percent open, or somewhere in between, ordinary social interaction in the workplace requires a series of on-the-spot evaluations and decisions:

- Does this person know I'm gay?
- Do they suspect?
- Are they comfortable with it if they know?
- Would they be comfortable if I told them?
- Is it possible they are gay themselves?
- Would they be threatened or happy if they knew I am gay?
- What would happen if I dropped hints?
- Should I lie or cover up some part of my life in front of this person?
- Should I talk openly about being gay in this context, right now?

Since most of us work in environments where more than one person is involved in any social interaction, the decision tree can grow quite large. If X knows but not Y, or if X is comfortable but Y isn't . . . The daily chitchat in a business environment poses choices for a gay person at every turn each day of their work life.

Most people, we found, develop some rules of thumb for situations they encounter at work. However, whether one is deeply in the closet or generally open, cases frequently come up that cause people to depart from their standard operating procedure. A closeted lesbian may reach out to someone she thinks is also gay. A gay man who is casually open with coworkers about being gay may avoid the subject when customers are present.

Life in the Closet

Just as it is highly unusual to be 100 percent out at work, it is virtually impossible to be 100 percent closeted. In the course of speaking to gay businesspeople on all points of the spectrum, we were able to identify some ways of handling a closeted career that seem to work better than others.

Some posed as heterosexuals at some time during their career. This strategy has obvious pitfalls and was ultimately abandoned by almost everyone we talked to; instead of maintaining a heterosexual facade, they simply stopped lying.

Others chose to avoid discussing their personal life at work, with mixed results. In many office environments this strategy was tantamount to coming out, yet some claimed it did not result in as much social awkwardness as explicit discussion. Some felt satisfied with ambiguity, while others hoped to achieve more openness in the future. Most in this group explained that while they had hoped to appear asexual or otherwise avoid the label "gay," their careers had suffered because they were seen as not fitting in.

People who sought to remain largely closeted found that there were certain office environments and personality types for whom this approach was more likely to be successful. We also identified ways that generally closeted people can begin being more open at work if they choose to.

Coming Out Successfully

One important conclusion of our study was that those who had a strategy for coming out fared much better than those who didn't. Many believe that these gay professionals succeeded due to some special circumstance. They were said to be lucky enough to possess unusual personal charm, to have selected gay-friendly business environments, or simply to have accidentally stumbled on a congenial, tolerant company.

Our surveys and interviews dispelled this myth. In almost every case, it was not merely luck. It wasn't always that the company was already gay friendly, either. Instead, each gay person usually paved his or her own way to success. Usually they themselves were responsible for the positive reception they received when they came out. In each case their strategy was congruent with their personality and their social values or political beliefs. While not a how-to book, this study analyzes the more commonly used methods for successfully coming out and being out at work. We also discuss common pitfalls and ways to avoid them.

Role Models, Being Mentored, and Mentoring

Today's theories of business success tout the significance of mentoring relationships and role models in achieving business success. These instrumental individuals provide inspiration that enable the visions we dare to dream to really come true. They give us examples of paths to success as well as wrong turns to avoid. Sometimes role models become mentors and have a personal influence on an individual's life: They grant favors, secure job interviews, and give advice. Without the presence of either a role model or mentor, the road to success can be threatening and exhausting. Had those gay businesspeople we interviewed been assisted by role models or mentors? Had they served as mentors to others, whether heterosexual or gay?

Annette says, "Growing up in a small farming town in Nebraska, I didn't have any gay role models. My goals were set on a career in business, but I didn't know any gay people, let alone anyone who was gay and in business. So I didn't comprehend what awaited me.

"I saw myself as a lone warrior riding into battle while trying to conceal my true colors. Fifteen years later, little has changed: Even though gay men and lesbians are receiving increased emphasis in the press today, minute amounts are written or known about high-level, successful gay men and lesbians in the business world."

Sharon explains, "Growing up gay in an affluent suburb of New York City, I was aware of gay people in the business world. Yet the price of living a closeted life seemed too high to me. I had openly gay role models in other careers, but none in business. Although today more gay people are open at work, they are often unwilling to have their stories told in the media. Thus the myth persists: People who are openly gay at work are a rare commodity."

There are few role models for gay people in business. Those who did have role models told us that just knowing there were other people out there like themselves was inspirational.

Sexual orientation seems to play less of a role in the mentoring process than we had imagined. Although a few gay businesspeople felt being gay kept them from being mentored, most did not share this sentiment.

The experience of being mentored was far from universal. While many have gone through their careers without developing such a relationship, this is also true of heterosexuals in business. It is not clear from our study whether gay people are less likely to establish mentoring relationships, although most articulated a sense that it would be especially helpful to have them.

Networking with Other Gay People

In contrast to our finding that sexual orientation made little difference in the mentoring relationship, almost everyone we interviewed sought to establish social relationships with other gay people in their company or field. The process of figuring out who was gay and of dropping prudent hints so as to establish the common bond was a subject that gay professionals returned to again and again.

A few insisted that they made it a rule to shy away from such relationships, particularly with subordinates. Most told us that they were always happy to make new gay friends where they worked; these relationships were a source of personal enjoyment and career support. One of the important findings shared later in the book is the unwritten social codes that seem to guide the formation and development of these relationships.

WHO THIS BOOK IS FOR

The findings in this book are based on the experiences of gay and lesbian graduates of the Harvard Business School. But the focus isn't just for gay men and lesbians pursuing business careers or careers with *For-*

tune 500 companies, investment banks, or consulting firms. It is for gay people working in any kind of job at any level in any business or service profession; it's also for businesspeople in the armed services, advertising, communications, computers, consulting, data management, education, engineering, financial services, government, health care, high tech, law, law enforcement, management, manufacturing, marketing, medicine, media, operations, publishing, retail sales, small businesses, and social services. Because Harvard Business School graduates are a diverse group of people who have held jobs in all of these fields before and after they received their MBAs, their experiences in these fields will be discussed and contrasted with their experiences in traditional corporate business fields.

As many pointed out, it remains an open question whether the experiences of Harvard MBAs are universally comparable to those of other lesbians and gay men in business. We do feel, however, that our findings can be of enormous benefit to gay people and heterosexuals alike.

A Resource for Gay Men and Lesbians

For lesbians and gay men, this book is an issue-by-issue guide to the challenges and rewards they are likely to encounter in business and it describes the critical trends that will affect them and their heterosexual peers in the future. Yet analysis and statistics go only so far. This book is about real people dealing with real issues. Because gay people have only recently begun to feel safe enough to make themselves visible in business, those who dream of business careers or seek job advancement have had few positive, successful role models to emulate. In the absence of proof to the contrary, the homophobia and discrimination they experience growing up gives young gay people every reason to believe that the road to business success will be difficult if not impossible, especially for those who are openly gay. It is our desire that the stories of the lesbians and gay men shared herein give other gay people the confidence that they too can overcome whatever obstacles being gay may place in their path. It is our hope that this book will provide a realistic balance between documenting dangers and celebrating successes, so that gay people in business can better cope with their reality-based fears as well as their habitual internal anxieties.

Insights for Heterosexuals

The findings in this book are important not only to gay people in business but also to their heterosexual associates, managers, and employees. For nongay people our findings offer unique insights into what has been until recently a largely invisible minority working alongside them. Our interviewees help pinpoint ways heterosexuals at every level in business can more successfully be supportive of gay colleagues in their midst.

Surveys of the American population show that many heterosexuals know there are gay people working among, with, and for them. But heterosexuals often feel uncertain about the etiquette of approaching gay colleagues or feel awkward because they fear they lack knowledge of gay issues. They would like to show their support for gay colleagues but don't know how.

Other heterosexuals are discovering that the presence of gay people working openly among them can bring their latent homophobia to the fore. Many may not have realized how much homophobia they had unconsciously absorbed from the culture around them until it is stirred by the revelation of a gay coworker's sexual orientation. Those who want to overcome this homophobia will discover they need to confront the negative beliefs and stereotypes they've learned over the years.

Both groups will find what they are looking for here. Heterosexuals will learn much about the important personal and workplace issues gay people wrestle with every day. They will also gain the kind of clear, realistic picture of gay people in business that is needed to dispel the homophobic myths and stereotypes that saturate our culture. This book may help all but the most homophobic to work productively with the gay colleagues in their midst.

Within these pages are suggestions to heterosexuals for achieving smooth working relationships with gay colleagues. There is advice on everything from etiquette to supporting gay colleagues by objecting to homophobic jokes and remarks to how to combat one's own heterocentrism by eliminating language that assumes all love is heterosexual.

Lessons for Managers

All managers, whether heterosexual or gay, are concerned with getting the best from their workers. Numerous studies have proven that happy workers are productive workers. Therefore, managers who are cognizant of their gay employees' issues can empower an important percentage of their corporate resources, adding to the company's overall competitive strength.

As our nation's workforce becomes increasingly diverse, a welcoming attitude toward this change will shift from a corporate virtue to a necessity. To ensure harmony and minimize disruptive outbursts of bigotry, more and more organizations are adopting nondiscrimination policies and diversity-training programs that include sexual orientation. As gay employees come increasingly under this protective umbrella, conscientious managers will want to be familiar with how workplace discrimination can be avoided. Companies are also increasingly adopting domestic partner benefits in order to compensate all their employees fairly.

Managers looking for insights regarding these changes will discover them in the chapters that follow, told in the voices of some of their own employees. They will also find suggestions and special insights on handling the most common forms of homophobia and reversing the heterocentric policies that harm the morale of gay employees.

LOOKING AHEAD

Our findings are certain to raise as many questions as they answer. Because they fly in the face of so many preconceptions, of gay people and heterosexuals alike, they are bound to prove controversial. Any questions our findings generate or any controversy they fan will spark a healthy debate that can only increase public awareness of the issues facing gay people in the workplace. We hope that increased visibility will result in an increasing dialogue between gay people and their heterosexual colleagues and lead to true equality for all.

A Note on Names

Over a third of those we interviewed gave us permission to use their real names; others have asked to be disguised with pseudonyms. In 1990, when we began, few chose to use their full name and place of business, no matter how out they were at work. Over the last few years, many we have interviewed have specifically requested that we use their name or other identifying information. Some in the original 1990 survey have also rescinded their request for anonymity and permitted us to use their names.

All of the people we have profiled are real people. None are composites. Some participants have asked that their company, title, location, or other identifying details be omitted. In a number of cases we have broken a single individual's story into several pseudonyms so as to further disguise their identity. Wherever company names, titles, or first and last names are given together, they are real.

Chapter 2

Gay Life at Harvard Business School

The Historical Context

In order to put our study in historical context when we began this project in 1989, we did a comprehensive search on the Baker Library computer system at Harvard Business School. We also visited various gay and lesbian archives in an attempt to learn about the history of gay men and women in the business world. In a search going back to the 1960s, the mainstream newspapers, newsmagazines, and business magazines offered very little. We found a few short news stories on lawsuits or legislation and a few impressionistic feature articles on gay business owners, with some speculation about the demographics and taste of the gay market.

Somewhat surprising, gay organizations, gay authors, and the gay press gave more attention to gay business professionals and gay workplace issues in the years immediately after Stonewall (June 1969) than they did during the late 1970s and the 1980s. In books now out of print, we noticed interviews with gay businessmen and read political analyses of issues affecting gay people on the job.

In the late 80s we found a few doctoral theses and studies for professional journals on gay people at work. Primarily these were small-scale studies (ten to fifteen interviewees) of gay professionals or technical articles by human resources specialists.

In the last few years there has been an explosion of interest in gay-workplace issues in both the mainstream and gay press as gay organizations have targeted the workplace as a locus for important social changes. Concomitantly, a few authors have penned popular works relating to the workplace, and a few historians have taken an interest in subjects that touch indirectly on the lives of gay businesspeople. Yet little has been added to the knowledge base about the changes in gay workplace issues over time.

THE HBS EXPERIENCE

As we began our interviews with gay HBS alumni of all ages, we realized we had an untapped resource. In addition to revealing important information about the lives of gay professionals today, these individuals, we hoped, could also help us reconstruct a history of their experience in the business world. As we interviewed more alumni, we realized that that ambition was too broad. Because those we interviewed worked in many cities and many different companies, it was impossible for us to distinguish individual impressions from broad social trends.

We concluded, however, that we would be able to assemble a reliable picture of our interviewees' experiences at Harvard Business School, at least from the 1970s. Additionally, written documention existed in back issues of the *Harbus,* the school newspaper, as well as other HBS publications. After looking at back issues of admissions materials, the student clubs book, the student *Prospectus* (commonly known as the Face Book), and *Net Present Value* (a student guide to the local area), we realized we could accurately describe several decades of the experience of gay men and lesbians at the Harvard Business School.

This project was useful for three reasons. First, knowing the context for their professional training helped us gain insight into the minds of those we interviewed. The business-school experience was particularly important to many of them, because their first or most important understanding of what it means to be gay among business peers was learned there. Until the last decade, many went directly from college to business school, so they had no business background besides their HBS experience. Recently, business school is where gay professionals first grapple with what it means to be approaching thirty and unmarried; thus, the issue of managing their gay identity became more salient at HBS. Interviewees of all ages came out to themselves at B-school or first made friends with other gay professionals there. Thus, for many, their experiences at HBS set the tone for their expectations of what being gay would mean in their business careers. Their experience there shaped their opinion on the value of finding gay peers and caused them to evaluate the issue of managing their gay identity at work. It also raised the question of what they could reasonably expect in terms of nondiscriminatory treatment from employers and peers.

A second reason for tracing the history of gay life at HBS is that in many ways HBS is a mirror of the business world. Looking at the cause and effect of changes at HBS provides a window into understanding how change has happened and will happen in large business organizations. The experiences of gay HBS students provides an interesting parallel to the situation of gay professionals in other tradition-bound business organizations. In some ways, we anticipated, gay life at HBS might be more repressed than gay life in some sectors of the American workplace, and gay people at HBS might be among the most conservative of gay people in business. Yet in other ways, we thought, gay life at HBS might be more progressive than gay life in much of American business, and some gay people at HBS might turn out to be part of the leading edge of equal-rights activism for gay people in business. As part of a highly trained, privileged elite, gay HBS students and alumni might produce institutional and social changes that other gay people did not have the ability or the self-confidence to implement.

Finally, we were also interested in studying the Harvard Business School experience in its own right, because HBS is the world's leading institution for business education. At HBS there is a frequent exchange of ideas with the business world. Faculty, students, and alumni are in constant contact with the cutting edge in the world of business. Business leaders often visit the school, recruiting, making presentations, giving lectures, or sitting in on classes that focus on their companies. HBS faculty frequently consult to large companies and a large cross section of world business leaders. When they graduate, HBS alumni fill the ranks of some of the world's largest and most prestigious companies. Therefore the on-campus lessons heterosexuals learn about what it means to be gay in business and how the campus administration treats gay students are the models they take with them into the business world.

HBS, by its very nature as an educational institution, touches the lives of many more people than a corporation, simply because every year a new group of students arrives and another leaves. Graduates take with them the collective experiences they encountered at HBS, such as sharing a locker room with a gay classmate, reading in the student newspaper that gay faculty's domestic partners receive health insurance benefits, or hearing discussions about gay issues from their gay classmates.

The HBS Curriculum

Founded in 1908, the MBA program at the Harvard Business School has remained largely unchanged since its inception. Incoming students are divided into sections, which form their primary academic and social focus. In the First Year the curriculum is the same for all, and students take all their classes with their section. In the Second Year there is only one assigned class; otherwise students take subjects that interest them. Each course is graded on a forced curve, with a small percentage making top grades (previously called "excellent," now called "getting a one") and a small percentage making what are essentially failing marks (previously called "low pass" or "loop," now called "getting a three"). Too many loops, or threes, mean a student may be asked to leave the program, also known as "hitting the screen."

MBA candidates pursue a two-year course of study using the case method in every class. Every night, a student has two to three cases to prepare, each involving roughly fifteen to thirty pages of reading and financial information or marketing statistics. In class the professor asks one student to open the case. Unlike the law-school case method, no one is interested in hearing a recitation of the case facts. Rather, the student is expected to answer the question "What would you do as the managerial protagonist in the case?" After a student presents his or her best interpersonal and financial option, the professor chooses among the sea of classmates' raised hands to either support or, more usually, critique the opening. Classes last an hour and twenty minutes, and most people try to speak at least once, because grades are based on both class participation and one or two exams. During First Year in particular, the competition and pressure are fierce. Students compete not only for grades but to land prestigious summer jobs that they hope will be the springboard to a lucrative career after graduation. Toward this end, students take leadership roles in various student clubs and vie against one another for student government positions such as Ed Rep (Education Representative) and GAC rep (General Assembly Committee representative).

Gay Life at HBS—to the 1970s

As historian George Chauncey has convincingly shown, homosexuality and homosexual culture were not completely hidden from public view before the 1970s. Yet aside from the Pansy Craze during Prohibition, when heterosexuals flocked to drag balls and clubs, it was rare for homosexuality to be discussed in mainstream news sources before Stonewall.

Perhaps the most frequent mention of homosexuality in tandem with workplace issues occurred when homosexuals were driven out of government and security-related fields by the McCarthy-era witch-hunts in the Cold War era of the 1950s. In other business contexts, the subject barely arose, except when an employer's name was published in the local newspaper after someone was arrested—for being caught in a raid of a gay bar, for public sex, or for soliciting. Yet we know from a multitude of sources that an active male homosexual social life existed in large cities since the turn of the century and that lesbian bar culture dates from at least the World War II era.

At HBS, not surprisingly, things were little different. It was a male-only school until the early 60s, and few interviewees recalled homosexuality ever being discussed by their classmates before the 1970s. Larry, who graduated from HBS in the 1940s, told us that when he was a young man, "Homosexuality was the sort of thing that was discussed by certain people under certain circumstances, but it wasn't the kind of thing that was discussed openly." He said, "It reminds me of when people who had cancer were whispered about." Lowering his voice to a whisper, he said, " 'You know, I understand he has cancer.' It was almost like that. And why did they talk about cancer in hushed tones? It was feared.

"There were certain people who talked about certain aspects of homosexuality, and they weren't always negative or condemning. But things that were stated as fact were based on a great deal of misunderstanding. I'm sure there were some people who had religious objections, but I didn't ever hear anything that would indicate that was the basis for large numbers of people to be disturbed. It was more a matter of 'isn't it too bad' that someone was homosexual."

Larry reminded us that until the 1970s psychiatrists labeled homosexuality a mental illness: "People who were readily identifiable by their actions might have been thought of as having a kind of disease or mental imbalance: men who were effeminate or women who wore mannish clothes or a severe haircut. If a woman was involved in sports or other typically masculine activities like disassembling a car engine, that could give them away. For either men or women, the extremes identified them. It was also very unusual for women to be in business unless they had family that owned the business. So a career woman might be stereotyped as a lesbian."

Yet most men in the 40s, 50s, and 60s who knew they were gay managed to meet other professional gay men like themselves by sexual pickups or in gay bars. Trevor, who graduated in the 1950s, recalls looking for other men along the banks of the Charles River. "I knew about that because there were songs about it. 'You can tell a Harvard man about a mile away, because he looks just like he'd fly away.' And the tag line is 'beyond the Boathouse.' I think anytime I went down there—dead of winter, middle of the summer, raining—there was always someone there." He laughed. Through cruising outdoors, Trevor told us, "I found someplace better to go. One of the men I picked up told me where to find a gay bar—the Napoleon Club in Boston. It's been open since I was in school, and it's still there." Several told us that the gay friends they made in those days played an important role in helping them accept being gay themselves. These role models also helped assure them that it was possible to be successful in business and to be gay. Of course, we were told, no one really questioned the idea that being gay was something you did privately, outside of your work life. "The main concern was not getting caught," Trevor said.

The gay men we interviewed from those years told us that the pressure to date women and to marry was very strong, and many succumbed or came close to succumbing, even if they were aware of their sexual interest in men. Herb, who graduated in the 50s, said, "I kept running into women whom I liked and had a certain amount of feeling for, with whom I could develop a certain amount of passion. I was actually engaged at various times to four different girls before the magic stopped working. With one, we had the whole thing planned. I gave her a ring, and the date was set and all that. But I just couldn't do it to her. We went for a trip across the country, and that is when I fell from grace and slept with yet another man. And I just couldn't face the idea of getting married to someone to whom I would have to lie to about what I was doing." While Herb never married, several other HBS gay men from that era did.

A number of the gay men from the 1940s to the 1960s whom we interviewed served in the military before or after attending HBS. The main lesson most of them learned from their military experience was the importance of "discretion," that is, being closeted. However, some said the atmosphere when they served was far more tolerant than it is now. Because of the draft, the military had a broader cross section of society, and this translated into more acceptance of homosexuals in the ranks. Yet all were aware of others who had been discharged for reasons of homosexuality. The other important lesson those who served in the military learned was how to find other people like themselves. This survival skill stood them in good stead as they went into business and needed to network with others who were also mostly closeted.

Before women were formally admitted to the HBS program, Roberta Lasley was one of the first women to attend classes at HBS, graduating in 1960. Before business school she had a girlfriend and was part of a circle of lesbian friends. Although all had college degrees, Roberta did not find the same support for her professional aspirations as the gay men we interviewed found from their peers. After business school, she said, "I certainly felt more in common with the people I met when I would go to the Harvard Business School Club in Philadelphia for a breakfast meeting on Friday morning than I felt many times when I was in the dyke bars. Because I had something to talk to them about, namely business. I found I was more interested in talking to them—these basically mainline Philadelphia WASP types, who I really had more in common with, despite being from a poor family in New Bedford—than I did with the butches and fems at the dyke bars." In part for this reason, Roberta said, she got married and raised a family for many years before coming out again. This lack of support for lesbians with career aspirations was typical in this era and accounted for many who chose to be very closeted or to marry.

As the 60s drew to a close, student activism began to grow, and gay groups also formed. Jason, who graduated in the late 60s, told us, "Back when I was at HBS there were no gay groups at any of the campuses. The closest thing was this group called the Student Homophile League. Thank God that word has gone out of fashion." He laughed. "It met at Boston University in a basement area with side doors. People sort of hovered around before they got the nerve to come in. It was sanctioned by BU but not part of BU. The goals of the organization at that time were primarily social. In fact, by charter the group was not political. After gay liberation began in New York, each of the schools developed specific groups. The first one at Harvard was in the graduate school of arts and sciences."

In the 1970s, while gay culture flourished in gay ghettos, the desire for privacy remained foremost in the minds of gay business students. Thus, only a few of those we interviewed came out to heterosexual classmates. It was also very difficult for them to find other gay students, although a few recalled doing so. In many cases, we learned, a sexual liaison was part of the relationship. In other cases, social activities like going to bars together were the focus.

Strikingly, even those who graduated in the mid-70s were not as out on campus as those who attended HBS a year or two later, when the gay student group was formed. And without backing from the group, none attempted on their own to seek changes in the administration policy with respect to gay students. In general, gay graduates from these years have come out only selectively at work, and many chose gay-friendly industries for their careers. However, some are completely out and are willing to be named in this book. Interestingly, most of those who are out at work were not out to themselves at business school and, hence, were less aware of the attitudes of their classmates, gay or heterosexual. Instead they learned about being gay in other contexts and have continued to adapt to the changes in the business world and in society.

Overview to the Present

The experiences of HBS gay students after the formation of a gay student group are especially interesting because of parallels to and differences from their experiences in the business world. From the late 1970s through the 1980s, business school was where many gay professionals received strong signals that being gay was going to be a problem in their careers. Despite gay students' generally favorable personal interaction with members of the HBS administration during those years, on-campus attitudes were often highly hostile. One reason may be that the administration announced no policy to prohibit discrimination against or harassment of gay students and faculty. In addition, gay students themselves feared that the workplace itself would penalize them for coming out at business school. Ironically, those who attended HBS during the late 1970s and the 1980s reported more overt discrimination against them at business school than in the workplace. One reason may be that their business-school experience convinced them it was best to keep a low profile about being gay. Many from that era who were closeted remain so today. Strikingly, they seem to have faced more workplace discrimination for being gay than those who are completely open.

Those who graduated in the 1990s have approached the issue of being openly gay on campus far differently. Recently, as a number of students have come out to their heterosexual peers, the atmosphere at HBS has been much more positive. Gay students see that those who are most out are the most respected and have achieved the greatest gains with the school administration. At the same time, the administration itself has initiated a number of policy changes that support those who are openly gay. As a result, many of those who have attended HBS in the 1990s are less fearful about being gay at work and are convinced that being out holds more benefits than disadvantages for their professional careers.

THE HBS GAY STUDENT ORGANIZATION

Since its inception, membership in the HBS gay student group has fluctuated dramatically from year to year, from a high of over twenty to a low of under five. Most club leaders also learn of other gay or bisexual students who never come to club meetings or parties. Lesbians have been actively involved in the organization almost since its beginning. While they are usually a minority and their numbers vary significantly from year to year, in some years lesbians have constituted half of the club's membership.

The Early Years (1978 Through Spring 1980)

The HBS gay student organization began in 1978 as a group called Alternative Executive Lifestyles. The idea came from a small number of gay men who were friends at HBS. Christian, who graduated in 1979, recalled: "Rupert, who was class of '78, had been at Stanford before coming to HBS, and that's where he got the name from. I heard about him from a gay friend in Boston and called him up. We got to be pretty good friends. There were five or six gay guys in his class who I got to know through him, as well as a few from my own class.

"The group of us got together and we decided there's got to be a lot more gay people out there. We wanted to find them, but it wasn't easy figuring out how. We rejected the idea of listing a P.O. box in the student newspaper, because it would be hard for the letter writer to stay anonymous. So we got a phone line and installed it literally in the closet of a student who lived off campus. Jeff Eisberg wasn't out to his roommate, so he hid the phone under a pile of his laundry! The fact that he lived off campus was important, because the on-campus phone numbers had a distinctive exchange. The other four digits could easily be traced," Christian explained. "We all chipped in and paid the monthly charge. We put up posters saying, 'Gay Men and Lesbians, Call Harvard Alternative Executive Lifestyles,' and gave the phone number. We started getting phone calls, and by the end of my first year we had about fifteen people in the group. We'd have monthly get-togethers and potluck dinners and that kind of stuff. Second Year I got pretty involved in the group. We had another ten people or so, and I had a couple of really tough meetings with the people after they'd call. Jeff would pass on their names and say, 'Take this person out to dinner and try to help him feel better about being gay.' I remember one guy was absolutely petrified. He'd never met anybody gay in his life."

He added, "Soon after we started the group, I started hearing a number of really antigay comments and jokes from section mates, both in and out of class. Everybody laughed, and nobody ever said anything about it. So I really got pissed off one night and wrote a two-page letter to the section, which became famous my year. I said that in every section there's eight to twelve gay people, and we are probably sitting next to you or in front of you. We're your friends and we just want the same respect everybody else was getting. So just cool it on the antigay comments.

"Well, it just caused an uproar in the section. One of the most macho guys in my class happened to be the best friend of my roommate, so it made it even more difficult for me. This guy went tromping through my room all the time talking about all this 'radical faggot' stuff, and he was very vociferous about it. He wrote a response to my letter and posted it on the class bulletin board. I told the other gay folks what I'd done and gave them copies of my letter. I was actually afraid that somebody would trace the typewriter somehow," Christian recalled. "I was actually shaking for days thinking how my classmates were going to come after me.

"One man in our group was on the *Harbus* staff, and he was able to put it in the school paper. There really was a backlash, with jokes about 'the eight to twelve' that were incredibly negative. The guy who wrote the response to my section wrote a response to the *Harbus,* naming the guy who worked on the *Harbus* as this gay radical who is trying to undermine our values and so on. So the poor *Harbus* guy took the brunt of this whole thing when it was really me who wrote the letter. Before that, there were a couple of people in my section who were just shaking in their boots because other people thought they had written this letter. One guy was gay, and that's why he was so afraid. The other guy was very straight, but he looked effeminate, so people picked on him too. It's funny; no one suspected me. Anyway, in one respect we made some inroads, because there was suddenly an awareness that gay people were around. But it did backfire in other ways," he concluded.

Although no early club members were completely out—none signed their letters to the editor or announced during class that they were gay—several interviewees recalled that some gay students were more out than others, which caused tension among the group. There was also conflict because some were highly concerned about portraying a "good image" of gay people to heterosexuals. Laurent recalls, "One of my classmates was extremely effeminate and I came down on him pretty hard. At the time, I told him he gave a bad image to gay people. He was really hurt and we didn't speak for many years. In the past I thought gay people had to put forward an image of being like anyone else. Over the years I've come to feel diversity is a good thing, and no one should be ashamed of anyone else," Laurent told us. "I've also apologized to him, and we've become friendly. I'm actually appalled at how narrow I once was."

In the early years of the club, some were politically active in terms of the school administration. Christian recalls that in 1979, the fledgling gay student group approached the faculty to put the nondiscrimination language in Placement Office materials. "The law school had just done it, so we had a precedent for making a proposal to the faculty. Two of us went in and submitted it. And we got back a series of questions that were very close to being homophobic. Their main argument was we can't 'force' this on everybody. In fact, they brought up Navy ships. You can't have gay men on Navy ships because they will wear dresses. We wrote back and said, 'Let us explain. Gay people are not transvestites, they are not transsexuals. That's something different.' We had to go through a very basic education process."

Although the HBS administration was not ready to establish a nondiscrimination policy, Christian told us he didn't suffer any personal discrimination as the result of coming out. "When the committee had their meeting to review the nondiscrimination policy I went representing the gay group. I looked around the room and didn't know a soul, so I felt very confident everything would be fine. They asked a few questions here and there before going to vote on it; then in walks my advisor on my independent research project. I just about died. I thought: There goes my project down the drain. So the committee voted on it and they voted it down.

"The next day I went up to my advisor's office and told him I wanted to talk to him. I said, 'If I had known you would be at the meeting, I would have said something to you beforehand.' He said, 'Christian, I voted against this, but I want you to know I respect the hell out of you for being there and saying the things you did. I may not agree with you, but you did a great job.' In the end, I got an Excellent in the course." Christian laughed.

Meryl recalled that she and a gay man in the group went to some of the HBS professors to seek changes in the curriculum. "Even though I was one of the founding mothers of Alternative Executive Lifestyles, I was not out at HBS. But I was out enough to tell a group of professors, 'Hey, we're here.' We wanted to get some cases into the curriculum. But nothing really came of it."

Jeff Eisberg, a 1979 graduate, told us another professor raised the issue himself by asking his entire class to write a one-page response to the following case situation: A client saw an advertising executive dancing with his male lover at a charitable event. He asked for the man to be removed from servicing his brand. As a manager at the ad agency, what do you do? Jeff said, "The results of the class's writings were never made public."

Jon Zimman, who graduated in 1980, was a First-Year student when the gay group started. He said, "I got involved with the gay student group my second semester, but I still considered myself closeted."

Jon and a few classmates set up the mechanism for the club that carried it for many years. Jon told us, "We didn't have a phone my Second Year, because everyone lived on campus. So we started having a listing in the school newspaper. We got a post office box off campus in Cambridge and held a few social meetings." Club meetings also continued to be advertised by posters put up in the dead of night, as the lesbians we interviewed remembered. Unfortunately, they were usually ripped down by morning. As a result, not all who attended HBS in the early years knew how to contact the group. However, Jon recalled, "We had about fifteen members. We'd put notices of our meeting in sealed envelopes. First Years didn't have student mailboxes at that time, so we'd have to hand them the notes in person. That was always scary for those who were most closeted."

The group did not seek status as an official student organization at the business school until quite a few years later. Jon said, "In order to find out the procedure for getting the group listed in the student clubs book, I came out to the assistant dean for student affairs who was the liaison for all the student organizations. But it didn't go in after all, because none of the new club copresidents wanted their names to go in there, which was the policy for all the clubs at that time."

Raul Companioni, a 1980 graduate, told us he was quite out on campus and had a number of close heterosexual friends. Jeff Eisberg was also somewhat out. Neither Raul nor Jeff reported any problems from classmates about being gay at HBS.

Isaac, however, did encounter some problems, perhaps because of his half-in-half-out status. Isaac says, "I made an enemy Second Year in the Management Consulting Club where we both were officers. I heard from a friend that this guy was making slurs about my sexual orientation to people at Boston Consulting Group, a blue chip firm."

In the following decade, gay students who attended HBS included those who were highly closeted and those who were relatively open. Those who were most open at HBS found personal and political benefits, despite the fears of their gay classmates that coming out to any heterosexuals could be damaging personally and professionally. Perhaps not surprising, they are also among those of their class who are the most open at work today. In contrast, those who were most closeted at HBS recalled more negative episodes from gay life there. Hence they are less willing to be open in their careers and are less optimistic about achieving protection from nondiscrimination policies or other kinds of equal treatment at work. Yet some, even if they are mostly closeted at work, have found ways to help other gay people behind the scenes by virtue of their strong networking ties. In many cases, they credit interactions with more open gay HBS alumni or gay people at work for their increased activism.

The 1980s

For about a decade, the primary accomplishment of the group was to advertise and hold social gatherings. The group held functions throughout the 80s, the first usually scheduled shortly after the beginning of the first term. Learning from their poster fiasco, the club realized the student newspaper could be an important tool in disseminating information. The main problem every year was how to get the information in the paper without having to come out. Fortunately, in most years, a club member was active on the newspaper staff. In those years, notices about the club's activities, anonymous articles about gay life on campus, and entertainment-related articles of interest to gay students made a regular appearance. In most years, the club held periodic gatherings, and at least occasionally the paper listed a phone number for gay students to call. Several told us that reading the paper in the privacy of their rooms was a lifeline that gave them the courage to reach out to other gay students. Although perhaps a majority stayed away from the gay student group, many made friends with those who were involved—as the result of meeting at a gay bar or because of various clues that they might be gay.

Although some people were out selectively to heterosexual classmates, Rosalie remembers, "The general consensus in the early 80s was it was not good to come out at all, because if you came out to your section, then you're out forever to everyone. You're marked. There was a woman a year ahead of me I figured was a lesbian when I went to visit the school before enrolling. I came out to her, and she told me how she had come out in her section and they did really bad things to her. I also remember one guy, Franklin, very vividly. He went on to become a real hotshot at McKinsey [a major consulting firm]. Another guy talked about having been on a train in Europe when some guy made a pass at him. And Franklin said, 'If that had happened to me, I would have murdered that guy.' The level of homophobia in the class was really creepy. There maybe were some people who were fairly open and didn't have any problems, but there were a lot of people who were very vocally homophobic, so I didn't feel safe about being out. Maybe I just focused on the negative stuff. But I even remember a case about some guy who was looking for work. Because he lived in San Francisco, was single and over thirty, there was a presumption he was gay, and that was a bad thing. The class advised he shouldn't have an address in San Francisco—he should rent a post office box in another city. Basically, I felt anything that identifies you as gay was dangerous."

Lucinda, who graduated in the early 80s, recalls, "In my First Year, the HBO [Human Behavior in the Organization] department got all the students to write something on being different, to get students to understand about diversity a little bit more. In the one I submitted, I essentially came out. It was about a business-school student and whether or not she should come out. I did it because I was at a point where being out was really important to me. It was very hard for me not to be out. Hearing everyone say she should not come out really colored my whole experience there, because it meant that I was very uptight a lot of the time about getting close to people."

Unfortunately, Lucinda did not get much support from the gay student organization either. "There were five lesbians who were part of the group one year, but we did not all get along," she told us. One reason is that many were sleeping with each other and each other's girlfriends. Maggie concurred, "The women weren't as much of a source of support as they might have been." In contrast, the four gay Black men who were at HBS at this same time were a group of buddies who went to the clubs and did other social things together, we learned.

Some of those who were active in the early years of the gay student group today are completely out at work, yet others who were active are almost completely closeted. One reason may be the memories of overt prejudice expressed against those who were rumored to be gay. Wynonna recalls her experience in the early 80s: "I was elected Ed Rep for my section. In January, some members of my section decided to ask for a new election on the basis of a whispering campaign: 'Do we really want our Ed Rep to be gay?' It was the only section to have a midsemester election. One person came up and told me what was going on, but otherwise no one explicitly discussed the reason for the challenge. Someone just stood up and said, 'I want to hold reelections,' and they did. So I had to get up and address the class. I admitted, 'I'm deeply ambivalent about this. If you want me to do the best job that I can, then reelect me.' I lost by one vote. Some people came up and said, 'We're really sorry. If you had really wanted to keep it, you should have been more aggressive about it.' And I said, 'Well, given what the topic was, they were going to decide what they were going to decide.' " While our conclusion from this experience was that it's better to come out and address the rumors head-on, Wynonna's conclusion even today is that the less said about being gay, the better.

Although a number of the lesbians who graduated in the 1980s did not feel they got much support from the gay student organization, almost all the gay men we interviewed from the early years of the club told us how much they valued the importance of gay networking. For Russell, gay networking at HBS was the start of a long history of working with a gay network to accomplish personal and, eventually, political goals. He recalls, "I had been living a very gay life up until business school. So when I was admitted, I was worried. I didn't want to have a straight roommate, because I wanted to be able to call my boyfriend back home. I had to be very resourceful, because I didn't know any gay people at HBS. But the Harvard College gay organization put me in touch with someone at the law school who had the name of an HBS alumnus in New York who knew someone who was currently at HBS, running the group, which was called the Gay Students Association by then. She and her friends were delighted that someone was coming to business school who was out enough to want to look for other gay people before coming to the school. They put me in touch with a straight woman in the administration who got me a single room."

Although the gay group had no official tie with the school in its early years, by the fall of 1983 at least one school psychologist was aware it existed and did not hesitate to recommend that gay students seek it out. Joshua recalls, "I had a hard time at business school in the beginning. Within the first few days, there was a case where we had to draw up a decision tree, and I had to open the class. I had the right answers in front of me, but I was so nervous I read all the wrong answers. I was humiliated, so humiliated. I was looking around thinking: No one is ever going to want to talk to me; no one is ever going to want to deal with me. Plus, I'm gay, so no one else is like me. I don't belong here. So I went back to my room and actually I cried. I felt really out of it. I felt too embarrassed to face anyone. The next day in class was so awful for me. I looked around, and they all looked different than me, they all sounded different than me, they all had names that were too fancy for me, like James

Worthington III. I felt completely like an outsider. By the third day I couldn't take it anymore. I was thinking I was going to get out of here or I'm going to do something about my attitude. So I went to the counseling service on campus.

"Of course, now in retrospect I realize, the counselor had seen many people like me. If not gay people, just people who were traumatized by the first day or two. So she was questioning me, 'Why haven't you reached out? Do you have any friends here, any support groups or anything?' And I basically said, 'No, I don't relate to these people.' And she kept challenging me, 'Why not?' Finally I said, 'Well, I'm gay.' And she said, 'Well, do you think you're the only one?' And I said, 'I think so.' And she said, 'There's actually a gay organization. Why don't you look around? There will be a notice about their first meeting coming up soon.' " Joshua went to the meeting and soon felt much more optimistic about his future at HBS. The name of this psychologist was passed down to club members for many years, but gay students not in the club were not in the know. Other school psychologists were less helpful, we learned. One was decidedly uncomfortable with a student who came out in a peer support group she offered, and we learned that she cautioned another student not to come out at school, warning that even joining the gay student group could mean being irrevocably labeled as gay.

While the gay student group was small during most of the mid-80s, the group often held events in conjunction with gay student groups from other Harvard professional schools. These were very well attended. Hugh, who graduated in the mid-80s, was an active participant in the gay student group at HBS. He recalled, "We didn't have a big group. There were maybe seven of us that really socialized—maybe even fewer. What we did is, we connected with the law-school group. And then people would invite their friends, so we used to have pretty big parties." We told Hugh that of all the classes until the 90s, his class has the largest number of gay HBS alumni we have identified. He laughed. "Yeah. I have been shocked at how many people didn't come out until afterwards. It seems like they've wasted an important part of their lives. Because I made some really good gay friends at HBS."

A number of those we interviewed were not actively involved in the gay student group but were friends with those who were. Ironically, some of them are as much out at work as some of the group leaders, and in some cases even more so. Xavier recalls, "Second Year, I lived with another gay guy, who I met at the gay student group. He was seeing a classmate, Wally, who I always thought of as very macho. First Year, at least, Wally lived straight; he only really started to go out to gay bars in the Second Year. Wally had an affair with my roommate, who was a leader of the gay student group. So Wally would come over every Wednesday night like clockwork and spend the night." Wally is now out to a number of heterosexuals at work, while Xavier and his former roommate are out to just a few.

In 1984, a gay student contributed to a case containing gay issues, which was taught in a Second-Year self-assessment course. Gordon told us, "I took the course because I was trying to figure what I wanted to do after business school. In my final paper, I talked about being gay. The professor was so taken with my story that he developed it into a case." Gordon added as postscript, "The case is no longer being taught. But I got exactly the kind of job I wrote about wanting: fifty to fifty-five hours a week, which is low by B-school standards, creative and independent, with plenty of opportunity for a private life."

By 1985, the group sought and won funding from the umbrella student organization. Ed recalls, "When I was at HBS I was fairly out, because I went to the B-school student association for funding for the lesbian and gay student group." He also established an ongoing liaison with the student affairs office so that the group could continue to be funded even if the leadership was closeted. However, we do not believe the group attempted to gain other forms of parity with the other student clubs until the late 80s.

Delila, who was at HBS in 1986, recalls that a number of her classmates were fairly openly gay on campus. "But there was still a lot of fear. When I wrote an article for the student paper interviewing all the gay student club members, none of them let me use their names. And I didn't sign the article either. Yet one of the men I interviewed said, 'Being gay is such a part of my personality I think it's impossible for me to hide.' He was outrageous, and everyone loved him for it. When people thought of him they thought: Black and gay. I mean, he was very open. And one of the women I interviewed was also really open. In fact, she was kind of irritated with the other gay students for not being more politically radical about being gay.'

"People I interviewed talked about how they would come out to their friends at school, and it was fine and people were supportive. But the closing quote was from this guy who said, 'Yeah, you can tell me that it's not a rational fear that I can't come out. But I'm telling you, it's not always an irrational fear. I mean, 70 percent of the time it's fine. But the other percent of the time it's so bad that it's not worth risking it.' "

Several students and faculty came out to many heterosexuals during the mid-80s. Yet public homophobia was fairly common, causing most to remain highly closeted. Benjamin, a graduate from the mid-80s, said, "I hadn't really focused on how bad it was going to be until I heard my classmates say so many evil things in response to one of these minicases written by a classmate. They really scared me into staying in the closet." Due to the climate on campus, many we interviewed from the mid-80s did not participate in the gay group. Yet the group and the friends outside it could be an important source of support. Wayne told us, "Part of the reason I think I've formed such tight friendships with the friends I go away with every New Year's was the sense of relief from the oppression of the heavily straight environment of the business school. I remember the number of wedding rings that were on raised hands in class. I mean, I grew up in New York, and even my straight friends aren't married. These are city kids and everybody marries at thirty-eight. So to sit in this room with all these married people there, and some of them had kids . . . I just couldn't relate to that. I think that's why I developed some really strong friendships with other gay men at business school."

Many others agreed that informal ties could be quite strong. Ed, who graduated in the mid-80s, recalls, "There weren't that many people who were out in my class. But we used to have some fairly large parties, including B-school students, their lovers and friends, and people from the other side of the river—Harvard University undergrads, law students, grad students from Kennedy public policy school, and medical students." During those years there were only one or two lesbians in the gay student group, and thus these parties were almost exclusively male.

During the late 80s, the gay student organization's numbers continued to dwindle. Those we interviewed suggested the increasingly conservative national political climate may have played a role. Rowan said, "Everyone wanted to be an investment banker in the go-go years. It was very macho and very competitive. Maybe fewer gay people were attracted to the idea of going to business school, and the ones who did go felt they had to hide. Maybe gay people were weeded out in the admissions office. Who knows?" The first two possibilities seem likely to us, but there is little evidence for the last. Otto told us, "I hit the screen in the early 80s and tried to get back in three times. Each time you reapply you have to write a fifteen-page story about why you screwed up and how you're so sorry and why it won't happen again. I got turned down twice. The essay that got me readmitted was the one where I came out. I said the real reason I was having so much trouble the first time was that I was alienated because I was gay. I talked about how I lived alone off campus and how a gay classmate's suicide affected me. Then I talked about the supportive gay relationship that I am in now and other things about how I'm much more confident now about being gay, because I've had some good experiences. That's the essay that got me readmitted."

In the late 80s, club activities were mainly informal. While the group usually held a beginning- and an end-of-year party to help gay people find one another, those we interviewed recalled going out to the gay bars with their friends as the most important aspect of their gay life at school. Few of those we interviewed were out to any heterosexual classmates.

For many closeted gay students, the atmosphere at HBS was frightening. Leonard, who graduated from HBS in the late 80s, provides anecdotal evidence for the climate of fear. "I have a terrible story from HBS. It's like a bad soap opera." During one of the first weeks at school, he went on the Booze Cruise, the first of many black-tie events of First Year. Because it is the first real break from studying after school begins, almost everyone attends and gets smashed. Leonard recalls, "There was this woman in our section from the Deep South. On the bus over she kept saying to me, 'I've just never met anyone like you. I don't understand you.' Later on she kept saying things like, 'I don't know, you're just not like other guys I know.' She proceeded to get more and more drunk throughout the course of the evening. Finally, late in the evening she asked me, 'Are you gay?' I said, 'Yes, I am.' I was surprised and horrified when she responded, 'I knew it. I could ruin you tomorrow if I wanted to.' That memory has just stayed with me—the look in her eye and how she thought she could ruin me because she knew I was gay. 'If I told the rest of our section tomorrow, I could ruin you.' I still remember her saying that.

"I was just totally freaked out. Because here I am, it's a few weeks into school, and someone has got my number already. So I was really freaked out by it. I still remember that. It was a really creepy, creepy, creepy thing. I was shocked. I felt like I was living in some really bad TV miniseries or something. I went from being kind of afraid of her initially to then being really resentful." Leonard admitted, "The rest of the time there, she was always kind of supernice to me, and I always tried to avoid her. I just felt this was a clear sign to keep a tight lid on being gay or butch it up."

David Stokes, who was president of the newly renamed Gay and Lesbian Students Association (GLSA) in 1989, remembers, "Individually people were very nice at HBS, but there's some group mentality that encouraged homophobic behavior. Peer pressure can work in either direction—homophobic or not. Frankly, I was not willing to be the test case for coming out publicly."

Emma recalls that the gay students she met all seemed to share a closeted philosophy. "Before I enrolled I heard through a gay HBS graduate there was a gay student group on campus. It was kind of hard to find the group at first. When I finally hooked up, I didn't meet any lesbians, and all the guys were closeted. They all advised me to stay closeted, as did the gay classmates I eventually met. I ended up being pretty closeted the whole time, and I really regret it."

Ironically, the struggle to protect their closets helped build the impression that HBS was a difficult place for gay students. Yet by the late 80s, a number of gay faculty and staff were out, at least to gay students on campus. In addition, the gay student group had heterosexual allies in the administration staff. As a result, gay students often had an ally somewhere who knew how to work the system to make day-to-day life easier. Like Russell, earlier in the decade, Leah contacted the gay student group before enrolling at HBS in the late 80s. Although it was late in the housing cycle, she was able to obtain an on-campus apartment through the intervention of members of the gay student group.

Also during the late 80s, the group found a faculty sponsor and began to include itself in business school publications. Along with other student groups, the gay student organization included a letter in the clubs handbook, which is sent to all incoming students in the summer. Until the 1990s, however, no one was willing to sign the letter or to put his or her picture as the head of the gay student organization in the *Prospectus,* which is distributed to incoming students and referred to constantly throughout the year.

Gay students took other steps toward seeking equal treatment, however. In 1989 a group of students in Section A wrote an anonymous letter to their classmates. The one-page letter was printed up on hot pink paper and put in the mailbox of every member of the section.

"Dear Sectionmates," it began. "As your gay and lesbian classmates, we want you to know that there have been homophobic comments and fag jokes made in class and we find them very offensive. We don't feel comfortable speaking individually when we hear these remarks, so we are writing you an anonymous letter as a group. . . . " It was signed, "Your Gay and Lesbian Sectionmates." David Schutte, one of the "signers," recalls, "We distributed it on October 11, National Coming Out Day, shortly after we met each other at the first GLSA meeting." Sharon recalls, "I really admire the man who wrote the letter. We all wanted to do it, and we all participated in editing it. But it was right at the beginning of school, and I remember being so overwhelmed with doing my cases that I didn't think I had time or the clarity of mind to write it. He did a great job."

Instead of an uproar, the result of the letter was that the comments stopped. A GLSA member had ties to the school paper, so it was also printed in the *Harbus.* Sharon recalled, "That was a very positive experience—first, because we stood up for ourselves, and second, because the negative jokes stopped. I know there was some speculation about who signed the letter, but that wasn't all negative. It fact, that's how Annette first heard that I might be gay." Annette remembered, "I followed the wrong woman around for months before meeting the real Sharon Silverstein at a recruiting function. A few months later I got up the nerve to call the anonymous phone number of the place where a GLSA party was being held. When I heard there was a woman there, I figured it was time to go and really get to know Sharon."

HBS alumni from the 1980s are interesting because most were highly closeted while they were at HBS. Yet a number have become much more open since graduation. One reason may be their ongoing association with students from later classes, who are increasingly open. Additionally, the changing political and social climate has given them hope that the business world is ready for openly gay professionals. Finally, those who were open in limited ways met with success. For example, Hannah recalls that a visiting professor from overseas made a comment in class that didn't sit right with her. "He said something about two people having children, laughed, and said 'a man and a woman, I hope.' It was an ignorant comment, more than a homophobic one. But I figured education at HBS should go two ways. So I went into his office and told him what he said wasn't right. Gay people can have children, and my classmates and I found his remarks offensive. To my surprise, he not only apologized to me, but he apologized to our entire section."

The 1990s

The tide began to turn with the class of 1990. One reason is that students in the early 90s became increasingly open about being gay and unwilling to let homophobic remarks from classmates stand. As in the business world outside, those who came out at HBS encountered the least discrimination. As the result of successfully resisting homophobia at business school or seeing their classmates successfully opposing discrimination, many graduates from the 1990s have come out at work.

During the early 90s the gay student group began to retain more of an organizational memory and built on previous successes. GLSA leaders contributed significantly to the climate of openness that has developed at HBS. By putting their name in the clubs book, their picture in the *Prospectus,* and by signing letters to the *Harbus* they have helped give gay life at HBS a recognizable face for both gay and heterosexual students. In some years almost every issue of the paper had an article by a gay student, and many of the articles were signed.

The first to sign his name to such an article, Stever Robbins, class of 1991, came out in a first-person opinion piece. He later included his name in the clubs-book letter from GLSA to incoming MBAs, included his picture in the class of 1992 *Prospectus* as president of GLSA, wrote an article about being a gay student in *Net Present Value,* and authored a guide to gay social life in Boston and Cambridge that was also printed in *Net Present Value.* He told us, "I had an incredibly favorable response to coming out at HBS. In fact, I had people coming up to me for weeks and months telling me how great they thought it was that I signed the article in the *Harbus.*" After Stever first included his name and picture in the *Prospectus,* almost every year one or more gay students have been named and had their picture there. GLSA leaders have also continued to sign the welcoming letter in the clubs book and to include an article about gay life at HBS in *Net Present Value.*

Stever's bravery also inspired other classmates to come out in the *Harbus.* Jim Sherman wrote an editorial in which he encouraged other gay students to come out instead of hiding in the closet and complaining about the lack of awareness of gay people on campus. Stever, Jim, and others encouraged members of the class of 1992 to combat homophobia during their First Year. Individuals who spoke up in class or signed letters to the editor helped end the atmosphere that allowed antigay remarks to flourish.

Alan Miles, class of 1992, told us he never really came out formally to his section, but as the result of his opposing homophobia in his first year, he was widely assumed to be gay. He reflects that he endured some of the negatives of being suspected of being gay without realizing all of the positives of coming out. "I had this incident at the very beginning of First Year. My section was supposed to divide itself up into homogeneous groups and write up a synopsis defining what our group was. It was really easy for a lot of groups. If you're a Black woman, that would have been really easy. But when you're a white guy, it was really hard to figure out what eight-person homogeneous group you're going to be in. Somehow in my group we had eight white, blond guys." He chuckled. "So we're writing we're white, Christian, all this stuff. And then this one military guy said, 'Heterosexual.' Before I could say anything, another guy says, 'Well, we don't know that everyone here is heterosexual.' I thought that was great. But then the military guy said, 'Well, if there's a faggot in this group, I think we should kick his ass out of here.' Just like that—and he was dead serious."

As Alan recalled, the previous speaker retorted, "Well, I guess we're not going to find out then, are we?" Alan said he was glad for the support, but he revealed, "It really sounds stupid, but that one guy really shook me up a little bit. And right then we had to go back to a full-class discussion. So I ruminated on it and ended up writing an article about it in the school paper. I'm usually not verbal about issues that I care about; I like to write about them. Of course the quote they blew up to forty-pica was 'If there's a faggot in this group . . .' Well, my section reacted pretty strongly to it, in a negative way.

"I talked some to my Ed Rep about it, and a few days later our professors in the class where we did the exercise made a kind of halfhearted attempt to talk about gay issues in the workplace. The example we used was a minicase written by someone in the class about how uncomfortable he was working with a guy he suspected of being gay. The workmate lived in Greenwich Village and was rumored to hang out on Christopher Street—stuff like that. And everyone was, like, 'Whoa.' The tone of the discussion class was that this is a professional environment and that people who are that way should stay out of the professional environment."

Alan recalls, "I was pretty shocked." But instead of retreating into silence as former HBS students had done, he confronted the bigotry. "I put my two cents in about how the same argument can be used about anything—people with long hair, women, Blacks . . ." Alan continued,

"Somebody from my section took me to lunch about a week later and said, 'I have to let you know that the section was really upset about this article that you wrote.' And I said, 'Yeah, I've picked that up.' He told me, 'We're upset because you really portrayed the section in a very negative light. It made the section look like we were a bunch of homophobes.' So I said, 'Well, if the shoe fits . . .' But I wasn't accusing the whole section, and in the article I didn't name the person who made the comment. But they sure proved their colors by the discussion in class. And I proved mine by standing up to them."

Douglas Plummer also opposed homophobia in his section by his remarks in class, and by Second Year he was completely open as the president of GLSA. "I was the gay student rep, on the HBS student clubs' diversity committee. Then, one day in my section, there was this video clip that some of my classmates had done about debt in Latin America, using a lot of really bad racial stereotypes. Then they did this spoof on this really effeminate gay man who wanted to open up an antique and flower shop, and everyone was laughing, including an African American classmate who was on the diversity committee with me. That just blew a circuit in me. I was just pissed beyond belief.

"So I raised my hand and waited for the professor to call on me. He asked, 'What do you think about gold prices in Latin America in the 1983 era?' I said, 'I don't have anything to say about that. I want to talk about the video. The stereotypes it portrayed of gay people was offensive to me, and to gay people in general, and I'm really upset by the fact that everyone in the section laughed at it and no one made any comments about it.'" Douglas further explained, "I said gay people would be offended and I am offended. I didn't say 'as a gay person, I am offended.'"

Douglas recalled, "Nonetheless, there was dead silence—you could have heard a pin drop for a long time. The professor was visiting from Canada, a really nice guy, but he just didn't know how to deal with it. He was trying, but all he could say was, 'Well, thank you for your opinion. Anyway, about gold prices in Latin America in 1976.'" But Douglas wasn't through. He said, "Wait a second. I have a legitimate issue here. I need you or someone else to either validate me or tell me I'm off the wall and it's not appropriate to bring up in the classroom. But I want some response." At that point the section leader stood up and said, "'Look, this is something we need to talk about after class. If it's all right with you, Douglas, we'll talk about this at the end of class.'"

"After class the two guys who did the video both got up. One of the guys was African American. He looked at me and said, 'I have seen this happen so many times where people have stereotyped Black people, and I've always been so bitter and angry about it, thinking, How could anyone do that? How could anyone do that and not realize how I feel about it? For the first time in my life, I know how it feels to have done something like that and just feel totally stupid.' Then he said, 'I'm sorry.' The other guy, who's from Colombia, got up and said, 'I had no idea, I am so sorry, I really apologize.' "

Douglas recalled, "The story ricocheted through the halls after class. My friends told me that people came pouring out of class saying, 'You won't believe what Douglas Plummer did. It was a scene.' One of the other gay guys in my section told me later, 'You know, you have a point, but this is not how I would deal with it. I would deal with it off-line. I would just talk to the two people privately.' I said to him, 'Well, maybe that's fine for you, but the problem is that it wasn't something he said just to me. It was something he said in front of all these people, and everyone heard and everyone responded to it. And because of that, I feel some right to respond back in that same forum. Not only do I feel a right, I feel a responsibility to respond back in public. I'm glad I did it.' "

As gay students began to come out to large numbers of classmates with no ill effect, others continued to take larger and more public strides. The friendship circles among the gay men in the early 90s seemed to foster their increased willingness to be out. During the 90s, the GLSA continued its tradition of socializing with students from other schools and continued to attract mostly men to these gatherings. There is a quarterly party sponsored by the Harvard graduate school gay groups that some go to. Even more popular are the gatherings that are organized informally. Beginning in 1992, for example, HBS GLSA members and their friends from the law school and other Harvard graduate schools have held a Thursday-night get-together at Club Café in Boston. Yet while we knew at least five women who participated in the gay student group in 1992, they were not as out as their gay male peers. One reason may be that, as in the early 80s, these women were not close friends. In addition, several of these women did not identify themselves as gay. They were affiliated with the group due to past lesbian relationships or because they were in a lesbian relationship; yet, they saw themselves as bisexual or unsure, and today a majority of these women are not in lesbian relationships.

Interestingly, in 1994 it was the friendship networks among the lesbians that set the tone for increasing visibility and activism. That year there were at least six lesbians in the club, all of whom had partners. As a result, some meetings and parties had more women than men—quite a feat at a school where women are less than 30 percent of the enrollment. Lesbians we interviewed from that year said they found one another a source of support, as did their partners. Gay men in relationships agreed. Ted Chapin, Torrence Boone's partner, told us, "Torrence signed me up for the HBS Partners' Club, but it was primarily oriented to the spouse who needed someone to have coffee with, which was not my scene at all. That and day-care issues. But the GLSA, I have to say, was wonderful. Here I was coming to Boston, didn't know anyone . . . and instantaneously I had a whole bunch of people I liked and I really looked forward to spending time with."

Institutional Change An important change at HBS in the mid-90s was the demise of the anonymous Gang of Nine. Dormant for a year and then revived, it has not achieved the popularity or venomousnesss of its earlier incarnation. The primary reason seems to be accountability—now all the gossip columns have to be signed. As a result, closeted gay students feel less fear of being picked on by classmates. In the past, this column caused terror for many gay students. An alumna from the 1980s, Deborah later learned the Gang of Nine was a relatively new tradition that she and her classmates all thought had been there forever. "Basically, it was an anonymous gossip column written about each section, and it could get pretty nasty. Like one time the Gang of Nine wrote some slam about me not liking men. Well, almost all my friends at the business school were men, straight men, as a matter of fact. That was just their way of insinuating I was a lesbian. That kind of thing got in all the time, and you never knew who was responsible until the end of the year, when it was too late."

In the 1990s, the HBS administration and the gay student group have worked together to improve the campus climate for gay students. In most cases, gay students found, all they had to do was come forward. Since the fall of 1992, the HBS administration has paid for other efforts to increase gay student visibility. In addition to starting the HBS audiotext hot line that students and people off campus can call for information about gay life, Jonathan Rottenberg, class of 1993, authored a multipage booklet titled *There Is Something a Bunch of Your Classmates Want You to Know*. Written shortly after he came out to himself and his classmates as a First-Year student, the pamphlet talks about the presence of gay students at the business school. Disseminated to all incoming students, this brochure informs heterosexual and gay students that a gay student group exists.

The administration has taken several other steps toward treating gay students, faculty, and staff equally. Long after the rest of the university had a policy of nondiscrimination based on sexual orientation, the business school did not. Beginning in the late 70s, students approached the administration to enact this change, but they were rebuffed. In the late 80s, the policy was included in the fine print on admission materials, but it was not widely noticed or promulgated throughout the school. In addition to pledging to judge gay applicants fairly by 1990, individual administrators were also cooperative about extending certain benefits to gay students on an informal basis. When Lydia wanted to get out of her Second-Year dorm contract, she was told the only way she could avoid paying was to die or get married. Laughing, she told us, "I did the next best thing. I went to the university official in charge of student life and told him I wanted to move in with my partner, Sheryl, another business-school student. He signed the release immediately. He also told us to let our friends know their partners were welcome to use the new athletic complex." Since it opened in late 1989, the business school's beautiful $10 million Shad Athletic Center became the mecca of campus social life for students and faculty. This sporting heaven helped transform the school's frigid atmosphere through the warm euphoria of shared athletic endeavors. In bathing suits, sweats, and exercise gear, everyone seems more approachable. At HBS—just as in the business world—on the racquetball courts, while bodybuilding, and in the sauna, students, faculty, and partners develop friendships that often work to the benefit of one another's careers.

Married spouses had the right to use Shad, and this benefit was widely publicized in registration materials. However, gay students and faculty were uncertain whether their partners were also eligible for passes allowing them use of the athletic center facilities. In 1990, Mitch, a young gay professor, wanted a pass for his partner. At the same time, Eldrich, a gay student, wanted one for his partner. Independently, only a few days apart, they each decided simply to apply for passes and see what would happen. Each went to the front desk of the center and asked to sign their partner up. Each was handed the list, wrote his male partner's name down, filled in the requested information, and received the pass. Neither experienced the refusal they had feared. A few months later, Mitch and a lesbian faculty member approached the business-school administration about domestic partner health care and other benefits. They were told the business school would cooperate with a universitywide study on the subject, and these perks were achieved the following year.

Benefits for faculty and staff partners now include health coverage, library privileges, and reduced fees for courses. Simultaneously, for the first time HBS informed students in writing that all partners, not just spouses, were eligible to use the gym and the campus libraries. Several of those we interviewed took advantage of these benefits. Mark, who graduated in 1993, told us, "In terms of being gay at HBS, I thought it was basically pretty easy. I brought my partner, Dennis, to class. He had all the spousal benefits except health insurance. A Harvard Coop card [a membership card for the campus bookstore] was really easy for him to get; the gym card was easy. The registration people seemed ready to deal with us." By 1994, students gained health coverage for their partners as well.

In 1994 gay students achieved another important political goal with the administration. In order to recruit on campus, companies now have to sign a statement that they do not discriminate on the basis of sexual orientation as well as other criteria like race and gender. It is not clear how or whether this policy will apply to military recruiters. Interestingly, the placement office had indicated a receptivity to the idea several years earlier, but until recently gay students did not pursue the issue. Once they did, they found it easy to accomplish. The campus nondiscrimination policy is now placed prominently in all HBS publications.

When we told Christian, class of 1979, about this, and that current students hadn't known about previous efforts, he laughed. "I'm sure they all thought they were doing it out of the blue. Yeah, they think that they just walked in off the street and got all this stuff settled. But that's not the way it happened at all. It's great that there are people who are openly gay on campus now, because the more people who come out, the easier it's going to be for everybody. The rest of society is going to realize that we are everywhere. The difficulty is that when you're all by yourself doing it, then the fear of what's going to happen can be pretty strong. A mass kind of thing is another story. I'm glad it's reaching that level at HBS. I hope that gay people take that with them and those kinds of things continue to happen more in the business world."

Although no case dealing with gay issues is being taught in the mandatory First-Year curriculum, several gay cases are included in the elective classes. Gay students and faculty played a role in the development of many of these cases, as well as cases that were taught in previous years. At the end of 1990, a First-Year AIDS case was introduced that contained a gay character. This case came up through the ranks of the postdoctoral program. Sharon sat in on a class where it was being discussed. "The level of AIDS phobia and homo-ignorance was surprisingly high. Fortunately, a number of people, both heterosexual and not quite openly gay, tried to do a lot of educating." The case was well received, but it was eliminated from the curriculum the following year in a major curriculum revamping. In some years there has also been an AIDS day, which brought speakers to campus. But for several years, the only place in the curriculum where AIDS is discussed is a Second-Year course, Managing in a Regulated Environment. The case, which is about Burroughs Wellcome and AZT, gives significant background about the gay community in the context of government regulation of AIDS research and testing. In 1995, a new Second-Year course also addresses AIDS issues.

At present there are several cases on discrimination and coming out that have been used in the Second-Year curriculum during the 1990s. Alan Miles told us, "First Year we wrote up these little minicases about diversity. I actually submitted two, because we had to sign them. This was like three or four weeks into school, and I didn't want to have my gay case discussed under my name. I sent in an unsigned one talking about being gay at work. We didn't discuss it in class, but it was later made into an HBS case in the Second-Year ethics module." He laughed. "I'm the protagonist in it, but they changed some of the particulars. I have a very faggy background—I was a singer and in drama and all that kind of stuff —but the case made me out to be this lady-killer jock who strutted around. That made me mad, because I thought this was negative stereotyping—like, it's OK to be gay in business if you're a jock, but not if you have an arts background." Another case that has been taught in past years deals with CBS's decision to suspend Andy Rooney, a television commentator who made racist jokes and homophobic remarks.

HBS is now undertaking yet another sweeping change of its curriculum, and additional cases dealing with the gay experience are being added, including one on Lotus and domestic partner benefits. Another case that has achieved wide acclaim among students is the groundbreaking *Harvard Business Review* article on coming out at work. Published in July 1993, this article was widely read in the fall of 1993, because the magazine was distributed free on campus. The article also continues to be circulated among gay students in the GLSA. Although no gay cases are currently being taught in the Second-Year elective Self-Assessment course, several of those we interviewed told us the course helped them clarify what kind of career would suit them as a gay professional.

Bill told us, "Some of my friends wondered why I wanted to take that touchy-feely course, but it was exactly what I needed. In my final paper, I wrote about being gay and how coming out to myself has been hard for me, and that the course really helped me through it. My life started rapidly changing after that point. I was feeling more comfortable with going out, not only to the bars but to the GLSA meetings, so I started meeting other gay people in my class. That was really important. It really helped, because I started to see that gay people weren't just perverts who hung out in back alleys." Bill ended up working for a mainstream company after graduation.

Other mid-90s grads said their involvement with the GLSA has also helped them gain the confidence to pursue mainstream careers. In addition to providing leadership by example, the GLSA instituted meetings with set discussion topics. Todd told us, "My impression is that for many years all the group did was drink and socialize. When I was a First Year, we wanted to do something in addition to having parties. A couple of us just took the bull by the horns and inaugurated what we called Section Q lunch meetings in the spring of 1993." He laughed. "When Ann Bilyew and I were elected club presidents our Second Year, we decided to continue that kind of leadership." We were told the meetings have proven very popular because they provide a formal way to share learning about being gay at the business school and at work.

Cassandra confirmed, "We don't have alcohol at the meetings. We have topics. Last week was coming out at HBS; this week is dating or having a relationship while at HBS. Having a special topic is great. There's a wealth of experience within the group that you really don't find out in conversations at bars."

The GLSA has recently undertaken another kind of political activism.

In 1994, the club wrote to the leading consulting firms and asked whether they had a written nondiscrimination policy and whether there were any openly gay partners or other consultants at their firms. The project was a success both in raising awareness and for networking, and the club plans to continue the letter-writing campaign to include other industries.

As a result of these various changes on campus, expectations are rising. Seivert told us, "I ended up being president of the GLSA—not so much because I'm a politically adept person, not so much it's something I really wanted to do, but because there was no one else in my class who would come out to the administration. I thought that was so weak. The administration are some of the easiest people to be out to! I also came out to my classmates by bringing Hal to the first black-tie dance, the European Club ball. Some people clearly figured it out, some people didn't, but it was not a problem either way. I formally introduced him in class around February or March, but by then they had all met him before. At the end of Second Year, my section had a big party. Everyone in the section showed up for a weekend at somebody's big house out in the country." Hal said, "Almost everyone was there in his section. People brought their spouses or partners, and Seivert brought me. it was obvious that we were together. And I was treated great. It wasn't condescending, like 'Oh, we're so glad you're here.' " Seivert reflected, "One guy was like that. This guy's so sincere you just want to puke. But he's that way with everybody. It wasn't just us. It's just, OK, we get the point; you're accepting. It's the 90s; it's not that big a deal that you're accepting."

In 1993–95, the gay student group had a column, "Out and About," in almost every issue of the paper, and most of the articles were signed. As important as administration and faculty support can be, the presence of openly gay students on campus has been an essential part of changing the atmosphere on campus from hostile to generally supportive. As individuals and groups of gay students continue to come out in class, in the *Harbus,* and in HBS publications, the atmosphere has changed dramatically in a short time. Samantha, who attended HBS in the mid-90s, told us, "It's interesting. The more open people are, the more respect they get. It seems to be the people who are more closeted who are the subject of the whispers and rumors. People love to talk about what they don't know."

CHANGING EXPECTATIONS Current HBS students were particularly interested in any workplace horror stories we uncovered, because their business-school experiences had generally been very positive. They were reassured that the most discriminatory incidents we found happened over ten years ago to people who were trying to be closeted. They were relieved to hear that people who chose to come out had almost universally positive experiences, because this confirmed their own experiences in business school. Although there are still a number of gay students who remain closeted, the success of the openly gay members of GLSA has inspired many to take the next step out of the closet.

Diane found that her exposure to openly gay students helped her cope with being gay at HBS. "After orientation I was opening my packet and saw the brochure Jonathan did." She laughed. "I was so paranoid I thought I was the only person to get it. So I closed it up and looked at it in my room. When I saw the notice for the club meeting in the *Harbus,* I decided to go, because it said bring partners. Anytime I can include my partner at HBS things, I want to do that." When we interviewed her, Diane was not sure that she wanted to come out to her classmates, although she admired those who did. "At one of our recent meetings, First Years and Second Years talked about coming out. A lot of the Second Years talked about how they weren't out, and then something occurred and they came out, and it was this big relief. They felt like they could finally be themselves. And a First Year, Torrence Boone, said, 'Well, I was out from day one, and it's really great. Because my boyfriend moved here from San Francisco with me, and it was a big commitment for him to do that. Now he is able to share my experience with me, because I brought him to the section parties and the schoolwide parties.' " By the end of her First Year Diane brought her partner to several section parties.

We also learned that Diane's experience was not uncommon. A number of those who were frightened and closeted have been inspired by their more open classmates. Some became open at HBS; others have begun to come out at work within a few months or a few years of exposure to these examples. One key to their increased willingness to be open is that no one feels pressure to come out more than they are comfortable with. Glenda said, "When I went to my first GLSA party, there were a couple of people there who were very open, who had told their whole section. That was so inspiring to me. I didn't feel any pressure at all. It was just awesome to have those choices. They really handled the issue very well. They made it very clear in all their documents and in what they said that this group is not focused on making everybody come out. They let us know they really respect where everybody's at. So I didn't feel any pressure to come out to everybody. But I was really impressed by some of the people who were so open. It was interesting to me that they handled it different ways. Ann Bilyew came out right at the beginning, and Ronnie Diaz didn't come out till the end of her second semester. So I didn't feel the pressure to make a big announcement in class right away. I can do what feels right to me."

Chris Hall, class of 1994, told us, "Five or six of us signed a letter in response to a homophobic letter someone wrote about the Roseanne Arnold lesbian kiss episode. Gay students had been writing a column all year, so it's actually kind of surprising there weren't any negative letters earlier. With that letter, everyone knows I'm gay. It's gone very well. There's a lot of people who congratulated me. I think by and large people our age are OK with it. The way the environment is now, no one's going to ever say anything negative to you. Networking is king, so it's not a confrontational environment. You never really know what people are thinking, but I think most people in our generation really don't care. Maybe there's that 10 or 20 or 30 percent or whatever it is that does. But they're not going to come up and say something to you and confront you with it."

While some might argue it is better for people who have negative opinions to express them, Chris does not agree. Rather, he reflects the changing expectation of gay professionals in their late twenties and early thirties. "Even in a job situation, I don't think anyone is going to be confrontational if you come out. They aren't going to say anything negative to you, and that's good, because who wants to work in a place where they do? I don't think you have to worry about losing your job if you're gay either. Anyway, if it is that kind of place, I don't think it's worth staying there. The great thing about being well educated—we have other options. You don't have to stay. Where I am interviewing, I think they are pretty open. There are 120 people there, and a good number of minorities and women. When they invited me to some social things, they never said, 'Bring your wife,' or, 'Do you have a spouse or a girlfriend?' They said, 'Do you have a partner?' They always used that language. I have talked to some other gay people who have worked there about how they perceive the environment, and they said, 'Fine.' It seems like it will be an OK place to come out. There'll be a period for six months to a year where I probably will hide it, I guess, just to build my credibility. And then there will probably be a period where I'll be increasingly open."

Ronnie Diaz and Ann Bilyew, who have been out and successful through their careers, agreed that women, ethnic minorities, and openly gay people will change the face of corporate America. Ann said, "Being out at business school has been great. In large corporations, I think it will eventually be fine too. Right now we're mostly seeing lip service; we're not seeing the rubber meet the road yet. But I think even the lip service is a big step. Now they just need to take that next step. It's very easy for the powers that be to say some of the things that are being said but not to act on them. We just need to get them to make that next jump. I think we will." Ronnie agreed, "It's happening already with respect to lower-level employees and managers. It's gonna happen at the higher levels too, and that's because more people are coming out. I learned an interesting lesson at business school. I'm completely open, and I get a lot of respect. Some of my classmates are trying to hide, and mutual friends tell me that they get talked about behind their back. It seems that doesn't happen much to me."

Torrence Boone, class of 1995, told us, "People in business respect someone who is willing to take risks. I have certainly found that to be the case at business school. A lot of my heterosexual classmates have gone out of their way to tell me how much they admire me for coming out, and I've gotten to know some of them really well because of it. Now that I've had a taste of how good it can be to be out, there's no way I'm going to be closeted at work after this!"

Many members of the class of 1996 have also been completely open since coming to campus and organized a sticker-wearing campaign for October 11, National Coming Out Day, that resulted in numerous students and faculty showing support for their gay friends and colleagues.

As those who have been open at business school continue to be open in the workplace, we expect others will follow their lead. In addition, for those who have been out all along, activism is natural. Both they and their peers are at the forefront of raised expectations for the treatment of gay people in business. In addition, as they continue to network with older gay colleagues, those above them are being increasingly challenged to help make changes. As a result of gay professionals living their lives at work openly and honestly, we expect that many of these changes will follow.

THE HBS GAY AND LESBIAN ALUMNI ORGANIZATION

Like the HBS GLSA, the HBS Gay and Lesbian Alumni Association (HBS GALA) began informally. Jon Zimman recalled, "In the early 80s there were no official HBS gay student-alumni parties; it was just a bunch of people getting together. The first gathering was in April of 1980, where about six students and thirty-five to forty-five alumni showed up. Jeff Eisberg set it up, and we tracked down the alumni by word of mouth. I think that is the one and only party that the author of *The Best Little Boy in the World* came to." [Andy Tobias has now publicly revealed that he wrote this book under the alias of John Reid.]

By the mid-80s, a formal steering committee was responsible for HBS GALA mailings and dues; in the late 80s a single president took over the reins of the organization. Today it has two copresidents, a membership of over one hundred, and a mailing list of over two hundred. This confidential mailing list contains the names of those who contact the organization, as well as those who become known to the club's leaders. Most often these are individuals they or their friends run into in gay bars or at gay events. In recent years, the HBS GLSA leaders have helped supplement the alumni mailing list with the names of gay students. Many of those who were active in the early years of HBS GLSA have also been the driving force behind HBS GALA. This group of alumni have always been closeted at work and have made confidentiality a priority for the alumni organization. Yet the group has also had an activist strain, and seeds are there for members to become more politically active.

For much of its history, the primary function of HBS GALA was to sponsor the spring alumni-student party. In many years, HBS GALA also marches behind its banner in the New York Gay Pride parade. Additionally, members of the group usually take a table at the New York and Boston Human Rights Campaign Fund dinners.

HBS GALA is also becoming more active in helping HBS gay alumni connect with one another. Recently the copresidents have sent more regular mailings to its members, including an update on club-member doings around the globe. These vignettes, supplied by the members themselves, follow the familiar format of HBS alumni Bulletin reports, listing the year and section of the member's class.

Although many we interviewed thought HBS GALA could be doing more to help alumni network, at least one told us he found a job by attending the annual party in New York. Wendell recalled, "I started my job search Second Year going through the names of HBS graduates on file at the Career Placement Office. I had the strategy of contacting the most senior person and the most junior person listed at each company I was interested in. I must have written one hundred to one hundred and fifty letters. Many of the people I wrote were very helpful. I reached one guy, Donny and he was also very friendly, although he said there probably wasn't anything at his company." Wendell laughed. "I decided to write him because of his address in the Village.

"So, that weekend, I came to New York for the HBS GALA alumni-student party. I was mostly socializing; I wasn't really focusing on trying to get a job. As I was leaving the party I noticed a list where people had signed in, and Donny's name was there. He had already left, so on Monday I called him and asked if he remembered me. He said yes, and I said, 'Well, I just wanted to let you know we were at the same party on Saturday night.' He said, 'What? What party?' I repeated, 'I was in New York and we were at the same party.' He named the address, and I confirmed it. He exclaimed, 'You were there?! I can't believe it! Well, the next time you're in town let's have a drink.' I was coming back to New York in a few days, so I went and had a drink. He again told me that there was very little chance that I could get a job at his company, but he would ask Human Resources if they would at least talk to me. I got the job, which was in Donny's area," Wendell concluded. "I think he was pretty influential in pulling for me behind the scenes."

Bart Rubenstein suggested there is quite a bit of networking occurring through HBS GALA. "I've faxed job descriptions to friends from the group and given headhunters names of people in it over the years. And through those people I've gotten some leads myself. So there's an awful lot of networking going on, if I think about it."

Personal Friendships Among Classmates

While most recent graduates of HBS are connected in some way with one or both HBS gay organizations, a significant number of those we interviewed are not. Alumni in their forties and older had no gay student organization when they were in school. Moreover, a good many came out to themselves only after graduation. Others, who were out to themselves when they were at HBS, admitted they stayed away from the group because they did not want to have classmates, even gay ones, know they were gay.

We were somewhat surprised to find that many of those we interviewed were not aware of the existence of HBS GALA. One reason is that the group is not listed in the bimonthly *HBS Bulletin,* where regional HBS alumni clubs are listed. Also, many gay HBS alumni have spent most of their careers outside of New York and Boston, where the HBS GALA leadership live and where all events take place.

Yet those we interviewed had other ways to find gay classmates and keep in touch. Some met by happenstance in gay bars or at gay community events. Others were put in touch with one another by mutual friends. Increasingly, gay alumni are also taking advantage of HBS-sponsored ways of networking. Some come out in the *HBS Bulletin,* much of which is composed of social and professional notes submitted by alumni to each section of every graduating class. The section class-notes representative has some leeway in the content and tone of these notes, and thus the column is also sometimes used to insinuate a section mate is gay. Jeremy told us, "The guy who wrote the class notes for our section for a long time is really bigoted. He has made quite a few comments at social functions, and he wrote about one of my classmates that he was one of the last ones in the group who was not married. To those reading between the lines—as you get into your thirties with men, either you're married or you're gay. We're all past thirty now, and Rupert isn't married. I know he's gay, but I doubt he wants the rest of the section to know."

Others have come out to classmates in the five-, ten-, or fifteen-year reunion books published by HBS before each class reunion. Each individual has a half page for a picture of themselves and their loved ones, as well as a synopsis of their personal and professional lives. Most of those we interviewed told us they read both publications avidly in the hopes of finding gay classmates previously unknown to them, and, increasingly, gay classmates have found one another as the result of such scrutiny. Jeff Baron, who graduated in 1979, said, "The five- and the ten-year reunion books for my class were all about careers, weddings, and babies—the external-status issues. By the fifteen-year mark, people's write-ups turn into real life. You see that in the class notes too. People write about what's going on with their marriages and kids; they talk about their health. Basically, they turn into real people. And when you talk to them, it's the same way. So you see a lot of people coming out in the fifteenth-year reunion book."

Jeff's theory was confirmed by several we interviewed, although more are coming out earlier to classmates. For example, several who graduated in the early 80s came out in their tenth-year reunion books. We expect that those from the 90s who were completely out at HBS will continue to be out in their fifth-year reunion books.

We found fewer networking ties among HBS lesbian graduates than among gay male alumni. One reason is that in most years there were only a handful of lesbian students in HBS GLSA, and lesbians who were not in GLSA largely remain unknown to GALA as well. We found a few lesbians who participated in the alumni organization as the result of meeting a gay male classmate after graduation but only one who joined as the result of knowing a lesbian classmate. Thus even after graduation, almost all lesbian networking stemmed from those who were in HBS GLSA or HBS GALA; none came from lesbians discovering other lesbians who were unknown to these organizations.

HBS GALA brought together a group of lesbians who graduated in the late 70s and early 80s, who threw well-attended parties in Manhattan in the early 80s. However, since those days there have been few occasions when large numbers of HBS lesbians gathered. As a result, we decided to organize a dinner in Cambridge in the fall of 1993 with local lesbian alumni and lesbian students at HBS. About twenty lesbians and their partners termed the event highly successful and looked forward to future get-togethers.

The authors also helped organize another HBS lesbian-bonding experience in the spring of 1994. A group of ten of us, including six HBS lesbians, a lesbian graduate of Harvard Law School, and assorted friends, went to Palm Springs for the Dinah Shore women's golf tournament and all the lesbian parties that surround that weekend. While we were there, we met another HBS lesbian, a lesbian from Harvard Medical School, a lesbian VP at a major retailer, a lesbian who is a highly successful Wall Street trader, and many other successful lesbian professionals.

In contrast to gay men, who have created many vacation gatherings for themselves, lesbians going en masse to Dinah Shore is only a recent development. Attendance has mushroomed from a few thousand women five years ago to fifteen to twenty thousand by the mid-90s. It has also become much more diverse in terms of age, ethnicity, and geographic origin, and is now a major party destination for lesbians around the country. All of our HBS lesbian friends agreed that it was a definite do-over, whether they were there for the golf, the networking, or to watch the bikini-clad beauties at the pool.

• • •

As in the world of business, organized groups of gay people seeking change from within are most effective when their members are out. Organized groups can also be an effective forum for gay professionals to find one another for personal support and career benefits. Students and administrators at HBS have effected numerous changes over the past few years and have significantly improved gay life on campus. As these young MBAs move into the workplace, they will not be content with unequal treatment of any kind.

Chapter 3

Discrimination Against Individuals at Work

Discrimination against gay people in the workplace can take many forms. In some cases, it is enshrined in corporate policy, as in the military, the Boy Scouts, or various right-wing religious organizations. More often discrimination takes the form of a hostile atmosphere, for example, where fag jokes are the norm. Discrimination can also take the form of diminished career opportunities for gay people—the subject those we interviewed were most deeply concerned about. And as many gay people are coming to realize, discrimination often exists in corporate benefits policies and company perks that do not apply to gay partners.

Discrimination can be pervasive throughout an organization or limited to a particular department. It may be rampant among upper management or manifest in a few isolated lower-level individuals. It may be directed generally against "those queers," or it may be targeted against a specific individual who is known to be or suspected of being gay. The first kind is what we call impersonal forms of discrimination—those that are not directed at any one gay individual. A lack of nondiscrimination policies, as well as certain types of behaviors, allow a hostile environment for gay employees to develop.

We also found a range of discrimination directed against individual gay people in business. In this chapter we discuss the forms of discrimination our interviewees encountered, the harm discrimination inflicts, the ways gay professionals react to it, and the changes it brought in their careers and work environments. We found that personal discrimination can have a broad range of impact, from career damaging to merely bothersome or irritating. Perhaps surprising, we found that those who attempted to be closeted suffered the most from discrimination against them. In contrast, those willing to be open were most able to effectively challenge both personal and general forms of discrimination.

A Problem of Definition

In our preliminary interviews we became aware that asking, "Have you ever been discriminated against at work based on your sexual orientation?" would elicit a large range of responses. All the gay professionals we initially interviewed took the question to include homophobic harassment directed at them personally. Most also described hostile work environments as discriminatory, citing examples in which they or others were subject to antigay jokes or comments.

In addition, many brought up what they termed subtle discrimination, like not being asked to join married couples for an evening of dinner and theater because coworkers believe they are single. Only a few mentioned formal corporate invitations to theater, dinners, retreats, or other gatherings that typically include spouses but exclude friends or significant others apart from spouses. None of those we interviewed in 1990 mentioned the lack of domestic partner benefits, which only a handful of employers had at that time. When we asked about it, most laughed at us, saying this form of discrimination was so entrenched they didn't see it changing anytime in the foreseeable future. (A few years later, in 1993 and 1994, the awareness of and reaction to systematic, formal kinds of discrimination was dramatically different. In our second and more comprehensive round of interviews, a number of gay professionals were quick to raise the domestic partner benefits issue and discuss how they hoped to end this form of inequality at work.)

Thus, as we formulated our questionnaire, we knew that inequality in benefits was endemic and that many workplaces tolerated antigay comments and jokes. Because we mistakenly believed that other researchers were covering this topic, documenting this truism wasn't our goal. Rather, we were interested in how individual gay professionals coped with discrimination and whether they felt their careers had been stalled by virtue of it. We also believed that each type of discrimination merited its own analysis, and we developed our questionnaire accordingly.

In the discrimination section of our survey we asked whether our respondents had personally experienced overt discrimination against them. As examples we included name calling, physical violence, threats, harassment, hostile jokes directed at them personally, being passed over for promotion, or being fired. Eighteen percent said they had, and another 16 percent said they were not sure. We had heard several anecdotal reports of an attempted blackmail incident, so we included a separate question on this topic and found that 12 percent said they had been blackmailed or threatened with blackmail regarding their sexual orientation.

To uncover more subtle forms of discrimination, we asked whether our survey respondents believed that their careers had ever been hurt because people at work knew or suspected they were gay. Thirty-seven percent said yes, and 21 percent said they did not know. We also asked how our respondents reacted when they heard antigay comments or jokes. We knew that almost none of our respondents had domestic partner benefits, so instead we asked whether our respondents had ever brought a member of the same sex to a business or social function sponsored by their employer. Thirty-four percent said they had.

From our survey data we had no way of telling when discriminatory events occurred or how serious were the repercussions on our respondents' careers. However, we were able to correlate the experience of overt and subtle discrimination with how out or closeted an individual was, both currently and in the past. As a general rule, the individuals who tried to be the most closeted and were the most worried about being outed felt they suffered the most discrimination.

In contrast, those who said that they were worried very little or not at all about the possible exposure of their sexual orientation and that most of their present heterosexual coworkers know, assume, or suspect that they are gay reported the least amount of discrimination. These individuals were also most likely to take advantage of the few corporate benefits for partners that were available at the time.

Taken aback by the apparent pervasiveness of blackmail and other overt discrimination, as well as its more subtle and general cousins, we set out to interview a number of those who had reported being discriminated against. What we found in our post-survey interviews in 1990 was more of a mixed picture. None of those who had been personally discriminated against were openly gay. Rather, we found repeatedly, it was closeted gay people who told us they suspected they were discriminated against because they didn't fit. Most of those who had written that they were passed over for promotion or were fired for being gay told us in the interviews that they saw the discrimination as ambiguous, because they didn't know if anyone actually knew they were gay.

In addition, a number whose survey responses led us to believe they were personally discriminated against or the victim of a blackmail attempt told us in the interviews that they meant only that their boss had told an antigay joke or that someone had tried to out them. Almost none who had detailed stories of attempted blackmail, outing, and other forms of harassment suffered short-term career damage, and none reported long-term harm.

Still unsure how pervasive or damaging personal discrimination was, we included questions about it in a second and more comprehensive round of interviews in 1993 and 1994. We found that this sort of discrimination is both less pervasive and less damaging than is commonly believed, at least among highly educated professionals. There is no doubt that discrimination, from the most personal and virulent to the most "benign" and general, is rampant in business today. Yet our evidence shows that while general discrimination is pervasive, the picture of personal discrimination is far less conclusive. Because almost all of those who felt they might have been discriminated against weren't out at work, it is difficult to substantiate their suspicions. While some might very well be discriminated against if they came out, it is also clear to us that others were stymied in their careers because they closed off ties with colleagues in an attempt to remain closeted. Lending credence to our analysis, many of those we interviewed raised this possibility themselves.

Some of the gay professionals we interviewed had heard horror stories from friends or read reports in the media about harassment or discrimination in the workplace. A number had heard homophobic comments or jokes from bosses or colleagues. These incidents served to frighten many away from coming out at work.

In addition, many of the instances of personal discrimination that gay professionals recounted happened years ago. While these stories continue to circulate among their friends, raising the level of fear about coming out, it is important to recognize that we found that no one who intentionally came out fully at work was discriminated against. Rather, it is those who sought to hide who were the victims of discrimination.

Finally, many of those who were faced with discriminatory circumstances refused to buckle under and quit. A number fought back, with highly positive results for their career. Others, who encountered short-term setbacks, told us that despite the personal turmoil, they suffered no lasting career damage. Rather, most of the costs of discrimination were to the companies that tolerated it. A few of those we interviewed pursued legal claims, based not on sexual orientation but on gender or race, that cost their companies hard dollars. Some changed jobs to find a more simpatico environment; this cost their companies time and money invested in seasoned managers. But most simply solved the problem themselves and went on working as dissatisfied employees for companies that don't even know what they've endured. There too the company suffers as much as, if not more than, the gay professional.

During the time these otherwise productive workers grappled with discrimination, no matter how minor, they paid less attention to company business. Even after the most pressing issue is resolved, the company continues to suffer losses. Though they have continued to rise through the ranks, these gay professionals told us, there is a bitter taste in their mouths. Although outwardly successful, they are more dissatisfied than their gay peers who have not faced discrimination. They feel less loyal to the company than they were before the discrimination occurred. This translates into a lower commitment to the job, including less team spirit, fewer hours worked, and more likelihood of jumping ship to a competitor. In the long term, most told us, they are planning their exit.

While the costs of discrimination may be most obvious when it is directed toward a specific individual, companies also bear costs for more general discrimination as well. Almost all of those we interviewed told us that they suffer from being closeted at work, and many said they would be more likely to come out if they knew their career would not be hurt. A number told us that despite their success at their present companies, they are looking for new jobs where they can be more open. A number of gay professionals also told us they resented not being able to include their partners on their health insurance plans. Further, we learned, companies without this benefit suffer a loss of managerial flexibility. Several highly placed executives mentioned that they were less willing to relocate because their partner would be without health insurance for a time in a new city before finding another job.

In contrast, those whose companies send a strong and consistent signal that discrimination in any form will not be tolerated told us that they are inclined to stay where they are and to be loyal and grateful employees. Even in the face of attractive offers from other companies, they say things are good where they work, and they expect to continue to be a team player. Several of those we interviewed told us that after feeling uncomfortable on the job, they saw their companies begin to take steps that signaled change. They also intend to stay on and see how fully the changes materialize.

This finding provides a note of hope for companies that have allowed discrimination in the past. Most gay professionals said it was not too late for their employers to change their ways. Companies can improve their external as well as internal image by adopting a nondiscrimination policy, establishing diversity training, supporting a gay employees group, granting domestic partner benefits, doing target marketing to gay people, and arranging philanthropic giving to gay groups. Most important, a clear message from the top that discrimination in any form will not be tolerated can help a company do a rapid about-face in just a few years.

The No-Discrimination Experience

Due to the discrepancy between our survey results and our 1990 interviews, as we continued to ask about discrimination in our interviews we framed the question as broadly as possible in an attempt to elicit even marginally relevant stories. For example, we asked Craig Ziskin, who is in his late thirties and works in telecommunications, "Have there ever been any instances when you felt you ran into discrimination or that other people in the company you knew were gay or suspected to be gay ran into any discrimination?" He replied, "No. None that I've been aware of." Frank, who is in his forties and works in computer software, racked his brain for a minute and came up with, "No, I don't think so." Jill, who is in her early thirties and works in manufacturing, told us, "I don't know of any. I just haven't been attuned to that."

Peter, who is in his forties and worked in the financial sector, told us, "I have never seen any overt antigay discrimination anyplace I worked. I didn't like working on Wall Street. It was too intense, too competitive, cutthroat; people were stabbing each other in the back. The politics were unbelievable. But I never saw anybody stab someone in the back because of gay rumors. The last time I heard people gossiping about that was probably back in college or something like that. I haven't heard any of that kind of stuff in years. People know better. It's not politically correct here to say anything. Just like you don't hear any anti-Semitic remarks, racist remarks. It's just not done, except in a very private conversation with two or three people joking about something. That's the only time I would ever hear anything. And then it would be a generalized joke, not a joke about a particular person."

Kenneth, who is in his mid-thirties and works in investment banking, told us, "Harassment I've never seen. Discrimination I've never seen. In fact, I argued with my friend this weekend. He said if I didn't think I had been discriminated against, I just haven't seen it." Kenneth added, "You know, intellectually it feels true to me, but if you ask people in the office, they would say that I had been the favorite child and been getting away with more than I should have—handoffs and favors and support. So to say that I've been discriminated against—nobody would buy it, you know, and I don't think it's true either."

Jon Zimman told us that when a previous employer starting laying people off, a receptionist started a rumor that if he was laid off he was going to sue based on discrimination because of sexual orientation. "When a gay subordinate asked me if that were true, I said, 'Absolutely not; tell the receptionist to knock off the bullshit.' "

Stan, who is in his forties, suggested, "The difference between us and people who are just squeaking by is, we don't have to put up with discrimination or abuse. Harvard Business School graduates might be in a better position to say, 'I'm not going to take it anymore.' Other types of middle managers might not have the mobility or the self-assurance to stand their ground." He reconsidered. "You know, I don't think it's just because I went to Harvard. It's because I've arranged my life in a way so that I will never be trapped by an employer financially. I will always be able to tell an employer, 'Hey, I don't need this. You're not a part of my life anymore.' And that's always been important to me to be able to do that."

Betty agreed. "If someone has a certain financial security, whether it's because they're from Harvard or they've arranged their life to have mobility, they're able to say, 'I'm not going to put up with this.' They are in a better position to say, 'I don't agree with this. That's not acceptable. I'm not going to tolerate it.' If they have a power base, they are in a better position. In the workplace, there's different ways to build your power bases, and how people do that is a personal decision. There's your age, your health, your financial situation—that all ties in to your comfort level."

There is no question that those we interviewed are exceptionally bright, skilled, and motivated. Throughout the various stages of their careers, they were flexible enough to leave a situation that might have turned into a dead end for them. Thus, although we found that the vast majority of those we interviewed have not personally been the victims of job discrimination, this should not be misunderstood. It does not mean that the business world generally does not discriminate against gay people. It also does not mean there is no need for antidiscrimination laws and policies. Rather, it highlights the importance of such measures. Many of those we interviewed worked in municipalities or companies that are bound by law or policy not to discriminate. In addition, the gay professionals in our study may have underreported personal discrimination against them for the following reasons:

- They may have minimized antigay discrimination they encountered, in comparison to more virulent discrimination they suffered as a member of a religious, racial, or ethnic minority or as a woman.
- They may have deliberately selected a company, industry, or job specialty known not to discriminate in the employment of gay people.
- They may have experienced subtle or ambiguous discrimination.
- They have no way of knowing why unfavorable decisions affecting their career were made.

Indeed, we heard far more examples of discrimination based on race or gender than on sexual orientation. Also, a number of those we interviewed told us they had intentionally sought employment in gay-friendly companies, industries, or professional specialties. Another group worked for themselves or primarily for or with other gay people. Other gay professionals were simply fortunate enough to be working in the right place at the right time and to have stumbled on companies run by open-minded heterosexuals. Thus their specific work environment, rather than the presence of a large number of liberal workplaces, may explain why their careers have not been harmed.

In addition, many of those in their forties and older were tightly closeted early in their careers. Thus the only discrimination they were likely to face was lack of fit for not being married. Recently, as gay professionals of all ages have come to be at least selectively open, many who work in large urban areas are protected by the nondiscrimination laws of their municipality. While the presence of such laws does not eradicate discrimination, at least it tends to make it less overt.

Whether personal discrimination against gay professionals is largely hidden or largely untested may be a source of some debate, but we feel it is primarily the latter. One encouraging finding comes from those we interviewed who work for America's largest and most prestigious companies and firms. Whether largely closeted or mostly open, the great majority told us that despite their fears they have not experienced personal discrimination at work. We are also optimistic about the changes that are happening in many workplaces. Some of those in their twenties and early thirties have chosen to be open with their employers from the beginning about being gay. If there were any conflicts or resistance, they could address these concerns up front. If these individuals later suffer harm to their careers, they will also be the most able to pinpoint how it is occurring and to combat it. Happily, we have not heard any cases where being openly gay has been a problem for them or their companies.

Hidden Discrimination?

It is also true, however, that a major reason gay professionals are not sure whether they have been victims of discriminatory practices in hiring or promotion is that they have no way of knowing what went on behind the scenes when decisions were made. If they fail to receive a job, a promotion, or a raise, they can never be sure it was because of their sexual orientation rather than their qualifications and performance—or their age, race, or gender. While openly gay professionals might also have this difficulty, this is most strongly a problem for those who are closeted. Without the issue of sexual orientation on the table, it is more difficult for them to be sure about the reason for their failure to rise.

Most cases of discrimination in hiring, promotion, and compensation leave no smoking gun. At the managerial level, gay professionals may wonder whether they are being treated differently from their peers, but they have no way of measuring the difference in their paycheck. Alternatively, they may know that they are being given diminished opportunities but cannot pinpoint the reason. Given possible legal consequences and shifting social attitudes, it is increasingly less likely that any company would acknowledge that an employee's sexual orientation had an influence on their performance evaluation. Those who are largely or completely closeted at work often felt they didn't fit in. But was it because they were perceived as hiding something or because they were gay? Was it because they were seen as a loner in a company where socializing was done in couples, or would they be excluded as part of an openly gay couple?

Those we interviewed told us of a number of instances of job discrimination based on sexual orientation that a court of law might not have recognized. They felt that discrimination occurred, whether or not there was an impact on their careers. In some cases this was based on "just a feeling." In others, a boss had made a specific comment about the importance of being married, but they could not tie their slowed career progression conclusively to this issue.

In most cases where gay professionals reported discrimination, it was not necessarily directed at them personally. Rather, it was the result of taking cues from offhand antigay comments made by management. Usually these remarks were not directed at anyone in particular, but nonetheless they created an atmosphere of homophobia that the gay professional took as a strong signal that he or she was not welcome at the company. In contrast to their reactions to similar remarks or jokes made by coworkers, few gay professionals had the courage to confront the boss. Most chose to leave the company rather than challenge the prevailing management attitudes.

Many were convinced that the real issue was that they were gay, although discrimination based on marital status or lack of children was the more obvious lack of fit. Janice said, "I live in the city; everyone else lives in the suburbs. Almost everyone in my department is married with kids, and I'm not. I guess it's more that we don't have much in common than homophobia per se, but I still suffer from it." When we asked her if she were to include her partner in company outings whether it would be better or worse, Janice admitted "I don't know."

As long as gay professionals are unwilling to come out at work they may be unable to show a direct cause-and-effect relationship between antigay discrimination and damage to their career. Thus they have no way to remedy the situation and little recourse to gain compensation for the damage it inflicts. Nonetheless, as we discuss in upcoming chapters, it is possible for closeted or semicloseted gay people to take a more proactive role in combating antigay attitudes and policies. By discussing gay issues at work, by coming out selectively to supportive managers, and by building alliances among open-minded coworkers, it is possible to lay the groundwork for coming out more broadly—or having a source of support if the threat of discrimination emerges.

Overt Personal Discrimination

This part of the chapter has the fewest stories in this book. In many cases we were able to discover only one example of discrimination or threatened discrimination per section. We have included virtually all of the examples we found in order to give the fullest possible picture of the kinds of discrimination that gay professionals we interviewed encountered. Surprisingly, while some of the threats came from homophobic heterosexuals, many came from other gay people—most often disgruntled ex-lovers. We have also detailed the often inspiring reactions of gay professionals who have been threatened with potentially career-damaging circumstances.

Those we surveyed experienced a variety of reactions to harassment or other discrimination around them, ranging from despair and anger to amusement and indifference. They also responded in a variety of ways. Some spoke up immediately and challenged the discrimination. Almost half sought redress from management, most successfully. Some simply ignored the whole situation. A few sued or handled the problem alone or with a coworker. Nine percent quit their job. All spoke ruefully of the pain and disappointment they felt when those they worked with and knew personally were hostile or abusive toward them or others.

Fear is the major enemy of gay professionals, we found. Those who summoned the courage to stand up to discrimination emerged with both their pride and their career intact. Thus, we believe, it is never too late to come out. Even after a discriminatory incident takes place, coming out may be a gay professional's best defense.

Violence

Ironically, the gay professionals we interviewed were more likely to have been physically attacked by their significant other than by a heterosexual. Unlike those in the military or the blue-collar macho professions like police or fire fighting, those we interviewed experienced no physical harm to their person from people at work. For most this wasn't even a serious fear. A few reported concern about damage to personal property, and one experienced this, as we will see in the next section. More feared sabotage to their work, as was dramatized in the movie *Philadelphia,* although none reported this happening to them.

Yet gay bashing on the street remains a real threat, which can have career ramifications. Jane, a heterosexual woman we interviewed, told us that her coworkers didn't know what to say when Anthony, a Harvard MBA in his mid-thirties, recently came to work with a black eye and a large bandage on his head. "He said that he had been mugged, but this story wasn't entirely convincing, because he admitted he had not filed a police report." She told us that when she questioned him privately, he admitted that he had been gay bashed by a group of young men. "He actually broke down in tears in his office," she told us. "I think part of it was he was so relieved that someone at work finally knew that he was gay."

Additionally, most educated white collar professionals have no reason to fear violence from their friends. But gay professionals may have particular reason to be wary. Bill, who is in his late twenties, encountered the specter of gay bashing when he came out to his HBS roommate. "The first thing he said was that his older brother and his friends would get drunk on weekends and take baseball bats and go out to hunt down faggots," Bill recalls. "I just kind of stared at him dumbfounded. Finally I asked, 'Well, what did you think of that?' " John said, 'Bill, he was my older brother, you know; I looked up to him. That's how I felt about it.' "

That night when Bill went to bed he locked the door because he was so afraid. "It was a really warm evening but I had on my sweats and covered myself with a blanket because I was shaking so much that I was freezing. I thought I was finished at school, my career, everything. Today, I know it's ridiculous to think that John would have done anything violent or even hurtful. But at the time I didn't know that."

Blackmail

Short of physical violence, blackmail is one of the most terrifying forms of harassment a gay professional can encounter. Above the threat to economic security, a blackmail threat is an assault to one's personal integrity. In the past, even when gay civilians were open with everyone about their sexual orientation, the government still perceived them to be a security risk and denied them jobs. Today it is those who are closeted who can be denied clearance. But old habits die hard on both sides, as those who work in sensitive industries told us.

Most companies working with the defense industry still do not have policies that protect their employees from discrimination based on their sexual orientation. And most in those industries remain afraid to come out at work. In the military, the government's policies continue to create the potential for blackmail.

Of course, not every gay person is equally vulnerable to blackmail or likely to be a victim of it. A number of factors seem to influence an individual's vulnerability. Among them is the career they choose. Some gay people deliberately avoid careers in specific conservative industries. They believe that by choosing careers where the rewards for blackmail are lower, they can avoid being targeted. Others choose industries with lots of gay people or companies that have policies opposing discrimination. In those situations there is less likelihood that a blackmail threat would have teeth.

Certainly, a company that fails to create a discrimination-free environment puts gay employees at risk for blackmail. And blackmail holds potential not only for personal loss to an individual but also for financial loss to the company. Thus, in failing to oppose discrimination, a company can unknowingly sabotage its own best efforts to optimize a productive and profitable business environment.

When we began our research project we wondered: How likely is it for a gay professional to encounter blackmail in the workplace? In years past, when both the nation and the workplace were even less tolerant of homosexuals, it seems that blackmail was a common fear. In today's relatively more tolerant climate, and with the increasing tendency for gay people to be open about their sexual orientation in the workplace, the opportunity for blackmail has decreased. Nonetheless, we anticipated that the high profile of many of the Harvard Business School alumni and the companies they work for might make them more susceptible blackmail targets.

Indeed, 12 percent of our survey respondents told us they had experienced blackmail or a blackmail threat during the course of their working careers. In our interviews, however, we found that some of those who said they had been victims of blackmail had in fact been harassed or outed, not blackmailed. While there were sometimes negative personal repercussions, there was no demand for money or other favors that characterizes blackmail. We did uncover at least one case of true attempted blackmail.

Fred Mann, a white executive in his late thirties, faced a difficult choice when he found himself being blackmailed by a dishonest vendor who had been cheating on a business contract. There was the potential loss of a prestigious and highly remunerative job if he refused to acquiesce. On the other hand, Fred reminded us, once you give in to blackmail, there really is no end in sight. The incident ended with unexpected results for the blackmailer when the tables were turned and his intended victim stood up to him. In addition, Fred survived this incident without any damage to his career. Fred chuckled. "You know, when you're gay, you're always prepared for somebody to confront you with it. But it really very, very rarely happens. Unfortunately, it happened to me." There was also an unexpected bonus—Fred discovered that his own willingness to come out at work was enhanced by the experience.

It is understandable that when a gay person feels vulnerable to the threat of blackmail, he or she wants to retreat more deeply into the closet. But Fred's story shows that the more someone is willing to be open about being gay, the easier it is for them to disarm the threat of blackmail.

Fred's Story

One of Fred's positions after Harvard Business School was with a large manufacturing company. He was not sure how management would handle his being gay, so he chose to keep his sexual orientation to himself. Fred recalled, "I don't think I ever had an outward appearance or mannerisms that bothered people in terms of my sexual orientation. Although I never tried to create stories to look straight, I also never volunteered any information about being gay to anybody."

Fred's career at corporate headquarters got off to a spectacular start. Dealing personally with customers and with company offices around the country, he found a way to save his employer $4–$5 million a year. After working two years in the corporate planning office in New York, he was rewarded with a promotion to senior manager and the job of heading up a subsidiary in the South. "It usually takes ten years to get that title, so it was a really big deal," he told us. Fred said that, shortly after arriving at the new position, he realized that while he could help the company become more profitable, it was not really a business the company should be in. "So I had been arguing from the day I was down there, 'Let's plan our exit from this business.' "

Partially for this reason, Fred found himself in conflict with "Bob," an outside contractor. In addition, shortly after Fred had arrived at the subsidiary, the company ran an audit on Bob. Because of the timing, "Bob got the distinct impression that I had been sent down there as a spy to get him." Bob, according to Fred, "was basically a scumbag. It was clear to me from the first meeting that this guy was not to be trusted."

Over a period of time, Fred learned about many of Bob's unethical business practices, one of which, Fred told us, Bob was ultimately indicted for. Fred explained, "If I had anything to do with it, he would have been gone on day one, but obviously it was out of my control. My division was corporate, and his contract came from another subsidiary. He thought that I was a threat to him, but I wasn't."

Not long after the audit, someone put sugar in Fred's gas tank, causing thousands of dollars' worth of damage to his car. Then Fred's house was broken into three times in one month. Once he found his car door open with a full gas can sitting on the ground next to it. "The gas had come from the garage—behind my house, across the street, and about four doors down from where my car was parked. So this was not coincidence. It was obvious that somebody went into my garage, took my gas can from my lawn mower, and put it by my car. They didn't want to torch the car; they just wanted to let me know that they could. Because it would have been very easily accomplished—another ten seconds and they could have poured the gas in the car and lit a match. That would have been no problem."

Fred suspected Bob was behind these incidents because Bob knew all of Fred's travel plans, and many of the people who worked for Bob were ex-convicts. This, according to Fred, "would have made it very easy for Bob to arrange such incidents." However, Fred had no conclusive evidence about who did these things, and when he talked to corporate headquarters, senior management refused to believe that Bob was behind the incidents. Fred laughed. "They preferred to think that I had gone out with some guy's wife or some crap like that."

One day Bob came to Fred's office. Fred explained, "I knew the minute he walked in my office that something was up because he never came to my office." Bob told Fred, "I just got a phone call from somebody who said that you'd been spreading rumors around that I was in the Mob." Fred laughed at this and said, "Bob, do you really think that I'd be stupid enough to say something like that?" Bob replied, "Well, I'm just telling you what somebody's told me. And I also heard that you're accusing me of putting the sugar in your gas tank." Fred told Bob this wasn't true. "No," he said, "I never did anything of the kind. It's just that whenever I told anybody what happened, they all asked me if I'd thought that you'd done it! Everybody knows you're a scumbag, including me. And I make no bones about it. But I didn't accuse you. I didn't have to."

Bob started to walk out of the office and then turned around, came back, and closed the door. At this point Fred realized, OK, now he's going to say what was really on his mind. "Well," Bob said, "what do you think if the New York office found out that you were queer and living with a Black man?"

Fred thought fast. He knew his whole future at the company might be at stake. He also knew what his life would be like if he ever gave in to blackmail over his sexual orientation. Fred decided there was only one reply he could make and keep his self-respect and peace of mind.

"Well, you're more than welcome to call them on my dime," Fred told Bob. "But frankly, I don't think they'd be shocked, first of all. And second, I don't think they would care, because I'm doing my job. So call them. But I would like to know how you're going to convince them that you aren't doing anything wrong and don't have anything to fear—yet you're having me followed. Because the only way you could be telling me this crap is if you're having me followed."

Bob never carried through with his threat. Fred explained, "I think that he had assumed that he had sufficiently scared me, and nothing ever came of it. At that time I never told anyone what happened, but I really meant what I said to him. I felt that I was professional enough and did my job well enough that the company would say, 'So what? That's really not an issue here.' I felt very confident. Now maybe I'm being naive and stupid there. I don't know, but that's the way I've always felt. And later I did come out to some people at corporate, and it wasn't a problem."

When we interviewed Fred, he was no longer with this company, but he was completely out to the entire staff in his office of roughly fifteen people. We asked him if he had always been so confident. He replied, "Yes, I think I have. I've always felt that if I did my job, then my sexual orientation wouldn't be an issue."

In our interviews we did not hear any other stories of attempted blackmail or giving in to threats of blackmail. In fact, we found, Fred's story has long been legendary among HBS gay alumni both for its singularity and his chutzpah in countering a blackmail threat. However, a few of those we interviewed were afraid that they too could be faced with blackmail. They said they would never give in, because it would mean living with shame, self-loathing, and a sense of profound despair about their work and their lives. But they were unsure whether they would be backed by the company they work for if they were forced to come out to preempt a blackmail attempt. Gay professionals reported that where they worked and who they worked with affected their confidence about standing up to potential blackmail threats.

Among those who felt the greatest fear about being blackmailed, one factor dominated all others: Discrimination creates a climate that encourages blackmail. Gay professionals who had heard senior managers make homophobic remarks or had seen them actively discriminate against other gay employees were especially afraid of being outed. Even some of those who had observed no such behavior in companies that had not taken tangible steps to preclude discrimination were worried. Thus they —and we—recommend that companies that want to keep this pernicious form of crime at bay can take steps to eradicate it. Adopting and enforcing a nondiscrimination policy that includes sexual orientation is an obvious first step.

Being Outed

Whether the motive is blackmail or simple harassment, those who are in the closet at work are subject to being outed. We were surprised that the motive for outing was simple homophobia in only a few cases. Rather, as with violence against gay professionals, the perpetrator of the outing was more likely to be someone gay. In some cases disgruntled ex-lovers did the outing. In others, gay activists who see outing as a political tool did the deed. A few of those we interviewed were outed inadvertently. Coming out in one forum, they found that others had information to out them more broadly. Interestingly enough, few of those who were outed, whether maliciously or inadvertently, suffered career damage. Even those who had a temporary setback at work say that they believe they incurred no long-term harm.

A few of those we interviewed have come out on television, on radio, or in published media but did not wish to be named in this book. One gay professional had not intended to be outed as part of a news story and did not want the incident recounted here. Another, a well-known public figure, came out to a room full of mainstream journalists and had his name reported in at least one gay newspaper. But his coming out has not been reported in any book or mainstream publication, nor was he willing to be quoted on the record in this one. (These last two individuals intend to write their own books on their experiences and gave that as the reason for not speaking on the record with us.) Another, Betty, intended to come out locally but not nationally. She found, however, that once you come out in the media, you cannot always control how out you become.

Betty's Story

Betty explained, "Lee Ann and I had a commitment ceremony a few years ago, and it was in the local papers. Well, somehow one of the sales managers I oversee in the South received a fax copy of the local newspaper article about our ceremony, which included a picture of our smiling faces."

Betty laughed, remembering how she found out about the incident. "Brian (a guy from another company who I work closely with) and I were at a press conference for the unveiling of a new project that both our companies were involved with. I had been out to Brian for some time, so as we were standing there melting in our suits in the hot sunshine, we began to tease each other. The camera crew was right in front of us and he began to ask me if I thought one of the female reporters was good looking. Now I know Brian is straight, but just to give him a bad time I asked him if he found the cameraman to be attractive. The question must have dislodged his memory, because he turned to me and said, 'Oh. I've been meaning to tell you, your sales manager called me up to ask me if I knew you very well. When I said I guess so, he asked, "Well, do you know anything about her personal life, living out there in California?" Brian responded, 'I know some things, yeah, like I know some things about everybody.' So the guy said, 'Well, so-and-so just faxed me this newspaper article—she got married to a *girl.*' So Brian told me he replied nonchalantly, 'Oh, yeah, that, yeah, I knew about that.' " Betty laughed again. "So I asked Brian what the sales manager's reaction was. He said, 'Herbert had no choice but to respond, "Well—oh, I don't have a problem with that. I just wanted to know if you knew about it." ' Eventually I learned that another colleague of mine had faxed to Herbert and said, 'You should know about this so you don't get surprised by it sometime. If we set the tone, it won't be a problem in the marketplace.' So, in hindsight, I think my colleague outed me with the best intentions, and there were no negative consequences to me or to the company."

Then Betty concluded, "You know, Brian and I travel together all the time. In fact, I learned that a lot of people thought we were having an affair, because we get along so well together. So in a way, I'm kind of relieved to have been outed, because I'd rather be known to be gay and stable than perceived as the industry slut."

A few of those we interviewed were thoughtlessly outed by a boss, colleague, or subordinate. They told us that no harm was meant and no harm was done. Oliver said, "When I joined the publishing company I came out to a few people who I worked with. But I was also outed by a couple of people who were my colleagues and subordinates. It reflected badly on them, because I was secure enough and willing to be open enough for it not to ruffle me. The way I found out was through a third party that they had made some casual comment to, like 'Oh by the way, Oliver's gay.' Now, it wasn't malicious, but it was still outing, and it was thoughtless."

Seth's Story

Seth also was the victim of outing when he worked at Time Inc. He reflected, "Although I'm not a big fan of outing, I think it was sort of a blessing in disguise. I still think it's the wrong thing to do. But in retrospect, it did take off a lot of the pressure of trying to be closeted." While Seth was there, he worked for his partner, Martin, who was dying of AIDS. Martin was openly gay at work, but Seth was not, and he did not want anyone to know about their relationship. But when Martin was rushed to the hospital, Seth took a couple days off from work to be with him. "Shortly thereafter, I learned that my direct boss, who was the second in command, outed me to some of my coworkers. She said something about why I had taken time off when Martin got sick and added, 'You know, Seth and Martin have something in common.' "

Seth related that his boss picked the wrong people to tell! "It turned out Jill was a lesbian, and Carl had gone to high school together with Martin and knew he was gay. You know, it was actually funny. The one woman she was speaking to was lesbian, and the guy had been hired by Martin and couldn't care less whether I was gay or not. But they really didn't feel that they should have been privileged to that information about me. They felt that my privacy was violated. So it really backfired for my boss, because they told me what she had done. And then a couple of other people also told me they had heard it from her.

"I reported her to the affirmative action committee and had her sent to management classes. When they gave me my options, they said you can file a formal complaint, you can file a complaint anonymously, you can have her sent to management classes anonymously, or you two can get together in a room and talk about this. There were a lot of different options. After Martin died, she was promoted to his position, but she's going nowhere. So my causing her any overt problems would just have added to her misery. But I figured it was worth it to have her 'stay after school' to become better educated. At least she would realize what she had done and the implications of it."

Seth said, "I'm not sure she was paying attention to the whole lesson though. When I got into Harvard, she took me out to lunch and asked, 'Are you excited about business school?' I told her, 'Yes, I'm excited, but also I'm a little concerned about really socializing.' She wondered, 'What do you mean?' When I told her I was referring to being gay at Harvard, she didn't want to get near that subject."

In contrast, Seth found that being openly gay at work was a plus with other coworkers. They could express their sympathy about his loss and also really get to know him. "You know, straight people say why do you have to bring being gay to work? But you know something? When straight people say, 'Mary and I went to the Catskills this weekend,' or 'Our little son, Johnny, is going to MIT,' and all that stuff, they're coming out about their sexual orientation to you. They don't realize that gay people aren't asking for anything special. We are just asking for equal time."

Being Outed by Ex-Lovers Several of those in our study were outed by malicious ex-lovers. Joanne told us that her boss called her late one night and asked her to meet him for an early breakfast. At the time she thought nothing of it and told her partner, Beth, that she could come home after the meeting before going in to work. She didn't end up having time to go home when she heard what her boss had to say. It turned out her ex-lover, Georgette, had called the boss in a fit of pique and outed her. Not caring for a minute that Joanne was gay, he was concerned that Georgette might be unstable enough to try another, more direct method of attempting to hurt her. Joanne told us that indeed Georgette was unbalanced, but she doubted that she posed any physical threat. Joanne revealed to us that for well over a year Georgette had managed to carry on simultaneous secret affairs with both Joanne and Beth. Joanne told us that when Georgette found that she was jilted by both women—for each other—it was more than she could bear. Despite their all working in the same small industry, Georgette was willing to damage her own reputation in order to retaliate. However, her tactics didn't work. Joanne emerged with an even stronger relationship with her boss. And Beth, who was motivated to come out at work because of this incident, has recently received a major promotion.

Whether or not they suffered a short-term setback, those we interviewed persevered in the long run. One factor that seemed to influence the short-term outcome was how the gay professional reacted to the threat. Those who ducked and ran for cover clearly had a worse time of it than those who acknowledged being gay with pride. The development of work relationships before the incident was another key factor. Those who had gained the support of a boss or key colleagues before the incident were the most able to put it behind them quickly.

Sexual Harassment

When the words "sexual harassment" are used, most think of heterosexual men harassing women. A few right-wingers think of gay men preying on innocent heterosexual men. Feminists and lawyers recognize that harassment includes an actionable offense on the part of those individuals, usually heterosexual men, who create a hostile environment in the workplace. But the reality of sexual harassment for many gay professionals is quite different from the stereotypes.

While our research did uncover a few cases of heterosexual men creating a hostile working environment for lesbian colleagues, none of the women regarded these men as anything more than an annoying nuisance. On the other hand, we found a number of cases where gay men turned their sexual attentions to subordinate gay men, and women who sexually pursued other women at work. In addition, we found that sexual banter is a common part of gay male culture, including in the workplace. A number of gay men we interviewed raised this issue as a problem they have specifically tried to avoid or change.

Two lesbians we interviewed were the target of hostile sexual harassment by men after coming out to colleagues. Another was harassed by a man with romantic intentions. Carrie, who runs a small high-tech startup, employs a cadre of young college students for part-time work. From time to time certain individuals fail to perform and have to be let go. Shortly after Carrie terminated Tim, the company began to receive obscenity-laden faxes. At first Carrie wrote them off as unimportant, but soon the faxes turned sexual and personal. One showed a woman labeled "Carrie" receiving oral sex from another woman. Another was addressed to another employee "from Carrie," and the picture depicted two women and a man in a three-way. After Carrie put a trace on the company fax line, the harassment stopped.

Looking back on the experience she says, "I'm glad I was already out to my secretary, who received the first fax. Otherwise I would have been pretty humiliated. I was a little concerned about whether this guy would try anything violent. We were never able to pin the faxes on Tim, although I'm sure he was the culprit. Anyway, he must have found another job, because we haven't had any trouble since."

Hope, who is in her late twenties, told us that coming out to her section at HBS seemed to have little to do with the hostile sexual harassment she encountered there. She said she and several other partnered women have been the targets of sexual harassment by a classmate whom she terms an "equal opportunity sleazebag." She said, "He's a married man with a little girl who is hitting on me and all these married women."

Kate's Story

Kate also had sexual-harassment problems before and after coming out at work. She was also pursued by a married man. But because she considers him a friend, she has not given him the clear message that his attentions are unwelcome. "We've always enjoyed each other's company. We get together every other month and go hiking for a day, and we send each other a lot of E-mail messages. We had gone hiking in Muir Woods back in October, and we had a wonderful hike. He brought me a bottle of wine; I brought the cheese. It was like going on a date. He's just a very affectionate person. He had always told me that if he weren't married, he'd want to date me. But I never took him that seriously."

Kate continued, "After I came out to myself and to him, he was in denial for a while, hoping that I would snap out of this. He just couldn't believe that I'm a lesbian, because he finds me very attractive. He told me that he doesn't think I'm really gay, because I have a lot of straight characteristics, and can be a very feminine and gentle, attractive person." She laughed.

"For a couple weeks afterward, every time I called, he was hoping that I would tell him that I changed my mind. I'm starting to realize he must have had some hope or some dream, maybe, that his marriage would dissolve one day soon and I'd be waiting for him." When we followed up with Kate several months later, this man was still sending her E-mail, hoping that she had reconsidered being gay, but she had stopped communicating with him.

Same-Gender Sexual Harassment As with opposite-gender sexual relations between colleagues, both parties may agree to be in a relationship and decide that by definition there is no sexual harassment involved in the sexual overtures of either party. But particularly when a boss-subordinate relationship is involved, both parties should exercise caution. In addition, as we learned, today's colleague can be tomorrow's boss or subordinate, so particular care should be taken with any workplace relationship. There are also dangers in getting sexually involved with people outside your company whom you have a business relationship with.

For anyone, gay or heterosexual, a sexual relationship at work opens the door to trouble. As a boss, one is open to the accusation of sexual harassment. As a subordinate, one may lose one's relationship and job at the same time. For closeted gay professionals, there is also the danger of being outed at the same time. Even a sexual affair with someone in the same industry poses danger, especially to a closeted gay person. There may be allegations of sharing secrets with a competitor. There is the risk of being outed, not only at work but to clients, suppliers, or vendors whom an ex-lover may know.

Those who are closeted are also at special risk when they are approached by someone at work. One woman we interviewed had been propositioned twice by female bosses. The first situation resulted in colleagues attempting to undermine her work; the second resulted in the loss of a mentor.

Trisha's Story

In one of her first positions out of college, Trisha told us, she was pursued by a married woman. "Before getting my MBA I worked for an investment bank, and I actually ended up living with my supervisor. She left her husband for me. That is, at first, she was my supervisor. As our careers developed, I was promoted over her. That was actually a pretty difficult thing in terms of the relationship dynamics."

Trisha also had problems at work. "During the divorce process, her coworker's husband would come in to work and start yelling and screaming at her in the middle of the day. Stuff like that. There were major scenes. Some of the people we worked with would go in and say bad things about her to my boss. One time he came to me and he asked me if she was doing drugs. He said that someone had told him that and that he had a responsibility to find out if that was the case. I said no, and that was the end of that. But it made me think that someone had probably told him they had suspicions about our relationship too.

"My boss was a great guy. He always dealt with their issues; people would go into his office who I knew were really pissed off at me, and they would come out looking chagrined. I would never have to interact with them about it."

Trisha acknowledged that the fact she was in a workplace relationship also contributed to her problems. "It made it harder for me to do my job."

Later in her career, Trisha had another putatively heterosexual woman come on to her. "When I was just starting my career, having my supervisor interested in me in this way was a big thrill. Now having my supervisor interested in me in that way is a real drag. It's just like sexual harassment from a male. It's really a problem. A big difference between that case and this case was that then I did it, and now I wouldn't even consider it. But I wouldn't report it either, because the legal system and the society is so screwed against me that I could never win. Secondly, I'm not sure why I would want to do that. It's easier just to stop working with her and segue into working with other people. But it's an extremely important problem in my life right now. In this situation, I second-guess myself all the time about whether it's really happening. The first time, the ambiguity wasn't as great, because we became lovers." Trisha added, "If I weren't doing well, it would be a bigger problem. If I didn't have other people that I could go to who can mentor me, it would be a big problem."

Another woman we interviewed told us of a much more clear case of sexual harassment by a woman she worked with but asked us not to report the story in detail. Another had sex with a partner in her firm, but we were unable to ascertain whether there were any negative repercussions. In addition, as we have attended various workplace conferences, other lesbian professionals have told us of being sexually harassed by other women. One lesbian told us of an incident that included an element of stalking.

Perhaps surprisingly, we found that sexual harassment was less of a problem for gay men in our study—only a few had been approached for sex by another man at work and none felt sexually harassed.

Sexual Harassment at HBS Most of the gay men we interviewed had never had sex with someone from work or even in their same line of business. However, we did hear a particularly egregious set of stories about one professor who taught at the Harvard Business School in the early 80s. This individual, whom we will call Professor X, abused his authority in many ways, including having affairs with his students.

Another professor from the mid-80s, whom we will call Professor Y, also used the Harvard Business School campus as his personal playground. Many of those who were in relationships with Professor Y had bad experiences with him and "went straight" afterward. One who remained gay also had a shockingly bad experience. Xavier and several other classmates told us Professor Y was openly gay and attended the gay student organization, where he became friends with Dominic, one of his students. The professor-student relationship became an affair, but soon another student caught Professor Y's eye. The night before the final exam, Professor Y told Dominic it was over. Dominic's response is now legendary among his peers. He was so distraught that he didn't write a word in his exam book except "If you flunk me, I'm going to tell everybody about our relationship."

Their relationship did become known among the other gay students. In fact, another gay student, Rory, who knew about Dominic's relationship with Professor Y, was in the professor's office for a meeting. Sticking out from under a cushion in the couch was a jockstrap, which he presumed to belong to his friend Dominic but may in fact have belonged to another student.

Not all gay Harvard Business School professors take advantage of their position, of course. In fact, a number of students mentioned several who were wonderful human beings and great role models. For example, the current advisor to HBS GLSA was cited for being equally friendly with lesbian and gay male students. He was also mentioned as being a real inspiration for many students in their coming-out process. Another, now no longer at the business school, who had been the target of student homophobia one year, was cited for his courage in coming out to a group of students on the first day of class the following term. This preventative action forestalled any further problems and also served as a model of courage for many students. A lesbian faculty member has also been an important figure in ensuring that gay issues are not overlooked in the curriculum.

Like these professors, many of those we interviewed were highly conscious of the need to maintain a strict separation between work and sexual play. Roberta Lasley admitted that when she was CFO of NutriSystem there were lots of nubile young women who might have been willing to give her a tumble. "After I'd give a speech at our sales meetings, all these women would applaud and come up afterward saying, 'I'd like to get to know you.' I'd break out in a sweat." She laughed. "Some of them were probably lesbians, others . . . It's not about gay or straight. It's about power. People are willing to kiss up to whoever has it. This one with green eyes from Virginia—I'll tell you—wow! But I was never really tempted. If any guy had ever put a finger on any of those women, he would have been fired in a minute. I don't care who it was. So I had a shield up, because I thought it was unethical. It's that simple."

Thus far we have examined the most overt forms of discrimination against gay professionals: violence, blackmail, and being outed. They have largely been revealed as paper tigers. Sexual harassment, while a major problem, seems most pernicious when directed against closeted individuals by those of their own gender. In the upcoming section we will focus on the other forms of personal discrimination gay professionals can encounter from colleagues and bosses—the forms it takes, the consequences for those who suffer from it, and how some highly successful gay men and women have coped with it.

PERSONAL DISCRIMINATION BY COLLEAGUES

Closeted gay professionals we interviewed observed or endured the following forms of discrimination by peers or subordinates: harassment directed at an individual; anti-gay comments or jokes directed at an individual; ostracism, exclusion, or avoidance; threats to the individual's reputation; and two-faced behavior by colleagues.

None of those we interviewed were victimized by antigay comments or jokes directed to them personally, although one gay man reported being the target of a phone call by a woman who he didn't know who came on to him; he believes colleagues put her up to it because they suspected he was gay.

But many had heard general homophobic remarks or had seen harassment directed at an openly gay colleague. Some of those who admitted they have a difficult time addressing general homophobic remarks told us they find it easy to assert themselves in defense of others. This was the case for Richard Stern, who told us about an incident that occurred when he was first coming out in the 1970s. Though he had been unable to respond to an earlier incident of harassment directed against himself, he found himself coming to the defense of a gay colleague, Pat, when a business associate made a homophobic comment against Pat. By personalizing the situation for the associate who made the remark, Richard helped the offender, who was himself a member of a minority group, to realize how offensive the comment was. This ultimately led to a change in his colleague's behavior.

One afternoon Pat, who was known to be gay, was walking down the hall ahead of Richard and Josh, a heterosexual associate, both of whom were Jewish. Suddenly Richard's colleague shouted down the hall, "Pat's queer." Richard was seriously disturbed by the incident.

After seeking the advice of a gay friend, Richard called Josh, who had made the offending comment, into his office and confronted him. "People who are gay don't like to be called queer," Richard told the man. Then he underscored it with a parallel that put his point across. "It's as bad as someone calling you or me a kike." That hit his Jewish colleague very hard. The man apologized and promised never to make a homophobic remark again.

Over the years Richard's work environment has changed, and most of those who have made homophobic comments or jokes have left. Yet Richard, like many others we interviewed, maintains a vivid memory of how powerless he felt in the face of such overt homophobia. He was also proud of his success at defusing such a difficult situation long before gay people had any protection from discrimination at work. Having encountered success, he was on his way to being more comfortable in his workplace environment.

Alan Miles also successfully came to the defense of a single-parent lesbian colleague without coming out himself, by pointing out that he couldn't think of anyone in the office who would be a better parent than she. But some who had heard similar remarks were less brave. They took such comments, even from subordinates, as a warning to stay closeted. As a result they felt unwelcome at work. In such cases, it seemed to us, their fear was out of proportion to the power dynamics of the situation. But as we heard, the habit of the closet and its attendant fear can be hard to overcome.

Ostracism is another form of harassment that homophobic colleagues can use to send gay professionals the very strong signal that their presence in the workplace is not wanted. When coworkers refuse to speak or work with them except on the most minimal level, the effect can be crushing. Many psychological studies have been done showing the damaging impact of isolation on individuals; and it is no coincidence that in the U.S. military academies, ostracism is considered the harshest punishment, reserved for those who have broken the honor code. Although we found gay professionals who resisted personalized antigay jokes or comments as well as discrimination by management, none cared to remain or fight when their own colleagues refused to talk to them.

Fortunately, our research uncovered only one case of ostracism. This happened to a lesbian professional who was inadvertently outed in the mid-1970s, early in her career, and she decided it would be better to leave the company as soon as possible. She has since gone on to a satisfying career elsewhere. Others who were outed found sympathetic coworkers rather than hostile ones. And despite the fears of many, we found no instances of ostracism among those who came out voluntarily. We also did not find intentional exclusion or individual avoidance of openly gay professionals. On the contrary, those who chose to come out almost always found that their relationships with work colleagues became closer. In other cases the relationships were unchanged.

We also found few incidents of ostracism's second cousin, exclusion of those suspected of being gay. While closeted gay professionals felt they were overlooked in some areas of workplace socializing, they attributed this to being unmarried. Many of those who told us they were excluded because of being suspected to be gay said the exclusion went both ways —on the assumption of different interests, gay professionals opted out of socializing with heterosexual peers as much as, if not more than, they were excluded from such interactions. Almost all of those who were openly gay reported a higher degree of inclusion since coming out; others reported no change.

We found that those who are selectively out may encounter some avoidance once the office gossip mill gets underway. However, we believe this is due less to homophobia than to social awkwardness. For example, after Becca came out to a few colleagues, trouble emerged. "I told one friend, and it turns out to have been the right friend to have told. It was a nonissue to her. But the second person I told, the only other person I told there, promptly told a whole mess of other people. I felt a change in other people's attitudes toward me after that.

"I don't know how many thousands of times I felt a change in someone's attitude. What gets to me about this whole thing is that you can understand why they changed their attitude about you," she said. "Because it's such an important thing, that for them to not have known it, means you weren't really nearly as good friends as both of you thought you were. So in some ways the fact that they're arrested by it is absolutely appropriate. But the fact that they don't stop being arrested by it is really disturbing." Becca saw this as evidence of homophobia. But we believe a less discriminatory motive is equally plausible: Because she was outed but not affirmatively out to these friends, they did not feel comfortable discussing the issue with her.

Thus our research disclosed a silver lining. Gay professionals themselves may be able to exert tremendous influence on whether homophobia drives the behavior of their colleagues. If someone encounters difficulty with bosses or colleagues as the result of being outed, the actions of the gay individual can play a significant role in affecting whether discrimination results. Those who challenged discrimination or ignorance were tremendously successful, we found. Additionally, the extent to which a newly outed gay individual is included or avoided by colleagues is influenced by the attitudes held by influential people in a company, both colleagues and bosses. The gay professional who addresses gay issues head-on can significantly influence those leaders and, in turn, the rest of the company. Thus the more a gay person has the self-confidence to object to homophobia, the more likely they will find acceptance, not rejection, from colleagues.

Management too has a role to play—before such problems develop. When management takes a strong public stand against discrimination, we found, employees are less likely to harass, ostracize, or avoid gay professionals.

Perhaps surprising, we found very little evidence of undermining work or reputation. Those who were openly gay told us they were not aware of any colleagues attempting to undermine them. However, a few closeted gay people described minor insults directed toward an openly gay colleague that reaffirmed their intention to remain closeted. In the few incidents we uncovered, it seems that no career damage resulted.

In sum, those who responded to homophobic comments by coming out were often pleasantly surprised. Having a colleague challenge them in this way usually led heterosexuals to rethink their hurtful behavior. Those who made general comments about opposing prejudice also felt good about themselves but reported they were less successful in changing hearts and minds.

PERSONAL DISCRIMINATION BY EMPLOYERS

Although gay professionals fear discrimination by coworkers, they are far more concerned about discrimination by owners or management. Antigay bias in hiring and promotion strikes directly at an individual's basic ability to maintain themselves and their loved ones, as well as their ability to advance and fulfill themselves through the work they have chosen. In locations where there are no laws protecting individuals from job discrimination on the basis of sexual orientation, discrimination by management is particularly terrifying.

Discrimination in Hiring

Some told us they didn't get certain jobs or promotions because they weren't married. When we asked whether being open about their gay relationship might have produced better results, they laughed derisively. Yet we believe that in many cases the issue of "lack of fit" can be challenged by openly gay professionals. Even some of those companies cited in this book for discrimination against closeted professionals have now begun to hire and promote openly gay professionals.

Other instances of discrimination are far less ambiguous. For example, some companies made their aversion to hiring gay employees obvious on the preemployment questionnaire. In the early 1980s at Harvard Business School, one of Tim's courses focused on the hiring and screening process used by a major telecommunications firm. The course materials included the company's preemployment screening questionnaire. Among the questions prospective employees were asked was "Do you ever feel attracted to, want to kiss, hold hands, or have sex with a person of the same sex?" Today this company has a nondiscrimination policy that includes sexual orientation, and the case has been dropped from the curriculum. But as recently as a few years ago, Dayton Hudson, a major discount retail chain, asked a similar question in screening prospective employees. After litigation, this company has also dropped the question from its application. But it is not always clear if the attitudes toward gay employees at previously discriminatory companies have changed.

In our interviews we found several well-substantiated examples of antigay bias in hiring—more than we found in any other phase of the work process. We also found many who suspected discrimination.

Marvin, who is in his late thirties, says he may have lost some jobs because of the perception that he is gay. "One time a friend told me, 'The person who interviewed you told me they thought you were gay right when you walked in the door, and I'm sure that's why you didn't get the offer.' " However, Marvin isn't convinced the discrimination actually occurred. "I don't know this person could know from just me walking in, other than I don't have a wedding ring on." But if he was discriminated against, he remains sanguine. "If that's the way that person felt, there's nothing I can do about it. And I certainly wouldn't want to work there. You know, one person can't change the world except the little world they're in, and that's only when they're already in it." After an experience with an overtly homophobic employer, Marvin sought a position with a firm that would be more comfortable whether he comes out or not.

Watson, who is in his forties, told us that when he worked for Bristol-Meyers many years ago, he was told they did a background check. "I don't know what they checked. I guess maybe they hired a private investigator. But my job offer was held up for quite a while after they had already made an offer verbally. I do remember it taking a long time, and the headhunter kept saying, 'Just be patient. They're doing your background check and they take longer than other companies.' So I don't know if they finally got anything out of the background check. And I have since had the occasion to hire a PI over a business lawsuit, so I'm acutely aware of how much information these guys can dig up. If you really want to know, you can find out just about anything you want. What you see in the movies or TV *is* true. So I don't know how extensive or expensive a company's background check on a prospective employee would be, but it was very consistent with the atmosphere there.

"There was a military attitude there that I found very uncomfortable, just in the way the company operated. It was very straight, especially compared to the advertising agencies. And it's funny, I have a gay friend who's still married. He is now at Bristol. He took a job change just about six months ago, and he also remembers it taking an unusually long while before they extended his offer in writing to him. He's still very much in the closet, so I don't imagine they would have picked much up. But in my case, I don't know. I had some gay friends at the time, but I hadn't gotten involved with any gay organizations yet." Despite the lengthy background check, Watson did get the job.

Delores also told us she believes large *Fortune* 500 companies keep dossiers on top managers' sexual orientation. "To this day I don't know what the official files in my previous company say. And I don't know what the official files in my current corporation said when I applied for this new job. I think they keep track of that sort of thing at my level. I'm not talking literally about a piece of paper. But I mean something more than a rumor mill. Something in between." Delores says, "Now that I'm coming out more and more at work and in the gay community, I think there are certain jobs that will be closed to me. But I've gotten comfortable with being as out as I am. I don't think I'd want to go back to hiding, even if they would hire me."

Two of the most blatant stories of antigay bias in hiring we encountered had positive endings; both job candidates ended up being hired and suffering no adverse career impact. Camille was maliciously outed by a former colleague before she went into a job interview, she later discovered. But, she said, that didn't stop her from getting an offer. Now affirmatively out, she says she's enjoyed a very good working relationship with her new boss and colleagues. She has received a number of promotions and expects to continue to rise at her company, where she is openly and comfortably gay. Aaron also had aspersions cast on his sexual orientation during the hiring process. While not as open as Camille, he too is thriving at his new job.

Aaron's Story

After working several years for a major consulting firm, Aaron, who is in his mid-thirties, sought a position with a large, diversified company. Two friends of his from the consulting company where he worked for many years were at the firm—Leo, a previous boss who was moving to another division and told him about the job opening, and Susan, a woman whom he had seen at a mixed (gay and heterosexual) party. "So I knew she'd be cool, and my ex-boss said he thought I'd be perfect for the position. So I figured that the job would be a very good situation.

"When I went there to interview, they put me though literally ten different interviews the first day. In a couple of interviews, I got some very weird questions." Despite his blue-chip background with a major consulting firm and a major consumer-goods company, Aaron admitted, "I'm insecure when I go through job interviews, because I just don't know how to answer those kind of uncomfortable questions, and I'm afraid they're going to come up. They usually don't. But in this case they did, and this was before my city had a nondiscrimination law. For example, a senior human resources manager really blew me away by asking me why I was not married and why I live where I live. At the time I had just sold my condo in the suburbs and had moved to a neighborhood where many gay people live. So I told him that. I said, 'One of the reasons I'm leaving consulting is because I have no social life due to traveling all the time.'

"I knew those questions were irregular, but I didn't think much of it. Toward the end of the day, just before I went back in to see Susan again, Leo called me in. He said, 'Aaron, I need to tell you something that has come up in the interviews. Susan got some feedback about you . . . And the feedback is everyone thinks you could do a good job, but a couple people are concerned about fit.'

"So I asked him what that meant. And he said, 'Well they used the word "feminine."' I said, 'What?' I was kind of taken aback, because I don't think I come off like that at all. Leo said, 'Well, I just needed to give you that feedback, and that's what Susan is dealing with right now.' So I said, 'OK, thanks very much for telling me.'"

We began to laugh during the interview, because Aaron was anything but feminine. His square jaw, athletic build, and deep voice fit the American conventions of masculinity to a T. He told us he never thought he came across as effeminate either, so he knew the real issue was the gay one. He continued, "Next I went back in to Susan, knowing exactly what was on her mind. When she asked me how I thought the day went, I said I think it went pretty well. And I asked her how she thought it went. She hemmed and hawed and said, 'I . . . I think it went well.' So I said, 'Hmm, it sounds like there's an issue. What could that issue be?' knowing full well what the issue was, but I wanted to hear it from her.

"She said, 'Well, OK, I'll tell you. You interviewed with ten people. All ten think you can do the job and all ten think you're incredibly smart and very well qualified, but two of them have brought up an issue . . . I have to tell you the word "feminine" was used.' And I said. 'OK. Well, gee, if my being feminine is a problem, I'm gay. Is that going to be a problem?'

"Of course she said it was completely cool with her. She also advised me she didn't really think it's an issue at the company, because they've treated her very well as a woman. And she thought being gay was kind of similar in terms of not being the same as all the rest of the managers.

"So I asked her who brought the issue up, and she told me. One was the HR manager, which just blows me away. You know, of all people . . . And the other one was a senior executive who'd had Susan's job before she had it. As I later understood, he was just so threatened by her he would do whatever he could do to lash out at her. But anyway, at the end of this day she also told me, 'You know you might face this wherever you go in corporate America, and at least you know exactly from what corners it's coming in this company, and so maybe that's a better opportunity for you.'"

Aaron continued, "You're not going to believe this, but at this point I started to cry, because I was so frustrated. I almost couldn't believe this was happening to me. I mean, at this point I was an engagement manager in consulting. I had been a brand manager of a major consumer products company. I had a Harvard MBA with distinction. I mean, my résumé was impeccable. And here I was, sitting here crying. I said, 'I cannot believe that this is the issue I'm facing.' I said, 'Susan, you know full well I could do this job and do it perfectly. I cannot believe that's being thrown in my face. It's just—it's simply not fair. It's such blatant discrimination.' I said, 'I deserve a shot at it. It's never been an issue anywhere I've worked, and I've gotten promoted.' She empathized and said she agreed it was horrible and she couldn't believe these people brought it up either. She was completely supportive. I mean, it's not every day that someone breaks down in tears in your office.

"So, at the end of it, she said 'go home and think about it.' I had to come back the next day to meet with the executive vice president, who was her boss, and he was the last person, the eleventh person, I had to meet. He did not want to hire me because I was coming from consulting and he thought there were too many former consultants already at the company. So Susan had already told me he was predisposed not to hire me because of that.

"I found out later Susan told him the feedback of all the managers. She reported that they all agreed I could do the job, and all but two wanted me to be hired. The other two argued, 'He's going to have enough baggage coming from corporate when he goes out in the field. Isn't it an added impediment that he has this other baggage of being gay?' When I interviewed with the final decision maker, he gave me a standard case interview, you know, where he presents a problem and you tell him how you would solve it.

"Well, I had just come out of four years of giving those kind of interviews myself at the consulting firm. So naturally, I just blew it away. I didn't know anything about the subject, and I told him that, but I explained how I'd analyze it. It probably wasn't a brilliant answer, but it was excellent compared to what other people had done. When I finished he was really impressed. Before I made it downstairs to meet back with Susan, he had already called her and said, 'Do whatever it takes to hire him; I will personally watch over his career to make sure that other thing is not an issue.'

"Aside from that horrible incident, there was enough good stuff about the company that made me want to take the job," Aaron explained. "It was an exciting company; it was an exciting business; and that's where I decided to go forward. In fact, everything's been fine ever since. Soon after getting there I really did some phenomenal work for them. I did a portfolio analysis on all their businesses, which I presented at a board meeting. Believe it or not, no one had ever done that for them before.

After the meeting, the chairman of the board came up to me and said, 'I want you to know that in all of my years of being on the board, this is the best board meeting I've ever attended.'

"At the time, Susan's boss came into my office and said, 'I want you to know you hit a complete home run today with a phenomenal analysis. It was just exactly what the company needed to hear. Blah, blah, blah, blah, blah.' We never had a very good working relationship, mostly because, I think, of his relationship with Susan, who was my boss. And on two other occasions, I did hear him make blatant homophobic, antigay remarks to other people.

"Once I was standing around the corner when I heard him say something about 'this fag' in this picture. I remember looking around the corner and seeing the other executive's face just kind of blanch, as if he just looked at this guy and thought, 'I can't believe you just said that. You're such an idiot. You're such an asshole.' I think a lot of people felt that way about him. So despite him kissing up to me, I know he is a bigoted person, and he's still at the company.

"I think I've established a good reputation at the company. I've gotten promoted since then, and I'm about to get promoted again. So I think I've moved beyond where he could hurt me. But he controls a third of the company. If I want to stay with the company, at some point I'd have to work for him and I'm sure he would try to slap me down.

"I'm convinced that even though he recognizes I'm a very strong player and a smart person for the company, he is bigoted enough that he would cut off his nose to spite his face.

"I mean, nobody at the top of a company makes those kinds of statements repeatedly, especially now that our city has a nondiscrimination law. I actually think making such publicly visible statements that are so blatantly wrong has torpedoed his career a little. Well, a lot of the things he's been doing have torpedoed his career a little bit. He was on the track to be one of the next chairmen of the board, and he's clearly been derailed from that.

"For the first two years, I almost left this company because of him. I had an entrepreneurial offer from this guy I used to work with at the consulting firm who I came out to, and at that time this guy was in the running for board chairman. I just wanted to go to the current chairman and say, 'Listen, I'm leaving the company. I have loved everything I've done. But the reason I'm leaving is because this guy is such a bigot and he's in such a powerful position in the company. It affects the whole company, because other straight people have seen him be a bigot, and I've been in conversations where he has carried on with his bigoted remarks. I appreciated the other straight people's reaction that they've been appalled when he says this kind of stuff. But they don't do anything about it because he's still in this position of power.'

"Eventually I decided to stay, and I'm going to be running a division myself now. But the way this guy behaves is still wrong. If he's going to be chairman of the board, I'll squawk bloody murder.

"The funny thing about the human resources manager is, he's my biggest fan now. In my second year there they had to go to the board to get a special dispensation for my bonus, because the company had done poorly that year and they were giving everybody small bonuses, and they wanted to be able to give me a large one. He helped me get that. Now, when I look back on it, he's such a fan of mine, I can't believe that there has been this huge turnaround. I'm sure it's not because he's embraced homosexuality as a viable lifestyle alternative. I think he just really respects my work because I've done phenomenally well there. While I don't think he is completely comfortable with me being gay, he isn't like he used to be either. He sees I can do the job, and that's affected his thinking."

Discrimination in Advancement

While some gay professionals reported willingness to put up with homophobic coworkers, most who felt management was homophobic saw an unavoidable threat to their future advancement. A number who saw their advancement blocked eventually quit and sought positions where being gay would not be an issue. This leaves the company to face the subsequent loss of a productive, caring employee, not to mention tens if not hundreds of thousands of dollars' worth of training, job skills, and job knowledge.

Some of those who quit went into business for themselves. Others found work in gay-owned or gay-sympathetic businesses. Many were careful to screen companies and joined them only after meeting management and prospective coworkers to minimize the possibility of repeating their previous encounters with discrimination in the workplace.

Almost every case of stifled advancement was about the question of fit, not explicitly about being gay. Some see these as interchangeable, but we believe that corporate culture can change as senior gay people begin to come out, whether selectively or completely. For example, McKinsey is one of the country's oldest, largest, and most prestigious consulting firms. Many gay HBS alumni have worked there at some point in their careers, and most told us that they felt their career was stymied because they were gay. Pointing to the profile of McKinsey partners—married, often more than once—they said being gay meant not fitting in. In addition, several reported hearing antigay jokes or comments from top management there. Many of those we interviewed left McKinsey or are planning their exit for these reasons.

Yet in our interviews we also discovered an extensive gay network at

McKinsey, which includes a number of very senior gay professionals, including partners. These individuals are not necessarily openly gay outside the firm but are well known to the up-and-coming gay professionals there. As a result, in some offices at least, corporate culture has begun to change. Barry Salzman was openly gay for a time while he worked at McKinsey after business school. He left not as the result of seeing closed doors ahead but to pursue a highly lucrative opportunity with a private investment firm. Alan Miles, who is currently an associate there, has been openly gay since he was hired and has alerted the personnel department that he is happy to talk to anyone who asks about being gay in the firm. We hope that as more gay people come out there, the climate will continue to improve, as it has in other companies we learned about.

Discrimination in Compensation

Because so few gay people are out of the closet, it is difficult to quantify their achievements versus that of others at their companies. In addition, those who are closeted and experience discrimination are never sure of the reason. Is it because they are gay, or has the issue of fit raised its head again?

Debby's Story

Although she was closeted when she worked at a major consulting firm before going to business school, Debby is sure she was discriminated against for being a lesbian. She says there was also an element of sexism involved, as in the case of the married woman at Price Waterhouse who won her partnership lawsuit about not wearing enough makeup or being charming enough.

Debby told us, "In consulting, performance evaluations are extremely subjective, because you're evaluated on the quality of your relationship with your clients. In my first review, I got the top performance evaluation, minus a little bit. And it cost me a couple of thousand dollars a year in salary. When I asked what for, I was told, 'Well you know, it's a lifestyle thing. It's hard to articulate. It's got nothing to do with the quality of your work.' "

Debby marvels, "I asked the guy who was reviewing me to actually write that down on a piece of paper and sign his name to it, which he did. And I asked him what specifically about my lifestyle he would change if he were me. There was one performance evaluator who told me to wear more makeup. When I complained they switched me to a new performance evaluator."

When we wondered whether sexism, rather than antigay bias, was the problem, Debby rebutted. "It's possible. But one of the senior managers took me aside and pointed out that all the partners at the firm were married." She continued, "I hated my job there. My work was OK, and I did OK there. In fact, retroactively they changed my ratings so that they were the highest. I think it's because they're afraid of a lawsuit or that I might be in a position to influence people's job decisions someday. I'm on leave right now, but I would take a job at Kmart before I went back to them. When you're slime dealing with clients, the fact that you're slime in dealing with your employees is not surprising."

Debby reflected, "There's a guy there who is in a very powerful position who is gay. He is not a partner, although he has been with the firm long enough to have made partner. But his career track is not for partnership. He's off-line—he doesn't do client work. And he is very, very clearly set up as the role model for gay associates."

Lance, who also worked for this firm, confirmed that the higher you go there, the more being unmarried is a problem. "I was on the partnership track for many years, but it's harder to be closeted the longer you are there and the older you get. It seemed my career prospects would be better if I left, which is what I did."

While neither is currently out at work, both Debby and Lance have chosen industries where they believe being gay is less of an issue. They told us that the decision to change industries had not necessarily hurt their careers long-term, a pattern we found repeatedly among those who said they experienced discrimination on the job. But given the tremendous income of successful consultants, they acknowledged, it will be difficult to match the earnings of their former colleagues in the short-term.

Termination

None of those we interviewed said they were fired for being gay, although the issue of fit came up at least once with respect to being fired. And we did find one likely instance of discrimination in the termination process itself, over a decade ago, when Watson left a major corporate employer. "They usually bent over backwards to get you out with as little pain and suffering as possible. I knew some people there who had been let go a year earlier and still had office space in the building and secretarial support and that sort of thing. Even for a junior weenie like myself, the usual arrangement, as I recall, was three months of time to work yourself out of there. In my case they offered me a month. At the end of the month, I asked for additional time and was given another two weeks. I think it's because they knew I was gay, which they could have found out from my after-hours copy-machine jams, which left behind photocopies with stuff about the Gay Men's Chorus."

NOT FITTING IN

Over a third of those in our survey group told us they believed their career had suffered because of their sexual orientation. Initially we were very concerned by this finding. But upon closer examination we found cause for hope. First, we were surprised to notice a high correlation between a desire to be closeted and overt personal discrimination. While we could not determine cause and effect from these statistics, the finding gave us pause for thought. Were gay professionals closeted in response to being discriminated against, or were they discriminated against because they were trying to be closeted?

In our interviews, we found, none who were 100 percent openly gay reported overt personal antigay discrimination. Surprisingly, the experience of this kind of discrimination was also highly unusual even among those who were completely closeted. Since we interviewed a number of those who reported overt personal discrimination in their surveys, what accounts for the disparity? Many of those we interviewed referred to homophobic jokes or comments, which created a hostile atmosphere. Thus they believed that surely their careers must have suffered in the face of such an environment. Even if they had only vague suspicions of personal discrimination, they checked "yes" on their survey forms. Others referred to being excluded from social networks that contribute indirectly to career success. Yet in interviews, almost all of those who were closeted agreed that they excluded themselves as much as, if not more than, they were excluded by others.

Julie told us, "If my partner and I were a married couple, we'd have social invitations coming out of our ears. But instead we know almost no one in town." Her partner provided some perspective. "Yeah, but if you came out and let them know you were in a relationship, I think we'd be invited to more things. And you're out to a number of people with no negative repercussions, so I don't think you're afraid to come out more. But when I suggest coming out to certain other people, you claim you don't want to, because then you'd have to waste time going to dinner parties. You can't have it both ways. Crying, 'Poor me, I'm a victim,' without giving them a chance to treat you equally doesn't really hold any weight."

Whether faced with the most pernicious case of overt homophobia or the most ambiguous case of failing to fit in, gay professionals must decide how to respond to discrimination in their work environment. Some we interviewed chose to ignore it; others chose to confront it head-on. Some chose to try to address it indirectly; others were going through painful soul-searching about how to react. Which approach gay professionals took depended on several factors. Most important was how comfortable they were with being openly gay at work. Usually a nondiscrimination policy was necessary but not sufficient for this feeling of comfort. Other considerations included whether they were out of the closet to friends and family, what type of professional support system they had developed, how well they were doing at work, and what type of company, industry, or city they were employed in.

In our interviews only a few told us they believed their careers had been hurt specifically because owners, managers, coworkers, clients, or others suspected that they were gay. Many felt their careers were not hurt despite their experience of antigay discrimination or lack of fit. But gay professionals in both groups often opted to seek new employment opportunities, usually in gay or gay-friendly environments. Whether or not these individuals felt that their ultimate career progress was damaged, the dislocation they suffered should not be minimized. Some were unemployed for a time; others had to move to a different part of the country; all endured significant internal turmoil during the period of change.

Those who said they weren't certain whether or not they had been the victims of discrimination based on their sexual orientation tended to feel somewhat dissatisfied with their career progress. But short of coming out, they saw no way to rectify the situation. If they were not willing to risk doing that, they were not in a position to formulate a decisive strategy to improve their work environment.

Perhaps ironically, those who knew they were being discriminated against for being gay were best able to confront and resolve whatever problems they faced. This may suggest that those who suspect they are being discriminated against should push the issue by coming out.

Fit and the Closet

Those who were closeted found most of their problems with being gay at work mostly stemmed from a lack of fit. Most who said they had problems of fit at their companies acknowledged there is a difference between being gay and being unmarried. However, some who were closeted insisted the two were virtually the same in terms of their impact on fit. For example, Jo worked for a company that was very trendy and socially driven. "Even though I was brought in as a thinker, it was really, who did you know, did you have a house in Capri, did you know where to stay in Hong Kong? Or did you do this, do that? What really mattered was who did you hang out with and did you go to all these kinds of parties and fund-raisers and that sort of thing. Which I was not prepared to do, because I hate that sort of thing. Also I had no connections. It was all nouveau riche and Eurotrash.

"I began to feel very quickly like this was a big mistake, that it wasn't enough for me to do my technical marketing job; what they really needed was someone who was a social PR butterfly. It was not me. And I began to feel that there was no way I could cut it. And I think my silence about what I did in my life began to really hurt me. I think that they may have figured out that I was gay. They thought there was just something weird about me, because I wasn't participating in things that they all wanted to do. It's what happens when you're silent.

"If you're silent and nobody cares, fine; then nobody cares. If you're silent and people care, then you're a weirdo. I knew all the dirt in their lives, even though I never talked about mine. I don't know if they really knew that I was gay, but I think they just felt like 'She's not one of us.' So I got fired."

Curtis told us about another HBS graduate who is a friend of his and works in retail. "He did retail before business school and did it afterwards, so he has a lot of experience, and he's at the buying level now. He's been a buyer for two years now. And he has a straight colleague without an MBA who joined his company who was a buyer for about a year and a half at another retailer before he came into this company. He went into the stores for about eight months, and now he's a division manager. They have comparable retail experience, but the straight guy is married; he has the wife. I don't know if this is in fact playing in. I don't know for sure, but I am starting to wonder. So now my friend is starting to think: Either I'm promoted within the next year or I'm going to leave. Because his business is good, he's extremely enthusiastic about retail. So if anyone would be a senior manager, you would think it would be him."

Curtis said that his friend is not out at work but he thinks others suspect he is gay. "I think it really takes someone pushing senior management to make that commitment. It has to be something that's decided at the top and then forced down on the organization. I mean, it's the same thing with me as being Black. I feel as if there are two ceilings that I confront. I have to find a company that's friendly to someone who's Black and also friendly to someone who's gay. And it's only the companies where the senior managers make the decision that this is a priority where that happens."

Holly said, "It's so easy in corporate America to find reasons to not promote or to fire people. I don't know offhand of any cases that are so clear-cut. But I think if you're not married and you're in a company where you're expected to socialize with other people, and you're not socializing with other people and you're keeping to yourself, that creates a distance. People like to spend time with people that they feel comfortable with. So you're in a company, as I was, where that whole family thing and socializing or partying together was very important; that's going to have an impact. People are going to start wondering and questioning and just seeing difference. That's one of the main reasons I left." She was pessimistic about whether coming out would be a good strategy to bridge the distance. "My advice would be to find a different company. Learn as much as you can there, but be looking for other companies to go to, because long-term it is not going to work."

The Lavender Ceiling

Many of those we interviewed, whether openly gay or closeted at work, were afraid of a lavender ceiling at their company. "I'm not sure I'd reach the inner circle of managing directors if I came out," Kenneth told us. Victor also "wants to avoid politics" by not coming out until he becomes an officer of his corporation. Until more openly gay managers come up through the ranks, the question of the lavender ceiling will remain unanswered.

For those who are openly gay and on the way up, the most pressing issue is how far the company will go to back up openly gay managers. Many gay professionals told us they were not very concerned about their company's internal reaction to their being gay. Rather, they were skeptical about how their bosses would view the capabilities of a gay manager in the marketplace—whether or not they intended to come out to clients, suppliers, or vendors.

Many of those we interviewed in large firms said their boss or company was not homophobic, and they had come out internally with great success. Fewer had taken the step of coming out to clients or other important contacts outside the firm. Even some of those who had done so successfully were afraid to tell their bosses that they had done so. They feared they would not be treated equally with respect to assignments outside the firm if they were seen as a loose cannon.

Ironically, having a track record of success with coming out to clients may be their best defense. Cindy, who works for a small company, told us her boss said to her openly, "I don't have a problem with you being gay. I know you're gay and always have. However, if I had a customer who said they had a problem with you, I'd have a problem with you." Cindy pointed out to her boss that being gay hadn't been an issue with any clients so far. She added, "He's Jewish, so I asked him, 'If I were a Jewish man and I wore a yarmulke and was working in the South and some customers said they had a problem with Jewish people, what would you do?' He said, 'I'd assign him to another client.'" Cindy rebutted, "What if that was our only client or your only employee?" Her boss responded, "I'd put him in a position where he's not dealing with clients."

Cindy expressed her concern that in those positions such a person would never become the president. Her boss retorted, "Then that's the answer."

Cindy was upset at the time but gave us a Cheshire smile. "I'm still working there and getting promoted. And the fact is, my boss hasn't hired anyone else who has a chance of replacing me. I'm in the middle of negotiating a key deal right now, and there is no one else in the world, including him, who could step up to the plate to close in the necessary time frame. So the truth is, I'm not all that worried. We have unique product, and if the customer wants it, they will deal with me to get it. I understand my boss's concern about getting business done, and I've got a damn good track record. The simple reality is that I'm the only one who can do what I'm doing right now. So he's making a kind of empty threat."

Cindy also told us she was taking the precaution of coming out to more suppliers, vendors, and clients to protect her position. "If my boss ever brings up the issue again, I'll be able to point to people in the industry who know I'm gay and haven't had any problem with it." Cindy also intends to do some educating. "He's made some other comments that are sexist, and I'll catch him on it and we'll discuss it. In fact, he is one of my biggest supporters out in the field. He'll introduce me as the decision maker to ensure that no one tries to go around me to get to him. As a result, men who were initially skeptical of my ability are some of my best customers. I think he could do the same thing on the gay issue if necessary."

While gay professionals who work for large firms may feel more replaceable, they can also build a track record by coming out successfully to colleagues, subordinates, and clients. Of course, they are more likely to feel comfortable doing this if their boss gives them explicit permission to do so and if the company policy is to stand behind their employees in the face of discrimination on any grounds.

BEYOND DISCRIMINATION

From a young age we begin to recognize that the world can be a cruel place to live. Bullies on the playground pick on anyone different from them or weak enough to be picked on—the fat kids, the skinny kids, the sissies, and the "four-eyes." But not all of them take it. The ones who fight back either alone or unified with their friends usually send the bullies packing.

In the workplace, gay people who confront their harassers head-on or with the help of their colleagues minimize the harassment. Being out of the closet also foils the potential of blackmail and allows the gay person to discover and develop sources of support. If a gay person is closeted and prefers to stay that way, a clear strategy of dealing with harassment is a necessity. Role playing and disaster planning are useful techniques in anticipating reactions to gay jokes, derogatory comments, prying questions, and even threats of blackmail.

Most gay professionals we interviewed told us that even having one ally they are out to at work can be a tremendous source of support. If harassment should occur, the ally can give advice, test the waters with upper management or the human resource department, and personally stand up in defense of their gay colleague.

Managers who truly wish to meet the needs of their employees while fully utilizing their talents and skills must recognize that an environment where harassment or other discrimination can occur fulfills neither goal. If employees spend their time worrying about roadblocks to effective performance or to their career, they cannot also be productive. To a significant degree, management has the power to set the precedent for acceptable forms of behavior. This can be done by personal action, company polices, and employee training programs. If discrimination against gay employees is to be eliminated in the workplace, everyone in the workplace needs to work to prevent it before it occurs.

• • •

In contrast to the existing literature, media coverage, and research available when we began, we found optimism where others had painted a very dismal forecast. Discrimination based on sexual orientation does occur in the workplace, but not in the epidemic proportions that we and those we interviewed have been led to fear.

No one should conclude that the relatively few examples of personal discrimination against gay professionals that we found means it is not a problem in the American workplace. On the contrary, discrimination in the form of a hostile atmosphere, corporate cowardice, and unequal benefits is rampant. This contributes to the climate of fear that keeps many in the closet.

Until more gay professionals come out at work, the prevalence of discrimination against individuals will remain largely unknown so long as no one wants to be the test case at his or her company. Fortunately, in many cases, gay professionals can take action to ensure that they will not be discriminated against, whether they choose to come out or remain closeted.

Few victims of discrimination that we interviewed simply ducked their tails and accepted injustice. Whether they faced blackmail, exposure, sexual harassment, or diminishment of their contributions to their employers, many stood up and fought. Contrary to their fears, this did not end their careers. The brave individuals who refused to be blackmailed or to deny being gay when they were outed earned not only their own self-respect but the respect of their employers as well.

Others, who felt the situation was beyond their power to rectify, left, taking with them valuable skills and contacts. In short, the companies that put an end to discrimination retained valuable and loyal employees; those that took no action often lost an employee and are stuck with environments that discourage diversity and continue to discriminate.

For business managers, this chapter should paint a picture of loss and the promise of gain. Companies that implement nondiscrimination policies and send other signals that they treat all equally have a role to play as well in helping gay professionals be free of fear at work.

For gay professionals, we hope this chapter offers a note of hope. The fact remains—we found very little evidence of discrimination against individual gay professionals. Most individuals who were discriminated against objected to it and succeeded in changing their work environment. As gay professionals' fears about discrimination are more realistically focused, they can learn to position themselves in order to be less vulnerable.

But the problem most faced was an amorphous lack of fit. We acknowledge that the fear of the lavender ceiling looms large for many. But on the basis of our interviews we believe that offense is the best defense. A well-developed plan for managing one's gay identity at work is far more likely to reap lasting rewards than the defensive posture of the closet. This does not necessarily mean coming out to everyone all the time. But it means having a plan and implementing it, rather than being caught off guard when trouble comes calling.

Chapter 4

Overcoming Impersonal Discrimination at Work

Even when individual gay people are not singled out for discrimination, companies can discriminate against gay people in general. One common form of impersonal discrimination is a hostile and unwelcoming environment. The gay individual is not the only one to bear the cost of such discrimination. Companies too suffer—from lower morale, higher turnover, and decreased loyalty.

In places where homophobic jokes or comments go unchecked, other forms of discrimination (against racial minorities or women, for example) are also likely to take root. In contrast, companies that are consistent in stamping out discrimination on every front are the most likely to have loyal employees. They are also the most likely to tap into profitable opportunities in a diversity of markets.

There are some organizations where discrimination against gay people has been institutionalized, such as the military, where the internal rules govern and justify discrimination against gay service members. There are also some corporate environments where the unwritten rules of conduct, the social norms, and the advancement criteria discriminate. Some institutionalized homophobia is blatant; some is less obvious. Most impersonal discrimination surfaces in jokes and antigay comments that create a hostile working environment. Today, racist and sexist jokes are widely known to be off-limits. However, homophobic jokes are often the last type of oppressive humor to be tolerated.

Times are changing, though. More and more gay people are gathering the courage to object to homophobia. They are no longer willing to sit silently and listen to antigay jokes or witness a gay colleague be ridiculed. They are also becoming more likely to object to unequal treatment of other kinds. A proliferation of gay and lesbian newspapers and magazines, as well as coverage in the mainstream press, has brought the news that many companies have implemented nondiscrimination policies and domestic partnership benefits and recognize gay employee groups within their organizations. Along with this, gay professionals' expectations have risen. In addition to objecting to overt homophobia, they are pressing for benefits their heterosexual peers take for granted.

As gay people object to antigay jokes, bring their same-sex dates and partners to company-sponsored social functions, and lobby management for domestic partner benefits, businesses find themselves in the midst of social change. Today being gay is not just whispered about. It is increasingly discussed in both the boardroom and the lunchroom. Through education, either as a part of diversity training or on a one-to-one basis, gay employees are letting it be known they object to any kind of discrimination against them. Companies too are setting new rules. Diversity-training programs increasingly include gay issues, and heterosexual executives are increasingly providing leadership in opposing discrimination of all kinds in their workplace. Some are acting out of a new awareness of gay friends, family, or work colleagues; for others this new approach is taken with an eye to the bottom line. For many companies, treating gay employees equally and reaching out to the gay community in marketing and philanthropy just make good business sense.

Discrimination as Corporate Policy

Over the years, some companies have been quite blatant in their disregard for gay employees, customers, or organizational members. Marvin worked in one such environment. Once he realized the pervasive nature of the discrimination there, he said, he bided his time and saved his money until he could get out. "Today, if I got an incredible job offer at a place that I knew was ultraconservative or homophobic, I would not accept that job, whereas five years ago, I might have, because I wouldn't have understood what homophobia in the workplace really means. Now I do; it takes a tremendous toll on you personally."

Marvin offered a strategy for surviving in that sort of environment—look for a job elsewhere. "If you work someplace that you didn't know was homophobic, but it turns out to be, you should plan to leave. Once you figure out that you need to move on, you still need good referrals.

So you build alliances with people who you know are going to be supportive of you. You try not to burn any bridges. Then, when you leave, you have allies who can give you a referral.

"I think that's a good strategy in any company. Because no matter where you are, you should try to hook up with people who are similar to you or most sympathetic to who you are. So if you can't find someone else who's gay, you find someone who's a woman or who's Jewish or who's Black or whatever. I think it's even more necessary when you're an island in an ocean of hatred."

Military Discrimination

A large number of people who attend the Harvard Business School come from the military. Thus we had the opportunity to discuss the special challenges of being gay in the military workplace. Employment discrimination in the military has continued unabated and has even increased over the years. Service members face the ever-present fear of being expelled or even court-martialed. This threat is especially potent for lesbians. Despite national attention to the issue of gay men in the showers, historically women in the service are investigated and terminated for being gay much more frequently than men, as we found in our own study. Ronnie Diaz was investigated three times in the 1980s, although she was never found "guilty" of being gay. Even with the new Clinton policy, gay service members continue to be drummed out.

Sinclair, who left the service a few years ago, posited that military specialties requiring a high level of education continue to attract gay people and more open-minded heterosexuals. After completing his ROTC obligations, Sinclair was assigned to an area which required a "Q" security clearance. "I never heard an antigay comment the entire time I was there. But a couple of people were discharged so quickly it made your head spin. One of them was a woman who was obviously gay, and I'm quite sure the man who was dismissed was gay too." Sinclair felt that lifting the ban on gay service members would result in very little day-to-day change in the military other than removing the fear that gay officers and recruits still have, despite "Don't ask, don't tell, don't pursue."

"People who are attracted to the military are similar to those who work for large corporations. They just want to do their job and get promoted. It's not like the barracks are going to be filled with sex—at least not any more than they are now. And it's unlikely that a gay man who wants to succeed in the military will be outrageously flamboyant or effeminate."

Donald was one of the few gay professionals we interviewed who had a number of gay friends while he was in the service. Most of the others remained tightly closeted; some didn't even acknowledge to themselves that they were gay. Kate told us the atmosphere when she served was so hostile it set back her coming-out process by many years. "As a woman, the choices were to be a virgin, a slut, or a dyke. I chose virgin. It was only after I got to business school that I found lesbians who I could identify with."

Amelia, who was not aware of being gay when she was at West Point, later found out that most of her closest friends from the military academy were lesbians. Most have left the service despite being top-notch officers. "The military itself admits that lesbians are some of their finest performers. But even with the new Clinton policy, highly qualified, fully trained contributors are being let go. It's an outrageous waste of taxpayer money and a detriment to military preparedness," she said.

"I was part of the trial of a woman who was being court-martialed for being a lesbian. I knew I was gay by then, so I had a real hard time with it. Had I been older and a little bit wiser, I think I could have swayed the group. I tried my damnedest. This was a star soldier. She must have had ten or fifteen people come in to speak for her, from colonel down to her people she served with. She was at the top of her unit. They all came in to support her. Everybody. But in the military the rule is, Don't say you are, you don't write you are, and you don't get caught doing anything by anybody. They can't throw you out unless you do one of those things. But they had intimidated her into signing a confession. They couldn't have done her in if she hadn't signed a confession. Once I learned that, I passed on that information to other, younger lesbians I got to know."

Before the Clinton administration changed the regulations, civilians who worked for defense industry employers could also be discriminated against. Gay professionals who worked for military contractors like General Dynamics and TRW had to be investigated and interrogated to receive security clearances. One gay professional we know was recently denied clearance but hopes this decision will be reversed under the new regulations. Others left the industry in order to continue to rise in their careers. While their careers were not damaged, their companies and the U.S. military lost out.

Corporate Homophobia

Outside the military, several other employers have gone to the mat over their right to discriminate against gay people. Companies in areas without nondiscrimination protections, like the Cracker Barrel restaurant chain, are free to discriminate by firing gay workers. Organizations run by religious institutions are also free to discriminate in most jurisdictions, and a number of them do so openly. In addition, the Boy Scouts have repeatedly gone to court to defend their right to discriminate against gay volunteers. Even gay people working for the Scouts for pay in areas with nondiscrimination-in-employment protection may have no protection.

Gay executives for the Scouts who otherwise believe in the Scouting mission have told us "Don't ask, don't tell" is their watchword for survival.

Companies with pernicious ad campaigns foster another sort of discriminatory environment. When the General Motors Company released a video sales tool that derided other companies for their little "faggot" trucks, no self-respecting gay person could have felt comfortable working in that environment. In fact, we know that a gay executive approved the ad campaign despite his own feelings of self-loathing.

Media entities that make homophobic movies or write homophobic articles exemplify another type of corporate homophobia. Jon Zimman told us he was glad to see the Fire Island Pines gay men's community covered by *Time* magazine in the early 80s. But the title of the piece, "Where the Boys Are," incurred his ire. "I didn't like being called a boy. So I wrote an anonymous in-house memo saying the headline was derogatory. I pointed out they wouldn't run an article called 'Where the Niggers Are.' There wasn't much reaction, but at least I did something." Those who work for other media giants have also become activists, both directly and indirectly. Some of those we interviewed go to bat internally, arguing it is important not to offend their gay consumers, readers, TV watchers, and moviegoers. Others feed leaks to gay media groups, such as the Gay and Lesbian Alliance Against Defamation, which monitors pending advertising, film, and television projects in an attempt to encourage unbiased portrayal of gay people.

TOLERATING A HOSTILE ATMOSPHERE

Outside the military and some "family values" companies, few businesses enshrine discrimination in their operating principles. But many more tolerate a hostile atmosphere toward gay people.

Antigay Comments

The most commonly reported form of discrimination by far that gay professionals reported took the form of a hostile atmosphere created by antigay jokes or comments. Dorothy, who is highly closeted at work, said, "You know, being antigay is the last prejudice that it's OK to have. It's politically incorrect to do all sorts of things, but it's OK to bash gays. It's still there. In some ways I'm still amazed everytime I hear someone say something like that."

At first we were inclined to see jokes and comments as the same. But as we sorted through the numerous references to antigay jokes versus antigay comments, we realized that comments were far less numerous. But this does not mean they can be ignored. They usually reflect a deep level of ignorance about gay people and, sometimes, even virulent hatred. Thus, without a well-thought-out plan, they may also be harder to counter effectively. For example, in 1993 the PG&E gay employee organization marched in the San Francisco Gay Pride parade for the first time. In response, thousands of antigay comments from employees flooded the PG&E internal E-mail system. Spencer, who responded to some of the remarks, told us, "There were a great deal of homophobic messages on the company electronic bulletin board. I printed out a stack once, and it was three-quarters-of-an-inch thick. Mostly it was antigay things, Bible-thumping things. The territory the utility serves is all of Northern California and the Central Valley. And there were things that were coming from those places that were very homophobic. I could tell where the messages were coming from because they signed their names to them. They had no shame about it at all.

"I wrote something on the electronic bulletin board when the homophobic comments came up. Basically it was in defense of the gay employees group marching in the parade, and trying to sort out the issues by putting an MBA mind to it, for what that was worth in an emotional debate. I just figured I should try to do my bit to bring a rational, business-school approach to a volatile discussion. I don't know if it did any good or not. I probably didn't change the mind of anyone who signed their name to homophobic messages. But maybe some people who read the messages learned something."

Another PG&E employee told us that in response to the vitriolic messages on the company E-mail system, this forum for intercompany discussion was shut down. "I don't know if that was a good solution. Just because people are precluded from expressing their opinion companywide doesn't mean they don't still have those opinions." Spencer disagreed. "I think if you don't give ignorance a voice, people have a chance to learn positive things instead. The problem is, PG&E cut back on diversity training just when it was needed the most."

The response of management can make a difference, we learned. Kyle, an employee of a major financial-services company, told us one of his colleagues was initially eager to participate in corporate outreach to the gay community. But after staffing a booth at the local Gay Pride festival in California, this colleague sang another tune. "He couldn't believe how 'sexual' the event was. All he saw were men running around 'half naked.' This made him conclude the people at the festival weren't to be taken seriously as potential clients," Kyle explained. "I tried to prep him ahead of time by explaining that Gay Pride festivals are kind of like Mardi Gras —a chance to party. But many of the people there *were* good prospects. I got a lot of new business from attending. Unfortunately, he couldn't see beyond his own stereotypes." Kyle said that due to support from management for ongoing outreach to gay clients, he is hopeful his colleague's opinions will remain the minority at his firm. "With some education, he may change his point of view."

While not usually career threatening, antigay comments can create an uncomfortable atmosphere for gay employees, especially if management does not set the proper tone itself. Karla told us, "When I was working for Price Waterhouse in New York, a partner was shot and murdered by a male prostitute in his apartment. This was in the mid-80s. At my level, we figured that all the partners had met and came up with this whole philosophy that they weren't going to talk about it. That just led to everyone else in the company making negative comments about the guy. For example, one of the senior auditors I worked closely with said, 'Well, if I knew there was a fag in this company, I'd have beat him up.' So that really made me not want to come out."

Whether antigay comments derive from ignorance or from someone's deeply held moral system, they are hard for many gay professionals to face head-on. One time Gary responded by openly disagreeing with his colleague on a political issue involving gay people. "Surprisingly, he backed right off," Gary said. "The conversation ended and it was done. I didn't have any problem working with the guy afterward, but he definitely avoids me more now," Gary concluded, "not just because of that issue, but because we part in our views a lot. He's an ultraconservative Rush Limbaugh supporter—one of those kind of guys—and I just don't have any patience for him. So, if anything, I'm the one that's shut him out."

Jonathan Rottenberg argued that rather than backing down in the face of homophobia or homo-ignorance, it's important to educate heterosexuals. He said, "Generally I believe that people have the capacity to grow. If you are thoughtful about how you craft your presentation to them, they can learn and change. It's not always that they're prejudiced. It's that literally no one has ever talked with them about this. You have to really give them the benefit of the doubt. Even people who voice homophobic opinions can change when you have a heart-to-heart conversation with them. Even people that are very thoughtful and sensitive about these issues really don't understand what gay people face and how gay people are oppressed and discriminated against, because gay people never talk about it. I don't think it's because no one wants to hear about it."

Jonathan continued, "I've had some really extraordinarily experiences talking to people about my experience of being gay and how it affects me. It usually started in not very positive ways—comments that were made that I wouldn't quite call homophobic but sort of homo-insensitive. I've called them on that, and they've been really surprised. I've ended up going out to lunch and then becoming really close friends with a couple of different people. So, as far as whether this has affected my success at Monitor, I think it definitely has. I think I've developed a lot of trust with people that I wouldn't have had otherwise."

Jonathan has brought his skills as a consultant to the table in this effort. "You can learn how to have productive one-on-one conversations with people. You don't know how to do it just because you are gay. But by systematically analyzing conversations, you can diagnose exactly what someone's homophobia is all about. Then you can sympathetically and supportively help them through a process of understanding it and work with them step by step to get over it. I use a lot of these situations at work to practice and develop my thinking on this.

"According to Chris Argyris, who teaches at Harvard Business School and the Harvard Graduate School of Education, across virtually all societies and cultures there is an almost universal pattern of behaviors that people adopt when they're facing issues that are embarrassing or threatening. He says people are usually unaware of doing these behaviors, but when someone is dealing with an issue that is embarrassing or threatening, the very nature of the associated behavior prevents us from learning why it is that we're feeling embarrassed or threatened." Jonathan added, "This works in a completely contrary fashion to learning and understanding. Fortunately, you can help people understand why they're embarrassed or threatened, and they can adapt their underlying beliefs in response to that knowledge."

Jonathan posited, "I believe everyone is trainable, although it takes a lot of work and effort to overcome your own defensiveness and to help others overcome theirs. But once you learn this, I believe it becomes the core for almost any other kind of change. In the end, I think it *is* the one-on-one conversation that truly creates change. When people understand us, they virtually never go back to their old way of thinking. They really understand the issue—and it is something that no longer stirs up fear and discomfort. It just makes sense. This is exactly the reason that coming out works. Polls show that people who know gay people, even if they don't like them, tend to support equal rights for gay people, at least in the abstract."

The next step Jonathan talked about is getting these people to become borderline activists. "Usually, people continue to move forward and care about the issue themselves."

By having the guts to come out and the willingness to educate, gay professionals found respect from others as well as for themselves. Of course, it is easier to be brave when one's city or company has an explicit policy against discrimination based on sexual orientation. Few came out in the absence of such protection. If management has a track record of supporting employee complaints based on gender or race, gay professionals were also more likely to take this risk.

Antigay Jokes

Most gay professionals believe jokes about gay men or lesbians stem from a deep-seated dislike of gay people. Often they see these jokes as hostile, a form of bullying that sends the message that gay people will not be tolerated in the organization. Some acknowledge that these jokes may be told out of ignorance or in the mistaken belief that they are really funny. Occasionally, they allege, the joke tellers are themselves gay, using jokes to mask their own sexual orientation.

Yet not all jokes people in the workforce tell about gay people are intended as attacks. Jokes about gay men and lesbians can be used to send a variety of signals. Sometimes we have seen open-minded coworkers trying to establish that they are in the know about a particular gay person in the news or an aspect of gay culture. Outside of diversity-training forums, many heterosexuals do not feel completely comfortable having serious, in-depth discussions on anything having to do with gay people. Joking can be their way, however indelicate, of indicating a willingness to talk about the subject. Clumsy yet sympathetic colleagues expect gay colleagues to laugh or banter back. Prematurely deciding that a coworker is homophobic can prevent the very bonds a potential ally is hoping to create.

"A woman I work with occasionally told me Michael Jackson jokes. One day, I retorted with a joke about Catholic priests," Carla said. "If I had jumped to the conclusion she was antigay, I wouldn't have made a valuable friend in another division. After I came out to her, I told her another joke: 'What did Michael Jackson say to O. J. Simpson? "I'll watch the kids!"' I don't know if these jokes are in the best of taste, but we have a rapport going that I think we both enjoy. And I certainly haven't experienced any homophobia on her part."

Other gay professionals told us they did not always feel it was necessary to object to jokes with gay themes. One factor is who the players are and why the joke is being told. Sybil told us that jokes about sex between men were a form of male bonding for the guys in the construction industry. "They would pound each other on the back and thank each other 'for last night' with an obvious leer. I guess what made it funny was that these guys were obviously not gay. But they were imitating some of the more macho gay men I know, not the effeminate, limp-wristed queens. I have to admit I thought it was funny to see them carry male bonding to its logical extreme. I also thought it was interesting that they were sure enough of their masculinity to joke about it in that way."

Sometimes the signals sent by jokes are difficult to decode. Bart Rubenstein recalled that in a former company he heard lots of gay jokes by senior management. "It was nothing vicious or mean, but the jokes were homophobic, nonetheless. Usually it was something inane and juvenile. Like somebody would raise their hand at a meeting or do something, and somebody else would say, 'Oh well, you know what it means if you do that? It means you're homosexual.' And everybody would laugh. There was one person who was kind of a ringleader for these jokes.

"He was the president of one of our divisions, and he was having a very hard time. In fact, at one point I think he was pretty sure that he was about to be canned. What I observed is that he decided he had to ingratiate himself to the rest of management. Making these jokes was a way he got laughs and approval. I noticed that over time he was starting to be accepted as part of the inner circle.

"Now the division that he's president of is actually much more progressive and open and liberal, to my observation, than the rest of the company. So I viewed that he had read the politics of the situation correctly and was stooping to the level of others, and it was working. It was a little scary. I felt disappointed, because I had spent a lot of time working with this division and always loved when I was working with them, because I felt more comfortable when I was there. And then I came into these senior management meetings and saw him acting like that . . . it was really a shame.

"The people who he was trying to cozy up to laughed, but I never heard them say anything like that. That's the irony here. The ones I was really nervous about were the ones who weren't saying anything. They are the ones who I was afraid of coming out to. The guy who was making the jokes—everything I know about him said being gay would not have affected anything in my relationship with him."

While many recalled painful incidents when they were forced to listen to gay jokes, few could recall the specific attempts at humor. Sometimes the jokes were situational and thus not jokes except in context. But many seemed to be the same tired old jokes we've all heard so many times they are no longer notable. In terms of content, almost all of the jokes were about gay men and involved sex. Many dealt with a seemingly universal source of heterosexual male anxiety—being treated like a woman in the act of sex. A number of others derived from an apparently widespread heterosexual male fantasy—that gay men are irresistibly attracted to heterosexual men. Only occasionally were lesbians the subject of jokes. The content of this brand of humor generally referred to stereotypes about lesbians' physical appearance.

A few of those we interviewed were able to recall the specific circumstances in which they heard antigay humor. When they recalled the incident to us, we often felt they wanted advice on how they should have handled the incident. Sometimes they explicitly asked us for our opinion. These reactions suggest the subject of antigay jokes is one that causes gay professionals a fair amount of anxiety. They do not want to feel they are letting down the gay community. Yet most are not confident that coming out will produce more good for the world than harm to themselves.

Strategies for Opposing Antigay Jokes

The gay professionals we interviewed were divided on how to respond to antigay jokes. The large majority of the gay men in our survey, and almost all of the lesbians, say they object to such jokes when told by their colleagues—but without necessarily revealing that they themselves are gay. Only 15 percent of our survey respondents said they reveal their own sexual orientation to the person who made the joke. A sizable minority, 25 percent, simply accept the joke in silence. Five percent said they show their displeasure by walking away. Sadly, 2 percent felt such a need to protect their jobs by concealing their sexual orientation that they laughed at jokes they found offensive.

The gay professionals we interviewed had tried many strategies for opposing antigay jokes. Because so few companies have made it clear that such jokes are not to be tolerated, both gay professionals and sympathetic heterosexuals are at times unsure of the best way to object. This climate of uncertainty only further alienates gay professionals. Most of those we interviewed felt strong enough to object in some fashion. But as with successfully opposing antigay comments, we found the most difficult as well as the most successful strategy was coming out.

Taking the High Ground While the lesbians in our survey and our interviews were more likely to object to antigay comments than the gay men, they almost always did so on political grounds. Loraine told us, "When I hear that sort of thing, I've always tried to say something that wouldn't give me away but still said, 'Look, you're too old to say stuff like that.' I try to quash that sort of thing, even if it isn't 100 percent offensive. But I actually hear very little of that around me. Very little women bashing, any kind of gay jokes, ethnic or racial jokes. I see very little of that. I think I sent a clear signal that I don't allow shit like that. I mean, why? You can laugh about a whole bunch of other things. You don't need to put other people down. I know some people get rattled when people make those kind of remarks, but I don't. People know not to get me going, because I'll go off on them."

Some men also made it clear they did not tolerate any questionable attempts at humor. Sebastian told us that when he was working with other engineers in the oil business, he heard very few antigay jokes or comments. "I always take the high ground with people. It's not that I am offended just by homophobic jokes but that I am offended by things in bad taste in general. So it got to the point where people would not make jokes like that around me. Now perhaps they didn't do it because they sensed I was gay and they knew that would upset me. But people didn't curse a lot around me; people didn't tell dirty jokes or sexist jokes. Of course, being Black, they didn't tell racist jokes. But in general there just wasn't a whole lot of that sort of thing.

"I always tried to position myself in a way so that people treat me with respect. I guess it means there's a certain distance that I keep away from everybody, although I'm quite chummy and friendly with people. But there's still this distance that I keep, and they can take that however they want to. I don't necessarily think people think it's because I'm gay. I think people take that as me being selective. The few people that I let in, I've sort of screened them. I know they can accept my being gay. I also know that they don't accept homophobic jokes or sexist attitudes. So I've chosen to befriend them because of that."

Unfortunately, in some cases, we found that politically correct sensitivity was not taken very seriously. Hannah explained, "They just thought I was being a do-gooder. Just like in the money markets, you get a lot more respect for your opinion if you personally have something at stake. When I've come out instead, I've found it works much better."

In addition, an attempt to take the high ground with respect to gay jokes can seem unusual if an individual does not also oppose other kinds of put-downs. Many of the gay professionals we interviewed admitted that they did not always act to quash racist or sexist comments at work. Hence they felt unable to oppose antigay jokes without casting suspicion on their closet.

Enlisting Management Support Some felt it was important to express their own disapproval of antigay jokes. Others felt the message would carry more weight if it came from management. Being willing to complain to a boss or to the human resources department can result in companywide changes, we learned. Gordon told us that when he worked at a large advertising agency in New York, he overheard a coworker make a homophobic joke. He recalls that a manager pulled his colleague aside to reprimand him so quickly it made the guy's head spin. This incident made an impression on Gordon, who saw how much power management has to enforce corporate culture, even at a time when nondiscrimination based on sexual orientation was not written in company policy.

Some companies cover antigay discrimination under general language. They say, "We do not discriminate based on race, gender, or any other non-work-related characteristic." However, the prevalence of antigay jokes suggests such an ambiguous policy is not enough. In the face of employee complaints, some companies have adopted more specific language against discrimination based on sexual orientation.

Such language sends an important message to gay professionals and heterosexuals alike. To the gay employee it says, "Your complaints will be taken seriously." To the heterosexual it warns, "Antigay jokes and comments are off-limits." Antigay jokes only continue because they are seldom opposed. Whether or not a comprehensive nondiscrimination policy is in place, gay employees who fail to counter these jokes allow this phenomenon to be perpetuated. The same applies to managers: A consistent and immediate response to antigay jokes is necessary to diminish hostility against gay people in the workplace.

When management sends a clear signal that discrimination will not be tolerated, it can be effective in shutting down antigay banter. Jonathan Rottenberg told us that Monitor has a very strong nondiscrimination policy that is reinforced by management. "It's actually one of the best ones I've ever seen. It prohibits discrimination with regard to hiring, promotion, performance reviews, based on sexual orientation and many other factors. It prohibits harassment and goes into a lot of detail in defining what is considered harassment. They talk about things like 'comments or jokes that directly or indirectly belittle a person's sexual orientation, age, gender, etc.' These are not tolerated."

Jonathan explained, "They communicate the policy to the employees as one of the company's six key policies that they discuss at the training program for every new consultant. Then it's discussed again in their professional-development reviews. They go through the six policies and see if there are any questions on them. They also set an example by never making those sorts of comments themselves. So I think people take it pretty seriously."

Fighting Humor with Humor Some felt it was necessary for gay people to maintain a sense of humor and laugh along with the jokes if they're funny, as they would if they were told in a group of gay men or lesbians. A few felt humor can be an effective weapon if it is wielded in response to an antigay joke or innuendo. Henry said, "If your goal is to change homophobic attitudes rather than just getting people to stop saying what they're thinking, it's always struck me that the best way to respond is with some sort of funny comment that makes your point explicitly but without entirely alienating the person. I have had situations where I have come up with something funny to respond with. A snappy comeback gets people to pay attention and sends the signal they can't mess with you." Henry admitted that it is difficult to think on your feet but says he sometimes pulls this off successfully.

In dealing with customers and vendors from the South, Carrie found herself hearing antigay as well as racist and anti-Semitic jokes virtually every day. She recalls her most successful response was humorous and spontaneous. "We were looking at a map of the United States, and one of my distributors was making cracks about California being the home of fruits and nuts—all the usual stuff. Then he pointed to the map which showed each state in a distinct color and said, 'Look, California is pink, that must be because of all those fruits.' Recalling that he was originally from Texas, I decided to respond obliquely by joshing, 'Look, Texas is pink too. I wonder why that is?' He looked flustered for a minute, but he rose to the challenge. 'It's because we have a woman governor,' he retorted. I had to laugh myself." Carrie chuckled. "I think we came out about even in the verbal duel."

The "Ouch" Technique Some of those we interviewed told us that diversity trainers for their companies recommended using the "ouch" technique. Brett explains, "That's what you say when someone says some general comment that hurts you." A workshop participant at a gay workplace conference held at Stanford University expanded: "It's a simple technique. When someone says something really offensive, you just say 'ouch.' Usually the other person will say 'What's wrong?' And then you just say, 'What you said offended me.' That leads into discussion and dialogue." But Brett and others commented it is easier to say "ouch" when someone is talking to you than when you just overhear the comments of others.

"I Don't Get It" A diversity trainer we know has another approach. "I've got one sure-fire answer that always stops jokes . . . People tell jokes because they want something back. People are looking for approval or they're looking for you to laugh. You know, it's a way of showing that they're hip, they're with it, or whatever. You pick and choose who you're going to tell jokes to. You don't tell a joke to somebody you don't think is going to think it's funny or isn't going to get it. What I have found is that the surest, most effective way to just shut the whole conversation up is right after the joke is told, you just look at everybody and say quite seriously, 'I don't get it.'

"It embarrasses people so much when I say, 'I don't get it. Was that a joke? Was that supposed to be funny? I don't get it.' All of a sudden, people stop. Nobody wants to be the one to have to explain. It's amazing, because it shuts down not only that person who told the joke but all the laughter. All of it stops. There's that pause where everybody has to think about why was that joke supposed to be so funny. And nobody has to come out. I've done it with coworkers, customers, and clients. It just cuts to the chase and it's over. And they're too embarrassed to do it again. *They're* the ones who are embarrassed."

Several lesbians we interviewed said they thought this technique would work for them and expressed interest in trying it. Yet this technique is less educational than confronting the joke teller directly. It can also create distance in the relationship rather than communication.

Coming Out While all of the above techniques for ending antigay jokes can be somewhat effective, those who came out found the jokes stopped automatically. One reason seems to be the corporate norm of getting along with coworkers. Very few white-collar workers want to insult someone to their face. So if a gay professional comes out, he or she gives a message that insulting gay people generally will be seen as a personal insult. Those who were out at work say this is one of the important side benefits to coming out. Not only do the jokes stop, but the underlying attitudes that give rise to the jokes change as well, because most people who know someone gay develop a more positive attitude toward gay people.

None of those we interviewed came out immediately in response to antigay jokes. But a number of those we interviewed felt coming out would help stop the jokes if they had the guts to try it. Annabel compared the situation to instances when ethnic jokes or racially based jokes are told in the workplace. She explained that in similar situations, Jews often choose to reveal they are Jewish. Or at a minimum, they feel comfortable asking a coworker to tell the person who told the joke something like, "You know, Sarah's Jewish. I think she was offended by what you said." Similarly, white people who hear racist jokes often say, "You know my husband/wife/child/best friend is Afro-American/Latin/Asian, and what you just said offends me." Annabel said she's sometimes tried to talk about loved ones who are gay and has seen some change in attitude. But she felt coming out had even greater benefits.

The Issue of Power

The major factor in how gay professionals react to antigay jokes is power. Generally those we interviewed said they had little compunction about chastising subordinates for homophobic comments. Antigay jokes from clients or customers, however, can be especially hard to combat. Donald recalls, "I put together a meeting of some potential customers the Friday before the 1993 March on Washington. It was the Germans' first trip to Washington, and they and the people from South Carolina wanted to stay in town. So they were making all kinds of comments about how they couldn't get a room. The conversation at dinner was very homophobic—every joke and stereotype that you can imagine, with one of the Germans and the president of the company in South Carolina leading the way.

"It would have been a lead balloon for me to contradict them. What I did was just not participate. Then afterwards I made some more neutral remark to the president of the German company, and he responded in kind. He said something about it being interesting that all these gay people were coming together, and that everyone would have to wonder:

Do you think he's gay or he's gay? And I said, 'Probably a lot more people around you are gay than you think.'

"I didn't want to shoot myself in the foot out of some noble aspiration to be gay first and a successful businessman second. I'd rather achieve success and in a few years say to them, 'Do you remember when we were all down there drinking wine and eating good food in Washington, and you guys were making comments about gay people? Well, I'm one too.' But I wouldn't do that until the deal was closed."

For those who are employed by others, the fear of discrimination or harassment can be mitigated by supportive management. Jonathan Rottenberg told us that when Monitor hired him, senior management told him that if any of their clients had a problem with him being openly gay, "They could go fuck themselves," as one partner put it. Douglas Plummer also recalled an occasion where his boss openly discussed his being gay in front of Japanese clients, although he is not sure if the men understood the reference. At a recent Out and Equal in the Workplace conference we also heard of other corporations that back their openly gay employees. One executive said, "For me, coming out to customers was very different than coming out in the workplace. The fear is that I am representing my company, and customers don't need an excuse not to do business with you. What I realized was that one of the things that allows me to be out in my own workplace is that the corporation has a culture and a norm and rules that say they will not discriminate on sexual orientation. The issue is—are they willing to lose business or gain business as a function of their principles?

"I was dealing with the Japanese customers back then. So, given the huge cultural differences, it was hard to look for common ground in the first place. What helped me come out to them was speaking to my boss and saying, 'Look, we all know that personal conversations are a part of doing business and all these situations will come up. My preference is to act honestly and nondeceptively. Is the company willing to abide by its standards and support me in doing that?' He had to stop and think and say yes, otherwise they're not living up to their own company's standards. At that point, if there's an acknowledgment they're willing to lose business rather than sacrifice their principles, that empowers me to be out to customers."

Gay professionals we interviewed said the most fear-inducing hostile atmosphere was created by an overtly homophobic remark by a boss or an antigay joke by a colleague that went unchecked by management. Rupert told us, "I've heard some of the partners, people who are on the partnership evaluation committee, make homophobic jokes. It's just not a very good environment. It's not as explicit as, 'We wouldn't want any fags being partners in our company.' It's just the sort of jokes that people put out. But yeah, it bothers me. I'd like to transition out." Rupert continued, "Also, there was another incident that really disturbed me. We have a real problem with retaining women in the firm. So they tried to address that by having a series of diversity seminars based on women's issues, and they had little breakout groups where you talked about things. One of the topics for discussion was a male client who puts in a request for a particular woman because he finds her attractive. And one of the senior people brought up jokingly, 'What if it was a gay client who said that about one of the men?' And everyone thought that was a great joke, people from all levels of the firm."

Sometimes the human resources department or others charged with monitoring the corporate environment are themselves the source of the hostile atmosphere. These individuals can also be very hard to challenge. Ethan told us, "Believe it or not, I hear more homophobic jokes and comments from corporate counsel than anyone else—the guy who's in charge of enforcing the antidiscrimination policy! We do have an antidiscrimination policy that includes nondiscrimination against gay people, but that fact is not widely known. It's part of the clause that's at the bottom of human-resources-type pamphlets. Some of them include sexual orientation and some of them don't. But I've heard it from the counsel's mouth that it is part of the policy."

Ethan continued, "Unfortunately he is one of the most homophobic and sexist people that I have ever encountered. He makes sexist jokes too, even though he's in charge of enforcing the nondiscrimination policy based on gender too, of course. If you were discriminated against, he would be involved in resolving the situation. I have to admit I'm fairly skeptical about how well equipped he is to handle these sorts of things. But there definitely is the sensitivity that the company wants to protect itself. So even just the threat of a lawsuit might have an impact."

An Atmosphere of Hyperheterosexuality

A final form of hostile atmosphere some encountered was what we term a hyperheterosexual workplace. Constant talk about heterosexual sex or dating can result in certain individuals' being targeted for abuse. Even if a gay professional is not personally attacked for failing to participate in such banter, this kind of environment can be harmful. Gay professionals often feel invisible, and such an environment makes them feel especially unwelcome. Most of those we interviewed said they tolerate jokes and comments based on an assumption of shared heterosexuality, which adds to their feeling of isolation and alienation. Many said they avoided social interactions with work colleagues because of such jokes or remarks.

The damage to company morale when such hyperheterosexuality is based on sexism is now beginning to be acknowledged. Although the modern rules of etiquette are often breached, discussions about whether women are married or likely to get married are increasingly off-limits in the workplace.

Many of those we interviewed wished that all personal subjects could be declared out of bounds at work. We found that several large companies have tried to implement this approach. For example, interviewees and their partners who worked at IBM said this policy has been in place there for many years. Amy told us, "When I worked there, my lover, who also worked there, was constantly getting promoted. I don't think not being married ever hurt her." Peter suggested this corporate culture applied to men as well. "Your private life is your private life. At IBM, it's the law. If you start asking someone too many personal questions, that is against company policy. My lover, who worked for IBM for thirty years, never had any problems there." Peter further pointed out that IBM was also one of the first companies to adopt a policy of nondiscrimination based on sexual orientation—back in 1972.

A few had pushed for a change in their companies' corporate culture to make personal conversations off-limits. Shamus told us, "One of the things I've managed to change in the corporation over the years is that we don't talk about those things that happen outside of work these days. That goes for me and all the people I work with. You go to work, you talk about work, you talk about a few things about your personal life because of how they might impact work, but there's not much of the prying. People don't ask. I don't care whether they're straight or gay; they don't ask. I think it's been a good change. Management policy is to support people who need time for their personal life, whatever they need time for. But you're not encouraged to discuss the content of your relationship with your spouse, partner, kids, whatever at work. You're there to focus on work."

While avoidance may be one way of solving the problem of a hyperheterosexual environment, it is not the only way. Playing dumb by refusing to react to the heterosexual allusion can also work. But plotting a reaction to a spur-of-the-moment joke-telling session may be difficult. Often those we interviewed told us, "What I should have said is . . ." Spencer told us that he finds the small joking references most difficult to deal with. "I don't think my boss ever figured out I was gay. If he did, maybe he was trying to bait me. He'd make comments like, 'It's too bad you didn't go to Stanford Business School because you could have played more.' And I fall into a trap by saying, 'Yeah, the weather's a little better than Boston and I probably could have improved my tennis game.' Because he'd say, 'Yeah, and you could have also hooked up with one of those hot chicks running around in shorts.' " Spencer laughed. "That's not quite what I had in mind. I should have told him, 'Well, it's a little bit closer to San Francisco than Boston is to New York.' But it's hard to think of that under pressure."

Coming out can also stop heterosexual teasing dead in its tracks. Those who have come out in the face of heterosexist joking say there are gains in personal respect as well as a changed atmosphere at work. Jonathan Rottenberg told us, "Last week I had a situation with this guy who joked about fixing me up with women. When I came out to him, he was kind of defensive at first. He said he didn't understand why gay people are so sensitive about people assuming that they're straight. I told him, 'I can answer that question for you on an intellectual level, but I'm not sure it would totally make sense. Because one of the things that's different about the two of us is that our lives have been shaped in very different ways because of who we are. If it were possible for you to imagine how your life would be today if you had grown up being gay and had dealt with all of the ramifications that had for almost every aspect of your life throughout your teenage years and onward into adulthood, it might begin to make sense to you why I have the perspective that I have."

Jonathan continued, "It was interesting, because he responded to that by saying, 'You know, I have to say that I have never considered the idea of what would it be like if I were gay, and I'm not even sure that I could imagine. But what you're saying does make some sense. I would see some things differently.' " Jonathan said that as the result of this conversation his colleague has indeed become more sensitive to Jonathan's perspective as a gay man.

None of the gay-owned businesses we know have a hostile environment toward heterosexuals. Yet just as a hyperheterosexual environment can cause difficulties for gay employees, a hyperhomosexual environment can create trouble in a gay-owned business, we learned.

James's Story

James owns a thriving business with twenty employees. Division one of his company primarily has heterosexual employees. Division two is staffed almost exclusively by gay men. James is now in a position of having to hire more skilled professionals in division two in response to customer demand. "I'm looking to hire the best-qualified person for the job, whether gay or heterosexual," he told us.

James has approached several heterosexual men, who have turned him down for the position. One was completely candid about his reason—the corporate culture of division two, where he would be working. James suspects this was an issue for other candidates as well. It's not that they were uncomfortable working with gay people, James believes. Rather, they are uncomfortable with aspects of gay culture, such as camp and sexual comments. "If heterosexual men or women were doing similar things," James said, "we might not say it was a hostile work environment but an inappropriate and unprofessional one."

So how does James intend to resolve this challenge? "It's my hope that, by bringing in two or three additional straight people at the same time, it will change the culture a little bit." He recognized that "I'll have to find the right sort of people. In a small company you need to find the right people anyway. It's hard to bring just anybody in, because there's a definite chemistry that happens when there's only a dozen people in the workforce. They're like a little family. And people do have to get along. It's not like a large company, where you can ignore the people you don't like and find other friends. The dynamics of a small company are a little different from that."

Another HBS graduate agreed that hiring more than one heterosexual at a time was a good idea, so no one person would feel isolated. He also suggested, "Try to hire a few straight women, because the women will feel more comfortable with all the gay men yet they will change the corporate culture some just by being there. Their presence will also make it easier to hire straight men in the future."

DISCRIMINATION IN PROTECTIONS AND BENEFITS

Changing Expectations

Since 1989 we have witnessed a rapid change in the expectations of gay professionals. When we began our research, the greatest hope of most of those we interviewed was to avoid hostile workplace environments. In just a few short years, many expect to find enforcement of nondiscrimination policies and access to equal benefits. Company behavior that gay people used to accept as "just the way things are" or as heterosexism is increasingly being labeled homophobia. Thus, companies must continue to adapt in order to be perceived as a fair place to work.

Small businesses are at the forefront of the private sector in offering domestic partner benefits. Yet most do not have them, nor do they have formal policies on nondiscrimination. Douglas Plummer told us that his otherwise progressive company does not have a policy of nondiscrimination based on sexual orientation. "That's something I really want to ask for, but I don't feel comfortable until I have been there for at least a year to start pressing for that. I think the chairman is a really moral person who would be concerned about something like that. There are people between me and him who might just say, 'Screw you, that's not my concern.' But it's his firm with his name on it, and I honestly feel like I could go and ask for it, and he would do it. That's the benefit of working for a smaller company. I'm going to do that in a few months after my one-year anniversary there."

Gay professionals we interviewed increasingly expect large companies as well to make changes. Already many large businesses have adopted nondiscrimination policies. A number have instituted diversity-training programs that include sexual orientation. Others sponsor gay employee groups. Some do target marketing to gay markets or make corporate gifts to gay organizations. Yet some continue to fund antigay groups or political candidates as well. Many told us, "Companies can't have it both ways anymore if they want to be seen as gay friendly."

Heterosexism or Homophobia?

Homophobia is a fear or hatred of homosexuals. When individuals or institutions are homophobic, this can lead directly to discrimination. Heterosexism is a view of life that assumes that everyone is or should be heterosexual. Heterosexist policies assume every worker's loved one is of the opposite sex and the only lifetime partnerships that count are those that can be legitimized in marriage. While heterosexism may be less obvious than homophobia, it has a more far-reaching impact. While not everyone encounters antigay hatred, almost every gay professional is discriminated against due to heterosexism at sometime in the course of their career.

Heterosexism means that the institutions in the workplace—benefits, company parties, and private social occasions—are based on the assumption of most heterosexual employers and managers that everyone is just like them. Therefore they assume all significant family relationships are between partners of the opposite sex and their children. This often results in discrimination because owners and managers extend benefits and privileges to the spouses of heterosexual employees that are not extended to the partners of their gay workers. Thus, the most frequent cause of heterosexism is not hatred or fear of gay people but the fact that those responsible for setting the company's policies in these areas have never had the motivation to change with the times. It can also be based on fear of potential higher costs or loss of customers. Usually, however, it is more a question of laziness than willful ignorance or hatred. Nonetheless, the result is often the same: Gay people are underpaid and feel unwelcome where they work.

As gay professionals become more aware of the injustice of such discrimination, the demarkation between homophobia and heterosexism becomes less obvious. Most gay professionals approach their companies with the stated expectation that the lack of equal treatment is caused by oversight or lack of knowledge; "the need to study the issue in depth" will increasingly be regarded as a defense for inaction. Information is increasingly available about the low costs and positives that accrue to companies that have eliminated discrimination in the benefits they offer. As more gay people come forward to seek specific changes, companies must respond, not stall, to achieve a reputation as nondiscriminatory.

Identifying Unequal Protections and Benefits

Most Americans agree that discrimination, whether caused by hatred or ignorance, is wrong. But until recently, discrimination against gay people was unnoticed and unremarkable. Today many companies still discriminate against their gay employees in the following ways: lack of a nondiscrimination policy that includes sexual orientation; not welcoming friends or partners to social events; diversity training that does not include sexual orientation; no support for gay employee organizations; and lack of domestic partner benefits.

Increasingly, forward-thinking companies are attempting to treat their employees equally in every way. In addition, they acknowledge gay people as their clients, customers, and members of the citizenry by doing target marketing in the gay community and directing corporate philanthropy to gay organizations. Previously, companies who did not do these things were excused as merely heterosexist. Today—as gay professionals are increasingly unwilling to accept unequal treatment of any kind—they are more often seen as homophobic.

The Importance of a Nondiscrimination Policy

For gay employees to do their best at work, a nondiscrimination policy is basic. Some companies think it is not necessary; they say discrimination is already covered by local ordinance or that they don't discriminate on any non-work-related attribute. Other companies say that that's their policy, but it's not written down. Some even have a written policy but do not disseminate it.

These approaches are completely wrong minded. A written nondiscrimination policy that is disseminated companywide is the basic step a company must take to communicate its desire to hire, promote, and compensate its workforce fairly on the basis of performance. The gay professionals we interviewed affirmed the importance of a company putting nondiscrimination in their corporatewide written policy. Harris said, "Some of our subsidiaries have the policy, but the head office in Orange County, where I work, does not. I can't believe they can still get away with that. And it makes me worried, because the state of California's nondiscrimination policy for gay people at work is very weak." Lisa, a current student at HBS, told us, "I definitely want to be in an open-minded environment that has a clause about no discrimination based on orientation. Even though I don't expect to be out at work at the beginning, it's important for me to know that I'm going to have an equal chance of success as anybody else." Several added, "If a company has gone through the thought process of adopting such a policy, it is definitely a good sign."

Both openly gay and closeted gay professionals told us the presence or absence of such a policy makes a tremendous difference in how comfortable they feel at work. After Jonathan Rottenberg accepted a full-time offer with the Monitor consulting firm, he came out in *Forbes* magazine. Although Jonathan was already protected from discrimination by local statute, he told us Monitor's decision to add sexual orientation to their nondiscrimination policy meant a great deal to him. "I don't think I was the only contributing factor to this. But they decided that they wanted to make a very specific policy in response to this situation," he said, "a very positive policy response."

Brett, who is mostly closeted at work, nonetheless banded together with several other New York–based gay executives and persuaded American Express to adopt a companywide nondiscrimination policy. "They had one in New York City, because they comply with local law. But we thought it was hypocritical that the subsidiaries all across the country were not covered," Brett told us. Because his company is doing target marketing to the gay community, the absence of such a policy was especially ironic. We learned that similar behind-the-scenes efforts have resulted in a companywide nondiscrimination policy at a few other large companies as well. Increasingly, we believe, competitive pressure will motivate companies within particular industries to come in line with one another on this basic aspect of fairness.

Some companies may avoid implementing a nondiscrimination policy for fear of lawsuits or for other spurious reasons, like fear of having to implement an affirmative-action plan for gay people. Joe Steele laughed. "It doesn't make any sense for companies to be worried about affirmative action for gay people. That's not the issue. Gay people just want to be treated right." And adopting a nondiscrimination policy may be a company's best protection against lawsuits. If a gay person has internal channels to bring a complaint, he or she will be less likely to file for damages under local ordinances. One reason is that company nondiscrimination policies are often far more comprehensive than local statutes. For example, local statutes may not protect against a hostile atmosphere or may have a narrow window of opportunity to bring complaints. A good corporate policy will have an enforcement mechanism that is not automatically adversarial. It may call for mediation or training, if appropriate, rather than fines or firings. Thus it can benefit both the gay employee as well as the company. A companywide nondiscrimination policy can also serve as preventative medicine, sending a strong message to both gay and heterosexual employees about company values. Increasingly, the absence of such a written and well-disseminated policy reflects that a company is behind the times.

Social Functions

At the Harvard Business School, professors emphasize the critical value of forming strong relationships with coworkers, peers, clients, vendors, and, in some cases, even competitors. Whether it is having drinks, playing golf, carpooling, exchanging weekend invitations to one another's homes, or going to formal dinner dances, socializing is often critical to cementing relationships that close deals, provide career advancement, and build goodwill. Yet, fearing discrimination, many gay professionals miss out on these opportunities. Sometimes their fear may be out of proportion to the possible risks. But at least equally often, the company fails to set the tone that assures gay professionals they will be treated equally if they choose to participate in social functions with their partners.

Informal Functions One of the first ways many companies signal an openness to its gay employees is with respect to informal social functions. Even companies that do not have a nondiscrimination policy in place may encourage their employees to bring family and friends to functions like the company picnic. While some organizations gear such events entirely toward nuclear families, most are happy to have employees bring anyone they want to enjoy the camaraderie of the day with. Another opportunity to include same-sex partners is when a small group of friends gets together in someone's home or at a bar after work.

Over half (57 percent) of the gay professionals in our written survey told us they had brought a person of the same sex to an informal social occasion involving people from work. Yet, as we learned in our interviews, most had done so without making the nature of the relationship explicit. One explanation for this is that companies have not done all they can to eliminate the fear of discrimination. Those we interviewed were especially reluctant to come out if their company had not adopted a nondiscrimination policy.

A nondiscrimination policy was not the only sign gay professionals looked for. Even with this protection, many felt just showing up together took a fair amount of courage. Betsy told us that, in her last relationship, "at first we were relatively cautious of exposure, and then there were too many opportunities to do things that were associated with my job that we wanted to do, that gradually . . . I felt, goddammit, Betsy, get over it. If we've got an opportunity to go to the theater with people from work, we go."

The more accepting the company and the less formal the company sponsorship, the more open gay professionals were willing to be. Art works at a company that has an active gay employee association and has promoted several openly gay executives to its top ranks. He told us, "My company participated in a promotional event where we were invited out to a ship for an overnight. The event wasn't company sponsored—it was sponsored by the ship. Two thousand people were invited, and of those two thousand people, maybe a hundred were from my company. The invitation was for you and a guest, so I brought my partner, and every other gay person I know at the company who has a partner brought their partner. It wasn't a planned thing. We didn't know who else was going to be there from the company, and we didn't really care. I figured it was a big enough ship that it didn't matter if I brought my partner, even though there was just one bed in our cabin."

Although so far the number of gay professionals who socialize with people from work in openly gay couples is relatively small, we expect that the number will continue to grow. Often being in a relationship was itself the impetus for coming out at least selectively at work. In other cases, the positive experience of friends or statements by bosses or coworkers contributed to the decision to include a partner in at least some work-related social functions.

A significant majority of the partnered gay professionals we interviewed told us they want to include their partners in work-related social activities and would prefer to do so as openly gay men and women. As companies become more aware of the importance of treating gay employees equally and as gay professionals themselves become more comfortable with being openly gay at work, we expect this trend will continue to grow.

FORMAL FUNCTIONS The importance of corporate policy is especially relevant with respect to formal company-sponsored social functions. We found that a third (34 percent) of those we surveyed had brought dates of the same sex to a company-sponsored business or social function such as a holiday party, industry dinner, or awards ceremony, but few were open about the nature of the relationship. In addition, some of those who are openly gay at work choose not to subject their partners to the scrutiny of workplace socializing. Other openly gay people are single; they told us they would bring a partner if they had one but did not feel comfortable bringing a date to such an event, as many heterosexuals do.

The most important reason, however, why gay professionals do not bring their partner to company functions is fear of discrimination. Perhaps inadvertently, many companies signal that heterosexuality is expected at such functions. Written invitations to formal events are common, and whether issued by the corporation or the boss, they often read "employee and spouse." Even when they read "and guest," gay professionals took this to mean a date of the opposite gender. Sometimes a gay professional's partner might be welcome, but how would anyone know unless they "pushed the envelope" and tried it? Many gay professionals fear that openly acknowledging their partner's presence could prove disruptive not only of the occasion but of their career.

Gay professionals fear that heterosexuals who seem comfortable working with a gay person may be uncomfortable in formal social settings with two gay men or two lesbians who they know are in a relationship. In general, those who raised this issue said they "didn't talk about being gay too much" or "had never talked about it," but claimed, "Everyone knows." In the absence of corporate clues to the contrary, they fear that introducing their partner as their partner would be going too far. Thus, many gay professionals told us they looked for ways to avoid such functions or went alone and left as early as possible. A few brought their partner but maintained a "Don't ask, don't tell" charade.

A few brave individuals openly brought their same-sex partners to business or social functions, generally with successful outcomes. Breaking past the initial discomfort takes persistence, but it can be done. Those who were most successful had previously built relationships with a number of close associates, both gay and heterosexual, who were looking forward to meeting or who already knew their partner. In addition, company management was supportive in both word and deed.

The risk and discomfort of taking such a step can be substantially reduced when a company takes an active role in treating all its employees equally before the first brave gay person seeks to break this boundary. Companies that offer domestic partner benefits are often in the forefront of this change, because many gay professionals look for tangible benefits before coming out at least selectively. Once their boss or coworkers know they have a partner, gay professionals are more likely to include a partner in corporate functions. Also, companies offering diversity training that discusses being gay in the workplace are more likely to find gay professionals willing to bring their partners to corporate events.

Diversity Training

Large companies are increasingly mandating diversity-training sessions for their employees and managers. In most cases, such training focuses almost entirely on gender and race. Increasingly, however, individual employees, heterosexual or gay, are requesting that sexual orientation be included in these sessions.

Simon's Story

Simon gave an example of such training. "The point of it wasn't why you should go out and hire gay people. It was, you should recognize that they're here already. So if you do anything that makes any of them feel like they're not part of the group, or if they are unhappy in any way, it affects the whole company. And you might not even know it.

"The story the trainer used was about a crew team, and the boat is the company. The crew team is in a boat rowing, and the boat moves forward. In the middle of the boat there are African Americans and Hispanic Americans, and they're upset because someone said something which made them feel they were being discriminated against. So while everyone else in the boat is trying to row ahead, they start jumping up and down." Simon laughed. "Then the trainer said, 'In the back of the boat there are some white heterosexual females. They don't feel like they fit either, and they've been unhappy for a long time, despite the fact that they're sitting there smiling. They don't jump up and down, because they're just not like that. But they sit there and smile, and as everyone else is rowing forward, they're rowing backwards,' " Simon said.

"Also in the boat there are some gay men and lesbians. You don't know they're there, because they're not comfortable letting you know they exist, but they're sitting there quietly. You think you've finally got everyone rowing forward, but as the boat is going, they're quietly drilling holes in the bottom of the boat," he explained.

"What happens is, the boat doesn't go anywhere. The point was, you have to be aware of who's in the boat and what they're feeling. You have to always make sure you don't do anything that can affect any of these groups in a negative way or make them feel excluded, because then they will not contribute to the overall mission of the company."

Although diversity training can be a significant factor in breaking down negative stereotypes, coming out is an important complement. By carrying out their daily jobs as openly gay individuals, gay professionals can play an important role in reinforcing the message of diversity trainers. In contrast, the closet is an ally of ignorance.

Joe Steele, a former international banker, now runs diversity-training programs for large corporations. "In response to market demands, I am increasingly including sexual orientation. Yet even when the clients themselves raise the subject with me and say they want it discussed, sexual orientation is the most difficult of all the issues. People tend to be incredibly uncomfortable. However, I think most are struggling for a forum to talk about it, because it is not something they can comfortably talk about otherwise. They often don't have the tools to know what's appropriate and what's not appropriate to talk about. They think about the sex. They don't usually know what other issues there are. They don't realize that being gay is also about identity, affiliation, and about relationships and so on. But when you point that out, they're usually open to listening and learning.

"I ask, 'To a gay man or a lesbian, what does coming out mean in the work environment?' A lot of times straight people say that it's about sex and add that talking about sex isn't appropriate in the work environment. I tell them I agree that work is not the place to talk about sexual activity. But I ask them, 'If you don't talk about sex at work, why do you think gay people are any different? Why do you think they want to talk about their sexual life?"

Joe told us management groups can often be his toughest audiences. "I've dealt with all levels, shop floor right through senior management. With management groups you can get some real adamant attitudes against discussing sexual orientation. Often management preaches nondiscrimination, but they don't necessarily want to do any diversity training on sexual orientation issues. I've dealt with several management teams where the minute the topic was brought up, they instantaneously tried to shut it down. Even in companies that have sexual orientation in their corporate policy around nondiscrimination. So we talk about their discomfort! Because if senior management is not comfortable with it, that really sends the wrong signal to the rest of the employees. After all, they are supposed to be the role models. I think that as society at large is increasingly becoming more exposed to gay people, it will improve. But we're not there yet. A lot of managers are still thinking of gay people as practicing some kind of deviant sexual behavior rather than thinking of gay people as having a sexual orientation that shouldn't be discriminated against."

Joe continued, "The good news is that in doing diversity training I find there are a lot more people in the middle than I had anticipated. I'm very pleased to see that. Because our society doesn't encourage dialogue around a lot of these issues, there is an underlying awkwardness for some people. Yet once people get in a forum that facilitates discussion, you can really see a lot of people are in the middle and just curious and want to learn."

When we asked him what is the most difficult issue he faces as a diversity trainer, Joe responded, "Being in diversity training, you see things you never would have even imagined. One thing I see is that a lot of people are very invested in how many gay people there are. For a long time gay people said gays were 10 percent of the population. So now there are studies that say there are a lot less, like 1 percent. And people will bring that up in kind of a whine: 'Well I understand it's only 1 percent now.' So I say, 'Does that make it less of an issue? If it's only one in two hundred, is it any less of an issue? If that gay man or lesbian is part of your team, don't they still have the right to be respected? Jews are only 3 percent of American society. Does that mean it isn't important to treat them equally?'

"The other part of that line of questioning is, sometimes I have people who will say gay people aren't a real minority. What's usually behind that question is, 'Shouldn't I have the right not to work with someone who's gay?' In most companies there are ways that you can get out of working with people for whatever reason, and they feel that sexual orientation should qualify as a reason not to work together. The way I've handled that is to take them through what their fears might be. Ultimately their concern seems to be: to work with a gay person, I have to condone the gay lifestyle. I try to get them to understand that these are not synonymous. That's the angle I try to come at it from because a lot of folks are resistant if they think they have to change their moral values or beliefs," Joe explained. "Folks are used to the tradition of being buddy-buddy at work—we work together, we play together. But American corporations are not buddy-buddy anymore. You don't have to approve of or even get along with someone to work effectively with them. You just have to treat them with respect."

Sheila, who participated in a diversity-training session, said, "I think there are a lot of parallels to religion. Like fundamentalist Christians have real problems with Mormons, because they don't think that Mormons are real Christians. But if they have to work together, they just work together. They don't have to get into the subtleties of each other's beliefs about religion. They just say, 'OK, you know, we have sales coming up this week. What do we have to do to get ready?' "

Joe agreed. "Part of the whole thing I try to do is help people understand, what's in it for me? Part of what motivates people, especially Americans, is: What do I get out of this? So I try to point out what's in it for them in working with a gay coworker and what they lose if they decide not to work with this person. Not working together usually means more work that you have to do alone, thus more stress. I try to help them understand that they get more out of the situation than they lose by working with someone. Once people get that it's win-win, I think that's how we'll see change."

Although not everyone will have the same point of view on political issues, familiarity with the terms of the debate can be important. Increasingly, gay professionals expect company management to be familiar with and careful of the language used. Just as most gay people today feel they have a sexual orientation, not a sexual preference, they resent hearing equal-rights legislation referred to as special rights for gays. Today it is almost always those who are part of the radical right who use terms like "sexual preference" or "special rights." Gay people see their sexual orientation as part of their inherent identity, not a preference, like a taste for certain kinds of ice cream. Even bisexuals usually think of themselves as having a bisexual orientation, not a bisexual preference.

Similarly, gay people note, there is nothing special about their desire to be free from discrimination. Thus, the battle to include language such as "There shall be no discrimination based on gender, race, sexual orientation, etc." is not an attempt to secure special rights. It is a struggle to achieve equal rights.

Gay Employee Groups

We found most gay employee groups formed only after a nondiscrimination policy was in place. But not all companies that have nondiscrimination policies sponsor gay employee groups. Some companies discourage all employee groups of any kind. Most claim they do so to avoid the development of cliques in their workforce. Ned said, "The company I worked at had this kind of policy. It was a stupid policy but a fair one." But women and most racial minorities can find each other informally based on appearance. Gay employees usually have no other way to identify or connect with one another outside formal channels.

In reality, most companies refuse to endorse any employee groups because they are afraid of the power of such networking. They fear that any socially oppressed group that wants to meet will hurt the company by backing discrimination suits or demanding "special rights," like day care, mentoring programs for minority managers, or domestic partner benefits. Some companies may prohibit such groups solely to prevent a gay group from using the company name, due to fear of consumer backlash. But such concerns are a smoke screen for discrimination. No gay group is seeking benefits that would be greater than those afforded to heterosexual employees. Rather, they are seeking benefits that would put gay employees on equal par with their heterosexual coworkers and peers.

Forward-thinking companies will constantly seek to keep pace with social changes and be the first to implement new policies and programs like those mentioned above. As a result, such companies will reap the benefits of a diverse and loyal workforce, including reaching and serving their markets more competitively. Rather than hurting companies, in reality gay employee groups are in a position to help their employers target gay markets more effectively. While, historically, mass marketers have shied away from marketing directly to gay customers, that is beginning to change. Clothing, entertainment, telecommunications, furniture, beer, alcohol, and cigarette companies now actively court the gay buyer. And the gay market has responded with raised expectations—they expect to see various brands in these industries competing for the patronage by advertising and underwriting gay sports and social events. Companies that can rely on their own employees to help them have a competitive advantage in reaching this market. Those that take the lead in this area reap another important benefit—they send the signal to their employees that they are willing to take some heat for making the right moral and economic decision. In contrast, companies and industries that do not follow suit now are losing an important way to reach potential customers.

Many we interviewed told us the presence of a gay employee group at their company was important to them, even if they did not attend the group themselves. "Just knowing it's there is a good sign," Amanda told us. "I don't want to come out yet, so I don't go. But it makes me feel better about the company to know it's there. Others, who have attended the gay employee group at their companies, said such groups can be important in career development, networking across departments, or socializing.

Some gay employee groups at large companies work closely with management to implement inclusive diversity-training programs. Increasingly, we found, forward-thinking companies realize that a nondiscriminatory working environment results in greater productivity for all. We also found the gay groups that consciously took management's bottom-line orientation into consideration when asking for recognition or funding were the most successful.

Many who are involved with employee groups recommend that the potential costs and benefits of any proposal should be addressed, even if they cannot be quantified in numbers. When it is possible to project dollar benefits, the likelihood of a win-win situation increases dramatically. Employee groups that are in a position to offer marketing or recruiting assistance have been especially successful in establishing credibility at their companies.

Victor's Story

Victor, an executive at a *Fortune* 500 company, told us, "I haven't joined the company's gay employee organization, but I did find a way to help them out—to give them support for their efforts by getting them management funding. It was really funny how it happened. One day I got this note from top-level management that said: 'The gay group within the company has asked us how they can help contribute to my marketing effort. What do you upper-level managers think?' And I thought: Oh, OK, this is an easy one. It's win-win. They get credibility as a group, and the company makes money.

"So I responded, 'I agree this is a market segment we should be paying attention to. After all, it's a group that has a profile as a high-income, high-profile, trend-setter community.' When you look at anything from a marketing perspective, you get results." He laughed. "I told them about the things that were starting to happen in the marketplace, in terms of the fact that the liquor companies, the beer companies were paying attention to the gay market. And I mentioned, 'Hey, maybe we should have somebody contact them and make sure they have the funding to help us reach that market.' "

As a result, Victor said, he was authorized to contact the group as well as to fund them. "The whole thing kind of happened through the fact that I control a lot of dollars." He laughed. "That's what it really comes down to. The budget I controlled last year is worth over $100 million. Senior management believes in my judgment. So I've been working with this group under the rubric of market development. They've helped us put together focus groups to evaluate the advertising we have placed in gay magazines. They helped us decide to sponsor social and athletic events within the gay community. We're also looking at implementing a trial run of direct mail to gay potential consumers."

Victor pointed out, "Gay employee groups probably have better chances of getting recognized if they're able think about what they can do for the company. For my company, that was the key issue. I was able to get money for the group because there is money for marketing initiatives. Once the group has the blessing of the company, of course, that gives them the credibility to do their own organizing around the social-policy issues."

Patricia also found that she is able to support target marketing to the gay community from behind the scenes. As in Victor's company, the question of how to reach gay potential consumers came down through the usual company channels. "Being new at my job, I don't know who initially decided to pursue this market," she told us. "But it makes perfect sense for us to advertise in gay magazines, from all the market research I've seen. So when my brand people give me their recommendations, I'm able to back them up all the way up to top management. If the business reason is there, great, do it.

"I don't need or want to take a more proactive role," Patricia explained, "because my philosophy as a manager is not to micromanage. I let my subordinates run with their brands so long as they are doing a good job. Fortunately I've been in the position where both gay and heterosexual brand managers have identified a compelling business reason to do that kind of advertising." She admitted, "I feel an obligation to separate out the emotional motivations from the business motivation. So at first I felt a little hesitant about the whole issue. But now I'm all the way on board."

Domestic Partner Benefits

Even when a gay person works for a company that actively welcomes a diverse workforce—by making it clear they will tolerate no discrimination in hiring or promotion of their workers, by offering diversity training, and by sponsoring a gay employees group—the odds are still overwhelming that the gay employee is being discriminated against in a very blatant way; few offer a full range of domestic partner benefits. Because discrimination in benefits is economic, it is easily quantifiable to the individual employee. The gay professionals we interviewed told us they increasingly resent being paid less for the same work as their heterosexual peers. If anything, the partners of those we interviewed were even more vehement on this issue.

Melvin says, "I'm in business for myself, and health insurance is really expensive as a self-insured person. If we were married, I'd be insured under his policy. You know, things like that just piss me off at this point. Also, Emery has a company car. If I were his wife I could drive the car, and I can't."

Some employers offer inexpensive perks to their employees' domestic partners, such as use of the company library or gym. But most gay professionals in a long-term relationship usually do not receive health, travel, or relocation benefits for their same-sex partner. Their loved one is also unlikely to receive retirement, pension, and other benefits their heterosexual colleagues' spouses enjoy. The company's failure to provide such benefits can be a major source of stress for the gay professional and thus significantly detracts from his or her ability to give 100 percent.

Historically, companies provide family benefits, such as medical, pension, and life insurance plans, that are extended to spouses and dependents to help their employees provide for their families. Additional compensation can also be a carrot to entice new hires or a reward for work well done. Companies often provide additional perks like moving costs, a company car, a vacation home, or travel benefits. For senior executives in particular, these perks can be highly personalized and substantial. Increasingly, gay professionals who do not receive benefits for their partners are coming to realize the true extent of their financial loss.

One recent trend in large companies is to give employees a choice of benefits. In the 80s, Donald told us, he recommended that his company adopt "cafeteria benefits" rather than just a standard package that was best suited to married people. "Take life insurance, for example. I had no one in particular who would suffer from my demise, so I could have traded life insurance for some more vacation or for better medical insurance or whatever. These proposed changes went up through the chain of command, starting with my boss. Unfortunately, he was not a particularly imaginative guy, and the company didn't adopt the plan."

Today things are beginning to change. Victor told us, "At my company, benefits are becoming much more tailored to the individual. They're not there on domestic partner health insurance yet, but it will happen because everybody doesn't have to fit into the same mold of being married with 2.4 kids. This is because the corporation's inherent goal is to save money. They can do that by offering a benefits plan where people can select and choose from a variety of options. I think at some point we will have domestic partnership coverage, because few people fit the married-with-kids profile anymore."

Some of the gay professionals we interviewed participated in their company's decision to evaluate or adopt domestic partner benefits. Judy was part of the evaluation committee that voted on benefits for her company. She told us, "When I was asked to be part of that committee, I knew I had to come out to the head of the company. I was out to my boss, but I hadn't told anyone else. So I decided I had to discuss this issue with the president. I told him, 'You know, I want to serve on this committee, but I don't want to be perceived as having any conflict of interest. I think I can bring a balanced view to this, but I happen to have a domestic partner.' I was kind of surprised when he responded, 'I know.' It turns out my boss had told him." She laughed.

"The other thing that made me feel uncomfortable initially," Judy added, "is that I knew I was on the committee to guard the bottom line. There was a considerable amount of fear that this could cost a fortune. So part of the reason I was asked to serve on the committee was that I was the financial representative of the largest department in the organization. The good news is, I was able to prove beyond a shadow of a doubt that the cost was going to be minuscule."

Louis, who is mostly closeted where he works, was recently named to run a new division of his large company. Despite the fact that the headquarters does not have a nondiscrimination policy, many of the subsidiaries do. Louis said he plans to implement both a nondiscrimination policy and seek domestic partner benefits for his subsidiary. "I've been there two years, and I've proved myself. Now I'm in that position where I can make things happen, change things."

Brent's Story

Brent told us that when he was a summer associate at the Monitor Company, he decided to press for domestic partner benefits. "One of the partners looked at it a couple of years ago, found out there were no insurance carriers (who would cover domestic partners as a spousal equivalent), and then they sort of dropped it," he told us. Brent was not in a relationship but realized that many of his gay friends at business school differentiate companies by the benefits they offer to gay employees. He said, "Companies that have domestic partnership benefits generally are viewed as more progressive. If a company offers those benefits, that's a good proxy for what the environment will be in the firm."

After doing research on the software industry, he realized that Lotus had a first-mover advantage by offering domestic partner benefits. "I thought that Monitor could obtain the same benefits by taking the stand of being the first out there. I also felt that at least the managing partner was very sympathetic to the issue. So I wrote a memo saying: 'From a business perspective, you're going to increase your applicant pull, you're going send the right signals out to people, and it shouldn't cost that much.' Harvard University did a comprehensive study of a bunch of different places that had domestic partner benefits, and I told them about that.

"The partner immediately left me a voice mail saying that one way or the other we're going to do this, and thank you so much for bringing this to our attention, because these are the kinds of things that we really want to do. He didn't have to appoint any committees or do any studies. He just appointed someone to handle it. They had a little trouble finding an insurance carrier, but eventually they were able to find one by engaging a consulting company to search for an insurer that would meet their needs."

Even those companies that are too small to find an amenable insurance carrier can take steps to equalize their treatment of valued gay employees. Of those who did approach their employers for spousal benefits, one story in particular demonstrates how a gay professional can gain much personally and financially, by daring to pursue equality. And it demonstrates how gay-friendly companies can win loyalty from valued gay employees.

Lydia's Story

When Lydia moved to a new city, she wanted to join a small company where she could obtain a high level of responsibility more quickly and work directly for the owner of the company. After a few meetings, the owner of the company presented Lydia with a shareholder agreement, since she was to receive equity in the company as part of her compensation package. In the event shareholders were married, there was a "spousal consent form" for their spouse to sign indicating they would abide by the terms of the agreement should the employee die or transfer shares to the marital partner. In addition, throughout the employment agreement itself, there were numerous references to a spouse for purposes of medical insurance coverage.

This job opportunity happened to come at a time when Lydia and her long-term partner, Ariel, were planning a commitment ceremony. Lydia had also decided that being honest and open about her sexual orientation had become an important goal and priority in her life. As a result, Lydia knew that eventually she would want to come out to her new employer.

Lydia had no way of knowing whether they were gay friendly or not, but the company was located in a city that has a nondiscrimination ordinance protecting employees from job discrimination on the basis of sexual orientation. From consulting with her own lawyer, Lydia knew that if the company rescinded their job offer, she would have a good case for a discrimination suit. Lydia hoped that she would not become involved with a protracted legal battle, but the very existence of the nondiscrimination ordinance gave her the confidence that she could not be harmed financially by letting the company know she was gay.

Lydia and her lawyer amended the language of the contract, replacing the word "spouse" with the phrase "domestic partner," and including a definition of domestic partner from the ACLU. In this definition, a domestic partner is someone who, among other things, is responsible for the person's well-being, shares a household with the person, and has been in such a capacity for at least six months. The ACLU definition deliberately avoids stating specifically whether the domestic partner is of the same or the opposite sex. However, in the contract, Lydia specifically named Ariel as her domestic partner and requested medical benefits for her.

Though she felt tremendous anxiety during the planning stages, by the time Lydia tendered her requests she presented herself very calmly. Lydia reports that her potential employers took in the request for benefits along with other details about the agreement calmly and noncommittally, as if they were nothing unusual, and said they would get back to her.

At her next meeting with management, the final language of the agreement contained the phrase "domestic partner" as Lydia had requested, rather than "spouse." Her employer's only hesitation was that he could not guarantee that the company's insurer would provide insurance for a domestic partner. They ultimately reached a compromise whereby the company would pay Lydia whatever it would have cost them to pay their insurance company to insure a spouse. Lydia could then apply the money toward an individual health policy for her domestic partner. Thus, Lydia's employers found a relatively inexpensive way to please their new employee. Although Lydia is responsible for taxes on this additional income, she told us she is happy to receive the additional compensation. In addition, the fact that her employer recognizes her relationship has made working there much more comfortable for her. Lydia confessed that this has tremendously increased her loyalty to her job and her employer.

Due to unfavorable tax implications or because their partners are already covered elsewhere, many gay professionals do not sign up for coverage that is available. But even those who have no need for it say it is important. "I'm single, so I don't have anyone to sign up. But the fact that my company has this policy sends me a strong message that they really mean what their nondiscrimination policy says," Jim Sherman said. "If I was in a relationship, it wouldn't be just the issue of monetary benefit that's meaningful, it's that they recognize my relationship."

Hard Benefits Of all the kinds of domestic partner benefits, major medical care has received the most attention. One reason is that it is a here-and-now issue relevant to a large group of relatively young, openly gay corporate employees. Yet other forms of health-care coverage, such as dental and vision-care, have been almost ignored by activists.

Other major benefits, such as stock transfer rights, disability benefits, pension plans, and death benefits, have also received less attention so far from younger and mostly junior gay activists. Yet their value can be substantial.

Also, a growing number of gay people share parenting responsibilities for their partners' children. While some companies informally cover any child living in their employees' home, few do so routinely. These benefits, which may include medical coverage, day care, or sick-child leave, can also be substantial, and few companies, whether public, private, or nonprofit, make provisions in this area.

Soft Benefits In terms of soft benefits there has been more progress. Due to AIDS, recognition of the need for sick leave to care for a partner and bereavement leave for the death of a partner are becoming increasingly common, although more often than not these benefits are available on a case-by-case basis. Other family responsibilities have been almost completely ignored on a formal level, such as sick leave to care for a partner's parent or bereavement leave for the death of a partner's parent; these are often available to those who are married.

Other soft benefits, like domestic partner discounts, access to company events and facilities, relocation assistance, counseling, and moving expenses, are also increasingly common. Yet family perks such as adoption benefits and reduced tuition at universities are often overlooked. We expect, as more senior-level gay people come out, they will increasingly push for these benefits as well.

Travel was the most common soft benefit offered by companies, we found. Most told us the use of travel benefits by partners was something they worked out for themselves, not an official part of company policy. Even before the current awareness of domestic partner benefits, some gay executives took advantage of this perk. Tony, an account manager at an advertising firm in the early 80s, discovered this opportunity shortly after starting work there. Tony, like the other account managers, was required to fly to faraway shoot locations to oversee commercials being made for his clients. He soon learned that because exotic locales were often involved, other executives' wives and husbands sometimes traveled along with them at the company's expense. Tony also knew there was a large presence of gay people in the organization, but he was still astonished and delighted to discover that the company's travel request form contained the word "other" rather than "spouse." He quickly realized many gay employees routinely took their same-sex partners along on company-paid trips, and he recounted with glee how his partner enjoyed such vacations as well.

In comparing the major airlines today, we found that some have discriminatory policies for their frequent-flyer consumers, while others have only recently abolished or modified immediate-family-only restrictions. We also learned that companies that discriminate against individual consumers also discriminate in their corporate programs. Clarence told us, "The programs for people in the travel industry vary. Some airlines let you bring one person; they don't care who it is. Others say it's only available to a family member." Because of his company's involvement in the travel industry, Clarence is often eligible for discounted airfare, hotel, and car-rental benefits, which his partner is also sometimes eligible for. "Tom has gotten great benefits from some of these companies, but it's not like you could say my company is giving us great benefits. They're not actually doing anything to help us as a gay couple. They leave it up to the companies we deal with."

Gay professionals face discrimination also with respect to sick and bereavement leave. Several told us they took the leave as necessary, despite the absence of gay relationships from the policy providing paid leave for immediate-family deaths.

Jon Zimman, who worked for a major corporation in the mid-80s, took sick and bereavement leave when his partner of many years was fighting and ultimately succumbed to AIDS. "At first I was reluctant to ask for time off, because I wasn't out to everyone at work," Jon told us. "But everyone could see that my mind wasn't on my work, and my productivity was really suffering. It was really meaningful for me to be with Peter at the end, and I got a lot of unexpected emotional support from people at work when I told them why I would be out of the office."

Others had similarly positive experiences when they found they needed to take time off due to a loved one's or a loved one's parent's illness. Those companies that have a written policy of offering sick and bereavement leave on an equal basis to gay and heterosexual employees have much to gain. By eliminating gay people's worry about whether they can attend to loved ones at such an emotional time, such companies can help an employee stay productive through one, rather than two, personal crises.

Some of those we interviewed told us they were reluctant to list their partner as a beneficiary on their employer-provided life-insurance policy for fear it would expose them to discrimination. Jordan told us he overcame this fear. "I don't want to tell too many people, because if you tell one person, the whole world knows. But I did list my partner as the beneficiary on my life insurance. So now I'm sure the office manager knows that. And I don't trust her one lick, so I'm sure other people know too."

Failing to list a partner as a beneficiary directly on a policy results in significant tax disadvantages. Even if the gay professional names their partner in their will as an heir, a significant portion of any insurance money will go to pay probate and estate taxes. This seriously diminishes the value of the bequest. In addition, given the time it takes to settle probate, the money may not be available when it is most needed.

How Change Happens

Many interviewees felt their company would never offer full domestic partner benefits until more gay professionals came out. Leonard said, "They won't do it until there is a critical mass of gay people trying to get them to change. The company would only decide to change if they were afraid of losing great people. Then they would realize discrimination is actually costing them money."

Pam concurred. She told us her employer, Met Life, has not been receptive so far to requests for domestic partner benefits. "It's been raised by another lesbian in my office. She met with management in New York on this. She brought up the fact that spouses are covered but gay partners aren't. The manager she met with basically belittled the issue by telling her there were more important things he had to work on before raising that. So I think Met is light-years away from that. I think the only thing that would make them feel it was a priority would be if a lot more gay people came out and pressed for it. They're not going to acknowledge anything unless there's enormous pressure to change."

Zackary admits his company, a prominent high-tech manufacturer, is likely to follow the lead of its competitors when it comes to benefits. "We have a really weak human resources organization, so I don't think they have the ability to actually create anything in terms of policy, on this or anything else. What they do is go out in the field and see what other companies are doing and copy bits and pieces of it." He laughed. "I think they benchmark because they are afraid to recommend anything. They don't really have any opinions of their own. I don't know if they recognize the importance of keeping pace with the industry. But they have a kind of 'me too' mentality. So if other companies do it, I think they will too."

While most felt large numbers were needed to effect change, individual gay managers who are willing to come out can also be an important catalyst for a company's implementing a full benefits program. For example, Conrad's company, which is in the entertainment industry, was thinking about implementing a domestic partner benefits package after a several-year period of careful study. But when they wanted to transfer him overseas, he said he and his partner wouldn't relocate unless they speeded up the process. They did and now have a strong and comprehensive companywide policy of domestic partner benefits. At the senior-management level, an extra perk was that they sent both Conrad and his partner overseas to find an apartment before taking the posting. Another HBS alumnus terms the apartment "stupendous and large, with a 360-degree view of the city."

Sometimes the actions of an individual can equally result in company inaction. This has been the case at AT&T, several of those we interviewed believed. For a number of years AT&T has been supportive of its gay employee group, but it has been unwilling to provide domestic partner benefits. After gay employees first raised the issue quietly, a lesbian employee died, leaving her partner and the children they raised together. Her partner applied for the death benefits AT&T ordinarily provides to spouses. When AT&T declined to pay and went to court to defend this position, the press had a field day—"How could a company that professes to treat all its employees equally do this?"

Although AT&T prevailed in the lawsuit, one AT&T employee told us she was glad the suit was finally over. "The entire benefit was only $50,000. It was a death benefit only. It didn't have anything to do with pensions or health insurance or anything else we want. Of course, the company should have paid her. But while the case was going on, they refused to talk to us about domestic partner benefits at all. Now they don't have that excuse anymore."

Several interviewees or their partners worked for AT&T. "I'm surprised you got anyone in the gay employee group to tell you that," one HBS alumnus said. "They really do like to work through channels. I keep trying to push my partner to be more radical, to push for domestic partner benefits and stuff like that. But they're very sensitive. They really don't want to criticize the company. In fact it's interesting, because right now there's another person apparently going to be pursuing a case on a similar issue. Obviously it will be a slightly different legal point. But the gay employee group is distancing themselves from that person, who is a member of the group—and it's for that exact reason." The company is quite serious "about cutting off all discussion on establishing domestic partner benefits when there is a lawsuit pending."

When company employee organizations are unable to achieve equal treatment, some have turned to outside groups, such as Lambda Legal Defense, the National Gay and Lesbian Task Force, the Human Rights Campaign Fund, the National Lesbian Rights Center, Hollywood Supports, and the Gay and Lesbian Alliance Against Defamation. Such groups can provide or recommend internal training, external encouragement, or external pressure to help companies adopt changes. In addition, they serve as a conduit for gay professionals who are unwilling to press for changes at work directly. Many told us they made financial donations to such organizations in the hopes of contributing indirectly to change at their company.

Overcoming Company Barriers

For owners and managers, making a decision to accord gay employees and their partners the same treatment they accord their heterosexual employees and spouses is not always easy. Even if management is aware that the potential costs would be low and is aware of the benefits of attracting and retaining a diverse workforce, it may be afraid to institute such a policy; some shareholders may oppose it, or it could ignite controversy, criticism, negative publicity, and consumer boycotts from the radical right.

However, there is every reason to believe the benefits more than justify the effort. Unequal benefits seriously undermine companies' efforts to build a cohesive team of employees. For companies that treat everyone equally, the resulting loyalty, productivity, teamwork, and morale can be enormous. In addition, despite the recent surge of companies adopting such measures, little consumer backlash has occurred. Despite an initial setback in Williamson County, Texas, where taxpayers opposed giving tax breaks to Apple Corporation due to their domestic partner benefits plan, Apple eventually gained the incentives it sought. The controversy also did not seem to hurt the sale of Apple computers. If anything, Apple has forged ahead with advertising in gay feature magazines and has thereby increased its customer base.

• • •

One of the most exciting trends in American management is the move toward embracing diversity in both internal and external policies. Increasingly, companies are recognizing the need to implement equal treatment for all, irrespective of sexual orientation. Domestic partner health insurance has gotten the most press attention but is only the tip of the iceberg. Large companies are addressing a panoply of issues—nondiscrimination policies, diversity training, gay employee groups, a full range of domestic partner benefits, inclusion of gay partners in workplace socializing, marketing to the gay community, and corporate philanthropy to gay organizations. Surprisingly, small companies too can be leaders in these areas, although many insurance companies continue to balk at extending coverage for smaller firms.

Openly gay individuals are at the forefront of some of these important changes. Yet those who are selectively open, and even some of those who are mostly closeted, have also played a positive role in bringing about workplace equality for gay people and helping their companies pursue the gay market. In many cases, gay employees farther down the career ladder are not aware of the steps being taken by those at higher levels they dismiss as closet cases, thus unfairly criticizing these gay executives for what they see as inaction on their part.

Due to market and competitive pressures, many gay professionals were optimistic that equal treatment is a battle that will be won in the long term. Gay employee associations at companies, unions, and government agencies are playing an increasingly important role in achieving such gains; their internal lobbying has been behind some of the major success stories in obtaining equal treatment. They have also been responsible for helping their companies to recruit and retain top talent, as well as to market successfully to the gay community.

Gay employee groups are just now beginning to work in concert to affect these changes. As gay senior managers work increasingly with such groups, whether openly or behind-the-scenes, we expect many more successes to follow.

Chapter 5

Being Closeted at Work

Perhaps the most encouraging news we obtained from our 1990 survey respondents was that less than 20 percent were completely closeted in their workplace. Rather, the vast majority had come out to a boss, coworker, or subordinate at their current or previous positions. Most had come out after being in a position for a few years. In our final round of interviews, concluded in 1994, we found that an even greater number were partially or completely open at work.

In a good number of cases, however, being selectively out at work meant coming out *only* to other gay people. Thus it is clear that a majority remain closeted to some degree, afraid of the consequences of coming out. While some may have good reason to be anxious about discrimination, in many cases fear of the unknown kept them closeted.

We were particularly interested in talking to the professionals who remained completely closeted at work even when they knew other high-level gay people in their companies or fields who are out successfully. Many said they thought most of their coworkers assumed they were gay, but they had not come out explicitly. We wondered: What is the difference between being *assumed* and being *known* to be gay? Is it better, or does it make things more difficult?

In addition, only 3 percent of our survey respondents said they worried a great deal about having their sexual orientation exposed. Another 25 percent said they worried somewhat. Thus, 72 percent were only very little or not at all worried about being outed or found out. After tabulating these responses, we wondered: What prevented respondents from coming out explicitly? In attempting to discover why some gay professionals are in the closet and why others have come out, we found our task complicated by the language gay people use.

"Coming out" may refer to a person's first glimmering of understanding that he or she is different—or the first time a person accepts his or her homosexuality. Alternatively, it may refer to the first time a person seeks the company of other gay people or habitually seeks out such company. Some use it to describe activities such as leaving clues or dropping hints about being gay. However, we found most who use the phrase in this way admit when pressed that they are not *really* out.

Finally, "coming out" refers to a range of behaviors that let heterosexuals know that one is gay. This range can be quite broad. Its scope ranges from pointed hints that are mutually acknowledged to direct statements about being gay or in a gay relationship. For example, coming out may include telling a coworker about belonging to the Gay Men's Chorus or playing tennis in the Gay Games. Courtney, who is in her thirties and is an executive with a media company, said she began "talking about my partner in the same way as my boss talks about his wife. He has asked me how the two of us met and how long we've been together, so it's clear to me that he knows." Some say outright, "I am gay" to people at work or have come out in the national media.

In our interviews we found each gay person has his or her own individual definition, often intuitive and largely unconscious, of what being in the closet and coming out mean in a particular context. Occasionally our interviewees stopped and asked us for clarification. More often we'd ask for additional information. The gay professionals we interviewed often said they were quite sure that various people at work "know." But when asked to describe how they could be sure someone else knew, they would give hazy descriptions. They'd fall back on feelings, or refer to remarks that could be interpreted very differently.

Even clues and hints that one person sees as signs of being open or of willingness to be open can be interpreted another way. For example, Dorothy told us, "The words have never been said," and she says she is closeted at work. On the other hand, Kurt said, "I'm thirty-five and have never been married. I don't talk about women, nor do I hide anything. They must think something. I think I'm pretty out."

Therefore we often asked direct questions: How do you identify that someone in particular knows? Have you told him or her in a concrete way? Do the two of you ever discuss the subject? After hearing the responses to these kinds of questions we were almost always able to evaluate whether our interviewee had really come out or was still hinting around the subject.

The challenge in evaluating whether a given individual was out or closeted at work was further compounded by the fact that many gay people are partly in and partly out of the closet at work. They may have revealed their sexual orientation selectively to some colleagues but not others. They may be out to their division but not to the entire company. And only a few have come out in the local or national media before coming out in this book.

In the vignettes that follow, we quote people who are closeted to varying degrees. Most haven't come out to anyone at work or are out to only a few heterosexuals. We've also included in this chapter some of those who are out only to other gay people at work.

WHY REMAIN CLOSETED?

According to the gay professionals interviewed, the primary reasons for remaining closeted are:

- fear of discrimination
- geographic location or specific knowledge about corporate homophobia
- a desire for privacy
- coming from a specific generation or culture that shaped their habit of hiding
- discomfort with the process of coming out to a heterosexual person
- HIV-related issues
- negative experiences with being out

Those who are closeted at work cited the following possible outcomes for being more open: harassment or ostracism from colleagues; poor performance reviews; fewer recommendations for raises, bonuses, and promotions; sidetracking to dead-end jobs; and termination of employment. But only one had seen any of these things happen to someone who was openly gay where they worked.

Most gay professionals we interviewed, whether mostly closeted or selectively open at work, admitted they didn't know what would happen if they were to become more open. However, they believed that the result couldn't possibly be good. A handful pointed to homophobic comments or discriminatory incidents at their companies. A number did not want to make themselves or their coworkers feel uncomfortable in an imagined coming-out conversation. A few thought specific colleagues would avoid them or that particular workplace friendships might suffer. But in general the fear was of the unknown.

Fear of Discrimination

The most common reason why gay professionals conceal their sexual orientation is fear of discrimination. People who have never come out at work almost always gave this explanation; even the respondents who are out to some people in the workplace gave this reason for coming out only partially.

Although few had personally experienced or witnessed discrimination, there were high levels of fear on this subject. Most were sure that being openly gay opens far fewer doors than it closes in the interview process. Not surprising, those who were open on their résumés or in interviews were in the minority and mostly under the age of thirty.

Once gay professionals were hired, their anxiety didn't end. Most continued to fear the consequences of coming out. Perhaps paradoxically, less than a third said they worried much about being *found out.* As we saw previously, the focus of these fears may be mistaken: For gay professionals in our study, the consequences of being found out were far worse than the consequences of coming out.

Few respondents were strongly concerned about physical violence, cruel pranks, direct insults, or harassment as a likely consequence of coming out. Most admitted that their real concerns were discrimination in advancement, lower status among peers, difficulties with key clients or suppliers, harm to relationships with mentors, loss of workplace friendships, or difficulty finding a new position.

Those employed by America's most prominent conservative companies almost universally believed they would be discriminated against in some fashion if they were completely open about their gay identity in their current work environment. These professionals include those working for *Fortune* 500 manufacturers (both industrial and consumer products companies) and in construction, energy, real estate, transportation, investment banks, and utilities. To a lesser degree this fear is shared by those employed by large banks, insurance companies, pension funds, and major consulting firms. Nicholas, a gay Black man, said, "I'm afraid to let people know I'm gay. In this business, if there's anything that can be used to gain a competitive advantage, people will use it. They'll say, 'Oh, you shouldn't send him to the client. Who knows what he's gonna do?' " Dorothy, a lesbian in her forties, agreed. "If one of my peers knew I was gay, I think they'd go in to my department head. I can hear it now. 'Lookit, you shouldn't send her out to the Midwest for that deal. You know how she is. And you know how they think about that out there. I'll keep the client happy. Send me to get the business.' I think, if they knew, the tendency would be to keep you at home, crunching numbers and stuff. Which is an absolutely essential part of the business, but it's not the kind where you get huge bonuses."

Most of those who had been and planned to continue to be largely closeted worked in these conservative fields, which they perceived to be especially hostile to promoting openly gay individuals. Not surprising, these are also the industries with the worst track record for promoting women, Jews, Blacks, Hispanics, and Asian Americans. In these industries there is strong pressure to be the same. Women and minorities in industries often try to maintain a low profile; few say their companies see difference as an asset.

There was a greater tendency toward openness in industries traditionally cited as more gay friendly. As a rule, those in advertising, the arts, communications, computers, smaller consulting concerns, cosmetics and fashion, education, entertainment, entrepreneurial enterprises, personal financial services, government, health care, high tech, journalism, marketing, music, publishing, retail, and travel—even in the largest companies—were out to more people than those who worked in more conservative industries. But even in these relatively gay-friendly industries, some gay professionals lived in fear.

Many companies in these industries deserve their open-minded reputations. But we also constantly heard: "My company/division is particularly homophobic." "It's different when you're a woman (Hispanic, Vietnamese, etc.)." "It's OK in the stores, but not in the executive suite." "The creative types are all gay, but hardly anyone on the business side is." "He's got it made, but I'm still on my way up." Most commonly we heard, "No one cares until you reach a certain level. Then you better not be open."

Gay professionals who worked in all industries frequently said, "I don't want to give them any reason to promote someone else instead of me." Those who were closeted in smaller-company environments or particular geographic locations most often cited potential customer reaction or the difficulty of getting another position in the future as their reason for keeping a low profile about being gay. A few also mentioned that they were not out to their family of origin. They worried the word might somehow get back to relatives or others in their hometown if they were more open at work.

It is important to remember that not everyone had the fears or is constrained by them to the same degree. A number in every industry have come out to one or more heterosexuals at work or have networked extensively with other gay people in their company; still others said, "I think people know and they don't care."

Patriotism, Radical Right, or Family Values Companies Those who work in companies that are associated with the defense industry, that serve children, or that are connected with conservative or fundamentalist religious groups face special challenges in the workplace. Gay professionals in these fields were the most likely to know of gay people who had been treated badly in their companies and to be aware of media reports about the homophobia that affects their company. Almost all are completely closeted.

Marvin, a Jewish man in his late thirties, told us about his experience with one such employer. "Right now, I'm the most militant and out workwise that I've ever been. That's because I've just left the most homophobic place I've ever worked. Now I will not go to work for a place that even hints at being homophobic. It's not that I have to have everyone know I'm gay or even have a picture of a lover on my desk, but I don't want it to matter if it should come out.

"Let's face it. It does come out. Someone who is of a certain age who's not married, who's not a troll . . . I mean, *I* assume people are gay in that context. I think anyone else would. I shouldn't say I assume they are, but it's very possible they are.

"Of course, when I worked at that company I'm not going to name, I never said I was gay. It turns out I also knew about a dozen other people there who were gay. I was in a position that was just intensely uncomfortable, and I made the decision to quit. I saved enough money to be able to be in a long-term unemployed job search, which is what I've just finished doing."

Many Harvard Business School students are active in the military or the military reserve, and the military is a career path for some. While we interviewed a number of gay people who had served or were still serving in the armed forces when they went to HBS, none returned to active service.

However, we were able to identify a number of gay professionals in the defense industry. Most have been heavily closeted throughout their careers. Now that security clearances favor those who are openly gay over those who are closeted, we expect to see some changes in these industries. In addition, many companies are shifting from military to commercial markets, which is also likely to contribute to more openness.

We were also fascinated by the number of gay people we found working for Disney, the ultimate milk-and-cookies company. We discovered an extensive gay network there, which is obvious even to some heterosexuals we know at the company. Rosa was able to accurately give names of many gay HBS alumni and other gay senior executives there. Most said that in the entertainment industry it was less an issue than one might think, but none was willing to use his or her name for publication.

Those in family businesses, whether owned by their families or someone else's, faced special challenges that led some to be closeted at work, yet this group contained both the most open and the most closeted individuals. Those who worked for another family's business often felt a close personal relationship with the owners. Those who were closeted felt particularly burdened by it; those who were open found a good deal of support. The major consideration for someone working for his or her own family was whether or not they were out to all their relatives. Other considerations were how accepting the family was and what industry and location they were in. Most allowed themselves to be guided by their family's level of comfort in determining how open they were to clients and others outside of work.

Large Manufacturers and Consumer Products Firms—Construction and Real Estate Companies—Transportation and Utilities

Corporate America well deserves its reputation as one of the most conservative parts of the business world. One reason is that many corporations do business in locations that are less than sophisticated about gay issues. Another is that these companies serve mass markets that include those who are homophobic. A third reason is that many companies' corporate cultures have long valued sameness, a habit that is proving hard to break. In many ways, the situation of gay people in corporate America mirrors the situation of Jews. Most try not to call attention to being distinctive and are able to hide the most conspicuous differences on a day-to-day basis.

Those who worked in these conservative industries were second only to those in patriotism/family-values workplaces in the number of homophobic remarks or jokes they heard from bosses and coworkers. Others reported that the word "gay" was never mentioned by anyone over the course of several decades.

Betsy, who left a large consumer-products company in a small city to join another large company in a more metropolitan area, said, "What is coming out and what is being closeted? My sexual orientation isn't on my business card. I'm not going to let you quote me and say this is the *Fortune* 50 company that she's a vice president of. Yet I certainly don't go out of my way to hide my lifestyle, like I did at my previous job. Now whether I needed to do that there or not, nobody will ever know. It may have also been a function of the time or a reflection of where I was about being gay.

"At my previous company—an ultraconservative one that all of America knows—the burden of duplicity was tremendously overwhelming. When I was first coming out, I lived in a neighborhood near a lot of the popular lesbian hangouts and hot spots. Almost every evening, some younger folks stopped by my place on the way home. It now seems crazy, but at that time my partner and I constantly made sure the curtains were closed and the doors were shut. We'd never just open the door but, rather, look through the peephole to make sure it was one of the crowd, rather than a straight friend.

"We both worked at the same company, and when we entertained heterosexual coworkers, my partner would pretend she was leaving with them, only to drive around the block and return home after the others left. We lived an inordinately closeted life. We became masters at contriving stories of why we were with each other or going to places together. That was really burdensome. The ordeal of always being on edge was also incredibly stressful."

Most gay people in conservative industries believe they must remain deeply closeted, both at work and in their personal lives, in order to function effectively in their jobs. However, those who were willing to risk being open even selectively usually met with success.

Many of the gay professionals we interviewed began their careers in these industries but left to go into more gay-friendly ones. Others followed the path of their heterosexual peers from HBS by moving from Corporate America to investment banking or to large consulting firms, thus jumping from the frying pan into the fire.

Finance and Investment Banking Many of our survey respondents worked in investment banking before business school but elected not to return. Was this because of homophobia they found there? Some who worked in investment banking after earning their MBAs, like Dorothy and Trisha, clearly left because of the homophobia. Many others also said yes to our question, although some added they also wanted a career that was more collegial in every way. A few said Harvard opened their eyes to new areas of interest and careers in other fields.

Peter, a white man who received his MBA in the late 1970s, worked in the financial sector for a decade, then left to enter an industry where he was openly gay. He now hopes to return to the world of finance at a senior level with one of the big firms and expects he will have to return to the closet again, although he does not intend to change his life outside the workplace. He described the fear he continues to observe in a former colleague who is still working in the industry. "A few times I invited him to go out to a gay bar with me, but he always declined. He'd come up to me and say, 'How do you deal with this . . . I mean, what if someone sees you?' I'd say, 'Look, Walter, it's a big city. Who'll see you?' I'd talk and try to help him. Maybe he wanted to be coaxed into going and doing things with my other gay friends, but he was so uptight about it that I stopped inviting him."

For Humphrey, who is Black, the issue of whether to be closeted or to come out in an investment banking milieu is not even a real question to him. "I've always been the only Black person in each work environment I've been in. I feel I am already at risk in whatever position I'm in. I can't think of any way that it would advance my career to come out."

Those currently in I-banking who say they are most comfortable with their strategy for managing a gay identity at work have generally chosen areas where they can avoid closeness with colleagues. While this is relatively exacting on the institutional-investing or deal-making sides, we were told there are other niches where a gay person can manage to avoid personal conversations more easily and certain divisions where the corporate culture is more congenial.

Although we heard many stories about investment banking as a terrible environment for gay people, we also found a few notes of hope. First, a number of the current HBS gay students have seriously thought about entering or returning to I-banking after hearing the stories of gay HBS grads currently coping successfully with the challenges of the field. Second, some of those we interviewed have come out more widely at work after becoming friendly with younger, more open HBS alumni or current students.

Third, as in every other industry, there are hidden friends in investment banking who plan to come out publicly after reaching a certain level of professional accomplishment. Jack told us, "If I had come out the first day or a few years ago, it might have had less impact. It seems like the longer I wait, the more visible I become and the more significant my coming out will be. I think that if I came out now it would have a lot of impact in the office, because I'm viewed as the most successful person in this job. To the extent people have biases or prejudices against gay people, it would be very disconcerting to them to have to reconcile those feelings with their respect for me.

"I think it would have a lot of impact through the entire division of the company, and that intrigues me. I've had very high visibility companywide due to my success in making money for the firm, so there would be ramifications. I would like to come out because I think I could really make a significant difference.

"My role is fairly broad companywide. I am integrally involved in MBA recruiting as well as in training new people. I regularly speak at regional conferences on the topic of how to do a better job. I'm not saying this to be cocky, just to relay how it is, so you know I'm kind of an example, a role model within the organization, and at a fairly young age. As I progress to a point where everyone worldwide in this job function knows who I am, then coming out would have even more impact.

"A separate issue is that in my job there are two choices. One is that I could do this job forever—it pays well, I'm good at it, and I like it. It gives me a great lifestyle, high income, control of my day, all that. I'm reluctant to leave it.

"On the other hand, there are not a lot of capable management types in my area at the bank. I could progress fairly easy through management and have a very good shot at becoming a managing director. Being a managing director is a big thing; you have extraordinarily high compensation, and it's very prestigious, because you are part of the team that runs the company.

"So I have to make a choice—either I stay where I'm at or I leave my current position to try to become a managing director. There are definitely gay issues involved in this decision. The major issue is: if I came out now, would that preclude me from making it? Because that's a subjective and exceedingly subtle process. It might be better to wait to come out if I want to go for that.

"If I decide I have no interest in becoming a managing director, then I could come out now and it wouldn't matter, since in my job I'm totally untouchable. Even if I thought they'd discriminate against gay people in general, they'd leave me alone. I'm in a very secure environment regarding my position."

As if calculating the possibilities, Jack locked and unlocked his fingers as he continued. "But if I waited to become a managing director and then I came out, that would be really interesting, because then I could be an openly gay managing director on Wall Street. I could have impact not only in just my division or firm, but probably within the entire industry. If I were openly gay before making it, I think the other managing directors' main concern would be: will this affect business relationships with clients? I think that that's their mind-set.

"It's inconceivable that it would be a problem with them personally. However, then I look at what's going on with the gays in the military, and I'm just blown away by how different my perception of how things should be is from others', such as those elected to the Senate. If our senators can be so out of touch with the way I feel, maybe the managing directors in the firm are too. Who knows, maybe I'm the one that's out of touch.

"So then I think: Well, since my situation now is so wonderful, why rock the boat just to come out now? Maybe I should come out in a few more years—either I'll be a worldwide star or a managing director. Since it's not that urgent to me on a personal level, I'm just sort of chewing on it; I'm not rushing it."

Banking and Institutional Investors Surprisingly, many Harvard MBAs said banks and institutional investors, such as insurance companies and pension funds, were "not such bad places to work" if one was gay, at least in major metropolitan areas. This group described themselves as semicloseted or selectively open in the workplace; nonetheless, all saw a lavender ceiling in their company as well as other obstacles to advancement.

Hope, a Jewish lesbian in her late twenties, was particularly surprised to find so many other gay people from junior to senior levels at a Japanese bank she worked for. "It has a reputation for being a staid, conventional, conservative bank. Only the most conservative students from the University of Tokyo go to this bank. So I never expected to work with so many diverse Americans.

"I wonder how many people realize the kind of a melting pot and an eclectic group that foreign banks draw. They pull together the 'misfits' from regular mainstream banking, like Chase Manhattan Bank and Chemical Bank and J. P. Morgan. Although there's tons of different people at those places, there seems to be a larger collection of ethnic and gay people at foreign banks. I didn't realize this fact when I started, but I quickly saw that was the case.

"There were Mexicans, Filipinos, Jewish, and Japanese people in our group. You'd think as a woman it would be very difficult, but I loved it there. I was the youngest person at my age to be promoted to my level, and I was definitely on the fast track at the bank. My boss was my mentor—he was great." In the course of this glowing conversation, Hope became serious. "The real roadblock for a career there is just being American. You don't hit a glass ceiling. You hit a cement ceiling."

Pam, who is in her late thirties and is out to all the people she works with daily, said, "As a lesbian, I'm an outsider. Add to the equation that I'm Asian. Here in the Northeast it's all very white. And the industry is very white too. There's a lot of personal connections that have to be made in order to succeed in this business. There are more women now, but we're still a minority. So I'm a woman, I'm Asian, a lesbian. It's a struggle to meet people and forge relationships. Considering who I am, I believe I'm three steps behind everyone else.

"One of the reasons I know I'm not going to be at this company forever is obvious every time I look around. Other than two women, all the VPs are men. There's a woman pretty high in the organization, but she's from personnel; she's not on the business side. Also, all the VPs are white, except for a token Black. So you see, it's filled with male, white, conservative leadership.

"It's a mutual insurance company, not a publicly traded company, so the company's not totally run for shareholder profit. They're going to make decisions in their own best interests with little motivation to change. They could also say, 'We don't have to worry about the shareholders backlashing against the gay-friendly policies or the employment diversity that we have.' But they haven't done that. They also have the freedom to be really reactionary."

Those who were white, male, older, and more senior were likely to be almost completely closeted in their work as institutional investors.

***FORTUNE* 50 SERVICE COMPANIES, TELECOMMUNICATIONS, AND FINANCIAL SERVICES** We found individuals in these industries were likely to be out selectively. Few were completely closeted, and while none were completely open, most had plans to continue to come out more broadly over time. Tyrone, a Black executive at a telecommunications company, is another who has a plan for coming out more openly after grabbing the gold ring. "I'm out to certain people at work and to my mentor. When I say 'out,' I guess it really depends on how it's defined. As far as I'm concerned, being out means being open about your life and sharing it with a certain set of people. That's happened for me with two bosses, one of whom has been my mentor for six of the eight years that I've been with the company.

"Of my direct report team, I'd say I'm out to three out of the four direct-report managers who work for me. They know not to talk about it to the fourth, because we kind of have this sense that her feelings would be a little bit different.

"I've also been mentoring people behind me, of which three are gay. With everyone else at the company, I've made no attempt to be out or any attempt to be closeted. I've not had to do anything like bring a woman to an event as sort of a cover-up. I've never found it necessary. It's been OK that I'd just show up.

"I thought when I joined this company it was going to be for only two years. I never thought I would stay this long. But I got hooked in with this set of people who I respect and I know respect me. We've all grown together, moved up through the corporation. We're all getting the tags and the titles right now. The big stamp is officer of the corporation; my mentor got it just last month. His boss got the big stamp two years ago.

"I now have four friends and mentors with the big stamp. I'm only two levels away from it myself, and I'll probably get it at the next level up from the job I'm currently in. So I'm right on the cusp of it. Out of three hundred thousand people, I'd be one of the hundred people who are running the business. Right now I'm in the top six hundred.

"That's my issue with anonymity—waiting for the big stamp. Because when I get it, I can tell you I will be out. My name will be everywhere. I won't give it a goddam thought. But right now, it's politics. I'm uncertain what would happen if I were out with more people. I'm in an environment where perception counts. There is performance, for sure. I'm bringing in hard dollars, but it's always part of a team. I'm making my profit-and-loss figures, I have profit-and-loss responsibilities for $800 million. I have a $5 billion product line with two thousand people on it. I'm bringing in my numbers and I'm showing leadership. But I'm working as part of the team. So it can be subjective about what I did versus what someone else contributed.

"That big stamp is like tenure. You become untouchable. You make seven digits. You work, but you don't work that hard. You're in. I'm on the fast track in terms of getting there. If I get it by age forty, which is when it looks like I'll get it, I'll be one of the youngest to have got it at that age. So it's a really big deal."

Brett, who is in his late thirties and who works at a large diversified financial services company, is out to only some heterosexuals in his immediate work group. Nonetheless, he has been instrumental in starting a large but informal network of senior-level gay executives at his company and obtaining certain domestic partner benefits.

"There are a few gay executives who are out throughout the company. I'm not one of them. On the other hand—even though I don't share this stuff with too many straight people in the company, I don't care if they know about me. In fact, I'm sure a lot of them do." Brett's willingness to be thought gay without coming out was typical of many in these industries.

Major Consulting Firms As a profession, consulting with large firms is ultracompetitive. You move up or you move out. We met a number of gay people at various levels of the consulting hierarchy, and almost all agreed being gay makes it harder the higher up you go. Alex, a white gay man in his mid-thirties, joined a major consulting firm after business school. He was a rising star for many years there and recently left consulting to pursue an opportunity he learned of through one of his clients. He said that while consulting can be a great training ground for young people in business, the more senior you get, the more being gay becomes an issue.

Alex told us, "Postcollege, pre-MBA, you are an analyst. After B-school you go from associate to engagement manager, which is rather like a project manager who holds everything together and makes sure everything is done by the due date. The next step up is senior engagement manager. About six or seven years out of business school you have a chance at making partner.

"This first level of partnership is the time when it starts to get much more difficult if you are gay. That's where your relationships with the senior clients are the primary issue: Do they trust you? Would they open up to you? That kind of stuff.

"In the early years, all that really counts is that you do good work and that you're smart, analytical, work hard, and crunch out the numbers while dealing with midlevel clients without being obnoxious and alienating them. But the more senior you get, the more you have to fit the senior-partners model. Your private life ends up starting to intertwine with your clients' private lives, and it becomes increasingly difficult to separate your private life from your work life.

"If there isn't a wife to bring to functions, no kids to talk about, there aren't the normal sets of things that you discuss with your CEOs. The role of the senior people is to become close personal advisors to CEOs, and CEOs are by and large straight white males. The question becomes, can anyone besides a straight white male become a close personal advisor to a CEO? Women and minorities face the same issues gay people do in this regard.

"There's a partner at my old firm who's gay but is not open about it. I'd say he is very heavily closeted, except some gay people know he is gay from running into him at gay social events. He does the staffing and assigns people to different projects. He's not exactly open about it, but I think most people know about him, both gay and straight. It's a nonclient job, so there is less of an issue there."

All of those we interviewed in the consulting industry concurred that it requires a herculean number of hours and much time away from home. Many heterosexuals leave the field precisely because the time and travel demands are so incompatible with family life. Thus it is rather incongruous that those without the competing demands of family responsibilities are made to feel unwelcome in the consulting profession; the very people best suited for it feel unwelcome. Single gay men or lesbians or those who are part of dual-career gay couples with no children are perfect candidates for this career, yet many are persuaded to leave.

Although most gay professionals at large consulting firms believe their careers would be jeopardized if they came out, some have come out to varying degrees over the last few years. A number of those in their twenties and thirties have been named in the press as openly gay or have consented for us to use their names here. We also interviewed others who are more senior and who are open within their firms, if not out to all their clients; thus they have asked us to use pseudonyms for their names.

Remaining Closeted in Gay-Friendly Companies or Industries We were surprised by the number of closeted gay professionals in industries that have the reputation for being gay friendly, such as retail, fashion, advertising, or high tech. Many explained there are important differences between the business side and the creative side of many companies.

In some cases we talked to more than one person in a company and confirmed the company's reputation as especially difficult for gay people. One company had employed two Harvard MBAs, one who wanted to be more out and one who was content to be completely closeted. Nathan, a Jewish man in his mid-thirties, explained, "We were in an industry where you would expect there would be a lot of gay people. There were. But what happened was the straight men in this company felt self-conscious that they were marketing products to women. So they overcompensated and they became ultramacho. There was little tolerance for gay people in the business, at least in certain job functions. In the art department it was OK. In management it was not. There were a few of us in management, but I did not feel comfortable there at all."

Those who were most closeted in these industries were women and racial minorities. They said that while white gay men could afford to come out, they were already unusual enough at their companies and didn't want to spend any more difference capital on the gay issue.

Independent consultants and entrepreneurs observed that their biggest issue was whether or not to come out to their clients. Some said they did most of their business over the phone and rarely met with clients, so it seemed especially awkward to come out. Many who developed personal relationships with clients have come out to them, but not all have done so, particularly to clients in very macho or conservative industries.

Medical and Legal Professions, Law Enforcement, Education Some of those we interviewed (or their partners) had significant experience in nonbusiness fields such as medicine and law. They confirmed our impression that these fields are generally similar to the gay-friendly industries described above.

Significant numbers of professional associations and a number of the large companies in these fields have adopted policies of nondiscrimination, active recruitment, or promotion of openly gay individuals within their ranks.

Universities and municipalities have in many ways taken the lead on the domestic partner benefits issue and have more leeway to implement nondiscriminatory employment and promotion practices. Many in academia and government have also been among the most visible gay spokesmen and -women. Gay teachers in New York City recently obtained domestic partner benefits and are starting to use this hard-earned perk in record numbers.

Even law enforcement, long notorious for being one of the most difficult career choices for gay men and lesbians, has begun to open its ranks in recent years, particularly in certain large urban centers.

While not every gay lawyer, doctor, nurse. professor, teacher, politician, cop, or civil servant has an easy time on the job, the business world has a lot to learn from strides that have been made in these fields.

Homophobic Locations or Companies

Most gay professionals who worked in small towns or cities in the South or Midwest were heavily closeted—and highly concerned with the repercussions of being suspected or found out to be gay. Generally, they believed they would receive little support if they decided to be open. At worst, they thought they would lose their job; this was a particularly strong concern in states that have employment "at will" law and cities that have no protection from discrimination. At best, they expected that their careers would grind to a halt and that they would have difficulty finding another position in their geographic area or industry.

Many who were more open in large cities became more closeted during the years they were posted in a less urbane environment. Most sought to avoid such postings or tried to transfer out just as soon as they could.

Some knew that their particular company was especially homophobic —from the media or their own experience. Obviously, employers that have explicit and well-publicized policies against hiring gay people, such as the Boy Scouts, the military, and organizations and ministries affiliated with the radical right, are not comfortable places for gay people to work. Additionally, some companies have received media attention for being accused of discriminating against particular gay men and lesbians—United Press International, the *Christian Science Monitor,* and Shell Oil, for example. Well-publicized incidents such as the Cracker Barrel Restaurant chain firing all its gay service employees, an advertising company creating the "Nuttin Honey" cereal ad that many saw as promoting gay bashing, and Dayton-Hudson (Target/Mervyn Stores) making its security personnel take tests to determine who was gay are similar clues that a company is unlikely to be a comfortable place to be gay. We also were able to confirm that companies that routinely pull ads from gay-themed TV episodes are some of the least desirable places for gay people to work.

Gilbert, a white man in his mid-thirties, received confirmation about the way he might be treated if he came out at work after he saw what had happened to an openly gay man in his company. "Basically, they found a way to fire him after he appeared on the cover of a nationally circulated gay magazine. I work in the corporate office on the business side and heard about their reaction. It's a very conservative company and doesn't really like publicity about itself in any form. The man who they fired was on the creative side of the business and had been fairly open before he came out to the public. I don't really take it that personally or anything. It just kind of confirmed the company culture to me, which is: Just don't discuss your personal life at work—if you're gay, that is."

The environment within a particular division or the attitude of a particular boss can also be a major concern. It is precisely this issue that kept Derek in the closet at a previous company. "Intense homophobia from a boss and from the boss of my boss made me feel I had to have a secret life in order to not be fired. This fear added a great deal of stress in my life." On the other hand, with certain bosses or divisions of a large company these concerns are less relevant.

Rick, who is now working happily at American Express, was originally contacted by a headhunter about a position in another division of the company. He didn't like the feeling he got from the people there and called a lesbian he had met through a gay professional organization who had worked there previously. She confirmed his impression. He told us, "The next day the headhunter called back and said, 'If you don't like that division of Am Ex, how about this division?' Then he started to explain about the other division of the company and why it's unique, and suggested I interview there.

"I told him, 'I'm sorry. I'm not interested.' I hung up the phone and called back my friend at Citibank to ask her about this other division. She gave me the scoop, saying it was a world apart from the other division and assured me I'd love it there." Rick chuckled and admitted, "I called the headhunter back immediately and told him, 'OK, I'll go to the interview.' "

Rick advised, "Don't write off a company because of one bad experience. Don't write off the whole company because of one section of it. Divisions change and times change; if you interviewed years ago, remember that it might be different now."

A Desire for Privacy

Not everyone said they stayed in the closet because of fear. Many claimed: "I prefer to keep my private life private, and I would feel the same way whether I was straight or gay." This was a more believable explanation from those who were single than those who were in committed relationships. For example, we asked all those who said they were private people whether they knew which of their heterosexual coworkers were married, and all replied that they did.

It was primarily our interviews with single gay men and women who are beginning to come out selectively at work that made us skeptical of the pat response about privacy. Their recognition of the change in their own philosophy on this subject gave us pause to doubt what now seems to be a rather facile explanations.

Sometimes what people meant by "keeping my private life private" is that they were not interested in socializing with people at work. Usually it also meant that they were reluctant to engage in even rather superficial water-cooler conversations during the course of the work day. Many of these individuals admitted that the difficulties of trying to hide being gay were at least partially behind this disinclination. Many also attributed their lack of interest to a related factor, that is, having a different lifestyle than their peers who lived in the suburbs and had children. They assumed that if they came out, there would be even less common ground for friendship or routine office chitchat.

When pressed, many who were closeted explicitly attributed their desire for privacy to a reluctance to expose their personal lives to the negative judgments of others or to their own lack of comfort with discussing the subject. We found that, universally, the more out people became, the more likely they were to integrate their work and personal lives, becoming more likely to divulge greater details in casual conversations and spending more time developing relationships with heterosexuals outside the office.

This was particularly easy to verify in the case of those few individuals we interviewed twice. It was also confirmed by those we interviewed a few years ago and have recently spent social time with. In each case, those who were not willing to admit to us (or themselves) that their desire for privacy was connected to their fears about coming out sang a different tune as they took steps toward becoming more open at work.

For example, David Stokes, a white gay man in his mid-thirties who is now a senior manager in the litigation-consulting practice at Price Waterhouse in Boston, told us in 1990: "I have always kept my private life and my professional life very separate. I don't really have a problem with that. I work hard when I'm at work. When I'm not working, everyone at work knows, I travel all the time on the weekends in the summer. They know that I have a fun house here in town and I have my own interests. I never talk about girlfriends or anything. When people ask if I'm dating anyone, I'll say, 'No, I'm not dating anyone now,' because I know they're asking me if I'm dating any women. I talk about my roommate. 'We're going to go here or do that. Yeah, we're good friends.' That kind of thing."

We reinterviewed David in 1993, and he told us that he planned to come out to some of the senior partners of the firm imminently and would follow by coming out gradually to others in the office. He summarized some of the clues and hints he has been leaving in preparation and the more pointed hints he would like to make: "There are an awful lot of folks who know that I live in the South End and I've been renovating the place with Darrin. If anyone were to ever ask me if I'm gay, like my secretary did two weeks ago, I'd say yeah. Once I realized what she was asking me, that is! Otherwise, I tend to be a lot more vague than I'd prefer.

"I'd like to be able to say that my partner and I are going to the Morning Party on Fire Island. Instead I'll say, 'I'm going down to meet some friends in the Hamptons for the weekend.' I say, 'I'm going to the Cape,' not, 'Darrin and I are going to Provincetown.' " We subsequently learned that David has come out to senior management without negative repercussions.

Age, Temperament, and Cultural Background

Some gay professionals choose to remain closeted at the office even after they question the need to. For some, keeping their personal life a secret has become so habitual they feel exposed and frightened by the prospect of change. Most of this group grew up in extremely homophobic times and still continue to harbor feelings of shame and embarrassment about being gay. In particular, they've convinced themselves that coming out would "shove" being gay in the face of colleagues who would have difficulty handling the information. A few of those we talked to seemed to have a hard time using the words "I am gay" in ordinary conversation, even with other gay people.

While this discomfort was more common with the older half of our interview group, some individuals of all ages referred to being gay as "my story" or "it," without ever mentioning the word "gay" throughout the entire interview, and some of all ages told us they viewed being openly gay at work as needlessly confrontational.

In general, gay people have developed a far more extensive terminology for hiding than for being open. We heard a large variety of circumlocutions used at work to avoid the simple statement "I'm gay." In contrast, interviewees described their closeted behavior in legions of highly descriptive ways. What follows is an ad hoc list of some harrowing ways people talk about being openly gay or describe their self-presentation in negative terms. Notice in particular, in many of the examples, that being gay is "it," an impersonal pronoun, rather than a descriptive noun or an adjective.

> I don't shove it down anyone's throat; I don't ram it down their throats; I don't rub it in their faces; I don't wave a banner; I don't bang it out on a drum; I don't make an issue of it; I don't put a sign up across my chest; I don't have a sign across my forehead; it's not tattooed anywhere; I don't wear it on my sleeve; I don't talk about my sex life at work; I don't discuss it explicitly; I don't flaunt it; we just don't talk about it; if anyone asked me, I'd tell them, but no one ever has; I don't use the "G" word; I don't use the "L" word; I don't volunteer anything; I don't deny anything; I keep my personal life private.

We pressed several of our closeted interviewees for concrete examples of some of the above. What specifc behavior would be going too far or flaunting it or shoving it down someone's throat? we queried. Very few rose to the challenge with examples. Instead most reverted back to generalities: "Well, I just don't carry a banner into work," or, "I just don't talk about it," or, "It's not that important to me," or, "I just don't want to make an issue of it."

When we discussed this phenomenon, many confirmed that they felt discussing being gay at work to be so anxiety producing they can't even imagine how they would do it.

Only a few who said they anticipated remaining closeted gave concrete examples of what confrontational versus nonconfrontational methods of coming out would be. They then added that they were afraid of or uncomfortable about implementing even the most nonconfrontational methods.

We found some differences with regard to cultural background. Respondents who are Black, Hispanic, or Asian American were slightly less open at work than white or Jewish professionals, primarily due to fear of double discrimination or because they did not want word to get back to their families. Similarly, those who grew up in a rural area or small town, the South, Texas, or the Midwest were less likely to come out, no matter where they live now. Many remarked, "At home, we didn't speak about anything personal, so I never learned how."

Among whites, those from high WASP, Baptist, or Catholic families described themselves as far more private than those from other religious or cultural backgrounds. They were also most likely to say that they had not had much practice coming out to heterosexuals and lacked confidence to do so.

Discomfort with the Process of Coming Out and Being Out

While fear of discrimination is real, and in some cases obviously justified, in other cases fear of the unknown is the real issue that prevents gay professionals from coming out. An important and often overlooked component of this fear is lack of practice and self-confidence, both of which can be overcome.

Many who attended Harvard Business School came out to themselves relatively late compared to others in the gay community. The pressure and distractions of pursuing academic and career success allowed many to ignore this critical aspect of their identity. In our survey, the average Harvard MBA first became aware of sexual feelings toward his or her own gender at age fifteen. The average age of coming out to oneself was twenty-one; to a gay friend, twenty-two; to a heterosexual friend, twenty-four; and to a family member, twenty-seven. Thus, the typical Harvard MBA missed the opportunity to be openly gay in all facets of life that many on college campuses are experiencing today. A mere 7 percent participated in a college gay student organization, and only 37 percent explored any off-campus gay social life in college.

Tellingly, many who had negotiated a coming-out conversation with family or heterosexual friends did not go on to actively manage the process of being openly gay in the ongoing relationship. At the first sign of discomfort, they dropped the subject. And many were simply unable to imagine just being out without having to go through the social awkwardness of coming out. They refused to even consider the possibility of such a world with such freedom. Others reported that they never tell anyone who doesn't already show signs of knowing or being open to the issue. Several summed it up by saying, "After I'm sure they know, then I tell them."

Given all that is written about the importance of effective communication, it seems rather amazing that some people actually communicate the fact that they are gay without ever saying the word. One interviewee said, "I know they know, and they know I know they know, but we never acknowledge they know in words." We were getting dizzy just trying to keep up.

This fear of open discussion has some validity; it can be difficult to come out in a workplace where there may be penalties for doing so. Also, coming out in certain ways and by using specific words may be better than using other ways and other words. For people who do not have a lot of practice in coming out and being out to heterosexual friends or family members, it can be hard to know which is which. There is another source of information, however. We found in reinterviews that those who have become closer to friends who are more open about being gay at work became more comfortable themselves with the language of coming out and being out.

HIV and the Closet

A significant percentage of our survey respondents were HIV-positive, and some were closeted at work, both about being gay and being HIV-positive. We repeatedly heard that health-care coverage was the primary reason these individuals remained closeted. However, others told us that as their health condition began to deteriorate they began to be more open about their HIV status. Whether closeted or open about being gay, these interviewees reported that their companies treated them with respect and accommodation during periods of illness.

Negative Experiences

Some closeted gay professionals were more out earlier in their careers and had negative experiences. Thus, they were reluctant to be out at work now or in the future. Most of this group were inadvertently discovered or outed, or used methods of coming out that we found can often lead to more negative experiences than coming out proactively.

Others were involved in workplace affairs that became the source of office gossip; some admitted they had mismanaged particular aspects of the coming-out process. While they hoped they had learned from their mistakes, the potential downside seemed too great as they moved up the career ladder.

Wanda catalogued what many others, even those who are openly and happily out at work, cautioned: "People can get too personal. Coworkers were always asking me about my love life and telling me about theirs. They believe you have trusted them with a great secret, and want to know all about it. Then they want to share their own secrets with you. They believe that if you are gay you automatically condone marital infidelity, group sex, or are comfortable discussing particular sex acts with them.

"It just became a distraction. It became something that made it harder for me to do my job. People didn't focus on work anymore. They just wanted to talk about coming out to parents, gay culture, gay politics, sex, their relationships, or their own secrets."

While all of these problems seemed fixable to us, those who justified their closet on this basis did not agree. Instead they interpreted these incidents as a mandate to remain closeted.

A RANGE OF CLOSETED AND OPEN BEHAVIORS

Similarly to those who are openly gay, those in the closet represent a range of behaviors. Gay people working in extremely homophobic fields and companies may go to extreme lengths to protect their jobs. Others simply make it a practice to not confirm or deny anything. Depending on how many clues are left, purposely or otherwise, coworkers may believe that they are heterosexual or that they are gay. However, these individuals remain closeted or quasicloseted at work; few or none of their coworkers know for sure.

Sebastin, a Black man who is a partner at a major consulting firm, confirmed, "I had a conversation with a colleague who I thought knew I was gay, but in the course of the discussion, it became apparent that he didn't. When I told him, he told me he was really surprised. He wasn't upset or annoyed or thought less of me or anything, but he said he was really surprised.

"I thought he knew because of how I dress sometimes. And when we have these various work-related events, I either go alone, come with a friend who's a woman that I make clear is not my girlfriend, or I bring a male friend or whoever I feel like. So it's not as though I have this pretense. When people talk about getting married, I'll say, 'Well, I don't think I'll ever get married to a woman,' and they don't ask me any questions about it.

"In spite of the fact that I haven't been deceptive, maybe I haven't been forthcoming either. There are still people that don't know or don't think or don't want to believe that I'm gay."

How They Hide

Being closeted or quasicloseted usually involves denying or mitigating clues and hints that might otherwise lead colleagues to suspect or assume one is gay. To stay closeted, gay professionals typically rely on a variety of techniques.

Those who are in the closet also often become expert at manipulating various clues about their sexual orientation in order to create an element of confusion.

Passing for Straight The presumption of heterosexuality seems to work best for gay men who are young or macho looking. Men over the age of thirty, in particular, are suspected of being gay if they do not do anything to suggest otherwise. However, in certain locations and industries there is the assumption that "no one could possibly be gay here because they would self-select out." Thus, gay men in the more macho fields, such as agribusiness, construction, energy, and investment banking, may be able to hide more easily. For most women, the heterosexual presumption seems to last a lifetime unless they actively challenge it.

Those who conform most closely to gay stereotypes—men who are sharp dressers and women who don't flirt—are more likely to be suspected of being gay. Most others are able to hide, at least for a few years. Since MBAs are notorious for job-hopping, it can be feasible to use this strategy quite successfully for a long time.

The heterosexual presumption is also one of the things most gay professionals agreed was the most difficult to deal with, even if they were willing to be out to some degree. In our survey, 46 percent said they never attempt to correct straight colleagues' misimpressions and assumptions about their sexual orientation, and 32 percent said they rarely do so. Some admitted they actively encouraged their colleagues to assume they were heterosexual by their coy remarks or flirtatious behavior, although they did not see such actions as outright lies.

Certain gay men seemed to be particularly adept at being social butterflies; thus they float along on the presumption of heterosexuality. Passive acceptance of the attentions of a member of the opposite sex can also help a gay person maintain the appearance of being heterosexual. Juan, a gay man in his fifties who worked for a family-values company in his small hometown, told us how one woman, deeply infatuated with him, helped him remain in the closet. The woman had a kind of "fatal attraction" to him and hung around him at every moment. His colleagues thought they were having an affair and focused their gossip on the supposed relationship, rather than on speculation about Juan's sexual orientation.

Avoiding the Topic Most gay professionals we interviewed don't feel comfortable with deception, and they are unwilling to mislead others about the gender of their dates or significant others. Instead, they have become very adroit at simply avoiding the subject altogether.

Doreen, a white executive for a manufacturing company, assured us, "If anyone asked I'd tell them I was gay. But no one asks, and I don't expect them to. I think people can tell when you have a wall up around you on a certain subject, and very few people want to try to breach that."

Generally, we found that for gay men to remain closeted, they had to avoid almost all casual conversations. Lesbians endured less casual quizzing but, if they wanted to stay closeted, found they had to steer far from the heart-to-heart conversations many heterosexual women in the workplace seem to love. As they rose in the ranks, however, this became less of a problem, simply because there were fewer women at their level in the company or industry.

Discussing Previous Heterosexual Relationships While referring to an ex-spouse or children from a previous heterosexual marriage would seem to be the perfect cover for remaining closeted, none of those we interviewed said they used it in that way.

Perhaps less believable, but more frequently used, is the dodge of dragging up stories about ex-girlfriends, ex-boyfriends, or ex-fiancés. Those we interviewed told us that this strategy could work short term and even for a few years. Eventually, however, heterosexuals are expected to evince interest in dating again.

Madeline explained, "Going to a company retreat, I drove up to the mountains with three women coworkers. They got into a conversation about oral sex and what their boyfriends liked. It was getting unbearably uncomfortable, because I knew they were about to ask me for my input, and I didn't want to be in the spotlight. I definitely did not want to come out while speeding along this curving mountain road at sixty miles per hour! Thank G-d, at least I had been with men in high school. Otherwise my naivete would have given me away as a lesbian or would have made me look like a prude or a total social outcast."

Particularly for men, who are assumed to have a wide choice of prospective dates and mates, the strategem of talking about old flames was difficult to maintain and most avoided it.

Wedding Rings Like a number of single heterosexual women, some lesbians attempt to avoid sexual harassment at work by wearing a wedding ring. Although this is not done specifically to hide being gay, the result may be that the woman is presumed to be heterosexual.

Marla, a white woman in her late thirties, told us she plans to be a single parent and have a child through artificial insemination. She intends to wear a plain band on her wedding finger when she does. Asked why, she responded, "Even though the company where I'm working is accepting of openly gay men and single mothers, I still think I'll need this added measure of normalcy to ward off questions by clients."

But very few of those we interviewed wore rings of any style, other than the omnipresent Harvard MBA class ring. A few wore a ring given to them by their partner, but only a handful wore a traditional wedding-style ring or one matched to their partner's.

Changing Pronouns and Making Up Stories It seems relatively easy to substitute pronouns when describing romantic partners in casual conversations with clients or acquaintances at work. Thus a lesbian would refer to her partner as 'he,' and a gay man would talk about his date that night as 'she.' " But none of the gay professionals we interviewed said they currently changed pronouns, although a number mentioned they had done so in the past.

Heidi, who was in a relationship with a woman at work before business school, made up stories about men throughout the relationship. She even went out on a few dates with men as a cover. Since she had dated men while trying to be heterosexual, she found it was easy to use this strategy in combination with talking about previous relationships. But mainly, she said, "I was vague. People would ask the usual questions about the weekend, and I'd make up something. Or they'd ask my vacation plans, and I'd create one that sounded feasible. Even with my family I'd do that. I don't feel like I've really come out either to my family or at work, but recently I just stopped lying. I don't know if that's the first step for coming out, but I like it a lot better."

A few went so far as inventing an entire persona for their heterosexual paramour. Nicholas, a Black man who has worked in several conservative industries, created a girlfriend he called Rebecca. With curious coworkers he even went into detail about this imaginary significant other. "I created a fictitious character whom they will never meet, whom they will never know, whom I never bring up unless asked about. It's that kind of game I was playing. She is a female; her name is Rebecca. I went the whole nine yards! Actually it varied. It was either Rebecca or Becky. Sometimes I'd get caught up. They'd say, 'Oh, I thought you said her name was Rebecca, and I'd say, 'Oh, yes, Rebecca. 'Becky' is kind of a nickname.'

"Occasionally when I run into people from before, she still lives. For example, last October I was invited to a wedding for someone who I worked with after business school. She called personally to say, 'Please bring Becky.'

"I thought: Oh God, here we go again. I showed up at the wedding alone after RSVPing for the two of us. The hostess asked, 'Where's Becky?' and I quickly said, 'Oh, she's got a major deal in the works—one that's big even for her. She sent her love.'

"Becky has had a very complicated life. Either she was doing real estate or consulting, and constantly on the road or out of the country. They'd say, 'Wow, she really works a lot.' Just after she left for a quick trip to

Venezuela, I've kind of lost track of her. I mean, it was exhausting trying to keep track of all that. Maybe she's moved on to another lucky guy. I don't need Becky anymore," he joked. "May she rest in peace."

Obviously this technique is most likely to succeed in business environments that do not place a value on attendance at corporate social events. In fact, few whom we interviewed reported that they were expected to actually have a date in tow for business functions. Rather, many said, they chose industries where work was the focus and socializing was less important.

Straight Dates A few of those we interviewed admitted they bring opposite-sex dates into the office or to office functions in order to convince colleagues they are heterosexual. Although it was common in the past, no one we interviewed currently deceives their date to implement this facade; rather, these dates are gay or straight friends, also in on the deception, who go along to lend credibility to the masquerade. For example, Kate and Skip are both Harvard MBAs in their early thirties who work for large companies in San Francisco. They use each other as cover for corporate events.

Kate talked about a recent office Christmas party they attended together. "Bringing a date brought me social validity. He was an attractive man, was sociable, and had his wits about him. I think people who are married are seen as more stable. Having a date also shows some social accomplishment, and that's reassuring to people. Not only are you accepted as a professional, but on a social level, you're viewed as an attractive person.

"Within my office, I know I'm seen as socially desirable, but people are always curious. They like to gossip. They like to meet your significant other, and Skip provided that stamp of approval. Lots of men friends visit with me in my office. It's a social validation that I think my colleagues find important."

While the issue for gay men is simply trying to stay closeted, for lesbians there can be another issue as well. Many women managers, whether gay or heterosexual, feel the need to prove they like men, whether as romantic partners or as people. The stereotype of the lesbian as a man hater lends an additional charge to this social pressure.

Of course, all of the above methods have their pitfalls. The heterosexual presumption works best for those who are young or change jobs a lot. Avoiding the topic works better as a strategy for tacitly communicating that you are gay than it does for remaining truly closeted. Having been married or talking about past relationships gets worn and unbelievable, particularly if the last opposite-sex date was ten years ago. Previous marriages work a little better but after a while people expect you to get back into the social circuit. If you are a woman, especially if you have children, you might be able to play that game indefinitely; if you are a man, you probably can't. Yet women who don't date men can pay another price, being seen as man haters or socially inept.

Most gay professionals who have used these techniques to hide told us that the longer they stay in a particular company and the older they get, the less they use these tactics. Eventually they become more willing to leave clues or even drop hints about being gay. While we found certain lesbians in their late thirties and their forties have become more closeted as they rise in the ranks, this was not true for all or even most in this age category. Meanwhile, a number of lesbians and gay men in their twenties and thirties are confident they will never be closeted at any time in their careers.

BENEFITS OF BEING CLOSETED?

Few claim any real benefits to being closeted. Most say, "It's not important to me to be out," or "It's not an issue," or some variation. Many report they think people at work assume they are gay. But they point out that there's a difference between assumptions and actual knowledge. While many gay professionals believe that it's better to be suspected of being gay, we found the opposite is usually true.

Some strategies for staying closeted can turn out to have highly negative side effects. A flirtatious relationship with a person of the opposite gender at work had harmful personal consequences for both Juan and Kate, though no career damage. Also, those who have come out at work tell us that flirtation with the opposite sex is a skill they have employed far more effectively *since* coming out. When it is apparent that flirting is used simply to smooth social relations, we found, it can be an effective tool; but when any question of actual sexual interest enters the picture, it is almost always damaging.

Some say escaping the uncomfortable result of forcing the issue is a benefit of remaining closeted. But avoiding the issue can also be negative and exhausting. Most justify their closet by saying it is a prerequisite to keep their job, and they see no alternative if they wish to continue to rise through the ranks. Since few openly gay role models exist in business, many believe they must be closeted on their way up the ladder.

Some acknowledge they "owe rent" on their closet space. They realize they continue to earn lots of money while being closeted at work, and they feel they have to give something back to the gay community. We met some closeted gay professionals who make significant contributions to gay causes; yet we found that most who contribute significant time or money to gay or AIDS causes are openly gay to some degree in all aspects of their lives.

Another supposed benefit of being closeted is being seen as a heterosexual ally of gay causes. Some think that in this role they can motivate other heterosexuals to adopt more positive attitudes toward gay people. We found that this can actually work and do some short-term good. But what happens later when the person comes out? The positive steps that the heterosexuals involved have taken seem to remain, but some have a feeling of being tricked or cheated.

Gay professionals fear that if they were known to be gay, their opinion on gay issues might be discounted as biased. Yet those who have come out in such situations say everything worked out just fine.

Most say that being closeted is a necessity at best. Many say it is an evil that they hope to overcome.

Costs of the Closet

Personal Losses

Gay professionals who remain closeted at work report they suffer a number of critical professional and personal losses.

Stress and Fear of Exposure While many who "don't lie, don't deny" say they are unconcerned about being suspected or assumed to be gay, 28 percent of our survey respondents acknowledge they are deeply or somewhat concerned. Time and energy spent worrying about how or whether to hide could be put to far better use. Employers lose out, because their employees have more on their minds than their job responsibilities. Our study shows a significant percentage of every workforce is underutilized in this way.

Vulnerability to Blackmail and Other Forms of Harassment Gay people who actively seek to conceal their sexual orientation are vulnerable. They are imperiled by homophobic employees who suspect or discover that they are gay. They are open to exposure by angry ex-lovers or future ex-lovers or politically radical acquaintances. They are also vulnerable to threats of blackmail from within and without their organization.

Throughout the years that they maintain their masquerade, they are constantly aware of how easily their house of cards could come tumbling down, and all too cognizant of the discrimination that could ensue. This fear may lead them to take certain actions in their personal or professional lives that are not truly in their best interests. For example, some avoid social relationships with clients or people in their company. This means they are out of the social loop so essential for most careers. They are also less likely to network with other gay people or to find mentors who can help them rise.

Some even cut themselves off from the gay community outside the workplace. This reduces social support in the event of being threatened or discovered. It also means they have fewer role models for how to become more open at work.

Discomfort with Socializing As long as business deals continue to be consummated at the dinner table, on the golf course, or over drinks, closeted gay men and lesbians will be at a disadvantage. Franklin, who works in banking, explained, "Events such as taking clients to Pebble Beach, U.S. Open, or the opera always involve the spouse of the client as well. It's nearly impossible to function in these environments with both clients and company executives without a spouse."

Many alleged that their company forced them to remain closeted and that the biggest obstacle in their career path was that they could not entertain at home, which was the norm for developing relationships with people at work. But as others found, being closeted, not being gay, prevents them from opening their homes for business functions.

Lack of Strong Support System After someone has consistently misled coworkers and bosses, he or she is less likely to have a wide base of personal support to turn to if outed. On the other hand, those who are out to at least some people are more likely to have some allies if discrimination is encountered. Those who are closeted and involuntarily outed are deprived of these potential sources of support.

Even in ordinary day-to-day work situations, those in the closet may unnecessarily deprive themselves of backing. We heard from a number of interviewees who are now more open about the opportunities they missed or almost missed for support from coworkers.

While working for a midsized public accounting firm in New York City, Sally was assigned to an out-of-town client for six weeks. "I was involved in a relationship and was not out at work. Rather, I was perceived to be a single woman by those in the office, and this was one of the reasons I was given the assignment." She explained that while she did not relish the thought of being out of town for such a long time, she felt she couldn't say anything except to express her desire to spend weekends back home in the city. "Later, I found out that the supervisor in this assignment was a gay man! And now I believe that being honest with straight people is important too."

Missing Out on Deepened Friendships with Heterosexuals Many who have come out told us they have enjoyed the friendships and support of heterosexuals. Closeted gay people deprive themselves of these relationships by assuming there will be a lack of support or no common ground. Some heterosexuals who would otherwise have been supportive may feel deceived, betrayed, or disappointed that their colleague lacked trust in them.

After Julianne was in the newspaper and her sexual orientation was revealed, she overheard a coworker express disappointment that she hadn't come out to her before. Her coworker had actually taken it as an insult to their relationship. "She said she was upset because she thought they were friends."

Less Networking with Other Gay People Many of those who are closeted at work also avoided friendships with other gay people, particularly those who are openly gay. Garrett laughingly told us how he and Alan didn't connect for a long time. "We hated each other, actually, at first. One of those 'on sight' things. Alan went to Yale at the same time I was in college. One of his friends from Yale started the same day that I did. So when I started, this friend of mine from Yale who knew Alan kept talking about, 'Oh, you gotta meet my friend Alan. You guys would really get along.' He had all these expectations about how we were exactly alike, and I knew what he was getting at was that we are both gay. He assumed we were going to have so much in common because all gay people are one big happy family.

"So when Alan showed up three months later, I was like, this is the guy I'm supposed to get along with? I was probably pretty rude, but so was Alan. We had our claws out for each other. Alan would come in to my office when I wasn't there and leave little notes for me and stuff, like 'How's it going, Miss Thing?' I just hated him because he was so comfortable and so out from day one. I could have just killed him.

"We eventually became friends, though. And if it hadn't been for Alan, it wouldn't have been the same for me working there. Alan is the kind of person that knows people worldwide. For instance, one time we were sitting in a gay bar in London, and somebody came up and asked, 'Alan?' I'd be like, no way is this happening. He knows people everywhere, including the other gay people in our firm."

Strains on Personal Relationships Many we interviewed mentioned the toll that being closeted has taken on their personal relationships. Being unable to include partners in social events involving coworkers or clients means these busy professionals have even less time together. Disagreements about how out to be also cause tension between some couples. Closeted couples may also remove themselves from participating fully in gay community activities, and this can seem burdensome to the one who is more of an activist. Another consideration is that, not having met people from work, partners are less able to offer concrete advice about handling specific people in the workplace.

A number of those we interviewed told us they now realize they avoided relationships for a period of time because of the added difficult-ies of remaining closeted while in a relationship. They didn't feel it was fair to potential partners to never be able to call them at work. They knew they were cheating their partners when they socialized with heterosexual friends and said they found it too emotionally taxing to hide being gay or to avoid the subject of their social life if they were seeing someone in particular.

Another strain on a committed relationship can come when one of the partners is offered a career opportunity in a new location. Difficult for any couple, the burden on a closeted member of a couple is far greater. Should they be reluctant to take the assignment, their bosses may fail to understand why the opportunity was turned down. If they want to pursue it, the partner will receive no assistance in finding a job in the new city as heterosexual spouses do. A particular problem with foreign postings, this can be a predicament with any move.

Even when none of these major issues are involved, being closeted can still rankle. Roberta Lasley was more than willing to accompany her partner, who is also an HBS graduate, to a new city. But since the women had not yet lived together, there was a question about how to move her belongings to Miami. She said, "I'm sure if it was a heterosexual relationship my partner would have said, 'I'm moving in with this guy and he lives on the way, so we'll stop there and pick up his stuff.' But we talked about it, and in the discussion it was obvious to me that she was not comfortable about doing that. I said, 'How much is this gonna cost, $2,000, $3,000? Don't jeopardize your own feeling of comfort for this.' "

Others, who could save this sum annually if they had domestic partner benefits, tend to feel a greater sense of injustice. Although most concur a partner should play it safe, some have pushed their partners to take a more activist role at work in order to obtain health or travel benefits. Usually, coming out is the first step to achieving these goals.

Lower Self-Esteem Perhaps one of the greatest losses as a result of being closeted is a by-product of fear. Fear that homophobia could be a barrier to one's career quickly translates to lower self-esteem. Whether this is expressed or internalized, one may believe, "If they really knew who I was, I wouldn't be in this position," or, "I'll never get to the top if they know that I'm gay." Living in fear that the rug could be pulled out from under places a person in a precarious position.

Such pessimism can undermine self-confidence and productivity. Although Harvard MBAs have many options, it can be crushing to feel one is unable to accomplish the goals so long worked for. While some would say, "Hey, so what if I don't become president? Vice president is still a worthy achievement," second best is not good enough for many individuals—or necessarily what's best for the company.

In addition, the higher up one goes in a particular field, the more specialized one's skills and résumé become and the better known one is throughout the industry. Ironically, it may be more difficult for Harvard MBAs to successfully change companies or professions if they run into a dead end at work, and this fear keeps many in the closet, afraid of being outed.

For those who wish to remain mostly closeted, moral support can be obtained from other gay professionals facing similar issues. Sympathetic coworkers and family can also be important sources of aid. Cultivating a basis of support and having a plan of action to come out proactively if necessary is the best strategy to combat the fear of being outed. Once a backup plan is in place, we found self-esteem exponentially improves.

Lessened Legal Grounds in Discrimination Suits As with the problem that Tom Hanks's character faced in the 1993 film *Philadelphia,* if you don't tell anyone at work you are gay, it is difficult to prove they discriminated against you on that basis. You may not even be sure yourself this was the reason for problems at work.

Being hired, promoted, or fired is a subjective process. The way you fit in, schmooze with clients, address your superiors, and play the corporate game of politics all determine if you succeed or fail. Even when business performance is measured by bottom-line results, subjective aspects of personality and working habits influence evaluations. Fortunately, the world is not completely left to people like J. R. Ewing on the TV show *Dallas.* Some states, cities, and large companies have set ground rules for a level playing field, outlawing discrimination on the basis of sexual orientation.

If a person is out and has witnesses to a hostile working environment, it is easier to claim discrimination as a factor in an evaluation. Realistically, few want to end up in court. Yet at least a quarter of the gay professionals in our study who have experienced discrimination based on sexual orientation have complained to a superior about it. Those who were not out were more likely to have ignored the problem.

Costs to the Company

The institution of the closet hurts not only gay people, but also the world of business.

The Best Person for the Job While heterosexuals often list on their résumés the collegiate and charitable organizations they served, prospective gay employees usually leave off important credentials and skills. Most chose to omit any gay, feminist, or AIDS organization activities from their résumés.

Many of those we interviewed had significant leadership roles in various gay organizations but felt they could not include this information on their résumé without danger of discrimination. Thus, by comparison to their heterosexual peers' résumés, theirs may have seemed devoid of outside activities and achievements, community involvement, or leadership skills. As Herman confided, "It looked sparse, but I didn't know what else to do." In an investment-banking interview in 1989, Sharon was asked: "Weren't you involved in any school clubs besides sports?" In fact, she had been an active copresident of both her undergraduate and HBS gay student group, neither of which was listed on her résumé.

Some lesbians admit they use the feminist rubric to disguise lesbian organizations. Many organizations have disguised their names themselves. For example, the San Diego Career Women is a lesbian organization. Most gay men's groups, on the other hand, cannot or do not choose to hide behind such innocuous titles. While some gay men see putting AIDS work on their résumés as a sure tip-off, others believe it is more of a clue than a direct hint regarding sexual orientation.

Perhaps so that they might have other résumé-building activities, many of those who were most active in gay community organizations were classic overachievers—president of both the Marketing Club at HBS as well as president of the Gay and Lesbian Student Association. But the companies they applied to knew only half their credentials and accomplishments.

Not One of the Team Most businesses run best when their employees work together like a team. But closeted gay professionals face almost insurmountable barriers to becoming members of the team. This can seriously impair effectiveness, productivity, and morale. Many gay professionals reported that hiding their sexual orientation forces them to avoid many after-hours social activities that other employees attend. Others told us that they participate to a limited extent but try to avoid the subject of relationships, recreational interests, where they went on their last vacation, and so forth. Ultimately, they felt this disrupted much of the bonding between colleagues.

As Pauline explained, "I feel I am not able to become part of the team at work like most others, because doing so in my workplace requires openness about spouse, family, dating, etc. And since I would never be dishonest, I have to close up in most cases when a friendly conversation with a coworker or boss warms up to that level of sharing.

"Since I'm unable to be open with my coworkers about my personal life, it not only prevents me from being one of the team, but creates some stress for me. My coworkers can let off steam or indicate when they have had problems and get support from others. I don't have that kind of relationship with my colleagues. Yet I'm afraid that being honest about my partner, Kathy, and our relationship would be more alienating than closing up is."

Others found fitting into the corporate mold to be problematic in itself. Steve, a white man in his late twenties, never thought he had a problem socializing with coworkers until he found himself working for a company that required more intimacy than he desired. Reflecting on his experiences in San Francisco, he told us that the trouble began in the summer shortly after he took a position with a management-consulting firm.

Most of his coworkers were about his age, and Steve discovered he had a lot in common with them, except that most of them were married or in long-term heterosexual relationships. As a company perk, the firm owned a mountain cabin at which employees were encouraged to spend weekends together in order to build their team's harmony.

"At first, I politely turned down invitations to the cabin, thinking it was not a big deal. I kept thinking there'd be opportunities closer to home to build those ties with coworkers." Eventually, he became the target of pointed questions asking why he never joined the others. "I always justified my absence in a tactful way with excuses like I was busy or expected out-of-town company." He knew from the others' stories that he would have to come up with a date of the opposite sex for the weekend and that she would come under scrutiny from the rest of the group.

"It became all too apparent that being married to or in a long-term relationship with a woman who would fit in was a prerequisite to winning acceptance from the team. And I also recognized I could deflect the pressuring questions only so long." At lunch one day, Steve remarked to a female coworker that he never intended to go to the cabin, because he preferred to keep his personal and professional lives separate.

"Her reaction was total dismay. To her, the question of when I might join them at the cabin was innocent, friendly, in fact. But to me, she was making it apparent that I'd never truly fit in unless I joined them or unless I took the chance of coming out to the group." Steve's insistence on keeping his privacy was interpreted by the rest of the group as rejection. "I finally had no other option than to chart my long-term career path elsewhere."

Other gay professionals echoed these remarks. Many felt that even if they came out, they would not feel completely part of the team. David Stokes told us a few years ago, "I never understood those who work with people all day long and then want to go out drinking with them or to spend the weekend with them. I have kept my private life and my professional life very separate. But I don't really have problems with that. I work hard when I'm at work. But when it comes time to leave work, I'm ready to move on."

When we recently talked with David, he reiterated that he doesn't expect to spend much more time with heterosexuals from work, even after coming out to them. But he acknowledged that coming out to other gay people, both at work and in the gay community, has had tremendous benefits for his career.

We heard this refrain from a host of different voices and in varying places throughout the interview process. Many said even if they came out they still wouldn't have a wife or children and thus would still be different. Those who have come out found this is not always the case. In particular those who have included their partners in social activities with heterosexual colleagues have found they enjoy these activities more than they ever would have imagined. Companies sending out strong messages that gay employees should stay closeted are depriving themselves of the synergies of this kind of teamwork.

MORALE AND PRODUCTIVITY A significant number of those we talked to had reservations about their long-term prospects with their company. This was far truer for those who were most deeply closeted. In addition, not feeling like a part of the team, most closeted gay professionals could not wait to leave work each day to begin their real lives. Those who were closeted and worked extremely long hours particularly resented the lack of time to socialize with other gay people, the only ones they felt they could be themselves with.

Although this issue is more pressing for those in the closet, even openly gay people can feel these morale problems, particularly if they are unwilling to include their partners in social activities with people from work. Preston, who is in his late twenties and openly gay at work, plans to stay in consulting for the near term. But he said, "Consulting demands a certain lifestyle in terms of the hours and travel you have to put in. For example, I have a meeting tomorrow at eight. Normally I would go out on a Thursday night and be with friends uptown. A lot of my friends don't work at professional jobs, so they go out whenever they want to. If you're young and single, a gay social life can be at odds with a professional lifestyle. People go to the bars pretty late, even during the week. If you're married with children, you want to be home to be with your kids. You're going to be up early because you're going to bed early. It's just a whole different thing.

"It's tough from that point of view, but it's also complex because, especially in professional services, so much depends upon schmoozing clients, socializing. I find some of these social events to be torturous, which is odd because a lot of straight people seem to really genuinely enjoy them. This was something that took me a long time to realize: Not everyone thought that a consulting retreat was a miserable experience. I would never subject my partner to them."

Being in the closet can also result in exposure to homophobic comments that put a damper on morale. Janet explained that after meeting a new boss, she was at first looking forward to working with him. "I remember at one point, a first vice president where I worked called me into his office. While talking about the case, I noticed a picture of his wife, Joanie. It turns out that we went to high school together. Within forty-eight hours I was sitting at his dining room table. Near the end of the evening, he blurted out, 'Hey, Joanie says you can really drink.' I said in a teasing way, 'Well, it's true, do you want to have a contest?' That's all it took. We drank for hours, matching drink for drink.

"About an hour into it, we were all laughing and having a great time and he said, 'I love to get a bunch of people together and go down to one of those gay piano bars after doing a big deal. Because, you know what? You never know who you're gonna see from your competition. All you gotta do is see 'em there and you've got 'em beat for the next job. You never know who might be a hidden faggot. It's so easy to start a whispering campaign,' and he took another swig of whiskey."

Unfortunately for many companies, not all of their gay employees have the courage to stand up to that kind of homophobia. Even if they do, the morale of those employees needs rejuvenating periodically. In companies that have instituted diversity training, there is a significant boost in morale among gay and lesbian employees. But this must be followed up with true commitment on the part of individual senior managers.

Loyalty Those who feel they have to be in the closet at work also tend to be less loyal to their companies. While none we spoke to have done anything to betray their company's trust in them, most feel strongly that they are looking out for number one—themselves—and would not hesitate to leave if they received an offer from a competitor.

In contrast, those who are open, as well as those who work at companies that have taken leadership roles on gay issues, report that they feel great loyalty to their company. Companies who take the lead in marketing to the gay community, offering domestic partner benefits, supporting openly gay managers, and making corporatewide statements in support of the company's gay employee groups are also the ones who benefit from their employees' loyalty.

Brain Drain A few of the gay professionals we talked with have left or are thinking about leaving companies where they cannot be open to at least some degree. Some plan merely to change to a division where they think life will be easier; the majority will leave the company and the industry altogether. A number have started their own businesses or now work somewhere they think will be more receptive to their being open. While many heterosexual Harvard MBAs and other successful professionals also eventually choose small companies or self-employment, we believe the gay brain drain represents a significant and unnecessary loss to the competitiveness of many companies and industries.

• • •

Fear of discrimination continues to drape its cloak around gay professionals from the lowest to the highest reaches of the business world. While gay people working in large companies, macho industries, and conservative environments were among those who were most closeted, we found people in every field who were afraid to come out.

Just as there is a broad range of coming out, there is a smorgasbord of ways to remain closeted. One can be closeted to all, or closeted to immediate coworkers except for gay ones. One can be closeted only to upper management or only to the conservative right-wingers in the office. Trying to pass for straight can mean simply avoiding social references to a personal life or can be as complicated as fabricating entirely fictitious opposite-gender significant others.

Most closeted gay professionals believe they are making a pragmatic decision as they weigh the costs of coming out against the benefits. This is the case even when the potential benefits are measurable in dollars and the possible costs are unknown. Despite this, those who have taken the risk and come out in a variety of industries, even conservative ones, have found tremendous rewards.

Companies are also realizing there are costs associated with an environment that requires gay employees to remain closeted. If the brilliant and vibrant light inside a closeted individual is allowed to emerge, the productivity of that employee is significantly enhanced. And if that light is welcomed, that person can truly flourish, and the rewards to the company will be exponential.

Individuals who are out—whether coming out means finding the other gay people in their company, coming out selectively, or coming out in the national media—are finding personal and career fulfillment they never dreamed possible. We explore these issues in the next chapter.

Chapter 6

Coming Out at Work

We have divided this chapter into three sections. First, we discuss role models and their impact on the coming-out process of those we interviewed. In the second section we discuss the coming-out strategies used by gay professionals and the reactions they encountered. In the final section we share the coming-out-at-work stories of nine of our interviewees.

ROLE MODELS

The presence or absence of role models can play an important part in the coming-out process of gay professionals. From the first time a success-oriented person realizes he or she is different, to the decisions a gay professional makes about what career to pursue and about coming out at work, role models can be an important influence. Conversely, the lack of role models often leaves high achievers feeling isolated and alone. Perhaps surprising, many of those we interviewed told us their peers or gay people younger than themselves served as their role models. In addition, we found, some gay professionals are willing to pave new ground in coming out about being gay, even without any role models to show them it can be done successfully.

COMING OUT TO SELF

Perhaps the most important function of role models in an individual's coming-out process is to expand the limits of the possible. Many of those we interviewed said they had known nothing about gay people except for the stereotypes. With no openly gay people in their families or communities, they relied on the media to provide images and information. While almost all of those we interviewed who had been out to themselves for at least a year had a "live-and-let-live" attitude toward effeminate men, drag queens, butch lesbians, gay men and women into leather, and street activists, many admitted that before they came out they made harsher judgments about these individuals.

Public Role Models

Bill, who is in his late twenties, told us it took him until a few years ago to come out to himself because the public image of gay people kept him from getting to know any. "It's really sad, because the only role models that I had were the freaks, gay men who were very stereotypical, which everybody saw negatively. Today it really pisses me off when I realize what a hard time effeminate men have. That really gets me going. But at that time, I saw it as being very negative too," he admitted. "The other thing I remember was that gay men were depicted as being into leather. Remember that movie *Cruising*? I remember it presented gay life in a very negative way—dark and secretive."

Adrienne, who is in her mid-thirties, said, "I was convinced all the lesbians in the U.S. were truck drivers or so closeted I'd never meet them. The sophisticated ones were in Europe, dead, or both. It seemed like there were tons of gay men everywhere, doing all kinds of things. But I had no idea how to meet any lesbians, or how to be one myself."

Jonathan Rottenberg told us he was less affected by negative images than by "a complete lack of positive role models." He said, "I guess I had some negative stereotypes, but mainly I had no idea how anyone could ever be gay and have any of the other things that you are supposed to be striving for in life, like family and being successful. I was never aware of gay people that I identified with in any way. The gay culture was never something that interested me. My impression was gay people were these very angry people on the fringe of society who were drawn together by being against the rest of the world, and I never identified with that. I mean, I never completely identified with the mainstream either, but I felt

I had a more constructive approach to the world than my impression of how the gay community dealt with it." He admitted, "I guess I didn't really know a lot about the gay community except through television. Also I think you tend to be most aware of gay people who are really unusual in one way or another, and the majority of gay people just blend in; you don't have a sense of who they are."

On the other hand, public role models can also play an important role in the coming-out process. Many we interviewed mentioned the personal significance of reading *The Best Little Boy in the World* by the pseudonymous John Reid. Several told us they learned through the HBS network that the author was a well-known HBS alumnus. "That helped me realize that there were gay people like me," Ethan said. Jared told us, "When I read that book, I identified with a lot of the passages in there. I was on this path of hyperachievement all through college, and a lot of that was about me being on a treadmill trying hard to avoid dealing with important internal issues."

Bill recalled, "The summer before business school, I found that book and read it in one day. I just cried my eyes out because there's just so much in it that seemed to tell my story. It was more important that people liked me than it was that I liked myself. Ultimately, by the end of that first year I just started questioning everything. And that summer I managed to write the words 'I am gay' in my diary."

Personal Role Models

Those who had positive role models in their personal life found coming out to themselves easiest. This was particularly important for the older professionals we interviewed. Robert Goldfarb, who is in his forties, told us that having worked in radio since he was a teenager helped him come out to himself. "There was really nothing special about the circumstances. When I was fifteen or sixteen, my first job was at a suburban radio talk station in Connecticut. An older coworker introduced me to some of his friends, and I got to know a little bit more about what the gay community was about. To me at the time, he was, of course, very worldly, wise, and mature, because he was twenty-three years old. He saved me the trouble of approaching him because he had me pegged as a gay youth. I never had to say I'm gay, because he knew that. So it was just a matter of taking something that came up in conversation a step further. He introduced me to his boyfriend or invited me to a party or something."

Robert reflected, "Knowing him demystified the whole thing for me, because it's one thing to have a private awareness that you're gay, that you're attracted to other guys. But it's something else to come into contact with the gay world and meet people who are long past that issue. I got to see people living a gay life."

Sol, who is now in his sixties, told us another HBS alumnus served as a role model for him. "I became friends with a classmate, Taylor, who lived off campus. His 'friend' was always there, a man who always played a domestic role and had no interest in professional activities. It was a real marriage. But I didn't figure it out until after graduation. After B-school, they invited me to come over and have a drink. I went and realized they were a couple. Taylor graduated and was going to be an executive, and his friend was going to go along when they left Boston. After I figured them out, they were convinced that I was gay too. Then, of course, everything was out. They even suggested, 'Why don't you go to this bar, this and that place, as a way to meet people socially?' So they kind of opened up the gay world to me. Yeah, they opened the closet for me. I mean, I knew what I wanted to do. I just didn't know where the hell to do it until I met them."

Personal role models could also be important to some of the younger gay professionals we interviewed. Burton, who is in his thirties, told us he had a very difficult time accepting being gay until he came to HBS. "I feel pretty blessed and fortunate to have had the Harvard experience, where I instantly came into a network of people who were dealing with being gay, and yet it wasn't the only thing in their lives. They showed me that being gay was just an element of all of the many challenges and successes and failures that we all face. It really helped for me to know successful gay people, for whom dealing with their homosexuality did not have to become all-consuming to their lives."

Burton told us he viewed both current students and recent business-school alumni as his role models. "In addition to HBS alumni, I knew some alumni of other business schools who are from the South, like me. One of the first gay guys I met was in a bar in Boston because I overheard him talking about a football game between two Southern schools. He helped me in the coming-out process, but, interestingly enough, I'd say I'm now much more comfortable with being gay than he is. Probably one reason is he moved to Atlanta, where people have to live with much more paranoia than one has to in Boston."

Burton added, "I also met a couple of lawyers, two guys who were both attorneys in Boston and had just bought this beautiful home together. I had thought being gay was a series of compromises. Suddenly I saw somebody having it all, which was what I wanted but had never imagined was possible if you were gay."

Several told us HBS peers served as role models. Brian Offutt said, "Going to the first HBS gay party my first year was a big step for me. I was out to my best friend, Mike Russell, who is straight, but I didn't have much of a gay life and didn't have any really close friends who were gay. One of the people I met that day was Jim Sherman, who was in my class, and I thought he was the most together person I'd ever met. I was just so impressed by Jim's comfort level with everything and the degree to which he was out. He just blew me away. That really helped me become more self-confident."

MANAGING A GAY IDENTITY AT WORK

Once our interviewees came out to themselves, both personal and public role models often continued to play an important role in shaping their career aspirations. Whether they chose to remain mostly closeted or to continue to come out, knowing other gay professionals was a factor in their career decisions.

Personal Role Models

Tad, who is white, told us an HBS gay alumnus at his company is a role model to him. "Wes is very close to breaking the lavender ceiling. I doubt if he'll make it this round, because he's very young, so maybe in two more years. That would be something, because all of the other senior people there are married with a couple of kids. So his success gives me hope for my career here."

Jana told us that several gay men have served as role models for her. "Where I work, there are so few women, period, that no one bothers to notice whether or not they're married." She laughed. "There are a few men I'm particularly thinking of who put themselves in the position of being role models to the younger people, including me. To us it's clear that they are gay. They don't hide it; they don't make any pretensions of being straight." She added, "I think one of the ways to be an effective role model as a gay person is simply to show that you can do your job and succeed at what you're doing."

Tess, who was in the middle of a career transition when we interviewed her, told us her older partner has been a role model for her. "I think she has a healthy, fuck-it attitude. It's funny, when Roberta was growing up, there were some role models out there for women being able to have a career, but not too many. Yet she was able to make it in business all along. Mostly by fear and hunger—there was no way she was going back where she came from. Whereas I became a teacher right after undergraduate school. As a middle-class woman, it was entirely logical that I did that because there weren't role models for doing other things. In fact, there were lots of barriers." Tess said, "Now, many years after business school, I've started to be less cautious about everything. Another reason is, it's less expensive for two people to live together than one; it means my costs are lower than they were. So there's a little bit of a financial safety net for me to be more daring about looking for what I want to do. She's real supportive."

Torrence Boone, who is Black, told us he has a role model at Bain & Co., the large and prestigious consulting firm where he worked before business school. "A very senior manager came out. He left for a while because he felt it was a difficult situation for him to be out there. Basically they said, 'Come back and come out and be yourself.' He did, and it all worked out wonderfully for him. He's back to where he wants to be, and he made this transition to make it all work for him. I just think he's great, and that would be a huge reason for me going back to Bain. The fact that he's there and that he's out and incredibly successful and very well respected is very significant to me. He's a tremendous role model."

David Schutte, who is white, cited an older Black HBS graduate as one of his role models. "He's been very successful in a very narrow kind of company. Being Black and gay and doing very well there—that's an inspiration. And I think more than anything, he loves being gay, he enjoys it. I think some people assume the victim role at work because they're carrying these issues on their shoulders that may really not make a difference to people around them. The way I see it, he's never let anything that other people in corporate America could perceive as a handicap hurt him. When people accept themselves and present themselves in a positive light to others, the reaction that they elicit is generally positive. I think that's an important reason why bad things have never happened to him."

Public Role Models

Public role models can also play a role in motivating gay professionals to come out at work. For example, many of those we interviewed mentioned the December 1991 *Fortune* magazine article "Gay in Corporate America" as comfirmation of their feeling that it might be possible to come out and be successful. Some who work in the entertainment industry also mentioned various gay executives, agents, and screenwriters as inspirations. In other cases, entertainment figures were cited as role models.

Media mogul David Geffen was cited by many for his business success and his candor about being gay. Also media stars with business empires, such as Madonna, were highly acclaimed. As one of the wealthiest and most astute businesswomen in America, Madonna is especially revered for her persistence in discussing sex, AIDS, and homoeroticism.

Jonathan Rottenberg, who is white, told us Ru Paul is a role model to him. "He is extraordinarily talented and just able to be himself. He's just able to truly be the person that he is. He's the best. I think it's something about being a Black man who is so totally the opposite of what the culture tries to force Black men to conform to. His message is, 'I'm different, and it's great that I'm different.' "

A few mentioned openly gay or closeted politicians as role models. Cora said, "Once a group of us were out drinking one night after working on a transaction and I was stunned to hear a particular politician's name brought up. The rumors have always been there about her, and she's been one of my heroes. Her name came up, and I said, 'Well it's always been a rumor, but I've never known if it was true, and what difference does it make?' My client said, 'Well, it doesn't make any difference, and it is true she is.' The client then went on to make some homophobic remarks, but I was glad to know about this woman."

Public Anti-Role Models

However, many more told us they could think of no gay public figures who might be a role model for them. Interestingly, those who complained most vociferously about the lack of openly gay role models were themselves closeted at work. Parker said, "Malcom Forbes's family is still denying it about him. The one good thing was that before he died he was supportive on AIDS issues and gave money. But he wasn't very supportive on gay issues. I remember once someone wrote an antigay editorial in *Forbes,* and then he retracted the whole thing the next week and wrote another one saying that this magazine does not feel this way. He was helpful there. But he would have been a lot more helpful if he had come out. I think it's actually very important for public figures of that magnitude to be out."

Spencer agreed that gay people in the public eye are not role models to him. "The thing that is missing is good gay role models. I mean, there are a few people in Hollywood who have shown up at AIDS benefits—some are openly gay, others aren't so openly gay. Some, I'm not even sure whether they're gay or not. There are so many closet cases. That's starting to change, but I wish more of them would come out."

Personal Anti-Role Models

Many also disdained personal contacts who might be role models for them. Scott knew a successful group of older gay men who were successful in the arts and related fields. "I was sort of a Eurofag, OK? I went out with the very attractive, very rich gay men. I was A-list for a while. Not to brag, but that was just sort of my thing. Summers in the Hamptons, all that. It was fun, because out there I was meeting some of the cultural-elite gay people." He laughed. "When I hooked up with my lover, who was in the arts, I was like the trophy husband to a certain extent. His friends were extremely openly gay when we were all together, but somewhat less so at work. These were very old-line guys, because that was their world, their generation."

Scott continued, "They were in their fifties and sixties, and after all, their world of years ago was fabulous. They threw fabulous dinner parties, and they just had the most fabulous, interesting people at their estates. I was sort of coming in at the twilight years of all of this fabulousness. I was a nice kid who was allowed in. They respected my background, because I was educated and accomplished on my own. So it was quite obvious that I was not in this for the money. But they were not role models for me, because they weren't really in business."

Jim Sherman said that the closeted gay men in his industry are not role models to him. "There is one senior guy I know about who may be responsible for supporting some AIDS-related events. He is quite successful in business, but I don't know if he's openly gay. I think being gay is less of an issue if you are not open. But that's not for me. I would rather be open about being gay." Brian Offutt agreed. "Do I have any role models? No, not really. I know of people. But everyone's sort of timid. There is one guy who is getting to be fairly senior and may become a hot shot. He's sort of at the point where a lot of people know about him, so he could become a role model. But even if I had to be the first, it would be OK."

Hope said she has some role models, but she would like to know more gay people who were out of the closet. "In New York I served on the board of directors of the Bankers Group, and I met a lot of gay women that way, like the women I go to the Dinah Shore golf tournament with. One of my lesbian friends is very successful on Wall Street, working for one of the biggest houses. She and her friends are role models, for sure. But they are all *extremely* closeted. Like one woman who is this Wall Street guru who I've met on several occasions. She out-and-out lies about her professional career. I've followed her career since I was eighteen, and she's been divorced three times in the papers, but I know she's never been married." Hope laughed. "And now the paper says she's going to have children—I don't know who with, but that's what the paper says. I could never live my life lying like that, no matter how much money I could earn. She's making $2 million or $3 million a year, but that's too high a price to pay for me. Maybe she can do that because she's from another generation. Her generation accepts that they have to live a lie. I don't accept that." Hope said that she doesn't expect to be completely out at work, but she never intends to lie about dating men.

Janis said, "I'd like to be more visible, but I wish that I had more role models to feel OK about doing that. I know some lesbians who are older than me, but they're not role models because they fit too many of the stereotypes. I haven't met a lot of women who are successful, attractive . . . I don't know. Maybe I just haven't met enough. That could be a possibility."

She added, "But I have to admit, I'm jealous, because I think a lot of my gay male peers do have role models. Where I used to work, there was a gay guy who was pretty open, and he was a great role model for gay men. In contrast, there was a lesbian there, but she wasn't comparable to him in terms of her career success. She's not the fast track. Not only that, but it's the whole package—his persona, his looks, everything. She's a very nice person, but she's not a lesbian to watch out for. He's very charismatic. He's great. Everyone loves him. The lesbians I know aren't like that. Give me a lesbian like that, and I think that it would really help."

Younger People or Peers as Role Models

Many said younger people or peers are their role models. We found that, quite often, younger partners provide the impetus for older people to become more open about being gay. Bart Rubenstein, who graduated from HBS in 1979, said, "The most important thing in terms of my progression in coming out has been being involved with somebody who's from a slightly different generation, where they're completely comfortable being gay. He's a role model for me and has helped me get comfortable with it. For younger people, things have changed so quickly, I think, in a huge way. The few years' difference between when I was at business school and when you were at business school, I suspect, were radically different, in terms of being out and being comfortable and figuring how being gay fits into your life. People in their twenties and up to around age thirty, I think, are way ahead of most people of my age."

Bart added that classmate Jeff Eisberg was also a role model for him. "I saw Jeff go through the process of coming out to his boss. I think he was really proud of the experience. This was quite a few years ago when he was doing it, so it was extremely unusual. I think he was crowing about it a little bit, which was fine. Before I met my partner, I certainly needed positive images, so that was important for me. It went very well for him, so that was interesting and good for me to learn about. It didn't have any direct or immediate impact on me, other than making me feel more comfortable that it's OK to be gay. It did affect me in one way, come to think of it . . . I only came out to a few straight B-school people right at the end of Second Year. And I have maintained a circle of straight alumni friends, and I came out to them over a longer period of time. And a lot of those people know Jeff, and I think seeing him being out and having it go so well helped me come out to straight B-school people, say three and four years after I got out of business school."

Ted Chapin said his younger partner, Torrence Boone, has been a role model for him. "Up until this latest job, at least one person everywhere I've worked has been gay. And I have to concede that my becoming an architect was partly my feeling that architecture was just a lot more friendly environment to be gay in. I majored in economics at Yale; I was ready to go to Wall Street. But I decided to go to architectural school for that reason. I think Torrence is really breaking new ground in the business world and is a great role model for his peers at HBS by being openly gay there."

Kimberly said Torrence has indeed been a role model for her. "He is like a knight in shining armor. He is probably the most articulate person in our section, and I will be shocked if he doesn't graduate a Baker scholar [top scholastic honors]. He gets so much respect. Everyone's scared of him. See, everything at Harvard is motivated by fear. He comes from Bain, a major consulting firm, and he's out about being gay. That makes a big difference. People respect him, you know. Professors have so much respect for him. Every word that comes out of his mouth is really a wonderful sound. Of course, I don't need to explain to you guys how much voice matters. I mean, 70 percent is presentation and 30 percent is what you actually say. Torrence happens to be A+ on both, and so no one would fuck with him. Everyone knows he's gay—he even brought his partner to orientation week. That's pretty damned ballsy, you know. I mean, he introduced him to the class and everything. Of course, he's bright and he's articulate and centered and self-confident as hell. No one would screw around with him. I don't think anyone could ever touch Torrence. People are too wowed by his charisma and his presence. You just can't touch him."

We asked Kimberly if Torrence was a hard act to follow or whether she was inspired by him. She answered candidly, "Well, I know I don't have to tell you that when you hear your classmates speak and they would say something so well, you think: Shit, why can't I say it that way?" She laughed. "But basically—I'm proud. I mean, I feel safer with him there, because I don't have the security that Torrence does. I feel good to have him in my section. Even though he's younger than me by a couple of years, I feel that I have this role model within my own class. I love that he is there. Another gay friend sits right next to me, and we're really good friends. He's incredibly bright and articulate as well, and people know about him too. They know about the three of us. And we all hang out together all the time. So I think the three of us are a force to be reckoned with in the section. No one's going to make a blatant homophobic remark in one of our sections and get away with it. I have no problems speaking out. And those guys even have less of a problem than I do."

Heterosexual Role Models

Jo said heterosexual women are her role models. "My role models are not gay women; they are straight women. Women who are nice and happen to have husbands." Eva had a similar point of view. "The reason I went into the health-care group was because there was a female managing director. That was important to me. I didn't know anything about health care whatsoever, but it was led by a woman. So it was interesting to me for that reason."

Several women cited male relatives as role models. In contrast, gay men who had role models almost always looked to other gay men for that function.

MORE ROLE MODELS IN THE PIPELINE?

Many said they felt things would be easier for the generation of gay people growing up now. Douglas Plummer, who is in his late twenties, exclaimed, "Openly gay people are in the movies, in popular music—even on television now! They've seen documentaries, news shows, feature films, you name it. Gay people are much better known in popular culture now. So they have some exposure to gay people, and maybe some role models growing up."

Ronnie Diaz, who is in her late twenties, agreed that the presence of public role models would make it easier for gay young people to come out. She said, "I think young people are going to start coming out now faster than they did before. There are starting to be a lot of positive role models, like people in politics, entertainment, and sports. Like Martina and k. d. lang and Melissa Etheridge! I don't think of them as role models for me, but I admire them. People like Rock Hudson and Liberace, who could have made momentous strides for our community, chose the weak way out. I mean, we could have been ahead a couple of years in the battle if people like that had the courage to do what they needed to do."

Peter, however, was frustrated with the relatively slow pace of change in the business world. "The more people who come out, the easier it's going to be for everybody, and the more the rest of society is going to realize that we are everywhere. The difficulty is trying to get across positive gay and lesbian images as opposed to the drag queens and the leather men and the man-boy lovers and all that kind of stuff. As my friend Craig Davidson, who was the head of GLAAD, said, it's that those people are willing to go on television. They have no fear of that. He had a house party for GLAAD, and people were debating this. These were folks who were fairly well off professionals. And Craig said, 'The reason that we're not getting anywhere is because you guys won't go on TV.' And of course, they wouldn't. They're petrified."

Peter continued, "You know, being out on Fire Island is one thing. But it's another thing to get people out on television or to do anything really public." Peter admitted, "I think the more people that can come out to mainstream America, the better it's going to be for everybody. But as I said, for one person to do it, for *me* to do it, it's something that takes a lot of courage. Because I'm afraid what the reaction is going to be. Even though it's probably not going to be real obvious. It's more likely to be the subtle stuff. But the truth is, I don't want to be treated differently."

Bill, who is in his late twenties, felt there are increasingly more role models for gay people in business. David Geller, also in his twenties, was also hopeful about the changes. "The cultural environment has changed in a lot of respects. Also, the young people coming up are role models in some ways. Older people begin to think: Maybe I really could come out and not ruin my life. In New York, anyway, you can see *Angels in America, The Wedding Banquet, Threesome,* things like that, which are all of a sudden developing in the popular culture. I don't think there are more gay people. But more have started to come out. I think the military opened the issue about gays in the popular culture, but there was coverage before that too, like about domestic partner benefits and other workplace issues."

Some older gay professionals were candid about the inability of their generation to serve as role models, and many of those we interviewed were not sure if they qualified as role models. Merton said, "Maybe some of our friends admire our professional success, but I don't think a lot is discussed. I think it's more that we set an example. Occasionally people will say something acknowledging that this is the way that they'd like it to be for themselves, but I don't think it's prescriptive. I don't think we're in a position to say this is what you should or shouldn't do."

On the other hand, some, especially those who are most out, recognize that they are role models and are proud of their accomplishments. Mitchell Adams, an openly gay senior executive in the state government of Massachusetts, told us he is glad that his friendship with the governor has led to a statewide nondiscrimination law. As for being in the press about being gay, he said, "I think that's important. I mean, I have a responsible job, and I am very pleased that I am a role model for young people who are struggling with the question, Is their life worth living? Also, I've spoken before the Boston Gay Professional Organization, so I suppose, in a sense, I am also a role model for young professionals who are hoping to have a successful career. I think it is so important—if all of the young people who are gay were aware of the highly successful professionals who are also gay, they would feel much better about themselves, and a lot of them would come out. I have no doubt of that, no question."

Mitchell told us that, in particular, he has been a role model for a gay friend of his. "There is a senior attorney in town, who I have known professionally for twenty years, who was married and is the father of four children. I was very much a part of his coming-out process. He knew I was in a leadership role at the AIDS Action Committee in terms of raising money, so he had lunch with me to ask how he could get involved in the AIDS Action Committee. I told him, and I helped make that happen. He used volunteer work for the AIDS Action Committee as a way of introducing himself into a whole new world he knew nothing about. He knew he was gay, but he did not know how to go about it. So he volunteered at the AIDS Action Committee, and one thing led to another. Now he has lived three or four years with a male partner, and they are happy and stable and great friends of ours. Recently we were at a Seder at their house with his four kids."

Jeff Baron mentioned being a role model for some of his HBS classmates at the fifteen-year reunion. "Several of us openly gay folks were at the business school show reunion party. There were a few closeted people there who were always hanging around us, kind of wistfully, busy checking out how everybody was responding to those of us who were out. Actually in terms of being role models it really worked, because they have all come out more since then."

Jim Sherman acknowledges that he was conscious of being a role model for some of his gay classmates at HBS. "When I first arrived we had a party for our section in Boston at a bar. The organizers said bring a date, and I brought a guy. I will never forget introducing him to a classmate as my date. I was very clear on that. I think it was the part of me that was rebelling against this society that I viewed as overwhelmingly conformist. My section mates responded just fine. I think part of me wanted to make a statement. I didn't have to bring him to this, but I wanted to make a statement that not everyone here is a well-dressed, business-oriented, heterosexual jock."

During his Second Year, Jim signed an article in the school paper about being gay at HBS. "A number of straight people came up to congratulate me. In fact, some of them were people who I never would have expected to have said anything. They not only congratulated me on writing it but told me they agreed with the point of the article. My article generated a lot of debate and subsequent letters to the editor and a whole debate on campus. Because one of the things I said was I was angry at the closeted gay people on campus. Not only because they were ignoring a part of their lives, but because I felt their inaction hindered those of us who are open from being more successful in the gay movement. Some of the closeted ones did not agree with certain parts of the article. But it's interesting, one person in particular who was very closeted there did come around a year or two later and told me he now agrees with what I was saying."

ROLE MODELS AS UNIQUE?

Several of those we interviewed mentioned Sebastin, a Black man in his late thirties, as a role model but then discounted their own ability to be like him because they saw him as so exceptional. Nicholas said of Sebastin, "He's out because I don't know any other way he could be. Actually," Nicholas reflected, "I don't know if he is openly gay at work or not, but when he walks in the room, you know something's a little different about him. And he's very, very successful. I haven't been able to figure it out. I mean, let's assume that because he's Black he's going to have more difficulty in being successful, even though he went to a prestigious college as an undergrad and as a grad student, and then went to Harvard Business School. So you have to assume he's also very intelligent. But he's either in a cat suit or something else very unconventional . . . I don't know how he gets away with it. Obviously he is very good at what he does at work. But it's hard for me to believe that's enough." Nicholas laughed. "Either he has pictures of someone with animals—forget about pictures of someone having sex with somebody else's wife or whatever—there have to be pictures of sex with animals for him to be able to prance around the office the way he does." When pressed, Nicholas was unsure that Sebastin wore these clothes to work. We learned from Sebastin that he sometimes wears highly stylish attire (once he wore leggings and a cape to the office on a weekend) but not during the week. Nicholas reflected, "Maybe one reason he is able to get away with it is that his consulting firm defines itself as being eclectic—they have all types, one of every kind. That's their whole thing. But maybe there's only room for one like him."

Marty, who is also Black, had similar stories about Sebastin's uniqueness but told us he did see him as a role model. "I think he should write a book on giving advice on climbing the corporate ladder. He's about as out as anyone I know, and he's very successful. I don't think he's gone as far as introducing his boyfriend as his lover to people at work, but I know he's brought him to the company Christmas party. And I've started to do that too. Not at work, but to parties with friends from HBS who are straight. If they have a party or a get-together at their house, I usually bring Ralph. I don't come in and say, 'Hi everybody, this is my lover,' but I think they know."

Jonathan Rottenberg's Story

Many of those we interviewed cited Jonathan Rottenberg, the founder of the Boston Computer Society, as a role model. He said, "People just see me as one of those people who always was out and doing all this work. They don't understand that my being out is the end point of a very long progression that actually started way, way behind where most people started. Most gay people I knew, if they weren't completely comfortable being gay in college, they were at least having gay sex. I was so repressed, I literally had difficulty saying the word 'gay.' "

Jonathan told us about an Outward Bound excursion that has shaped the way he psychs himself up to come out, even today. "One day, they took us to a place we'd never been to before. There was a pier jutting out from where we were standing, and then a thirty-foot drop to the Atlantic Ocean crashing on the rocks below. And they said, 'What you're going to do is walk to the end of the pier and jump.' And everyone's immediate reaction was there is no way they're going to do this. It feels absolutely impossible. What they said is, 'There's basically one way to do this. You walk to the end of the pier, you click your mind off, and you keep walking. The one thing you do not do is think about what you're doing. You just do it.' " Jonathan said, "If you look at it carefully you would realize that you can't get hurt. But you still see the sinister-looking ocean and these rocks or whatever.

"Somehow, though, I just walked to the end of the pier, literally clicked my mind off, and just went. It was a phenomenally intense thing. And by the fourth day, we were doing this every morning. And we were actually at the point where we would run and yell our favorite ice cream flavor."

So when Jonathan began to come out, he said, "I would get together with someone for dinner or lunch, and we'd just talk about a lot of things. And we would always reach a point in the conversation that I'd realize I now have an opportunity, and if I don't take the opportunity, our meeting is going to be over and that would be it. At that point I would just sort of close my eyes a little bit and, in my mind, drift back to standing at that pier and just mentally calm myself down and start walking to the end of the pier and just click my mind off and say, 'I have to tell you that I'm gay.'

"You might be choking on your potatoes while the other person is going on about their kids, and they have no idea what's going on in your head. But when the opportunity opens up, if you don't go for it, you've lost your chance, and you have to go through all the fear another time." Jonathan recalled, "Like with jumping off a pier, each time I come out I have felt an incredibly intense sensation of falling through the air and not knowing what's going to happen. But in every case it worked out really well."

Jonathan added, "The other thing about coming out is that it's an incremental process. My Outward Bound experience also helped me internalize that philosophy. They brought us to the base of a ninety-foot granite cliff and said, 'This afternoon you are going to climb to the top of this cliff.' And of course, everyone is totally freaked out, because we've never done anything like this in our lives. They taught us a lot of different climbing techniques, which we did one after another. Eventually they brought us back to the cliff. What you realize is, you don't look up at the cliff. You look directly in front of you and you think about what situations you have seen before.

"When you get about two thirds of the way up, you come to a ledge about two feet deep; there you can stand very comfortably and sort of relax there. You realize, looking in front of you, that there is absolutely smooth rock in front of you, above you, and all the way to both sides. There is nothing apparent that you can grab on to. There's nothing that this is like that you've seen that you can do. I was kind of looking at it for a while, and finally realized I can't do anything. There is no place to go.

"Finally I think: Well, all right, I'm going to try jumping up to the right. So I jump up to the right and I come sliding down, and I feel really stupid. So I thought: All right, I'll just try it again. I jump up to the right, I come slamming down, nothing happens. I'll try jumping to the left. I jump up, I come sliding down. I probably did this twenty times, feeling like an absolute idiot. I think it was about the twenty-first time when something hits me. I realize when I'm jumping, I'm seeing a different angle on the situation. And I suddenly realized that there is another ledge around the corner that I couldn't see from where I was standing. We had learned a technique that morning, a dynamic move, where you use the motion of swinging to hold your foot onto something that you could not hold your foot to long enough without swinging.

"All of a sudden it comes together. I figured it out, and I swing around and got up to the next ledge, and in a few minutes I'm up at the top. The lesson that experience taught me is that when you're stuck on a ledge, the one thing not to do is just sit there. You just have to keep doing things. It's in the process of doing things that new possibilities become apparent to you. And that, to me, is very much like what happens in the coming-out process.

"You get to these ledges where it's just very safe and secure and it seems like there's no place to go. So you either stay where you are or you fall back off the cliff. I really think that that's where so many people are at. They tell one or two coworkers, and that's enough, that's it. But if they move off that ledge, the benefits to them would be greater than sitting on the ledge. There are benefits there, but they are just not seeing them because they're not doing enough."

We asked Jonathan what personal benefits of coming out might outweigh the potential negatives other gay professionals fear. "I believe that it is precisely this process of overcoming their fear that will build their self-confidence in many other work situations," he said. "I feel that the process of coming to terms with being gay and talking with people about it and not backing down from it has done more to build my capabilities as a consultant than almost anything else that I have done so far. I think that when you have self-confidence, your sense of your own capabilities expands. When someone realizes that they can take on a risky situation and manage it and be effective and turn it into something successful, they can transfer that to many other challenges that they face."

Jonathan believes that "even if the reaction is negative, there are benefits. To me, a successful coming-out experience is one that you learn from and take action from as a result. Whether it goes well or goes poorly, whether it gives you warm fuzzies or makes you uncomfortable . . . that's not the measure of success. I think that fundamentally people are afraid of having a massive disaster in which they will be mortally embarrassed or where terrible things will happen to them. And I think it's not impossible that something like that could happen if you did something really, really stupid. But I actually think that the people who worry the most about those things happening are so much smarter than they'll give themselves credit for, that the chance that they would actually do something to create that level of mistake is very, very unlikely.

"People who really think it through recognize their fears about coming out may be grounded in reality. But they are willing to test their fears and become tactical in the way that they approach the issues that they're dealing with. They are constantly moving themselves to take action. It doesn't matter if it's a big action or small action, it's just that they're always doing something. If you can look back each week and point to the specific actions you took that helped advance you forward personally and helped the cause—you're on the right track."

• • •

Many gay professionals spoke of the importance of role models in their coming-out process. Most said they wished they knew more gay professionals who could help pave the way for them in becoming comfortable with their own gay identity or in coming out at work. However, while role models can play an important role in helping gay professionals become comfortable with their gay identity, the presence or absence of role models is not the whole story behind why some have come out at work and others do not. Rather, it seems to be the willingness to *be* a role model that makes the most important difference. Whether or not they knew anyone else who was openly gay at work, it was those who had the courage of their own convictions and faith in their own abilities who were willing to come out there.

COMING-OUT STRATEGIES

There is no one particular *kind* of gay professional who comes out at work. Gay men and lesbians of all ages, races, and backgrounds are among those who have come out at work. Additionally, we found, gay professionals are coming out in a variety of industries. A decade ago, gay professionals who came out at work were usually self-employed or in gay-friendly industries. In those days, a gay professional in a mainstream business career had two options: stay closeted or leave. Today gay professionals are breaking new ground—coming out in corporations, financial institutions, and large consulting firms, as well as in many other fields, both before and after pursuing an MBA.

We found that those who are the most out at work have encountered the least difficulties professionally and have had the greatest success in overcoming the difficulties they did encounter. One reason, we believe, is that these professionals had a well-thought-out and consistently executed strategy for coming out and being out on the job. Not all used the same approach, however. In this section of the chapter we identify and examine four successful coming-out-at-work strategies that can be used by any gay professional.

While Harvard MBAs are generally bright, capable, and highly skilled, those are not the sole reasons for their success in coming out at work. Rather, we believe, their success is the result of their courage and persistence. Those who employed one or more of these strategies have been able to achieve their career goals in both gay-friendly and conservative industries.

A CHANGING WORKPLACE

Those we interviewed told us that before the 1970s, coming out at work was unthinkable in any white-collar profession. In the 1970s gay men and lesbians started to come out in fields like advertising, communications, art, music, design, architecture, retail, and fashion. Most who came out were on the creative side, but some business professionals began to come out as well. In the 1980s gay professionals began to come out more broadly in these industries and to test the waters in other fields. Those we interviewed recalled coming out at least selectively in health care, government, entertainment, the media, publishing, banking, and financial services during that decade, often without knowing anyone else in their field who had done so. Today professionals are beginning to come out in many large corporations, consulting firms, and investment banks.

On a sociological level, it is easy to see why these changes have occurred. Though prejudice and discrimination remain, there has been a significant change for the better in the way gay people are viewed in American workplaces. Some states and cities have passed laws against discrimination based on sexual orientation in employment. A number of major companies have enacted corporate policies to the same effect. And a number of opinion polls show that a large majority of Americans believe that gay people should not be discriminated against at work (so long as no children, touching, or sharing close quarters is involved).

Yet on an individual level, the reasons why gay professionals are coming out now are not so obvious. Most companies still have a long way to go in ensuring equal treatment of gay people. While increasing numbers of gay people are coming out selectively at work, few companies have publicized their willingness to hire or promote fully open gay senior managers. While many municipalities and universities have begun to offer full domestic partner benefits, the number of private companies that do so has remained relatively small. While many large companies have diversity-training programs, the issues of gay employees are usually given short shrift if they are mentioned at all. Few companies do target marketing to gay men and lesbians or contribute philanthropy dollars to gay community causes. And most heterosexuals in the workplace continue to assume everyone they work with is also heterosexual, and some display ignorance or hostility toward gay people generally.

Thus we need to look more closely at the reasons why gay professionals come out at work, whom they come out to, and how they come out. First, however, we need to define some terms. What exactly is coming out at work? This seemingly simple question gave us no end of difficulty in conducting our early interviews.

WHAT IS COMING OUT?

When we started this project, we asked, "Are you out at work?" This turned out to be an inappropriate way to get information, for two very different reasons. One is that many people interpreted this question to mean, "Are you out to every single person you ever encounter at work, as well as to people you do not personally know?" Thus they answered, "No," or, "Not really." But when we asked, "Have you come out to anyone at work?" we found the vast majority of our interviewees had told at least one and often more than one person at work that they were gay. Sometimes we found gay professionals who were out to their entire work group, including bosses and secretaries, but did not consider themselves "really" out because they had not come out to people in different divisions, or to people several levels above and below them, or in the company newsletter!

A second problem was the contradictory assertions we encountered quite frequently. "People at work know," but "I haven't actually told them," some said. For example, George told us he felt he was out at work because "I never lie about dating women or try to hide anything." However, we learned, George had also never actually told anyone at work he was gay. Neither had he had a conversation with anyone at work who specifically acknowledged what he thought they knew. "No one ever asks me about getting married or anything," he said, "so I think they've figured it out. But no, no one's ever literally told me, 'I know you're gay.' "

Thus for some gay professionals, the idea of being out at work seems so radical they do not want to attribute that behavior to themselves, even if they had in fact come out selectively. On the other hand, some felt so brave about dropping hints and so eager to claim the mantle of respect that comes from being out that they considered themselves out at work even though they had never actually told anyone they were gay.

In addition, as we explored the ways people came out, we found few used the simple declarative statement "I am gay." Rather, many relied on the ability of their listener to infer the meaning from more oblique statements, such as "my partner and I" or "at my summer share in the Pines" or "when I was at the March on Washington." Thus, we constantly asked our interviewees who claimed someone knew to clarify for us, "How do you know they understood what you were telling them?" In most cases, we heard, "Oh, because she asked me how long my partner and I had been together," or, "He asked me if I had come out to anyone else at work." But sometimes we heard, "They must know, because how could they miss the point?" or, "It might have flown right over them," or, "The truth is, I don't know if they get it."

Thus, in our definition of coming out at work, the defining factor was a verbal exchange in which the heterosexual obviously has no doubt as to what he or she has been told—not how many people probably knew. This definition proved to be important, because we found great differences between those who are out, even to a few, and those who had hinted to many but had told none. One difference is that those who are suspected of being gay but are not out seemed to suffer the greatest amount of discrimination against them. Another difference is that those who hint but do not come out remain unable to take advantage of the benefits of being out, including increased self-confidence, improved networking opportunities, and tangible corporate benefits and protections.

We also found differences based on how broadly a person was out. The more someone was out, the more optimistic they felt about their ability to succeed in their career. One reason may be that those who have come out most broadly usually employed a conscious coming-out strategy, while those who came out only selectively usually came out in reaction to the behavior of others. Thus those who were most out felt a sense of agency in their approach. Whether they met immediate success or encountered setbacks, they saw themselves as having choices in their workplace relationships. In contrast, those who were out selectively and intended to come out no further tended to feel more fear and uncertainty about their future.

For those who are out selectively, doubts and questions remain. Many wonder: Is coming out to anyone else worth the risk? Or they assume: Everyone kind of knows anyway. Why bother to actually tell them? Others worry: Is there such a thing as being too out? For those who are completely closeted at work, there are other questions: How can I really know whether it is safe to come out? Is there a right time to come out? Will my career suffer? Will people's attitudes toward me change? What will people say or do behind my back?

FINDINGS

An encouraging discovery is that the willingness of gay professionals to actively hide their sexual orientation has decreased over time. In our 1990 survey, we learned that in previous jobs almost 50 percent led their coworkers or bosses to believe that they were dating heterosexually, and almost a third did so actively. Yet only 10 percent said that they have actively done so at one time in their present jobs, while an additional 13 percent said that they "sort of" did so. In our interviews conducted in 1993 and 1994, we found a number of individuals who said they had made up stories at their job in the past, but none who said that they now did so. In addition, many of those who said that they "sort of" misled coworkers in the past have stopped doing so, and some have even come out at work. Finally, a large majority of 1990s graduates report they have never actively attempted to conceal their sexual orientation and never intend to.

Rather than hiding their sexual orientation at work, we learned from our survey, most gay professionals come out at work at least selectively. Of those who do not work for themselves, 40 percent are out to a boss, more than half are out to one or more subordinates, and three fourths have come out to at least one coworker in their present job. Even more have come out to bosses, colleagues, and subordinates in the past. (This does not mean gay professionals are getting more closeted; rather, MBAs change jobs fairly frequently, and most do not come out at new jobs right away.) In our interviews we discovered a significant trend in favor of coming out earlier and more broadly.

In developing our survey, we anticipated that selective coming out may mean coming out only to other gay people. Thus we also asked how widely gay professionals were out at work. About a third told us that most of their heterosexual coworkers know that they are gay. In addition, another third said they believe that their heterosexual coworkers assume or suspect that they are gay.

Some of these findings appear to paint a fairly positive picture of progress. But these gay professionals are far less out at work than they are with their friends, family, or even neighbors. While most said they don't hide anything or are completely open about themselves and their sexual orientation when the subject of homosexuality comes up, for many these are empty boasts. As we learned in our interviews, it means that most never discuss the subject at all. A telling statistic is that when heterosexual colleagues assume they are heterosexual, almost half do nothing to correct the mistake.

Another sign of the degree to which gay employees are out of the closet is language. Almost half of those we surveyed say they discuss their partner or dates at work. But most discuss such a person as a friend or in gender-neutral terms. And the overwhelming majority say that they never hug, hold hands, walk arm in arm, or kiss their lover or date at or near work the way their heterosexual colleagues often do. These are the things that many saw as too out. Yet, ironically, many of these same people say their goal is to be treated exactly like everyone else, or for others to treat being gay as a simple fact of life.

Those who talk openly about a same-sex partner or date, come out when someone assumes they are heterosexual, and display casual affection to their partner in front of people from work sing a different tune. They suggest that it is difficult to be treated as equal unless one acts equal. Thus they expect a higher level of nonchalance about being gay from both themselves and from people at work.

From a corporate viewpoint there is also a significant difference between having gay employees and having openly gay employees. Those who tolerate gay employees as long as they don't talk about it must do little. On the other hand, management that really has a place for those who are openly gay may have some changes to make. Openly gay professionals are far more likely to demand respect for their identity as well as to ask to be treated equally with heterosexuals. They expect their companies to treat them fairly as individuals, which means a nondiscrimination policy. They expect management to treat them equally with other employees with family relationships, which means domestic partner benefits. They also expect management to treat their relationships equally in social invitations and casual conversation. Finally, they may want to know they have management support for being out about being gay to clients, vendors, and suppliers.

The gay professionals who come out at work recognize they—and their companies—are breaking new ground. Even for those who are most open, deciding to come out in the workplace was one of the single most important decisions they faced in their business career. No matter how secure they felt about the company's probable response, gay professionals knew they were traveling uncharted waters. As a result, even those who have never hidden being gay from family, friends, or fellow students did not lightly make a decision to come out at work. Even younger gay professionals who have been out at work from the beginning of their careers told us that continuing to be open about their sexual orientation is not always an easy decision.

The most common reason for not coming out at work was fear of negative career ramifications. But none who are completely open reported suffering any. Instead they say it is well worth it and they would do it all over again.

A few expressed some concern about hitting a lavender ceiling. Yet they pointed out that closeted peers faced the same hurdles unless they married or otherwise actively pretended to be like everyone else. Those who are open add that if their companies do not continue to promote them, at least they'll know why and can move on. Some said their ultimate goal was entrepreneurial anyway, so their aim was to get as much experience as they could before striking out on their own. Others said that an important component of career success to them was progressing as high as they could as an openly gay individual—by definition they couldn't achieve this if they were closeted.

WHO COMES OUT AT WORK?

Gay professionals who decided to come out at work, whether selectively or broadly, usually shared the following profile:

- They were comfortable with their sexual orientation.
- They were out to heterosexual friends and family.
- They had a partner or gay friends who encouraged them to come out at work.
- They did not consider their workplace a hostile environment.

Those who rated themselves the happiest with being out at work, usually those who were most out, shared another characteristic:

- They had a coming-out plan.

For fairly obvious reasons, the gay professionals we interviewed told us they did not come out at work until they were comfortable with being gay themselves. But, interestingly, we found no correlation between length of time an individual was out to him- or herself and being out at work. Nor, surprisingly, did we find any correlation between the difficulty of the coming-out-to-self process and being open at work.

At first we were puzzled by finding that being out to oneself longer does not mean coming out more at work. Much of the literature describes coming out as a series of developmental stages that occur over time. But we found the role of a support system and practice were generally far more important. Coming out is like anything else that you try to be good at—it takes practice. Most people who successfully come out at work have a history of practicing coming out with heterosexual friends and family. For any given individual, it is important to find out what works and what doesn't work.

Thus, being out to family was another typical precondition for coming out at work. Almost every gay professional who came out at work had already come out to siblings, parents, or other relatives. The experience of coming out to heterosexual friends was also a usual precondition for coming out at work. Most told us they did not have the self-confidence to face the responses of work colleagues until they first handled coming out to family and heterosexual friends.

Those who were most out at work shared the belief that they were in control of the coming-out process. Whatever the reaction of heterosexual friends and family, they felt they had done the right thing by telling them. Even those who encountered rough spots along the way maintained their self-confidence about coming out at work. As Shawn joked, "Yeah, I'm a pioneer, and the pioneers get the arrows. But you know what? I've taken so many arrows by now, it's no big deal anymore." Some who had problems with heterosexual friends or family shied away from coming out at work because they felt even less safe about coming out to strangers. But Ryan disagreed. "It's easier to come out to people at work. They don't have any of the psychological issues that parents or even friends do about their identity being wrapped up with who you are."

Most who came out at work discussed the issue with a supportive partner or friends. Being in a relationship significantly increased the desire of gay professionals to come out at work and having a partner to refer to made the actual process of coming out at work easier. While partners were most often neutral or encouraging about coming out at work, gay friends, perhaps surprisingly, were often naysayers. Often this was because they had not come out at work themselves and thus had their own fears and rationalizations.

Gay professionals who had been out to themselves for years or decades were sometimes so used to living their personal and professional lives in separate worlds that they had surrounded themselves with gay friends who took the same approach. In contrast, those who came out at work were more likely to have friends who had come out at work themselves and to have found their example and feedback very valuable.

While some of those who came out, whether selectively or broadly, worked in gay-friendly industries, others worked in a wide variety of other businesses, and not everyone in gay-friendly industries was out to anyone. Gay professionals who came out selectively were most often guided by the tone set by management. Awareness of others within the company or industry who have come out successfully also sometimes played a pivotal role. But more often gay professionals who came out selectively reported testing the waters on their own via clues and hints to try to assess the implications of coming out. In contrast, those who were out most broadly told us they intended to come out irrespective of the obstacles they found. While they might have modified their strategy to take circumstances into account, they always intended to come out no matter what.

For some, the initial experiences of coming out selectively determined whether or not they continued on a path of coming out at work. But this reactive approach may not be the best strategy, we learned. Those who continued to come out sometimes met setbacks. But they also usually had a conscious plan for coming out at work. They were able to implement their plan, whether or not it faced roadblocks, because they had confidence in their long-term vision. By evaluating their performance and continuing to sharpen their coming-out skills, they were confident they would continue to succeed not only in coming out but in their careers as well.

Thus a composite picture of the typical MBA coming-out process was not in itself revealing. On average, gay professionals in our survey recognized they had gay feelings around age fifteen. They identified themselves as being gay by age twenty-one and came out to a gay friend by age twenty-two. By age twenty-four they came out to a heterosexual friend, and by age twenty-seven they came out to a family member. Of those who worked before attending HBS, almost half came out to someone on the job, usually a work colleague. At HBS, most came out to a heterosexual friend on campus. The standard coming-out model would predict that gay professionals would continue to come out during the course of their career.

But as we analyzed our data more closely we saw other findings that seemed important. Forty percent considered themselves gay while they were in college, and almost all of these individuals participated in gay life as an undergraduate by going to gay bars. But only 8 percent of those whose colleges had a gay student organization participated in it. Coming out to others as a college student can occur in a relatively safe environment. Yet we learned that many of those who go into business did not practice this skill as ardently as they learned to crunch numbers or analyze facts. Thus, many of those who came out to themselves in college did not have a sizable gay peer group to trade job-hunting strategies with, nor did most have much practice coming out to heterosexuals. A large majority assumed all career choices would be equally difficult, as only 18 percent who knew they were gay in college said being gay affected their choice of industry or job function. Although a number came out to someone at a pre-HBS job, in our interviews we confirmed that this was often an act done in isolation. It was not until business school that most in our sample had an opportunity to put their dreams and experiences about coming out at work in context.

At HBS, we found, almost 75 percent of our survey respondents considered themselves gay, and again, all these individuals participated in gay life by going to gay bars. In marked difference to their behavior in college, however, almost all who attended HBS when the gay student organization was in existence participated in it. In our interviews we confirmed that the business school experience was formative, and many found themselves in for a rude shock. Of those who graduated before 1990, the vast majority listed campus homophobia as a major problem, and over half recalled specific homophobic comments, jokes, and actions of their classmates. Some of those who were most out before business school had a different experience—they recalled the fear and paranoia of their gay classmates most distinctly. For both reasons, upon graduation from HBS, almost half of those we surveyed said their sexual orientation affected their choice of industry or job function. In most cases, this meant selecting careers they perceived as gay friendly directly out of business school.

The coming-out experience at business school in particular left a deep impression on many. In general, we learned, those who were successful coming out to heterosexual peers at business school developed strategies they would continue to use in the workplace, whatever career they pursued. In contrast, those who had negative experiences with peers often retreated from coming out at work at least temporarily.

Although most of our sample came out to themselves in college, we were also struck by the number of all ages who did not come to terms with their gay identity until business school or later. Stever Robbins had a theory about this. "Nerds come out in undergrad. Businesspeople come out in grad school and beyond. I don't know all the reasons why, but I think most of the people who want to go into business are just too uptight about things. I mean, businesspeople are not exactly the most forward-thinking, risk-taking, daring, creative people in the country. Which is a shame, because if they were, we would have one hell of an economy." He laughed. "In contrast, I think most technical people . . . You know, in our society, the technical people are really looked down upon anyway. Certainly at business school the attitude was, they're all interchangeable. And that is not true at all. If you know anything about technical stuff, you know the right or the wrong engineer can make or break your product. We geeks are oppressed and put down from a very early age. You know, we're the last ones chosen for the football teams and the baseball teams, and we're made fun of and we're teased, and so on and so forth. Just like homosexuals. So I think a lot of the gay geeks say, 'So I'm gay, too. Fine. Big deal.' Coming out is no big deal. I mean, what are they gonna do, ostracize me? Oh boy. There's nothing to lose; geeks are already ostracized."

In many ways, our research confirmed Stever's hypothesis. Many of those who came out to themselves in their late twenties had the most tormented experiences of coming out to themselves. But only some of these were the most fearful about coming out at work. A number told us coming out was such a fundamentally life-changing event they saw no need to hide any longer. "Once I do something, I do it all out, all the way," several told us.

Those we interviewed who were at HBS in the 1990s seem to be coming out to themselves and others far earlier. In part due to the increasing presence of openly gay people in the media and on campus, today's youth and young adults have more information available to them to assess and accept their sexual orientation in their teens. They are also more likely to have social support at an earlier age from heterosexual friends and family members as well as gay friends. As a result, they are coming out earlier and more broadly at work. When they reach business school, they are more likely to have a track record of coming out successfully to heterosexuals throughout their entire adult lives. For them, coming out to HBS classmates was a final testing ground for coming out in their professional career. Unlike their predecessors, many termed their experience successful and thus left business school with renewed confidence about being out at work. Many told us they expect to continue to come out to people at work over the course of their careers, in whatever industries they choose.

While many are still fearful, the example of those who have come out successfully at business school and at work shows that the biggest barrier for many gay professionals may be internal. Usually, those of all ages who were most out at work had a reserve of self-confidence based on a long-established pattern of coming out successfully outside work. Yet still, most felt that they were traveling without a map by coming out at work.

Knowing no one else who had come out as broadly as they wanted to was not a barrier, however. Instead, those who are most out say what separates them from their peers is the willingness to move beyond their fears.

WHY COME OUT?

Why do gay professionals choose to come out despite the possible difficulties? Those who are out, whether selectively or completely, told us that while revealing their sexual orientation may have dangers, it also has strong potential rewards. Gay professionals cited many motives for coming out, including personal reasons, career reasons, and political reasons.

It would be naive to fail to acknowledge the occasional negative reactions and setbacks that some gay professionals have encountered after coming out. Yet, for those who were most out, these incidents were rare and relatively inconsequential. One difference between those who had a plan for coming out at work and those who tried a more hit-or-miss approach was their reactions to obstacles. For some, the minute they encountered resistance, they backed off and never dared come out to another person at work. But for those who are most out, these stumbling blocks were problems to be overcome or mitigated. They did not detract from the big-picture idea "I want to be out at work."

Some who are out say that they still have some fears about what goes on behind their backs. But they also report that by being true to themselves, they found a sense of inner peace and wholeness that has propelled them to excel at work and in other aspects of their lives. Thus, on balance, the identifiable benefits far outweighed their vague fears. Alan Miles said, "My parents didn't go to college, and they worked very hard their whole lives so me and my siblings could go to college. They have been fine with me being gay and have always been very proud of everything I've done. But in their minds, being out at work risks it all. Their big worry is, 'Won't being openly gay hurt your career?' And all I can say to them is, 'Well, you know it might. But what am I supposed to do about it? If I try to hide it, then people will find out in some way. Or I'll just seem like this strange person with no life. That won't help my career either. And if I hide it I'll feel terrible about myself.' "

Personal Reasons

Another reason for coming out at work was in response to a personal crisis, such as illness or death of a loved one, a breakup, or an outing threat. Most who came out for personal reasons, however, did so proactively. Even those who were not actively dissembling about being gay found that the accommodations they had to make in trying to hide were just too draining. The need to live, communicate, and be recognized by their coworkers as a full person—with a professional and a personal life, just like their heterosexual colleagues—was a powerful motivator. Whatever fear and misgivings they experienced beforehand, gay professionals who came out to someone at work felt that a great burden was lifted from their shoulders. Jane said, "I was so relieved. I realized how much being closeted affected the way I performed in my job. Now I can just be me. I changed my whole orientation from trying to hide or not discuss things to being completely natural about my weekend plans or the fact that my partner and I are moving in together or whatever. All the time I used to spend worrying I now spend working."

The need to be a complete, integrated person is almost always cited by those in committed relationships. Some of those who are single also felt this need. Joel said, "After you pass thirty, if you're not married and not dating, people begin to assume you're gay anyway. It just gets harder to pull off that ambiguity. It's actually easier just to tell them." He laughed. "Then you actually have something to talk about with them."

Some say they come out simply because there is no more reason to hide. As Torrence Boone told us matter-of-factly, "I made a choice that I'm not going back into the closet because I think it's infinitely easier to just be out. Also I think that a lot of people just don't care. One thing that I've learned is that this isn't such a big deal to most people. Most people are not that wrapped up in knowing what your sexual identity is."

For many, there is the hope or expectation of making new friends, both gay and heterosexual, by coming out at work. Another reason to come out is to forestall awkward situations with heterosexuals. Several told us removing the heterosexual assumption from their relationships with the opposite sex can be a professional advantage. Many gay men say that it is easier to be friends with women who know they are not out for something. Several lesbians told us it is easier to go on business trips with married men when their wives know they are gay. Both gay men and lesbians who are out at work say they find it easier to engage in the casual flirting that greases workplace relationships with the opposite sex, because no one ever takes it too seriously.

Professional Reasons

Some of those we interviewed said they were uncomfortable having people who work for them know too much about their personal life because they think that it will undermine their authority, but those who are completely open disagree, pointing to closer bonds with heterosexuals. Others who have come out at work found it has enhanced their ability to network with other gay people. At first, most feared that a consequence of being fully out was that more closeted gay people would stay away from them. But this was not always the result short-term and was rarely the case long-term. Some we interviewed told us more closeted colleagues kept their distance at first. But eventually the knowledge that someone else at work was gay opened a pathway to friendship. Often, those who are out told us, their success at being openly gay led others to consider taking the step out. Steven told us, "There's a woman I worked with who was struggling with coming out until she met me. I was her role model as an intelligent Ivy-educated person who is also gay. She had never met anybody like that before. Just seeing me being me helped her come out."

We also found some evidence that those most deeply in the closet might stay away from those who are merely thought to be gay more than from those who are openly gay. We asked Chip for an explanation. He said, "Hector, who is out, is friendly with everyone at work, so it's no big thing for us to be friends too. On the other hand Travis, who is more ambiguous, is also more of a loner. So for the two of us to suddenly start going out to lunch together—well, everyone would start to put two and two together about me, and I'm not ready for that yet."

Political Reasons

Another reason some gay professionals come out is to educate. Mitch, a professor at Harvard Business School, told us, "There is more homo-ignorance here than homophobia. The more I come out, the more being gay becomes a nonissue. But that doesn't happen if you don't come out. People respect you if you stand up for what you believe." Barry Salzman, who has worked in consulting and leveraged buyouts, agreed. "Because it's just been such an incredibly positive experience for me to come out to myself, I really do feel I have a responsibility to the gay community to keep educating people, whether it is friends, family, or people in the workplace. It's something I talk about very openly, and I think that's a good thing, because a lot of straight people have questions about things they don't understand."

A gay man in his mid-thirties, Barry told us he thinks coming out at unexpected times, in particular, can have a great impact. Others agreed that being matter-of-fact about coming out can be tremendously positive in terms of its educational impact. Ann Bilyew told us, "People respect you when you come out. They cannot help but respect you. Even if they don't agree with a particular point of view that you have, they respect you and respect your honesty with them. And when it comes to getting to know you personally, you let them know you expect to be treated like anyone else. That's also an important method of education. It's not always necessary to make a big speech to get your message across."

Jim Sherman also told us he is more likely to come out when someone assumes he is heterosexual. He laughed, saying, "I see why it's almost the opposite of what you might expect. Because if someone says, 'Are you seeing anyone?' you might think that they're broadminded and they're leaving you an opportunity to come out. Whereas, if they ask 'Do you have a girlfriend?' then you really have to be proactive to come out. You have to flip over their assumptions. But that's what I usually do. I sometimes wonder why I do that. I mean, I'm single, so I could obviously choose to answer both questions in the same way, right? I could say, 'No, I'm not seeing anyone,' to either one. But I think maybe the difference is that I'm kind of offended that someone is assuming that I should be seeing a woman. It's an opportunity to educate them, an opportunity to shatter assumptions, and maybe a part of me is angered by it, and that is driving the more open response."

Another important reason to come out is to secure particular protections or benefits. Interestingly, we found it is not always those who are out to the most people who are the most political in this sense. In addition, some who are out to very few heterosexuals are among those who have done important work behind the scenes to achieve benefits. Yet in most cases, being willing to come out at least selectively is a necessary precondition for changing corporate policy.

METHODS OF COMING OUT

Perhaps surprising, we discovered that for this group of highly successful business professionals the decision to come out at work was rarely the result of careful planning. This finding is also in striking contrast to their behavior outside work. With heterosexual friends and family, most of those we interviewed had implemented very specific plans for coming out or not coming out to particular people. Yet very few had specific strategies in mind for managing their gay identity at work. Those who were most tightly closeted often had a plan and kept to it, namely, to tell no one, gay or heterosexual. But their numbers were small. The vast majority of the gay professionals we interviewed had come out to someone at work.

Coming Out Selectively

Few who came out selectively had thoroughly evaluated the pros and cons of using one method versus another to come out at work. Rather, by default they ended up with a strategy we nicknamed "Don't do anything until you're sure." Those who used this strategy said things like, "I would only want to tell someone whom I have a sufficiently close relationship with" or "I'd only tell someone who basically already knows." Those who were out selectively were hardly ever sure of the outcome; hence they rarely came out. Instead of actively looking for opportunities to come out, most who were out selectively looked for ways to avoid doing so. Additionally, we found, many of those who are out selectively came out defensively rather than strategically. For example, they came out if someone asked them, but they did not initiate the coming-out conversation themselves. In a number of cases, the decision to come out was triggered by a crisis event. Those who faced sudden illness, an outing threat, or a direct question were usually forced to make an on-the-spot decision about whom to tell and how to tell them. Interestingly, many reported they were glad that this pressure made them come out to a given person or group of people.

In the absence of such pressure, most had no order or timetable for whom and when to tell. In addition, we found, most who were out selectively were unable to envision how they wanted to be treated by coworkers. Instead, they articulated both a desire for privacy and a desire to be treated like everyone else.

There are two major disadvantages to coming out selectively. First, the coming-out conversation itself is usually framed as "I've got a secret to tell you." As a result, those who are out selectively sometimes find they are sending the wrong message about how they want their sexual orientation to be viewed. Additionally, they must rely on the other party to keep their secret or to keep track of who else knows. Second, those who are out selectively feel safer because they have told a few people. But without coming out more widely, they still suffer most of the disadvantages of the closet.

Not surprising, those who had a plan for coming out judged themselves more successful than those who did not. For some the plan involved a particular chain of scripted conversations. For others it meant being out spontaneously from day one. A few chose to come out in the local or national media, which helped them come out to those at work.

We learned that even those who are most out do not necessarily use the same strategy in all aspects of their work life. Many differentiated between short-term and long-term assignments or between people in their home office and clients. Most of those who were out to everyone they personally worked with agreed it was harder to find ways of coming out to those they did not interact with on a daily basis; they agreed that coming out to a stranger in casual conversation was the most difficult kind of coming out to do. Even some of those who have come out in the media told us they do not always come out to strangers or clients. But generally those who are most out said they are always looking for opportunities to come out. Torrence Boone said, "Once you're sort of over that hump it's like . . . now you can be real. Otherwise you really hit a barrier in terms of how close you can be with people. As human beings, the way that we relate to others and our sense of intimacy and our sense of commitment to relationships and love is important. All of those things are so interwoven into the things that bond people as friends. How can you have a natural conversation as a human being and not broach the issue of the person that you love or the person who you're committed to?"

While most of those we interviewed told us they looked for signs that certain protections exist and that social attitudes are fairly benign before coming out at work, few came out fully confident of the results. Instead, most chose the strategy or strategies best suited to their personality and situation.

Always Out

The few who used an always-out approach all termed the experience highly successful. No less than the other strategies, it required careful thought in advance to employ successfully. Those who used this approach told us they had thought long and hard about the best way to phrase things and how to initiate various kinds of coming-out conversations.

Some, like Ann Bilyew, came out on their résumé or in their interview. "If they don't want to hire me because I'm gay, I don't want to work there anyway," she said. Ann told us that despite her being listed as copresident of the HBS Gay and Lesbian Student Organization on her résumé, none of those who interviewed her and ultimately offered her a job asked her any questions about her role there. Marcy, who was part of a training session for managers with hiring authority, had a suggestion for why that might be. "At this session, someone brought up a question about why someone would list gay activities on their résumé. And someone else said it was so that they could claim discrimination based on sexual orientation if they weren't hired. I shot that remark down by pointing out that they probably listed it because they were proud of their accomplishments in a community organization, just like anyone in any other group would be."

Some came out before accepting a job offer. "You're in a position of strength then like you'll never be again," several pointed out. "So it's a good time to get that issue out of the way." Others came out the first day on the job as part of the getting-to-know-you conversations, usually as the result of having to rebut the presumption of heterosexuality. Some said they waited for their coworkers' inevitable questions about marital or romantic status, and if they did not ask, some initiated the conversation themselves. Generally, they said, rather than talking about themselves first, they asked their colleagues about their personal lives in order to elicit reciprocal questions.

Those who preferred the always-out strategy told us they were uncomfortable with having to go through a period of deception before telling the truth. "I'd rather just be myself from the beginning without waiting for the right moment or waiting until we're such good friends that it seems like a slap in the face that they don't know already. Or having that awkward 'I have something to tell you' conversation, when they have to say something back right then and there. I'd rather tell new people I work with as soon as I have a chance," Shawn said. "When your primary orientation is to be closeted, you are always looking for ways to avoid talking about yourself. Instead, I look for opportunities to come out."

Some dropped strong hints within a few days or weeks of coming to work and came out concretely shortly thereafter. Such hints could be verbal or take symbolic forms, such as a picture of a loved one on the desk or a gay symbol or slogan. In some ways this is similar to the strategic approach described below, although the gay person has not had a chance to build up professional credibility or a team of allies before launching into a coming-out conversation.

Those who are always out are most likely to continue being out. This means they keep coming out to new people, and they continue to be out in conversation with the people they have already told. This way of instantly breaking down distinctions between their lives and the lives of heterosexuals around them reflects a strong political perspective also shared by those who came to be all the way out by different means.

Another kind of instant coming out came in response to a personal crisis or being asked or outed. Those who found themselves on the spot were usually the least prepared to handle the coming-out conversation with aplomb. Yet a number laughingly said that they did their best thinking on their feet and admitted they would never have come out otherwise. In contrast to those who chose the always-out strategy, those who were forced to "shoot from the hip" usually came out far less broadly. Some tell once and never discuss it again, while others continue to be out in conversation to those they have come out to. In general, those who have come out most broadly and integrate being out into their daily lives at work report the highest level of happiness with coming out.

Coming Out in the Media

A number of the gay professionals in our study have come out in the local or national media. For some, this kind of coming out was unplanned. Those who participate in gay public events are aware of the risk of being photographed or videotaped, but few expect to end up being featured in the news. Yet those who make an attractive media target should be aware that this is always a possibility, as one HBS alumna learned when she was inadvertently outed.

Others came out publicly but assumed their names would not be noticed very widely. Two of those we interviewed appeared as domestic partners in a book celebrating Gay Pride. Coming out in this book was a more difficult decision for them, but ultimately, David Schutte and Rob Levy agreed to be named here as well. Similarly, Andrew Tobias, a well-known Harvard Business School graduate, came out in a short speech to his industry peers at an event well attended by both gay and mainstream press. But to date coverage of his coming out was mentioned only in the gay press, and since he plans to write about his own experiences, we did not interview him at length.

While sometimes coming out in the mainstream media can mean being out at work, at other times, people at work never make the connection. Thus, the primary consideration about coming out publicly is the *willingness* to be out at work at any time. But in actuality, this does not mean that one is out at work at all times or even out at all to any heterosexuals.

For example, Connie signed a petition originated by classmate Jeff Baron that came out as a full-page ad in the *New York Times* to support statewide legislation protection for nondiscrimination based on sexual orientation in employment. She also encouraged several of her gay subordinates to put their names in the paper, which they did. She told us she was nervous at work the next day, but no heterosexual mentioned seeing the ad. She said, "For me, this was the next big step out of the closet. I was ready for whatever came, and I still am. Am I possibly cutting off some career opportunities somewhere by being as out as I'm getting to be? Maybe. But at this point, I don't want to work anywhere being gay is going to be an issue. I wouldn't say I'm out at work, although I think some straight people know. But my company is really strong on its nondiscrimination policy, and the fact there is that safety net there makes me feel safer doing what I did."

In addition to these fairly low-key media appearances, a number of gay professionals in our study consciously decided to come out in local and national mainstream-media interviews. A few attracted attention for newsworthy events in their private lives; most came out in the context of business or political articles.

Surprisingly, some of those who have come out in this very public fashion say they still sometimes encounter people at work who assume they are heterosexual. These situations occasionally catch the gay person off guard. Coming out is indeed a process, not an accomplishment!

Strategic Planning

The most common way gay professionals come out at work is to first scout the territory and then artfully prepare the way. Whether they intended to come out to a few people or to many, they helped lay the foundation for a positive reception with four interlocking components:

- Developing strong credentials relating to their job performance
- Identifying allies
- Testing the waters
- The coming-out conversation

Those who used this strategy least consciously generally did not continue to come out over the course of their career. Rather, they came out to a few individuals and had no plans to come out more broadly. In contrast, those who used this strategy most consciously were more likely to go through the steps deliberately within a few years until it covered everyone they worked with on a day-to-day basis.

In general, gay professionals who used this strategy reported satisfaction with it. But a few who had tried it as their primary methodology concluded it is not suitable for their personality. Those who use it most successfully report they are able to tolerate ambiguity for a period of time that seems too long to others. Many of those who were most comfortable with this strategy are single. While some in coupled relationships also used this strategy successfully, more reported feeling the strategy took too much time to implement.

Developing Job Credentials A necessary step in using this strategy is to develop a strong reputation for work quality and performance. As many put it, "If you are different, you have to be very good." Sometimes the possession of even a single critical skill was enough to establish that reputation. Steven, who is in his late thirties, recalled that he was the lone computer expert at a major bank in the early 80s. "When I first went there, there was one computer and it was in a closet." He laughed. "People were swapping green spreadsheets among each other to correct their mistakes. I had been using a PC for two years by then." Steven's name became known throughout the company, "just by virtue of the fact that I could run the computer." When a new department head was sent over from a different division, this man had already heard about Steven and realized how valuable a resource Steven would be in making the department a success. Steven said his new boss's first move was to assure him that he would not be swept out with the old administration. "He took me aside and said, 'Don't worry, I want you to stay, and I'm going to make it good for you, because I need you.' And he became my mentor. He's a wonderful man. Married with children, he took me under his wing; he promoted me and gave me lots of responsibility. I love him dearly." After a while, Steven felt comfortable coming out to his boss. "I began to trust him, businesswise as well as personally, so I came out to him."

Gordon found himself in a similar position after he won a prestigious award and found himself in high demand by his firm's clients. His first assignment was high profile: developing a campaign for a major entertainment personality. Gordon did so well that within seven months he was promoted and put in charge of another important account. Then Gordon was given responsibility for the company's first international ad. It was shot in Europe, and his work earned a Clio, the highest award in advertising. It was while he worked on this account that Gordon finally decided to come out to his boss. According to Gordon, his boss "was totally cool about it." Today they are still in touch, and just recently Gordon went to the man's five-year-old daughter's birthday party. Eventually Gordon felt confident enough of his position to come out to selected heterosexual clients as well. He became close friends with many. Gordon and his boss would even triple-date with a client and his wife.

Those who are using this strategy consciously have usually had a specific career goal to reach or time frame after which they began to come out at work. They felt their colleagues would understand their short-term lack of openness so long as they did not play the game of let's pretend or let's avoid for too long. Yet others we interviewed seemed to be using the need for professional credibility as an excuse for staying closeted. Their time, title, or dollar targets kept moving, seemingly indefinitely.

Thus those who truly intend to come out at work using this method usually set realistic and easily achievable professional goals that they meet enroute to taking steps toward making both gay and heterosexual allies.

Identifying Allies There are politics to coming out—just as to most other aspects of office life. Those who have come out successfully told us they attempt to identify allies before coming out to them or others. This can be difficult, because not everyone who will turn out to be an ally has ever said anything about gay people. In particular, other gay people at work may avoid voicing an opinion on the local Gay Pride parade or the question of gays in the military. Some may be so afraid for their own closet, they will not make effective allies. Thus, identifying those who can be allies, whether gay or heterosexual, can be a challenge.

Interestingly, we found the process of identifying allies, whether they were gay or heterosexual, was much the same. First the gay professional looked for clues that an individual would be a safe person to tell. Those who intended to come out selectively often agonized over the meaning of the slenderest hints that a heterosexual would be open minded or that another person was gay.

Others sent signals that were more overt. For example, using neutral language such as "Do you have a partner?" rather than "Are you married?" can signal that the individual is aware not everyone is heterosexual. Gay professionals also had their ears peeled for comments on subjects like gays in the military or movies and plays with a gay theme. Discussions of a gay family member or friend can also reveal that a colleague is open minded on the subject. If someone at work actively opposes a homophobic joke, this also sends a strong signal that they will not have a problem with a coworker coming out to them.

Some of those we interviewed said they felt uncomfortable approaching someone else at work who they suspect is gay. But seeking gay allies early can be a double win. One benefit is that a gay professional can sometimes obtain specific information about which heterosexuals at the company are gay friendly or hidden homophobes. Thus they can tailor their coming-out plan to a more complete set of facts. This does not always mean avoiding those who might not be supportive, but it may mean coming out to them later and with a better-developed conversational plan. In addition, gay professionals may learn about a previously hidden network of gay professionals at their company. These individuals can be an important source of support in both the coming-out process and in one's career in general.

Gay professionals who intend to come out broadly told us that having allies was an important source of psychological support before implementing their plan. Bob explained that after he had accepted a new job, he worked hard to develop a strong nucleus of people who cared about him before coming out to his boss. This way, he felt, "If my boss finds out I'm gay, people will say, 'So what?! He's good at his job.' "

TESTING THE WATERS WITH CLUES AND HINTS Many came out after leaving clues and dropping hints that they are gay. Sometimes this included making comments that are supportive of gay issues or gay people. But most seek a more personal approach. Many discuss their living arrangements, social life, or leisure preferences in such a way as to leave somewhat subtle clues. Others use strong nonverbal hints, such as leaving photos of their lover on a desk. In our first round of interviews, Craig Ziskin described using verbal clues before coming out to some of his colleagues at work. "They all know that I live with Roger, that I bought the house with Roger. And then in some cases it got a little more explicit. Right now there are four people that I'm specifically out to. I've had them over to my home and I would go to theirs, and Roger would join us. There's another group who know Roger and I own a house together, but I don't know what else they know."

Bernie told us his lesbian boss used a strong nonverbal hint that she was gay before she came out to him. "I visited my boss in her home, which she shares with another woman, and saw there was only one bedroom and only one bed in it; I knew that this was her way of trying to come out to me. As a result, I stopped talking to her about my 'roommate' and started using Reid's name. Now we get along even better than ever, and the atmosphere in the department is much more relaxed."

While both gay and heterosexual colleagues may be similarly adept at interpreting strong clues, heterosexuals are often less capable of interpreting more subtle hints. Because the hints gay people drop at work are exactly that—hints that require noticing and deciphering—heterosexual colleagues sometimes fail to read them. Some gay colleagues also don't seem to get the message. It can be frustrating for gay professionals when this happens. They can never be sure if the person is deliberately ignoring their signals or simply doesn't understand them. In particular, we found, gay men can miss the meaning of hints lesbian colleagues sometimes try to use.

There are many reasons why heterosexuals may fail to respond to the hints gay people drop. Some are unsure how to respond without giving offense, and as a result they say nothing. Others know next to nothing about gay people and are simply oblivious of the fact that someone gay might be working beside them.

In the course of our interviews we realized that many of those who told us they were out without saying it were not necessarily as out as they thought. While it was clear to us the gay person had left clues and dropped hints, it was not always obvious that they had in fact come out. Many had convinced themselves that leaving clues and dropping hints about being gay is the same as coming out. Often what they meant was that they wanted savvy heterosexuals to figure out that they were gay and stop asking them questions that presumed that they were heterosexual; they didn't really want to talk openly about being gay.

Some insisted they were out at work because they brought a partner to company functions just as straight people would. But we found that most introduced their partner as "my friend" or with some other circumlocution. Even the word "partner" is not always clearly understood by heterosexuals. For example, Toni brought Lois, her partner of many years, to a social function at the Harvard Business School and thought she was coming out by using the word "partner" to introduce Lois to everyone. One man in particular seemed confused by the term or by how open Toni and Lois were about being gay. "So you two are business partners? Law partners? Partners in crime?" he asked. "You mean to tell me that you relocated from across the country and gave up your job to be here with her? You must be a *really* good friend." Thus, for everyone who said he or she was out to someone, we asked for specific ways the heterosexual person acknowledged that the message was understood.

Those who acknowledged that clues and hints weren't really coming out usually admitted they were uncomfortable with being out to heterosexuals or were afraid of the repercussions. Ironically, some of the same people who insist, "People at work know, so why come out?" also admit their heart was in their throat when someone at work asked them to confirm that they are gay. "Despite promising myself I would never lie, I found myself thinking desperately for ways to avoid saying yes," Wayne said. "But I finally did."

Many who have not come out yet despite years of leaving clues and dropping hints said that they want to find a setting that is comfortable for them. "I have to find the right time and place." But most of those who have come out say that there is not one perfect moment. While some carefully selected the setting for a coming-out conversation, those who are most out said they looked for any remotely acceptable time to *just do it.*

The Coming-Out Conversation There are as many different ways of coming out as there are gay people. No two people we talked to were alike, and no two conversations we heard were the same. As with other important workplace communications, their way of informing their colleagues they were gay were dictated by their personalities.

In many cases, we found, when a heterosexual person wonders if a colleague is gay, they say or do something to try to verify their hunch. Mel Glapion told us that when he worked in investment banking, he moved from lying about being gay to coming out to someone he worked for. "Early in my first year there I had made up a name of a woman I was supposedly seeing. I was actually dating this guy who had a female cousin who also lived in New York, and I used her name as my girlfriend. It was easier to remember that way." Mel laughed. "Then I started telling people: 'Oh, it's over with the woman.' And slowly, people would start getting that I might be gay. One of them even asked me about it directly. One time a director and I were in a car together, and she was very nervous. At the strangest moment in the conversation she said to me, 'Maybe I am totally wrong, and if this causes a strain in our relationship we will have to work it out, but I am going to ask you a question.'" Mel told us, "Because she is usually very forthright, I always thought that she would have just come out and said it. But when she started getting flustered, I knew for sure what the question was. And I was sitting there thinking, How are you going to answer the question? And she finished, and I said, 'Yeah, I'm gay.' And then she went into this whole story about her gay family member. Her family was from the islands, and she told me about how they were dealing with it. Basically, she said, 'We don't really talk about it,' which seemed kind of hard on her. The car ride was brief, so we discussed me being gay just a little. But from then on I felt more comfortable about being open," Mel told us.

A number told us they went to lunch or on a business trip with a colleague and engaged in a tightly orchestrated series of hints until the colleague asked, "Are you trying to tell me you are gay?" Others said they prefaced their coming-out announcement by saying, "I'm sure you probably know I'm gay, but I just wanted to make sure that was out on the table." Some said that after a long period of hinting, they finally dropped the bomb in the midst of casual conversation on other matters.

COMING OUT SELECTIVELY VERSUS BROADLY

Many we spoke with were out selectively—to one boss but not another, to most colleagues but not all, to some staff but not others. The reasons for coming out to one person at work versus another are several. For some, coming out is driven by a deep internal need to talk openly with a friend about this important part of their life. Thus, one important consideration is how personally close the relationship is. For others, the motivation to come out to anyone is more heavily driven by an analysis of the possible rewards and risks. In those cases, the decision to come out is based on an assessment of the individual's likely response.

Often, we found, those who came out selectively continued this pattern for many years. Coming out at work was often the culmination of a largely unplanned pattern of coming out to an increasingly wider circle. In other cases, we learned, gay professionals came out only to another gay person or to a close heterosexual friend, boss, or subordinate. Sometimes those who have told only a few people do not ever discuss the issue again. Thus they reach a dead end in the coming-out process.

Many of those we interviewed have come out selectively to a few trusted heterosexual confidants. In some cases, this disclosure is coupled with a request not to spread the news. Surprisingly often, the heterosexual colleague is the instigator of such a suggestion. "I'm fine with it, but I don't think others here would be, so don't tell them," several told us their heterosexual peers advised. But those who disregarded this advice reported no negative outcomes. It seems that heterosexuals who have less experience with the issues involved in coming out at work may be flattering themselves too much and assessing their peers too harshly! In addition, they may not be as attuned to the psychic costs of remaining closeted.

In other cases, gay professionals are happy to have others do the work of coming out for them. We found this strategy works best when the gay person goes on to discuss the matter openly with those who have heard secondhand. Otherwise those who have not been told directly can feel awkward about their indirect knowledge. Avi said coming out to some heterosexual peers was also a good way to start coming out to others. "I would talk openly about going to Gay Pride or something like that with the people I'm out to, and then the others would overhear it. Then they could ask me something about the entertainment or the weather or whatever, and we could move seamlessly into them knowing that I'm gay."

A number of those we interviewed were out to no heterosexuals at work besides their boss. Coming out to a boss or mentor can be an important component of workplace satisfaction and success. Even some of those who came out to a boss under the most difficult personal circumstances reported positive experiences.

One surprising finding was that very few are out to subordinates—with the exception of the support staff, like secretaries or copy-machine operators. (Many are out to their support staff even if they are not out to any other professionals at work.) One reason for not being out to subordinates is an unwillingness to compromise the professional distance between boss and subordinate. Some of those we interviewed felt that being gay, whether an open secret or a closely held one, was enough of an issue that it would require an "I have something to tell you" conversation, which felt too personal for them to have with a subordinate far below them in rank.

In contrast, many said their support staff were the gatekeepers to their lives and needed to be among the first to know. "In fact," Spencer said, "if my secretary can't figure out that I'm gay within the first few weeks, I should probably fire her, because she isn't doing her job." Several cited day-to-day matters and the need to have phone calls from loved ones given top priority among the reasons to come out to immediate subordinates.

Some also mentioned the need to entertain their team at home as both a need and a way of coming out to subordinates. Victor told us, "I have been on a fast track at my company, and I have moved up very quickly. For various reasons—education, background, creativity, the whole thing. And I had pulled a lot of people along with me. So at a certain point I felt that these are people that I like, these are people that I share a lot in common with, and we had developed a real sense of partnership together, and I want to invite them to my home.

"So at various times during different points of my career, I invited them to my home. So once that happened, you kind of have to say, 'Hey, here's the deal. And are you comfortable with it or not?' And in each case I already knew they were comfortable with it, and they reciprocated by inviting me and my partner to their homes. I used to have them and their spouses to parties. One of them is gay and finally admitting it to me. And I thought: How do we go four years, five years without admitting it to each other? But it happens! It happened to me before, in fact."

For others, coming out to subordinates is part of a process of coming out to others at the company. Brian Offutt told us about a previous position. "One of the support staff at my company was the blood-drive coordinator, and she wanted me to give blood, and I couldn't, because they don't let gay men give blood. I just said I wasn't going to give blood, and my secretary never understood why. So after I came out to her, I said to my secretary, 'Now do you understand why I couldn't give blood?' And she says, 'Yeah, oh my God, I'm so sorry I was so pushy.' "

Brian explained how he came out to her. "My secretary and I had become very close. She is Black like me, had a kid when she was sixteen and raised him very successfully. I liked everything about her, although she is a born-again Christian, so because of that I thought, I'm not going to say anything. One day I took her out to lunch. We talked about her for a long time, and then at the end she said, 'Well, you know, we talked about me a lot. Can we talk about you?' But I was afraid to tell her.

"Then my colleague had met a boyfriend, and I had met a guy at the same time, and we were both very excited about it. My secretary overheard us talking . . . She was always asking us, 'What are you guys talking about?' I said, 'Oh, we're just talking about her new boyfriend.' She said, 'I know, but I thought I heard you say you met someone too.' I said, 'Oh, no, no, no. Just teasing.' She said, 'I really want you to tell me about it—who is this person you've met? You've been so happy and so excited lately.' I'm like, 'Oh, you know, just someone I met.'

"She persisted: 'Well, what kind of people do you like?' And I said, 'Well, I like funny, beautiful, intelligent people.' And she said, 'OK, fine, you're not going to tell me anything. Well, fine.' So I said, 'What are you asking?' And she said, 'You know what I'm asking!' So finally I said, 'OK,' and I told her." Brian explained, "Once my boyfriend had come to visit in the office, and after he'd left my secretary had said, 'God, he is really cute, he's really, really beautiful.' So I came out by saying, 'Remember that guy who you thought was really hot?' She goes, 'Yeah.' I said, 'That's my ex-boyfriend.' She said, 'I thought so.' And she added, 'I'm so glad you told me.'

"I said, 'Well, you know, you're a born-again Christian, I didn't want to tell you.' And she said, 'Yes, but my Christianity is the kind that says love people, let them be who they are.' And then she revealed to me . . . she'd always told me about this friend of hers who was sick, her best friend growing up. And it turned out he was a gay man who had AIDS. She then revealed that a family member to whom she was close was gay. So two of the most important people in her life were gay men. In fact, she had been out dancing the previous weekend at the Monster with a gay man who is a friend of hers. And she had said to this friend, 'I hope we don't run into Brian here because he might get me fired.'

"I told her I would never do that. But she didn't know, because she thought I was trying to hide something. And so she didn't want to ever run into me socially, until we had this discussion. And I said, 'Well, first of all, you know I would never do anything like that. Second of all, you know, there's no closet to protect!' So it was really good that I came out. Because we bonded and have become even closer since then. And of course, she said she always knew, because only guys ever called me." Brian concluded, "With her being born-again and my best friend Mike being Catholic, I've had people in my life who you would think would not be supportive, and yet they have been. Good people get beyond the dogma of religious teachings and stick to the heart."

RESULTS OF COMING OUT AT WORK

Overwhelmingly, those we interviewed reported positive reactions when they came out to heterosexuals at work. We found that almost no one who came out intentionally suffered negative consequences, even in fairly conservative industries. Rather, we heard many inspiring accounts of heterosexuals who responded with openness, support, help, advice, and time. Most said the reactions they faced were positive from the beginning. Robert Goldfarb's experience is quite common. "In terms of telling people I was gay, whether with family, friends, or at work, I can't remember ever having a negative experience." Those who encountered a strongly or unexpectedly positive response to coming out at work often felt encouraged to come out even further. Yet we learned that giving up in the face of a negative reaction can be a mistake. As Jonathan Rottenberg pointed out, "Most people are basically willing to learn if you personalize the issues by talking about your own experiences."

Whether they were always out or just starting to come out many years after working with the same people, those we interviewed had few regrets. Jeff Baron posited, "I'm the most political person a lot of my friends know, and a lot of people assume that I've been this way my whole life. I haven't been. But I'm someone who, when I hear a good idea, I just embrace it and don't look back. In terms of coming out, I think that's true for almost everyone. I don't know anyone who wishes they were a little more in the closet after they've come out. It's such a relief to be out."

Some but not all of those who have had a negative experience being out at work are determined to conceal their sexual orientation more strongly in the future. In general, those who had a negative experience were outed or inadvertently discovered to be gay and tried to avoid discussing the subject.

Several lesbians admitted they had handled being open badly and didn't want to risk trying again. Rowena admits candidly, "I was immature.

I didn't know what was appropriate to talk about and what wasn't. I didn't set good boundaries." Several told us it was a mistake to have talked so explicitly about sex or to give so many personal details about their relationship. Several also told us they resented becoming their coworkers' confidants about secrets such as eating disorders, alcoholism, or surviving child abuse. It seemed to us that some of these errors could easily be corrected in the future. But most of those who had bad experiences told us they were reluctant to try, attributing their reticence to sexism at work. "I don't want to risk being doubly different anymore," Diana said. "It's not that big a deal to be an unmarried woman at my age, so I don't really stand out for that. Why should I make problems for myself when I can just as easily blend in?"

Coming out can be one of the greatest challenges a gay person faces in the workplace. As we have seen, having role models can provide tremendous inspiration, information, and motivation in a gay person's process of coming out to themself and at work. Increasingly, as role models become more visible and prominent, gay people will benefit from the leadership and experiences of others. However, having a role model does not in itself provide gay people the skills and judgment to come out successfully in the workplace.

Planning and implementing a strategy which is tailored specifically to the individual and their work setting is essential, whether one desires to be completely or selectively out. As many of the people we interviewed learned, coming out takes practice. Not surprising, those who took proactive steps in coming out were most able to successfully manage being gay at work. Those who let others set the tone or spread information to coworkers were less comfortable and met more harassment, discrimination, and speculation behind their backs and were seen as weak.

Further, many were more out than they realized yet immobilized by fear. Those who came out saw in hindsight that they could have built closer relationships with coworkers earlier. In sum: those who were most open reported the greatest overall satisfaction with their decision about managing their gay identity at work.

COMING-OUT STORIES

Most of this book presents short excerpts from the experiences of gay professionals. In this section we have elected to present somewhat longer portraits in order to convey the message that people who are out at work can be found in a variety of fields, come from a variety of backgrounds, and take various routes to coming out to themselves. They had various reasons for coming out at work and used various strategies for doing so. Some are out selectively, while others are out more broadly. What they have in common is courage and a belief in themselves.

We are able to present in the most detail the experiences of those who are willing to be named, and in most cases, these are white men. In other cases the level of detail reflects the amount of time we had to interview a particular individual. We also faced certain constraints in our selection of stories for this section due to requests for anonymity in identifying details. Not all of these individuals are the most out of their peers. We have selected them to provide a balanced picture of the reasons why and ways in which gay professionals today are coming out at work.

Mitchell Adams's Story

Mitchell Adams, a white man in his fifties, has been openly gay to his boss, Governor Weld of Massachusetts, since the early 1980s. The two were close friends at Harvard College and even roommates for a time in the early 1970s. In the early 90s Mitchell became the leader of Weld's gubernatorial campaign and was rewarded with a position heading the state's Department of Revenue. With his partner, who also holds a senior position in the Weld administration, Mitchell came out in the Boston press in 1992.

Like many other openly gay business professionals we interviewed, Mitchell spoke of the various thresholds of coming out. Mitchell said that he began the process of coming out to himself at age nineteen but did not complete it until he graduated from business school in 1969. Next was the threshold of coming out to other gay people, finding a partner, and living together. He met his partner, Kevin Smith, over fifteen years ago and credits the relationship with nudging him into more and more openness.

The last two thresholds involved coming out to heterosexual friends, including Bill Weld, and coming out selectively at work. Mitchell remembers using the roll-out plan to come out to his old friend. "There was not a moment at which I revealed this. He learned it just because I was open about it to other mutual friends, and people talk. He was part of the circle of people in Boston who have known me for years. So just by osmosis he came to know that I was gay. And then at some point, after it was becoming known among my friends that I was gay, I was having lunch with Bill.

And I knew by that time he would have known, and we just launched into open discussions about the matter. It was not necessary ever to say, 'Hey, Bill, by the way, I am gay.' "

The final threshold for Mitchell was willingness to come out through the media. He said that one reason he wanted to do it is that he believes he has a responsibility to be a role model for young people. "If all of the young people who are gay were aware of the highly successful professionals who are also gay, they would feel much better about themselves, and a lot more of them would come out earlier, both to themselves and to others."

For Mitchell himself, finding a role model who was gay was an important breakthrough in his own coming-out process. After seven years of group therapy in the 1960s to try to change his sexual orientation, Mitchell endured several months of aversion therapy in the form of electrical shocks. He recalls painfully, "It didn't work. I think I broke the machine. By the grace of God I was able to cope and manage, but it was enormously stressful, really enormously. That pain has passed now. Interestingly, a lot of it came back to me a year and a half ago. I went through it again for a blessedly short period of time, three months or so. But one of the things that happened to me in that time was a visitation of all the pain that I felt as an adolescent gay person and as a young adult. It all came back. That was awful, just awful. I felt as if I couldn't bear to be in my own skin.

"The way I first got past hating myself for being gay in the 1970s was that there was a man whom I had known for more than a year, looked up to, admired, respected, and thought was the neatest person around. I was also very attracted to him. I was sure he was straight, but he was absolutely the most attractive person I knew. Well, what happened was that one day I saw him in a gay bar. So it turns out that he is not straight. We had a short and fiery relationship. That's when I quit therapy rather abruptly. All of a sudden it was OK for me to be gay.

"Why was it OK? Because of the role model. Here was this person I had on a pedestal. He was bright, capable, articulate, effective, and widely respected. When I found out that he was gay too, I realized that being gay is not the end of the world. Even though he wasn't very much more accepting of himself than I was, just the fact that he was gay was enough for me to change the way I felt. I had met other gay people by then, but none of them were business professionals like myself. They weren't role models to me. All of a sudden a role model comes along who is gay, and bang, that did it."

Mitchell also feels a debt of gratitude for those who came out publicly in the 1991 *Fortune* magazine article. "That really registered with me. It was a cover story, and I thought it was a very positive article. That article showed me that press coverage of this subject can be handled tastefully and appropriately. It started me thinking about coming out openly gay in the press myself."

Mitchell volunteered that he had heard that Jack Sansolo, who was on the cover of *Fortune* for that issue, suffered some short-term career problems after coming out. However, Mitchell felt that his position in the Weld administration was secure. During the gubernatorial campaign, Weld called a meeting with the leaders of various local gay organizations. He asked Mitchell and several other selectively open gay members of his campaign staff to attend. Mitchell recalls that the meeting went very well. One participant commented that the previous governor had a pro–gay rights position but that many had the distinct impression that personally it made his skin crawl to be in the presence of a gay person. She said, "In contrast, Mr. Weld, it is clear that you are totally comfortable." Weld agreed and pointed to various people who are close to him, including Mitchell, who are gay.

Mitchell acknowledged, "Of course I was happy to participate in the meeting. But that was another little minithreshold of coming out publicly for me. I had previously shown up at the meetings of various gay groups that the governor was talking to. But there was never any kind of public announcement about me being gay. It was probably clear to everyone, but it was unsaid."

Mitchell said that he had a project in mind since he saw the *Fortune* article. "I wanted to be part of a massive coming out of professional people. The idea was that twenty-five or fifty or a hundred individuals like me would come out together. People who are reasonably well known, because they are established in their field. Gay businesspeople, doctors, lawyers, and so on who may be out among their heterosexual peers but are not on the record to the general public.

"My idea was that everyone would come out in one fell swoop at a press conference. The governor thought it was a terrific idea, by the way. He even gave me the names of some prominent gay people to talk to. So I began to develop this plan by calling up friends who were in the same boat I was—selectively out at work and in the gay community, but not out on the record. I guess I talked with ten or fifteen people, trying to develop interest in this. Basically what I found was that it was a doable thing, but I would have to twist people's arms to do it. In other words, people would not simply flock to the podium; they would have to be dragged. But they *could* be dragged. I just felt that I did not have the time to make this happen. It would have been a full-time job for three to six months to get twenty-five high-level people to do this.

"And it wasn't the kind of thing I could find someone else to do. The only kind of person who could pull this off would be someone who the others felt had something similar to lose by taking this risk."

While Mitchell's plan to come out as part of a group was on hold, he found that events moved faster than he had anticipated. His plan was preempted. Instead, he decided to come out publicly as part of an offensive strategy against a whispering campaign in the local paper.

By the 1990s, both Mitchell and Kevin held senior positions in the Weld administrations, and their relationship attracted the attention of an anti-Weld columnist for the *Boston Herald,* who penned several columns with insinuating references to them as a couple. Mitchell recalled, "He did not cross the line of saying Kevin Smith and Mitchell Adams are gay, but he went about as far as he could." From public records, the reporter discovered that the two owned a house in Dedham together, as well as a vacation home in Maine. Mitchell recalls, "He did a whole story around that. Oh, it was awful. He talked about how romantic it was that we have set up housekeeping together. There was absolutely no news value to the piece. It was just a bald-faced attempt at outing."

Then, about a year later, the same columnist struck again according to Mitchell. "The focus of this piece was maligning Barney Frank's partner, Herb Moses, who lives with Barney in Washington. At the end of it, he threw in a gratuitous slam at us. He said, 'Herb, listen. You really ought to come up to Boston. We'll get you a job at the Department of Revenue; you'll love it there.' That kind of thing."

Finally, Mitchell said, he and Kevin had enough of rumors and innuendos. "Everyone we worked with knew we were a couple. We were out 99 percent. Why not come out all the way? So we decided to call a sympathetic reporter we knew at the *Boston Globe* and give him a scoop—the real scoop."

Mitchell smiled victoriously. "The *Herald* columnist has been completely silent since the *Globe* article. He has nothing more to write about!"

Mitchell has found that being completely open at work has benefits, both expected and unanticipated. "In the first month after we came out in the *Globe,* a number of other gay people came up, revealed themselves, and said, 'I just want you to know how good it makes me feel to know that you have done what you have done. I just want you to know that you have made my life easier.' It was really quite wonderful and gratifying to hear how good and empowered they felt because we had done this. They felt legitimized. One of them was a person way, way down in the organization at the Department of Revenue. There are a number of people like that who had obviously been suffering and uncomfortable. It made them feel really good to know that the commissioner was gay. It was a breath of fresh air to them. They really felt better about their working environment.

"The Department of Revenue is a very hierarchal, conventional organization of straitlaced accountants, lawyers, and tax professionals. It is not the Boston Ballet. You would expect that it would be an environment that would be less conducive than many others for the head person to make such a revelation. But it has been a zero issue. I don't think it's been a problem at all.

"In my perception, there has been no compromise whatsoever in my ability to lead, to make change, to get cooperation and support. What's funny is that, as I am doing my job at the Department of Revenue, working with all of the people that work for me, I can honestly say that I have finally been able to forget that I am a gay person. It's not on my mind as a secret I'm trying to hide, and I am getting no signals whatever that it is on anyone else's mind. It is gone as an issue.

"On the other hand, I now get all of the normal social questions like, 'How's Kevin?' or, 'How was your weekend in Maine?'—which is very nice. I didn't know what I was missing before. Now I feel completely normal.

"I've also been able to do some of the socializing that is important politically. Now that we're officially out, we've been able to host a number of parties at our house for senior members of the governor's staff. Everyone comes—the governor, the lieutenant governor, and the cabinet. As a matter of fact we recently held a congratulations reception in honor of Priscilla Douglas, who is the first Black woman ever to be appointed to a cabinet position in the Commonwealth. It was a great success. No one thinks twice about coming into our house and joining us for a party. We don't worry about whether or not to do it anymore either. We just do it.

"The other thing that has been wonderful about coming out so openly is that we've had a wonderful reception at our church, which is almost all upper-middle-class and rich old-line Yankees. Although I have been active in the church for many years, I never came out to the parish as such before coming out in the press. Right after the new rector arrived, five years ago, I had a long sit-down with him and I just told him I am gay. He had no problem with it. We just took it from there. Some people knew, and some people did not. It took the *Globe* article to make it all clear to everyone.

"I have been absolutely delighted that the response has been so positive in that environment, because I would not have thought so. I would have thought that they would be pretty frosted. They have not been. There's been no problem. There may be some people in the parish who are not comfortable, but they are not making any noise that I am hearing. There has been no problem whatever.

"Moreover, I have been suggested as one of a small number of individuals to be considered to be one of the wardens of the church. The way Episcopal churches work, there are two wardens, elected by the parish, who have the executive control over everything that the rector doesn't.

They are very powerful. So that's an important sign that the parish is OK with it.

"The other thing that's been nice is that we've been able to make some connections with the other people in the congregation who are not openly gay. When the article came out, they didn't approach us, but the parents of one of them did! His parents are absolute mainstays in the whole WASP hegemony out there, very rich, very established, and active in the church for ten generations. They came up to us and said, " 'Look, I just want you to know that our son and his friend live down the street and have been together for a long, long time, and we must get you all together.' " It was wonderful, really nice, absolutely. Really super."

Coming out in the press also gave Mitchell and Kevin the opportunity to come out to Kevin's mother, who has lived with them for many years. "She makes our bed every morning but claims she never knew until one of Kevin's siblings showed her the article in the paper!" The couple continues to host gatherings of Kevin's large Catholic family.

The Story of Two Lesbians

Two of the lesbian MBAs in our study who are among the most out at work first came out in the media. Linda, a white woman in her early thirties, served in the military before attending business school and has been active in both political and legal attempts to reverse the military's policy against openly gay service members. As a result, she was constantly in the media spotlight during and immediately after business school. She told us about a full schedule of testifying in her own case, giving interviews to both the gay and the mainstream media, and speaking to virtually any group that invited her. She said she especially tried to make time for university engagements near military posts, since members of the military often attended.

While she did not intend to come out right away to everyone at work, having her name and picture featured in a major newsmagazine during the gays-in-the-military debate helped change her mind. It turned out to be a pretty easy way to come out to a large number of people at work, she told us. She told us that while appearing in the media helped her come out to colleagues, clients do not always associate her picture in the paper with a live person in front of them. Just starting her job, she does not always come out to clients, although her goal is to do so eventually.

Pam, who is in her late thirties, came out to her colleagues in the insurance industry after being featured in an early 1980s television program on gay families. "Our son is Black and deaf, my partner is Jewish and deaf, and I'm Asian American. So we are quite a rainbow family as well as being part of the early lesbian baby boom. The show was conceived of as a local broadcast, but turned out to be shown nationally. That was actually a very convenient way to come out to a lot of the upper management. It was also a good experience because it made me stand out in their minds more. Without exception, the reaction was incredibly positive."

Desmond's Story

Desmond, a white man in his early thirties, is in the process of coming out selectively at work. He said, "I was just like a madman all through college as far as grades but, more importantly, extracurricular activities; I just poured myself into some major campus positions. I left that campus with this growing sense of terror that all I was doing was just building myself up for a bigger and bigger fall, which is ultimately what actually happened. I had a history of sneaking out to bars that dates back to that time . . . always these tortured, greatly regretted, almost psychotic trips that I would look back on the next day with self-torture.

"I finally began to do some reading in psychology and in other fields, trying to understand a full range of the big issues one faces in life. I thought about everything from religious belief to who am I and why am I. The good things, but also the things that are harder to accept and understand about myself. And the central one was, I was finally even beginning to articulate to myself that I might be gay. While studying overseas, I was finally able to get away from all the glaring eyes of people and my excessively Peyton Place kind of hometown.

"I began to deal with it, but not in a healthy way. I found a psychotherapist who promised me that he could change me in an American-based school of counseling theory that was long since discredited in the U.S. Anyway, I came back to the U.S. hoping to God that I had achieved what I set out to do, and in a way believing it. But when I got back home, within four weeks I began to feel like nothing was different. In a way it felt like I was decompressing from a brainwashing.

"I spent three years trying to screw myself into being straight. I began to date women more aggressively than I ever had. Eventually I realized it was just not there. So I was really looking forward to going to a large city away from all the glaring eyes of my hometown, where people know everyone, and go with what feels right. But when I got into Harvard I ended up being in a bit of a housing crunch, so when an opportunity presented itself to room with an undergraduate friend, I thought I'd better grab it. I knew he was a pretty progressive guy, so I thought, well maybe he can deal with it. But what happened was, he had this one big blind spot in his progressive worldview. He was pretty homophobic."

Desmond continued, "I truly withdrew in the Harvard environment. I think it's an insulting environment in many ways. It's hard to feel secure when you're judged by lots of judgmental people. I just did not want to have to deal with other people's ideas and opinions about anything. I just wanted to try and deal with my own. So the two years at Harvard for me were a time when I was just beginning to incorporate being gay into my life. I went by myself to a gay bar every couple of months and decided that I absolutely hated it. I hated the whole gay world, the whole gay "lifestyle," which is an expression that I cannot stand now. I ran into classmates from HBS a few times, and that was always very traumatic, because I just didn't know how to deal with that.

"Finally, though, in the spring of First Year I got up the nerve to go to a GLSA meeting. That was the biggest thing that I had ever done at that point in time. Also, I realized I needed to live alone Second Year. That's when I began to finally live the life of being gay. I had my first boyfriend from January to late March of my Second Year. But I still wasn't really comfortable with being gay. I remember going home in April of that year and telling my parents I just still could not see myself being happy living a gay life, and they encouraged that.

"The way I finally managed to come out to myself is I sought gay people out, and I was lucky to find a lot of smart, insightful people who were willing to tolerate my naivete. They understood that we all walk in different shoes and that you just can't judge where people are in their process. I found some people who were pretty patient with me. You know you can't be told, you have to experience. They can't tell you to get over it. You just have to experience the process of getting over it." Today Desmond is happily out to friends and family, as well as to some people at work.

Referring to his final year at HBS, Desmond said, "I interviewed with some of the more standard HBS marketing interviewers, like Kraft and Quaker Oats and the like. The position I finally accepted is with a nonprofit. It was a choice that not a single one of my section mates could understand. But my family and people that knew me responded immediately that it was a great thing for me personally. I consciously knew I had to get in a situation where achievement wasn't going to so consume my life so I could finally deal with other, more important issues. Ultimately, getting your life together has got to be positive for your career.

"I've really struggled with that choice ever since I've made it, because of the sacrifices and compromises in terms of my long-term career goals. I think there have been some big ones. But at the same time it was a life-led decision, not a career-led decision, that I ultimately made, and I would make the same decision again. I guess knowing what I know now, I probably would have tried to position things so that I could have found an opportunity that would have put me in an environment where I was doing more skill development. But on the other hand, I'm one of the few MBAs I know who are actually happy with their job.

One of the significant benefits Desmond enjoys is that he is comfortable coming out selectively. "I've come out explicitly to three people. The rest I've just not hidden things from and I think they've finally gotten it. I have never had a bad experience coming out with someone, largely because I think I am cautious about taking that risk. But then again, I'm not always completely cautious. One guy I came out to was a colleague of mine who I just really liked a lot, and I was involved in getting him to take the job. He's a guy who I was friends with and we would play squash together. He used to call me a faggot when I got a good shot. Then I noticed he stopped doing that at a certain point in time. I also noticed that he disengaged from an office discussion about my personal life that was excessively uncomfortable for me. I just noticed that he didn't want to be in on that discussion, and that told me he knew. So when I figured he knew, I told him." Desmond laughed. "And it made us better friends."

Desmond went on to describe his career outlook. "The thing about this job is, it isn't going to lead anywhere. It's what it is. It's never going to be more, it's never going to be less. Now that I have dealt with my personal life, I want to get back to focusing on my career and find more challenge and growth from it. I still haven't gotten terribly focused. I've been looking for a while, and the gay thing still figures in it prominently, because I can't go backwards now. Last summer I had a great opportunity to work for a small company that had developed into a money machine.

"It was a spectacular opportunity to happen into. I could learn a lot about analyzing investment opportunities and possibly position myself for that entrepreneurial dive I might want to make someday. We started talking, and it was just going great. It was rounds and rounds of discussions and it got closer and closer to the point where I needed to start using stronger language about whether I would commit to them, and I just couldn't do it. I just felt the heebie-jeebies about the culture of this very small company. It was made up of men from the 1950s generation, and they kept talking about how this was a marriage, and how we didn't want to rush into anything. They kept saying it was more important for me to be sure that this is exactly right for me, because they were a small company and it wasn't like they hired any people very often, so that they had to be sure that we were right for each other. They were just sending me signals that kept making me more nervous about the idea of going in there being different in any way, let alone in the way of being gay.

"It sounded like a hot job, a great opportunity, yet it meant working up in one of these glass shell buildings in an office of only twelve people. I was already worrying about the fact that I don't play golf, and what are they going to think about me not being married? In the end, I had already decided in my mind I was not going to take the job without first saying, 'I'm gay. Does that matter to you?' As things came down to it they sensed my hesitation. They were getting down to the brass tacks, and I was getting more and more nervous, and we both just sort of at one point just disengaged and said, 'You know, let's not do this.'

"Then another situation . . . I interviewed with a company that called me through a friend of a friend. It was an executive-search firm, and they wanted to hire another associate. Again, I basically felt, this is not a bad job. But the main reason I decided to disengage with them was culture. Every person I talked with felt it important to mention to me that he voted for George Bush. I was, like, that's fine. I don't understand why . . . maybe they're telling me that this is how it is here. The last person I talked to was a guy who had just come back from having been in the Bush administration, was an ex-marine, and he really turned me off to the idea of working there. I wasn't going to go into an environment where being gay was going to be an issue. So again I disengaged from a job possibility that was there.

"I keep being in this position of passing on lots of possibilities that come and go because I screen them heavily on the front end: Is this an environment where I can be myself?"

Alistair Williamson's Story

Alistair Williamson, a white man in his mid-thirties, came out within the first months of his career in publishing. He came out to himself when he was a senior in college, and came to be open to others since his days at the Harvard Business School. He remembers, "Business school was wonderful for me because I had never lived away from home before, and I had never lived outside Canada. The business school is quite an interesting microcosm of American business. I had made up my mind when I got here that I was not going to scream 'I'm gay' from the rooftops, but I was never going to lie about it. I was still not out to my family at this point. But I made a decision not to lie to people.

"Three weeks into the school year I'm at the Hong Kong doing scorpion bowls [a potent mixed drink at a famous eatery beloved by HBS students], and this woman in my section asked if she could ask me a question. I said yes. She asked me, 'Are you gay or what?' I replied tongue-in-cheek, 'What are the other choices?' When she repeated, 'Are you gay?' I said yes. She said, 'Cool. I had a feeling you were.' From then on I began to come out selectively to friends at school."

After receiving his MBA, Alistair joined a joint doctoral program with HBS and the psychology department of Harvard University. His advisor there was not openly gay at the time, although he and Alistair traded many hints back and forth. Finally, when Alistair approached him with a thesis topic on diversity in the workplace, his advisor finally said, "Come on, let's just cut the crap. I know you know, and you know I know. Wouldn't you rather do something on being gay in the workplace?" Alistair agreed that he would and his mentor gave him some starting resources.

Eventually Alistair realized, "Being an academic isn't what I'm cut out to do. However, several years of academic training have given me a good set of skills to use in publishing, where I was meant to be."

For a number of years Alistair had been courted by a friend of his to join the Harvard Business School Press. So when he took her up on her offer, he was already out to her but not to anyone else there. Over the first few months he began to come out to some of his colleagues in an ad hoc fashion, as it felt appropriate. But he was still not out to people in other departments.

Within six months of working at the HBSP, however, he came out at a meeting attended by most of his colleagues from the entire organization. As each of the twenty people in the room went around the table introducing themselves, and talked about their backgrounds, Alistair drew a deep breath and waited for his turn. When he spoke, he casually included the title of his unfinished doctoral thesis: "Determinants of White Gay Males Coming Out in the Workplace."

Alistair noticed that the woman sitting next to him, one of the senior editors of the *Harvard Business Review,* was trying to communicate something with her body language, but he couldn't quite interpret it. Alistair recalls, "The meeting moved on, and I didn't think anything of it. The next day she called me to go out to lunch. She told me that she was thrilled to hear about my thesis topic and wanted me to write an *HBR* case for publication."

"Is This the Right Time to Come Out?" was featured in the July-August 1993 issue of the *HBR.* It presented the dilemma of a senior executive faced with a rising-star performer who comes out to him. The younger man also told his boss that he intends to bring his partner to the client dinner honoring the team for their work. In standard *HBR* style, the case poses the question: What, if anything, should the senior executive do? This question was given to a number of business experts, who presented their individual decisions about how the executive should respond. All the experts agreed that the executive should do nothing other than to inform this young star that his partner would be entirely welcome to attend the dinner.

Alistair notes, "It was the first *HBR* article on homosexuality that didn't have an AIDS component. I felt very good about the fact that I was invited to write this first article on the subject for what is the second-most-influential business publication of its kind in the world. Number one is the *Wall Street Journal*. Number two is the *Harvard Business Review*. So I was given this unique opportunity.

"The *HBR* recognized that they were doing something groundbreaking as well. We really tried to get a range of responses, but nobody would sign off on a homophobic response in front of a quarter of a million business leaders. The editors put the entire publicity machinery of the organization behind this, because they felt it was a threshold. It was an event. It was an accomplishment that they had broken this barrier. And it was important to them that the world know that they had broken down this wall.

"I've seen press coverage about the article in a lot of the important newspapers. For example, it appeared the July Fourth weekend on the front of the business section of the *Washington Post*. And I was subsequently interviewed by Madge Kaplan of National Public Radio for a *Marketplace* segment. So I have been given many platforms to talk about these issues.

"The article is a pretty big kind of national coming out for me. I mean, I didn't sign it, 'Alistair Williamson is a gay man,' but I think that's what everyone who read the article assumed."

Alistair said that coming out has only improved his relationships with colleagues at work. "As an editor at the Harvard Business School Press, I'm enmeshed in a network of relationships. We all rely upon each other to get work done. Publishing a book takes many steps, and I interact with all the different departments throughout. I'm like a brand manager at P&G. That's how I describe my job as an editor. I don't blue-pencil. Blue-penciling is one of the tasks I manage. I make sure it gets edited. I'm like the brand manager, making sure it gets the right advertising and placement and so on."

He received independent confirmation of the success of his way of coming out and being out from his friends at work. He said, "I have a lot of sources for news on what's going on in the organization. They don't quite repeat gossip, but it's close. I learned that a group of employees was getting together for lunch every couple of weeks. One of my friends told me that at one of these lunches everyone was going through and dissecting everybody in the organization, and I got unanimous points for being funny and charming. That's important to me, because I want to be liked by the people I work with. I'm very friendly. We joke around a lot. I mean, it's a fun workplace for the most part. Sure we work full-tilt, and sometimes there's a lot of stress and tension. But I feel like I've developed good relationships with everybody at work."

Recently Alistair accepted an offer to run Alyson Press, the world's oldest and largest publisher of books for gay men and lesbians.

Laura's Story

Laura, who is in her early thirties, told us she hadn't planned on coming out at work. "What happened is, my boss at the time was a coke addict, and she crashed and burned one Friday morning and gave me a call at work. Since I'm the kind of person who usually responds to a call for help, I went to where she lives and basically scraped her off the floor." Laura continued, "During this whole process of trying to help her through a major alcohol-and-coke hangover, she grabbed me by the shoulders and said, 'Are you gay? Are you gay?' Just like that, out of the blue." She told us, "It was completely inappropriate, because we weren't talking about me at all, we were talking about her coke problem. So I didn't answer right away. I asked, 'Why do you want to know? Why do you care?' And she said, 'I've been curious since the day you walked in for your interview. A simple "yes" or "no" will do.' "

Laura said, "I kind of sat back and said to myself: OK, you can tell her it's none of her business or you can just be honest. And I decided to be honest. So I said, 'Yes, I am.' " Laura added, "It was really interesting—I felt so empowered by saying it! It was like: *Yes!* So my boss jumps off the bed and gets me a book about a model named Gia who was like the Cindy Crawford of the seventies. A total babe who was a lesbian and a major drug addict and had AIDS." Laura laughed. "I guess that was her way of trying to bond with me." Laura added, "I'm sure she probably asked me if I was gay because she wanted something on me, since now I had something on her. She probably wanted to have some point of vulnerability on me. But I wasn't going to let that happen. When I got to work, I went into the office of another woman I work with really closely and said, 'I just want you to know that Shelley just asked if I was gay and I told her yes, and I want you to know too.' " Laura explained, "I figured she should hear it from me. One reason is, I was afraid she would feel hurt that it came from someone else, that I didn't feel close enough to her to tell her myself."

Laura told us this woman responded, "Oh my God! I didn't know today was going to be like this. All right. Well, it's not relevant to anything." Laura responded, "But it's important to me that you know so I can be open with you." Laura told us, "Her response almost didn't matter, because I was so pumped up with the courage of having come out to someone so quickly and so directly." She added, "It was really interesting driving to work the next day, when I knew my boss would be back, because she has the biggest mouth ever. I went in knowing full well that the word that I'm gay could be all over the company and probably would be. So I was driving and thinking: OK, I'm gay and they know. So what? So I work with 1970s Olympic athletes, old men who have probably never met a gay person in their life. Hey, so what? I can deal with it. I just started building up my own armor. I was nervous. But it's turned out to be fine. I had lunch with our marketing manager, and she proceeded to tell me her sister is a lesbian and she knows all about Olivia Records and the Michigan Women's Music Festival. The word has definitely gotten out."

Laura reflected, "This is really different from my previous job, where I really led a double life. There my entire personal life was gay women and my entire work life was completely closeted. I was sort of asexual in what I talked about. Nobody knew who I was dating, and I didn't seem to have much of a life. It's been really nice for me to be able to talk about my personal life at work, even if it is just with a few people. I feel a lot closer to some of my work friends than I ever have before, and that's given me a lot more passion for my job. It's better to feel able to be more open. It's just a lot more comfortable to be able to talk about what's going on in my life or to be able to make jokes with some gay content. Some of the women I work with even make those kind of jokes to me now. It makes a much nicer working environment."

John Wurster's Story

John Wurster, a white man in his fifties, grew up in a rural and conservative Southern Baptist family and came out to himself years after being married and having a son. He is perhaps unique among the gay professionals we interviewed in having been in the same business for the last twenty years. His coming out process was long, but he is now out in every aspect of his life.

John recalls intense friendships with men in college but says that the thought of being sexual together never crossed his mind. Things changed the summer after graduating from college. First, he received a Dear John letter from the woman he thought he was going to marry.

"After learning that we weren't going to get married, I spent the summer alone hitchhiking around Europe," John said. "I vividly remember getting a ride from the German soldier who seduced me. Afterward, I remember walking around Munich to get away from this guy as fast as I could, just feeling like I had been run over by a truck. The next day I felt so ashamed. I felt sick to my stomach. I felt horrible for weeks because I had allowed this to happen. I kept thinking that it was a sign of great weakness, that I had just done something revolting."

John joined the Peace Corps after business school to avoid being sent to Vietnam. He said that going overseas was an eye-opening experience for him. "In Tunisia I saw a culture where men's friendships were very heavily laced with an erotic component. And I read French literature by Gide and Proust. So I finally saw there was more than just that one way of being a man than I had seen growing up."

John continued to struggle with his sexual orientation in those years and began dating a Canadian woman who was also working in Tunisia. "It was an incredibly romantic environment there," he recalled. "I fell in love." He and his bride moved to New York, where he took a job at American Express in the travel-planning area. John recalls, "When I was in New York those three years, just after I was married, I started seeing more and more gay people around Brooklyn Heights, where we were living, and in the travel field where I was working for American Express, and I just starting feeling that there was a lot more to life than being in a heterosexual relationship."

Shortly after their son was born in 1973, John decided that he didn't want to be working for a large company in an urban environment for the rest of his life. So he and his family moved to Amherst, Massachusetts, a location John had scouted out while looking for a place to start a travel agency. John said proudly, "That's what I've been doing for the last twenty years, running a travel agency. I now have a branch in Northampton also. The Valley is a very pleasant place to live, and business is good."

Recalling how he got from being a married man with a small child to the gay man he is today, John said, "In the 70s, as the whole sexual revolution was exploding, I was living a very traditional married person's life here in Amherst. Only the reading I was doing was keeping me in touch with gay life. I was still reading like crazy. It seemed like every book I would pick up would be another description of homosexuality. That was all I had to go by. I didn't know a single gay person in town; there were no gay bars. There was nothing. What liberated me was all the reading I was doing on my own.

"I felt an enormous responsibility toward my wife and son. To me, divorce was out of the question for a very long time. I just didn't imagine that I would or could do that. I felt I had to raise my son and that I had obligations that would last a lifetime. It was difficult because I loved my wife. But it wasn't enough, once I saw other dimensions to life. We divorced in 1981."

Work was the one thing that stayed consistent through this whole coming-out process. "The travel agency was very successful. In the beginning of the 70s I specialized in travel for students. We had spring break trips that would attract thousands and thousands of students to go to Fort Lauderdale and Bermuda, and ski trips to Vermont, and it was very lucrative.

"But I didn't want to spend my whole life running these college trips. It was insane; it was like being in the middle of the movie *Animal House.*" John laughed. "By the end of the 70s I'd had enough, because I was thirty-five, and you can't be on location all winter in Fort Lauderdale with these drunken eighteen- to twenty-year-olds and not go crazy after a while.

"So by the end of the 70s I was doing more adult travel, which was a lot less lucrative and a lot harder work. But I liked living in Amherst rather than traveling all the time."

Once he came out, John faced some business problems at first. "I had two employees that left my company shortly after my divorce. It was two older women who were married to professors, who had less than accepting ideas about homosexuality. They saw a business opportunity for themselves to open a travel agency across the street and take the clientele with them that they had cultivated while working for me. That was very expensive for my agency; it took a big chunk of my business away, and it greatly enriched them.

"I don't think they would have done it if they had really respected me. They left at the toughest time of the year for me to continue without them. I was surprised and very hurt. I think they were surprised that I was able to survive and actually come back stronger.

"This happened about eight years ago. Of course, the last laugh is on them. I'm busy developing the gay travel market here in the Valley, and they don't even acknowledge that it exists. It's not as easy as you might think, though. It's actually harder to earn money in the gay community here than from the academics. Most gay people here are not very affluent. In the big cities you might get two men or two women who are making $60,000 each in high-paying professional jobs, but here in the Valley you don't have those lucrative career possibilities."

John said that while work was fulfilling, it also was not enough. "All this time since my divorce I was looking for a man to share my life with. The idea of just going out and partying at discotheques didn't appeal to me long-term, although it was fun for a while. I wanted to have a significant other, I wanted to have a partner.

"In 1983 I bought this house, and shortly afterward I met a man that I was in a relationship with for five wonderful years. At the end of that time, he needed to leave, because he didn't have any career possibilities here. And although we really had affection for each other we weren't compatible in a lot of ways. We had completely different tastes in so many aspects of life, from the food we liked to eat to the fact that he absolutely detests travel.

"I was very lonely again from 1988 until 1990, when I caught a glimpse of my current partner, Keith Woodruff, one evening in Northampton. I guess we actually started living together in 1991. In addition to my travel business, we opened our bed-and-breakfast two years ago, and that's doing well also."

The B&B serves gay people as well as heterosexuals, which John says, 150 bookings later, has never been a problem. "Most people find it rather difficult to be rude to somebody in their own home. And at the travel agency also I don't separate gay travel from straight travel. One of our agents will be talking on the phone to somebody about a gay bed-and-breakfast in San Francisco, and there will be a straight person sitting at their desk, and they'll overhear the conversation. We don't try to have different departments. Most of my agents are not gay people. But they're all capable and comfortable booking gay clients and gay destinations."

Keith added, "Here at the bed-and-breakfast we receive gay news magazines like the *Advocate* and *10 PERCENT*." John confirmed, "We are not going to de-gay each room when there is a straight person checking in. So these parents of these straight students will pick up these magazines and see that being gay isn't just about sex. Also, we don't know from one day to the next who will be staying with us. We'll have a lesbian couple in one day and a straight couple the next. We could also have a gay couple and a straight couple in the house at the same time.

"We sit down to breakfast with our guests and talk. It's great. I love it. You know, you get into all these different topics and it's really wonderful."

The couple is also active in both mainstream and gay organizations in town. John said, "We go to the Rotary Club together when it's a function that members typically take their spouses to. The stereotype that they're mostly fifty- to sixty-five-year-old conservative guys is pretty valid. But we're very out, and no one seems to have a problem with that. There are lots of gay organizations that have started up around here in the last five years, and we're active in almost all of them. Keith is in the gay chorus, we're in the gay and lesbian outdoor adventure group."

Keith added, "We're members of the Chamber of Commerce too. We feel that the best way to do business is to be a businessperson first and then be who you are. And as long as you're accepted as a businessperson, you will be accepted as who you are. That's the way I feel I have to be. I can't think because I'm gay that I can't run a business or that I can't be accepted in our society. I just expect others to accept it. We don't give them an alternative.

"I think that some people think if they're gay or lesbian that they can't be mainstream. They think that they should only do gay/lesbian business and have gay/lesbian staff, because they won't be accepted by the rest of the population. But I'm saying give the whole population a chance. I think you'll be much more successful."

Jonathan Rottenberg's Story

Jonathan first attracted the attention of the media when he was still in high school. At age thirteen, he founded the Boston Computer Society, which soon became the world's largest computer users organization. *Wall Street Journal, Business Week,* and *Boston Herald* articles from 1982 to 1987 charted the meteoric rise of this young high-tech superstar. Jonathan told us that he was struggling to accept his sexual orientation even as an undergraduate. "I came from a very happy, traditional, *Leave It to Beaver* kind of family, and I wanted that sort of life for myself," he remembered. "I went to see a therapist to try to sort things out." The therapist's advice was, "Go on about your life, meet as many people as you can, and at some point you'll meet somebody who is very special. And if that person turns out to be a woman, you're straight, and if it's a man, you're gay. Don't worry about the gender of the person, just focus on the relationship. Basically, don't worry so much about it."

Jonathan said that at the time he thought this was good advice, and he operated according to it for almost a decade. He said that it wasn't until he was at Harvard Business School that he realized that this strategy had a basic flaw in it. "It's very easy to meet straight women in mainstream society; it's extremely difficult to meet gay men unless you make an effort at it," Jonathan now recognizes.

He admits, "I had a particularly difficult time coming out, even to myself, because of being in the public limelight so much. I noticed that people recognized me whenever I would go out to restaurants. I didn't feel like I had a lot of privacy. The fear of public exposure made coming out really difficult for me. I reasoned it was very likely that I would continue to be interesting to the press. I felt that I had to go one way or the other, straight or gay. Being undecided and experimenting wasn't really an option. Even at that time, I thought if you're gay and you're open about it, that will be OK. But if I left behind an audit trail of sexual relationships with men and then got married, there was a potential for scandal. That really concerned me."

The first week of business school, Jonathan remembers, he looked around the amphitheater-style classroom and realized something he had never noticed before. "People my age were starting to look older. Adult, mature features were beginning to emerge. For the first time I could see my classmates being fifty or sixty years old. It suddenly struck me that I'm not going to have my youth and vitality forever. I began to wonder—how old do I have to be before I figure out whether or not I'm gay? I remembered a button I saw someone wearing that admonished, 'Don't die wondering!' It was literally at that moment that I decided I was going to get to know some gay people. So that afternoon when I got home from class I called the HBS gay student association. It turned out that they were having a meeting in a few days, and I anxiously awaited the weekend."

Jonathan found, somewhat to his dismay, that his worst fears were realized. Within seconds of stepping into the apartment where the meeting was being held, he heard a classmate say, "That's Jonathan Rottenberg. He's the president of the Boston Computer Society." Jonathan laughed. "It turns out that there were at least three people there who were Boston Computer Society members."

Jonathan admitted, "I was a little bit mortified. My hope that I could explore being gay in a low-key way was instantly forgotten. I was pretty uncomfortable at that meeting. But at the same time I thought it seemed like a nice group of people. Everyone looked and acted so normal. I don't know what I was expecting, but the only gay people I had ever seen before were the ones on TV, people who are really unusual in one way or another. But this group wasn't very different from any other HBS cocktail party.

"At the end of the meeting a bunch of people were going out to a gay bar called Buddies. Well, I had never been to a gay bar before, so I thought this would be a good time to give it a try. It was really a lot nicer than I had expected. It wasn't seedy at all. It was more preppy than anything else. I remember standing at the bar looking around and thinking: Boy, this is really nice. This is a very nice place."

Jonathan admits, "It's funny, but what happened next is that I suddenly realized that every single person there was a man, and they were dancing with one another and touching each other. I don't know what else I would have expected at a gay bar, but it was just the strangest thing for me to see. I had never really thought of the idea before, and it actually . . . it started to make me very uncomfortable. The whole idea of it seemed very strange.

"But I didn't let that stop me. The next month I went to another GLSA meeting and went out again to another gay bar. By Thanksgiving break, I realized that something was beginning to change. I had become curious. I had heard there were twenty-two gay bars in Boston, and I began to wonder what they were like."

Applying a methodological and analytical approach to coming out, Jonathan discovered a parallel universe. "It had always existed all around me, but I never saw it; I never knew it was there. As I began coming out, this whole world began to materialize all around me. I realized that there were gay bars, gay health clubs, gay video-rental stores, gay restaurants, gay political organizations, everything." After taking his first tentative steps out of the closet, Jonathan never looked back. In December 1991 he and Harvard Business School alumnus Paul Kowal were among those featured in *Fortune* magazine's ground-breaking cover story "Gay in Corporate America."

A few months later Jonathan was the subject of HBS alumnus Andrew Tobias's article in *Time* titled "Three-Dollar Bills." There was nothing queer about the article, which congratulated the business school and its students for its positive reception to Jonathan's visibility and accomplishments as an openly gay man on campus. Soon after, Jonathan was again the focus of a new article. This time it was a *USA Today* profile, which lauded Jonathan's accomplishments in the computer industry as well as his perspectives on ending homophobia.

Jonathan worked at the Monitor Company, a prestigious management and strategic consulting firm, during the summer between his First and Second Years of business school. Based on his excellent work during the summer, he had an offer to return there full-time after graduation. Jonathan pointed out that he had come out quite publicly without discussing the matter with anyone from the company. Jonathan confessed, "After the *Fortune* article came out in December, I felt very awkward about the whole situation, because I wondered if I should have told them what I was going to do.

"After the New Year, they started wining and dining me to get me to accept their offer to return to the firm. At first I wondered if they really wanted me to come back or if they were just trying to do what they thought was the right thing. By that time I had done the interview with *Time,* also. And I had been on the local TV news by then as well. I knew I had to talk some things out with a partner of the firm before I made any decisions.

"I planned what I was going to say very carefully. I pretty much delivered a speech when we finally had dinner together." Several years later, Jonathan could still recall the conversation word for word.

He told the partner, "I recognize that management consulting is one of the most conservative professions and our clients are some of the most conservative companies in corporate America. And I realize that it's very unusual for a management consultant to be involved in any kind of high-profile controversial public activity outside of work. As I find myself being more and more a person in the media talking about gay and lesbian issues, I want to understand whether you see my involvement in these matters becoming a problem for the firm or for any of the firm's clients."

Jonathan recalled, "I had a range of answers in my mind that I thought he might have. So I was prepared to counter whatever he might say with a well-thought-out response. I had also thought about what would be my bottom line. I knew which answers would have been acceptable to me and which answers would have given me reason to pause about accepting the offer. Basically I assumed that he would come back with some kind of caveat about 'what you need to keep in mind.' "

Jonathan set the stage for us. "There we were, this partner and me, having dinner in one of Boston's most luxurious restaurants. I delivered my speech without a hitch, just as I planned. But I sure didn't expect his response! He went so far beyond what I would have even said myself if I were in his shoes. The partner was absolutely unequivocal. 'As far as the firm is concerned, all that matters is that you're doing good work for the clients. We really don't consider it any of our business what you do on your own time. It's exactly the same as if you were active in feeding the homeless or raising money for the Red Cross and got on TV for that.' And he added, 'If any of our clients has a problem with your being gay, we'll just tell them to fuck themselves!' "

Jonathan beamed. "It was absolutely extraordinary. We ended up talking quite a bit about this subject. That was the point that he told me that the board of directors had seen the article in *Fortune* and had talked about it at a board meeting. They decided that they wanted to make a very specific policy in response to the situation of me being out. A month later, they instituted a very strong brand-new policy of nondiscrimination based on sexual orientation, which was a total surprise to me. I don't think I was the only contributing factor to this, but I'm sure I helped push them along that path."

Jonathan points out that not everyone he works with day to day read about him coming out in the media. "There have been a number of occasions where coworkers assume that I'm heterosexual. A few have even made insensitive remarks about gay people in front of me. Those I always challenge right away. But sometimes there are ambiguous situations that require a little more tact. Usually I find a way to come out to them within a short time. I find that when I come out to someone, we become much better friends," he concluded.

Elizabeth's Story

Elizabeth, who is in her forties, came out in response to a personal crisis. She said, "When I first moved to this job, which was about eight years ago, it coincided with Bonnie's father being terminally ill. And so at the same moment that I was starting a very large, very new, very high-pressure visible job, I knew that I was going to be seen as behaving erratically if I didn't come out. I was going to be taking off and going to the hospital to be with my 'roommate's' dying father at times that you would only do that if it was more than a roommate. So I could see the need to come out imminently.

"In the first month I was in this job, I decided just to go to my boss, who I had worked with in the past and whom I trusted a lot, but to whom I had not come out. I just went downstairs and said, 'Look, life is too short. I can't deal with playing games anymore. There is too much going on. Bonnie's father is dying; we are a couple. You probably figured that out before, but if you hadn't figured it out before, you have to know it now, because I'm going to start behaving like the spouse of a person whose father is dying.' So, you know, it was one of those things where I was in such a panic that I didn't care.

"Well of course it went great. It was something that in retrospect I wish I had done earlier. That was the real icebreaker. From that point on, I've come out to some, and I don't care what the others think. I don't go out of my way to tell people, nor do I go out of my way to decline to talk about Bonnie. I have my entire office to our vacation home every spring for a day, and she is there. If they have any eyes, they see that we wear matching rings. And they know, if she calls, to treat it like they ought to treat the spousal phone call. So although I haven't told my staff, I think they've all figured it out." Elizabeth has come out to all of her bosses and most of her colleagues, she told us.

Ann Bilyew's Story

Ann Bilyew, a white woman in her late twenties, has been completely out at every job she's ever held, right from the beginning, and at every school, and intends to continue in the same path. She said, "I've been out since I was about fifteen. A long time. It seems like my whole life. I didn't ever go through that whole agony that people go through about coming out to your parents, because they walked in on me and my girlfriend. So they knew almost simultaneously with me. I never thought it was a phase; it just felt so right. When I was sixteen, I had a fake ID and started sneaking into gay bars in New London. I guess I was always kind of outrageous. I don't know why, it's just I can't be any other way. It's a matter of happiness, but I think to me it's also a matter of personal integrity."

Ann was a deferred admit to HBS. "I applied when I was still an undergrad. A big chunk of what I had done as an undergraduate was gay related, so of course I included that on my admissions application. Being accepted under the deferred-admit program meant I had to work for two years before enrolling. I worked in an advertising agency for a year, and I was out there. Then I knew that I had one year left before I came to HBS, so I was interested in some different stuff. I'm really attracted to nonprofit, saving-the-world sorts of things."

She explained how she found her next post. "At the advertising agency I worked with a guy who also ended up going to Harvard. It turns out his mother was a vice president of a health center, and they were starting a fund-raising drive for a new building. So he talked to his mom and said, 'Hey, Ann would work out really well,' because they needed somebody for one year to get the capital campaign started. So I went to work at this place called Swope Parkway Health Center, which is an inner-city health center in Kansas City. So she already knew I was gay before I even started working there. She also told me there was already someone gay there who had gotten insurance coverage for his partner. So when I showed up, I just told her I wanted health insurance for Kelly, and she sent me down the hall to sign up. Kelly was on the insurance plan and got glasses and eye exams, whatever. She had full medical benefits."

When Ann got to HBS she continued being completely out right from the beginning. "I signed Kelly up to use the athletic center at HBS, and I brought her to the section orientation. She came to visit the class the second week, and we go to section parties and social events together. The only reason her picture wasn't in the Face Book was because she wouldn't get her picture taken. That wasn't my doing. I would have had her picture in there. I introduce her to everyone as my partner. I guess that's the word I use. People understand that means we're in a relationship, because I say it with a certain emphasis, and that's the word people use here to talk about spouses. So I think people are pretty quick to pick up on that. If they're not, I tell them. Everyone's been fine about it. I think if you send ambiguous signals, you're unconsciously telling people that you're personally having some problem with it and that's why you can't just come all the way out and say it—that's the signal you're sending out. I've never seen anybody attack somebody who looked somebody in the eye and says, 'I'm gay' or I'm 'lesbian.' I've only seen people be attacked once they've been found out or discovered. I think it's a function of the fact that people cannot help but respect you if you come out."

Ann told us she worked as a management consultant between her two years at HBS. Ann also told us she listed being copresident of the Gay and Lesbian Student Association on her summer job résumés. She also came out during the various recruiting dinners as part of explaining her geographic preferences over the long term. "I talked about the fact that Kelly is applying to graduate school. Sometimes they thought Kelly was a man, so I corrected them."

She explained, "See, for me, it's definitely a criterion how they deal with that, because I would never go to work for a place where I couldn't feel comfortable. If I felt that would be an issue in terms of my ability to move up the ladder or achieve whatever goals I had in terms of my career . . . if I felt that was an impediment because of the atmosphere or the environment of the firm, I wouldn't work there. I think being out in the recruiting process is a good way to do some screening. At the firm I worked for this summer, I felt totally comfortable talking about Kelly and being out at work. Again, sometimes people would assume that Kelly is a man, and I'd just correct them. It was no big deal. I think it's very easy to come out when you're in a relationship. I think it's somewhat harder to come out when you're single. The strongest reaction I'll get is people will blink a couple of times. I think I'll probably go back into consulting full-time, because I really liked it."

We told Ann we saw her as a pioneer in being out on campus and in her career. She replied, "Gosh, you know, I hadn't ever thought of it like that. I guess it's just natural to me to do what I do, it's just who I am."

Chapter 7

Networking

Many successful business professionals recommend getting to know other people who can be helpful in one's career. Whether the association leads directly to a new position or consists primarily of advice about managing one's career path, networking can be an important component of job satisfaction and career success. Business professionals have long used networking—often based on personal commonalities or similar interests—to achieve business goals. For gay professionals who may be cut off from some of the more traditional networking opportunities in business, networking with other gay people can be especially important.

In the first part of this chapter we discuss the importance of networking in the lives of gay professionals we studied, looking at the ties they developed with gay work colleagues, industry contacts, clients, vendors, subordinates. We also discuss the emerging role of formal organizations in networking. The second part of this chapter contains a discussion of gay networking outside the company.

NETWORKING WITH PEOPLE INSIDE THE COMPANY

In our survey we learned many gay professionals knew of other gay people in their current work environment. The vast majority knew of at least one gay coworker, and 21 percent knew of five or more. The average respondent knew of three other gay people at his or her current job, and four at all their post-MBA positions combined. Gay professionals were somewhat less likely to know a gay boss, but the average respondent knew at least one at a current or previous position. Almost half knew at least one gay subordinate at their present job, and respondents knew an average of three gay subordinates at previous jobs.

At the time we developed our survey, gay employee organizations were uncommon, but we found that some belonged to such associations. In analyzing the data from our interviews, we distinguished between networking through formal organizations and networking through person-to-person contracts. For those in formal gay employee organizations, the question of how to meet other gay professionals is less pressing, but for those without access to such a network, the problem of discovering these hidden allies is extremely important. Hence, we devote a portion of this section of the chapter to "gaydar," gender differences in networking, and the unwritten rules governing gay networking. Finally we look at the ramifications of gay networking on our interviewees' personal lives.

In our interviews we found gay professionals were able to find others in almost every industry, from the more gay friendly to the most conservative. Those in more creative industries often told us they felt little risk in dropping hints that would lead them to others, while for those in more conservative industries, the risk was usually more pronounced.

GAY EMPLOYEE ORGANIZATIONS

The vast majority of those we interviewed work for companies that do not have gay employee organizations. Most gay employee organizations have been formed in *Fortune* 500 companies, government, civil service, media, or the high-tech industry. Such organizations are far less common in industries like consulting, investment banking, banking, real estate, publishing, advertising, retail, or small business—where many of those we interviewed are currently employed.

Those Who Do Not Join

Some of those who work for companies with gay employee organizations felt the personal risk of joining was too high. None told us they were afraid of management crashing the meetings; rather, they were afraid that other gay people would out them or pressure them to come out.

Kelly told us, "My company, Pacific Gas & Electric, has a corporate policy of nondiscrimination based on sexual orientation. We haven't gone so far as to offer benefits to domestic partners or same-sex couples. But the company is very open in the sense that they have a gay and lesbian employee association. The group includes both white-collar management and blue-collar union members." However, Kelly has not attended any of the group's functions. "One reason is, I don't want them to expose my sexual orientation to my colleagues. My other fear is—once the employee association finds out you are gay, I think they would start going after you and almost insisting that you join the organization and get involved in public events like marching in the Gay Pride parade, and I don't want that kind of pressure."

Some said their impression was the gay employee group at their company was primarily social, and oriented toward lower-level employees, so they saw no benefit in participating. Charlie, who has thought about organizing a gay group at his company, said he saw no potential for personal gain from it. "For me, organizing a group would be something to do for the sake of doing it because no one can impact my job at all. It would just be something nice to do. And if my goal is to just do something nice, I think it's better to be more of a mentor to gay people at HBS, to help them think about their job search and what it means to be gay in investment banking. There I can really have impact and really help someone, as opposed to just getting together at a cocktail party with no purpose, which is the way I would see a gay employee group."

Stever Robbins laughed at this perspective. "I don't understand how anyone can go to HBS and not appreciate the value of networking simply for the sake of networking." Sheila added, "Besides, what about helping to organize for protections or benefits for gay people? It seems that a lot of groups started out as primarily social but eventually accomplished a great deal more."

Those Who Join

Those who have joined their company's gay employee association have found the benefits to be primarily social, but some have found networking benefits or political gains as well. David Geller told us he initially went to Time Inc.'s gay employee association events "to try to meet men to date—without much success." But the group led to a source of career support for him when he became friendly with a lesbian executive. "I think we clicked partly because we're both gay. She's an HBS alumna and wrote my recommendation for Harvard Business School. She also really helped prepare me emotionally for what it was going to be like there the first year." The group also served to introduce him to another HBS graduate, a gay man who has become part of his social network.

Brian Offutt participates in the gay employee association at his company, the New York Times. "Most people in it are editors, not businesspeople. But I still enjoy it." Similarly, Jim Sherman told us he attends the meetings of the gay employee organization that serves Time Inc, HBO, and Time Warner Corporation.

Many gay employee groups are difficult to find. In some cases this seems to be because leadership wants to keep the group underground, while in others it seems to be due to ineffective marketing by the group's leadership. In general, we found, when a group is less visible, white men are more likely to be the main participants, because they are most connected to one another through social ties.

In contrast, other gay employee groups announce their existence to all employees through companywide E-mail announcements, company newsletters, or flyers on bulletin boards and attract a greater diversity of participants. In addition, some groups keep their membership informed via blind E-mail, which allows them to disseminate up-to-the-minute information and mobilize large numbers of people for quick action while maintaining the anonymity of their members.

QUASIFORMAL GAY MANAGEMENT NETWORKS

We found relatively sizable informal networks of gay executives at many companies. Some are very loosely organized, while others are becoming more formal. In general, the more organized the group is, the more likely it will achieve specific protections and benefits for its members. However, we know of one rather small informal network at a major investment-banking firm that recently got the company to adopt a nondiscrimination clause and is working on getting domestic partner benefits.

Financial Services

Several of those we interviewed confirmed the existence of informal networks among gay execs at financial services companies.

Brett's Story

Perhaps one of the largest informal gay management network exists at American Express in New York City. Now boasting over one hundred members, the group has met monthly for several years. Brett, one of the founders, told us, "I'd say it is mostly an executive-level group of people. The vice presidents who come are people who are completely out at the company, whereas everyone else is not completely out."

How had such a group developed, we wondered? Brett recalled, "One summer in the Pines [on Fire Island, a gay resort town outside New York City], I bumped into a guy that I worked with who I didn't know was gay. He was actually kind of upset about being found out—and it turned out I was the third person from work he'd seen that day. Over that summer I kept bumping into more and more people from work at the Pines. Except this first guy, everyone was really thrilled to meet other people from work," Brett was happy to learn. "We would meet every week at the tea dance on Fire Island. We'd talk and have drinks, and we would share stories about work and the people there—who was gay, who was gay friendly, who was homophobic."

When the summer was over, everyone wanted to continue meeting, so Brett and another colleague decided to make it happen. "Ultimately we decided to just spread the word that on Thursday after work if you are gay and you're interested come to Splash [a gay men's bar]." Most of the initial group were white men, Brett said, but over time it has become more diverse.

"The first time we went, we were so nervous on the way over there, wondering if anyone was going to be there." Brett was delighted to find that about thirty people from his division showed up. "Many of them were people I work with or talk to on the phone, but I had no idea they were gay. Everyone was really thrilled with the turnout and said that they knew people from other divisions who should be here."

The group continued to grow to over one hundred people, but keeping the group going has taken some effort. "What I've found is that you have to call people and remind them. People love coming, people are thrilled about meeting each other, but you have to encourage them to go."

Brett said the purpose of the group has changed over time. "At first the group was purely social. I still think that's an important function, because now we have friends across the company who have things in common. I see the little enclaves of gay people having lunch together; it's mostly men, but there are some women too. People of all different races. And there are a lot of different job functions represented. So it's been good for networking."

Once the social function of the group was established, it was possible to move to political activism. Brett's partner and some of the group regulars began to talk about approaching management for specific protections and benefits. "Some people, particularly one of the vice presidents, said that they weren't really interested in continuing to meet in a bar without a purpose. And some of the women said, 'We would be more interested in coming if we weren't going to a male bar all the time.' We haven't resolved all the issues yet, but we came up with some specific goals that we want to achieve.

"First we brought the nondiscrimination policy to Human Resources. A group of four of us—including a director and a vice president—went to the head of Human Resources and said sexual orientation should be included companywide." And they changed it.

"Then there was another thing. We're in the travel business, and the company offers special travel deals to the employees. Like there were special travel packages for you and your spouse. So we challenged that, and they changed it. So now it's you and a companion.

"Now we want domestic partner benefits. And I honestly believe that will happen. The company is making extreme efforts at embracing diversity, and including gay men and lesbians in that. They're saying the right things, and they're starting to do a lot of the right things. We self-insure the whole company. So it shouldn't really be a problem."

Brett told us he personally has benefited from the organization in many ways: workplace protections, travel benefits, networking, and social friendships. We asked Brett, Does it ever get too close? Many people, both gay and heterosexual, say they prefer to separate their work life from their personal life. He responded. "No, that hasn't been a problem at all. There are some people in the group that I really like and I really feel they are my close friends, and there are some that I just know and I don't really care to get to know too much better. Just like with anybody that I meet from work, either I choose to share personal things with them or I choose not to. It's entirely up to me."

Today, Am Ex officially recognizes its gay employee group.

Brian Offutt's Story

Another sizable network of gay executives exists at Morgan Guaranty Trust, we learned from Brian Offutt. Unlike the group at American Express, however, it does not hold regular meetings. While Brian was not out to himself while he worked at Morgan, he has stayed in touch with a former colleague whose partner is a vice president. "My friend also left Morgan, but his partner is still there. It turns out that there's this extensive

Morgan gay life, which I have come to know through them, which I didn't know about at the time I worked there. Everyone knows each other. There are a number of people who are now vice presidents, and even a few managing directors, who are gay, who socialize together with a few other guys. I never would have dreamed it possible when I was there. I also have a good friend who's a star entry-level person. And through him I met some of his friends, who are also gay Morgan bankers. So I know this whole younger set as well. If the two groups don't know about each other yet, I'm sure they will eventually—maybe at one of my parties. They don't really socialize now, but I'm sure they will at some point."

We asked Brian if he thought gay people were especially attracted to Morgan for some reason. "Well, it's a meritocracy. And among all the Wall Street banks, it might be the most civilized. So the macho swaggering is not as prevalent there as it might be at some other banks. You don't hear as many homophobic jokes, and you might not feel as pressured to conform. I mean, it's still a tough place, relative to other industries, but relative to other banks, I think it might be better. That came through in that there were more women and more minorities in Morgan than there were in other banks, also. I think if you're twenty-one or twenty-two, even if you're not out to yourself yet . . . even if you can't quite articulate why you're more comfortable there, yeah, it is more comfortable to go to a place like that."

Hope's Story

Hope also got to know a rather sizable group of gay executives at a major Japanese-owned bank. "There were nine of us, including one of the senior managers from Japan. I ran into one assistant vice president on New Year's in the Village, and he told me about the other gay men at the bank. And then a friend of mine met a gay woman who mentioned where she worked, so my friend told me about this other woman, and we became good friends as well. There was a whole little network of us from all the different levels. It was so comfortable for me there. It's funny though," Hope recalled. "The gay men weren't so friendly with each other. I mean, I think I probably had a better connection with each of them individually than any of them did with each other. We certainly weren't a cohesive group. We were afraid to all go out to lunch together —that would make it too damned obvious, you know."

Although the group itself was not out, Hope told us, some of the individuals in the group were quite out. "The other lesbian there—she would have all these gay groups like GLAAD [Gay and Lesbian Alliance Against Defamation] fax her things. One time she faxed something down to me on my floor, and I found out later that a lot of the Japanese men found out that I was gay that way. Even before that, there was definitely a guilt-by-association factor. Because I was friends with her and people saw us together, pretty much everyone suspected that I was gay—which I didn't know until just before I left. I just blinded myself to it, because I liked having that friendship and I wanted to maintain it." Also, Hope told us, "A couple of us told some straight people. One of my best friends was promoted to vice president and men called him all the time, so some people figured it out. Then he told his team leader, his boss, that he was gay. And I know that his boss told the junior member on their team, who probably told some other people. People love to gossip, and talking about who is gay is good gossip material. Since my friend and I went to lunch together all the time, I think that also confirmed people's suspicions about me."

Yet despite some of the gay men's fears about being too out, Hope pointed out, her gay male friend, the other lesbian, and she herself suffered no career damage. "He kept getting promoted, at least as much as any non-Japanese person could. She's now working at another bank, where she doubled her salary and is in a bonus position, making a damned good living for what she does. So obviously it hasn't hurt her too much either."

Hope also continued to receive tremendous opportunities while she was there. "You would think as a woman that it would be very difficult, but I loved it there when I was there. I was the youngest person at my age to be promoted to my level, and I was definitely on the fast track. They were flying me all over the country to meet with all these leveraged-buyout groups, and I was the lead person on the account. No one my age got that kind of experience and independence at American banks. My American boss was my mentor, and he was great to me. I ended up coming out to him before I went to business school."

Carmen's Story

In a previous position, Carmen was part of a sizable gay group at a leading investment bank. "We had a whole mess of gay people there. We turned out to kind of be a focal point for socializing in some ways, because I think most of the people who were working there who were gay and were willing to come out to someone came out to us. So it didn't take long before we developed a nice group of friends. Once it became clear to the people who weren't in the group that it was safe to be in the group, more and more people started coming out to the other people at work who were in this circle of friends. Over a couple of years, it became quite a cohesive group. Because we mostly did things outside work, none of the straight people at work really knew that we were gay or that we all know each other.

"There were straight people in the group, too," Carmen added. "But they tended to not be entirely straight. That is—they occasionally had their forays into gay relationships or gay sex. I wouldn't say this was the first time for them or that they were experimenting. I think it's more that sexuality isn't such a black-and-white thing all the time," she pointed out.

The Consulting Industry

Those we spoke with in the consulting industry also felt a strong need to network. One reason was for personal comfort and safety in developing friendships. But several told us they wanted to develop a network that would enable more gay consultants to be free to come out at work and to obtain domestic partner benefits.

While there are no formal gay employee associations at any of the major consulting firms, several of our interviewees confirmed there is an extensive informal network at McKinsey, one of the largest and most prestigious firms. Several told us, "There are actually a number of gay partners at McKinsey. None of them are completely out. One of them is sort of out."

We asked Alan Miles how he got to know the other gay people there. "When I was offered a position there after business school, I looked up Barry Salzman. I had met him once or twice a long time ago and knew he was gay. I didn't know how out he was there, but I soon found out. At one point when we were walking down the hall I asked casually, 'Well, what's it like being gay here?' And he said rather loudly, 'Oh, it's great being gay at McKinsey. Everyone knows I'm gay.' " Alan laughed. "Secretaries are turning their heads and everything, and I was wildly impressed. Then Barry told me about one of the partners.

"I had a good discussion with the partner. He told me it doesn't matter at McKinsey if you're gay or not. And I really don't think it does. But he says appearances have to be maintained. For example, he doesn't have his lover listed as a spouse in the firm directory, although he makes a big deal about how they have been together for twelve years now, which, by McKinsey's standard, is epochal." Alan laughed.

"Then there's another partner who I called up one day to get a copy of a paper he had written a while ago, and he was incredibly animated and just talked my ear off, and every day for the next week just called up to talk. So I thought: This guy's got to be queer. And sure enough, I guess the other partner had told him about me at some point, so he was really eager to get to know me better.

"And then there's this other partner who I met at a party, who used to go out with a friend of mine. Another one I just kind of figured and sort of came out to him. He didn't come out to me for a long time, but finally he did." After Alan told us about yet another gay partner at McKinsey, we began to wonder: Did all the gay people there know about one another? "Until recently, no. I have to say I was kind of the catalyst, because I had met a lot of them, and I kind of forced us all to get together at a recent company retreat. Eight of us, three partners and a bunch of associates, piled into two rental cars and tore off away from this retreat for one night and had this wild evening out in town. It was great."

Glenn, a former McKinsey consultant in his late thirties, had the opportunity to be on both levels of the McKinsey network, as an associate coming in and then, by the time he left, as a more senior consultant. He said, "It's interesting, because some of the new associates are far more open than most of my generation. It's less than a decade, but there really are differences. The younger people are becoming more visible. I know there was one guy who was toying with bringing his significant other to a function, and that's the kind of thing that those of us who went to business school in the mid-80s or before never conceived of. The feeling was, Oh that'll be interesting to watch." He laughed. "We all felt the environment was relatively tolerant, but nobody's ever pushed it that far before. With the people who were more out, they were doing a lot of pushing of the limits. I don't think it impaired their job assignments or ability to work for the most prestigious clients. But they were still in the early years of their careers, where it's not as much an issue.

"I don't think the older guys found them threatening, like guilt by association or anything. I think I found it more amusing—and inspiring. It's kind of like, gee, I wish I would have the guts to do that, and it'll be interesting to see what happens, but I'm glad someone else is taking the lead on this." Glenn laughed. "But I didn't worry about guilt by association, because there was still a high contingent of people, much like at business school, who were just simply absolutely oblivious. The whole issue never crossed their minds. They either assumed you were straight or didn't think about what your personal preferences were."

A number of those we interviewed are taking action to foster a climate of receptivity to openly gay executives in the consulting industry. This is a fairly new development for this industry, which most gay professionals saw as one of the most conservative industries until recently. But emboldened by the successes they heard about from gay classmates or other HBS gay alumni, several of those we interviewed took additional steps. For example, Grant, a current student, wrote all the consulting firms that recruit at HBS saying, "You're always talking about diversity, but never once has the word 'gay' been mentioned. Do you have any openly gay partners?" "The replies were fascinating," he told us. "Some of the smaller firms wrote back, saying 'Gee, this has never been an issue; we really have no idea. As far as we know, we don't even know if we have gay people here. We don't discriminate; we basically don't care.' " Grant told us one large firm offered money to support the gay student organization. At another large company the head of human resources contacted the group, saying, "Well, I'm out at work and I'd be willing to come by and talk to you," which he did. A number we interviewed in consulting have taken bold steps out of the closet at work, to no ill effect. This has inspired some of them to pursue additional gains at their companies and to seek and foster industrywide gay networking ties.

Other Industries

Gay industry networks can pave the way for increased networking within a given company. When Ginger accepted a position in a media company, she was unaware of the existence of other gay people at her firm. But after she asked for and received relocation assistance for her partner, information about her spread rapidly. The first day she came into the office she found a newsletter from the Gay and Lesbian Journalists Association on her desk, and she soon met the other gay people in her office. Corporate employees in other industries also told us of industry gay associations that they tapped into leading to greater networking at their companies.

Personal Networking

Where a formal or even quasiformal gay organization does not exist within a company, some found networking with other gay people difficult. Most said they relied on "gaydar"—the ability of gay people to find one another, much as ships use radar to locate other vessels. In particular, we found, lesbians often had a harder time forming such bonds than gay men. One reason may be that an important component of gaydar for men is sexual. For lesbians, on the other hand, the sexual component of gaydar is far less important; they rely on other methods for identifying both gay men and lesbians.

The Components of Gaydar for Gay Men Many gay men told us they were able to figure out other men were gay within minutes of meeting them, based on "a certain look in his eye." Others said that whom a man looks at and for how long is a key component in their gaydar. As they do with heterosexuals, many gay men also rely on clues and hints to begin the process of coming out to one another. Living in certain neighborhoods or having a male roommate past age thirty were seen as very strong clues; so, many did not reveal this information indiscriminately. Other clues, such as going to vacation locations like Provincetown or Fire Island, were used far more often. An interest in the arts, having a number of close male friends, or a lack of any evident physical attraction to women were additional signs gay men looked for and used in establishing rapport. These clues were often substantially reinforced by a slightly longer than usual glance between men or a comfort with male-to-male physical touch. We often heard that heterosexual signs such as marriage or a girlfriend could be overridden by these subtle signals of a sexual commonality. "Gaydar is never wrong, although it sometimes takes time," Gilbert said. "That is, sometimes the guy isn't willing to acknowledge that he is gay to himself, let alone to you. But I've seen it happen a lot of times where a guy I've suspected eventually comes out."

Gay men who were out the longest seemed to have the best-developed sense of gaydar. Those who had not been an active part of the gay community tended to rely more on the same clues that most heterosexuals use to figure out who is gay. Thus, the sexual aspect of gaydar may be something gay men learn as they participate in the gay community.

Leonard, who has his own business, told us gaydar has been important to his career success. "How do you define gaydar? If they're single, over thirty, well dressed, attractive. Prolonged eye contact. I think there are a lot of components. I think it is a sense that you establish out of survival when you are growing up. And then you refine it as an adult, more for convenience than for survival. It's kind of a social skill that facilitates other skills, like making friends and establishing business relationships."

After gaydar has sent up a flag, the next step is to make the bond explicit, Leonard told us. "It's pretty easy, really. You kind of talk about your life and you just listen for the clues about where they vacation, where they live, the type of interests that they have. As biased as it sounds, I definitely find gay people more interesting than straight people. Because they're very externally focused, I find their social lives and their interests are more eclectic. Maybe because they don't have families, generally speaking, gay people spend more time engaging in the world around them. Whereas once you're on the family track, everything becomes much more introspective and much more about the family unit. Because most gay people don't have families, even now, I think there is this connectedness to the larger world that stays with us longer and later into life than it does for straight people who go into the family structure."

Yet even those who have been gay for many years can have difficulty. Patrick, who is in his forties, said he has had a hard time picking out the gay people in his work environment. "You try to put two and two together: They're single, they're cute, you've got eye contact, they seem to be interested in more artsy kinds of things. But that doesn't always work.

Somebody exactly like that who I worked with married a woman at our company. He was a prime candidate. And I still think in the back of my mind that if he had just met the right guy first . . ."

Patrick laughed and said, "I don't know of an easy way to do it. I mean, you can't exactly leave a copy of the *Advocate* lying around. I myself can drop some hints about 'my friend' and 'we' do this and this and this, and I don't ever talk about women, but unless somebody else does the same thing . . . I don't know how you find each other. There's no easy way because of the risk factor. If they're trying to stay in the closet, it's almost impossible. Sure, you can tell the fey ones and whatever, but that's not somebody I'm necessarily going to be clicking with. And I apologize for my political incorrectness, but I get along with people who are like me."

Components of Gaydar for Lesbians For lesbians, it seems, the components of gaydar are far more often limited to clues and hints, some of which may be unfamiliar to gay men or even to other lesbians. Lesbian vacation destinations—such as the Dinah Shore golf tournament, the Virginia Slims tennis tournament events, Provincetown, Fire Island, and the Hamptons—have only very recently gained prominence among lesbians themselves. And since many heterosexuals also attend these events and summer at these retreats, these clues carry much less weight than they do for gay men.

To the dismay of the single lesbians we interviewed, the primary component of gaydar for lesbians seems to be who a woman lives with or whether she is in a close intimate relationship with another woman. Thus, we found, lesbians in a relationship had a slightly better track record in finding other lesbians as well as being found by gay men. Single lesbians more often suffered social isolation at work, unless they were willing to be proactive about befriending those they suspected of being gay. In many cases, single lesbians who found other lesbians at work entered into romantic relationships with them. (We will explore this issue further in the chapter on gender.) Otherwise, most lesbian networking was with gay men. One reason is that there are fewer executive women than men. Thus it is likely there are fewer lesbians than gay men to be found in business. Also, lesbians seem to be more likely than gay men to feel there is more to lose than to gain by being openly gay. Hence the likelihood of two lesbians networking may be lower than that of two gay men or a gay man and a lesbian networking.

We asked Cecilia whether she ever found any gay people in investment banking who were a source of support to her. She responded that she was friendly with a man who worked for her who she thought was gay, but otherwise, "Never, not one. Not one. Now, there was a woman who worked for a competing company who I would see around at things. Since there were so few of us, you remembered who all the women were. She never struck me as being really either way. But I was once in the Village coming home from the grocery store with both of my hands full of stuff from Balducci's, and she was in front of me on the street. I stopped and looked, and she was clearly with her lover; they had their arms around each other. I thought: It never occurred to me, but I guess it could be. So I watched her a little more carefully the next few times we were together, and she was even more closeted than I was. So I never made any overtures to her to try to let her know that I knew. I think it would have freaked her out."

Susan only learned of the existence of another lesbian at her investment banking firm after she stopped working there. "I didn't socialize with her when we were working together because I just wanted to separate my real life from my working experience. My feeling was always that I had my outside life, where I can act like myself, and then there is my life at work. I knew that investment banking wasn't a job that I took because I wanted to become friends with the people there. In fact, I already knew that I didn't want to associate with them at all."

Susan recalls, "But toward the end I dropped a lot of really conspicuous hints to this one woman. And a week before I left she took me out to dinner, and we played this kind of cat-and-mouse game because I had it clear in my mind that I was not going to say anything until I left the office. Once I left, I called her up and we started hanging out, and then I told her about me and she told me about her. After I left the firm I found out that a very senior-level investment banker came out. She's living with her girlfriend, and she is basically out in the bank. But I didn't know that when I was there either," Susan added regretfully.

Nancy had a different perspective. "I'm trying to find out where all the lesbians are at my company, and it's not that easy," she told us. "I actually met one lesbian who is no longer with the company. She was in another department, the marketing department. The way we came out to each other was that I told her I had a friend who was dying of AIDS, so I used to go to the Castro a lot. So she knew I was gay friendly, because I told her my friend was gay and I had a lot of gay friends. First she came out to me, and we became really good friends. She had gaydar; she had this sense about her that I was gay. I don't know how, but she did. And I kind of sensed it about her too. So we developed this wonderful friendship, and that meant a lot to me. But otherwise, I think these women are few and far between."

We asked Elizabeth what the components of gaydar for lesbians were. "How do you describe antennae? You know, it's what people talk about, what they did on the weekend . . . " She said that over time she has become more bold about testing the clues by dropping follow-up hints. "In the early years I would be extremely tentative, and would say things like . . . 'My roommate has taken such good care of me while I've been in business school. I mean she does everything. She cooks, she cleans, she washes . . . ' And I would wait to see if I could get a glimmer of understanding in someone's eye. In fact, in one case, the person who ended up to be truly one of Bonnie's and my very best friends said, 'Gee you know, it's funny. My roommate did that for me too, but actually she's a little more than a roommate.' So that would be sort of an early-years conversation. But more recently what I do is, I just say to somebody, 'I don't even remember whether I've given you any clues before, but I really am tired of talking about myself as an *I,* because I'm a part of a *we.'* And inevitably at this point the person says, 'Well, I know that.' And if they don't say, 'What's your husband's name?' or 'What does your husband do?' you know that they understand. If they don't, I usually tell them. And if they're gay, they'll usually come out to me too."

Lesbians and Gay Men Networking Perhaps because gaydar is less effective in identifying lesbians, most lesbians who networked with other gay people did so with gay men, and only a minority of gay men we interviewed told us they had networked with lesbians at work. Yet we believe other factors are also at play. Gay men seem far less aware of lesbian culture, and hence of lesbian hints, than lesbians are of gay male culture, and thus of gay male hints. Additionally, lesbians may be less willing than gay men to engage in the mutual dance of leaving clues and dropping hints. As a result, more lesbians we interviewed felt isolated at work.

Sally's Story

Sally told us, "Until someone outright says that they are gay, I didn't feel comfortable saying anything explicitly about me being gay. While I was working at a public accounting firm, I invited a supervisor to my birthday party. Almost everyone at the party was gay, but still, neither of us said anything. After I left the company I invited him to a New Year's party at another friend's. He showed up at 4 A.M. with his boyfriend and two other guys in drag. He later became a partner at the firm. Later I told him that I was angry that we never talked about being gay back then—it would have made my life so much easier. I guess he was so in the closet then that nothing I said when I worked there would have made a difference. But since then, I've been much more forward about gay networking and open at work."

Gloria had better luck networking with a gay man in her company, perhaps because she was familiar with gay men's hangouts. "One guy, who was a senior person there, two levels above me, would say stuff like, 'I went to the Monster last night.' And if you're familiar with New York City, you know it's a gay men's bar. So we sort of talked in these codes. He would say, 'I went and danced at USA last night.' And I know that Sunday night is gay men's night. He had it figured out about me too, probably because I understood what he was saying. So he'd ask me, 'Did you go to Washington last weekend?' and I'd answer, 'Yeah, I went to the March.' "

Oliver told us that getting to know a few lesbians has led him to befriend others at work. "We don't go on endlessly about our sexuality, but it's what brought us together in the first place. And we discovered lots of other interests and just genuinely like each other. I mean, that's really what it comes down to. One of them I've only known for six weeks, and she took me out to dinner for my birthday, and she wants to introduce me to some of her friends outside work. It just happens that I've got these thriving relationships with three different women in my workplace who are gay. I don't eliminate the possibility of relationships with other people in the workplace, but that hasn't happened. There's a couple of straight people that I would like to be friends with, and I have lunch with them from time to time. But I feel I have a stronger social bond with my gay coworkers than my straight ones. And the bond is stronger than the other straight people seem to have. I guess it's natural that the people you have interests in common with are the people you like to socialize with, both inside and outside the workplace."

In industries where gay men predominate, it is even more likely for lesbians and gay men to network. Ricki told us her partner is a director of a modeling agency. "There's only one straight person in her office of twenty people. The models are mostly women, and most of them aren't gay. But the agents and the administrative people and one of the owners of the agency are all gay. So are the hairdressers and the makeup artists. So I go with her to company events, and I think that's been good for her professionally."

Laura posited that networking between lesbians and gay men is limited by sexism in many cases. "There's certainly a gay network in many industries, but you have to be a certain kind of woman. Not too dykey. Men don't like that. Even gay men." Sheila agreed: "Also, men have vacation places like the Pines where they go and they network. Lesbians don't really have that. Even if they're out there for the summer, lesbians tend to go their own way by default, because gay men don't invite them to their fancy dinner parties. A lot of times it's because they all want to cruise each other or feel free to have explicit discussions about sex, but it turns out that some pretty strong business bonds get formed in those kind of environments."

Eric, a man in his forties, concurred that some gay men don't feel they have much in common with lesbians. "There are things like camp humor that I have never encountered with a gay woman. I am friends with a few lesbians, but not close friends, no. I think gay men and gay women don't mix well in general. My lover and I have a house in East Hampton, where there is a large gay population. And on the gay beach, the women are at one end of the beach and the men at the other. Gay women in general think the gay men's promiscuity, vanity, and materialism silly. Maybe they're right about it being silly, but I find the scene at the gay [men's] beach fun. Nobody's there discussing Bosnia. People are talking about having seen Calvin Klein at the bar the night before. Things like that. That's what I want on the weekend."

We asked Eric for the gay male stereotypes of lesbians. "I guess the stereotypical lesbian is a lousy cook, has a home decorator from Kmart, and has no appreciation for the finer things in life, in culture. I'm not close with any really successful lesbians, so maybe it is different if they are making a good living. But on the beach, I figure they're talking about a softball game or feminist rights or abortion. More politically correct conversation. I mean, there's no question a lot of gay males get silly. Especially in an environment of crisis, there's a need to laugh through the tears."

Eric told us there are two lesbians where he works. "I don't think they're friends. I don't think they ever socialize. And one of them isn't really good at her job, so I just try to avoid her. The other doesn't look like a lesbian, so I wouldn't have known if someone hadn't told me. So I don't feel free to approach her."

Many gay men told us they have a hard time picking out lesbians, as do most lesbians. Both gay men and lesbians agreed they had an easier time picking out gay men. Yet, just as participating in social activities with other gay men can sharpen gay men's gaydar about each other, exposure to lesbians can sharpen gay men's gaydar for lesbians and debunk their stereotypes.

Cultural differences can also confuse gaydar. Pam said, "As an Asian lesbian, most of the clues that gay people rely on as part of gaydar don't seem to have me on their screen. I usually have to be proactive about coming out to them. When I worked at the Boston Consulting Group, there were a bunch of guys there that were gay. It was very funny, because although he wasn't gay himself, it turns out that the manager of that office, the guy that did all the hiring, just happened to hire all these gay guys. Once I tapped into that group, it was fun. But I had to come out to them first." As with gay men identifying lesbians, Lucy, another Asian lesbian, added, "The more gay Asians someone knows, the better they get at picking us out."

The Unwritten Rules of Gay Networking We learned that gay professionals operate under several unwritten rules about divulging the sexual orientation of another gay person. Many delighted in revealing to us names of celebrities or notable people in business whom they knew to be gay. Most were also happy to name other Harvard Business School classmates we might want to talk to. Many told us they were glad when gay friends or colleagues hooked them up with other gay people by telling others about them. Yet all were careful to ask us to avoid naming friends and colleagues they told us about without their express permission to do so. And most said they would never out someone they knew unless that person was in a position of power and actively doing harm to other gay people. The bottom line for most seemed to be: It's OK to tell another gay person that someone is gay, so long as they can be relied upon to keep that information within gay circles. Yet for some, we learned, even that level of disclosure is too much.

Earl's Story

Earl told us, "There was this woman that I worked with who I had no idea was gay. But then we went on a business trip together, and she came out to me. She made it clear that she was totally closeted at work. She did make that clear. But I thought that I could tell other gay people to start a little network of us. She was also very friendly with another gay guy at work who I was friends with too. It turns out she knew he was gay, but she hadn't come out to him. I caught holy hell because I made the mistake of saying something about her to him. I figured it was cool, because everyone was gay, so who cares? But when she found out she was ready to kill me. She had told me her lover was also a person we worked with. I didn't say anything about her lover, about the fact she was seeing someone in the company or any of that. But she was really upset with me. She took me into a conference room and yelled at me and screamed at me, 'How dare you let my secret out?' Where I've always come from, gay people always felt it's great to know about each other."

While many gay people are willing to be outed to other gay people, it's always best to ask. And most are upset to be outed to heterosexuals, even open-minded ones. Yet others told us they were happy to learn that heterosexual colleagues knew and were supportive. Some even told us they were glad to be outed to heterosexual colleagues because this contributed to their feeling a greater sense of comfort and freedom at work. But the rule of thumb seems to be: Don't tell heterosexuals, even if they ask.

Networking with Gay Colleagues

The most common form of networking we found was between gay male colleagues. Many men we interviewed met colleagues at bars or through friends, avenues that were less fruitful for lesbians.

David Geller, a Jewish man in his late twenties, said that when he worked for Time Inc., "I ran into this one guy at a bar who worked at *Time,* and I went over and said, 'Hey, how are you?' We became instant buddies after that. Men are funny, you know. They don't approach each other too much as friends. I know I don't really go out of my way to have straight male friends. It's just too uncomfortable. With gay men, granted, still, you have to work to maintain a friendship, but you feel like you have this big thing in common, which is being part of a sort of an underground network."

Tony, a Black man in his late thirties, told us gay people are prominent in the advertising business, especially on the creative side. "Gay men are vital in producing virtually every commercial made in the United States, but every firm is different. I was with one firm for eight years—and a vice president for three of those years—that was great. They hire lots of gay men. The director of personnel was a lesbian; maybe that had something to do with it. At another firm I worked for there was a gay man who was director of research, and he used to bring his lover into work all the time. So it was a really nice atmosphere there too."

Lewis, a white man in his late 30s, told us, "There are a number of gay people where I work, including several buyers and a senior executive. That has been the case virtually everywhere I've worked in retail. With the second in command, I didn't realize he was gay when I interviewed with him, but afterwards I was talking to a friend who knew him, and my friend told me he knew for sure that he was gay. There's definitely a camaraderie there because we share that. He's quite a bit older than me, but there's a bonding. In fact, some of it is quite humorous. He'll make some comment about some good-looking guy, kind of playing at being a dirty old man. I enjoy that sort of humor, so it's fun."

Herschel, a Jewish man in his sixties who has worked in New York City, said, "I meet a fairly large number of other gay people in music and the arts. Now it's much more out there than it used to be. I mean, there's no hiding it really. I mean, you say hello to somebody, and after two sentences you know whether it's a totally straight party or whether it's a gay party. I mean, you just simply know. Or a gay friend of mine will come over and say, 'Isn't that so and so. He's a lawyer for so and so and such and such.' And the assumption is, unless he says he not's gay . . . he is. Especially if he's attractive." Herschel laughed. "If he's not gay, he'll set the record straight, so to speak."

Daniel, a Jewish man in his late twenties, works for a major high-tech firm. He learned from a mutual gay friend that an HBS classmate of his was gay. "I was really glad to learn about him, and we have ended up spending a reasonable amount of time together. I travel a lot, but if I'm in town on the weekend, I'll probably see him at least one night for dinner. We go to gay bars together too. I decided I'm not going to be paranoid about the fact that this is a reasonably small town and it's very conceivable that somebody could be driving down the main street of town as I was entering a gay bar. If it happens, it happens. I'm not going to stop living my life just because somebody might find out that I'm gay." We learned that for Daniel, getting to know other gay people at work isn't a priority. "I've run into a couple of people from work at the bars, but I don't automatically try to get to know them. Like I ran into this one woman in our product group. She's probably gay, but maybe she was just there with friends. I'm not really ready to come out to any more people at work so I haven't pursued it. Nothing's changed at the office. I say hi to her, she says hi to me. And that's fine with me."

Peter's Story

Peter, who is in his forties, told us he met two other gay men at his company shortly after starting work, one receptive to networking and the other not. "I had just gotten out of business school and took a job in finance. One gay guy was a senior manager there for over ten years. I knew him beforehand socially, so that's how I knew about him. I called him before I started the job and said, 'I just want you to know that I accepted a job at your company and I'll be looking forward to seeing you there. I guess we won't be working together, but we may bump into each other, and I just want you to know so it's not a big surprise.' I thought that was the courteous thing to do. We weren't really friendly, but I just didn't want to shock the guy in the hallway sometime. When I started, it turned out he was on the same floor. So within the first day or two I walked down to his office and said, 'Hi.' He looked at me and said, 'Uh-huh, good to see you.' And he invited me to come in and sit down, so I did. I was certain that there was no way anybody could hear our conversation, so I said, 'It's really nice working here. There are a lot of cute guys here.' And he just erupted at me. 'Don't you ever say anything like that in this office!' he fumed.

Peter laughed. "The ironic thing is, the only time he would ever talk to me about anything social was in the bathroom when we were alone.

He'd be all friendly and make chitchat like, 'Oh, did you know Miles and Whitey went up to Nantucket this weekend?' But as soon as we left the bathroom, it was a complete change of character. He was absolutely petrified. I asked him if there were any other gay people there. But if he knew anybody, he wouldn't introduce me to them.

"My experience with the other fellow was quite different," Peter said. "When I got to the company, I approached everybody to see if I got a reaction, hoping I could meet a friend. And I was lucky enough that about a month later, I was visiting a friend who told me he had a gay friend at the company and gave me his name and asked me if he could tell his friend that I was one of the new people there. 'Sure,' I replied. 'That would be terrific.' This guy was in the legal department. And before we had a chance to call each other, we had a series of seminars and training programs. It turned out he was leading one of them, so I knew who he was as soon as the session started. And he knew I was in the room but didn't know which one I was initially, because there were about twenty other people there. So I kept looking at him, hoping that he would pick up that I was the guy he was supposed to be looking for." Peter laughed.

"Afterward, I went up and introduced myself. He responded instantly, 'Oh, glad to meet you. Let's have lunch.' You know, it was funny, because the other people were looking at me thinking: Gee, why's he being so nice to you? It was great. Here was somebody who was much more senior than me, and he wanted to meet me. It turned out he was a bit more hooked in than the senior manager. He knew a couple of other gay people there. Most of the people there were pretty much closeted, but yet we had a nice little group."

Jamie's Story

Jamie, a Black man in his late twenties, had several very positive networking experiences in investment banking. "Soon after I got to my company's analyst program, I heard all the secretarial staff talking about a young Black associate, Al, who had arrived at the same time as me. At first I just steered clear of him; as a matter of fact, he kind of scared me. But then I noticed him looking at me, even when he was talking to someone else."

Jamie said that he was too worried about his closet to pursue the connection, but Al made the first move. "One night when we were both working late he kept walking by my area, even though he really didn't have any reason to stop. Finally he came over and said hi. We chatted awhile, and Al suggested, 'You know, we should hang out.' And he asked me, 'Where do you go out?' " Jamie explained to us, "I didn't think that he was really interested in hanging out with me. I just thought he wanted to find out for sure that I was gay so he would have something on me. So I answered, 'I hang out at all kinds of places, very strange places—leather places, places with people who are head bangers, and stuff like that. You wouldn't like them.' " Al was unwilling to be rebuffed, however.

"A few days later," Jamie told us, "Al got my phone number out of the company directory and he called me at home one Friday night. I told him I had company in town, so the first weekend I got out of it. But sure enough, he called me again. And this time I just couldn't make up another lie, so I said, 'OK, if you want to go, I'll meet you at the subway, and we'll ride into the city together.' When we met, he was very well dressed, nothing that would make you think he was ready for some leather and wild partying—which these clubs I went to really weren't." When Al asked, "Well, where are we going?" Jamie answered, "Don't worry about it, it's a surprise." Al persisted, "Well, any particular area of the city that we're going to?" Jamie replied vaguely, "Oh, downtown." Jamie told us, "So we were on the train, just chitchatting, and we get off at the West Fourth stop. And I didn't notice then but he was grinning. We made a left onto Christopher Street and he said, 'I don't know, could we happen to be going to Two Potato [a Black gay men's bar]?" Jamie confessed, "Yeah." And Al admitted, "Oh, good, I've been there before." Jamie said, "That broke the ice."

Jamie also became friendly with another gay man at his firm. "One guy I got to be friends with was an ex-football-player type who was part of the support staff for the traders. I saw him in a gay club one night, and he just started talking to me from then on." Jamie found that Terry was able to help him identify the people who were gay friendly as well as gay. "He just went down the list for me, including telling me about a gay managing director." Based on Terry's recommendation, Jamie found a way to befriend this man, who was very helpful to his career.

Those who worked in the more macho industries, like sports, told us they had a harder time networking with other gay people. However, some were able to make connections. Dale, who worked for the Summer Olympics committee in Los Angeles, told us, "I couldn't have been happier because I was in Los Angeles, and that summer, that place was the best place to be in the whole world. And I've always liked athletics and I've always like athletic men. So I couldn't have been happier. I didn't find the environment homophobic. Anyway, several of the sports are known for having their team members [gay people] too. I really had no bad experiences. The whole experience was good for me."

Bill worked for another mainstream sports organization. At first he enjoyed it very much. He explained, "What people think about an organization and what it actually is can very often be different. I know for a fact that somebody in a very high position in another major sports organization is gay. There were several at my firm I suspect were gay, and the president that hired me was certainly gay friendly. When I came in to interview, I never let them pay for a hotel. He knew I was staying with a friend, Mike. And when I took the job, he asked me very politely, 'Will you be needing a hotel or will you be staying with Mike?' So I think he got it. But he was let go, and the people that took over were very different. Really harsh. They were what you would think a sports organization would be like. As a result, I didn't come out to a single person when I was there or try to find any other gay people. I made that conscious choice. But in retrospect I think that I was too afraid to network at all, and that was stupid of me. I didn't really create friends. I didn't go to lunch with one single colleague. In a year's time I took the people that worked for me to lunch a couple of times, but I never grabbed somebody in the hallway and said, 'Hey, you wanna grab some lunch?' So I was outside the whole friendship-networking type of thing."

Marvin also worked for an organization where coming out would have been career suicide because of his organization's well-publicized opposition to homosexuality. Nonetheless, he said, there were many gay executives where he worked. "One friend comes to mind. He walked out during lunch one day and was carrying a book to read in the park. It was Edmund White's *A Boy's Own Story,* so that was a pretty good clue." He laughed. "I had no idea the organization was so homophobic when I started. I knew they were conservative, but then I had been working for conservative companies. I mean, we all have to do that; corporate America's conservative. But it was homophobic all the way. I challenged them on that, but I never said I was gay. And neither did anybody else, even to each other. I knew about a dozen other people there who were gay, but no one would ever admit it to each other. I mean, you or I looking at them would say, 'How could people not know?' But no, no one was out. They don't want to know who's gay there. It's like the military. They're so homophobic—they know there are some gay people there, but they don't want to hear about it; they just don't want to know about it. It was very, very uncomfortable for me. It didn't affect my life outside of work. I still went to gay bars and so on. But what it did affect was just my living with myself and being happy about myself. That's what it affected."

Those who were able to establish relationships with other gay people in their workplace rated their job satisfaction far higher than those who did not. Having gay friends and allies gave them a feeling of security and comfort on the day-to-day level. In addition, some also obtained career advice, inside information about others at work, and news of job openings.

Don Bickford, a white man in his fifties who works in city government, told us, "One of the things that happened to me in the transition between the two administrations is that my new boss decided that there was a personal friend of his that he wanted to appoint to some senior-level position. And in the process of elimination, he decided that he was going to have to use my position to appoint this friend of his. So he asked me to start looking for a different assignment somewhere, somehow. There was a couple of months' period where I was sending out résumés and trying to get interviews. And given the mayor's pronouncement about wanting to appoint diverse people in the senior levels, I did decide that it was the right thing to do to make it clear on my résumé that I was gay. The way I did that was by listing my affiliation with various gay organizations like my college's gay and lesbian alumni association and my church's committee on lesbian and gay concerns, stuff like that.

"I got a couple of interviews. One in particular that I can think of was set through the commissioner of human rights, who was openly gay. My memory of the interview was that we really didn't dwell on gay things at all; we really just talked about professional qualifications and interests and job possibilities. But it was through gay networking that I got that interview. As things ended up, I got asked to take a different assignment in my original department, and the guy who fired me got fired in about two months. So he's now long since gone, and I'm back in the thick of running things." Don laughed.

Networking with Gay Subordinates

In contrast to networking with colleagues and bosses, gay professionals were less likely to network with their subordinates. Although some were willing to serve as role models or mentors for gay subordinates, most were primarily interested in networking with people who are at a similar professional level.

Elizabeth acknowledged it was more usual for her to befriend gay colleagues than subordinates. "Certainly, over the years, people with whom I've worked would figure each other out. That's happened, and some of these people now are my very best friends. Offhand I can't remember somebody who had worked for me who has told me they are gay. However, I have an increasingly bad memory." She laughed. "At least, it hasn't happened lately."

Several told us they had reservations about becoming too close to gay subordinates. Stan, a white man in his forties, told us that when men much younger than he attempt to approach him on the basis of their both being gay, "I feel uncomfortable in situations like that. I had a situation in a previous position where I supervised a group of people, and one of the guys who was just out of college was gay. I have to admit, I was afraid it would injure my credibility and my position of power if I explicitly acknowledged I was gay. You know, could he blackmail me? Could he . . . whatever . . . That was a fear that I had. I wasn't so afraid he would try to use our being gay as a way of getting ahead of the others. It was more my fear about my own vulnerability. As it turned out, we did come out to each other and became friendly. Once we came out to each other, we went to the bar for a drink after work on a Friday night a few times, that kind of thing. That was something I didn't do with anyone else that reported to me, but it was kind of a guarded friendship. In a certain way I suppose I wanted there to be a friendship, but I felt it was wrong, because I was his supervisor. I honestly don't know what he could have done to allay my fear that it wasn't good for us to be friends."

On the other hand, Robert Goldfarb told us he was unconcerned about befriending subordinates. "I think some people are afraid to have people who work for them know too much about their personal life because they think that it will undermine their authority in some fashion. Some people operate on keeping people guessing. And part of their power comes from their unpredictability. They don't want people to know them very well. I'm afraid I couldn't work that way; I couldn't function that way myself. I can't make the choice for someone else. But for myself, I like the people who work for me to know me as a human being. One thing that has made me most proud is that I have worked in a lot of jobs and I'm still on friendly terms with an awful lot of the people that I have worked with in the past. I don't mean to be patting myself on the back, but a lot of the times when I leave a job, people say to me, 'You know, I would love to work for you again.' So I must be doing something right. It's not to say that everybody else should follow my model. But for me it makes the most sense to be a complete human being with the people that I'm working with."

Networking with Gay Clients, Vendors, and Suppliers

Being gay can also create a common bond between gay professionals and their clients; we learned of several deals that were made on the basis of such relationships. Networking with vendors or suppliers can similarly result in important benefits.

Andrea, who works in the high-tech industry, credited her network of gay contacts at her company's principal vendor for many of her successes. She said, "At first I thought it was just really nice to know other gay people and to build friendships with people I could chat about work with. Pretty quickly I learned just how valuable my network had become. If I needed a part shipped out ASAP I knew who to call. If I had a technical question, bang! I could get answers. Since my gay contacts worked across a number of departments and levels, I became much more effective in my job. I'm also told that I get better terms and more favors than other customers."

Peter told us, "While I was working in finance, I ran into two clients at a gay bar one night. I was down in Washington visiting two of my accounts. At the end of the day I went to Rascals, which is the after-work bar for business professionals. One was just this kid who I bumped into and started talking to him. We really had nothing in common, but he was interested in talking, so we chatted for a while."

Peter continued, "Then I turned around and saw my client Tad from the other company. It was so funny! Within the same half hour, I ran into two clients. Tad and I had known each other for about a year or so, because he's also a Harvard MBA, and we had hit it off as customer and advisor, but knowing he was gay made our relationship even better. Over the next couple of years we did a couple of things socially together with my partner. The two of us also tried to do a joint venture together."

Cynthia's Story

Cynthia told us she almost never met gay people in her line of work, but recently she met a very powerful gay man. "I've been doing a lot of work for the Clinton administration. So far some of it's been pro bono and some of it's been referral. So I was in Washington talking to some important people in the government, and I was coming back on a plane with a very senior member of the administration who I had heard was gay. We were just chatting back and forth, and I was trying to be as bright and witty as possible, because I wanted him to recommend my firm for some work. At some point he said, 'Oh, this weekend's gonna be tough. I'm gonna put my house up for rent.' I commiserated, 'It's pretty difficult running back between Washington and Boston, isn't it?' And he said, 'Yeah, it is. And besides that, I just had a seventeen-year relationship end.' I said, 'Ooh, that's tough.' So as we were talking, I decided to send a subtle kind of signal that I understood. So, I said something about 'you guys.' Now, 'you guys' can be interpreted any way you want. I mean, a lot of people use it to refer to women too in casual conversation. But he turned and looked at me and said, 'What does that mean?' And I said, 'Whatever you think it means.' He said, 'That was pretty cheeky, wasn't it?' and sort of grinned. So I said, 'I think I'm on safe ground.' So then he started talking about his ex. And I started talking about Ramona. Being in a couple is kind of a useful tool, I find." Cynthia laughed. "Before the plane landed, we were both absolutely out to each other. And this person will be helpful to me. I think the key is that nobody put anybody on the spot. I just said, 'you guys,' and he chose to follow up on it. In a conversation with someone who wasn't gay, 'you guys' would have meant nothing. But with him, it was a signal."

Victor's Story

Victor, who is Black, told us networking with other gay people has aided his success. "I benefit because my gay peers are such movers and shakers that I'm really able get big things done. Others at my company socialize only with people in the company. I've got networks in a lot of companies. My contacts surprise the hell out of them.

"Just to tell you about a few of the HBS gay people I've done business with: Gordon, a Black gay man who does target advertising to ethnic minorities; Joe Steele, a Black gay man who does diversity training; Raphael, a Jewish gay man who is an executive at a major financial services corporation. In fact," Victor continued, "via Raphael, I was able to pitch a really big sale to his company, one that represents over $150 million to our company. Now his company is one of our largest customers. When I landed the account, all of our bigwigs were amazed. They knew we went to business school together. But the real truth was: This is the gay connection. My mentor knows, though. Another thing is that we're in an environment that's heavily regulated, and one of the regulators is in my gay social circle. And sure, I let my mentor know that too.

"Every appraisal review I've gotten says things like 'one of the most creative managers and leaders we've ever seen.' They don't mean 'creative' like 'artistic.' They mean 'creative' in the sense of problem solving. They're not used to people having a peer group where they can go to discuss a lot of distinctive, interesting experiences. Having such a diverse group of gay peers really helps me."

GOING INTO BUSINESS WITH GAY PEOPLE

Several of those we interviewed had gone into business with other gay people. Some, like Frank, had a positive experience. "I went into business with a straight colleague from my previous position, along with my lover, and a guy who wasn't really straight or gay at the time. We hired a lesbian HBS alumna who was also more of a colleague than a subordinate. Now there's just me and my lover. The whole thing has been great. I'm still friends with everyone who left the business."

Marvin was one of the few who had a bad experience. "I got involved with some dishonest people, and I lost a lot of money. I hooked up with these people, one gay and one straight, by networking through a mutual friend who put us together. Their sexual orientation had nothing to do with anything, other than the fact that it was really very comfortable, because obviously it didn't matter about me being gay. But other than that, it was a horrible experience to be involved with something where you really hate the people you're working with. It's very important to be working in a place where you're comfortable, whether it's about your sexual orientation or anything else, because you spend so much time working. I have to admit, that whole experience made me really gun-shy at this point about entrepreneurial opportunities. I don't have the nerve to do that again. Not for a while, anyway."

PARTNERS AND NETWORKING

Whether open or closeted, many of those we interviewed did not include their partners in networking with heterosexual colleagues, subordinates, clients, vendors, suppliers, or customers. Slightly more included their partners in socializing with their bosses.

Some of those we interviewed told us they preferred not to mix business and their personal lives. While for many this assertion was an excuse for remaining closeted at work, for others it meant they really preferred not to spend leisure time with people from work, including gay people. Rather, they preferred to maintain the boundaries between work time and personal time, so as not to have the added pressure of maintaining a professional persona in their time away from work. Another factor, more common among gay men than lesbians, was that some preferred to have a diverse mix of friends, rather than socializing only with other professionals. Thus they did not regularly include gay people from work in their social circles.

Some of the partners we interviewed found networking burdensome whether among heterosexuals or gay people. For example, Gerard's partner is part of an extensive circle of gay people from work. Gerard admits he sometimes resents the constant talk about business because he feels excluded from the conversation. Although he did not attend HBS, he is also a business-school graduate now working in another field. Thus, it is not a lack of knowledge about business that makes him feel alienated at times but, rather, the specific company-related subjects being discussed.

Heidi shared a similar perspective. Despite graduating from HBS and working in business herself, she sometimes wishes she could avoid socializing with her partner's heterosexual colleagues. "My partner does a lot of entertaining of people who work for her. Some of the people you really like, and others you don't like being around—you don't want to have these people over. They talk about their business all the time, and it's kind of boring. I just kind of try to sound interested. There are some people I actually want to do stuff with, and we go to shows and things like that. That's more fun," she said.

On the other hand, some told us they enjoyed socializing with their partner's business friends, particularly if they are gay. David Stokes told us, "This Friday night, a gay attorney and his lover are having us over for dinner. The way we met was, I was down in New Orleans for a seminar, and this man got on the elevator and was staring at me. When we got off the elevator in the lobby, he came up to me and asked, 'Don't you live in Boston?' and I said, 'Yeah I do. Who are you?' And he said, 'Well, I live there too, and I thought I had seen you before at one of the gay clubs.' He introduced himself to me, and it turns out that he was in New Orleans on a legal case. So I said, 'You're a lawyer. Great! I work with lawyers. We should get together and talk.' So we did, and got to be friends." David's partner, Darrin, added, "This guy's lover is really nice too, so it works out really well to have us all get together."

David continued, "And then we're having a couple of other gay lawyers that I know over for dinner in a couple weeks. So there's a network that goes on that's fun. It's not only business; it's social too." We asked David how he met these other lawyers. "The one I'm having dinner with tomorrow night, I met at a gay fund-raising breakfast for a local political candidate. I happened to sit next to this guy that I had seen at Fire Island before. We started talking, and it turns out that he's in-house counsel at a big biotech company that does a lot of litigation, primarily patent litigation, which is what I do. So we got into an extended conversation, and ultimately I suggested that we should get together. So it can happen—you can bring in business from the gay community. You just have to be pretty actively involved in the community activities."

NETWORKING WITH PEOPLE OUTSIDE THE COMPANY

Harvard Business School inculcates its students with the importance of networking, and those we interviewed adhered to this teaching. Most relied on personal contacts with other gay people for their most successful networking experiences outside work. While many hoped to network through gay organizations, a majority were disappointed with the results of their efforts in this area. Those we interviewed also occasionally networked with heterosexual friends; however, we did not study this issue in detail. Gay men reported that on average, over 80 percent of their male friends and about a quarter of their women friends were also gay; lesbians were somewhat more likely to have heterosexual friends of both genders.

FINDINGS

Almost 50 percent of our survey respondents told us they had received career assistance from a gay individual unconnected to HBS, while 25 percent had received such assistance from HBS gay alumni. Seventy-five percent participated in a gay organization outside work (not including the HBS Gay and Lesbian Alumni Association), and 25 percent of those who belonged to a gay group told us they had received some career benefit from that association. This data seems to suggest that gay professionals are well connected, both personally and organizationally, to one another. Our interviews revealed a somewhat less rosy picture.

While a number of those we interviewed confirmed that they received assistance in their career from another gay person, such aid was often fairly intangible. Most often, gay professionals told us, gay friends served as sounding boards for business or career issues they faced. Only a small percentage reported learning of a job, receiving a promotion, or being mentored by a gay individual. Fortunately, personal relationships with gay professionals were often important in other ways. Gay professionals often served as role models during the internal coming-out process of those we interviewed. They also served as role models in the process of coming out at work. Others mentioned feeling less alone as the result of knowing other gay professionals. In contrast, those who had not been able to develop a strong network of gay professional friends often felt less satisfied with their social and professional lives.

The qualitative data from our interviews also revealed far less direct career benefit from participation in gay organizations than our survey led us to anticipate. Gay professionals told us they networked far less frequently through formal organizations than they did through friends and friends of friends, and the most important networking contacts came through personal ties to other gay HBS alumni or other gay professionals they knew personally. Only a small percentage found gay or mainstream organizations personally or professionally rewarding. One reason may be that few had made a concerted effort to network in this way. Most were leery of mainstream organizations, which they saw as exclusively heterosexual. With respect to gay organizations, we found the reasons for shying away from involvement were more complex. Some claim disinterest; others cite fear of being outed; still others were skeptical about meeting anyone worth befriending at a gay organization.

This finding is disturbing, because gay individuals who fail to make use of social opportunities in gay organizations may be depriving themselves of important networking contacts and exposure to new ideas that could benefit their careers. For example, most of the gay men in our study told us their friends were usually people like themselves—other highly educated gay professionals of their own race and gender. Many lesbians and gay men also gravitated toward those who were equally closeted or equally out at work as they were. Thus, they usually received reinforcement, rather than challenge and new suggestions, for how they were managing their identity as a gay person in the workplace.

We believe the best gay organizations create a climate for cross-fertilization between people. Such interaction produces personal and career growth, which ultimately leads to political change. One reason is that formal networks may provide the best opportunity for women and racial minorities to break into friendship circles that otherwise include only white men. Indeed, a number of the gay men we interviewed told us they would like to have lesbian friends but don't happen to know any. Socializing or working together with people of common interests yet different backgrounds can remove this insularity.

In other cultures, like Japanese society, networking with classmates and fellow club members or hobbyists is the norm. In portions of American society, like fraternities, it is also common to socialize with others who share an organizational affiliation. Such networks may be primarily social, but they often provide important career assistance to those who use their networks extensively. In contrast, many gay professionals do not utilize gay organizations for forming such networks. But those who persisted until they found the right groups for them say both personal and professional gains can be the fruit of ongoing involvement. Their experience also shows that those affiliated with organizations are more likely to seek political gains than those whose involvement in the gay community is limited to smaller friendship circles.

Felix argued that gay professional groups are only beginning to meet their potential: "The Greater Boston Business Council and the Boston Professional Alliance in about three years have grown from a few hundred people to seven hundred people each. So you can imagine the demand there that wasn't tapped. The BPA has a dinner for 250 people every month, and it's sold out all the time. The New York Advertising and Communications Network has well over a thousand people. That's a huge number for a locally based gay group. And it's part of a network of other professional organizations in New York that have a few thousand more members. Those are very successful groups in some ways. But obviously, that is just the tip of the iceberg in terms of the number of gay professionals in those cities. I don't know if the answer is more specialized groups or just for more of the right people to start showing up at these things."

Ursula suggested another issue: The existing organizations may not be doing all they can to encourage interaction between members. She said, "My partner and I keep trying to go to the meetings or mixers or whatever they have scheduled. What happens is . . . we'll go for a couple meetings to see if we can strike up some conversations. We've never been too successful. As a result, we haven't really done anything with those groups in the last year. Networking isn't really a critical component for success at my job, but my partner and I really want to do it for social reasons. We just haven't found the mechanism to really get involved like that. Business connections would be nice, but social needs are a priority, because we live in a pretty rural area. We get some social activity at our jobs, but you really want a little bit more variety than just those people that you're working with."

GAY PROFESSIONAL ORGANIZATIONS

Gay business owners we interviewed were far more satisfied with the organizations serving them than the other gay professionals we interviewed. Several were active in starting such groups or helping them grow. In general, gay business owners felt such organizations contributed positively to their lives. For some, that meant a place to discuss professional issues; for others, the opportunity to develop social camaraderie was most important. Some told us they participated in order to give something back to the gay community.

In contrast, those who worked for others told us their needs were generally not being met by gay professional organizations. This is unfortunate, because most of those we interviewed expressed interest in joining such an organization if they felt it could help them in their career. Only a handful of those we interviewed told us they were not interested in doing business networking with gay people outside of work.

Some said no gay professional organization of any kind existed in their city. But most did not participate for other reasons. Part of the issue may be an image problem. The vast majority of those we interviewed had never actually attended a meeting of a gay professional organization; rather, they based their opinion of such organizations on the advice of friends who said these groups were a waste of time.

Yet many of those who had participated in gay professional organizations also reported significant disappointment with the difficulty of meeting other high-level gay professionals, whether for social or professional purposes. Even some who were active in founding or maintaining such groups agreed these organizations often fell short in creating professional networking opportunities.

Most gay men who had attended gay professional organizations felt they functioned best as a social network for single men. For this same reason, lesbians were often critical of these organizations; and many lesbians felt uncomfortable or unwelcome because of the low number of women at such groups. Lesbians were generally more positive about their experiences with the lesbian-only professional organizations, although some also expressed highly negative views regarding the level of professional accomplishment among the lesbians they met.

In general, kudos went to organizations that held a variety of regular meetings. These were either social-only gatherings, those which attracted a large audience to events by sponsoring interesting speakers, or those which provided a semistructured way for people with similar interests to find one another. In particular, our interviewees lauded groups that provided an opportunity for new people to introduce themselves to the group, for job seekers, and for people with job openings to make short business-related announcements. Several also suggested that group organizers could play a more active role in helping people get to know each other.

By far the most common complaint of those who attended such gatherings is that the right people weren't there. Of course, whether the criticism comes from lesbians about the lack of women, or from young gay men about the lack of young gay men, or from senior executives about the lack of senior executives, it poses a bit of a chicken-and-egg problem. In general, we heard, success breeds success. The more a given individual brought friends to a professional gathering, the more likely they were to attract others like themselves to attend.

Our interviewees' cited additional barriers to their involvement with gay professional organizations such as lack of time, lack of need, lack of fit, and inability to find a job despite previous participation.

One reason some were not involved in gay professional organizations was lack of time. But of course, the more interesting and personally beneficial a group appears, the higher priority participation in it is ranked. The fact very few chose to be active in gay professional organizations suggests that for most, participation was simply not a priority.

Only a few we interviewed told us they were uninterested in meeting other gay professionals in their field. Most who worked in gay-friendly industries and didn't participate in gay professional groups told us their networking needs were already being met at work and they felt no need for a gay-specific organization. However, others who worked in gay-friendly industries said they wished there were gay professional groups they could go to, because most of the gay people they met at work were on the design side of the industry, not the business side.

Many of those we interviewed believed the existing gay professional groups in their area were not useful for them because of the specific industry or job function they held. As Hilton pointed out, "New York has many gay professional groups, but none of them seem to be right for me. As a consultant, you don't really know what to join. For a while, I was a member of the New York Bankers Group, which is more for people in finance. I like the idea of being involved in some way in a professional organization and meeting my peers in other places. But I haven't figured out a way to do it yet."

Job Hunting at Gay Professional Organizations Many of those we interviewed were down on gay professional organizations because they didn't help them find a better job. Certain professions, such as medicine and law, had strong groups in most cities, and do regular outreach to students doing their summer internships or residences. But business groups tend to be less connected in this way, making job hunting more difficult.

One group that gained kudos in this area was the New York Advertising and Communications Group. David Schutte, a marketing professional, initially told us he attends the group only for socializing. He added, "I do like the speakers programs though. Even though it's not a springboard for my career, it can be entertaining and even motivating. Because you go there and see that you can be out and be really successful." He continued, "I don't know. There may be more top-level people there than I think. There are over a thousand members, and I know some of them are Harvard MBAs or MBAs from other schools, because they are friends of mine. And I have heard people make job announcements for some pretty decent jobs. But you don't always know who the real professional people are, because there's sort of a democracy of fashion involved there—Levi's and T-shirts and boots, whether someone's making twenty thousand dollars a year or a hundred thousand dollars a year. It's like it's more important to advertise your body than your success. I admit, I try to run home and change into casual clothes. But it's kind of neat to go into a room and see all these gay people in suits and realize they all have professional jobs of some kind. The whole body thing in gay male culture kind of makes business professionals invisible otherwise."

Hope, who is in her late twenties, told us she had benefited from working with a number of lesbians in the Bankers Group. "I'm still in touch with a lot of them. It's been great to know other lesbians with successful careers. And they've introduced me to some of their friends, which has also expanded my social circle and given me some job leads."

Some cities had a mixed gay professionals group and a separate group for lesbian professionals only. Those we interviewed in Atlanta, where the lesbian group has been in existence for a long time, and in New York, where a new group has just formed, expressed satisfaction with their groups. Dita, who is in her forties and lives in New York, said, "Lesbians simply won't go to the existing gay professional groups because there are so many men at them. One or two will show up, but they'll never come back. I'm glad someone finally figured out that all these women really want is to meet each other. I've been really impressed by the caliber of the women at these events. They come from a variety of fields too, which is good whether you're there for business networking or looking for a girlfriend." However, those we interviewed in other cities had more mixed feelings.

Joan, who lives in Southern California, said, "It's like pulling teeth to find out what anybody does for a living. I guess it's a California thing—work isn't the first thing you talk about. But the other reason is, most of these women don't really work in what I think of as business—they are massage therapists, color consultants, or things like that. I've certainly never found a job there."

Gay men sometimes registered similar complaints. Randall said, "Now that I'm in a career transition, I would like to go to a gay professional organization to do some networking. But I have found the gay community is not a good source of things like that. I used to go to the gay professional organization here when I had a job and I wasn't looking. But even so, I never really met anyone who was doing anything that I would want to do or be part of." He lamented, "I haven't been able to figure out how to meet any gay people appropriately placed in organizations to bring me in to do the kind of stuff I want to do. I can meet retail queens with no problem," he said disparagingly. We asked if the group had a job bank as part of its program. Randall laughed. "They do. In fact, I was the one who maintained it for many years. But a lot of jobs listed weren't professional jobs. Or they were professional but in areas that I wasn't interested in. Or where ten years of prior experience in a specific area was required, which I didn't have."

Despite the claims of many gay professionals we interviewed that gay professional groups were no good for job hunting, some had found positions through contacts made at such groups. Marvin was also job hunting when we interviewed him. "I've joined the business organizations here. I've enjoyed them, but I get more out of them socially than I do professionally. It hasn't been that great for networking. I went through the membership book and called a bunch of people and met some of them. I've made a few contacts, but nothing's really panned out." We subsequently learned Marvin found a position through a personal friend whom he met through an acquaintance at a gay professional organization several years ago. Perhaps the benefits of organizational networking aren't always immediately apparent!

Going into our study we speculated that gay professionals might avoid gay professional organizations for fear of jeopardizing their career. This proved to be far less an issue than we anticipated. Few of those we interviewed told us they stayed away from gay professional organizations due to fear of being too out. Rather, most told us, based on either experience or hearsay, that such groups did not attract the other high-level gay professionals they wanted to meet. Instead, many told us, they joined other kinds of gay organizations or made friends through friends and let their networking grow more organically out of these friendship ties.

Gay Political Organizations

About half of those we interviewed participated in gay political organizations in some way. While most participated primarily on the financial level as donors, some had devoted numerous hours to various organizations. In general, those who were most involved were most enthusiastic about the networking benefits they achieved as the result of such involvement. But even those who wrote checks and attended benefits felt they had gotten added value for their money in terms of the group of people they interacted with.

Reasons for Involvement

Many told us they contributed to or participated in gay organizations out of a desire to make the world a better place to live. Several cited the obligation they felt to upcoming generations of gay men and lesbians and the debt of gratitude they felt to those who had made it possible for them to come out.

Personal connections to the organizational leadership were important to some in choosing causes. Lyle told us, "I belong to the Federal Club of the Human Rights Campaign Fund. I like the work they do, and I know Tim McFeeley, the executive director, from Harvard College. The former director of Gays and Lesbians Against Defamation was from Harvard Law; I also gave money there, because I think he gathered a good group around himself."

Personal connections to other contributors or peer pressure can also result in involvement. For example, an HBS group has taken at least one table at the major Human Rights Campaign Fund dinners in New York and Boston for the last several years. In many years older alumni offer current students complimentary tickets as a way of encouraging the tradition to continue.

For some, the impetus for making financial contributions to gay causes was unabashedly social. "You meet a more professional sort of people at the more pricey gatherings," Harvey told us. Amanda agreed. "Most of the lesbians you meet in gay community organizations are the whiners and complainers, not the movers and shakers. At the black-tie dinners, it's more likely for my partner and me to meet women we have something in common with." Yet even for Harvey and Amanda, the ultimate goal for participation was not purely self-interest but a desire to contribute to larger social and political change. "The more successful and accomplished gay people begin to get involved in these organizations, even if it is only financially, the more good these groups can do," Amanda said. "And hopefully you can corral some of their managerial skills to help the organization expand its influence by growing in a prudent and strategic way." Harvey also pointed out that he didn't contribute money just so he could attend dinners. "Sometimes the leadership of these various organizations gets carried away by their desire to get everyone in the community to agree with each other. One thing I think I do to help these groups is to provide some ideological balance. Yes, of course it's important to represent the disenfranchised in the gay community. But it's also important to represent the needs of gay people who have careers and own property."

Some admitted they were more likely to get actively involved in organizations that didn't have the word "gay" in the name. For example, Alvin is active with the Human Rights Campaign Fund but says he probably wouldn't join the National Gay & Lesbian Task Force. "Apart from the political content of the group, I just wouldn't feel as comfortable with the affiliation. With the Human Rights Campaign Fund, I feel I can put it on my résumé; it just sounds like a general civil rights organization." As such organizations become better known, however, this generalization may hold less true. Several younger gay professionals told us they preferred to get involved with groups that had the word "gay" in them. "It's a matter of pride, for one thing," Gina said. "Also, it helps me come out. When I talk about developing the budget for the Lesbian and Gay Community Center, the person I'm talking to hears the name, knows what it is, but doesn't have to react to that right away. We can just go on discussing the issue of fund-raising or accountability. If I talk about doing the budget for 'the community center,' they sometimes want to know which one. Then I tell them. Then they have to react to the news. I think it's better politics to just assume they can deal with it than to put them on the spot like that."

Kinds of Organizations

The causes favored by our interviewees tend to be rather mainstream in terms of the spectrum of the gay community. They are partial to large national gay organizations (Human Rights Campaign Fund, National Gay & Lesbian Task Force or Lambda Legal Defense Fund). They support organizations that strive to present a diverse image of gay people (Gay & Lesbian Alliance Against Defamation, the Gay Games). They are also involved in the national and local electoral process, working to elect Democratic or Republican candidates who are supportive of gay issues (various gay Democratic clubs and the Republican Log Cabin Club). Some are also active in local political or social service organizations (gay community centers or AIDS groups).

Yet, particularly with respect to AIDS issues, some also support more radical or unconventional groups with their money, time, or both. For example, we found gay men from their twenties to their sixties involved with ACT UP, perhaps the most radical of AIDS organizations. Others devoted time and energy to leading safe-sex workshops or staffing AIDS information switchboards. In addition, several of those in our study group left mainstream business careers to take leadership roles in AIDS organizations.

Many lesbians were significant donors and activists in local AIDS organizations. In general, however, lesbians were somewhat less likely than gay men to contribute to national or local gay organizations. In some cases, we believe, this is because the lesbian fund-raising network is less developed than the gay male networks. However, another reason several lesbians suggested is that they feel less affinity than gay men do with the issues traditionally addressed by gay groups, such as battling sodomy laws or police entrapment. In contrast, issues important to lesbians, such as partnership benefits, have until recently taken a backseat in the agendas of many gay organizations.

Kinds of Involvement

For the gay professionals in our study, donating money and attending political benefits were perhaps the most common forms of involvement in the organized gay community. While some might scoff at such checkbook activism, we do not share this view. Most of those we interviewed devoted significant hours and organizational energy to managing their careers and had little personal time or patience for the often fractious world of gay community activism. The fact that they nonetheless contribute in the way they feel they are best able—through their dollars—is a testament to their belief in the importance of such causes.

For a significant number of those interviewed, involvement in the gay community meant primarily friends, bars, dance clubs, restaurants, gyms, vacation spots, and an occasional Gay Pride march. Deciding to attend an event sponsored by a gay organization meant committing, however briefly, to being part of a group with an ideology. This required a level of seriousness in attending the event.

In addition, it is important to realize that until recently, gay organizations could not draw sizable crowds to their upscale events. For some we interviewed, attendance at organization fund-raisers represented the first time they are willing to merge their gay and professional identities. Simply by attending a gay event in a business suit or evening wear made the fusion real to some. As these are also the sort of functions at which it is expected to introduce oneself formally, by first and last name, and it is common to carry and offer business cards, these events can foster another level of coming out for many.

Some we interviewed also contributed more actively to gay political organizations by fund-raising or by taking a role in budgeting or finance functions. Other gay professionals felt personal example was an important component of their political activism. For example, Paul Kowal has served as president of the Gay, Lesbian, and Bisexual Speakers Bureau in Boston, which sends speakers to high schools and colleges. "I think it's important to have businesspeople be a part of that educational process," he said. Nadine, who has also done speakers bureau work agreed. "Some of it is role modeling for gay young people, and some of it is personalizing another kind of gay person than the ones they are more likely to see in the media," she said.

Although we did not investigate gay professionals' involvement in election campaigns as extensively as we asked about involvement in issue-based organizations, we found many we interviewed during local elections were well aware of the various candidates' positions on issues of interest to them as gay people. Some worked as openly gay volunteers on the campaigns of friends who were running for public office, while others were considering running themselves.

Closeted at Work, Closeted in Giving? In general, those who were most open about being gay at work were also the most highly affiliated with gay organizations, whether professional, political, or social. It seems this participation serves as a reinforcement and support system for their often groundbreaking personal strides in the workplace. Yet a few of those who were fairly out at work told us they didn't participate in gay organizations of any kind because they are not joiners or preferred to work in mainstream organizations. And some of those who are quite closeted at work said they made significant financial contributions behind the scenes. Kenneth told us, "I'm in the Federal Club [which honors significant donors] for the Human Rights Campaign Fund, and I went to their dinner for the first time last fall. It was hard for me to decide if I wanted my name in the program or not. I decided no, that I didn't want my name in the program. I rationalized to myself that it was because I just didn't want it to be a high-profile, ego kind of thing. I wanted to be discreetly anonymous. But in reality," Kenneth admitted, "I was a bit afraid to have my name on the program, because of the possible ramifications at work. But this year my name is in there. So I can see myself progressing along in terms of my willingness to be out, both in the gay community and at work. I think it's inevitable for me to come out in the workplace. But I'm not really sure of the timing on that."

We learned from one of our interviewees who contributes significantly to a variety of gay and AIDS causes that his wealthy employer, now deceased, was also a significant contributor. Herman told us, "He did a lot to get AIDS groups off the ground and for gay youth. He also provided money to keep the major gay publications, like the *Advocate,* the *New York Native,* and *Christopher Street,* open for a long time." Herman admits, "It was also a good way to keep them from blowing open his closet. He was terrified that if he were too open he would somehow be thought of by the press as being a spokesperson. And the idea of getting called up about every gay issue coming down the pike is something that he thought was a waste of time. He wasn't a professional politician and didn't want to be one."

Networking at Gay-Organization Benefits We asked those we interviewed about the networking value of participation in gay-organization fund-raisers. Perhaps because they had lower expectations for doing business at these functions, those we interviewed were more satisfied with them than they were with the events held by gay professional organizations. It may also be that gay organization galas attract a better-heeled crowd than gay business functions.

Several of our interviewees told us the most direct personal benefit of attending such fund-raisers was the affirmation that other successful gay professionals existed and were willing to be out at least enough to attend. Moti, a Jewish gay man in his sixties, said, "I've attended several fund-raisers for Lambda Legal Defense Fund at the home of a gay friend in the Greenwich, Connecticut, area. He and his partner have been together thirty-five years. They are active in the gay community and the local political community—the mayor, the governor have both been to their rather palatial house. They're doers, they're makers, they're shakers, they're breakers. They just do everything you can think of. They're involved with the ballet; they're involved with the opera; they're involved with the city; they're involved with the gay movement; they're involved with politics." As Moti points out, "But that's just one couple. Imagine a hundred gay people, men and women, at one of these benefits. And they all live in suburban communities there. I never imagined anything like that when I was a kid. In fact," Moti continued, "two of the men I've met at the parties have had a child with one of their close friends, and they are all raising the child together. The kid's about seven years old now. The last time I saw him, he was a toddler, sitting on one of his daddy's shoulders at a very elegant Christmas affair. It's quite a different world from when I was a kid."

For some of the younger gay professionals we interviewed, fund-raisers also served an important function in bringing gay professionals together. "Even if I don't meet more than a few, it's important to me to see a room full of achievers," Shawn said. "At the gay professional organizations you tend to get more of the young people who are up and coming but don't really earn that much yet. At pricey fund-raisers you are more likely to meet people who have accomplished something."

Charleen posited that things are changing in terms of lesbian involvement in gay political organizations. She told us AIDS has played a sad but significant role in her ability to network. "I find I meet the serious lesbian professionals in two places. One is at the hospital or the memorial service for our mutual gay male friends. AIDS has been a major factor in my industry, and a lot of my friends have died. So I meet a lot of people at the hospital, both lesbians and gay men. It's really a painful way to meet. But it happens a lot, especially in my age group. Because all of these men who were party boys in Fire Island in 1981, their time is up now.

"The other place I meet lesbian professionals is at fund-raisers for the Gay and Lesbian Community Center or the Human Rights Campaign Fund. HRCF has gone from being 5 percent women to being almost half and half in New York. The women have just sort of come in because the men are dying. The board at the Gay Community Center is like that too. It's radically different than it was, say, five years ago."

GAY SOCIAL ORGANIZATIONS

In general, our interviewees were more actively involved in gay social or cultural organizations than they were involved in gay political organizations. As a result of their more committed involvement, they told us, they made numerous friends, some of whom were also useful professional contacts.

A number of those we interviewed participated in gay sports or outdoor-activities organizations. Several helped produce the Gay Games and Cultural Festival held in New York City in 1994, while others came from all over the country to compete in a particular sport. "I enjoy the camaraderie of doing sports with other gay men," Philippe told us. "I know that quite a few of my professional friends are also participating. It's a way that ordinary gay people can meet, as well as get their chance in the spotlight." He continued, "I think the Games are a good opportunity to present a wholesome side of gay life to the straight people who read about the Gay Games in the media or see all of us in town for the two weeks, or for the kid who thinks he might be gay."

Quentin is involved in a gay sports-and-social group in Milwaukee. "I complained to a friend of mine that I don't really like the bars and that whole scene, and he suggested I get involved in this group called Gamma." He laughed. "It's funny, because the president turns out to be another Harvard MBA. The group is quite active—they do ten to fifteen things a month—and has 225 gay men in it. It began with a touch football game once a year during the fall over a decade ago, and it grew to include touch football in the fall, volleyball in the winter, water skiing in the summer, and hiking. The core of the group is a sports orientation." Quentin continued, "Meeting the president of the group was important for another reason—he's the one who told me about the gay and lesbian bulletin boards like America Online, and that's how I got in touch with the two of you and ultimately with the HBS Gay and Lesbian Alumni Association."

One of the most common organizations gay professionals joined was the local gay men's, lesbian, or mixed chorus. Most who participated joined after business school as they were in the midst of seriously developing their professional careers. For a number of those we interviewed, a chorus was the first gay organization they joined, the most meaningful personally, and a source of networking for several.

Paul Kowal, who worked in advertising and then for a corporation early in his career, told us, "I ended up serving on the board of the chorus for several years, and singing with them for several years when I lived in New York. That's what really got me solidly out to myself and into the gay community. It became harder and harder to be in the closet when you were standing on the stage at Carnegie Hall as part of a gay men's group." Paul laughed.

Gay choral events regularly bring together groups from around the country, and this can also aid networking. Beverly told us, "The Gay and Lesbian Choral Association is a huge organization with about eighty gay choirs in the U.S. I went with my women's chorus to a national conference, and that's how I found out two of my business-school classmates are gay. Neither of them ended up being there, but their names were in the program. So I reinitiated contact and we all met up again at our HBS class reunion, which was great. Now that I've moved to the same city as Rupert, I have ready-made friends here, all due to the chorus connection. And I've ended up doing business with Leo."

MAINSTREAM ORGANIZATIONS

Less frequently than they joined gay organizations of any kind, gay professionals participated in mainstream organizations. Some joined in the hopes of meeting other gay people; others joined specifically for career reasons.

Finding Gay People in Mainstream Organizations

Don Bickford told us that he joined a mainstream church because he knew the minister from college. Joining had an unexpected result; he found himself networked into an increasingly large circle of gay peers. "My coming out to myself kind of coincided with my getting involved in Riverside Church in New York, which had a very public and very visible gay/lesbian caucus. Discovering the church I was getting involved in had a task force and welcomed gay members really helped facilitate my coming out. That felt like a comfortable group to get involved with to meet other gay people. That was a positive experience for me, and fairly soon I got active in the leadership of that group and I started attending some meetings in the New York City community where representatives from many different groups would come together."

He continued, "One of the things that happened in getting involved in the community council was, I discovered that there was a Harvard gay alumni group. Their treasurer was a B-school graduate, and he knew about the B-school group, so it was through him that I learned about the Harvard Business School gay group, which I also got actively involved with when it was first forming."

Mitchell Adams also met gay peers through a mainstream church. "I joined the Church of the Advent in 1979. I started going there because it was at the base of Beacon Hill, and it was one of these parishes where there were a lot of gay people. It was a great place and I made many friends there. I really needed to meet other gay professionals at that point in my life, so it was very positive. As a matter of fact that's how I met my partner Kevin."

Robert Goldfarb attends B'nai Jerushan, a mainstream synagogue in New York affiliated with the Conservative movement. "There are about thirty of us gay people there, and we participate fully in the services and the ongoing life of the congregation as a whole. We also have our own separate meetings. I really feel at home there. It accomplishes a lot for a straight congregation to be able to see that there are accomplished gay people in their midst. Instead of perpetuating whatever stereotypes there are about the kind of work that gay people do, it allows them to see that there are gay people in all sorts of workplaces. In my synagogue there's really no surprise left in this. But the really heartwarming thing is that it is happening in other congregations that are not necessarily that progressive. Gay synagogues are important too, but they are usually so liberal religiously, they don't meet all of my needs. If you're lucky, you find a synagogue, as I have, that is fully accepting of being observant as a Jew and being out as a gay person. If there are other gay Jews there—even better," he said.

Those who joined public membership mainstream organizations for career purposes were generally satisfied with the results and were often out there. Such organization tended to be local real estate organizations, chambers of commerce, Rotary clubs, and other similar groups related to their field or community interests. In contrast, those who participated in minority community organizations or women's groups tended not to be out in them.

BUSINESS NETWORKING IN PERSONAL FRIENDSHIP CIRCLES

In contrast to our interviewees' dissatisfaction with most gay organizations, we found most quite satisfied with their circle of gay friends. Such friends often served as an important source of emotional and professional support. Whether by role modeling, conversation, or business leads, gay professionals reaped the benefits of participating in rather extended friendship networks of others like themselves.

Sebastin was part of a large nationwide network of friends and acquaintances. "I travel a lot, so whenever I'm in a city, I try to connect with people. When I'd go to Chicago, there are five or six people I would always call. Last time they brought together fifty of us. Two nights ago, there was a party of about sixty-five people in New York, and about twenty of them were from out of town."

While many others were part of smaller circles, most gay men we interviewed had a group of ten to twenty gay friends and a larger circle of acquaintances, most of whom were other gay professionals. Even those who had many other kinds of friends generally sought close ties with at least a few gay professionals. Lawrence said, "Part of the reason I think I've gotten closer to two particular guys in my circle of friends is that we're the only ones who can relate to each other's careers. We work long hours and make more money, and we also have kind of different stresses than our other friends have."

White gay men in their thirties who lived in large cities usually had the largest circle of professional gay friends. But even some of them had complaints—in particular, those who were single. Lance told us, "New York is very arts driven. Everyone I meet is a dancer or a model or whatever, and there's a limit as to how much in common you can have with someone like that."

Simone, who is single, also told us she had a hard time meeting lesbian professionals she could relate to. "I see myself as so different from most lesbians. I haven't met a lot of women who are successful, attractive . . . I've found lesbian professional organizations are the worst to meet women. They have the most boring women with no social skills, women who get on these career paths that are really boring, but they stay, because they are making some money, and they feel somewhat powerful . . . But it's like, get a life. They don't have any women like me or my lesbian friends from HBS who have really interesting lives, people I feel empowered around. I find that self-confidence breeds more self-confidence, and unfortunately, most lesbian professionals I meet don't have any."

Usually, at least for gay men, hooking up with a few gay professionals was the entrée into meeting many more. Lesbians could also take advantage of this network if they were willing to be one of the only lesbians in a given gay professional social set. But many lesbians, particularly if they were in a relationship, told us they preferred to spend their social time with their partner or other lesbians.

Several of those we interviewed told us about discussing specific business deals within their gay professional social circle. Rich revealed, "Maybe I'm operating under a false sense of security, but I do trade confidences with other gay men in my business. For instance, I'll have gay friends who call me and say, 'Hey, this is the latest on that company that you're going to deal with.' It's stuff that they probably shouldn't tell me. But because we have this other bond, they trust me. They trust that I won't use the information in a way that will get them in trouble."

Rich told us, "I really do think that the gay network is very small and very tightly knit. So any time I go out to another town or something or other, I just ask any of my friends, 'Do you know anybody who lives in that city?' At this point I'm sure I know someone gay in almost every city across the nation. You know, once you know one person, then they hook you up with others. Like if you're out on a business trip and you want to have fun at night. It works for jobs too, I think. You know, I get a lot of calls from friends of mine who want my advice on their next career move or on a company that I know something about."

Gay Networking and the Job Search

Several told us about receiving assistance in their job search from gay friends. Seth learned of a job opening for his most recent position from a man he first met on the subway and later ran into at a gay bar. "He didn't make the hiring decision. But he certainly told me about the position because we were both gay." Seth added, "I also received career assistance from a gay person in getting into business school. A good friend looked at my essays, just like somebody who was gay had looked at his essays. I think gay people really look out for each other because of that bond we have."

Nichole also learned of her previous position through a gay personal contact. "In the past I tried to use the gay community for job networking without success. So I stopped trying for a while. But recently I've reached out and found that things are changing. Maybe it's my perception that is changing, or maybe the people I know now are more hooked into the business world. Anyway, a friend of mine is the one that I heard about my most recent corporate job from."

Robert Goldfarb, who was looking for a position in the classical music industry when we interviewed him, said, "I'm calling all my gay friends for referrals. People do move around a lot in this business. So you always look for referrals about things that aren't officially posted from people you know in the business. And it has been helpful to talk to my gay friends, as well as my straight friends, of course. But with the gay friends there is the extra opportunity for networking, precisely because there is that extra thing we have in common."

HBS Gay Alumni Private Friendships The common bond of being gay does not always translate into friendship or a job offer. We expected to hear that closeted individuals might avoid hiring gay people who they were afraid would be too out, but we did not hear any such stories. Rather, other issues played a more prominent role. Stephen told us, "I was a finalist at one company to be director of stores, and the president was a gay man. I didn't get the job. I think he ended up hiring a woman instead. I think, in the end, I was far more educated than he was, and that intimidated him."

Perhaps for this reason, for many we interviewed, other HBS gay alumni were an important part of their social and professional networks. In Chapter 2 we explored the value of formal organizational affiliation with the HBS gay student organization or the HBS gay alumni association. Those who did not or could not take advantage of such organizational ties also managed to come out to one another on campus and after graduation. Informal networks of gay alumni exist at many other business schools as well.

Generally, friendships formed among classmates often led to greater involvement in larger gay circles during school and afterward. In some cases, the friendship started out as a sexual one but quickly became more—sometimes lifelong friends or partners. Having common business interests, some continue to network or do business together.

Valerie recalled, "When I met Denise, we were at a Merrill Lynch recruiting dinner, all gussied up in our suits. I had been introduced to her one time before, but I considered myself straight at the time; I had never been with a woman. At one point during the recruiting briefing, I remember, she turned to me and said something like, 'You're beautiful.' " Valerie laughed. "You know, I don't care who tells you you're beautiful, if someone tells you you're beautiful, you like that person." They ended up in a sexual relationship during school. Although the two women are no longer together, they have remained friends and are part of a bicoastal network of other HBS gay friends. A number of gay men we interviewed also told of meeting classmates through a sexual pickup, usually at the gym or library, which often led to ongoing ties.

No lesbian we interviewed recalled meeting another lesbian classmate in a gay bar. One reason may be that with far fewer women per class, there are fewer HBS lesbians than gay men. Another seems to be that lesbians at HBS went out far less often than their gay male counterparts. Even those lesbians who described themselves as big party animals told us they never ran into any classmates. Ariel said, "I went out a lot, and considering there's only a handful of bars lesbians ever went to, you'd think I'd run into someone eventually. The truth is, I'm kind of jealous of my male gay friends, who had a much larger social world of other gay men than I did at business school with other lesbians."

In contrast, many gay men we interviewed had met classmates at a gay bar. Additionally, many gay men continue to run into other HBS alumni, at bars or gay events long after graduation, who provide an on going source of networking; lesbians recalled meeting only gay male classmates in this way.

While those who belonged to the HBS gay student association and the HBS gay alumni association reap many networking rewards, those who meet classmates privately also report career benefits can follow. Ira told us he recently visited a classmate who works in the entertainment industry. "There's a pretty strong group of gay HBS alumni in West Hollywood. When I was there I ran into a group of about seven or eight guys from HBS at this bar called Revolver. Most of them are in entertainment, of course. A whole bunch at Disney, a whole bunch at the studios. Probably four or five were from within a year of each other at business school. The others were a bit older or a bit younger, but they had all hooked up with each other and I know some have helped each other job-wise."

• • •

"Networking" is not just a tired buzzword from the 80s. Instead, networking is a way to leverage being gay in the workplace. Networking with other gay people at work and outside of work can be very valuable to gay professionals. Whether assistance comes in direct job leads or in general advice about approaching various career issues, the gay professionals we interviewed found these ties important. We expect that as gay professionals continue to be more willing to be visible, they will find the opportunities for networking continue to expand. Gay employee groups and gay professional organizations increasingly are looking for ways to facilitate networking and as a result are attracting more members and gaining strength. Additionally, interaction among these groups as they come together in umbrella organizations is leading to important gains for gay professionals in companies of all sizes.

Gay professionals at all levels are learning the benefits of having a network of gay friends, confidants, supporters, and informants throughout their companies. Whether they network with people above or below them or with people laterally throughout many different departments, these contacts will continue to gain in value. This trend will not go unrecognized by management.

Perhaps the greatest gains yet to be realized are through networking with gay clients, vendors, and suppliers. Such ties will yield benefits to individuals' careers as well as to their companies. Also, as more gay professionals come out at work, they will facilitate further networking through their visibility.

Chapter 8

Success

How successful are gay professionals?

Before we can adequately answer that question, we first have to define success. For many of those we interviewed, success means meeting personal goals or being on the road to achieving them. Others measured success in comparison to the achievements of their peers. In general, those who saw themselves as successful said they had achieved financial security, satisfaction in their personal lives, and a sense of accomplishment in their career.

WHAT IS SUCCESS?

In our initial interviews we asked gay professionals if they were as successful as their heterosexual peers from business school. It seemed like a simple enough question. But often the answers ran for hours! What exactly is success? our interviewees pondered. In whose eyes? On what scale—monetary wealth? personal happiness? Most gay professionals felt success has many components. There is material success; there is success relative to power, prestige, and a corporate title. We heard that for many, success involves working at something challenging and enjoyable. For most, success includes personal happiness in relationships—with a loved one, friends, and family of origin. And, importantly, we found that success includes self-acceptance as a gay person and being comfortable with how one manages a gay identity in the workplace. For many, success also includes a sense of making a difference by working for a cause or helping others.

In our interviews and our survey, certain components of success continued to surface: *traditional measures of success,* including net worth, compensation, power, control, and influence; and *success and happiness,* including self-acceptance as a gay person, management of gay identity at work, balance, flexibility, and doing good for others.

We discuss the components of success in this chapter. But first, to set the background, we present some findings on class and discuss our methodology for measuring the success of gay professionals.

Class Background and Status

In our interviews, sex, race, religion, health, or politics were not taboo topics. Money and class were. We often asked the gay professionals we interviewed rather personal questions about work and personal relationships, sex, HIV status, race, ethnicity, or politics. But we felt somewhat constrained in asking pointed questions about money or class face-to-face. One way we obtained information on these subjects was by broaching the question of career success, which many understood to contain a financial component, although this was not the sole criterion sought by our questions. Moreover, in our written questionnaire, the option of anonymity allowed us to get answers about income, wealth, and other related topics.

The relationship between class background and nonmaterial benefits such as power, influence, prestige, and leisure time were difficult to measure. In addition to our survey, which attempted to quantify some of these data points, we relied on a subjective assessment of our interviewees' own self-reports. Interestingly, we found that those who came from the most privileged economic backgrounds often opted out of pursuing high-powered careers or living lavish lifestyles. While some heterosexuals from wealthy backgrounds also spurn the opportunities afforded them by family connections, we believe gay professionals do so at a higher rate. Otherwise, we found no correlation between sexual orientation and pre-HBS class status.

We also asked interviewees about their partners' professions, which gave us a sense of their income, and although we generally did not verbally seek information on their net worth or class background, some volunteered this information. Again, the written questionnaire provides the largest basis for information on this subject. As we expected, partners usually earned less money and had less wealth than those who went to HBS: Only 8 percent of the partners earned over $100,000, and only 14 percent had personal net worth over $250,000.

We were interested in the impact of economic disparity on couples' relationships, although we found it much easier to ask about racial, ethnic, or religious differences, and monogamy. Sometimes we could infer certain insights about how financial differences affected the relationship by tracing the career path of the HBS graduate and his or her partner. For example, we found many instances where a non-HBS partner moved to another city due to the academic or career opportunity of the HBS partner, while we know of only one case where the reverse occurred. When both partners attended HBS, the considerations were different, and the partners were likely to take turns following each other.

Benchmarking

Outsiders see HBS students as uniformly privileged, both academically and financially. HBS graduates themselves have in part created the myth of an HBS degree as a Golden Passport that magically transports its holder into realms of undreamed fortune. Both these perceptions obviously have a component of truth, but they can gloss over important differences. Not all HBS graduates are equally successful financially.

Both companies and individuals benchmark, that is, compare themselves to others or to their own goals in trying to measure their success. Companies measure their success in terms of market share, stock price, ability to raise funds, and their bottom-line results. But whereas business performance can usually be tracked quarterly, gathering data to benchmark individuals can be very difficult.

For alumni of the Harvard Business School, it is relatively easy to compare oneself to others. One way is through the bimonthly *HBS Bulletin,* which is sent to all graduates. Its primary purpose is to help classmates stay in touch. Each section of ninety people has a column filled with tidbits of career and personal information. Most of this is provided by the individual, but occasionally class secretaries add their own gossip to the narrative. Usually the column announces promotions, new business ventures, weddings, and births. Many describe their new responsibilities in some detail and purposely attempt to make their lives as glamorous as possible. Thus, the *Bulletin* is a major vehicle by which alumni compare and measure their success versus that of their peers.

In addition to the *HBS Bulletin,* HBS mails out class-reunion books every five years. Each graduate has the opportunity to send a picture and a half-page of narrative or reflections about career, family, and personal interests. Since the rate of contribution is very high, HBS alumni often have a very accurate understanding of what their classmates have achieved both personally and professionally. Many also attend the reunions, which supplement their information. For members of the HBS gay alumni association, the quarterly newsletter and yearly get-together perform a similar function. In addition, the social circles of HBS gay alumni often intersect. Thus personal social networks help keep the gay professionals we interviewed posted on others' career changes, accomplishments, and personal relationships. Finally, on occasion, gay people from HBS read about one another or their heterosexual classmates in newspapers or business magazines. Thus, those who care to benchmark have many ways of doing so.

TRADITIONAL MEASURES OF SUCCESS

Quantification is important to HBS graduates. While almost all of those we interviewed hastened to add that, for them, success equaled personal happiness, they were still eager to hear how gay professionals stacked up numerically in comparison to heterosexuals. We have several ways of answering that question.

Relative Measures

The first is a relative answer. In our survey we asked: "In comparison to the careers of your heterosexual classmates of the same gender and race, how successful do you consider yourself?" Thirty percent believe they are more successful; 43 percent say they are equally successful; 26 percent say they are less successful; while the remaining 18 percent don't know (and probably don't care). We were extremely heartened to learn that the majority, 56 percent, of gay professionals saw themselves as equally as successful or more successful than their classmates.

Of course, our findings do not mean gay people don't need laws protecting them from discrimination at work. It simply means that much of this particular group of gay business professionals has found ways to overcome barriers to success. Perhaps the true meaning of our findings is that most gay professionals are determined to succeed despite the obstacles in their path.

In our survey we also asked people to rank their happiness on a scale of one to five (with one being "extremely happy") in their present job, company, and career progress. In all three areas, a large majority—almost 85 percent—ranked their happiness at a one or two on the scale.

Confirming our survey findings, the majority of those we interviewed said they were more successful than or as successful as their heterosexual peers. Most mentioned a combination of the most commonly desired components of success: self-acceptance, balance, happiness, income, rank in the corporate hierarchy, flexibility, and doing good for others. As few people focused on just one criterion of success, we will not discuss how successful they were in each of these areas. Rather, we present a chorus of voices of various ages and from various industries.

We hypothesized that those who were most successful at HBS and closeted at work would be the most successful financially, while those who were most out about being gay would be the happiest but least well off. But there were no hard-and-fast rules about financial success, although ambition and willingness to work hard usually played an important role. Some people who were out were wildly successful, as were some who were closeted. Some who were average in their scholastics were very successful financially, while some who graduated at the top of their class pursued other forms of success besides material success. However, we did find that those who were most out were the happiest with their lives in general.

Less Successful Some felt being gay has negatively affected their career success. Tammy told us, "If you're closeted at work, people don't get to know you, so you become alienated from your peer group, and you don't really like your experience there. In the closet you get paranoid. You lose confidence, and it's much more difficult to succeed."

Those who felt less successful often attributed it to their lack of self-confidence or low self-esteem. The mere fact they admitted this to us was remarkable. People in business are often guarded in admitting their shortcomings; just as in sports, you don't want to reveal your weakness to your opponents. However, they were frank with us because they hoped their truth would help others. Because gay people face hostility and negative sentiments throughout society, it is important to realize that the repercussions can be significant to individuals and their careers.

Today, we found, fewer gay professionals are self-selecting out of mainstream careers. Gay professionals are choosing their career paths based on what they want to do in life and based on what is inherently interesting to them. They are aware that being gay may make their road more difficult, but they are not giving up their dreams for success in their business careers. Many still fear being gay can hinder their career, but we believe that the future they face is promising. More and more young gay people are entering the business world, and they are not going to settle for second best.

Equally Successful Many said that as far as they could tell, they were equally as successful as their classmates. The longer HBS alumni are out of business school, the more most leave typical MBA career paths in investment banking or consulting to pursue other opportunities, and gay professionals are no different. Duane, who is in his mid-thirties and works in the media industry, said, "I feel I'm equally successful. I mean, I don't feel like there's anything different about my career progression compared to my straight friends. I'm comfortable that I would have left consulting even if I were straight. It was not a sexuality issue; it was a career-change issue. And I'm quite happy with the position I ended up with. I've ended with a great job. Actually," he reflected, "I've landed a better job than some of my peers who came out of consulting." We asked Duane why that was. He replied, "I had a little good old-fashioned luck. These kinds of jobs only open up at certain times, so you have to be there when that happens. I happened to be there and have the right skills match. So in a career sense, I feel pretty much on a par with other people I went to business school with. If I went back to a business-school reunion, I wouldn't be embarrassed, nor would I be gloating. It would be, 'I'm at peace with my career progression at the moment.' "

MORE SUCCESSFUL Had we not written this book, we probably would never have had the chance to tour as many beautiful homes as we did. We often joked that if we took a video camera, we could have made a film called something like *Lifestyles of the Rich and Powerful Gay and Lesbian Professionals.* Probably only real estate agents have seen the diversity of property that we have from coast to coast. In addition, many of those we interviewed had their brushes with fame, if they were not well known themselves. In one interview we were told we just missed Barbra Streisand leaving the building. As we arrived for another interview, Placido Domingo was leaving a meeting with the man we interviewed. And in the business world, we interviewed some corporate household names. The common threads of being gay and being from Harvard helped us open the doors to their glamorous and wealthy gay lives.

Ross, who works with a firm that helps companies find top-level managers, told us he was more successful than others at his company because of his HBS connections. "As a headhunter, I pretty much rely on the Harvard network. I'm able to get into the major investment banks because I call up the people I know from school and say, 'You'll never believe what I'm doing now. I'm a headhunter. Do you know of any positions that are open or do you know anyone who's looking to move?' And they say, 'Oh I'm looking,' or, 'I know of something,' or whatever. It's real easy. I would never have gotten a Harvard degree to become a headhunter. But I'll tell you, having those contacts are priceless. My boss hasn't been able to penetrate those kinds of accounts on his own. But since I've been at this firm, we've moved into new offices because the business has just been incredible. Absolutely incredible. I can call these people up just because I know them."

Yet many who seemed highly successful to us pointed out that success is still relative. Whether their basis of measurement is their peers or their personal goals, what counts as success for one person may be less important to another. Several also pointed out that, even if they were more successful than their average classmate, they were still not the most successful. For example, Aaron said, "I'm about to get this next promotion, so I'll be president of one of the operating divisions. I can only think of a handful who are at my level by their mid-thirties. So I think I've done better than most of my classmates." But he added, "There are people in my class who have done phenomenally well. One guy in my class is senior vice president and CFO of a major corporation. And there are some people who are in investment banking, and those kinds of things, who are just richer than shit—but they have to be investment bankers to get it." He laughed.

When we asked Bill if he was as successful as his heterosexual peers, he replied, "It's really tough, because it depends on how you measure success. If you're talking about a position in a corporation or financially, yeah. I think most people would say a manager with a salary in the six figures is very successful for somebody two or three years out of business school." But, he said, "I know investment bankers who are making a lot more than me. Like one friend is already a vice president and just got an $800,000 bonus. So he's doing phenomenally well."

Absolute Numbers

The second answer to the question "How successful are they?" comes in the form of absolute numbers. At the Harvard Business School, gay people seem to be successful in greater numbers than their heterosexual peers. Through our survey we learned that 9 percent of our group were Baker Scholars—that is, ranked in the top 5 percent of their class. So the percentage of gay students who were Baker Scholars was larger than the percentage of heterosexuals who had achieved that distinction.

We are not alone in recognizing that there are high-achieving gay MBA students. Jonathan Rottenberg told us his employer, Monitor Company, a consulting firm based in Boston, now offers domestic partner benefits to attract top gay graduates. They perceive the downside of failure to attract gay professionals to be that their competitors could be hiring the best and brightest.

Total Compensation Another quantifiable measure of success is total compensation. While Annette was studying at Harvard as an undergraduate, she recalled seeing a greeting card at the Harvard Coop Bookstore. It was a "Happy Reunion" card. On the outside it had a drawing of middle-aged couples at a class reunion having cocktails. One alumnus boasted,

"I made six figures this year." Inside it read, "After you graduate, salaries replace report cards." So just like grades, salaries are generally not disclosed except by the boastful few. But salaries can be misleading if a significant portion of a person's compensation comes in the form of shares, options, or bonuses.

While HBS does not compile compensation statistics of its alumni, the average salary for a 1990 graduate exceeded $55,000, not including signing bonuses or school-loan payments, which brought total compensation closer to $100,000. Of course, compensation varies by industry, with consultants and investment bankers earning the most and almost everyone else earning far less. So we knew industry choice would play an important role in compensation—and that years out of school could play an important role in earning power. But we also knew that many HBS graduates, both gay and heterosexual, step off the high-earning career track to go into business for themselves or to pursue a more balanced life. Thus we need to tally the numbers in aggregate as well as to analyze them more closely.

Income level was somewhat less tied to age than we had anticipated. A number of gay professionals in their forties and older were using their cushion of savings to strike out in business for themselves; this accounts for some of the lower figures among the older businesspeople. Some of the young graduates were tremendously successful in traditional MBA jobs, such as investment banking and consulting; this accounts for their high incomes. Some of all ages worked in gay-friendly industries, which are traditionally lower paying than other fields.

In our 1990 survey we found 21 percent earned less than $50,000 a year. Most of these alumni were recent graduates, had recently gone into business for themselves, were semiretired, or had taken positions in education or the nonprofit world. Forty-three percent of our respondents had a total annual compensation between $50,000 and $100,000.

The rest of our respondents were living examples of why many choose to go to business school. Twenty-nine percent earned between $100,000 and $250,000—including some who had been out of business school only a few years. Six percent received between a quarter of and half a million dollars. In addition, a few individuals earned over $500,000 a year.

Most people would perceive the high-wage earners as extremely successful, but some of the high earners felt they were at a disadvantage in comparison to their peers. Of those earning between $100,000 and $250,000, the majority felt they were equally as successful as their peers. Yet in this range the number who felt less successful was greater than the number who felt more successful.

Those making over a quarter of a million dollars a year felt more successful than their peers. Of those making under $100,000, 41 percent felt equally successful, 31 percent felt less successful, and less than 5 percent felt more successful. It is also interesting to note that, throughout all of the ranges, about 20 percent said they had no idea how successful they were compared to their peers. Similarly, in our interviews, a number in all professions told us they didn't care about how well their peers were doing; they measured their successes against their own objectives. For most in this group, nontraditional measures of success were usually paramount. For example, Warren said, "What is success to me? That's a tough question. Self-actualization, I guess. How fulfilled do I feel? What kind of sense of accomplishment do I feel about some of the things that I have done? While some of that is career related, certainly not all is. Do I compare myself to business-school classmates? Not much."

Net Worth Because we anticipated that some of those we surveyed would choose lower-paying jobs, semiretire, or retire after accumulating a nest egg, we also asked gay professionals to reveal their net worth. Over 9 percent had a net worth of over $1 million; another 9 percent had accumulated between $500,000 and $1 million. Eighteen percent had a net worth of $250–500,000; 19 percent had a net worth of $100–250,000; 26 percent had a net worth of $50–100,000; and the remainder had a net worth from negative to $50,000.

Most of those who had negative net worths were recent graduates still paying off their student loans. In 1990, a student attending Harvard Business School could easily spend $60,000 on tuition, housing, cases, and other living expenses. Graduates who had a negative net worth had put all of their assets on the line to go into business for themselves.

Some of those who have extremely high net worths may have inherited it. But in our interviews we learned that at least some had amassed their wealth as a result of their own business endeavors as senior managers or business owners or by having equity in their companies. Most with a net worth in the middle of our scale multiplied their savings by investing it in real estate, stocks, and bonds; this resulted in significant appreciation over the years.

Based on the information available, the wealth of many gay professionals seems to be in line with or exceed their peers', and gay professionals enjoyed many of the fruits of success. For some this meant savings, a nice place to live, a vacation home, a fancy car, or exotic travel; for others, the time or money for non-work-related activities or the ability to retire early to pursue other interests. In particular, our interviewees who had no dependents agreed they were able to enjoy a fairly high standard of living.

Power, Control, and Influence Another measure of success is to quantify the resources and people gay professionals manage. We found most gay professionals had power and influence over a significant amount of dollars but not over a significant number of people. This corresponded with a question on our survey to rank the components of career success. Autonomy and responsibility ranked the highest, with total compensation following, while level in the hierarchy and number of subordinates were in the middle of the criteria.

Another straightforward measure of success is the dollar value of the revenues that gay professionals are responsible for. The majority of gay professionals in our survey are responsible for between $100,000 and $5 million worth of revenues. At the high end of the scale, 13 percent were accountable for over $20 million. Thus, we found, gay professionals control a significant amount of money. However, given the types of business they go into, most didn't also manage large numbers of people. Rather than seeking careers in large corporations or staying with consulting or investment banking for the long term, most gay professionals sought careers that are not people intensive. Fewer than 12 percent manage more than twenty people. In fact, 73 percent of our respondents had five or fewer people reporting to them.

THE ROLE OF BEING GAY IN ASSESSING SUCCESS

Except for the necessity to come out, at least to oneself, much of the foregoing could have been said by heterosexuals. Yet many of those we interviewed said being gay has had an important influence on the way they think about success. Some said being gay made traditional forms of success more important to them, while others said the opposite.

Traditional Success More Important

It would be an understatement to say that those who go to Harvard Business School have ambition. Simply by going to Harvard, they manifested a drive to succeed in at least some traditional areas. Thus, it is no surprise that a number sought success in terms of income, amount of responsibility, level on the corporate ladder, prestige, and power. Many were hard-driving people who put career first.

But Harvard didn't make them that way. Rather, they had to be that way to get admitted. Both at college and at HBS, they pushed themselves to excel academically. Many also sought recognition as leaders in their student government, campus organizations, and athletics.

For many gay people, the drive to succeed in traditional ways is particularly important. For some, it is a way to sublimate feelings of being different; by throwing themselves into academics or career, many tried to convince themselves that their gay feelings were insignificant.

For others, achieving traditional forms of success was a way to prove to themselves and to the world that being different would not stand in their way. Roberta Lasley told us, "I knew I was different from a very early age. In fact, I was marked as an illegitimate kid in a town where everybody knew it, and it was something to be ashamed of. So figuring out I was a dyke when I was a teenager was nothing. I was trained for that. I'm talking about knowing how to handle inner pain. I learned about being excluded in ways that are unfair—because you are illegitimate, because you are fat, because you are a lesbian, because you're whatever the hell it is. Those are the kinds of things that really forge your own personality. The only place you can go is inside, to hear your own voice, because those outside voices are not your voices—they're not real. From a young age, I knew one thing—I was going to do whatever I had to do to get out of that environment."

Drive like this to prove oneself can sometimes be seen by others as having a chip on one's shoulder. Mordecai told us he thinks this drive to succeed is common to many gay people. He said, "I think the typical gay man's profile is, not into sports and they got picked on. Well, I did get picked on as a kid all the time. So I look back on it and I think, Yeah, I do have a chip on my shoulder that says, 'Fuck all you straight people. I'm going to be more successful than all the rest of you. I will do whatever it takes. I will rely only on my sheer brainpower to make sure that it happens. And I'll stop at nothing until it does happen.' When I look at my gay friends who are successful, I think that's why they're driven." He added, "I think a lot of straight people have a hard time understanding. They think it's some kind of superior attitude, but I think it's because they don't understand the context that we're coming from. Every day we're reminded that we're different. And we feel we have to prove something —to ourselves and to other people."

In explaining why traditional forms of success were important to her, Delores said, "I think that everybody needs to find their own spot and their own comfort level. But I personally believe in playing to win. And if you're not playing to win, not competing to win, then maybe if that's fine with you, that's fine. But, for myself, I believe in playing to win. Being gay is just one of those factors that works against you. You just have to play as strategically as you possibly can."

Traditional Success Less Important

Many we interviewed said that being gay gave them more choices about whether or not to pursue traditional forms of career success. Betsy prefaced her remarks by saying, "As an officer of a *Fortune* 50 company,

I'd have to say I'm more successful than my heterosexual female classmates; I'm in the top third, for sure. Lots of my female classmates dropped out—either totally dropped out to raise families or semi dropped out to take on small business or consultant sorts of things. I think that's a function of society's expectations for women. If you're married and you're not wildly successful, you don't have to keep competing. Whereas a Harvard Business School guy can't drop out—at least if he's straight, because he has to work to support his family. Gay guys have more choices, I think. I wouldn't be surprised if there aren't too many gay men in the middle either. My perception is that a fair number of them have opted out of the rat race too, because they don't have to stay in it."

Cory agreed. "Unlike most of the guys I went to business school with, I don't have a mortgage in the suburbs and wife and kids to support. Or in the case of a lot of them, an ex-wife and kids to support too." He laughed. "My partner and I both make a pretty decent living, so I don't feel the same pressure to earn money. I don't have country-club friends to impress. We like to travel, but that doesn't require tons of money—it requires time." He concluded, "So I have different priorities than a lot of people I went to school with."

Barry Salzman told us, "The way I quantify success has changed a lot over time. In the beginning, the way I quantified success was the status and prestige of the job. It was about how I was succeeding in the eyes of other people. That's why I left McKinsey and went to a leveraged buyout firm—it was incredibly prestigious, and I was earning an unbelievable fortune at my age, more than I ever imagined. They were giving me equity in their deals, too." Barry told us, "In the eyes of other people, everything was great. But once I had all that, I realized everything I had accomplished was based on the standards of everyone else. Having succeeded by those standards gave me an enormous amount of confidence to be able to put that aside, because no one could ever say, 'He's gay and that's why he couldn't make it.' "

Barry told us being gay allowed him to change careers at a relatively young age. "Had I been straight with two kids, I would have gone to another job that paid me half a million dollars a year very quickly. For the most part, being gay, we can afford to take some bigger risks with our lives. Certainly I can afford to start doing things that I really want to do . . . for reasons that make me happy as opposed to needing the stability or the money. Once I realized that, it was real easy to give it up."

Success as Happiness For many gay professionals, success in terms of money, power, or prestige was not the primary goal. Instead, success meant achieving a balance between other priorities and earning a living. These individuals were unwilling to sacrifice personal happiness in the short term to achieve conventional forms of success.

For some, free time was a priority. Having worked in fast-paced careers ourselves in New York City, we know it's hard to maintain balance in your life when you are spending seventy to ninety hours a week at the office or with clients. From our peers at business school, we knew the most lucrative careers routinely demanded those kind of hours, and a number of the people we interviewed stayed out of these fields for that reason. It turns out that gay professionals also seem to value their private time more than their heterosexual peers. Fifty-six percent of gay professionals said they spent between forty-five and sixty hours a week working, a very reasonable amount of time for business-school graduates. Another 19 percent were working only about twenty-five to forty-five hours a week, a fairly low number of hours. Of course there were some workaholics, about 17 percent, who spent from sixty to ninety hours toiling away. Another 10 percent were not working at the time they filled out the survey; some were retired, others had stopped working due to AIDS, and some were unemployed.

Those who were working twenty-five to forty-five hours a week also told us they were somewhat less committed to their jobs and far less satisfied with their careers than the other gay professionals in our survey. Yet they also told us they valued time with their partners, friends, and outside interests over career goals. In our interviews a number of them told us, "the only thing money can't buy is time."

Others sought to do work that they love with people they enjoy or to contribute to a cause they have passion for. Arlene was in the midst of a career transition when we interviewed her. She told us, "I used to think success was about getting a high-level managerial position and managing lots of people. It's nice to have money. But it's really more important to me to be doing work I enjoy and work I love. It's hard to find work that I'm passionate about and to sustain that passion. If you do, I think that's what makes you successful. A mistake I made in the past is not remembering that. Accepting situations I wasn't that interested in, staying when the passion wasn't there, or losing my passion for what I was doing—those were not successful situations. My goal now is to be more proactive about doing things I really care about."

Paths to Success The gay people we interviewed were successful in many fields and in various aspects of their lives. The paths they took and the time it took them was highly individualized to suit their abilities, drive, and priorities. Yet those we interviewed who considered themselves most successful also had a common method for achieving their goals: They had high expectations of themselves for achieving their short- and long-term career goals; they were comfortable with being gay and had a strategy for managing their gay identity at work; they did their homework before entering a particular company or industry; and no matter what their current job, they had an exit strategy.

Who are those people who see themselves as having it all—financial success and comfort with the way they are handling their gay identity at work? Those who felt most successful, both financially and as gay people, suggested two ways of being selective when choosing career paths. The first is to choose an industry or job function one is passionate about, no matter how conservative the industry. The second is to select an industry or job function based on one's perception about how gay people are treated there.

A majority of the gay professionals we surveyed chose the first route, saying their sexual orientation did not influence their current job or industry selection. In our interviews we learned that most of this group had originally intended to be fairly closeted at work, although some were so determined to go into the field of their choice they had no intention of letting being gay stand in their way.

The others, almost half, who said their job choice was affected by their sexual orientation, gave several criteria by which industries and employers can be judged. In addition to companies or industries known to be gay friendly, gay professionals looked for companies that offered an objective basis of measure or a collegial environment, or a small company where people get to know each other as individuals.

Objective Measures of Performance

Whether closeted or open, gay professionals often prefer companies that measure employees in quantifiable ways. If their results can be tallied at the end of the day, quarter, or year and compared to their peers' results, they always know where they stand. Michael used this as his criterion for selecting his career and employer. He said, "I work in investment banking, which is as conservative as it gets. I came out to myself near the end of business school, and because I was still uncomfortable with being gay myself, it didn't occur to me that I could find a gay-friendly business environment. So my approach was to find a job that I would enjoy doing and one where the judgment about whether I was good or not was not subjective. If I was good at it, it would be clear. And if people figured out I was gay before I came out to them, it would be a nonissue because of my quantitative performance.

"That ruled out a lot of alternatives. I did not see going to work for a *Fortune* 500 company, rising for fifteen years, and then being shunted into a know-nothing, retire-early job—without the gay issues ever being discussed, but just because I didn't have a wife who was friendly with the wife of the guy who ran my division. I was also concerned about environments where it was sort of an amorphous team environment, and so consulting was out. First of all, I don't think I could be a good consultant, but even if I was, I was afraid of working as part of a big group where my contribution could not be measured. I was afraid it would be very easy to suddenly discriminate against me by assigning me to low-level clients, people that were hard to work with, on things that didn't get you the right kind of background. I could see working my heart out at the beginning and then being shut down later. I was determined not to get in that situation.

"Happily I found a job where you build a base of clients so that you really have measurability. After your first couple of years, you switch from salary plus bonus to a compensation system that is tied to how much money you bring in. Because the criterion for success is so clear, the computer just ranks who's the best—there's no subjective aspect to the bonuses. For me that is a very safe and comfortable environment, and I feel comfortable being gay there, even though I'm not out to anyone." He added, "It's also a comfortable place to be because of the office environment itself. Everyone has a little franchise that competes with each other, so there's a certain professional distance and lack of human interaction that characterizes the culture. It's not like everyone else is going to dinner at each other's houses. No one is doing that. No one makes personal calls. It's very much come to work, crank it out, and go home."

Those who were selectively or completely open at work also lauded investment banking and other finance-related industries for their quantifiability. "If I see I'm getting shafted, at least I can sue or leave," Kim said. Julian told us, "I remember when I was at business school, we were advised to get jobs where our accomplishments are measured, not evaluated. I thought that was very good advice, especially for gay people. If you're in a situation where your productivity is measured, then there's no chance for anything discriminatory to creep in."

The trouble with using this criterion alone is that few jobs are measured purely objectively. Even in investment banking, where an important part of job performance is measured by the amount of money made for clients, few people work in isolation. Most positions require some teamwork, entertainment of clients, development of relationships, and personal interactions. In other finance jobs, some criteria can be quantified, but promotion and compensation often have other, highly subjective criteria. Some banks and investment banks stress the team approach and require team members to participate in significant amounts of after-work socializing. Thus they have more in common with collegial environments. In some of these firms, the approach is truly collegial, while in others, macho forms of bonding are de rigueur. Thus it is important to research the particular company or division before pursuing or ruling out a career there.

Collegial Environments

Many gay professionals feel that by working in a place where teamwork and cooperation are part of the ethos, they will be able to develop a close bond with their coworkers. Whether they come out at work or their sexual orientation remains unstated, they hoped the "get along to get ahead" mentality would protect them. In addition, gay professionals said, the expectation of building personal relationships meant they could make allies. Thus, if they encountered any problems being gay, their allies would come to their defense.

A number of gay professionals were drawn to consulting for this reason. The goal of working in teams with other highly intelligent people is to utilize the skills of each individual to the maximum benefit for the group. Therefore there is a strong incentive for everyone to accept one another and smooth over differences. Of course, many cautioned, competition was alive and well even in collegial environments, and some felt being gay could be used against them. Interestingly, those who were most open felt they enjoyed the most success in collegial environments. Perhaps the stress on closeness and teamwork meant that those who were more reserved had a harder time fitting in.

But we also found a wide range of collegial environments. There were those where all of the team players and their wives were expected to go off on weekends together. Other teams were governed by more polite, arm's-length interaction. Naturally, where discussions of personal lives were more infrequent, and closeted gay people found it easier to stay safely hidden in the closet. The type of teamwork can vary within an industry, a company, and between departments. Only by interviewing the people with whom you will be working can you determine the type of environment in any potential job.

Small Companies

A significant number of gay professionals we interviewed sought to work in smaller environments. They perceived such environments as more collegial due to the more frequent personal interaction among everyone. In addition to the opportunity to make allies, they felt they had more opportunity to become significant players in a smaller firm. As big fish in a small pond, they would more likely be able to call some of the shots, both professionally and with respect to company culture. Not only would the value of their contributions insulate them against possible discrimination, but they would be able to set the tone regarding how they wanted to be treated on a day-to-day basis.

Zev has come to the conclusion that being out and being successful might best be achieved in a small-business environment. He told us, "I used to be really driven to rise to the top of a big company. That's really started to change since I've started to come out to myself." Reflecting on his choices if he were to leave consulting, he said, "I'm not sure I can accomplish the goals I want in the corporate environment. In some companies, being gay—whether I was closeted or out—would stigmatize me from the word 'go.' In some, I could rise to a certain level but no further. So I'm really starting to think more about the small to medium-sized companies where I can have more control and freedom. If I had a personal relationship with coworkers, it might be easier to be out."

While small companies are less likely to have policies or benefits that explicitly treat gay people equally, this is not always the case, because owners of small companies often have greater flexibility in tailoring their policies and benefits to meet the needs of their employees. Again, in every case, it comes down to the people involved. Only by doing their homework were gay professionals able to determine their likelihood of fitting successfully into a small or medium-sized organization.

Commission Positions

For some, sales positions that pay a commission are a happy compromise between starting their own businesses and life as a corporate manager. In these positions they had considerable flexibility and control of their destiny, without the risk of capital. Some went into venture capital, stock brokerage, executive recruiting, and real estate sales, just to name a few. For some, these quasientrepreneurial opportunities also provided an opportunity to test the waters of striking out on their own. For others, such a position in a small firm was virtually akin to owning their own company. This was the case for Chuck, who said, "If I were straight, I don't know if I would be more or less successful. Depending on how senior you get in the ranks, they like to see a spouse by your side—but I don't see myself in that arena. Those aren't my aspirations. My aspiration is to be able to do what I want when I want to do it. With the job I have now, I said, 'Okay I'm gonna leave today, and that's that.' Last week, I took Wednesday and Thursday and Friday off, just because I wanted to. I didn't have that flexibility before. And fortunately I'm earning more money than I did when I was traveling 150,000 miles a year. To me, the trade-off is in the prestige. At one point in my life, it would have been important for me to say, 'I'm a senior person at a major corporation.' But now I laugh at myself that I ever thought that. I mean, who really cares? I would prefer to say that I work for myself and I call my own shots. I'm shocked that I'm saying this now, because coming out of HBS my goal was to go to the top and all that. But now I don't care one way or the other. Going after the brass ring of the corporation is not for me anymore."

Exit Strategies and Entrepreneurial Aspirations

Many gay professionals who worked in mainstream companies had an exit strategy or entrepreneurial aspirations. Exit strategies were their backup plans. If they ran into barriers hindering their career progress or a hostile environment that was making their lives miserable, they had a plan to move on. In practice, those who left mainstream positions were almost always closeted. Rather than standing up for themselves in a conflict situation, they chose to leave. However, we also found that openly gay professionals had exit plans. For some, these plans were a backup strategy. "If I don't keep getting promotions and pay raises, I have the option to leave," Brandon told us. For others, mainstream positions were a stopping point along a long-term goal to be entrepreneurs. Openly gay professionals and those who were closeted were little different in this regard—many at all points along the spectrum of openness wanted to have their own business.

Exit Strategies

Fear of the lavender ceiling was probably the most significant reason people in mainstream business careers had exit strategies. After surveying their industries and companies, looking for gay role models in upper-level positions, many saw only obstacles and no role models. That's when they began to develop a backup plan. Just because they had exit strategies, it didn't mean that they were any less loyal or committed to their jobs. Rather, exit strategies were a psychological and financial safety plan if their current jobs came to a dead end. They hoped to continue to rise in their current industry, company, and profession, but in case they encounter a career dead end, they feel the need to have an alternative lined up. For some, this means simply keeping the résumé current and in the hands of recruiters. For others, this means actively cultivating contacts and networking in the alternative area.

Although Devin was openly gay at work and continued to be promoted, an exit strategy was always at the back of his mind. He said, "When I had this discussion with a friend at my firm, I told her that I firmly don't believe there is a glass ceiling here. Yet in the back of my mind, I really wonder, Would I ever be promoted to a partner level? It's hard for me to say what the main reason is why I question this. Is it because I'm openly gay, or is it because I'm a really expressive person in a buttoned-down industry? I think those factors are intertwined to people where I work. I mean, how do you separate those things that are such a part of my personality? Do I worry about it? Does it depress me? No. When I was talking to my friend I said, 'Look, if it ever comes to the point where I'm convinced that I'm not getting promoted because I'm gay, then I don't want to work there anymore.' And I won't be upset about that. I'll just go somewhere else. I have enough confidence in myself and my abilities that I know I can get a good job anywhere else. So, if it ever does get to that point . . . and in the back of my mind I think it might, then I'll just find some other place where being gay and being a fun person is not an issue."

A few intended to exit into other mainstream businesses that they hoped would be more hospitable than their present positions.

Reilly told us, "I've always thought that I'd wanted to run a big company. But you move up the hierarchy; it's much less of a meritocracy. If you don't look like everybody else, it becomes questionable whether you'll ever make that last step. If you're not going to be able to make the last step, is it worth investing the twenty years to get there? I feel this way partially because I'm gay, but more because I've come to realize that I'm not willing to stick it out for twenty years of corporate life, even if I had been heterosexual. The opportunity costs are too high and the lifestyle cost is too high. I prefer something where I have a lot more control over my life. I hope to be able to make a lot of capital so that if I decide that I really don't want to work anymore, I can stop. The corporate life doesn't really ever give you that kind of capital, so you've got to keep working."

Jay told us he was accumulating skills and contacts before exiting corporate America for entrepreneurial opportunities. Employed by a large and successful corporation, he intends eventually to strike out on his own. But he said, "I can see several years in this job before I ever even worry about what the next step is. It's enjoyable, and there are growth challenges. I've got fifty people in my combined departments, so managing something of that size is going to allow me to work on my management skills. I can see spending several years in the position I'm in before I worry about where I go next."

Others intend to pay off school loans and establish a financial security net for themselves before leaving. Some also hope to line up investors or partners before they exit. In this way they are little different from their heterosexual peers. Being gay, however, added an extra dimension—many were acutely conscious of having less time to make it work on the traditional career track. "I'd say five or so years out of business school, you have to be all the way out at work or start making plans to leave," Tim said. "If you're closeted, you are certainly going to face a stalled career. So I want to make sure I'm out of there before then, because I don't see myself trying to make it work as an openly gay person in a traditional field."

Walter told us that instead of exiting, one option for him was to feel comfortable in a no-growth position. He said, "One of these things I've figured out in the last few years is you get this kind of brainwashing in business school that you need to be a *Fortune* 100 CEO; that must be your goal in life, a priority, if you came to the business school. Now I sit back and say, 'I have absolutely no desire whatsoever to be a *Fortune* 100 CEO.' It just doesn't look like a fun job, by and large. They're too big, they're too unwieldy, they're too bureaucratic as organizations. I think you would lose a lot of freedom along the way if you go the corporate route." He admitted candidly, "I'm still grappling with, Where on the way there do you choose to stop? It's clear to me I'm not planning to run the race to CEO. But it's hard to know where along the way you decide you're comfortable. Most of us have been achievers our whole lives. At what point do you say, 'Gee, I kind of like it here, and I could just hang out'? Even internally, it's not that easy to define success in other ways than being able to write about a promotion in the class notes."

However, Walter was a relatively rare exception. Most gay professionals who encountered a career dead end or saw one looming on the horizon decided to exit the mainstream. With so many gay people leaving the corporate pipeline to the top, we wondered, who would be left to break through the lavender ceiling?

With so many gay people opting out of the mainstream corporate route, it will be longer before gay people are visible at the top of corporate America. Before significant numbers of gay people break through the lavender ceiling, there will have to be many gay people who make it to that level. With only a certain percentage who are willing to keep playing the mainstream game, it may take many years before this happens. Until then, gay professionals who reach the pinnacle of success in mainstream careers will continue to be few and far between. Although many told us their sexual orientation has nothing to do with their decision to pursue noncorporate alternatives, this doesn't seem strictly true in every case.

Rather, gay professionals often have a different definition of success than heterosexuals because the struggle to come out to themselves and to others means personal happiness is often more important to them than money, power, or glory. At a minimum, they often have personal lives and social interests that are different from their heterosexual peers'. Thus they are often more willing to explore alternative routes to career success.

Entrepreneurial Aspirations

In our survey we found many gay professionals who have been able to achieve a dream held by many heterosexual and gay Harvard graduates alike—owning their own business. Most said they wanted to be in control of their own destiny, work at something they are interested in, and structure their work schedule in accord with their other priorities in life. In these ways they are similar to their heterosexual classmates. Thus, most said they did not go into entrepreneurial ventures solely because they are gay. Many admitted, however, that being gay was an important factor in the ultimate decision to go into business for themselves. A number added that having no dependents gave them the flexibility most of their heterosexual classmates did not have. Finally, they said, having a social circle that was more diverse than their heterosexual peers' meant they also enjoyed more emotional support for their decision.

Very few of our interviewees had gone into business for themselves directly out of business school. Generally they felt the need to gain experience and contacts by first working for someone else. Additionally, many had significant student loans to repay or didn't have the capital to start up their businesses right away. Many who were in business for themselves told us they selected their first jobs with the goal of positioning themselves for their own endeavors down the line. Just a few felt forced into working on their own as the result of reaching a dead end in mainstream careers.

One third of the people we surveyed were self-employed at some point in their careers. Twenty-seven percent of these gay entrepreneurs went into business for themselves somewhere between one and four years after graduation. Forty-one percent worked five to nine years first. The remaining individuals waited for ten or more years before striking out on their own.

We interviewed gay entrepreneurs in a wide variety of businesses, including advertising, travel, investment advisory, financial advisory, strategic planning, competitive analysis, management consulting, software development, gift wholesale, retail, radio station ownership, and information services. Many said they went into business for themselves as a way to be in control of their own destiny and write their own rules.

Guy said, "I'd worked for a *Fortune* 500 firm before I went to business school, and I saw that if I wanted to run the company, there were certain things I had to do. Not because people were forcing me to, but there were things you just had to do, like go to the country club and things like that, and I didn't want to do that. I self-selected out of that. If you wanted to run the company, you had to spend time running divisions in small towns in the Midwest. You know, that could be great if you have four kids and you want public schools, but if you're gay, it's not that attractive. So there's sort of a self-selection process." Guy added, "After doing consulting as a summer job at HBS, I thought, it's really going to be stifling, despite how much money they make. They work all the time, then you have to go to certain restaurants and spend all your time with people that you're stuck with at work, not people you select on your own. I didn't find it all that attractive, which is why I started my own business right out of school."

Flexibility and happiness were two very strong goals for gay entrepreneurs. We asked Leon: If he were to sit down with the next graduating class, what type of advice would he give them? Leon told us, "The things that seem really important when you leave business school are irrelevant two years later. What your business-school classmates think of you . . . two years later it really doesn't matter, to tell you the truth. So accepting a prestigious job because you can impress your section mates is not a very good criterion on which to base your job selection." He continued, "I remember reading an article in the *Harbus* written by one of the professors, which said, 'You're not as flexible as you think you are.' So in terms of geography and other aspects, don't take anything that you won't be happy with. A job is only one aspect of life. Of course, it depends on what sort of person they are, but I would recommend that they run their own business. It's a lot less security and possibly a lot less money, but there's a lot more flexibility."

Barney, who also started his own business soon after graduation, recommended getting some experience with a large firm if you have the kind of personality that can handle it and if you're the kind of person who can leave that kind of security. He said, "If you can, go work for someone for three or four years. Go ahead and take a job out of B-school, make some money, and then go out on your own." Reflecting on his own experience, he said, "I would have been better off if I had worked for McKinsey for two or three years. I could have paid off some loans, put some money in the bank, had a nice wardrobe. Whether I could have said good-bye is another story. I'm not so sure I could. Once you get into it, it's very hard to get out."

We asked Barney, "Of the people that you know who went out on their own, do you view them as being successful financially?" He said, "From what I can tell, they seem OK. In the long term, happiness is what matters anyway."

Being able to be out at work was important to many gay entrepreneurs we interviewed. Paul Kowal told us in 1993, "I now have a small consulting firm with a couple of million dollars in revenues and twenty employees. It wasn't necessarily easy, but it wasn't like the first time I was trying to start a business and it just wasn't getting there. I've been out at both of my businesses to the other people at the company. Now I am out to a number of clients as well, including my largest client, Philip Morris. There may be some risk to being out, but I've decided it doesn't matter

—I would rather be hired for who I am than trying to hide. I think it's pretty easy for me to be out. Once a company hires us, our work speaks for itself." We asked Paul whether he felt being out was a barrier to attracting new clients. He responded, "You know, I have a relatively small company. We have a limited client base, and there are a lot of potential clients. So if there are people who can't deal with it, I can go find other business. If you're in an organization, if there are people there who have a problem with you being gay, I think that's a harder position to be in." When we spoke to Paul in 1995 his company had grown to 91 employees; he attributed much of the growth to marketing to the gay and lesbian community.

One-Person Operations Many of those who owned their own business were in one-man or one-woman shops, usually serving as consultants or financial advisors. For some, this was a way to make a living while looking for something more interesting. Elroy told us, "Even though I have been able to come out to some of my clients, I have found I don't really enjoy independent consulting." Now, looking for other work, he said, "I may end up doing it again for a while, but that is not what I really want to do. It's a viable alternative that I've got, though. It's something I know I can do. It's just that I don't have the passion for it. It's not what I want to be doing in five years."

Others have found working for themselves meets their needs perfectly. For some this is because they can be out. Sam told us he had always been closeted at work until he started working as an investment manager to a high-net-worth individual. "She was the one who first made me realize, 'What's the big deal?' This was back in the 1970s, and she was very cool about it. We were on a long flight one night, having dinner on the plane and talking about everything in the world, and she brought up the names of several men in the cultural circles she moved in. She asked me if I knew they lived together, and I said I did. She laughed and said everyone else did too." Sam explained, "This was at the time I was living with my first lover. I used to bring him to various society events, and he always used to sit separately from me. But no one was fooled. So my client took another sip of champagne, and asked, 'Who's Winston, by the way?' Well, I came out to her, and the rest of the flight we talked openly about everything. It's been great since."

For others, it was easier to be closeted when they worked alone, which they cited as an advantage of self-employment. Colin said, "In my information service, most of my business is done on the telephone or by mail. I've never met any of my clients face-to-face. So there's no natural way for being gay to come up. If it did I'd talk about it," he claimed. "But the truth is, it's hard to come out in that context." Wanda agreed. "I fly in, work for a few weeks all day and night, make a presentation, and fly out. There's no time to go to social dinners or anything like that. When I'm working, I'm working pretty much full-time."

Barriers to Entrepreneurial Entry

For some of those we interviewed, lack of capital was the reason they had not yet become entrepreneurs. Bert said, "Right now, I'm just working on getting rid of my Harvard debt and building enough capital so I can eventually start my own firm. After that, I can go wherever I want and set up where I want to be."

Yet for many, this was not the main problem. Barry Salzman, who is in his mid-thirties, told us, "When I resigned from my last job, my intention was to find a small business to buy. I have some equity capital committed, and my intention was to embark on an acquisition search. I've just started it, and it's been challenging, because there's a lot of garbage out there. Also, I don't want to relocate, and finding something within commuting distance of New York has been fairly tough. A lot of the attractive-sounding opportunities are out in the Midwest or on the West Coast." He told us, "In the interim I've just been doing freelance consulting for some of my old companies. But that is sort of frustrating, because it's really not what I want to do, and it's a very easy trap to fall into. So I'm just doing that in the interim. But every time I put on a suit and tie I feel like I'm selling out." He laughed.

Oscar, who is in his late twenties, also felt confident about his access to investment capital. "I think if my partners and I had a plan, the financing part of it would be the least of our worries, really. Maybe that's being a little naive, but I don't think it is. We have contacts through a quasi–business-school connection. Haven't you found out that it's a real small world where everybody sort of knows everybody at this level? I know some people who are not direct business-school contacts, but it's people from HBS who know other people."

Many others who intend to be entrepreneurs also told us they were waiting to figure out what they want to do. Heidi explained, "That's the challenge right now for me. Once I have a path, boom, I'm there. I can name six people from my HBS section that I would go into business with, but none of us has an idea of what they want to do. Right now we're all trying to come up with a great idea."

Some who tried the entrepreneurial role have concluded they are better suited to corporate life. Asher told us, "I went through a period where I wanted to be in business for myself. But that experience made me realize I'd rather work for a company and get a paycheck and benefits, even though it's very glamorous to think about being your own boss. I found I don't have the emotional makeup to worry about where the income is going to come from."

• • •

In our interviews with gay professionals, we learned success means many different things. For most, success meant achieving their own goals. While most of our interviewees also compared themselves to others based on traditional measures of success, they said it was more important to feel happy in their work and in their life outside of work. Perhaps for many heterosexuals as well, the 1980s emphasis on power, money, and control are diminishing. But for gay people, the struggle to come to terms with their own gay identity and to figure out how to deal with being gay at work means the question of possible trade-offs was always on their minds.

Whether in mainstream businesses, gay-friendly industries, or as entrepreneurs, those we interviewed had a strong desire for balance in their lives. No one defined a successful life as having a lucrative career with no regard for their personal lives. While some were willing to sacrifice their personal life for a few years, most were unwilling to do this for long. In the short term, some made a priority of succeeding in material ways, but an equal number said their first priority was to seek work that was inherently interesting or to do good for others. For many, the needs of loved ones or community interests were a priority, and their primary career concern was to have enough time and energy to do things outside of work. Most hoped they could eventually have it all—money, fun, and time. In this respect, they are very similar to their heterosexual peers.

A unique concern of gay people in business was the possibility of discrimination. Whether they were out or closeted, this issue loomed in the background for everyone we interviewed. Why spend a lifetime striving to reach the top of an organization when someone else could deny them the recognition they deserve? As a result, many went into business for themselves or pursued careers in gay-friendly industries. Even those who sought success in the mainstream defined their goals and arranged their priorities with an awareness of discrimination. Many who pursued mainstream careers did so to glean experience they could put to use in another setting or in their own business. Although some hoped to be the first to break through the lavender ceiling in the mainstream, most had well-thought-out backup plans.

For many, entrepreneurial ventures were an attractive first choice or backup plan. Autonomy, control, flexibility, the possibility of striking it rich, and the ability to be out at work made independent opportunities attractive.

Whether you intend to be closeted or out in your business career, there are lessons to be learned from those who have already been there. The gay professionals we interviewed did not have a road map. Their methodology was to try for what they wanted and have a backup plan in the event it didn't work out. To us, the results are cause for optimism. Given the personal and professional successes our interviewees have achieved, we believe gay professionals today have many choices in terms of industry and how out to be at work.

While gay business professionals in retail, marketing, and advertising may be most visible outside their companies, there are successful people in investment banking, consulting, and finance, as well as some of the more conservative industries throughout corporate America—and not all are in the closet at work. It is our hope that this research will be useful to gay people of all ages in planning their careers—it certainly has affected our own thinking. We now have reason to hope that gay professionals in all fields can achieve all the success they aspire to.

Due to social and economic forces, the business world is changing. Specific companies and industries are also changing, particularly in response to openly gay business professionals. Many companies are waking up to the contributions their gay employees have made, and some are beginning to hire and promote openly gay professionals, a trend we believe will continue. Thus we have every reason to believe gay businesspeople, whether open or closeted, will continue to have an increasing range of choices in planning and achieving their professional and personal goals.

A NOTE ON MENTORS

Many gay professionals told us having a mentor was a significant factor in their success. Their mentors gave them career, political, and personal advice and helped them to move up the corporate ladder or to find new opportunities.

FINDINGS

On our survey we asked: "Has any person in your present or former work organization after HBS taken a greater than usual interest in guiding or assisting you in your career?" Thirty-seven percent felt their boss had. Nine percent felt another higher-up at work had. Three percent felt a coworker had. Another 3 percent had received assistance from someone else in the organization. Just under half answered no.

Those who had mentors told us they had a significant advantage in the workplace. Mentors are individuals who take a personal interest in helping others along their career paths. They give advice, insight, and leadership on personal and professional matters. Most often, mentors are senior people in the same company. But mentors can also be successful people in other companies or even other industries.

Gay professionals without mentors often said they wished they had one. Not having mentors means that no one higher up, more experienced, and more wise is looking out for their careers. No one is giving them little inside tips and strategies on the fast track to the top. No one is taking them to country clubs and posh lunches and introducing them to key players. Some gay professionals have succeeded in business without the help of mentors. But unquestionably, the road to success can be easier with the help of mentors.

Whether or not they have mentors, many gay professionals we interviewed seek to mentor others. While some say they mentor all kinds of subordinates, a number spoke specifically about their desire to help other gay people. In doing so, they hope younger gay professionals will go even further than they have.

Benefits of Having a Mentor

Career Advice It is often said that two minds are better than one, and that certainly is the case with career advice—mentors can be important sounding boards. When Randy was in the middle of an important career decision, he was fortunate enough to meet a gay mentor. He said, "I bumped into a guy in the gym who was wearing a T-shirt from a company I was thinking of working for." Randy introduced himself, and Vito ended up opening up a world of opportunities for him. "I had narrowed down my job search to wanting to be in investment banking and had been thinking about three or four firms, and two of the firms were Goldman and Solomon. The first or second time I was at the Metropolitan Health Club, which is the gay gym in Boston, someone was working out there who had on a long-sleeve shirt—and one sleeve said Goldman and the other sleeve said Solomon," Randy said with a laugh. On the back, the T-shirt had some real estate deal. I was just blown away. So I went up and introduced myself.

"Vito told me he worked at Goldman and told me to call him when I was in New York." Randy took him up on the offer. "We had dinner and talked about my career options. It was great for me to meet someone who was gay in investment banking. He helped reassure me that just because I was gay, I wasn't forced to go into retail or something like that," Randy said. "Talking with Vito was enormously helpful to me, just because it let me realize that there was a gay person in investment banking who was having a good career. I think most people that you talk to who are gay in investment banking will say that by far the most important thing is performance, and that whether you're gay or straight doesn't really make that big a difference. That's what I've found, anyway."

A number of those who had mentors said they relied on them for career advice. For Trent, a mentor was a frequent sounding board for career decisions before attending HBS when he worked for a large agribusiness company. He said, "It's a very large family business, and the person who hired me is a partner who married into the family. He had a very big role early in my career path. I talk to him maybe once or twice a year now that I'm at business school."

Not everyone we interviewed took the advice of their mentors, however. Colleen told us, "I was seeing a woman whose father, Ned, was head of a major securities firm. She was out to her father, and he knew we were a couple. In fact, he treated me like a son-in-law or daughter-in-law. I visited him at work one day to ask for career advice. He suggested, 'You have the right background for it—have you considered public finance?' " Colleen told us, "Although I had government experience and an HBS degree, I really hadn't thought about it. So I said, 'No, I really haven't.' "

"Ned said, 'Well, why don't you do some interviews around town, but there's definitely a place for you here.' " Colleen said, "I was a bit taken aback by his offer, but thought it was a good opportunity to ask him directly, 'What's it like to be gay on Wall Street?' He said, 'Well, I don't really know, but I fear for my daughter, and in many ways I fear for you too. But if you are here, I will fear for you less than if you are someplace else.' "

Colleen said, "At the time I was also thinking about going to work in the broadcasting industry. Ned advised, 'I suspect you will find many more like-minded and sympathetic people in that industry. But if you want to work on Wall Street,' he reiterated, 'don't hesitate to work here.' " Colleen told us, "After getting a bunch of recruiting letters from various investment banks, I finally decided I wanted to work on Wall Street. But being stubborn, I decided that I would not go to work for Ned's firm. I decided that I should do it on my own."

"In many ways," we said, "this is kind of the mentor most gay people would hope for—to have a top insider watching out for you. How could you turn down such an opportunity?" Colleen said, "One reason was I was a little uncomfortable about the nepotism aspect. But the main reason was I had not been particularly good in finance; I felt I was just too far behind to compete properly. As it turned out, I'm actually very good in finance now."

She speculated, "If I had known that I was going to turn out to be really good at finance, I would have felt more comfortable going there. But I wasn't sure that I was going to be any good at it, and I did not want to go in as Ned's daughter-in-law and not have to function on my own. That little streak of independence is just the way I've lived my life. And sometimes it's hurt me, but it's the way that I have to do things."

Political Advice Brent told us his mentor advised him on gay issues and, in essence, paved the way for his own efforts toward achieving equal rights for gay people at work. He said, "I knew Jonathan Rottenberg before he was at Monitor, because he was active in the HBS GLSA. I ended up working there last summer, and Jonathan was pretty instrumental in helping me think about the role I wanted to play in gay and lesbian issues there. I wanted to do some things about getting domestic partnership benefits, but I was pretty nervous and I didn't exactly know how to go about it. With Jonathan having been very open and having dealt with some of the issues that I was dealing with, he was a great resource. We could talk about finding information and about who to approach."

Personal Advice Although most mentors were mentors in the context of business and their careers, they also gave extensive personal advice. As gay professionals became friendly with their mentors, the topic of their conversations often shifted from business to personal issues.

Many told us that having balance in their lives was critical. Such advice coming from a mentor took on added significance. Marvin told us, "One of my very first bosses right after I got out of business school was a woman who I think the world of. Actually, she's also a Harvard Business School graduate. She said to me, 'The most important thing in your life is your personal life. No career or anything is more important than you being happy.' And this is coming from someone from Harvard Business School, remember, where it's career first. I've always remembered that, because I think she's right."

Career Advancement Mentors are like friends in that it is difficult to count the ways they benefit you. Benefits ranged from simple gestures of kindness to saving or making someone's career. Most commonly, mentors are responsible for seeing that their mentorees' careers stay on track and that they continue to be promoted.

Often mentors are like heavy hitters who carry their team to victory. Oswald told us, "I'm friends with a lesbian at work who is much more open about being gay than I am, although I'm also out to quite a few people, including my mentor. Neither she nor I really fit the corporate mold, but we've both done very well." He added, "We're peers now, although I got to where I got to faster. I don't think it has anything to do with how out she is. My perception is that at an earlier point in her career she was really thwarted, but then she hooked into a star as her mentor. If there's anything I learned from her, it's the fact that cream rises, but it doesn't rise alone. There's almost always other cream there with it, moving as a team. Now she's on the team of a star, so she's rising, just as my mentor is a star, and I've been rising with him. And my mentor is following somebody else, who is following someone else." Oswald added, "I've also been bringing people along, including three gay mentorees."

Mentors can also be like coaches, parents, or older siblings watching over their mentorees' careers. One of the principal ways a mentor can assist a person's career is by saving it in times of downsizing. Joy described a time when she found a mentor and that relationship literally saved her position with the company. She told us, "When my company was bought out, they sold off all the little companies. They just called us and said, 'Hello. We've bought all your assets. You can have thirty days to shut it down.' I was really traumatized, because this was my third traumatic workplace experience, and this time I had put my whole heart and soul into it.

"The purchasing company sent this manager down to see if there was anything worth salvaging, people or accounts or anything else. She's wonderful—one of the few other women MBAs in our industry. She and I just totally clicked for all the right reasons, and I had enough business to bring with me to pay my salary, so she saved me from the bloodbath."

Less dramatic than saving someone's job was writing recommendations and giving referrals for their next endeavors. In the company where Lisa worked before attending HBS, she said, "There was definitely an old boys' network, so it was difficult for me there. My mentor was a woman vice president, and she is why that experience was so good for me. She also wrote one of the recommendations for me to go to business school. She has been really great."

Who Their Mentors Are

The gay professionals we interviewed sought various kinds of mentors. Some sought mentors for their careers, others for managing their sexual orientation in the workplace. Not all mentors were people at work. Gay professionals found mentors outside work in many different ways—through gay professional groups, the HBS gay alumni associations, women's groups, race-based organizations, and the media. Sometimes friends, partners, parents, or professors also played a mentoring role.

Mentors were not always older than their mentorees. Close friends of all ages played the role of mentor to many we interviewed. What made these friendships mentoring relationships as opposed to networking is that one person was usually in the role of helper and the other helpee.

For some, there was an age reversal in whom they sought for advice. In particular, older gay professionals referred to younger friends or partners as their mentors in the process of coming out at work.

But most of those who had mentors told us their boss was their mentor. Elizabeth told us, "I've always had very good people to work for—straight people, gay people, men, women. Eventually some of them have become my mentors as well." Because bosses are typically the most common type of mentors people have, Elizabeth wisely advised gay people to choose their boss well. In doing so, they might also find a good mentor.

Heterosexual Mentors

Most had heterosexual mentors. Steven, who works in banking, said ever since his new boss was appointed, this man has been his mentor. "He took me under his wing and gave me a lot of responsibility. We've also written a couple of chapters in a book together, and we've given several talks together. He loves having protégés, and I'm glad to be one of them. I've been promoted several times under him—including after I came out to him."

Alumni ties were often the lead-in to mentoring relationships at work. The HBS connection was Victor's primary source of mentors and mentorees. Victor said, "My mentor is an HBS alum. And of the people that I mentor, there are three or four HBS alumni."

Gender or race commonalities were also important for many. Nicholas, who is Black, said, "As far as mentoring goes, I'm unaware of anyone who was gay. Everyone who has mentored me has been married or divorced. A couple of mentors come to mind, and I think it was race that outweighed anything related to sexual orientation."

Coming Out to Heterosexual Mentors Precisely because mentors are so valuable for advice and career assistance, they are among the most difficult people for gay professionals to come out to. Also, because good mentors are so difficult to find, many feared that a replacement would not be easy to come by.

A significant number of those we interviewed formed their mentor relationships at a time when they were not out to themselves. Not all had the desire to come out to their mentors, but most did. They had built close personal bonds with these people and they wished to be honest with them. Additionally, they reasoned, if their mentor truly knew them, they would receive better advice and cement the bonds of friendship.

For some gay professionals, coming out to heterosexual mentors was no big deal, while others struggled with the decision for months or years. Many told us they came out to a mentor when their mentor sent signals that their being gay wasn't going to be a problem. Several said their mentors' advice after coming out was, "Get over it, it's no big deal. Accept yourself as you are, and get on with your life!" Yet in many of these cases, it seems the mentor was not completely comfortable with the information, because they never discussed the issue again, although the mentoring relationship continued as strongly as before. In contrast, those whose mentors said, "I'm so glad you told me," and began to occasionally ask about the mentoree's partner relationship or social life termed their coming-out experience most successful.

Gay Mentors

Gay professionals often sought gay mentors who could give them advice in managing their sexual orientation and their careers. Yet forming these mentoring relationships at work can be difficult, some gay professionals told us, because they feared the more senior gay person would not want to acknowledge their shared sexual orientation. Claude said, "There's another guy at work I have heard is gay, but he's pretty closeted. I'm afraid if I approached him he would flip out. He's going to be promoted soon anyway and sent overseas. Eventually, I will be too. So I'm sure we'll connect over there." Others said they thought older gay people might not want to show favoritism to a younger gay person just because they were both gay.

This can be a real fear, whether or not the mentor is openly gay. Greg told us, "At one point at Gillette, the head of my entire division was gay, and kind of openly gay. He and I became friends. We actually became kind of suspect to everyone else, who didn't understand how someone at my level could be friends with the head of the entire division. When they figured it out, they resented it."

We asked, "Is there anything that the mentor or the protégé could do to make the relationship less threatening for heterosexuals?" Greg replied, "I don't think so. Anyway, I'm not into doing things so that the straight people will be less freaked out." While Greg's gay pride is admirable, companies must take the charge of reverse discrimination seriously; one lesbian professional we talked briefly with was party to a lawsuit on exactly these grounds.

Coming Out to Gay Mentors Coming out to someone who is gay themself may seem like a moot point, but that wasn't necessarily the case. Especially if there is a great age difference, coming out may not be automatic. Furthermore, if there is a great disparity between rank, which is most often the case with mentors, there may be no appropriate foray into a personal conversation.

Alistair Williamson told us at first he was unsure how to approach his mentor about their both being gay. But he found that simply acknowledging his mentor's relationship opened the door. Alistair said, "When I heard that his lover of thirty-five years died after a long illness, I didn't know how to approach it, because he wasn't really out at that time. But I wrote him a little card saying, 'I'm very sorry to hear about your recent loss, and if there's anything I can do, please let me know.' He saw me in the elevator a couple of weeks later and said, 'I really appreciated your note. Thank you.'

"Two years later, I learned that I was one of the few people to acknowledge his loss—other people didn't know how to approach it. When other people's wives or spouses died, there were flowers and letters—he knew that, because he had been kicking in for flowers for years; but there was nothing for him, and none of them came to the funeral. They just didn't know how to deal with it since he wasn't openly gay at the time."

Some of our interviewees' gaydar failed them, and they formed mentor relationships with people who they didn't even suspect were gay. Others were drawn to people they thought might be gay, but nonetheless experienced great anxiety in coming out. In many cases, gay professionals were so adept at shifting the focus of conversations away from sexual orientation at work that they habitually did this even with other gay people.

Generally gay people in their twenties and thirties came out within the first few years of the formation of workplace mentoring relationships, especially if they had reason to assume the other person was also gay, while older gay professionals typically waited longer. Mel Glapion, who is in his late twenties, said, "When a big restructuring came about, that gave me a chance to pursue the mentoring relationship with Jake. In working with him, I realized he had a great deal of power within this organization. He was one of the oldest people there, so he had contacts all over the firm, and all of the clients loved him, so he had a lot of power. The younger investment bankers were incredibly careful around him. And as I began to work with him more closely, people started associating his power with me, so they were more fearful of me as well."

Mel told us, "I really respected him, because it was pretty obvious to people at work that he was gay. He just sort of left this trail of popcorn which was fairly easy to figure out. His boyfriend called five times a day, and they would leave early in the afternoon of Friday to go to their weekend home together. He even brought his partner to a fund-raising event that one of his clients invited him to."

On a business trip, during dinner, according to Mel, "Jake brought up what went on during the restructuring and how homophobic one of our senior bosses was and how that influenced things at the company. Jake told me he eventually told this guy off, and from then on, their relationship has been very good. That was pretty eye opening for me. Then he asked me about my experiences there and the people that I had encountered and how working for him was as opposed to working for a heterosexual managing director. He also talked a lot about his partner and what he wants to do in retirement, which was coming around soon." Mel met other senior gay people at work through Jake, which has given him renewed hope that being gay in investment banking would not be a career dead end.

LACK OF MENTORS

While many had mentors, almost half the gay professionals in our survey did not have a mentor. In our interviews, disappointment with their inability to find a mentor was a frequent theme. Often those we interviewed were caught up in the day-to-day rigors of their jobs and didn't have the time or the opportunity to try to develop relationships with potential mentors. A few sought mentoring relationships that failed to develop.

Many expressed a mixture of pride and disappointment over the lack of potential mentors. But most said that sexual orientation had nothing to do with their inability to find a mentor. For example, Wayne told us about the lack of suitable mentors in the fashion field. "I've had some heterosexual mentors when I was in consulting. But after business school, in my job search in the retail industry, I kept looking for a mentor that I could latch on to. I thought: OK, this is a totally new industry for me, so who can I learn from? What I found is that there were no mentors out there for me. Maybe that's a really arrogant statement, but everybody that I met was looking to me to be the innovative one—the one that was going to drive the company into a new era. The people I met really didn't view themselves as having a lot to offer me. Instead, they were putting a lot of responsibility and a lot of hope in me being able to help them."

Dick, who also worked in retail, mentioned a gay man in senior management who he had thought might be a potential mentor for him. He explained, "When I joined the company, I was hoping for that to happen, but I haven't had a lot to do with Roman. At this point, I don't think it will happen. He has a house in the Hamptons, and I thought my partner and I would get invited there this summer, but we never did." Since Roman was openly gay, Dick concluded sexual orientation was not the reason a relationship was not formed. Rather, he pointed out, the company was in the process of a major restructuring, so senior management was under considerable pressure. But it also seemed to Dick that Roman didn't have his eye on the ball with regard to business. Dick said, "Roman and I have great camaraderie, but he doesn't always return my phone calls. And I'm his number-one store! So that is something that really surprises me."

Stever Robbins said he no longer expects to find one person to serve as his mentor. He told us, "I've had a few mentors. During high school, a friend of mine's mother was a self-made real estate mogul, and a few of my HBS professors were mentors. They're all straight, and I'm out to all of them. But recently, I've stopped looking for a principal mentor relationship. It's pretty clear to me from the work experiences I've had that the traditional corporate route is not for me, and I don't know how one finds a mentor for a nontraditional career pattern. So now I'm more likely to try to get to know different people for the different aspects of the things I'm interested in."

Lesbian professionals had an even more difficult time finding mentors than gay men, which they usually attributed to sexism. Gloria said, "I haven't been able to find any mentors. A lot of my male peers from college have been able to establish that kind of relationship with male bosses, and I'm at a disadvantage because I haven't been able to do that."

Even when they sought female mentors, lesbian professionals were often disappointed. Often, they said, sexism was to blame here as well. One reason is that women feel they have to work twice as hard to achieve the same recognition as their male peers. Because of this, they have less time available to mentor and develop others. Another reason is that due to sexism, some women are insecure about their place in the business world and seem to be threatened by the credentials and success of younger women. Thus, they did not want to serve as their mentors. Several also suggested that senior women might be putting them through a kind of hazing ritual by ignoring them.

Some felt locked out of mentoring relationships because they were gay. When they took a look above them in the ranks of their organizations, they saw few gay mentors. Yet when they tried to develop a mentoring relationship with a heterosexual, many of those who were closeted found it difficult to surmount the distance the closet imposes. Others simply assumed that their sexual orientation would be in the way of building a mentoring relationship, so they didn't try to form one.

It may be that some of these individuals had not made enough of an effort to seek out and develop mentor relationships. For example, Susie said, "I haven't formally approached anyone. Maybe I was waiting for it to evolve naturally, but it's never occurred." It also seemed some shied away from trying to develop mentoring relationships in order to protect their closet. Perhaps they would have been better served by coming out strategically in order to foster mentoring ties.

Alternatively, it seems possible that closeted gay people may have certain advantages in getting along with more senior people in their work environment. By being silent about their own personal lives, they could allow their mentors to set the tone for conversations, thus building rapport. Over time, then, they could begin to share more of themselves with their mentors, with an increased likelihood that the relationship would continue after they revealed their sexual orientation.

MENTORING OTHERS

Many of those we interviewed were in a position to mentor others, and they got tremendous personal satisfaction out of helping others along in their careers. Additionally, because they generally mentored people who were younger than themselves, they said they enjoyed having contact with younger people whose fresh outlook on life they found inspirational. Most people we interviewed felt proud enough of their accomplishments to feel they had something to offer others. They mentored others because they hoped to help others where they had struggled themselves.

Mentoring Outside Work

A number of gay men we interviewed told us they served as mentors to younger men they were in sexual relationships with. Some were happy with this role, while others were dissatisfied. None of the lesbians we interviewed said they had this kind of relationship.

Mentoring at Work

Most commonly, gay professionals mentor students or business associates at work. Nearly all of those we interviewed desired to mentor other gay people, although they said they did not always know which of their mentorees was gay. A number told us they mentored or hoped to mentor gay HBS students. With busy work schedules and lack of contact with students, it was difficult to become involved. However, many found the time and ways to help.

Randy, who had benefited from mentoring himself, told us, "I want to be more of a mentor to gay people at HBS, to help them think about what it means to be gay in investment banking. Because the thing that would have made my coming out the easiest would have been to have access to more gay alumni." We learned later that Randy did help an HBS gay student find a summer job in his department.

Others, who had not had mentors themselves, were reversing this trend for others. Betsy, one of the first women to go to HBS and one of the first women to break into the upper reaches of corporate America, told us, "I've never had a mentor. But I have probably served as mentor for any number of people—both men and women, straight and gay. Because somebody has got to be the first to take the body blows, and it always seems to be that it's me."

She explained, "In the corporate environment that I am in, I'm not really out, but I don't try to hide anything either. I'm sure my whole staff knows—I suspect it took them less than two weeks to figure it out. I realize I'm in a position where I'm a role model to younger gay people, because there are people who work for me and who work in associated departments who are gay, and I've come out to them." She reflected, "It's interesting. Most of those I mentored in my last job were women, and now it's all guys. I think I've set a good example, because the young gay men in the company who were incredibly scared to let anyone know they're gay are now more comfortable and more out because they see somebody up the line being that way. I'm really satisfied that I have improved the quality of life for some of the gay guys in the company."

She added, "That feels as good and as satisfying as being able to develop women, which I did a lot of at my previous company. There I made it a point to hire at least one woman from Harvard Business School every year, so I had quite a family tree of women that I have developed as my career has progressed."

Lesbian professionals often made a point of mentoring other women. Elizabeth said, "I've paid most attention to helping women. I get a lot of requests to do informational interviews, and I've had to sort of confine it, because it got out of control. So what I do now is, I only do information interviews for women. And I've helped women get jobs and make inquiries; I like to do that. The odds are that some of them must have been lesbians, but I'm not necessarily sure I knew who."

Other lesbians also often told us they tried to mentor other women and racial minorities. Sebastin mentioned mentoring a number of people at his consulting firm, none of whom was gay. He said, "I mentor four people, a woman and three men. Two of the men are Black, and the other man and the woman are white. I go to lunch with them, we go out to dinner, we go to the movies, they've been here to the apartment, and I invite them to my parties. I like them. I know there are gay people in the firm, but I just happen not to be close friends with them. But if they were to come to me with some sort of problem or something, then I would certainly try to help them."

Not everyone made a priority of helping people like themselves, however. In answer to our question "Have you been a mentor to anyone?" Roberta Lasley said, "Sure, tons of people. It didn't matter if they were gay or straight. I always had a lot of people who I mentored. Women especially always sought me out for mentoring, but there were a lot of men I mentored too."

A number told us they didn't see being gay as a strong bond on which to base a mentoring relationship. When we asked Harold if he had formed any mentoring relationships in the company where he works, he said, "I knew people who were gay, but no one that I ever really looked at as a mentor. And there were people who I knew were gay, no one that I viewed as a potential mentoree. I reject the notion that just because two people are gay, there needs to be a special connection. I mean, when I first came out, being gay was enough of a reason to be friends with people or to interact with them professionally. But at this stage of my life, it's just not a good enough reason to connect with people. I mean, if it's not someone that I would have connected with otherwise, then the gay issue is not particularly relevant to me."

Charley, a gay Black man who has both gay and Black mentorees, nonetheless told us, "The toughest issue I've faced as a manager has been people who sense that I'm gay or know that I'm gay and see that as a reason why I should give them special treatment. I think that has been the toughest thing about being both a gay manager and a minority manager—there are people who naturally assume a commonality that I don't, because I operate very much on an individual basis."

Others also said ability to do the work was the only priority in developing mentoring relationships. Yet we wondered whether for many the desire to stay closeted at work was not at least equally strong. When we asked Coleen if she has been approached by gay people for jobs or job assistance, she admitted, "I really hate to say this in a way, but I look at most gay people and say, 'Is this the kind of person who I think would be good at this and can they work well with me?' And usually the answer is no."

Earlier she had led us to believe the gay people she had met in business made her uncomfortable because they brought personal issues to the forefront—issues she didn't want to surface in the workplace. So we asked her if she prefers to keep her working relationships focused on business. She agreed that she did. "I like to keep it to business, not on people's personal lives."

MENTORING AND THE CLOSET Typically we found that the people who didn't mentor others were closeted and drew a solid line between their personal and professional lives. Thus they were not comfortable in getting close to others at work, including potential mentorees. Most of those who were mentors said they came out to their mentorees, whether heterosexual or gay, as the bond between them grew. Many gay professionals we interviewed told us they would be glad to mentor other gay people, but often in the same breath said they found it hard to come out at work, even to someone else who was gay. Thus getting prospective mentor and mentoree to acknowledge their shared gay identity could be a difficult challenge. While most said that they would not be threatened by a younger gay person coming out to them, they also said they might not come out right away in return.

We asked nearly everyone we interviewed, "What advice would you give to someone who wanted to approach you as a potential mentor?" Bart Rubenstein replied, "I would have been extremely happy if someone gay would have approached me at work, but I would have wondered how they figured me out." He said, "I guess I'm inconsistent. I put out signals that I'm gay, and then when people get them I'm kind of taken aback." He told us, "For many years I've wanted to be more out at work, but I've felt incapable of taking the necessary steps. So I would have been thrilled to know of other gay people at work. I guess the best approach would be to come into my office and close the door and say, 'We've got to talk.'" But then he reconsidered, "But what if they were wrong and they approached someone who was really heterosexual? Or what if the closeted person really flipped out? Maybe walking into someone's office and closing the door wouldn't be the right thing. I'd suggest asking someone to go out to lunch. Then sitting across a table in a more informal way, you could start dropping pointed hints."

Jo, who is closeted at work, advised not raising the gay issue at all in the beginning. She suggested, "Keep it business at first. Keep it as a business mentoring thing and wait for the other person to open up. Be very patient and don't push." Norman told us even subtle signs that the younger person was gay could threaten his closet. He told us, "Gay people can't wear pink triangles to find each other anymore, because a lot of people know what it means. There aren't too many discreet signals left. Everyone wears red ribbons now. Until we're all willing to be more open, you can't really use those ways of approaching someone."

When we told gay professionals in their twenties and thirties these comments, many felt frustrated. Whether mostly closeted or openly gay, many said they'd like to approach a gay mentor just as women or minorities approach mentors based on their commonalities. But older professionals cautioned that the time may not yet be ripe for such a forthright approach. Instead, they advise younger gay professionals to continue to focus on business; to network, to build their professional relationships, to drop hints, and to participate in organizations that can lead to fostering mentoring relationships.

• • •

In this note we have attempted to give gay professionals a sales pitch! Mentors can play an important role in your career progression. At the same time, you can help up-and-coming gay professionals by mentoring them. Although heterosexuals can also be valuable mentors for gay professionals, having a gay mentoring relationship can produce a very close bond and significant career advantages.

Having a sounding board who understands your crises and your daily working challenges can be a significant boost. Besides, many of the people we spoke to had a lot of fun knowing their mentors and considered them friends. Unlike a partner who may be tired of hearing the latest twist in a political battle at the office or unable to give good advice, a mentor is probably someone who is interested in listening and can provide valuable advice as well.

Most successful gay professionals have had at least one mentor during the course of their career. The bottom line is: If gay people help one another we'll all get further ahead.

Chapter 9

Gender

Some have asked us, "Is it easier to be a gay man or a lesbian? a gay person or a heterosexual?" We find this question funny, because it's not as if anyone really has a choice. However, we find the similarities and differences informative in shedding light on how gay professionals understand the challenges they face in life while managing their home lives and professional careers. What gay professionals do have a choice about, of course, is whether or not to come out at work. Lesbians often find it easier than gay men to slip under the "gaydar" screens of many heterosexuals. Yet ironically, they seem to have advantages in the workplace over both gay men and heterosexual women when they come out.

Social Expectations for Men and Women

Typically, male MBAs face significant societal and financial pressure to pursue mainstream business careers, in large part due to family obligations. Without the responsibility for supporting a wife and children, the gay men we interviewed told us, they felt far more free than their heterosexual male peers to take risks and pursue careers that interest them. In addition, since the vast majority of their friends are also gay, most face little social pressure to fit in to the country-club lifestyle of their heterosexual peers. For gay men who choose to buck social convention by parenting children, the road is more difficult than it is for lesbians. But most have sufficient capital to make this dream came true.

The messages society sends professional women are mixed. Although heterosexual women are constantly reminded that economically they must be able to earn a living, they are also expected to marry and raise children. Lesbians who go to business school have a significant advantage over their heterosexual peers—they don't have to subjugate their career to a man. They are also not constantly in fear of losing their partner to a younger version of themselves, as some of their heterosexual peers are. Thus, the lesbians we interviewed are basically free to chart their own career path. Lesbians who want children have an easier time than gay men. Yet without a man's salary in the household, lesbian couples usually plan to juggle two full-time careers in order to maintain the standard of living they desire.

Parental expectations for male and female offspring often differ significantly, which can have important implications for the relationships between parents and gay children. Many agree that social condemnation is stronger against gay men than against lesbians and that fathers have an especially difficult time relating to gay sons. In contrast, mothers are often the strongest champions of their gay sons, and at least one study suggests that the relationship between parents and their gay sons is stronger than the relationship between parents and their lesbian daughters (*Parents Matter,* Naiad Press). This study suggests that because gay men usually fulfill the primary male gender role of being breadwinners and successful in their chosen professions, parents can be proud of them and talk about their accomplishments to friends and family members. In contrast, the primary gender role for women is marriage and raising children, which most lesbians do not fulfill.

The vast majority of both lesbians and gay men we interviewed said their parents were proud of their career accomplishments; lesbians did not report any more difficulty in their current relationships with their parents than the gay men. Hence, for this group of high-achieving lesbians, at least, parents seem to have redefined the expectations they hold for their daughters.

FINDINGS

Educational Background and Job Selection

For both gay men and lesbians, there has been a change in the career-selection process during the 1990s. For gay men this change has largely had to do with how they intend to manage their sexual orientation at work; for lesbians it seems to have more to do with expanding opportunities for women.

Gay men who attended HBS have had undergraduate and pre-business-school backgrounds very similar to those of their heterosexual male peers. Many studied engineering, finance, or accounting and took positions with large corporations, financial institutions, or large consulting firms before HBS. After receiving their MBAs, however, the gay men in our study showed some important differences compared to heterosexual men.

Through the 1980s, gay men who hadn't come to terms with their sexual orientation often went into traditional MBA careers after HBS: corporations, finance, and large consulting firms. These fields were also chosen by those who knew they were gay but intended to remain highly closeted at work. Those who recognized they were gay and wanted to be more open about it were often keen on careers in more gay-friendly industries, such as marketing, retail, the arts, music, advertising, and the media—in fact, many told us they went to HBS for the express purpose of transitioning into these fields.

Recently, a new trend has begun. Men who know they are gay are less often self-selecting out of historically conservative fields for the more creative professions or job functions. Instead they are going into whatever industry and type of work they are interested in—and they expect to be able to come out at work, even in traditional business positions. They still choose their employer carefully, but they are not limiting their industry or career options to the same degree as previous generations of gay male professionals. As a result, openly gay men are now working in an increasingly large number of fields.

While, even a decade ago, gay men and lesbians often went into different industries, today they can increasingly be found making the same career choices. A major reason is that the educational background of women admitted to HBS and throughout the business world is changing.

Like their heterosexual female classmates admitted to HBS from the 1960s to the 1980s, nearly all of the lesbian HBS alumnae we interviewed from those years pursued liberal arts or humanities degrees as undergraduates. Their pre-HBS job experiences most often included publishing, education, government, leadership experience in the women's movement, or other nonprofit work; only a few had finance backgrounds or experience in mainstream business careers. In general, women from this era, whether gay or heterosexual, went to business school to further their skills and to transition into higher-paying positions. In large part, the lesbians in our study succeeded, although the types of careers they initially sought—in marketing, publishing, or academia—usually required fewer quantitative skills, and thus were lower paying than typical male MBA positions. Those who sought careers in corporations, consulting, investment banking, or investment firms were often the first women to arrive on the scene and had to be brilliant to be seen as merely smart. Those who have remained in these industries have often risen higher than heterosexual women classmates.

Today the scales between women and men MBAs are more evenly balanced at the beginning of their careers. Women are coming to business school with a variety of educational backgrounds that more closely match the profile of their male classmates. They often have a few years' business experience in investment banking, consulting, the military, or corporate life—again, just like their male classmates. As a result, lesbians are now working in a diverse range of post-MBA industries.

Younger lesbians we interviewed have gained parity to heterosexual men in another way—through athletics. While few of the lesbians older than their mid-thirties were athletes, most of the younger lesbians were. In addition to several who had played college basketball, we met a former tennis pro and numerous avid golfers. Many participated in the highly competitive HBS intramural and interscholastic soccer, basketball, and ice hockey leagues, as well as pursuing their own individual athletic interests, seemingly at much higher rates than heterosexual women.

While gay men were most attracted to individual recreational sports, such as swimming, the lesbians we interviewed have often been competitive athletes, which gave them the drive and skills to become leaders. Peggy, who is in her late twenties, was typical of these go-getters. She told us, "I was a very active athlete in college, and I like competitive experiences. When interview time came around in my senior year of college, the industries that people were talking about the whole time were investment banking and consulting. I thought: Well, this is the hardest thing to get into, so I'm going to interview and get more offers than anyone else around. So that's what I did. It was like a big game to me. That's still kind of how I see interviewing for post-HBS jobs."

Investment banks, in particular, seek to hire college athletes because of their perception that these individuals have the stamina to survive rigorous hours, the teamwork orientation required to fulfill the organizational mission, and the self-confidence to succeed.

Location

For the most part, gay professionals choose to live in large metropolitan areas. Yet while many gay men preferred to live in safe harbors like gay neighborhoods, lesbians were more willing to go outside these havens. Gay men often told us that living in the center of the action was an important factor in choosing their career. Many also sought positions that would allow them to travel to other large cities that have a significant gay population. While living near a large city was often important to the lesbians we interviewed, lesbians were more likely to select jobs that gave them the best career opportunity, even if it was located in an outlying suburban area. With an increasing number of lesbians who are planning to raise children, lesbian professionals were more interested than gay men in finding a position that allows them the income, flexibility, and time to be parents.

Friends and Social Life

Lesbians' friends were more diverse in terms of gender and sexual orientation than gay men's friends. Most gay men socialize with heterosexual women and gay male friends, while lesbians were likely to have all kinds of friends—gay, heterosexual, male and female. But lesbians were less likely than gay men to have friends of different ages and socioeconomic status.

Many gay men we interviewed told us they wished they had more lesbian friends, but only a few reported actively taking steps to meet some. Ironically, we found that gay men who might be tagged with the "neoconservative" label were more likely to have lesbian friends than gay men who were heavily enmeshed in the gay male subculture of their cities. "It makes sense," Bruce explained. "My partner and I don't live in a gay neighborhood, we have a monogamous relationship, we're committed to our careers, and we want to have children—just like a lot of the lesbians we know. A lot of gay men—including a lot of gay professionals—are running around the gay ghetto thinking they are advancing gay liberation by drinking, drugging, dancing, and having sex with lots of men. Of course they're not going to meet any lesbians."

Gay men often had an extensive social network of gay male friends, while lesbians more usually had just a few lesbian friends. A typical house party for gay men in their twenties, thirties, or forties could include upward of fifty revelers—both invitees and their guests—and eventually it moved out into the clubs. Older gay men often had an equally extensive circle of guests at dinner parties or brunches.

From the parties they throw to the clubs they frequent, gay men were much more comfortable being out there and fabulous. Having boundless energy, some gay men told us that they and gay classmates who are now working in very high-level positions go out frequently to the hippest gay clubs and draw attention to themselves as the center of the action. In contrast, most lesbian professionals were far less willing or interested in taking such risks in their personal lives. Some felt it would be unseemly or they might tarnish their professional reputation or be outed. Gay men rarely had these fears. Even if they were indulging in wild behavior in public, most were out to have a good time when they weren't working.

The emphasis on socializing had career ramifications for some. Rupert traded the demands of a high-paced career for the chance to spend more time having fun. He said, "What I was getting in my professional life was not adequate to compensate for what I was giving up on a personal dimension. I think the phenomenon of age may be a bigger issue for a gay man than for a lesbian. There's a real premium on youth among gay men. So the notion that I should spend until I'm sixty working crazy hours for some retirement—it's ridiculous. I mean, I would almost rather incur massive debt now and start working when I'm fifty," he said with a laugh. "As a gay man, my whole set of values is different."

Partners

Lesbians have a more difficult time meeting potential partners than gay men do, most often meeting through friends or mutual interests. Few met each other through a sexual pickup or in a bar, as many gay men did. Most lesbian professionals said they followed the typical lesbian pattern of pursuing a friendship first and then a sexual relationship—usually without actually dating in between. Many had been in a relationship with a woman who today does not consider herself gay. In contrast, most gay men said their relationship started as a romantic or sexual one, and while many had sex with a man who did not consider himself gay, few had been in a relationship with one.

Also in contrast to gay men, who had a more diverse group of partners, lesbian professionals tended to select partners who were quite similar to themselves with respect to age and income. One reason may be that their partner serves as an important source of personal support. Many lesbians we interviewed mentioned that they felt alienated from or unwelcomed by other lesbians because of their professional pursuits. Thus they sought a soul mate who could understand and share their interests.

But lesbians were less likely to have a well-defined erotic type they were looking for than gay men did. Gay men who consciously sought difference in sexual or romantic partners had mostly positive experiences, but a few pointed to a darker side. One gay man in his early thirties found himself stood up one evening and later learned his date was unavoidably detained—and in jail for knifing someone in a bar fight. Another gay man in his early thirties wondered why his new boyfriend seemed so possessive and did a search for his name on an on-line database. He found his boyfriend had just got out of prison for murdering his last partner. Another gay man in his early thirties dated a coke addict who was literally unable to practice safe sex. Other gay men reported seeking sexual partners in parks or other public locations, which put them in danger of being arrested, mugged, or gay-bashed.

In general, gay men had multiple opportunities to meet other single gay men, but many complained they had a hard time settling down with

Mr. Right. Gay men often said they or their dates had the idea that someone better might come along, and thus were reluctant to commit to a relationship. Yet most told us that being in a committed relationship was their goal. A number of gay men complained that so much of the emphasis of the gay men's community is focused on sex, they find little support for their long-term relationships.

With the emphasis on bars and sexual activities in gay male population centers, gay men faced more challenges to building and maintaining long-term relationships than lesbians faced. However, the men and women in our study were equally likely to be involved in a relationship—over half of both had a long-term partner.

Gay male couples we interviewed were more likely to have open, or nonmonogamous, relationships, while lesbian couples uniformly expected monogamy. Gay men said that the main difference between them and their heterosexual peers was that both partners had fun on the side. We suggested that such open relationships could be very confusing for heterosexuals at work. For example, if Dan's boss knew he was gay and saw him at a restaurant making eyes at a man who wasn't his partner, the boss is going to perceive that he's cheating. Would Dan say anything to help him understand that he defines his relationship differently than a heterosexual couple would define their relationship? Dan replied, "That would depend upon the relationship with the boss. I might be able to explain it so that he would be envious, if not jealous," he said with a laugh.

While lesbians did not actively seek open relationships, a number complained that, with so few suitable single lesbians available, the practice of serial monogamy was common. In theory this means dropping one partner and moving on to the next. But in practice, for many lesbian professionals, it meant that their relationship was monogamous—until the relationship was broken up by an affair that quickly turned into the next relationship. We believe the frequency of serial monogamy among lesbians is changing. As socializing options for lesbians expand, more of the lesbians in their late twenties told us of dating, rather than jumping from relationship to relationship. In a parallel shift, many of the gay men in their late twenties and early thirties told us their relationships are monogamous.

Sex at Work

The final and in some ways most significant difference between gay men and lesbians was their sexual activities at work. Gay men seldom had sex with anyone from work and almost never had a relationship with someone at work; they viewed the potential downside as not worth the risk. Also, gay men said, they have so many avenues to meet potential partners, they could easily afford to write off men at work as being out of bounds. If men did have sexual encounters with men from work, they typically were just that. A longer-term relationship usually did not ensue.

Lewis told us, "I don't think whether you're gay or straight that sleeping with people you work with is ever a good idea. I don't think I would do it because of my reputation. I wouldn't want the owner of my company to find out."

Will was one who had sex with someone at work—primarily in order to find out who the other gay people were. "I had an agenda, and it wasn't just sex." Will laughed. "He ultimately did tell me who most of the other gay people there were, and I ultimately met and became friends with most of them."

Stephen had a brief affair with someone from another division whom he never expected to see again and was chagrined to find the man now reports to him. He advised leaving fun outside the office door. "You never know who is going to be reassigned to your area. It's really awkward. I don't recommend fooling around with anyone you work with."

Lesbians and Sex at Work In striking contrast, almost half of the lesbians we interviewed had sex with a woman they met at work, and almost always, this affair became a long-term relationship. Primarily, we attribute this to the fact that lesbians have far fewer opportunities to meet women, especially lesbians who are intellectually and educationally equivalent to themselves. These workplace romances with a boss, a coworker, a subordinate, or a woman in the same industry typically began as friendships; the bond continued to grow and eventually became a secret affair.

Betsy, who was heterosexual until she met her first partner at work, said, "I was in a relationship with a woman whom I had helped to recruit to work for my firm—and then she did some recruiting of her own! It was three or four months of lots of social interaction and a good bottle of scotch one night before anything happened. She came out to me and said those wonderfully quotable lines, 'If you're ever curious, I'd be interested.' Then she passed out on my couch drunker than a skunk. I went to my room and pretended to sleep. But I stayed awake all night thinking: Oh my God, what's going on, what's going on here? After we started seeing each other, I was just totally traumatized. It was kind of like: Oh my God, are the curtains all closed and the doors all shut? We lived a very, very closeted life."

After having been in a lesbian relationship in high school, Rochelle dated men while working at a *Fortune* 500 corporation and became friendly with another woman at work. "She was a peer of my boss. Somewhere along the line when we were friends, she made it obvious to me that she was gay. I can remember that all of a sudden we started electronic-mailing notes to each other all the time; it was something I looked forward to. We went out to dinner a couple times, and then I suggested, 'Let's go away for the weekend,' and that was it." Rochelle laughed. "She moved in four days later and we were together for five years."

Some finessed their job assignments so they were not working closely together with their partner. But others were unsuccessful in charting their career progress separately and found themselves working for or with or managing their partner.

Sherri said, "There were a couple of years that we were working in the same department and that was fine. There was only about a year or so when I was manager in the department that she was working in. I wasn't her direct manager, but it was still a little bit uncomfortable in that I was privy to her performance reviews. If we had been open about our relationship, the company would've moved us so that the reporting relationship wasn't there."

Lesbian professionals who broke off workplace relationships typically had little support for their misery, because they were so closeted about their relationship. And if the former couple had to work together, they were forced to be amiable even though they were at odds with each other.

Dot said, "When we parted ways, we were working in different divisions. We were close enough that we still had to see and deal with each other, but the business issues were minimal for three or four years. Then one day we woke up and we were both being promoted into new jobs where we were working together. It turned out that even people we thought had figured out we had been together didn't really know." There was one manager who Dot was pretty sure knew about their past relationship, but, she explained, "The only way he could have stopped it would have been to betray our confidence." They endured the arrangement until Dot's ex-partner worked her way into another assignment.

Dot added, "In hindsight, and after many years of therapy, I realize that this relationship wasn't very healthy for me. Because I just knew the gay world through this one individual—I didn't know anyone else who was gay, and I was completely closeted to everyone who was straight." Dot eventually started meeting other lesbians—also at work. "My partner and I had always speculated about the women in the sales force, and sure enough, we were right about some of them. I know, because I got involved with one of them, the highest-ranking woman there. She and I became friends, because we were two of the few women at that level in the company.

"When I went to visit her city, I truly believe that my call suggesting dinner was innocent. As it turned out, in the conversation, we both revealed that we had each just left relationships with women, and the relationship between the two of us kind of went from there. It was a short-term thing, but it helped get me hooked into the fact that there were other lesbian professionals in the world. If you asked how I would find other lesbians at work today—you know, if I had to pick up the phone and start that conversation, I have no idea how I'd get to that. I mean, that's the kind of thing that you kind of say, Hey, let fate carry that through. That's how I see what happened to me."

None of the lesbians we interviewed came out to coworkers about their interoffice romance, although some suspected that others knew what was going on. Jo said she met her partner at work, although they no longer work at the same company. "She wasn't out when she was there, but I think everybody knew about her. She said to me, 'If you get seen with me too much, people will figure it out.' It didn't actually end up hurting her, but I still have some reservations about coming out. I don't take so many calls from her at work, because everybody knows who she is, and if I'm getting tons of calls from her, they'll figure me out."

Jo added that she is concerned about being seen with her partner outside work as well. "As soon as we started going out, on our first big date, we came around the corner arm and arm, and there was my chief rival at work and her husband, right there, figuring it out. She hasn't actually used it against me, as far as I know. I guess it's OK, but I'm still kind of worried."

Sexual Harassment of Lesbians by Lesbians In addition to secretive workplace affairs, we found a significant amount of same-sex sexual harassment by women. In contrast, reports of male-male sexual harassment were rare. Ironically, in most respects the behavior of women who sexually harass other women is not much different from women who attempt to initiate a mutually desired relationship. One lesbian acknowledged that the difference between a workplace affair and sexual harassment primarily consists of whether or not she is interested in reciprocating. Yet this is a sad commentary. Gay people no less than heterosexuals should be free of sexual harassment at work, as well as free to meet potential partners there. Once a romantic relationship ensues, gay people, like heterosexuals, should be able to be open about the relationship so as to avoid conflicts of interest.

Interestingly, not all of those women doing the harassing identified themselves as gay—some saw themselves as bisexual, experimenting, or unsure. Assuredly, finding ways to meet lesbians can be a challenge in some areas of the country, and those who are closeted have additional difficulty meeting potential partners, as lesbian couples seem to meet primarily through friendship circles. Women can avoid potential pitfalls in the office if they expand their social circles and find other venues besides the office for meeting potential partners.

Interestingly, only those who were closeted at work reported being sexually harassed there. Those who are open speculated that they are not targets because women who harass typically rely on secrecy to protect them. Those who have been harassed said they were afraid blowing the whistle would mean drawing attention to their own sexual orientation, and thus they would not be believed. Sexual harassment by other women is particularly damaging to lesbians' careers, since most worked in fields where there were few other potential female mentors.

GAY MALE ADVANTAGES

Gay men have many advantages over lesbians in the workplace. Some of these derive directly from sexism, while others have more to do with the larger strides gay men have made in forming a gay community that meets their professional as well as social needs.

Gay Men Compared to Heterosexual Men

Openly gay men also have certain advantages over heterosexual men, including facility in befriending heterosexual women. Many gay men we interviewed said their female colleagues were hesitant to build close relationships with heterosexual men because they could be seen as inviting a sexual relationship. In contrast, Sebastin told us, "I have a number of really close friends who are straight women, because they know I'm not out for anything."

Additionally, their female colleagues' husbands and boyfriends were not jealous of their friendship with a gay man. Marvin explained, "A lot of my bosses have been women, and I've become really good friends with some of them. We'd go out drinking until late at night, and their boyfriends or husbands have never cared. But women would never do that with a straight guy."

Another advantage some openly gay men said they had was that they were seen as more creative by virtue of their exposure to a greater diversity of ideas, opinions, and trends than the average person. Gay men who have a reputation of being creative found it has opened many doors for them, particularly in fields like marketing or advertising, but also in more traditional fields where there is an increased need for creative problem solving. Gay men often said their connection to gay friends in many different fields contributed to their ability to help their companies look at things in new ways, develop new markets, and take advantage of new business opportunities.

Some final advantages open and closeted gay men share have to do with living in gay neighborhoods. Not having to worry about school districts, many gay men choose to live in gentrifying areas of a city and thus spend less of their lives commuting to and from the suburbs than heterosexual men. This is especially significant in large cities, where commutes can be quite long. This leaves more time for work—and for play. Most gay men we interviewed exercise regularly, and most say they work and play equally hard.

Gay Men Compared to Lesbians

In general, gay men were more open about being gay at work than lesbian professionals were. In addition, while gay men tended to become more open as their careers progressed, a number of lesbians became more closeted. Many lesbians defended their need to stay closeted by saying, "Of course they can be more out; they're men. It's easier for them." We did not find this argument persuasive, for two reasons. One is that heterosexual men, who control most businesses, are more threatened by gay men than by lesbians. Second, we draw a parallel to race. Closeted minority professionals often said it was easier for white gay people to come out. Yet other minority professionals told us they felt that it was actually easier for them to be out than for white gay people, since they were already seen as different. So why should lesbians think it was easier for gay men to come out at work?

This feeling comes from a number of advantages gay men, whether open or closeted at work, have over lesbians. These include earning more money, feeling more secure about their career, and the fact that the gay community meets their needs better.

More Money Although our data is sketchy on this point, most studies show that gay men of comparable age outearn lesbians and have a greater net worth. Additionally, gay male professionals who are coupled have the benefit of two male incomes, whereas lesbian couples earn somewhat less and are more likely to have or want children.

More Secure The gay men we interviewed said that as they accumulated career successes they were more willing to be out about being gay at work. Gay men usually felt less vulnerable to discrimination as they gained seniority, while as lesbian professionals rose, they became acutely aware of being one of the few women at their level in the hierarchy and often the only lesbian they knew with such a degree of professional success. In contrast, gay men took advantage of abundant networking opportunities with other successful gay men, who gave them the feeling that they were not the only ones. These factors combined to give gay men the confidence that if they were suspected of being gay, were outed, or came out voluntarily and faced negative repercussions, they would be able to find comparable jobs. Lesbians were much less optimistic about their futures and were therefore much more concerned with staying in the closet that they saw as protecting them.

The gay men we interviewed also seemed to be more social with coworkers than lesbian professionals were, and thus enjoyed stronger workplace ties with both heterosexuals and other gay people. Perhaps because of the security they feel as men, they were not so guarded as the lesbians in building both close and casual relationships with coworkers. Many of the gay men we interviewed also have the kind of outgoing personalities that naturally lead to social ties, while a number of the lesbians we interviewed described themselves as more reserved.

Gay Community Meets Men's Needs Better For both social and professional needs, gay men find the gay community has much to offer them, while lesbians often feel alienated and invisible. One reason may be, as several recent studies suggest, there may be almost twice as many men as women who identify as gay. Certainly, gay men have far more venues catering to them, perhaps as a result of men making more money, but also because gay men and lesbians seem to enjoy rather different social activities.

While lesbian professionals socialized with circles of close friends and did a lot of entertaining in one another's homes, the gay men were more likely to socialize at gay bars, gay fund-raisers, gay resorts, and gay organizations, where they met a wider spectrum of people. As a result, gay men were more likely to meet other gay professionals who could be of assistance to their careers both directly and indirectly. And when they talk to friends who have taken steps out of the closet, they gain confidence that they too can make such a move. Another way the gay community fits gay men's needs better than lesbians' is that far more gay men are featured in magazines, newspapers, and books. The vast majority of the gay media covers gay men's lives, interests, and issues. This is tremendously reinforcing for their self-pride and their access to information about other gay men. Lesbians often have to cull through pages of irrelevant information to find one article, ad, or announcement that is of interest to them, and many do not make the effort.

We asked both gay men and lesbians what they read to keep in touch with the gay community. Many of the men ran off a whole list of national publications, including the *Advocate, 10 PERCENT, Out, Genre,* and *Out and About*—in addition to the local gay newspapers that they pick up in gay bars on a regular basis. In contrast, far fewer lesbians were even aware that such publications exist.

The presence of gay men in literature is also an advantage for gay men of all ages. When referring to their coming-out process, they told us they were able to find novels that included gay male characters. Most lesbians were not able to find or learn about other lesbians so easily.

While most lesbians had read or heard of *The Well of Loneliness* or *Rubyfruit Jungle,* what they took away from these books was that while lesbians existed, a lesbian community didn't. Rather, lesbians were fated to seek liaisons with previously heterosexual women or to live as independent iconoclasts. None could think of a title that focused on a lesbian professional, and only one had read *The Best Little Boy in the World,* which focuses on a gay man in business. In contrast, numerous gay men told us this book helped them accept themselves as gay men who wanted to go into business, and in addition many gay men had read Larry Kramer's *Faggots,* Andrew Holleran's *Dancer from the Dance,* or works by David Leavitt. Although Kramer and Holleran offer a searing indictment of the gay male community in New York, their books were evidence that a large and visible gay male population existed there and that gay male professionals were part of it; while Leavitt, writing a decade later, also shed light on the lives of professional gay men and their ability to integrate into the American mainstream.

Additionally, we found that gay men are more likely to contribute financially to gay groups than lesbian professionals were. While lesbians were equally likely to contribute their time to gay groups, they were somewhat less likely to contribute money. As a result of their regular appearance on the gay fund-raising circuit, gay men were more strongly connected to other successful gay people, which provided both socializing and networking opportunities for them.

As a result, among those who are closeted at work, none of the men—but a significant portion of the women—reported they worried about the revelation of their sexual orientation "a great deal." In general, gay men were more open and less worried about being found out to be gay than lesbian professionals. However, we found signs that the picture may be changing. As more lesbians come out successfully at work, we believe their example will inspire others to do the same.

LESBIAN HURDLES

One of the most puzzling findings to emerge from our study is that a number of the lesbian professionals we interviewed started out in their careers being somewhat open about being gay and have become more closeted over the years—while the opposite is the case for gay men.

Lesbians attributed their gradual retreat to the closet to the negative experiences they had with being gay at work—whether they were outed, suspected of being gay, or the subject of a whispering campaign. One said that she had a bad experience because she was too willing to gossip and discuss her sex life with certain colleagues—things that one might expect she could change at her next job. Interestingly, none of the lesbian professionals who were completely open about being gay reported a negative experience. Yet those who had suffered ridicule or ostracism as the result of their half-in, half-out experience were convinced they were right to become more closeted rather than more open.

As they rose in their organizations, these women increasingly felt that fitting in was critical to their success, and they perceived that being gay would cause them not to fit in. Yet, ironically, the lesson we learned from lesbian professionals who were openly gay was that they were more successful in fitting in than those who were closeted, because they were better able to develop strong ties with colleagues. Instead of cutting off personal relationships and friendships in order to protect their closets, they were able to be more relaxed and open to bonding with others. Additionally, they were freed from the negative stereotypes about single heterosexual women at work. While lesbians, like all other women, face sexism, we found that coming out can help them overcome some of its sting. Thus, remaining closeted may actually do more harm than good for a lesbian's career.

For lesbians who have always been completely closeted or are afraid to come out more broadly, there are three principal career hurdles to face that gay men have gotten over or do not face. These hurdles are the lesbian-community norm of political correctness, the lack of visible lesbians, and the misconceptions and exaggerated fears about coming out that many lesbians have.

Lesbian Norms and Political Correctness

While lesbian cultural norms are changing, the expectation that lesbians should be politically correct—that is, anticapitalist, downwardly mobile do-gooders—remains an obstacle for those who wish to pursue careers in business. The pressure to be politically correct and the fear of discrimination combine to make lesbian professionals invisible—which results in even fewer being willing to be test cases for coming out at work.

Many of the lesbian professionals we interviewed told us their careers had been affected by going against the grain of the lesbian world they knew.

Roberta Lasley told us that when she lived in New York in the 1960s, she and her friends formed one of the lone outposts of educated women in the lesbian bars. Yet Roberta was also different from her own crowd of friends. "Most of my lesbian friends were in the traditional women's professions. They were in publishing. They were editors, photographers, artists. They did things that smart women did. But no one else was in business, per se."

Roberta said that in some ways that was advantageous. "The lesbian community was very much a mix, and I think that's still true today. You get a socioeconomic mix that you do not get in straight society, which is one of the rich things about the lesbian and gay community—that it's not so stratified." But she also said that having more in common with other businesspeople led her to get married soon after graduating from HBS.

Roberta's partner, also an HBS graduate, told us her decision to go into business a decade later was even more difficult, due to the emergence of lesbian feminism. Tess said, "I've been lesbian identified very strongly for most of the past twenty years. Certainly, I've always participated very regularly in gay and lesbian groups—as well as feminist and socialist groups. In the mid-70s I was real involved with the women's community where I lived—I helped cofound the women's newspaper and was also involved with some socialist groups. In fact, in those days if somebody had said to me that I was going to go to Harvard Business School, I would have thought they were crazy. In fact, I would have been highly insulted. I would have said, 'No way, I would never sell out like that.' Political correctness was the law for lesbians in those days. In the cities I lived in and visited, you didn't put on a skirt or a dress; you didn't go into business. The thinking was, if you're earning real money, you're not a true lesbian. That was the residue from when I went to college in the late 60s, the whole antiwar movement. It was anti–big business, anti–military industrial complex."

We asked Tess what changed for her. She said, "What changed is, I got real tired of not earning very much money. In working with those groups I realized that I am bright and capable and have a lot of ambition, managerial skills, and financial skills, and I wanted the credentials to be able to do something with those—I really felt that I was unable to make it without the credentials. Also, I really didn't believe in a socialist philosophy, I realized, and the world was changing. Even in the women's movement there were all these women going out and getting advanced degrees and trying to create opportunities for themselves, and I started meeting a lot more women—straight women mostly—who had done that stuff. So I started having some role models for women being able to grow and develop. Roberta broke out of the traditional women's role by fear and hunger and not wanting to go back to her roots. Whereas I became a teacher right after undergraduate school, just like a nice middle-class girl should. It was entirely logical that I did that, because there weren't role models for women doing other things. In fact, there were lots of barriers."

We asked Tess about the reaction of her socialist-feminist friends when they learned she was going to HBS. "Some of them turned their back on me," she said, "including the woman I was seeing at the time." She added, "It's funny, last summer, when I was in Provincetown, I ran into a woman I knew from those days who is now doing diversity training for Wall Street firms—and she still feels she's sold out. So there still is a lot of that sentiment."

Judith, who graduated from college in the early 80s, told us, "There was a big division at my college between the lesbian-feminists, who were generally very serious, very out about being gay, and went into nonprofits. Then there were the lesbian athletes, who were all very closeted but had great parties and went into business. I was kind of in the middle. I played sports and had fun, and I was out. I felt like I never fit anywhere."

Hope found that in the late 80s, when she graduated from college, the pressure by other lesbians for a lesbian to be politically correct remained strong. "At college I was always kind of on the fence. I would be really involved in these radical feminist groups, and then I'd be interviewing for banking jobs. So they nicknamed me the Republican lesbian." She laughed. "But the fact of the matter was that we got great benefits from having me be a translator for both groups. I sit on both sides. I can't commit to one or the other. And I'm sure I'll continue to encounter this, because I don't want to have to separate feminism from whatever I do professionally. It's too important to me." Her partner Alissa added, "Often I found boredom or sometimes horror that I was from a professional world among lesbians, and that was really a hard thing when I was first coming out."

When many of the lesbian professionals in our study began their careers, they were ostracized and put down by other lesbians for doing so. While today there is more positive acclaim for lesbians who are making it in business, the notion of what is politically correct is still very much alive in many lesbian communities.

Additionally, a number we interviewed mentioned encountering jealousy or distancing from other lesbians when they reveal what they do for a living, where they live, or what they own. Gigi said, "When I started to get to know this group of lesbians in California, I rarely spoke about my job or my education. It was really kind of funny—nobody really knew what I was doing or the kind of job I had. I mean, they knew that I had a nice apartment and I was driving a pretty nice car—you know, that kind of stuff. But I didn't want to be regarded as a capitalist tool. That always bugged me. I believe you can work in the system and do a lot of good for women and for gay people.

"Actually, my first girlfriend, the one that I broke up with last year, was pretty radical. We were the biggest mismatch. I didn't get overwhelming support for choosing to go to HBS from the lesbians I knew. My closest friends definitely gave me support, but overall it was more . . . kind of ambivalence."

Political sensitivity has been a bond that has given the lesbian community identity and cohesion. However, many lesbian professionals feel alienated by the tenets of political correctness. A number of the lesbians we interviewed smoked cigarettes, voted Republican, served veal, wore furs, watched MTV, bought Exxon stock, ate green grapes, bought erotic magazines, and shaved their legs—not out of ignorance of the issues involved but out of personal choice after weighing all the considerations. Though their behavior may be offensive to nonsmoking liberals or radicals, antipornography activists, ardent vegetarians, animal-rights activists, environmentalists, union supporters, advocates of "natural is beautiful," or even those with different esthetics, they see no need to toe the line of political doctrines formed by a group of lesbians with whom they have little interaction.

When Winnie was coming out to herself a few years ago, she didn't want to be a lesbian because she thought it would mean that she would have to conform to the lesbian community and "alter my appearance in a way I didn't find aesthetically pleasing." Winnie also had difficulty coming out because she thought she would be required to ascribe to the political correctness and norms of the lesbian community. She said, "Had I been to or known about the Dinah Shore golf tournament in Palm Springs and all those beautiful lesbians who obviously have jobs, I would have had a much easier time coming out!"

As more lesbians become visible in the business world, it will be easier for other lesbians to see that coming out does not mean marching in lockstep with whatever is on the politically correct agenda for today.

Some lesbians say, "Who cares what assimilationist, male-identified, capitalist, closeted lesbians do and whether or not they figure out they're gay?" But we feel this view is misguided—especially because more mainstream lesbians are coming out at work and in other segments of society. Hence, those who consider themselves more radical will no longer have the opportunity—or the burden—of speaking for all lesbians. Further, all the lesbian professionals we interviewed identified as feminists and supporters of equal rights for gay people. Thus they actually do have common ground with their more radical sisters and deeper pockets for such causes as well.

Over time, some of the stringency of political correctness among lesbians has faded, but it continues to be part of the lesbian stereotype—among gay men too. Many gay men we interviewed for this book would catch themselves making a critical comment about the lesbians they know and say, "Oh, I don't know if that's politically correct," or, "Well, I apologize if this isn't PC." We put them at ease and they were relieved to find that simply stating their opinion would not lead to World War III, since we had often had similar experiences ourselves. As lesbian professionals continue to create bonds with gay men, we hope that stilted, politically correct conversation on both sides can give way to true friendship and sharing.

Lack of Visible Lesbians

One evening, while we were visiting two lesbian professionals—both are attorneys and one is an MBA—they played some old Alex Dobkin records. In one song she sings, "Here come the lesbians, here come the leaping lesbians." Our MBA/JD friend cracked us up by leaping around the living room singing along with the record. Whatever became of these leaping lesbians who were supposed to take over the world? Did they leap from the 1970s and land in the business world?

We can assure you that we found successful and powerful lesbians. However, it is rare to find a lesbian professional who is fully openly gay. For example, only two HBS women who graduated before the mid-90s let us name them in this book—Roberta Lasley, who is semiretired, and Fran Henry, who was in a gay relationship at HBS, is now married and does not consider herself a lesbian. Today, things are beginning to change —younger lesbians are beginning to leap out of the closet, whatever field they are in, and we expect that as more do so, others will follow.

A number of reasons explain the low numbers of visible lesbian professionals in contrast to the number of openly gay male professionals. Lesbians are not easy to spot—even by other lesbians. Some lack time and energy to be role models or mentors. Some are actively trying to hide, while others are unwilling to be the first to come out.

Contrary to popular belief, lesbians come in many varieties. They don't all look or act in accordance with most heterosexuals'—or most gay people's—stereotype of a lesbian. Often stereotypes about lesbians keep them from being identified, even by other lesbians. Both the mainstream and the gay media show us images of lesbians who are far removed from the business world. Thus, when you walk down the street and run into a woman with short hair wearing Doc Martens and a black leather jacket, you might think she's a lesbian (although today many teenagers have adopted the same look). Despite "lesbian chic," "Oh, she's gay!" probably would not be your first assumption if you met the vast majority of the lesbians in our study, who wear hose and heels, have long hair, dress fashionably, and wear makeup. As more lesbians come out of the closet, the idea about the lesbian look will be expanded, and lesbian professionals will not be so easily overlooked.

Also, we were told by many highly successful lesbians that they had to work more hours than their male peers to get ahead. Most chose to devote their remaining time to their partner. Therefore, they had little time or energy remaining to be mentors and politically or socially active. We believe this will change, however, as many lesbians we interviewed plan to get involved in activities that will result in their being leaders in the gay community.

One reason we wrote this book is that so many lesbian professionals are invisible. We had the selfish motive to seek and find other lesbians who are leading interesting lives and succeeding in their careers. We succeeded in finding them and befriending some. Our goal is to entice more to come out and be more visible so that others might not feel as isolated and ignorant as we did.

Most of the lesbian professionals we interviewed shared a distinct disinclination to be the first lesbian to come out at work. Rather, they preferred to wait until lesbian friends, colleagues, or others came out first before engaging in a behavior they saw as very risky. "Pioneers get the arrows," Lacey said. "I'd rather let someone else go first and then learn from her mistakes." Many also waited for heterosexuals to drop strong hints that they knew, rather than initiate the coming-out process themselves.

One result of there being few visible lesbians is that lesbian professionals see coming out as carrying a lot of responsibility—to be role models to other gay people and to educate heterosexuals—and some shy away from this responsibility. Lorraine said, "I don't know enough about the gay community to be expected to be the expert in my office."

Second, those who don't come out continue to place the responsibility of representing lesbians on the shoulders of a few women—yet many are dissatisfied with what they see. Theresa said, "My problem with the ones who are visible is that they are the ones I don't want to be visible. I want some of us to be visible. It's always the lesbians who fit the negative stereotypes who are out. So straight people believe that all lesbians are these really tough women who have no sense of humor. There is a segment of the lesbian community that's so damn . . . oppressed. But I don't want those people representing me—the big dykes with the big breasts hanging out in the parade, with no hair on their head and hair everywhere else." However, Theresa acknowledged, she was unwilling to come out at work, let alone in the media.

While gay men also made similar comments about stereotypical gay men, most also saw the contradiction—if they weren't willing to come out themselves, they shouldn't really criticize those who do. In contrast, more lesbians were content to make critical remarks about other lesbians without acknowledging their own responsibility to solve the problem they identified. Until more mainstream lesbian professionals are willing to come out at work, they are by default electing more courageous, yet often more marginal lesbians to be their representatives.

Misconceptions and Exaggerated Fears

The most important reason why lesbian professionals stay closeted, and thus why lesbians lack visible role models, is lesbian misconceptions and exaggerated fears about coming out at work. Writing in England in 1966, Bryan Magee commented in his book *One in Twenty: A Study of Homosexuality in Men and Women*:

> Lesbians quite often have a fear of exposure in their jobs which broods over them all their lives. . . . At first I listened with sympathy to these fears and stories, but after a while I became suspicious, then positively skeptical. . . . the truth is the opposite of what I was told. . . . People . . . are not describing what actually happens, they are giving voice to their private anxieties, objectifying them, talking about them as if they were realities. . . . In their minds they ridiculously inflate the danger of the one eventuality against which they have no defense, just as many people board an airplane convinced it is going to crash—in both cases the fear runs flatly counter to probability, but every crash or sacking that does occur serves to keep it well-nourished. . . . It is natural for people's fears and insecurities to focus sharply on the one thing that would be disastrous for them if it happened, with the result that they vastly overestimate not only the likelihood of its happening but the frequency with which it actually does happen. Their fears distort not only their judgement but their view of reality. Of course there is prejudice against lesbians . . . and . . . cases of lesbians being sacked because their lesbianism came to light (just as there are plane crashes). I am not denying that it happens. What I am denying is that it is what normally happens.
>
> I know of many cases in which someone's colleagues at work know she is a lesbian, or have a shrewd suspicion. . . . when cruelty does occur it is, in almost every case I can think of, on the part of one person among many. . . . When I took to pursuing this question I asked every lesbian I talked to if she had ever lost a job because of her lesbianism. None had, and when forced to the point none was able to say that any of her friends had lost a job unequivocally for this reason—but nearly all of them knew of friends of friends who had. It is rather like the experience of having seen a ghost. . . .
>
> I have come to the conclusion that most of them could afford to be more open than they are. This would have disadvantages as well as advantages, but these would be a balance of advantage. The amounts of concealment, hypocrisy and tension in their lives would be instantly reduced. They would be helping to educate the public in elementary tolerance. And they would find, I'm sure, that most of the public cared a great deal less about the whole business than they had always supposed. (From the Chapter "Lesbians at Work," pp. 164–167)

Although the world has changed in many ways in almost thirty years, generally for the better with respect to gay people, Magee's findings and advice for lesbians, sad to say, still holds true today. Even though few fear being fired, most are afraid that their careers would come to a standstill. Yet we believe they vastly overestimate the likelihood of that happening —while the likelihood of something positive arising from coming out at work is far higher.

Fears In general, lesbian professionals believe they have to be closeted because they fear that the costs of being out are greater than the benefits. We believe they fail to give sufficient weight to the fact that being out means freedom from the fear of exposure and an increased ability to bond with others, both heterosexual and gay, while being closeted seems to almost completely thwart their ability to bond with others. By being closeted, lesbian professionals are often closed off from potential sources of support for their careers—which can be especially important to women in business.

The most closeted lesbians seemed paralyzed by fear, spending untold hours of anxiety worrying about being outed, while gay men gave far less weight to these worries. Lesbian professionals were also more likely to discount the experiences of others in their company who are out successfully.

Misconceptions Both gay men and lesbian professionals often justify being closeted with many of the same misconceptions. Yet lesbian professionals were more likely to believe these misperceptions more strongly and defend them more tenaciously.

One misconception that gay men are more likely to hold is that coming out at work equals "talking about what I do in bed," although some lesbians also said this. The vast majority of lesbians saw being gay as much more than sex. So when contemplating coming out, they saw it as a chance to discuss their whole life more openly, rather than as a forum to discuss sex, as many of the gay men did. However, many lesbians were still paralyzed by the misconception that they would be forced to share all of the details of their personal lives, rather than defining their own boundaries.

Additionally, lesbian professionals are more likely to suffer from certain other misconceptions. For example, many lesbians seem to believe that, based on seniority in the hierarchy alone, they deserve credit for leading the way for other gay people at work. In reality, those who are open are usually doing far more.

More so than gay men, lesbian professionals told us they are waiting for a time when it is safe to come out. Many of the lesbian professionals we interviewed had been in their jobs and working with the same people for years, and they still didn't think they had gotten to know them enough to come out to them. The reason they hadn't gotten to know anybody at work was that they hadn't socialized with them! Their lives were a closed book, and so their coworkers saw them as standoffish and unfriendly. Gay men, on the other hand, are more accepting that there will never be a perfect time to come out, and more willing to do so.

Some lesbians asserted they felt little need to come out at work because being gay is only one small piece of their lives. In comparison to gay men, at least, they may be right. Yet really, the belief that being gay is a piece of their lives that can be excluded from the workplace is no more true for lesbians than for gay men. If heterosexuals never discussed their families, spouses, or dates, closeted lesbians would be no exception. But in the business world, having a life outside work is critical to establish one's individuality and social acceptability, and since many lesbians' after-work activities are little different from most heterosexuals', it should be even easier for them to talk openly about being gay than it is for gay men.

Some lesbians believe that coming out as a lesbian will be seen as analogous to being a man-hater. In reality, lesbians who come out report that they are no longer seen as antisocial and standoffish when they fail to respond to male flirtation or others' attempts to set them up with eligible men. Instead, lesbian professionals who come out at work generally feel more free to be sociable with men as a result of lessening the chances of the men misinterpreting friendly social gestures.

Lesbians who actively try to pass as heterosexual may end up hurting themselves even more than gay men who do so. Fake dates or talk about a boyfriend can be misleading and damaging traps. In particular, heterosexual women often insist on sharing intimate secrets, which can get the lesbian professional in over her head. Lesbians who try to pass by inventing heterosexual romances may also be seen as pitiable losers, if the relationship does not lead to marriage, or sluts, if they continue to bring different men to social events.

Lesbians face fewer barriers when they begin to be more open. After years of hiding being a lesbian, Bonnie came to the conclusion that hiding was pointless once she hit the glass ceiling. "I realized that it had nothing to do with my sexual orientation—it had everything to do with the fact that no woman had ever gone beyond my level. So I developed an attitude of: whether I go to the party alone or bring my significant other, it didn't really matter much."

As Bonnie began becoming more comfortable in leaving clues about being gay, the social interaction with coworkers proved to be a benefit to her career. Now working at a new company, she has come out to a number of gay colleagues and suspects that most heterosexuals suspect she is gay. As a result of her first steps out of the corporate closet, her expectations from the workplace have risen. She expects heterosexual colleagues to accept her and her partner at company functions just as they would a heterosexual spouse. Furthermore, she expects that her performance will continue to be fairly evaluated or she will leave for a place where the lavender ceiling is at least no lower than the glass ceiling for women. "To be honest, I expect sexism will be a limit before being gay is a problem," she told us.

Getting Beyond Sexism In the business world, sexism was a far greater problem for lesbians than problems related to their sexual orientation. However, those who cite sexism as a reason for remaining closeted fail to see the advantages of coming out as a lesbian in overcoming sexism.

Even more so than heterosexual women, lesbian professionals are well placed to confront, combat, resist, and succeed despite sexism.

The lesbian professionals we interviewed saw the need for obtaining impeccable credentials to overcome discrimination based on their gender and sexual orientation. Fear of being hit with a double whammy also drove them to work especially hard and to choose a company on the basis of its treatment of women—or to strike out on their own. As lesbians, they usually find it easy to turn down sexual advances from men at work, thus building a reputation as someone with a clear regard for the professional boundaries of appropriate social interaction.

They may also be particularly attuned to the need to align themselves with others who have the power to help them succeed. As Roberta Lasley pointed out, "There is never any problem about promoting a Black or a woman or a gay person if the people who are making the bucks and making the decisions and the career choices for other people—if the ones who have power and influence say so, everybody says 'Yessir, boss.' They fall into line just like that, in seconds," she said with a snap of her fingers. "The only time there's any doubt is if people see wavering at the top."

Finally, lesbian professionals tend to be focused with respect to their career goals and willing to put in the work necessary to attain them. Without conflicting demands from husbands and children, which place an especially strong burden on heterosexual women, lesbians enjoy more freedom to make choices that serve their own best interests, because lesbian couples are more likely to take turns in pursuing career opportunities than any other kind of couple. While many lesbian professionals we interviewed intend to be parents, we also expect this same role sharing and turn taking will characterize many of their domestic arrangements as well.

In summary, sexism is one of the greatest hurdles lesbians face in the workplace, yet remaining closeted is not necessarily the solution. As companies increasingly realize the economic benefits for opening up opportunities to women, lesbians are well positioned to take advantage of them. As they fight the battle to succeed in business, they will have a less difficult time doing so out of the closet.

THE LESBIAN ADVANTAGE

Although no one told us being a lesbian professional was a stroll in the park, lesbians have a few advantages in the workplace over gay men and heterosexual women.

Lesbians Compared to Gay Men

STEREOTYPES OF GAY MEN AND LESBIANS Gay men are the subject of numerous negative stereotypes. Many heterosexuals perceive gay men as being effeminate, silly, emotional, weak party boys—not the authoritative traits companies are looking for in executives. Gay men who come out have the opportunity to refute these stereotypes by being seen as brave. But the stereotypes of lesbians, whether closeted or open, are far more positive. Lesbians are seen as being aggressive, non-emotional, tough, and reliable—in short, ideal management timber.

Lesbian professionals who are openly gay are in the best position to reap the benefits of this stereotype. Brooke, who is openly gay at work, said, "People at work view me as appropriately aggressive and dedicated to my work. Men don't misread my attempts to build relationships as having sexual connotations—which they might if I were a straight woman or a gay man."

But even those who are suspected of being lesbians can also find career advantages. Jody, who is closeted at work but believes coworkers suspect she is gay, said, "I never talk about men, which is pretty unusual for a woman in my office. Whether or not they think I'm gay—they assume I'm completely dedicated to my career and don't mix business with pleasure."

While closeted lesbian professionals can be seen as cold or impersonal, they may still be taken more seriously than heterosexual women, who are often viewed as inappropriately social. Other lesbian stereotypes also work to lesbians' advantage. In the 1960s and 1970s, lesbians in the feminist movement were press items as man-haters. Those images have faded, and now the press is full of lesbian chic and lesbians having children—very normative images of looking good, finding a mate, settling down, having and raising children that are closely aligned to the values of many heterosexuals. Yet in general, the stereotype of lesbians is that they do not have children—which means that, in the eyes of management, they have more time available to devote to a career. Perhaps most important, lesbians are seen as independent women who will not put a man or a man's career ahead of their own.

We still wondered about the stereotype of lesbians as tough. Weren't lesbian professionals threatening to heterosexual men? Rosalyn, who is in her late thirties, said, "I don't think anybody who heard I'm gay was surprised, just by virtue of the fact that I was a woman at HBS. They thought all HBS women were tough, you know. So being a lesbian just wasn't really a big deal either way." Barbara said, "I feel being gay has been an advantage. Although I have never been out at work, the role and style freedom that comes with lesbianism puts me head and shoulders over most heterosexual women."

Sexual Issues In addition to the personal stereotypes of gay men, the sexual stereotypes—and fears of gay men—remain strong. In fact, for most heterosexuals, a gay man is someone who has sex with other men, nothing more and nothing less. Lloyd said, "It's the 'ick' factor. When straight people think about gay men, they immediately think about him having gay sex, and they're uncomfortable with that. They don't think of him falling in love, buying a house, or doing all the things they do. They might think of two women doing that. But with a gay man, they instantly think *sex.*" Heterosexuals tend to view gay male identity to be sex-based only while overlooking other aspects of their lives. Meanwhile the notion that two women would desire to nest together is less alien because a woman's role in society traditionally has been to build a home for the family.

Often seen as inherently wild and promiscuous, gay men are stereotyped as unstable employees who are unsuitable for managerial positions. "The people I work with associate gay men with wild, seminaked, gyrating torsos on parade floats. If I come out, they'll see me as the exception—if I'm lucky," Stuart said. "Otherwise they'll think I have this wild hidden life. I only wish," he joked.

While many blamed the mainstream or the gay media for the sexual image of gay men, some gay professionals felt gay people themselves deserved some of the blame for the sexualization of gay identity. Harvey said, "I'm horrified by what I see in the Gay Pride parades. Guys running around in jockstraps and women without their tops on. It's unbelievable." However, not all of those we interviewed shared this perspective. "Gay parades are the gay Mardi Gras," Hannah said. "The truth is, I found Stonewall 25 really boring—precisely because it didn't have any drag queens or disco floats. If that's the only image of gay people straight people have—that's the problem. The only answer is for more of us 'boring' homosexuals to come out—at work, in the press, at the dry cleaner's, wherever."

As part of this sexual image, gay men are often blamed for the AIDS crisis. Mary said, "I think that in general, straight people aren't as threatened by lesbians as they are gay men, particularly since the AIDS epidemic."

Finally, the sexual stereotypes about gay men are at the heart of the homophobia of many heterosexual men. Stan said, "I think gay men have a harder time at work than lesbians, because men make a lot of power decisions in society. I don't think they care too much if a woman is gay or straight. But if a man is gay, it can threaten them. It's a macho thing more than anything else. They feel like it says something about them as a man if they tolerate someone who is gay. They're also flattering themselves that the gay guy is going to come on to them, which would—oh, no—make them feel like a woman."

In contrast, there are fewer sexual stereotypes about lesbians, and lesbians are not defined only by their sexuality. As a result, lesbians who were openly gay at work told us, heterosexuals did not find it threatening to work with them. Yolanda said, "Straight men are less threatened by lesbians than gay men. Also, straight women are far less threatened by lesbians than heterosexual men are threatened by gay men. So it's really not a big deal to come out if you are a lesbian."

The Closet Gay men found that as they aged, it was harder to avoid the suspicion that they were gay. In contrast, lesbian professionals said they did not find it harder to stay closeted as they grew older. In fact, some told us they found it easier, since coworkers were reluctant to embarrass a woman they assumed to be heterosexual by drawing attention to her single status. In addition, with more women remaining single longer, divorcing, or never marrying in order to pursue professional careers, it is far more socially acceptable for women professionals to be unmarried. While some are pitied or seen as socially inept, most are simply seen as unlucky. Men who are unmarried past age thirty-five are judged more definitively. They are seen as losers, playboys, or gay.

Thus lesbians find it easier to stay closeted at work than gay men do, despite a greater incidence of living with their partners. While a number of gay male couples maintained separate residences in part to maintain their closet, none of the lesbian couples we interviewed did. Some believed they were pulling the wool over the eyes of neighbors, families, or work colleagues. "Maybe they think we're living together to cut down on expenses," Adele said. But most said that whatever others assumed, the rumors about them were low key compared to the talk that would ensue at work if two men lived together. "Lesbians are basically invisible, no matter what we do," Cheryl said.

While some of the ways lesbians take advantage of this invisibility are trivial, we believe they make day-to-day life easier for lesbians, especially those who are out to friends and family but not at work. For example, Karl said, "Our message on the phone is in the singular." Stan added, "Yeah, it says *I'm* not home right now." Meanwhile, no one would think it was odd if a single woman were to put 'we're not home right now' on her answering machine. They would assume she did so for safety reasons —so that strangers would think she had a man living with her. Thus, this gives lesbian couples a perfect cover to be open about their relationship without being understood as coming out. "Since my partner and I sound more or less the same on the phone," Cheryl said, "whoever calls figures the voice they hear is the person they are calling for."

UNIQUENESS While gay men had more access to other gay men for networking, a few said meeting other gay men was so commonplace that being gay was not a significant bond. In contrast, lesbians often told us that meeting an openly lesbian professional was a novel experience and the basis for a strong connection.

Some gay men also felt that gay women had an advantage in getting plum positions. Tip told us, "I think it's much easier for women today than men, because firms need women so badly." In comparison to a closeted gay man, who might be seen as just another John Doe, lesbians had the opportunity, as women, to stand out at work. Lane said of her previous position, "There were so few women in my industry, we all knew who each other was, and so did all the men. Being in the spotlight meant better networking—people approached me—and more opportunities, because people knew who I was."

Lesbians Compared to Heterosexual Women

By definition, lesbians do not have the choice to be gay men. Their choice is to be seen as heterosexual women or to come out as a lesbian. Despite what many believe, it is only by coming out that lesbians can fully enjoy their advantages over heterosexual women.

CAREER FOCUS Kellie said, "To most people, being a lesbian means you are focused on your career, not your husband and children, and you have a strong, aggressive style—just like other top executives." Most senior businessmen have sacrificed their personal lives for their careers and believe that being tough and aggressive is what took them to the top. Thus their picture of lesbians has a lot in common with the profile of successful business leaders."

The lesbians we interviewed agreed that they were aggressive, tough, and not afraid to stand their ground. In listening to them talk about their personal stories and professional pursuits, it was apparent to us that these women had no trouble deciding on courses of action, executing plans, and standing behind their actions. In many cases, they are the women who will break through the glass ceiling. But being aggressive and smart is not enough, as many women have learned. Darleen said, "Women in their twenties and thirties have this stigma that they're married or they're going to get married, and they're going to leave their career to go have children—they're not going to be long-term employees. If they know you're a lesbian, they don't think that—whether or not your plans include children, that stereotype can work to your advantage." Wanda agreed. "Lesbians make great employees. They're dependable; they're reliable. They're not going to follow their husbands' careers; they're not going to make babies all the time. They make good hires."

Natalie, a senior executive, said, "My theory is that in a corporate environment, the percentage of lesbians versus heterosexual women is probably higher the higher you go, because lesbians don't opt out. If you take a universe of women that, at eighteen years old, their goal is to marry their high school sweetheart and make babies, you cut the population down. Others go to college and then get married and have babies. So as you make the population smaller and smaller, the number of lesbians increases."

Studies of the educational achievements of lesbians would seem to confirm Natalie's theory. Several studies, most recently *Sex in America,* confirm that self-identified lesbians have more education than heterosexual women, while gay men and heterosexual men have similar educational attainments. If a higher percentage of lesbians are seeking higher education than heterosexual women, they are also better positioned to attain greater professional success.

While heterosexual women today are also learning that they have to depend on themselves, it seems lesbians may internalize this message earlier and more fully. Certainly, at whatever age they realized they were gay, lesbians knew they would have to take care of themselves throughout life. Marrying a man who could bankroll them was not an option. Betsy said, "Lesbians have a belief deep down inside that you have to be able to take care of yourselves. And that isn't a deep belief held by every female in America."

While women have always worked, it is only recently that they have gotten a crack at upper-management jobs. Lesbian professionals in their mid-thirties and older are pioneers in the workforce. Their hard work, persistence, and sheer brainpower often won them acceptance and advancement. While heterosexual women often pursued the mommy track, most of these lesbians never saw children in their plans. Consequently, they have always made a priority of career success—even though many didn't have the strong business background and training of their male peers. Helen, who received her MBA in the early eighties, told us, "I was working in the public sector and I did very well. But it was clear to me that if I was going to take the next step up in terms of managerial jobs, a woman not yet in her thirties with soft degrees like I have was not going anywhere. So I said, " 'All right, well, fine. I'll just go get business training at the best place I can find.' " She continued, "I think that has worked pretty consistently. You know, when I decide what I want to do, I just do it."

Younger lesbians continue to chart new roads in traditionally male-dominated industries and companies. While many intend to have children, they have another advantage over more senior lesbians—most have always planned to go into business. As a result, they find themselves on equal footing with men at the beginning of their careers. Hope told us, "I planned far in advance. When I went into banking I knew that eventually I'd want to go to B-school and get my MBA."

Additionally, a number of the lesbian professionals we interviewed went into business for themselves. Because they hadn't sacrificed their early wage-earning years to raising a family, they had the financial base from which they could launch their own business. Others told us they are waiting to identify the right opportunity to go into business for themselves.

Seen as Independent Women Another advantage lesbian professionals have over heterosexual women is that they are seen as strong, independent women. Because they do not bring a husband or boyfriend into daily conversation or into workplace socializing, they establish their own authority. Further, heterosexual women face special difficulty in entertaining colleagues and clients. If their husband or boyfriend is another accomplished professional, they may be overshadowed. Yet if he is less successful, others may disparage him—and consequently her, for having chosen him. In contrast, single women or lesbian couples are free from these gender stereotypes. While many lesbian professionals told us they thought being married would be a career asset, we believe they overlook how often having a husband is a career liability.

In addition to the interpersonal dynamics, there is another issue. Wives follow husbands' careers far more often than the reverse—while lesbians are more free to make their own decisions. Compared to gay men, lesbians are also more likely to take turns in planning career moves. Thus any given lesbian professional is likely to have more individual autonomy than a heterosexual woman and more parity with her partner than a member of any other kind of couple.

Finally, unlike heterosexual women, lesbians do not see their value in the relationship market decline while their partner's increases with time. Thus while heterosexual women fear—and often encounter—their husbands' leaving them for a younger model, lesbian relationships are far less likely to be fraught with this inherent inequality. As a result, lesbian professionals may have a stronger sense of their own self-worth.

Emotionally Reserved "Being a vulnerable female is not an image that you want as a senior executive," Judy told us. As lesbians, the women we interviewed have had to be tough in the face of both sexism and homophobia. Especially if they have been closeted, they have learned to hide their emotions well. Many avoided personal subjects or shifted conversations away from themselves to avoid discussing being gay. Additionally, even if they are out, they didn't tend to share the intimate details of their relationships around the office. Meanwhile, heterosexual women who put all of their personal lives out in the open were seen as more emotional and, hence, less professional. Because of this, men who are uncomfortable working with women who are outwardly emotional or who like to dwell on personal conversations tend to be more comfortable working with lesbians.

Especially when dealing with a breakup, lesbians may be less vulnerable and less likely to express distress than heterosexual women. Dalia, who is in her forties, suggested, "The woman of a straight couple would have far more visible things to deal with. Usually the man is the higher-income person. So the woman would have a lot of financial worries." Referring to her own breakup, Dalia continued, "Over my dead body would I let my boss know that I am emotionally vulnerable. And in a lot of ways, I wasn't as vulnerable as a straight woman would be. I had the higher income, there were no kids involved . . . Yeah, I had to refinance the house, but I wasn't in a tough financial situation where I had to wonder, How am I going to pay the bills? Am I going to have to move out? The typical heterosexual woman my age would be dealing with those things. It's another reason why lesbians make good employees."

Seen as Less Sexual Much has been written on the subject of gender relations at work, and generally the conclusion is that female sexuality is seen as disruptive to the male power structure. When a man and a woman have an affair, it is almost always the less senior woman who gets fired or reassigned. Even when the pair are colleagues, it is the woman who gets the demeaning reputation of being a slut or sleeping her way to the top, while men who bed women at work may be ignored or seen as manly. Although our findings show that lesbians are in fact quite likely to have sex with female coworkers, most heterosexuals are not aware of this. Rather, they are likely to see lesbians as having a clean interoffice record; thus lesbians benefit from a reputation as solid professionals.

As one might expect, lesbians are far less likely to have sex with men at work. Additionally, lesbians are less likely to engage in serious or casual flirting, which can also be disruptive in the workplace. Trisha told us there may be times when men flirt with her, but she literally doesn't notice. "That's really the only advantage I can think of in being gay," she told us. Lesbian professionals who kept their attention on business told us they are often spared male workplace come-ons and are easily able to deflect any they did encounter by simply not flirting back.

This benefited their careers, because women who were not known to flirt to get ahead were known instead for their solid achievements. Meanwhile, the heterosexual women they worked with got more attention for their clothing, smiles, and casual touching. In contrast, lesbian professionals did not come across as flirtatious. Their demeanor was friendly and professional, not overtly attentive to the men at work.

Networking with Gay Men A final advantage some lesbians told us they have over heterosexual women is the ability to tap into a gay network. Many gay men befriend heterosexual women as individuals, but lesbians are able to tap into a larger circle of gay professionals, some of whom are quite senior to them and able to serve as mentors. As lesbians become more willing to come out at work, at least to other gay people, we believe they will increasingly discover the power of gay networking, with both men and women.

• • •

While many lesbian professionals claim that being gay in business is easier for men, we believe this is not generally true. The primary advantage gay male professionals have over lesbians is their more developed network—which lesbians can often tap into or help create if they are willing to be more visible at work and outside of work. And compared to gay men, lesbians are more likely to encounter a positive reaction to coming out. In addition, lesbians have much to gain by coming out at work, rather than being seen as single heterosexual women. In comparison to both gay men and to heterosexual women, there truly is a lesbian advantage.

Chapter 10

Race and Ethnicity

This chapter focuses on the experiences of Black, Hispanic, and Asian American gay people in the workplace, also discussing Jews and others who have maintained their distinctive ethnic identification in American society. According to the gay men and lesbians we interviewed, being a member of a racial or ethnic minority *and* being gay can be a double whammy or a double blessing, depending on the situation and what a person makes of it. Members of two minorities in American society can be twice as likely as other professionals to encounter prejudice and discrimination. But as members of two potentially highly supportive communities, they may be able to draw on twice as much assistance.

Many minority gay professionals told us they faced race-based prejudice in the course of their careers. A number also cited career and social obstacles due to being gay. However, as with white gay professionals, this was far more the case for those who were closeted. Interestingly, many suggested that being different can be a foundation for personal resilience and career effectiveness. In particular, those who were openly gay told us that belonging to a minority can sometimes be an advantage for them.

Repeatedly we were told that being a minority gay professional presented unique challenges and opportunities that white gay professionals did not encounter. We also found many similarities between minorities and whites. As a result, this chapter is not the only place to read about the lives of minority gay professionals; we have interspersed their stories throughout this book.

As we are both white, we were initially not sure whether we would be able to achieve a representative sampling of these professionals. Fortunately, we were met with tremendous cooperation from everyone we approached. Several were also especially instrumental in referring us to other minority HBS graduates. Thus we were able to discern common themes and trends in addition to individual perspectives. To our knowledge, this is the largest study of professional gay people who belong to racial minorities.

When we asked for referrals to classmates, we did not always know the race of people we were referred to. But by looking at pictures in the HBS Face Books, we were able to identify the race of most of those on our master list. Unfortunately we did not have access to Face Books dated before 1979, so most of the minority professionals we were able to identify are in their twenties and thirties. Hopefully the issues raised by this chapter will be studied in greater depth by other researchers, with special attention to the issue of age.

By far, gay Black men form the largest subgroup in our minority sample. While we met our goal of interviewing Black lesbians and gay Hispanics and Asian Americans roughly in proportion to their presence in the HBS alumni population, we were not able to oversample these groups.

While we did not initially foresee a need to oversample Jewish gay professionals, we eventually did make this effort. Although Jews have been admitted to HBS for many years, far more Jews attend law or medical schools than business school. In addition, some of those who attend business school are quite assimilated in terms of surname and consciousness of Jewish identity. Thus, halfway through our interviews we realized that we had interviewed far fewer people we knew to be Jewish than our best guess of the percentage of Jews in the business-school alumni population. As a result, based on last name or personal knowledge, we targeted Jews for oversampling as well.

Our Jewish interviewees ran the spectrum from self-identified "lox and bagels" cultural Jews to deeply committed religious Jews. In general, we found, the more traditionally observant the Jew, the more similar being Jewish was to being Black, Hispanic, or Asian American. We regret that we did not have the opportunity to interview any gay Mormons or gay Moslems; it is likely these individuals would have posed an interesting counterpoint to the cultural and religious issues faced by gay Jews in the U.S. workplace. This study did not delve deeply into the issue of religion itself, apart from the cultural issues. While we interviewed numerous Catholic gay professionals and gay Protestants from most of the American denominations, none raised specific issues that related to their workplace experiences.

FINDINGS

Black, Hispanic, and Asian American gay professionals told us that there are important differences between being part of a minority racial group and being gay. Almost all mentioned the most significant as visibility. A number reported that they never encountered discrimination because of their sexual orientation but had frequently encountered it because of their race. As many pointed out, racial background is often obvious whereas it is almost impossible to know somebody's sexual orientation at a glance.

Jordan told us, "I can pass for straight if I want to, but no matter how I feel or what I do, I can't disguise being Black." Tony told us, "I've encountered more racial issues than gay issues. Racial issues I've run into all the time."

Another difference cited by some minority gay professionals is the degree of support they feel from their minority community as compared with the gay community. "I find the gay community to be incredibly racist," several commented. Others disagreed, saying they felt more comfortable in the gay community due to the homophobia of their own racial group. In the workplace, this means that minority gay professionals are often deprived of natural sources of support. Whether alienated from other gay people or from other minority professionals, minority gay men and women can feel very much alone in facing the business world.

While Black professionals expressed their sentiments most vehemently, these remarks were echoed by Hispanics and Asian Americans. Jews often compared being Jewish to being gay: It is possible for most to hide. Nonetheless, Jews often felt alienated by the cultural assumptions of their overwhelmingly Christian coworkers and angry at other Jews who did not seem to notice slights such as assuming that everyone came from a Christian background, which they paralleled to the assumption that everyone is heterosexual.

Some mixed-race or light-skinned Black and Hispanic Americans also told us they had to deal with the issue of coming out about their racial background. Joe Steele, a light-skinned Black man, told us, "My mother is Polish and my father is Black and German. I was adopted and raised by a Black household, so my culture is Black. Yet looking the way I do, most people don't immediately assume I'm Black. I'm not a very typical gay person either, so people I work with don't immediately assume that either. So I'm treated to a lot of comments about race and sexual orientation that a lot of people don't hear."

CHALLENGES AT WORK

We found these career turning points to pose the greatest challenges in the career of minority gay professionals: getting hired, getting promoted, and coming out at work.

Getting Hired

Those who are Black, Hispanic, or Asian American generally agreed that race is far less an issue for them in the hiring process than later on. Often trailblazers as the first member of a racial minority in their company or industry at their level, most felt they had received a fair shot at being hired.

Some told us they felt being a minority can even be an advantage for getting hired by certain companies. But both white and minority professionals we interviewed agreed it was unusual for an unqualified applicant to be offered a position. Hence, Tammy quipped, "I'd rather get the job because I'm Asian than *not* get the job because I'm Asian."

Most minority gay professionals felt that gay issues are irrelevant in the interview phase. Kenny, a Black gay man who is involved in hiring decisions at his company, told us that as far as he can tell, "race doesn't matter. It really does not matter. And I have my antenna up looking for it, believe you me. I realize that in my position I have a unique opportunity to see really what's going on behind the scenes. And I have just not come across it. As for sexual orientation, I have not had anyone come to me and say, 'Well I have this skill, that skill, and I'm gay, and I can do this and this.' No one says that."

However, like their white peers, several minority gay professionals mentioned the question of fit surfacing in an interview. Curtis, who is also Black, told us one firm asked him if he was married during an interview; he also knew of an even more blatant case involving a friend. He said, "A friend from HBS who's also gay recently interviewed with a Wall Street investment company, one of the boutique firms, and he told me that they asked him at the interview if he was gay. He told me he answered no. At the time, he was without work and he wanted to break into this area, and he needed to get the experience. So he said he wasn't gay. And the interviewer warned him, 'Well, let me tell you, if you are, you will not fit in here.' " Curtis told us his friend still ended up taking a consulting assignment there.

Some of those we interviewed said they themselves looked for companies where they would find people like themselves. Many felt that looking at the number of women and minorities in management positions was a good indicator of how comfortable they would be there—both as a minority and as a gay person. Pam, who is Asian American, said, "Definitely, if I was trying to figure out whether a company was going to be a good place to work as a gay person, I would look at the number of minorities, look at the number of women in management in the company. I think it's very telling."

Similarly, Marvin, who is Jewish, said he would "look at the names in the company directory to see if there are Jews there, if there are women there. I would look around and see if I see any women, any Black people in the executive ranks. My guess is that bastions of white Christian maleness are probably the same places that would be homophobic."

Getting Promoted

Once they begin to work at a company, many of those we interviewed agreed, both race and sexual orientation can become issues, and a number of minority professionals attempted to hide being gay. Joseph, who works in investment baking, told us, "You have to work so hard to make them forget that you're Black. OK, now I've got to make them forget that I'm Black *and* gay? You know, my job is already rough enough here. Let's keep certain things that people don't need to know away from them."

Cecil, who is also Black and works alongside an overwhelming majority of white people, including many gay men and lesbians, agreed with the job-search strategy of looking for racial, ethnic, and gender diversity. "If you see that a company has minorities, then you know that they are willing to accept at least that amount of diversity. It's the same principle if there's women there." But he feared: "Being gay could be the last whammy. If you're more than one or two of those things—watch out!"

Some of those who are openly gay at work have also concluded that race is more of an issue. Gordon, who is Black, took a job with a major advertising company, where he worked alongside many white gay men and several white lesbians and came out without incident to several major corporate clients. But he wondered what kind of future he could expect with the firm, because he was the only Black professional there. He suspected he had been hired because his employers felt they needed a token Black to present an image as a liberal firm.

He told us that certain prospective clients required an integrated staff, an experience that Lamar, another Black gay man working in advertising, also reported. "The group I was in always had to have three Blacks. There were always three Blacks in certain groups because certain clients dictate you have to have Blacks," Lamar told us. "McDonald's always says you have to have Blacks. P & G says you have to have Blacks. Philip Morris says you have to have Blacks. Therefore, that's where the most Blacks work. And if the client doesn't dictate it, the company is not going to do it."

Although P & G is one of the companies that demanded Black advertising executives, Marc says he found P & G to be "a very oppressive place to work." Others echoed that large Midwestern employers that hire multitudes of MBAs and have a very regimented up-and-out corporate culture is deadly for diversity, even when a company tries to hire and promote a diverse workforce.

For example, Andre took a position with another company in the Midwest. He told us, "I sort of entered the firm with a few problems to begin with. The Harvard thing even worked against me, because this company is very homegrown. It's what I call the 'aw shucks' mentality. 'Aw, we're jut good old hayseeds trying to do our best, and we work really hard.' I'm not blond, blue eyed, and Midwestern, OK? I'm a wise-ass Black guy from New York. Pretty quickly I realized that things were really not working out for me there.

"Fortunately, there was someone there, a Black guy, who was a mentor to me to the extent that he could be. He was hired to be in the executive corps and oversee minority affairs—which means he had no power whatsoever. As much as he could be a mentor, he was. But he didn't have enough power to combat what was happening to me. He did, however, know a headhunter, who knew of a company that was looking for someone to handle European business, and he recommended me. So my friend recognized that I was getting the shaft there and helped me move out. It was the best thing in the world for me."

Gordon also doubted whether what he described as his "WASP-nest" advertising employer was really likely to consider him as serious candidate for promotion into the upper echelons, and he ultimately left the firm. He recalled two incidents that seemed symbolic. He had stepped out into a hallway for a breath of fresh air before a luncheon meeting. An executive Gordon didn't know came out of another meeting room and told Gordon that they were ready to be served. Despite Gordon's Brooks Brothers attire, the man assumed that a Black man in that building must be one of the caterers! Another time, again dressed in a business suit, Gordon was waiting outside for his colleagues and a potential client. The client arrived first and asked Gordon if he was the limo driver! He left because he saw little future as the token Black professional there.

A number of Black gay professionals told us that while they haven't encountered any direct prejudice based on their race, they felt that it was a significant component of the problems they had at work. Marty told us, "I have no specifics but a definite impression that I remained on the outside looking in, since so much business success is based on those in power promoting others that are like them, who they are comfortable with and socialize with. I don't play golf, or go to the same night clubs, social clubs, beaches, or have the same family-oriented concerns that they do—and I have no intention of pretending that I do in order to get ahead.

As a gay Black man, I feel that my ability to be like them was doubly difficult.

Difficulties faced by heterosexual Black executives have been extensively documented and are confirmed by many of those we interviewed. Denzel told us that membership in every country club in his suburb was restricted in some way. "There are WASP clubs, Italian clubs, and Jewish clubs. My Black peers and I are limited to the public golf courses and tennis courts or to being invited as somebody's guest. That means we can't reciprocate when clients include us, like our white peers can, and that hurts professionally." While he was not sure whether gay or unmarried people would be eligible for membership, he pointed out that if his married Black friends were members, he could at least bring clients when we went golfing with them.

Only a few felt that being gay was a bigger barrier in their careers than being Black. Clark said that while being Black has also been a major liability for him, the gay issue loomed larger. "Interestingly enough, while I ran into blatant examples of racism where I worked, and no homophobic incidents other than the occasional fag joke, nevertheless I feel that being gay was probably a bigger obstacle to my success than being Black. I knew that I would never continue to rise if they knew I was gay or even if I failed to get married soon." Those who voiced this opinion were all highly closeted at work. Those who were open generally told us they were aware of little discrimination against them based on either race or sexual orientation.

Coming Out at Work

Various studies we've read and the speculation of our peers suggested that minority gay professionals would be more closeted at work than their white peers. Members of other ethnic groups also drew parallels between the experience of being gay and being a minority, usually to justify remaining closeted at work. Anton said, "I do know that bad things can happen to you out there for reasons that are a lot smaller than being gay. It can be for being a woman; it can be for having Black hair; it can be for being Greek. I mean, there are so many things out there that can get you, because there are so many things that you can be that are so politically charged. Why give somebody any more ammunition against me?"

In fact, we found racial minorities to be somewhat more closeted than their white peers but far less closeted than we had anticipated. Although some minority professionals and current business students are among the most closeted of the gay people in our database, others are also among the most willing to be out.

We also found that many minority professionals were among those who felt most strongly about the importance of openly gay role models, which led a number of them to be at least selectively open at work, and led a few to be willing to have their names included in these pages. To the best of our knowledge, this book is the first place where a number of minority business professionals have elected to be named in print. Perhaps one reason is that other studies of gay professionals did not have an extensive network base of minorities to draw from. Another may be that times are starting to change. Younger gay minorities, like their white peers, seem to be increasingly willing to come out.

Torrence Boone told us, "Racism is incredibly subtle on a lot of levels and is dangerous and awful because it is so subtle. But I think it's been easier to wage the battle, in a sense. I mean, first of all, you have a whole structure of legal precedent that's behind you. For me, being Black and gay, I feel the gay issue is so much more important, because you don't have the explicitness and you don't have the history and you don't have the legal superstructure helping you out. You don't have a lot of things to make the battle easier. And that's why, in terms of the Black/gay thing, I'm probably more active on the gay front."

Those who are open say they have learned from their families and their ethnic or racial community to take pride in who they are and have applied that sense of pride to being gay as well. Brian Offutt told us, "The issue of racism has never been a big deal for me; it's never been a problem. I've never felt held back, and certainly no one ever says anti-Black things to my face, whereas people have said antigay things, because they haven't known I'm gay. People who know I'm gay don't say antigay things either." While Brian acknowledged that having people keep their prejudice to themselves is only the first step on a very long road to true acceptance, it may be a necessary one.

Despite significant commonalities, there are also some unique issues regarding coming out related by Blacks, Hispanics, Asian Americans, and Jews.

Black Gay Professionals Some Black gay professionals were among those who were most adamant about their desire to be completely closeted at work—often the same individuals who had encountered the most difficulty being Black in the workplace. Nicholas told us, "As a result of difficulty of being Black in American business, we oftentimes feel that we're at risk already in any position we're in, so you don't feel secure enough to say, 'OK, you know it's obvious that I'm Black. On top of that, I'm gay. So deal with me.' "

He posited, "I don't know if you've come across Blacks who are comfortable being out. In general, my Black friends from Harvard Business School are not out at work. I don't know if you've interviewed any of those people or not, but they would be hard pressed, I would think, to come out and say, 'Yes, I'm gay.' Because it doesn't advance your career in any arena I can think of for a Black person to do that." Yet we found a number of openly gay Black professionals, as well as many who are selectively open, who have not found being gay a barrier.

Deidre told us that she is out to her boss and several others at work and has not had any problems. She fully expects to continue to receive promotions, as does Sandra, another openly gay Black lesbian we spoke with. The particular circumstances of these women meant they were not able to participate in full-length interviews with us, but their experiences regarding coming out were similar in many respects to those voiced in this chapter and the chapter on gender. Gay Black men such as Brian Offutt, Joe Steele, Torrence Boone, Mel Glapion, Gordon, an advertising executive, Sebastin, a partner at a major consulting firm, and Victor, a high-ranking corporate executive, are all at least selectively open at work.

Hispanic Americans Harvard Business School admits far more Hispanics from Puerto Rico, Mexico, Latin America, and South America than it does from the United States; thus limiting our study to the fifty states narrowed our sample considerably. Two Cuban Americans were among the most open of our entire study. While others were less open, most said they thought others knew they were gay.

While at business school in the early 80s, Raul Companioni encouraged his peers to pursue political as well as social goals for the gay student group, a cause that was not tremendously popular at the time. After graduating from HBS, Raul joined Christopher Street Financial, a money management firm specializing in tax-exempt securities and oriented almost exclusively toward gay clients. Raul enjoyed a successful career there before succumbing to AIDS in 1990. At the time we met him, he was also extensively involved in organizing for the Gay Games, an international sporting event for gay athletes in virtually every competitive sport.

Ronnie Diaz, who was out at Coca-Cola and Taco Bell before coming to Harvard Business School, came out to her classmates and future professional peers during her First Year there. "In a human relations class we were doing the Xerox case about the Black caucus group. We had just seen this inspirational film about how the Black caucus group had moved from being kind of an alienated side organization in the 1960s to now being a big national organization where they had a convention and the president of Xerox came to talk to them. And there was a conversation in the class about whether the corporate liaison to the group should be whoever the vice president of employee relations is or whether it should be a Black person.

"A Black guy raised his hand and said it has to be somebody that understands the issues and knows what it's like, because you're really alienated as a Black person in most corporations. You have to have someone who understands what it feels like to not belong. I just raised my hand and said that I can relate to that as a gay person in the workplace. I gave examples of how you feel kind of alienated, how sometimes you don't fit in, and that type of thing. That was it. Then afterwards I started shaking a little bit. It was around the third- or fourth-to-last comment of the class.

"Afterwards about twenty people rushed up and hugged me and said, 'Oh, that's great, and we're behind you.' And then, periodically over the next week, people would come up to me and say it's great and everything. Both men and women were extremely supportive. Very, very supportive. I had the Ed Rep post, so I felt like I already had a little bit of respect from them by doing that. I already had a little bit of credibility. I think that helped quite a bit.

"People have actually been really glad to be able to talk about it," Ronnie told us. "A bunch have come up and asked me about different things. Some folks want me to give a talk about what it's like to be gay. Our section is really big on diversity, so being gay kind of fits right in with that. It's interesting though. One of my classmates made some comment about straight white males, which led everyone to assume that he was gay. Friends have told me about comments made behind his back, but no one ever says anything like that about me. He was treated totally differently than I was, and I think it's because I'm openly gay." Having graduated, Ronnie had her pick of numerous job offers and intends to continue being openly gay in her career.

ASIAN AMERICANS The Asian Americans we interviewed, as the so-called model minority, said they found promotions easy to come by through the middle-management levels. But they worried that the stereotypes of Asians as technically oriented and unaggressive might prove a barrier in obtaining the big-picture management jobs at the top. Many were at least selectively open about being gay and felt that this was not a major issue by itself. Rather, they saw the combination of race and sexual orientation as making them too different.

Ty told us that he left the company he worked for previously because he knew that at some point he'd hit a glass ceiling—both because of being gay and because of being Asian. He also felt that his political views were not in sync with the rest of the company. He said, "All the senior execs went to the same church and lived in the same suburb. So I realized that I wasn't too sure that I'd fit in there."

Cathy said that she too is thinking about leaving her company. "I've been restless for about a year or so. The job has been great because it's been really interesting, and I've learned a lot. But I've sort of done the rounds at this point, and there isn't a lot of advancement opportunity unless I want to live in New York, and I don't. It's also a very male, very white, very conservative company, and I'm a woman, I'm Asian, and a lesbian. It's really tough. Personally it's hard for me to integrate the corporate hierarchy with my own lifestyle—being gay and all my other interests—because it's just so different from who I am, and not everybody is open minded. You have to fight a certain amount in life, but I don't want to have to be working uphill my whole life, every day. You know it would be nice to just feel comfortable about the gay issue, because you have to fight in so many other ways.

"Sure, I can go off on my own and be successful and be happy. But on the other hand, if I did that, I wouldn't be doing anything for the general good. A part of me feels that if you give up, you're letting them beat you. You can't let that happen. I know I'm good professionally. It's just that you have to make a lot of personal sacrifices along the way. So there are all of these conflicting things. I want to set an example and make things easier for the people who come after me. But sometimes I think there's only so much I can do."

Matt originally had hoped that consulting would be a hospitable place to be gay and Asian. At a recruiting briefing sponsored by the Boston Consulting Group, he said, "One of the senior partners gave a speech about how BCG prides itself on the diversity of its workforce. I thought, Oh, diversity. OK. And they're proud of it. Well, maybe I might fit in." But Matt's hopes were dashed when he attended the reception after the talk. "I went up to a woman from the New York office and I said, 'I'm interested to know how many gay people you have in your office?' She kind of thought about it for a long time, and said, 'Well, there was one gay associate, or maybe it was a partner, but he left. So basically, right now, nobody that I know of.' "

Matt then went over to a woman from BCG's Los Angeles office. Instead of going directly to the gay question, he asked, "How many Asians do you have at BCG Los Angeles?" Matt told us, "She kind of thought about it for a while and it looked like she was counting up all the people. And she said, 'None'!" Matt exclaimed. "I thought, Oh, well, you know, even though Los Angeles has a huge Asian population, Asians are a small minority group at business school. So I asked, 'Well, how many Black professionals do you have?' And she thought about it for a while, and said, 'None'!"

By now Matt was seriously beginning to have doubts about whether there was any meaningful diversity at the firm. But he continued to ask. "Well, I don't suppose there are any gay people there?" Matt said, "She kind of thought about it for a while, and answered, 'Well, there's this one guy we think is gay, but he's kind of closeted.' " Matt ended up accepting a position in another industry.

Jews Being gay and being Jewish are parallel experiences in many ways. Most Jewish gay professionals felt they were able to conceal their Jewish identity just as they could conceal their sexual orientation if they chose to. Also, both gay people and Jews are accused of being a secret cabal with great wealth and immense power, despite their small numbers in the American population. Additionally, being gay and being Jewish are said by some to contain an element of choice, in comparison to "real" minority groups. After all, it is said, Jews can convert, and gay people can choose abstinence or pretend to be heterosexual or get married.

Gay Jews told us that such arguments make them really furious. "I wouldn't take a magic pill to become heterosexual, even if I could," Hannah told us. "And I certainly don't intend to give up being Jewish either, even though I'm not especially religious. To me, this whole issue of choice and numbers is ridiculous! Whether there's six thousand or six million Jews, we deserve political equality and protection from discrimination; so do gay people, whether there are a hundred or a hundred million of us."

Some Jewish lesbians and gay men report they too encountered job discrimination or cultural alienation at work because of their ethnicity. They agreed, however, that being gay was usually far more of an issue for them in business. We found this interesting, because the number of openly Jewish business professionals in the upper ranks of many industries, whether gay or heterosexual, remains relatively small.

Jews who worked in ethnically diverse workplaces and described themselves as not very religious found being Jewish was far less an issue for them than being gay. However, there were major differences on this issue based on industry and geographic location. Several pointed out that corporate America has made strides in hiring and promoting Black managers. Asian Americans and Latin Americans have also made inroads into corporate environments in certain cities. But there are few openly Jewish executives at the higher levels of many large manufacturing or industrial companies, despite the large numbers of Jews who have sought higher education. While corporations are quick to hire Jewish accountants and attorneys, we learned, this did not mean that Jews were well represented throughout corporate America itself.

Jacob, who worked for a major New York City bank, told us that he saw fewer Jews than gay people rise through the ranks of his company, a comment that was echoed by others in banking and other fields, such as the oil industry, utilities, transportation, and large manufacturing companies. Consulting firms, on the other hand, seemed to vary considerably from firm to firm.

Industries like investment banking and financial services employ a large number of Jews, but this too can significantly vary from company to company. In contrast, the media and the entertainment and fashion industries employ many Jewish as well as many openly gay professionals. Gay Jews in all these industries usually told us that being Jewish did not set them apart from their coworkers, particularly if they were willing to assimilate culturally. Those who were actively Jewish year-round found being a Jew most similar to being gay.

Robert Goldfarb, who is religiously observant, compared coming out as a Jew to coming out as a gay. "I don't remember any hostility toward gay people at HBS. If anything, I felt like an outsider because I was a Jew. I remember I made a comment once in a class, with overtly Jewish content, and all heads turned instantly. It was as if I had crossed some sort of boundary by revealing myself to be openly Jewish. With a name like 'Goldfarb' it shouldn't have been much of a surprise. I'm sure it wasn't a surprise on an unconscious level, but maybe it was the fact that I was articulating it in that environment."

Robert has found "You often feel your way with being observant as a Jew in much the way you feel your way with being out as a gay person. You have to test the limits as you go. You can't assume how understanding somebody is going to be. You can be wrong either way—fearing the worst or assuming the best. As much drama as there can be in a coming-out experience, I prefer to think of it as part of life. It's like when people discover that I don't work on Shemini Atzeret [a less-known Jewish holiday]," he told us. "Usually people are surprised, just as some are when they find out I'm gay. But it's usually not a problem."

Robert told us, "I also don't work on Shabbat. I have never found anyone sneer at this. But I have had some bosses who are literally uncomprehending. It's almost as if they're asking, 'Why on earth would you want to go to synagogue that much?' " Robert said that he has also found colleagues, clients, and bosses to be open to his being gay.

Many told us they felt that being Jewish prepared them for being gay. Bart Rubenstein reflected, "I suppose, if you want to be philosophical, I could relate my gay identity to my identification as a Jew. I always viewed the community at large as different from me. And while I want to live and be successful in the mainstream, my own friendships and my own community are very distinct and apart from the people who were in my class at school or in my office at work. Those are not where I choose to spend most of my off-duty time and effort."

Deborah, who also describes herself as more of a cultural Jew than a religious one, said that being a politically aware Jew helped her learn to voice unpopular opinions, both in the mainstream society and within the Jewish community. "This ended up being good training for being openly gay at work and taking unpopular positions in the gay community as well." She laughed as she told us.

However, some said they had more difficulty standing up for themselves as gay people than as Jews. Richard Stern explained, "I grew up as a Jewish youngster being a part of a minority in a majority world. When I worked for Control Data in Minneapolis, I had a young man who worked for me who used the expression 'Don't jew 'em down' to me. I spoke to him afterward and asked, 'Do you know what that means?' He told me that he didn't realize that the term 'jew' in that expression referred to a person who is Jewish. I believed him, but I made sure to tell him that I was Jewish, that's what that word refers to, and that I was offended by that. I was the first Jewish person that he'd ever known."

In contrast to his aplomb in dealing with anti-Semitism, Richard admitted he had a more difficult time dealing with antigay comments and jokes. "Maybe it's because it took me so long to come to terms with being comfortable with being gay myself," he told us.

CHALLENGES OUTSIDE WORK

In addition to discrimination in the mainstream, minority gay professionals may face discrimination from their own culture as well as in the gay community. Instead of being a source of support, these communities may raise barriers that leave minority gay professionals isolated. In other cases, it is possible to surmount those barriers.

Being Gay in a Minority Community

One reason gay minorities can have a difficult time at work is that they do not always receive the support of their racial or ethnic community, either inside or outside the workplace. At work they may encounter isolation or rejection by colleagues and employers of the same background. Thus, from the very people in whom these professionals hoped to find strength or at least neutrality, some found additional trials.

Both Jordan and Gordon joined ethnically diverse companies after leaving primarily white ones. Jordan says that people where he worked may suspect that he's gay because he doesn't talk about women that much. He added that his male partner is the beneficiary on his life insurance, and "I don't trust the office manager to keep that confidential." But he is worried about coming out at work because of the homophobia he has experienced in the Black community.

Gordon, who is out where he works, told us, "This is the first time I've tried to integrate being gay and a racial minority. Now I work for a very ethnically diverse company, and being gay is more of an issue than it ever was before. The owner isn't great on gay issues. But I'm trying to educate people. They just have to deal with it. I've already got my credibility with them. And what the boss doesn't know is that I've had a drink with his son at a gay bar here in town."

Although selectively out at his previous mainstream employer, Gordon told us, "I'm actually more out now. Just recently I told my boss that I learned Italian from an ex-lover and went on to use the pronoun 'he.' I said that in the divorce I got custody of the language, and *he* got the apartment. At least I made him laugh."

Many gay minorities told us they felt the need to be closeted within their racial or ethnic group's business and social groups. Those who were closeted to family or at work feel this way even more strongly. Jeffery, who says he sees no need to come out to family or at work, although he believes that both know he is gay, received many invitations to the Black power-elite social circles in Chicago. He said that socializing with the most prominent and powerful Black leadership in town could lead to many career opportunities, but going without a female date has closed most doors.

Yet Torrence Boone suggests that coming out can produce change. "For example, at HBS most African Americans come from the traditionally Black colleges, and these schools don't tend to have as active a gay organization as the large research universities. You also don't have as diverse a mix of people. So I think in terms of exposure to gay things, there is a limit there, and that plays itself out at HBS. But Black people there have been fine about it, once I came out to them."

Being a Minority in the Gay Community

Until recently, minority gay people were almost completely excluded from white gay networks. While some believe that things are changing rapidly, others point out that prejudice still remains. Emil told us that some dance clubs in New York continue the practice of asking Blacks, Hispanics, and Asians for three pieces of ID or using a selective door policy based on a patron's look, which often results in a very white crowd with a few drag queens thrown in for color.

Joe Steele concurred. "To be perfectly honest with you, I have a real issue with the gay community. The bulk of the power is with white gay men, who are incredibly racist. I think they feel that, being gay, they're shit on enough, so they want to just shit on somebody else for a change. It's hard to be involved in something when you don't have respect for the leadership or some of the underlying folks running it. Maybe some of this is just me, but I don't feel very welcome in a lot of gay community activities. I find them to be more exclusionary than inclusionary. So I don't go out of my way to be involved in gay causes, because quite often the powerful individuals in them are the problem themselves."

Emil went further, charging, "Gay groups are just not as accepting of Black people as straight ones are. And while I have straight Black friends who accept me for being gay, I have very few white gay friends who accept me as Black." He added, "I am not actively involved in the gay and lesbian community, because Black issues are more important to me.

"In college," Emil said, "white students always wanted to know why most of the Black students ate lunch together. Well, it's because it's the only hour of the day we could just be ourselves. The rest of the day, we're doing what everybody else is doing. It's like that now with work. When I go home, I just want to be myself." Although he has a white partner, most of Emil's close friends are Black. He is also active in a Black professional organization, where, as far as he knows, he is the only gay man.

Gordon felt that things were changing. He told us, "The greatest change in the shortest period of my life is the degree of racial acceptance in the gay community." But there is still discrimination, he told us, and not only against racial minorities. "I overheard two men at a party deciding to exclude one of my friends from their get-together because he is 'Swiss,' which was their code word for 'Jewish.' "

Mel Glapion said that he felt there was still racial prejudice but that it was more complicated now. He said, "Being gay and Black in Boston is very strange for me. Here I've found that prejudice is along different lines than race per se. It's not along the race line so much; it's along social status and economic status much more. Because Blacks have had a hard time out there, they don't meet some of the status requirements that white gay men have for friends and lovers. So you will find some Blacks who will go around constantly saying, 'Oh, I went to Harvard.' And the truth is, once you meet that level of socioeconomic status, you are fine. Then you're in, and you're invited to all the parties, and you can go to all the clubs and meet anyone that you want. But until you achieve that status stratum, you're sort of locked out. White men here are more standoffish —as well as more nosy in a certain way. They want to know what I have going on that I meet so many people without being introduced. They think: If you're not introduced, then, God knows, don't talk to someone Black."

These issues can also arise in the workplace. Some told us that they felt a certain distance from their gay and lesbian coworkers and even chose to disassociate themselves from those coworkers—for one or several reasons. Cecil said, "There was a group of gay men where I worked who were in a bitchy little social clique. They all hung out together at work and in the bars. A little bit of the reason I wasn't part of their group was by choice. They weren't the type of people that I wanted to associate with, whether they were gay or not. I just don't like them, and I didn't want to have to deal with them." Another gay man at Cecil's company also divorced himself from that group. He told Cecil, "You know, these guys wanted me to play their [silly little] reindeer games, and I just didn't want to be part of that." Cecil said, "They kind of ostracized him a little bit for that."

When we asked the racial makeup of the group, Cecil told us, "They were all white, except for one who was Black. He was a very senior person there, and he was on the creative side, where he could probably get away with being more 'fabulous' at work. Cecil told us, "I didn't really want to be part of that group—first of all, it would have marked me as gay at work. Second, gossiping about other people in bars is not how I want to spend my social time. I'd rather be home with my partner."

While most gay Jews said they haven't experienced personal discrimination in the gay community, many noted that they sometimes feel culturally excluded. "One of the largest gay groups in my city did a major fund-raiser on the first night of Passover. That's only the most widely observed Jewish holiday." Reuben exploded. "They sure didn't raise any funds from me. In response, the gay Jewish group here sent out a calendar that highlighted the major Jewish holidays for the next decade. So far, so good, but I'm sure they'll have to send out the same calendar over and over, even though the major Jewish holidays are also noted on most secular calendars."

Joan told us, "The gay professional organization in my city throws a Christmas party every year. Finally I got fed up and pointed out that many of us are Jewish. So now it's a holiday party. But the decorations are still red-and-green, and they still do a Secret Santa gift exchange. Unless I was willing to be on every party planning committee in town, I don't think things are going to change," she said in frustration.

Others decried gay friends and work colleagues who saw them as too sensitive about Jewish issues. "It's like being gay," Dean asserted. "If everyone constantly assumed that you are the same as them, and you don't speak up, your point of view is going to be completely overlooked. Jews have been around for thousands of years under conditions ranging from horrible oppression to almost total assimilation. You'd think gay people would be more aware of the parallels between being gay and being Jewish, but in my experience, I always have to be the one who educates them."

UNIQUE ADVANTAGES

Happily, in addition to the many pressures minority gay professionals face, there are compensatory advantages. We found that the ability to take advantage of these benefits was not limited to those in a particular industry or from a particular family background. Instead, at least for this relatively privileged group of minority gay professionals, these advantages were more or less available to all who sought them.

The Legal Advantage

One advantage enjoyed by gay minority-group members over white gay peers is that they have legal protection against lack-of-fit issues under race or ethnicity statutes. As a result, some of those we interviewed felt their companies tend to tread more lightly around all of their differences, including being gay.

License to Be Different

We found that if a person is accepted for being different in any way, they often are given license to be different in other ways as well. Ray told us that being a Black man caused people in the oil industry to give him a wide berth. He said, "In those sort of environments, it's already strange because you're Black. My observation is that it made things easier for me. Once I was accepted in the first place, they just see everything as part of a package. Here's this Black person who went to MIT—that's plenty for them right there. Then when you throw in the gay stuff, it's sort of inconsequential. My behavior is seen as sort of an enigma to people anyway, and so they accept the gay or the flamboyant stuff with everything else. That's my take on the way things go. I've observed that, and I use that wherever I can. So, whereas other people are trying to downplay being Black or trying to hide being gay, I play it to my advantage. I capitalize on that sense of difference. I don't hide, and it works for me."

After business school, Cameron chose a company that has had a longstanding commitment to diversity. He told us, "We have a number of women at the top, we have a number of Black people in the top ranks, and we have a number of senior Hispanic executives. And there's a pipeline coming up, so that will continue to be the case. It's different than most other firms in the industry, I think. I think it really is more diverse than others, because for years they've always hired people from different business schools, not just from Harvard, and people who are MBAs and some non-MBAs. So there are all sorts of different backgrounds there.

"The firm is generally full of people who are a little more accepting of 'You do your thing, I do my thing.' We come in and do our work and give value to the clients, but most of us also have a whole personal life outside of work. Whereas at some other companies you have to do a lot with people you work with. I have a friend who is a senior executive at another company in the same industry, and he feels he has had to be completely closeted all the time. And something like 80 percent of his friends are people for the company. That's almost a requirement there."

Sebastin is out selectively with clients and to some of those he works with at his consulting firm. He also has a well-deserved reputation among his friends for his flamboyance in the way he dresses. "You know, at some point I probably should not be so risk taking. I mean, it's one thing to feel as though you can be yourself and you don't have to hide things. It's another thing just to be blatant, and I'm getting close to really just doing stuff just to see how far I can push it." Having recently made partner, Sebastin seems more than justified in feeling that being unconventional has worked well for him.

"I've also opened up some opportunities for other guys to dress and act a little more creatively at work," he noted. "As a matter of fact, I've had a couple of junior colleagues who are gay compared to me by some of my peers. Or they'll say things like, 'You know, I just interviewed this guy and he was another Sebastin,' that sort of thing. And they'll hire him. You know, it's interesting. At first when I would hear that, I thought: Oh, it must have been somebody Black, but it's not always somebody Black. I don't know if all of them are gay. But it's always somebody who was kind of a unique individual."

Others echoed Sebastin's sentiments, although most were far more conventional in their appearance and demeanor. Torrence Boone told us "Being marginal has its problems and negative aspects, but it also allows you to define things on your own terms."

Mel Glapion told us that being gay can even be an asset in forging social and professional relationships with heterosexuals. He said, "In New York, it's almost like straight people want to meet gay people, because they are going to be the most exciting people and know the best clubs, the best parties, and they have the most money, the best jobs. New Orleans wasn't like that. I just love New York!"

Calvin admitted that he uses his caustic tongue and quick wit to intimidate. As a Black man, he intimated, he found this strategy particularly successful. "People don't want to mess with me," he exulted.

While none of the Black, Hispanic, or Asian lesbians we interviewed directly addressed the issue of being different as an asset, a few of the Jewish women did. Sybil suggested, "I think that when people see that you are not afraid to be who you are, they tend to respect that. A lot of Jews try to assimilate and never talk about being Jewish, just like a lot of gay people try to downplay being gay. I talk about what I want to when I want to." In addition, lesbians of all backgrounds mentioned that being a woman in a traditionally male profession gives them visibility throughout their company or industry, even at fairly young ages, and some were able to capitalize on that advantage.

Extra Support

Support from Minority Heterosexuals Because minority gay professionals often come from close-knit ethnic or racial communities, they often have support from parents, siblings, and other relatives for their career success. Even after coming out as gay, many found that their families were no less proud and supportive of them. For Jewish gay people in particular, we found that family support was the norm and surpassed the level of acceptance that white Christian families afforded their gay offspring. Many Black, Hispanic, and Asian American families were also supportive.

At work, minority gay professionals often looked for support from coworkers of the same background. Some felt this support would be jeopardized if they came out. However, others found support from such colleagues, especially if there was a shared difference. For example, Torrence Boone, who is in an interracial relationship, told us, 'At business school there's this one straight couple, where the white woman is the student and she is married to a Black fellow. At the section picnic, it was interesting how they gravitated toward us." He laughed. "They could identify."

Some told us of establishing successful mentor relationships with others from their same background, even after coming out to them. While these informal social ties may help pave the way for a few, they are hardly developed to the extent of providing top-level corporate access that the entrenched old-boy network has. Age is one factor—relatively fewer minority executives have attained positions of power, and thus there are usually not many in the position to offer career opportunities to other minorities.

But we saw evidence that times are changing here too. A number of gay minority professionals mentioned serving as role models and mentors for those who are coming up behind them. Of those who were in a position to serve as mentors, many had made a conscious effort to mentor other minority employees, whether gay or heterosexual.

Support from White Gay People After coming out, some minority professionals felt distancing from heterosexual friends and family. For them, support for their sexual orientation came primarily from ties with white gay people. Troy admitted, "In my social life, I very much identify as a gay man first. Socially, that's been the most important thing for me, the most important part of who I am. After identifying myself as a human being, an individual, I see myself as a gay man—before I see myself as Black. I think it's because I didn't have any trouble being Black. But being gay was the hardest thing I had to figure out how to deal with."

Some also established bonds with white gay people at work. For example, Gordon discovered his sexual orientation has been a commonality allowing him to bond with others with whom otherwise he would have little in common. He told us, "Being gay was a way in for me. Out of twenty-five floors of people, there were two other Black people; one secretary and one mail-room person. But there were lots of gay people there, both gay men and lesbians, who I became friendly with."

Extra Networking

While many of those we interviewed networked extensively with white gay professionals, almost all had also sought out friends of their same background. Pam spoke at length about how important it was for her to finally get to know other Asian lesbians. She said, "When I first moved to Boston, I was one of the founding members of the Boston Asian Gay and Lesbian Community. There was an Asian guy that worked in the local gay bookstore at the time. He talked to me, and we found a couple of other lesbians and men and made a group. So that was a really good thing, because I had never met any Asian lesbians before that. I never saw any in bars. Never. It's somewhat better now. But back in the 70s there were none. I was the only one. It was hard to be the only one.

"I was recently at the funeral of one of the first Asian lesbians I ever met. She was my age and from a very similar background. Just like me, after she went to college, she got a lot more distant from her family. In her family, like my family, talking about your personal life, especially your lesbian personal life . . . it was just not something anyone wanted to hear. So the way that her family perceived her was kind of strange. They had stopped knowing her after high school. She was almost a stranger to them.

"It was so enlightening, hearing her friends talk about her at the funeral service, because her family sort of got to know her a little better again. It was so surreal—it was like being at my own funeral. It made me try to be closer to my family after seeing that. Also, she did so much to help people, as well as professionally, that it also made me vow that in my own life I need to worry about something other than making money or being successful professionally. I need also to help people in some way."

Black Gay Networking For some, the support that minority gay people receive from their peer networks goes well beyond emotional support and constitutes what might be called an "old gays network." Black gay men, in particular, told us about such social ties that have been important career networks for them. Many said that at business school and afterward, many of their close personal friends were career-oriented Black professionals like themselves. A number of Black gay professional men told us there is a large yet informal series of holiday-weekend get-togethers in various cities, like Memorial Day in Washington, D.C., and Fourth of July in L.A.

Victor told us that he had a group of Black friends from the HBS gay student group in the early 1980s who were also active as academic tutors in the Black student group. "We were all rebels in a way. Almost none of us thought of Harvard as a struggle. I figured out day one what Harvard was all about. It was all about communicating. It was communicating who you are and what difference you make and how you're going to influence the situation; getting other people to buy into it and getting somebody else to follow up and say, 'That was a great idea; let me feed off of that too.' When it was necessary I was making tons of notes, but I was looking for the nugget that I wanted to communicate. That was the approach that I took into class every day: What was my nugget and how did it relate to what others were discussing?

"Because of that approach I had a lot of extra time that I was able to devote to doing some other things. My friends and I were playing big-time, even first semester of First Year. I was part of the bad-boys set. We went off every day second semester and played Risk. The guys that I hung out with at that time are all super-duper millionaires at this point, because they figured out some things in terms of how to play the game within the various industries they went into." Victor himself is well on his way to achieving spectacular career success at a young age.

Many of the more recent Black gay graduates have hooked into an existing network of gay Black Harvard Business School alumni and their friends, thus extending the network into another generation. One of the nicest parts of our research was our ability to make introductions that fostered such ties.

Since most gay minority professional networks are informal, the ability to network sometimes requires downplaying one's education and income. Mel Glapion explained that in contrast to the demands placed on him by the white gay social scene, in the Black gay community the rules are different. He said, "When I'm in Boston, if I meet someone, especially if they're white, the first thing they'll ask me is, 'Where do you go to school or what do you do here?' And that's very normal. In the Black gay community, it's definitely preferable that you have more money than less, but it isn't a big deal. It can actually work in your favor if you have more money and you're cool about it, that is, you don't discuss it.

"In fact, in New York in the Black gay community, if you were to offer that kind of information, you are just ostracized, because you are putting it in somebody else's face who may not be as wealthy or have as many options as you. So what happens is . . . if they find out over time, or if they find out from a third-party source, it makes you look that much better. Because somebody met you and you didn't put it in their face. And then, when they find out, 'Oh, he's very bright and has money,' you are highly regarded."

He explained, "Black gay people have to meet a certain status threshold to be accepted among white gay men. They resent that, and they don't want someone Black to do the same thing to them." He elaborated, "There's a certain group of gay Black people who have made it, but you also have to show the rest of the Black community that you don't want to exclude yourself from them. So you don't want to become a Black man who dates only white men, for example."

For Torrence Boone, who is in an interracial relationship, the issues are complex, he told us. "I know a lot of Black gay professional men who are dealing with this issue. You know, what does it mean to be in a relationship with a white person as opposed to a Black person? What does that mean in terms of loyalty and commitment to your race? A lot of people have the stereotype that Black men are with white men because they are not proud of who they are or they're trying to diminish their racial identity by embracing the dominant culture on that most intimate level. There are a lot of Black gay men who will only date other Black gay men because of the cultural issues.

"I think a lot of Black men think of those things, or at least deal with the discrimination that you get by being in an interracial relationship. But my friends transcend that. You know, at some point you just have to say, 'Look, I'm just gonna live my life, and if you can't deal with it, fine.' In general, I think the Black gay men that I socialize with are more open-minded than the general Black gay population. The Black gay men who are my closest friends . . . I guess that's why they're my closest friends."

Extra Strength as Individuals

The openly gay minority professionals we interviewed all highly impressed us with their inner strength and personal fortitude. As Torrence Boone told us, "I'm already different because I'm Black, so why not just be fabulous?!" With a grin and a laugh he poured out his charm which we knew opened many doors to his success.

Sebastin, another highly successful Black man who is widely known for his fabulous behavior, hesitated only for a second in answering our question "What accounts for your success?" He said with a Southern drawl from his childhood, "My mamma taught me that nobody could make me think they were better than me."

Minority gay men and women told us repeatedly: Those who do not accept defeat are met with success. People who are able to be fully themselves are the most productive, successful, and happy people in today's society, and minority gay professionals are no exception.

When we reviewed our master list of potential interviewees, we were struck by the number of Black gay men who were on the list. Some of the numbers came from an excellent referral network—but Black gay men were also among those who were most protective of their friends' identities. More often we were referred to these individuals by classmates of other races.

In some final interviews, we wondered aloud whether Black gay men were particularly driven to attend HBS and, more generally, to succeed in business. Emil shared his theory. "I think when you're Black, whether straight or gay, male or female, you are being pulled in one of two directions. You can go up or you can go down. And if you're gay and have figured it out young enough, you also have to decide real early which way you are going to go. For a Black male, if you realize that sports or entertainment is not going to be your ticket, you try to excel in school. I suspect that a good number of Black gay people from middle-class homes decide that they are going to go up from a very early age and that they have to focus on academics and achievement in business. So I'm not surprised by the disproportionate number of gay Black men at HBS."

Mel Glapion told us, "People sometimes say how you may have to do a lot more because you're gay. For me it was: You're going to have to do a lot more, because you're gay, you're Black, you're from the South, and you're Catholic. So I thought: I'd better work my butt off."

Although being gay and being a member of a minority can be doubly difficult, we also conclude that many such individuals have developed an unusual strength or fortitude. In a study done by the *Wall Street Journal* and reported on March 6, 1994, one woman says, "Black women are taught from a young age to be multitalented, multifaceted, and to be able to be a chameleon. And for industry that's very crucial. You need people you can put into a particular environment and know they'll thrive."

Successful minority gay professionals have also managed to integrate many valuable experiences as the result of being part of many communities. Sheryl, who is Jewish, said, "I've learned to translate from one to the other and back. It's like speaking two languages."

Some have taken the skills acquired in the mainstream to benefit minorities and the gay community. Raul Companioni took his mainstream business experience to Christopher Street Financial, where he served a largely gay investor base in the first financial-services company to seek gay clients in the early 1980s. For Gordon, being gay gained him entry into the upper ranks of an almost exclusively white organization after graduating from Harvard Business School. Eventually he went on to achieve many successes based on his own very considerable talents during his years with a prestigious New York advertising firm, winning a Cleo award for his advertisements. Now that he is working on his own, doing targeted marketing to Blacks and Hispanic Americans, the talent, skills, track record, and expertise he has developed are also being put to use in the gay community, as large corporations have begun target marketing there.

CROSS-CULTURAL BRIDGES AND TIES

In our research we found that the intersection of race and gay identity is important to many of all races.

Diversity in the Gay Community

Although the gay community is not as open to diversity as it could be, diversity is far more visible in the gay community than in society in general. People of all races, classes, ethnicities, ages, and religions who come to terms with being gay gravitate to gay bars, organizations, and social groups for support, friends, and a good time. As a result, those who otherwise might not come into personal contact with people unlike themselves find themselves part of a community with a wealth of differences. "It makes life very exciting. I wouldn't trade it for the world," Dale, who is white, ruminated about the diversity of the gay community. Jill, who is also white, said, "I think there is more interreligious mixing, more interracial mixing, and more people from different social-economic backgrounds together than among heterosexual social communities. As gay people we can more easily shake off the prejudices of society because we have been outcasts as well."

In many ways, the gay community is a catalyst of change that is breaking down the barriers between races, ethnicities, religions, ages, and classes. Nonetheless, as many pointed out, the gay community, like mainstream American culture, still has a long way to go.

In pointing out how segregated most white people's lives are, Nicholas told us angrily, "People I know from undergrad, people I know from business school, people I know from previous jobs—in some instances I'm the only Black person that they know. I tell them, 'Get off of it. You should really know other Black professional people, because I'm not the exception. There are a lot of people out there who are like me.' And they say, 'Well, I just never come across them.' A white friend of mine said something very interesting. He said, 'You know, I can live my entire life without having to deal with a Black person.' Which is true. Now if you're Black you can't say that. It's just a different set of circumstances."

Although white and minority gay professionals sometimes feel especially close to one another, a number told us that hoped-for commonalities failed to materialize, as the gay community remains largely stratified by gender, race, class, and age.

Minority Gay People as Cultural Bridges

As gay minority professionals are gaining visibility in the business world, the gay community, and in their home communities, one important role some play is that of a cultural bridge. For example, when a Black gay person comes out to his or her family and friends within the Black community, that person has the opportunity to educate them and to demystify the gay community. When that same person socializes or becomes politically active in the gay community, he or she has the opportunity to educate other gay people about the Black community.

Thus openly gay minority professionals play a leading role in paving the way for acceptance of diversity throughout society. Playing the role of cultural translator can be beneficial to both communities and to American society, but there are also dividends to the individual. Minority gay professionals who took advantage of networking opportunities in the mainstream gay community had access to a wide network of professional and social contacts, which in many cases were beneficial to their careers.

White Gay Professionals' Ties to Minority Peers

A number of white gay men and lesbians saw heterosexual minority colleagues as their natural allies. Alistair Williamson told us that one of his closest friends at business school was a woman with an interracial background. "Because she's had to confront a lot of things some very zealous types don't approve of, I sensed a potential alliance. In fact, that's what happened. She was able to put herself in my shoes a little bit, see that I was the kind of person that she could still respect, despite being gay, which her church says is bad."

Douglas Plummer told us he felt the commonality of difference is recognized by many of his minority peers. "I was on the Diversity Committee at HBS. Last year, when Jim Sherman was the representative of the gay group, he walked into the diversity club meeting, and he was the only white man. Everyone sits down and they're about to start, but there's this tension. Finally, someone asked him right out, 'Why are you here?' When Jim answered, 'I'm representing the Gay and Lesbian Student Association at the business school,' everyone relaxed, because they realized, Oh, it's OK, he's persecuted too."

Other white gay professionals told us of their increased sensitivity to racial issues as the result of having gay friends who were people of color. Ian told us, "As a white person, until you see it happen to someone you know, you really don't see racism. I think it's the same thing with gay people and heterosexuals. If heterosexuals see a blatant case of discrimination, they realize that it happens. It doesn't have to occur over and over."

Also making a parallel to his own situation as a gay man, Alan Miles told us, "My theory is that if you're Black and if you have any sort of political consciousness, at some point you're going to be perceived as radical. It's similar to what I experience in being open about being gay and expecting to be treated equally."

LOOKING TO THE FUTURE

Many heterosexuals fail to realize that functioning in the gay community can be like living in a different culture. Whatever background they come from, when gay people come out, most become part of a gay community. There they learn behaviors, cultural references, and humor that they enjoy in their nonworking hours. Whether they socialize primarily with other gay people or not, gay people learn a series of behaviors, words, symbols, and gestures that few heterosexuals in business understand. Thus gay people of all backgrounds sometimes experience cultural distance from their heterosexual coworkers, even if they share other important life experiences.

For the most part, gay people who wish to succeed in business adopt the behavior, vocabulary, and appearance of the mainstream during working hours. Whether closeted or openly gay, many abandon gay cultural signifiers during working hours, just as some Black professionals of all class backgrounds switch between Black English and standard English in order to succeed at work.

In many cases, even the most sophisticated heterosexuals in the business world are unfamiliar with the jokes, lingo, and cultural works of gay people. White heterosexuals are also often ignorant of minority gay life. Unfortunately, many white gay men and women are as well. Thus, minority gay professionals have become especially adept at culture surfing. This skill may serve them well in many ways, but it also has hidden costs. Some of the costs are to the individual, who may never feel truly comfortable at work. Another cost is to their company, which is deprived of a fully functioning worker and is not able to tap into the creativity that flows from being a whole person at work. Another cost to companies comes from the fact that a gay minority person may be their best resource in reaching a rather hidden pool of talent and customers—gay people of all races. As most companies realize, those who are bicultural have a unique opportunity to help make bridges between dissimilar colleagues. In many ways, gay minorities, who are tricultural, are best suited to foster this kind of understanding. But if that person is closeted, the company may never know what it is missing.

As we write this, many changes are taking place. As more people throughout society are interacting with gay people in their everyday lives, the general populace is being educated about various gay cultures. In addition, both the mainstream and gay media are beginning to do a better job of covering the political issues and cultural accomplishments of an increasingly diverse group of gay people. As individuals of all backgrounds come out to nongay people in their lives, there will increasingly be more awareness and, ultimately, equal treatment of gay people everywhere.

• • •

Ties to multiple communities can give minority gay people role models and support as they build their careers and structure their own personal lives. Depending upon the individual and the circumstances, being different from the majority of one's coworkers can bring certain advantages as well as challenges. The combination of personal fortitude, carefully choosing the places one works, and having a plan to combat discrimination can be even more important for minority gay professionals than others.

Perhaps surprising, gay professionals who stood out from others because of their race, ethnicity, or religion were often the most successful at standing out due to their sexual orientation as well. One reason is that, from an early age, they have practiced being different. Additionally, the support many received from their parents, friends, and communities strengthened their sense of self-worth and pride. Persevering in the face of the challenges they faced as minorities helped bolster their personal fortitude to object to situations that could have otherwise defeated them as gay people.

Many of the minority professionals we interviewed were well on their way to achieving their business and personal goals. They are also paving the way toward greater acceptance of all kinds of diversity in the companies and industries they work in. Whether or not they have benefited from networking with and mentoring by others of their own racial or ethnic group or from other gay people, many feel a sense of obligation to serve as mentors themselves for women, minorities, or gay people.

Diversity is one of our nation's greatest strengths. The more people are able to express their culture and identity and the more others are able to understand them, rather than be alienated by them, the more competitive American industry will become. Increasingly, companies are finding economic justification to embrace diversity. Those that fail to do so should realize they face economic peril. Forcing valued employees to conceal their identity, whether based on ethnicity, race, or sexual orientation, impairs their performance by making their lives difficult, distracting, and defeating. Companies where individuals are free to contribute their full selves to their career will reap the largest gains.

Just as the business world has a long way to go in order to fully embrace diversity, the gay community is still growing in this area. Minority cultures within the gay community continue to suffer from lack of visibility and understanding. However, individuals who are both gay and members of a minority group are bridging the cultures they participate in.

Although some white gay people are just as racist and nonaccepting as heterosexuals, the gay community has made many strides in encompassing a wide range of diversity. As the gay community often creates as well as mirrors important social trends, we are hopeful that the education process between gay people of all ages, races, ethnicities, economic backgrounds, and religious beliefs will help fuel the necessary changes in the business world as well.

Chapter 11

Parents, Partners, and Children

When we began this project, we did not intend to include a chapter on parents, partners, and children. This was a book for businesspeople; a book about how to balance a gay life and a mainstream job, with the focus on work life.

Yet as we compiled the interviews and examined the results, several glaring facts kept coming to the surface: People who are more comfortable with being gay and more confident about discussing the issue with heterosexuals are significantly more comfortable with being gay at work. Additionally, those who are partnered tend to be more open, and those who are or plan to be parents also tend to be more open at work. Finally, a growing number of gay professionals have or want children, and this has important repercussions for the workplace.

PARENTS

Most of the successful people we spoke with attributed part of their success to their parents. Through parental words or deeds, they learned ethics, leadership, and values. Many gay professionals credited their parents for presenting opportunities for personal growth. Coming out to parents was a pressing issue for interviewees well into their forties. Gay men and women in their fifties and beyond also spoke with passion about the roles their parents play and have played in their lives—and perhaps surprising, were just as likely to be out to their parents as their younger counterparts.

FINDINGS

Most gay professionals in our study, even those who remain closeted at work, have come out to some or most of their family of origin. Many said that coming out to family was one of the most difficult challenges of their lives. Nonetheless, 80 percent of those with living parents are out to them. The large majority of those who had not come out to their parents told us that they had fairly immediate plans to do so. Almost every gay professional in our study has come out to at least one family member, and only a few said they did not intend to come out to a specific family member.

Despite heartrending stories of their fears about how their families would take the news, and of the years of work involved in helping parents cope, most eventually have found love and some degree of acceptance. This does not come automatically, nor does it always mean a full integration of the knowledge that a son or daughter is gay into ordinary social interaction. Acceptance by family members generally consisted of a gradual transition from shock, denial, or guilt, to the phases of acceptance or welcoming.

Whether closeted or open with family, most gay professionals hoped that their families could make peace with their being gay, and most believed this was possible, based on their knowledge of others' experiences. This is in striking contrast to their perception of the situation at work, where most, even those who were out, saw coming out as uncharted territory.

Most who were closeted at home or at work told us that the issues of coming out to family and coming out at work were distinct decisions. One was based on the strong emotional ties of family, the other on the hard economic realities of work. But a number of those who have done both say that they acknowledge the connection in retrospect. In both cases, they say, they overcame fear to achieve an increased level of personal comfort and happiness. And as with being out at work, those who continued *being out* to family after the initial *coming out* conversation reported the most happiness with their decision.

Race Initially, we hypothesized that Black, Hispanic, and Asian Americans might be less likely to come out to parents than Jews and other whites. This proved to be the case, but only slightly. The interviews were far more revealing than the statistics in any case. We were happy to find that many minority families fully accepted their gay son or daughter.

Gender A majority of both lesbians and gay men interviewed said that homophobia is less an issue for women. They felt it was easier for a family to accept a lesbian daughter than a gay son. They also said that mothers were more accepting than fathers. Those in the minority strongly opposed both arguments.

We found that lesbians were no more likely to have come out to their families than gay men. Neither were gay professionals more likely to have come out to their mothers than to their fathers. However, we did find that over time, mothers were slightly more likely than fathers to fully accept gay children. Mothers were also slightly more likely to accept gay sons than lesbian daughters right from the beginning.

Why Come Out?

We found that the following are the primary reasons gay professionals come out to their parents and other family members: Not telling them places a barrier in their relationship; they feel it's better to tell them than for them to find out from others; and they feel strongly that they want to be out in all aspects of their lives. Some gay men come out because they need family support in dealing with AIDS.

The Coming-out Plan

Those who have gone through the rigors of the Harvard Business School training have internalized the concept of creating a plan of action for any given situation, almost in their sleep. In the "case method" used at HBS, the professor asks one student, usually without warning, to "open" the case for the class. That student is expected to have assimilated the facts of the case the previous night, and to draw upon his or her analysis of those facts in presenting a plan of action for the case protagonist.

We found that with respect to coming out to their parents, Harvard MBAs have thought thoroughly about the ramifications of various courses of action, similar to the way they approach a business challenge—they formulate a plan of action. Most of those we interviewed had clear opinions on the issue of coming out to their parents. They had already done so, planned to do so, or did not want to come out to them. Those who planned to come out had given much thought to coming-out methods: "Should I just come out and say that I'm gay? Would dropping little hints be better? Should I tell my brother first? When is the best time to tell them? Should I say it this way or that way?"

In striking contrast to their thoughts about coming out at work, almost everyone we interviewed had a well-reasoned, considered approach to the issue of coming out to their parents, and most had acted consciously in accordance with their plan. And they were very well prepared to handle the reactions they encountered. If they encountered a negative reaction from their families, they took steps to ameliorate it.

In any case, the removal of uncertainty gave them a feeling of comfort that translated into other aspects of their lives. Having come out, they could also move on to give full attention to other matters of importance, including their careers.

Methods of Coming Out

Except for a few who were found out as teenagers, those we interviewed generally had come out to gay friends, and often heterosexual friends, before coming out to their parents. Gay professionals who came out to their parents primarily used the rollout method of leaving clues, then dropping hints, and finally saying the words "I am gay."

Most gay people in business are emotionally conservative by nature. They prefer to come out by testing the waters before finally coming out. While many report saying the words "I am gay" to their parents was the single most difficult conversation of their lives, they all agree that it was worth it. The freedom from ambiguity and the self-respect that came from being able to say the words "I am gay" meant they were liberated from fear. They no longer had to devise elaborate plans and counter plans to come out. They could move on with *being* openly gay.

Responses to Being Out

Whether it be with family, or with friends, or at work, being out is a process, not an event. Whether the initial reaction is positive or negative, there are bound to be changes in the relationship immediately and throughout the subsequent years.

Although the gay person is liberated from the confines of the closet by saying the words "I'm gay," parents and other family members may resist a change from their habitual method of dealing with this issue—namely, by ignoring it. Some have been explicitly asked by their parents to continue the closet game. Fear of telling the rest of the relatives or family friends is the reason many parents give. Others acknowledge that they are uncomfortable discussing the issue themselves.

Even those whose parents said that they had suspected and that they were fine with it found they usually had some educating to do. Most parents were ill informed about a variety of issues that are important to gay professionals. They relied on their offspring to help them learn what they needed to know. To move to the fullest level of acceptance, parents were usually prodded by their gay offspring. Often they needed time and their own support system to become fully comfortable with it.

One important finding, which we believe is equally applicable at work, is that the willingness of the gay person to discuss the issue improved the chance of a positive response. Those who persisted in comfortably and openly discussing their identity as a gay man or woman found that their families were more willing to embrace the issue. Those in committed relationships also found that when they clearly communicated the tangible ways that they expected their parents to acknowledge the sanctity of their partner relationship, their parents rose to the occasion and treated their relationship with respect.

THE WORK-FAMILY CONNECTION

Some gay professionals said they waited to come out at work until after telling their parents because they didn't want their parents to hear from others that they are gay. More important, however, coming out to one's family means engaging in conversations with heterosexuals, perhaps discussing the intimate details of one's life. For some we interviewed, coming out to a family member is the only time they have broached the issue with anyone who is not gay. With family, the conversation may delve deeply into personal issues, from health to sex to partner relationships to fundamental moral issues. Questions in the workplace can be equally forthright. The practice of discussing gay issues with someone who doesn't necessarily know the "politically correct" responses is an invaluable role-play for situations gay professionals might encounter at work.

Those who have gone through the soul-searching process of coming out to their families have a strong sense of self and profit tremendously by being better prepared to handle delicate conversations loaded with emotional significance. As Carrie said, "After I dealt with my family, I'd done so much self-assessment that I have a much more balanced head on my shoulders than a lot of my straight coworkers."

OUT TO FAMILY, OUT AT WORK

We found that, overwhelmingly, parental acceptance has led those we interviewed to be more willing to be out to work colleagues. Jim Sherman drew the clearest picture about being comfortable with being out in all aspects of his life. He explained, "I think you have to be comfortable with yourself, and secure with your sexuality or sexual orientation first and foremost. That's clearly the most important thing. If you haven't reached a level of peace with yourself, then it's immensely more difficult to be at ease telling others, whether that's in the work environment or with parents and straight friends."

Although there are similarities between being out to family and being out at work, there are also important differences. Most people do not stay at the same job for their entire lifetimes. Yet, at any given job, they probably interact with people at work more frequently than they spend time with their parents. Although coworkers and bosses usually have less invested in developing a deep and meaningful relationship with those they work with, they also have less invested in judging or trying to change people at work.

Therefore, while it can take parents many years to accept having gay children, the process continues to evolve toward greater and greater acceptance over time. In the workplace, we have found, it is possible to compress this time frame significantly.

PARTNERS

If we were to describe the typical profile of a gay professional who wants to be out at work, that person would most likely be in a long-term relationship. Having the common ground of relationships to talk about can make both gay people and heterosexuals more comfortable. Work environments that are social can help move talking about relationships to a new level. When partners and spouses meet, there is another common bond in the form of real people to react to, rather than mere references to a person's name. However, it would be a mistake to assume that gay and heterosexual relationships are identical. This mistake may lead to misunderstandings and unmet expectations on both sides.

FINDINGS

Who Is Partnered?

Based on stereotypes about gay men, we were surprised to find in our survey that slightly more gay men (61 percent), were involved in partner relationships than lesbians (50 percent). This finding was not replicated in our interviews, however, where the 75 percent of the women were partnered while 62 percent of the men were.

We were also interested to find that virtually all the lesbians in both our survey and interview groups have been in committed relationships in the past. This was not always the case with the gay men we surveyed or interviewed; a number of them have never been in a serious relationship.

Of the couples in our survey, almost a third have been together for more than five years, and 10 percent have been together for over 10 years. Of male survey respondents who are in relationships, 36 percent are in a relationship of six to 10 years, and 20 percent have been together over 10 years. This finding was replicated in our interviews.

Significantly more gay men than lesbians are in these longer-lasting relationships. One reason is that our gay male sample includes a number of individuals who are many years older than any lesbian who is part of our study. There may also be some important differences between lesbian and gay male relationship patterns, particularly with respect to the issue of monogamy, which some say has a bearing on relationship longevity.

Universally, the gay professionals we surveyed and interviewed say their relationships bring them the most happiness in life.

On a scale of 1 to 5, with 1 as the highest, our coupled survey respondents rated their relationships at 1.2. Satisfaction with their relationship was rated higher than satisfaction with their careers, friends, money, and other choices. For those who have children, their happiness in their relationships with their children outranked their partner relationship by a slender margin.

We also found significant benefits for couples' attitudes towards their work. Gay professionals who thought of their heterosexual coworkers as friends were more likely to find fulfillment in and enjoy work. If they were able to openly discuss their same-sex partner, they were more likely to see their workplace as an extended family or team.

Differences from Heterosexual Norms

How They Met In general, gay male couples meet in different ways than heterosexual married couples do, while lesbian couples have more similarity to their heterosexual peers in this regard.

Gay male survey respondents met their partners in a variety of ways, with more than a third meeting at a bar or club. Some of the other places men met their partners were on the elevator, on the street cruising, at a bathhouse, through a personal ad, skiing, and at church. Another 11 percent of the gay men met through participation in a gay organization.

Lesbians generally met their partners through friends, school, or at work. By way of contrast, none of the men met their current partner at work. Sixteen percent of male survey respondents also met their partners through friends.

Career Flexibility One way gay couples experience more freedom than most heterosexuals is with respect to the vocational choices available to the couple. While the situation of young gay couples without children is parallel to that of young heterosexual couples without children, the majority of heterosexual couples have or intend to have children at some point. Particularly for the gay male couples we interviewed, freedom from child-raising responsibilities meant career flexibility throughout their lifetimes.

Separate Households We were not initially puzzled by the fact that 16 percent of survey respondents said that they were involved in a relationship, but not living together. We attributed this figure to dating and other new relationships. But as we examined the data more closely, we found that a number of gay men who were not living with their partners were involved in relationships of many years' standing. This finding was confirmed in our interviews as we talked with a number of gay men who did not live with their long-term partners. This arrangement of maintaining separate residences in the same city did not exist among lesbians in relationships longer than a year.

Some older gay men told us they have never lived with a partner. They said living together long-term wasn't possible because there was too much likelihood of being suspected of being gay. Another reason for separate households is to maintain sexual independence.

Monogamy Versus Nonmonogamy While we were conducting the interviews it became apparent that just because gay men are in a long-term relationship, they are not necessarily monogamous. This is conspicuously the largest difference between gay male couples and heterosexual couples. Lesbians almost universally sought monogamy in their relationships.

Symbols of Commitment Tangible forms of commitment are a focal point in any relationship. For heterosexuals, the script is largely written, and one departs from it at his or her own peril. For gay couples, there is more leeway to develop unique symbols of commitment. Many chose to utilize familiar expressions from the mainstream culture. However, those who took this path noted that while some of these symbols of commitment may look the same as those used by heterosexuals, the timing and significance of each can be different.

For example, most heterosexuals exchange rings as one of the first tangible symbols of their commitment to each other, but many gay couples do so almost as an afterthought. And while many young middle-class professional heterosexual couples often live together, generally they buy property together only after getting married. For many gay couples, the timing is reversed. They may own a home together for many years before taking any public step to acknowledge their relationship.

For the gay professionals we interviewed, property ownership, rather than rings, union ceremonies, domestic partner registration, and legal documents, was the most common public symbol of their commitment. But an increasing number have or intend to employ symbolic ways of formalizing their relationship.

WORK AND PARTNER RELATIONSHIPS

Gay relationships, like gay individuals, generally face more challenges in life. Nonetheless, many gay people have loving, long-term, supportive, and joyful relationships. The benefits to the individuals involved are immeasurable, and the benefits to their employers are just beginning to surface.

Change does not occur overnight, but tremendous strides have been made in the last twenty-five years of gay liberation. Gay professionals desiring to be in long-term relationships now have role models who have been together for many years. Most are increasingly unwilling to stay in the closet about loving someone.

Although there are some differences between gay and heterosexual professionals in long-term relationships, there are numerous similarities. When gay partners are included in company social functions and benefits packages, not only do the gay people feel welcome; they become more effective employees. Furthermore, companies can send a clear signal that homophobic attitudes will not be tolerated.

When a company extends benefits to its employees' gay partners, it is communicating full acceptance of its gay employees. Even if only a few gay couples use the benefits, the signal is sent. Gay employees feel welcomed and heterosexual employees know upper management intends to treat all equally. Additionally, prospective employees who desire to work in a diverse workplace will be drawn to the company.

Benefits to the Individual

Socially, partners are an equalizing factor between heterosexuals and gay people at work. As demonstrated by the Employee Paradigm, throughout a person's life, an individual strives to integrate three primary components: Individuality, Family, and Work.

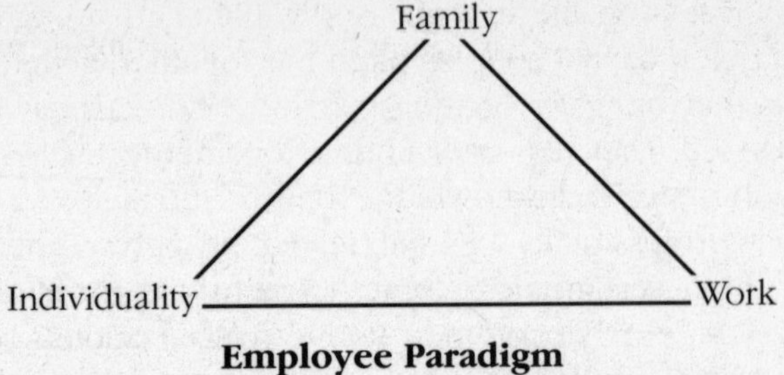

Employee Paradigm

The more a person is able to fully integrate all three aspects at the same time, the happier and better balanced that individual will be. For example, someone who is able to express his or her individuality and is recognized as having a family or a partner will be a more whole person at work. Thus, he or she is a more productive manager or employee.

Viewing the triangle from the individual's point of view, the closer the person's work and family or partner fit with a person's individual interests, the more the person will feel complete and at peace with their lives. And the more a family or partner can understand, appreciate, and lend support for the person's individuality as well as the person's career, the stronger that relationship will be. If any of these pieces are repressed or are out of sync, that person will be less fulfilled.

From a corporate point of view, the individual who is the most stable, loyal, and productive is the most desirable. We found that openly gay people in committed relationships contribute the most to their employers. They are the ones who are highly motivated to help the company succeed, and are willing to stay long enough to make sure that happens.

It's easy to understand why partners are significant to one's professional career and to the employer's business. Choosing a partner who can respect and understand one's work can be critical to career success. And being able to be out about being gay and having a partner is essential for an individual to be a whole person at his or her job. An employer who recognizes an employee's whole life can greatly enhance the behavioral fit. Therefore, there is an increase in performance by the employee.

The responsibility is not only on the employer. The individual who wishes to incorporate all aspects of his or her life must recognize that more education is needed. Not all companies are ready to roll out the lavender carpet and change their corporate culture overnight.

Because the subject of partners has proven to be a litmus test for truly welcoming gay employees, we have explored some of the similarities and differences between gay and heterosexual relationships here. Gay professionals will find it useful to understand these similarities and differences in order to decide how to best present themselves in a corporate environment. Heterosexual managers and coworkers also need to understand these issues in order to achieve a smooth transformation to a diverse workplace.

Benefits to the Company

Business schools have traditionally taught that hiring people who fit into the corporate culture achieves a strong organization based on shared traditions. A homogeneous culture promotes consensus and minimal conflicts so the wheel of business can roll onward.

Recently, firms are recognizing the world isn't so vanilla. If companies exclude diversity, they miss market opportunities because of their narrow views. They also fail to hire the best and the brightest, because they draw from a smaller pool of applicants. Additionally, they fail to utilize the talent they have within.

The incentive for a company to recognize gay couples is simple. The more an employee is welcome in an organization, the more his or her results will be acknowledged. The following matrix (adapted from *Managing Human Assets* by Michael Beer, Bert Spector, Paul R. Lawrence, D. Quinn Mills, and Richard E. Walton, Free Press, New York, 1984) demonstrates this.

Measurable Performance

		High	Low
Behavior fit	High	Effective	?
	Low	?	Ineffective

Effectiveness Dimensions

This matrix shows how high performing employees are judged as effective if their behavioral fit with the corporate culture is high. If there isn't a fit, the employee is perceived as an ineffective or questionable performer. Instead of hiring and promoting only people who automatically fit the culture, some companies are changing to welcome and applaud the diversity that the person brings.

The more that companies understand their employees, the better they will be in creating this welcoming culture. And since having more effective performers ultimately results in a more competent company, companies who value diversity come out ahead.

Experience has shown that the downside to adopting domestic partner benefits is minimal. Once a decision has been made by management, there is usually little difficulty or dollar cost in implementing such policies. Recognizing gay employees and treating their relationships equally does not take away any "goodies" from others.

CHILDREN

One of our most exciting discoveries, and one with far-reaching implications for the workplace, is that increasing numbers of gay people in business have or are planning to have children. While only a handful of our survey population told us they have children, we found this number to be somewhat higher in our interviews. Additionally, 16 percent of our survey population said that they planned to have children, and an additional 26 percent said they weren't sure. This finding was more than confirmed by our interviews.

In the course of our study we interviewed gay fathers and mothers from their thirties to their fifties. About a third of those who are parents have children from heterosexual marriages. Another third intentionally raised children as gay parents. The last third became informal stepparents via their relationship with a gay partner.

In addition, a significant number of those we interviewed also look forward to becoming parents. Most of these gay professionals are in their twenties and thirties. The expectation of being able to "have it all" (i.e., a career, a relationship, and children) is unique to this new generation of gay professionals.

None of the gay men in their forties told us they intended to be fathers. They said that when they came out they made their peace with being childless, and it was too late to change their minds. A handful of lesbians in their forties are considering motherhood, but only one is actively pursuing it. Most of the lesbians in their forties expressed little interest in parenting. They often told us that the pressures involved in being among the first women to "make it" in a business career were enough trailblazing for them. Others were simply not interested.

In contrast, a number of lesbians in their twenties and thirties have begun to make specific plans for parenting, and some have taken tangible steps in that direction. Most plan to become parents through pregnancy, although a few intend to adopt. While some of the women had decided to have children whether or not they were in a relationship, all of the men who expressed interest in having children said that they would only do so if partnered.

Generally, gay men in their twenties and thirties placed a higher priority on meeting Mr. Right, deepening their relationships, or developing their careers than on planning for children. But a surprisingly high number of these gay men also expressed interest in parenting, usually through adoption or by hiring a surrogate mother.

While the women's plans were often quite specific with respect to timing and how they expected to juggle work and family commitments, the men's plans were generally in the formative thinking-about-it-and-acquiring-more-information stage. However, many of the men reminded us, "Our biological clocks aren't ticking. We have plenty of time to establish ourselves in our careers and our relationships—or even to find relationships in the first place." They fully expected that the option of raising children will be open to them if and when they are ready to pursue it.

Those who are contemplating parenthood realistically anticipate the rigors of balancing careers, relationships, and children. They are also taking concrete steps to attain their goals, including moving to neighborhoods where they intend to raise children. Career-oriented gay parents may not have any more time with their children than heterosexual parents, but being constantly emotionally available may be even more important. Thus gay prospective parents are also implementing career strategies that will allow them time to focus on their children.

While heterosexual couples usually choose to maximize the income of one partner, usually the man, gay couples may be more likely to seek equality in home responsibilities when it comes to children. Even career-driven Harvard Business School graduates saw themselves taking time away from work to be parents.

Gay Parents and Workplace Issues

The decision to have children can be the final factor in motivating gay professionals to come out of the closet. Most gay prospective parents we interviewed were already out at work to some degree. Of those who were not, most expected to be fully out about being a gay parent. Based on our interviews and our knowledge of other gay parents who are business professionals, we expect that increasing numbers of openly gay employees will be bringing their children to the company day care center or the company picnic—and seeking benefits for them.

Companies that are ill prepared for these new social realities will find severely disgruntled employees on their hands. Management can't control every interaction between employees, let alone kids of employees. But just as they do with respect to race, companies can create a tone that lets everyone know that prejudice will not be tolerated.

Many of those we interviewed anticipated prying questions from coworkers, and they planned to seize the bull by the horns and answer them up front. Gay men expected questions about whether two men could be adequate parents. Lesbians whose partners planned to get pregnant expected questions like "Did you adopt?" Most said they would give short and straightforward answers from the beginning.

The increasing numbers of gay parents, like the tidal wave of single mothers, will have a profound impact on the workplace. As gay parents and prospective parents in business, those we interviewed need medical benefits and other safeguards to protect their families. The gay professionals we interviewed expect to place increasing pressure on businesses to provide the same kind of benefits routinely accorded to heterosexual married parents, including parental leave for birth, adoption, or children's illness, as well as health-care coverage. The companies that measure up to their expectations glean their support and loyalty. Companies who are cowed by the radical right's allegation that gay people seek "special rights" need only look at the issue of parenting to realize the inanity of this phraseology. Like all parents, gay parents need equal rights. Those companies that recognize this obvious truth will be able to draw from the largest possible pool of applicants, in addition to keeping the gay parents they currently employ happy and productive.

• • •

It was not possible within the scope of this book to share the full richness of gay professionals' relationships with their parents, partners, and children. But these relationships often have workplace implications that managers would be wise to consider. Because of their relationships with loved ones, we expect, an increasing number of gay professionals will come out at work and seek full equality there. Gay professionals will increasingly expect both equal material benefits and equal recognition of their relationships in social interaction with heterosexual bosses, colleagues, subordinates, clients, and vendors.

Chapter 12

HIV, AIDS, and Gay Professionals

AIDS is a subject that many books are devoted to. It is difficult if not impossible to cover all the issues relating to HIV in a single chapter. However, omitting AIDS from this book would be an injustice. Most people today are aware of the void left by gay men who have died of AIDS in certain industries like the arts, fashion, and design. Losses to the business world of so many talented managers and entrepreneurs have been largely overlooked. HBS alumni are not immune to HIV infection and its impact. Whether they are infected or merely affected, there has been a dramatic impact on their careers, their daily lives, and their priorities in life.

Many of those we interviewed were coping with HIV infection or AIDS —their own or that of partners, mentors, and friends. Many said the AIDS crisis has policitized them. As a result, many lesbians and gay men we interviewed are active in AIDS organizations—fund-raising, managing; providing direct service, education, and street activism. For some it is no doubt safer to be involved with an AIDS organization than a gay one. But we find it admirable that so many are helping others in need.

The gay professionals we interviewed also generally participate in the cultural changes in the gay community that have come about due to AIDS. One change, which has transformed the world of gay men, is with respect to safer sex and the increasing importance of relationships. Perhaps less noticed are the cultural changes that have occurred as lesbians become caregivers for gay men with AIDS and step in to fill the void left by dying gay men in gay organizations.

Whether HIV-positive or HIV-negative, gay professionals we interviewed have strong feelings about the way AIDS awareness has changed or should change the business world. By profiling different types of companies, we give just a few examples of how large businesses are managing AIDS in their workplaces. We also look at the strides small businesses have made and briefly discuss the way information about AIDS is and is not taught at the Harvard Business School.

FINDINGS

In our 1990 survey, almost three fourths of our respondents had lost at least one friend to AIDS, and 20 percent of the gay men had lost a lover. Of those who have lost a friend, the average number of friends lost is almost seven. Of those who have lost colleagues or acquaintances, the average number lost is over twelve. Almost all of the men we surveyed in 1990 had been tested for HIV infection, and 20 percent reported they had tested positive. Thirteen percent of our respondents say the AIDS crisis has resulted in their taking more time to be with partners and friends; 35 percent said it has resulted in their becoming active in gay rights organizations; and 43 percent say it has resulted in their getting involved in AIDS organizations.

In tabulating the results of our survey, we were saddened at the numbers some had lost. One gay man reported losing over fifty friends and lovers, in addition to countless acquaintances. In our interviews, gay professionals elaborated on how such catastrophic losses have affected their lives, career choices, workplaces, and relationships. Torrence Boone's partner, Ted Chapin, who is in his forties, told us sadly, "Of course . . . I lived in San Francisco all those years . . . I've lost numerous friends and associates. I know two hundred . . . three hundred people who died from AIDS. I felt when I was leaving San Francisco that I was closing a chapter and that there wasn't really that much left there for me. Literally so many people had died that the Rolodex was getting thin. The hardest thing about moving to Boston is saying good-bye to people who were HIV-positive, thinking about how many more times I would see them, maybe once or twice, maybe never again."

In contrast, Torrence, who is in his twenties, told us he has personally known very few who have fallen. We found this generation gap repeatedly through our interviews. Yet even those who have not lost anyone close to them told us the impact of AIDS has been devastating. "I think about all the people who could have been role models for me, or mentors, or trailblazers. And a lot of them are dead or dying," Spencer reflected sadly.

In the course of our interviews, we learned of over fifteen HBS gay men who had died of AIDS. Their loss to partners, friends, and workplaces is great, and they are sorely missed. We also asked those we interviewed to tell us about partners, friends, bosses, mentors, and co-workers they have lost to AIDS. Their memories were rich with detail, and they were glad to tell us their recollections. Sadly, a lot of their wisdom is left only with the people whose lives they touched.

Gay Professionals at Less Risk?

A few we interviewed posited that gay professionals were less affected by AIDS than other gay men. Neal hypothesized, "I think AIDS did not hit the more well-off professional people as much. To be honest, I think a lot of it has to do with sexual priorities. A lot of my gay friends have been together ten, fifteen, twenty, thirty years. They may not have been completely monogamous all along, but they didn't have as many opportunities to be infected. It may sound snobby and I apologize for that, but a lot of the people who had AIDS were not in that same category. People who went to the baths all the time or who almost made a profession out of getting laid—not being involved in long-term relationships meant they were having a lot more unsafe sex."

Neal's theory may explain the lower infection rate among the gay male professionals in our study who were most closeted at work during that critical era. That is, it seems those who were most willing to identify as gay in the late 1970s and early 1980s were also often deeply involved in the gay male world of parties, drugs, and multiple sex partners, which put them at greatest risk in the early years of the AIDS crisis. Sadly, this includes many of the gay professionals in our study who were pioneers in terms of being out at work. This means that AIDS has dealt a double blow to the gay professional world—first, the lives that are lost, and, second, the loss of role models for being openly gay and successful in business.

Jan remembers quite specifically when many of her gay male friends became infected in the early 80s. Jan told us she remembers her boss, who was an HBS graduate, coming into work with the infection and the rash and the fever that people get a couple of weeks after being exposed to HIV. She said that it's the same thing for virtually every one of her friends who died; in retrospect, she can remember when they got infected. But then again, she said, "What could you expect? They were all getting so many sexually transmitted diseases in those days, getting them treated, going right out and getting some new ones." She said, "The early 80s was a never-ending cycle of guys getting laid and getting sick."

She also told us there wasn't really the awareness of the need for safer sex until the mid-80s, when it was simply way too late. "Also," she said, "there were just so many opportunities for sex—the toilets, the meat rack in the Pines, the Ramble in Central Park, the West Side piers, the bathhouses and dungeons, the sex in the dance clubs themselves. A lot of gay men saw all that as a playground—a place to have fun with no consequences or responsibilities. Professionals were no exception."

Yet even those who were deeply closeted could also be infected. Neal told us one of his closeted professional friends had an especially difficult time accepting being gay. "We have been friends for about twenty-five years—since HBS—but until recently I wasn't even sure he was gay. What's really sad is, here's a guy who never really explored being gay. He never had any gay community, gay friends or anything. He just had sex with the wrong person or people at the wrong time. I confronted him after he had been on disability for a year. He was just so relieved. Because he had gone to some gay community organizations and he just couldn't relate to the crowd there. It was alienating for him to see a bunch of kids with long hair and earrings and whatever. This guy was a vice president at a major investment firm. He couldn't relate to any of that stuff, so he didn't have much of a support network."

We asked our interviewees when they became aware of the idea of safer sex. Typically, we found those who lived in larger cities were aware far earlier than those in smaller cities, some as early as 1981. Typically, those who were not connected to other gay people except through sex had less awareness and thus were also at tremendous risk in the early years of the disease. By the mid-80s, most of those we interviewed told us their awareness had increased. Yet some acknowledged they continued to be at risk for infection, due to slipping on safer-sex practices. Thus, gay professionals told us, it is important to continue reinforcing the message that whom one has sex with and how many people one has sex with is less important than how one has sex. Open dialogue with a partner who may not be strictly monogamous is also important in reducing risk, many told us, as it is common to drop certain safer-sex precautions when in a relationship. Finally, there was much disagreement about the riskiness of unprotected oral sex, which some suggest might continue to put gay men at risk.

AIDS AND THE WORKPLACE

These days, AIDS is in the news; it's being discussed in the schools; it claims lives throughout every sector of society. AIDS has also gotten a fair amount of airtime in the workplace; certainly, AIDS is discussed more frequently than gay issues. Yet ironically, we found, AIDS is almost always discussed in conjunction with gay issues or with gay issues as an unspoken subtext. Both gay professionals and their heterosexual colleagues often treat AIDS issues in this fashion.

Heterosexuals usually discuss AIDS at work either as a way to put gay people down or as a way of acknowledging gay-friendliness. Gay professionals usually discuss AIDS at work as a way to test the ground before coming out. Sometimes, however, they don't intend to come out but inadvertently cast suspicion on themselves. Additionally, some believe that by mentioning AIDS they have come out, when in fact they have not. Those who are HIV-positive usually have an internal time line for coming out at work, usually tied to their time line for coming out about being HIV-positive. Yet some come out about their HIV status without coming out about being gay.

We found AIDS awareness among heterosexuals is often at odds with the facts. Especially in the Midwest and in the South, we were told, AIDS continues to be labeled a gay disease. Some blame the increase in their health insurance premiums on gay men dying of AIDS. Others talk about how unnatural sex is responsible for AIDS. Most of those we interviewed told us they try to provide accurate information about AIDS in a calm, rational manner, despite their inner fury. They point out that, today, AIDS does not discriminate. Robin says, "I tell them unprotected sex, not the kind of sex or the number of partners, is the cause of HIV transmission. Sometimes they actually listen." Spencer exploded at the notion that AIDS is responsible for increased insurance premiums. "The single greatest health expense at my present company is pregnancy-related costs. And a lot more women get pregnant than men get AIDS. Having a baby in certain hospitals can cost $8,000! I mean, give me a break. Putting someone in a hospice is a hell of a lot cheaper than that. Even if someone is on AZT, which is not cheap, it's not that much either, compared to all the pregnancy complications the company now pays for."

As with stopping homophobic jokes, we were told, revealing a personal stake in the discussion—being gay, HIV-positive, or having an HIV-positive friend or loved one—can stop AIDS-phobic remarks or jokes. Management-sponsored education can also play an important role in ending AIDS phobia at work.

Companies Managing AIDS

The purpose of our research was not to quantify the losses of people to AIDS by specific industry. However, we did find a strong correlation between the gay-friendliness of the workplace and the AIDS losses experienced. It is no revelation that industries with a large concentration of gay men have been more affected by AIDS. Fashion, retail, music, and the arts, all of which involve some creative expression, were industries that those we interviewed mentioned most frequently in connection with deaths from AIDS. An important result is that managers in these industries had more experience in handling employees with AIDS than those in other industries.

When an employee develops AIDS, there are significant ramifications for employers. One issue is the question of training and support for managers who are faced with losing an employee. Managers have to determine not only how to adequately shift that person's workload to other employees but how to do so in a manner that leaves that person with self-respect, pride, and an active role—health permitting. Another issue is how to acknowledge the loss of an employee. Happily, we found many managers who represented the human face of the corporation by being supportive while HIV-positive employees continued to work, as well as being present at retirement parties and funerals.

Aside from the personal responsibilities managers carry, they may also have legal accountability. Discrimination based on health status is against the law, and this includes illness caused by HIV infection. Yet, few management-training hours are spent on the subject of managing people with terminal illness, and even today, not all managers are adequately prepared to deal with HIV and AIDS.

Ill-Prepared Managers

Barry Salzman told us a story that clearly demonstrates the lack of training managers have received when it comes to dealing AIDS. He said, "I had a straight friend of mine from business school call me a couple of weeks ago because somebody who reported to him had come to him and said he was HIV-positive. This friend of mine just flipped out. He didn't know how to deal with it; he didn't know what it meant, and he didn't know if what the person was asking for was reasonable. I think that's a huge issue that management of corporate America is completely unprepared for—even in 1994. Some of the professional firms and the law firms are being great with employees who are HIV-positive. Like, I know McKinsey has had HIV-positive employees that they've been very, very good with. But for the most part, corporate America has not really learned how to deal with this issue."

He reflected, "I think most business-school graduates will tell you they feel ill prepared to deal with personal issues. Hiring people, firing people, dealing with personal problems like divorce—these are issues that for the most part we're not exposed to at business school, and they're critical issues for a successful manager."

David Stokes confirmed, "I was recently at a management-training meeting with an HBS classmate of mine who used to work at my company. I could hardly believe it when she said, 'If I thought anyone in my office was HIV-positive, I would quit in a minute.' And I'm sitting right next to her. I challenged her. 'That's pretty extreme. Why do you say that?' And she said, 'I don't know, I just . . .' " David told us, "It was obvious she didn't know anything about it. She was speaking from an ignorant position. But it's kind of scary that she went all the way through business school with that attitude. You would think that if she didn't learn at business school, she would have learned about it somewhere outside of class. With all those bright, educated people, you would think that she would have learned it somewhere, even if it wasn't taught in the program."

David continued, "You'd like to think folks are educated enough now to know that it's not easy to get. I mean, Darrin and I have been together for many years, and he's still negative. And we don't sleep on opposite sides of the bed." He laughed. Turning somber, he reflected, "It's remarks like that which make me so nervous about coming out as HIV-positive at work. I think maybe sometimes . . . as gay people we're so used to AIDS, and we're surrounded by it so often, that sometimes we forget that there are other people who are just clueless." He pointed out, "Part of the goal of telling people about my HIV status is to try to decrease the level of stress that I'm under. But with remarks like that, that's certainly not going to do anything to decrease my stress level." David has now successfully come out about being HIV-positive to senior management.

Surprisingly, few of those we interviewed told us their companies had formal AIDS-education programs for employees or managers. We asked Stu how his previous employers had handled his coworkers with AIDS. He recalled, "Each case, the usual thing, someone starts going on medical disability at some point. Then you don't really see them again. You never knew what happened." Sometimes this secretiveness is at the request of a sick employee. But equally often it is management that does not want to face the issue head-on, we were told. This can add to an HIV-positive employee's anxiety; in contrast, employees were more loyal to their employers if the company policy was spelled out. An inclusive corporate policy on family and bereavement leave is equally important, yet most companies still handle this informally.

Jon Zimman said, "In September of 1985, Peter started getting rashes that wouldn't go away. In October of 1985, he went for an HIV test and tested positive. We didn't discuss it much; we just came to an understanding to go on living our lives as best we could. In June of 1986, Peter got a job in Chicago. We talked about his health and that he should try to get a deferral so that he could stay in New York. He got the deferral and moved into my apartment in July of 1986. Peter got sick and took a leave of absence in December of 1986 and never went back. It's fortunate that he had disability insurance through work. It was the first time his company had to work through the benefits for someone with AIDS, and they were fine about it. I cut back my hours at work and started coming in late a lot. About two to three weeks before Peter died, my boss finally asked what was going on, because I was missing so much work. When I came back after the funeral, he said how sorry he was, and asked if there was anything he could do. I was pleasantly surprised by his reaction—I didn't expect it."

A decade later, little has changed in many companies, despite the rising losses. While most bosses are humane about leave, companies are better served by policy that assures equal treatment.

Large Companies and AIDS

The way that companies treat their employees who have AIDS sends a strong signal to those we interviewed. In this section we tell the stories of five gay managers who gave positive evaluations to the way leaders in their corporations dealt with employees who developed AIDS. Simply by implementing their policy of treating gay employees like anyone else, as having feelings and loved ones, management can earn tremendous respect from other gay employees who are watching from behind the scenes.

THE *NEW YORK TIMES* Brian Offutt, who worked at the *New York Times* when we interviewed him, told us he feels the company set an important precedent in its treatment of star journalist Jeffrey Schmaltz. "Jeff had been a deputy national editor at the *Times* and was on the track to the top. He was the rising star. Before he collapsed at his desk, no one knew he was gay. *Times* management was there for him throughout his illness. He devoted the last three years of his life to writing about AIDS and gay issues, like the ones during the election and some cover stories for the *New York Times Magazine.*" Brian said, "Arthur Sulzberger Jr., the head of the *Times,* was very supportive of Jeff through his entire illness, and last week, when Jeff passed away, Arthur was there at his memorial gathering."

Although some have criticized the *Times* for its human, rather than political or scientific, coverage of the AIDS crisis, there is no doubt its attention to gay issues has improved since Schmaltz came out. Brian agreed. "That was really the turning point."

AMERICAN EXPRESS Brett, who works for American Express in New York City, told us how his employer has also done a good job managing people affected by AIDS. "There have been some vice presidents that have lost their partners to AIDS, and the company has been extremely understanding in giving them the space they need to deal with it while their partners were sick. And when the partners died, the company was there; senior management went to the funerals."

He added, "There was one vice president who had AIDS himself. The company recognized him for his achievements without saying anything about his illness. Everyone pretty much knew he had AIDS, but he didn't want the company to make a big announcement about it. So they did this party so he could be recognized and appreciated in a public forum without saying this is the reason why we're doing this now. It didn't come across as a cover-up. He did deserve it for his achievements. So it was a good solution. The company dealt with it the right way." We asked if this sort of retirement parties for employees with AIDS was commonplace at American Express. He replied, "Yes, that's happened a few times, actually."

A *Fortune* 50 Corporation We asked Jerome how he felt his telecommunications employer dealt with people with AIDS. He responded, "About the best any company could. They've been very flexible. Nobody has gone into the poorhouse. The company really has stepped up to take responsibility from a health-care perspective, from a caregiver perspective."

We asked how AIDS was treated as a management issue. "When it happens, we don't talk about it, because we have a corporate policy—we're not allowed to share with anybody what anyone's health status is." We found that many companies have such policies to protect their employees. "Even if you're a manager, human resources won't give you one iota of information. They simply say the employee is out on disability." He explained, "You can't find out what the disability is unless the individual tells you. However, they will give you an expected return date. As a manager, you are allowed to talk to the individual during the intervening time period, but it's really up to the individual to discuss the AIDS issue. It's their choice."

He said, "In big corporations you see a lot of illness of every kind. And you go to a lot of funerals. As a manager you represent the corporation. I don't care whether you're going to Brooklyn to an AIDS-related funeral or you're going to Queens to an Irish Catholic family that lost someone to a heart attack—you're representing the face of the company. As part of the supervisory structure, that's what you are supposed to do, and you do it."

Jerome told us, "I had an employee, a gay Black man from Brooklyn, who died of AIDS three months ago. I was there, and my senior management team below me was there, and their teams were there for the funeral too. It's the culture. It wasn't like we said beforehand, 'Are you going to be there?' I didn't make it mandatory. But everybody who he had worked for at one point was there; it was their expectation that they would go." He added, "Actually, this was like a family event for me, because all the offices I'd ever managed and all the people I'd always known, they were all there. And everybody knew he had died of AIDS."

Jerome continued, "I didn't make it out to some of the others' funerals . . . I always felt bad when I had people who had worked for me who died in other cities and I couldn't go. Even if I really didn't know them very closely, it's always an expectation that the management team shows up at funerals."

A Canadian Company Roland also had a positive take-away from his experience working for a company in Canada. He said, "There were several gay executives in the company, including one who died of AIDS. This was 1988—so, relatively early in the AIDS crisis. When he became sick, not a lot of people knew what was the matter with him. There was a suspicion, because he took a long time off.

"He was disliked by the rank and file, so they didn't have a lot to do with him. But I know the president of the company liked him very much and had great respect for his ability. When he died, his partner threw a massive party in his apartment, and we drank champagne until seven in the morning, and my boss was there, at least for part of it. That environment I would say was largely positive."

Thompson Many managers try to be as flexible as possible in order to keep an employee. Until his retirement, Bart Rubenstein worked for Medical Economics Data, a $125 million subsidiary of Thompson, its $6 billion parent company. He recalled that when he told his boss he was diagnosed with AIDS, "It was the most humane, positive response I could have imagined on the spectrum. I had considered all scenarios before I went in. I had some fears, because this company was not the most progressive company, so I was afraid the reaction would be very bad. But it was honestly very good. My boss's reaction was very humane and supportive. His first words were, 'What can I do for you?' So on a human level he was right there. He was also kind of stunned, as I recall. I'd only been working for him for maybe three months at that point. And it was just clear that the whole subject totally blew him away, that he had never considered the possibility."

Bart told us his boss was anxious to keep him on as long as possible. "The company is the most stress-producing company I've ever worked for. The president of the company believes that unless he's giving you more work and quicker deadlines than you can possibly imagine, you're not working hard enough. And so he consciously creates huge levels of stress. After I told my boss of my health status, he would still put a lot of work on with some ridiculous deadlines, but when I didn't do it, or when I backed off or eased up, there was no problem. He was very compassionate; he was doing everything he could to encourage me to keep on, on whatever schedule."

Whether the policy comes from the top or from line management, it is often up to middle managers to carry out the fair treatment of sick employees. As a person's health deteriorates, many companies have been able to find ways to shift the person's workload to match their ability to contribute. Many professionals with AIDS try to work as long as they can to keep their mind productively employed and not dwelling on their ailing health. Another, probably more important reason is health insurance. Bart acknowledged, "I'm fortunate, because I have private disability, which I bought more than ten years ago. When I started reading about this health crisis and mystery ailments, I got as much disability insurance as I could. In addition to my company plan, I've been able to retire as soon as I needed to." In contrast, David Stokes, who is in his thirties, admitted frankly, "Basically, as long as I can work, I can't leave. I need the health insurance provided by my company. And I'm counting on the company's disability policy for the future."

A middle course taken by some large companies is to have former employees with AIDS consult for them on an on-call basis after retirement. Although these professionals acknowledged they were physically unable to make it into the office on a regular basis, their input was still valuable to their former companies. So long as they do not run afoul of income limitations on their disability policy, this solution can work well for both sides.

Although we found strikingly positive responses from large companies dealing with AIDS, many of those we interviewed remained skeptical about their own companies. Skip said, "Straight people get a lot of leeway if they're sick or when they're going through a divorce or when their wife is dying of cancer. If I was HIV-positive or had a lover that's dying of AIDS or I'm trying to sell the house because of a breakup, I'm afraid I won't be treated the same way." Closeted at work and not aware of how his company has handled top managers who are gay or who are sick, Skip sees only the way his company treats those who fit the heterosexual norm.

When asked what would make them more optimistic about gay issues at their companies, some we interviewed recommended strong antidiscrimination policies. Many counseled visible leadership from top management that is strongly monitored all the way down the line. Others hoped gay employee groups would eventually gain their employers' attention in this area. But the common thread through all of their recommendations was that gay professionals should be prepared to ask for what they want.

Like gay professionals, professionals affected by AIDS usually have to ask to get. In return, their companies get not only a loyal and grateful employee but an employee who is more willing to trust management with information about personal health or home-life responsibilities. This has important ramifications for a company's ability to plan ahead.

Small Companies and AIDS

By now, most large companies have suffered a number of AIDS-related management issues. In contrast, we heard, small companies usually have less experience dealing with the issue. Like large companies a few years ago, small-company management usually does not deal with AIDS until the first employee comes forward and asks for benefits or is unable to perform the functions of the job. Sometimes the actions of an AIDS-phobic employee also causes management to act.

Management can take two courses of action. One, they can do nothing and let their lower and middle managers deal with the situation. But with increased legal liability, they may be passing off a tremendous responsibility. High legal costs and negative publicity are forcing senior management and owners to rethink their willingness to delegate such responsibilities. Thus, more commonly these days small companies create ad hoc policies for handling their employees who become ill. In a number of cases, we were told, these policies are strikingly supportive.

Without the resources to provide for fully funded disability or retirement packages, small companies can find it rough-going. The constant absence and reappearance of a valued manager can put a serious crimp in the company's ability to carry on work day to day. Nonetheless, small companies can also take advantage of their size and flexibility in managing their employees with AIDS. While large companies often have very specialized job functions, top professionals in small firms tend to wear many hats. Thus, perhaps more easily than in large companies, small-business management has the option of continuously shifting responsibilities among its top team when the health of one of its members dictates a change. Ironically, in addition, small companies may also have more flexibility to help employees with AIDS get top-notch medical coverage.

Fred Mann's Story

Shortly before his death in 1990, Fred Mann told us his experience at Rentek had been very positive. He said, "I discovered in January of 1988 that I was HIV-positive. Soon after, I sat down with one of the partners and told him what was going on. I sensed that he would be very open to it, and he was. I suggested that I tell everyone at the company, and they've all handled it extremely well on a personal level."

Fred added that the company also handled it extremely well on a management level. "When I told the president of the company, he just said flat out, 'Look, as far as medical care or whatever—whatever it takes, do it. If the insurance company doesn't cover it, the company will cover it.' I had carte blanche to do anything I wanted or needed. I think that's very unusual." He thought again for a moment and said, "I say it is unusual, but I'm not so sure, because I really do think if you're dealing with people in the right fashion—you are up front with them—most of them would like to be able to do that. Now, when you get into a larger organization, they may not be able to do that. Bureaucracy might prevent them. But when you're the president of the company, you can make whatever policy you want right on the spot." Fred continued, "It even got to the point that when we decided to change our insurance company, the president said, 'You're in charge of this, because I know you have more concerns about this than anybody. So, you get comfortable with what plan you want.' "

Fred told us management had also handled the complications of his declining health very well. "The company's been very accommodating on the progression of my health problems. I started deteriorating and was in pretty bad condition about a year ago. It was all stress related. One of the ways I learned to handle stress was to lie down and take a nap in the middle of the day. Now that I'm feeling better, I still do take a nap every day—they even bitch at me here if I don't do it."

Others also pointed to the flexibility of smaller firms, which facilitates options like telecommuting or variable hours.

AIDS ACTIVISM AND GAY PROFESSIONALS

Although the demographics of AIDS in the United States is shifting rapidly, gay men still comprise the largest number of those infected. As a result, gay male professionals are likely to care about this issue very deeply and tend to be well informed about AIDS organizations in their city and the issues needing attention.

Lesbian professionals, who have also seen the loss of many friends, were only slightly less active in AIDS work than their gay male peers. Gay professionals assisted AIDS organizations in a number of ways: cooking and preparing meals, serving as AIDS buddies, volunteering for medical tests, answering AIDS hotlines, demonstrating, writing checks, fund-raising, keeping the books, and serving as board members of AIDS organizations. Others have made AIDS work their full-time career.

Some see involvement in AIDS activism as a central part of their gay identity. Others see AIDS issues and gay issues as completely different but are nonetheless involved in AIDS prevention or relief in some way. Bill, who is in his twenties, said, "Is it enough anymore just to say you're gay? I think more of a political statement is necessary. One reason is the AIDS epidemic. I don't know if this has always been going on, or if I just finally saw it. But I feel there's a movement going on. Gay people are more of a community. And I feel, more and more, it's not just enough to say, 'I'm gay.' I need to take part in things, in helping make things better."

Sometimes the motivation to become involved in an AIDS organization came from a kind of peer pressure. Harvey said, "All my friends are doing something, and I began to feel a little out of it if I didn't get involved too." Others cited the example of role models as a reason for their involvement. For many, AIDS organizations provide a way to be connected to other gay people and to socialize away from the bar scene.

With so many avenues of involvement to choose from, the gay professionals we interviewed had many different personal philosophies about selecting an AIDS organization to become involved with. Some favored a civil-rights approach, while others pursued more radical forms of direct action. Most fell somewhere in between.

Barry Salzman believes a brash and forceful approach is necessary. Addressing ACT UP, he said, "Having acknowledged that a lot of their activities are controversial, I am frankly a very big supporter of everything they do. Including demonstrating outside St. Patrick's Cathedral. That was a demonstration I was part of. I recognize that it may have offended a lot of people and done some damage. But I think it's important to continue drawing attention to AIDS and protesting those who are contributing to the problem, and I think ACT UP does that."

Age and economic standing had no direct relationship to political philosophy. Both Barry, who is in his thirties, and Hans, who is in his sixties, are tremendously financially successful ACT UP supporters. Yet others who were equally successful were far more conservative and avoided participating in groups that supported ACT UP even indirectly.

Bart Rubenstein had a more pragmatic view of ACT UP. He said, "Early on I thought their tactics were interesting, but I thought they were naive in terms of their expectations from the system. I think it's evolved into something very different now, where it's a lot more mainstream. The people who started sitting on FDA committees and becoming really knowledgeable about drugs became very much a part of the system, and for the good, I think. The fact is, they created some great changes."

AIDS Activism at Work

A number of those we interviewed told us they are helping people with AIDS in their business careers. Richard Stern, who is a financial planner, explained, "One of my good friends and I have developed a series of seminars that we are giving on finances and insurance for people with HIV infection. We bring together financial planners, but also attorneys, CPAs, nurses, health care providers, and psychiatrists. Basically, I feel that people like myself, people who are intelligent and who have gotten a lot out of our society through our education at Harvard and elsewhere, if we can't help people who have AIDS or who have HIV infection, who will? Why rely on the mainstream when we have the ability to provide?"

Sally, an accountant, found her business responding to the needs of her clients who have AIDS. She commented about the turn in focus her business has taken. She said, "I didn't think I'd have to be learning about trusts and estates until I was sixty. Now, unfortunately, I'm doing them all the time. Like many in the community, we've lost several colleagues as well as clients to AIDS. It's rough on the survivors, too, picking up the slack while caretaking and mourning."

A number of those employed by mainstream companies also took their AIDS activism to work with them. Sometimes this meant discussing their outside involvements or their politics. As heartless and AIDS phobic as business seems to some people, gay professionals in a cross section of industries told us they have found tremendous respect and support for their involvements.

In some cases, gay professionals have led the company itself to contribute to AIDS causes. A number we interviewed solicited work colleagues for pledges to the local AIDS walk, just as they in turn are solicited to buy Girl Scout cookies. David Schutte found his colleagues were only too happy to sign up for his AIDS Walk pledge. "It's getting to be a very mainstream thing to support, so they're totally fine with it," he explained.

Participation in fund-raising for AIDS organizations is also a fairly common way of testing the waters before coming out about being gay at work, we found. David Stokes told us his affiliation with AIDS organizations was also a way he has started taking steps out of the closet at work about his HIV status.

Some told us fund-raising for AIDS causes has helped them network with other gay professionals. By seeking pledges from those who are more closeted, the workplace activist sometimes developed close personal friendships that could cross many levels in organizational hierarchy, thus leading to networking and even mentoring relationships.

Involvement in AIDS fund-raisers could also translate into industrywide networking. Jim told us he has met a number of gay people in the cable television industry at AIDS fund-raisers. "I was at a benefit for one of the AIDS groups and I recognized a couple of guys I previously figured were gay. A friend of mine at another company in our industry confirmed it. You know how it is—one person knows another who knows another. I was pretty surprised to see one particular guy there. But it turns out he's getting to be pretty out. He's been speaking to gay professional organizations in California and everything. I've known him for many years. But until that night, I didn't know he was gay. And I'm sure it was the same for him with me."

AIDS Activism Versus Gay Activism?

While some come out about being gay while doing AIDS work, many feel they can contribute without putting their closet in jeopardy or coming out in so many words. Ironically, a few gay professionals pointed out, the respectability of AIDS activism among gay businesspeople has made fund-raising for gay issues much more challenging. Gay people who contribute openly and in large amounts to AIDS causes are generally fearful of having their names identified with a gay cause. And since charitable pockets are only so deep, even for the very affluent, it can be hard to tap the same well twice. In addition, the very visibility and social acceptability of AIDS charities is a self-perpetuating draw, some said.

Peter points out that the work of groups like the Gay and Lesbian Alliance Against Defamation is critical. "Public education and image making are so important, and gay groups are not doing it as well as it should be done. One reason is that GLAAD and groups like it don't have the resources. Someone who is very active in that group told me flat out he is competing with AIDS as a fund-raiser. He said he's lucky to get $20,000 from a foundation when the Gay Men's Health Crisis is getting half a million dollars. And he said, 'You know, it's hard to argue with it because people are dying. How can you afford to spend money on public relations? But yet we have to, because the reason that people are dying is because we didn't do this ten years ago.' " Even wealthy gay individuals are more likely to support AIDS groups than gay ones, Peter asserted.

One reason he suggested, is the closet. We found strong evidence to suggest this is true among gay professionals. Yet when we asked people what type of organizations they were involved in, they often explained to us that initially they got involved in AIDS organizations. Then, later on, they were more willing to be associated with gay organizations. Thus for many gay professionals, AIDS work can be a bridge to increased contributions and visibility in gay causes.

CHANGES IN LIFE GOALS

For many gay professionals, goals for their careers and their lives have changed because of AIDS. Many who are HIV-infected themselves or have watched friends and loved ones become progressively sicker and eventually lose the battle against AIDS have significantly rethought their outlook on life. For some, this meant that making money in Wall Street, growing businesses, or bringing new products to market were no longer as meaningful.

Gay Men

Those who had lost a partner or were HIV-positive themselves are the most likely to make significant career changes. They are also most specific about how AIDS has impacted their personal relationships. Shane told us, "Kent is HIV-positive. So there is that intensity with him and our relationship. He's been healthy so far, but we've known for two years. It just makes us more conscious of the moment." Most have concluded that career and financial success is not as important as time with the ones they love.

Many who have lost friends also report feeling that life outside of work has become more precious. Sebastin told us, "I have had a number of close friends with AIDS who I've seen go through all the stages. I've always been kind of balanced in the way I think about life; I never wanted to spend all my hours with people from work. But the AIDS situation has caused me to appreciate my home life even more, because, you know, tomorrow isn't a sure thing. At the end of the day, all that I ask for is my health and my sanity; everything else will take care of itself." Motioning around his luxurious condo, he said, "Of course, I love this apartment and I would hate to lose it, but if I lost it, I think I could deal with that. What I can't deal with is if I lose my mind or if I lose my health. Knowing people who aren't here anymore, I can just imagine if they could trade having to live on the street but being alive, versus being where they are, I'm sure they would rather be alive. To me, the fear about anything at work, like coming out or not, or being discriminated against is not nearly as important as the fear of AIDS."

Bo, who stepped off the fast track in banking, said, "The AIDS epidemic is what made me more comfortable with coming out and being who I am." He explained that after losing so many friends to AIDS, he has reassessed "what's important. I no longer accept the training of Harvard Business School, where someone else is defining for you what success is, as opposed to you defining for yourself what success should be. This

AIDS thing really pushed the whole thought process in my mind to the forefront, because it's a matter of life and death."

Lesbians

Many of the lesbian professionals we interviewed had also lost close friends to AIDS. Like gay men, they told us, they often experienced a renewed appreciation for life and the importance of making the fullest use of their time on earth. Many also sought increased involvement in gay and AIDS causes. Yet some were skeptical about the longevity of personal and political ties between gay men and lesbians as the result of AIDS. Wanda, who is in her late thirties, said that virtually all of the gay men her age she knows are HIV-positive. She added wryly, "Gay men need the lesbians now. They know that they're gonna get sick and really actively cultivate their relationships with lesbians, because lesbians are the ones who are healthy enough and emotionally strong enough to keep doing the hospital visits, bringing the food . . . the men are just so shaken by their own being ill, their lovers dying, all their friends being decimated by AIDS, that the men have really come to see the importance of their friendships with lesbians. But are they really there for us?" she wondered. Many lesbians pondered whether enough lesbian time and money were being spent on breast cancer and other female health concerns in comparison to AIDS.

Another change many mentioned is that, as the result of AIDS, lesbians are now beginning to gain access to the political and economic roles held previously by gay men. Rachel told us a friend of hers was considering buying a gay-owned company. "All the owners are dying, and someone's going to buy them out eventually." Candidly she told us, "It would be a great opportunity for me if she did buy it. It would be great to go work there. Because who the hell wants to work at an investment bank their whole life and be a little toy soldier?"

The effect of shifting demographics is especially apparent in areas that have predominately gay-owned businesses. A new business owner in Provincetown, Massachusetts, Roberta Lasley said, "In the past, men and women really kept their separate social circles. Even their politics, what they cared about was very separate. But today, because of AIDS, and a common commercial interest in tourism, that's begun to change. P-town's always been fifty-fifty gay-straight. Now it's also fifty-fifty lesbians and gay men." A similar phenomenon that creates investment opportunities for women can be found in Cherry Grove and elsewhere, which used to have very few lesbians.

AIDS EDUCATION AT HBS

During our two years at HBS, 1988–1990, well into the AIDS crisis, not one case dealt with the issue of managing an employee who is HIV-positive or who has AIDS. Nor did we have any case dealing with any terminal illness. In the spring of 1990, a well-written case was taught as part of the First-Year curriculum, but it was never used again. In 1991, and a few other years, HBS sponsored an AIDS Awareness Day with a series of panel discussions. However, since then there has been no AIDS instruction as part of the mandatory First-Year curriculum. We understand that the MBA program is undergoing some significant retooling, and we hope that AIDS cases will once again be included.

The need for this kind of education was mentioned by virtually everyone we interviewed as the result of their experiences in the workplace. It is underscored by our experience with the shocking ignorance we encountered among HBS students in 1990, when the case was taught. There were some in the class who were well prepared to manage someone with AIDS, but they were by no means the majority. While AIDS awareness continues to grow, there has really been no new information about transmission since 1985. Thus we fear that some of the same ignorance displayed by future business professionals in 1990 may still be prevalent today.

The HBS AIDS Case

In 1990, Sharon sat in on an HBS class in which an AIDS case was taught. The central character in the case was Paul Cronan, a gay man employed in a blue-collar capacity at New England Telephone. In 1985, his boss, O'Brian, noticed that Cronan has been home sick a lot and asked him if he had AIDS.

Cronan obtained O'Brian's promise of confidentiality and told him he is HIV-positive, although he has not been diagnosed with AIDS and is capable of continuing to work as a lineman. O'Brian does not keep his promise of confidentiality; he tells his own boss and other company managers what he has learned. Soon the entire workforce knows about Cronan, and his fellow crew members refuse to be in close physical proximity to him, even to collect their job orders. In response, O'Brian arranges for the crew to get their orders while sitting in their trucks. But the crew continues to barrage Paul with homophobic insults. The question posed at the end of the case is: "If you are O'Brian, how do you manage the situation?"

Some of the more troublesome student comments included these: "The other employees could get AIDS from him, so he should be fired after consultation with medical personnel." "You have to take into account how the other workers feel about working with Paul, even though you feel sorry for him. It's like having the flu—it's possible to be contagious even if you are not sick." "Cronan should have told someone in the company six months ago that he had a dangerous disease." "The managers should keep quiet and not do anything. Profitability for the shareholders is the purpose of the company. It is utopian to consider human resources management before possible legal risks from Cronan's coworkers."

Next, additional information about the case was revealed to the students by a film clip from the local news. It talks about Paul Cronan's lawsuit against NE Tel and shows a lawyer from the company discussing the termination package they offered him. The clip then cuts back to Paul, who says that he wants to work for his own sense of dignity and because he needs the money. The professor again asks: "Now what should the senior management do?"

The troublesome comments continued: "Some of you want to take the moral high ground. But if someone had AIDS at work, I don't know what I'd do. I have children. What if I infect them?" "Yeah, that's still a real fear." "Doctors still can't give absolute assurance that it's safe." "The legal position is unclear. Wasting a whole day talking about it isn't responsible to the customers and the shareholders. The company should isolate Cronan from this environment." "Company-sponsored education creates a potential liability if it turns out that you can get AIDS by casual contact. There is a great downside for the company to continue employing Cronan, and no upside."

The professor interrupted with a request that members of the class do a little role playing on the subject of how they would handle the situation. Unlike the typical class, in which people volunteer in all seriousness to boost their grade by their class participation, students jokingly volunteered one another to act out the roles. Finally, the professor selected several students at random. The man playing the company management said to the workers: "I'm on your side" and refused to participate in the role play, forcing the professor to select a new manager.

After bringing the role playing to an end, the professor introduced additional information about the case, in which the company put a program in place to educate the workers and made it clear that discrimination against people who are HIV-positive and disruption of the workplace will not be accepted. The professor asks: "Was this response by the company responsible?"

The troublesome remarks continued: "It is wrong to discipline a worker about this. People have religious beliefs about this. There are religious groups that are against contact with people with AIDS on a religious basis."

Time was up, and the professor summed up: "The company's lack of early problem solving and talking to each other led to the original problem. Then the management engaged in too much legal thinking. It took a crisis to force them to act. They originally thought they could keep quiet and that this disease was like any other. But the emotions of the workers—homophobia, fear of disease, and Paul Cronan's anger—would not let this tactic work. And management did not attend to these emotions. Furthermore, regardless of challenges to managerial authority—the constraints are established by law: It is illegal to discriminate based on health status."

When it was over, Sharon remembers feeling stunned by beliefs of many supposedly well-educated people. Many were still unsure that HIV could not be spread by casual contact; many felt management's best response to AIDS was to try to get rid of anyone who had it, and many believed that prejudice should be accommodated. While we have reason to believe that HBS students today are somewhat better prepared to manage employees who are HIV-positive or have AIDS, the depth of ignorance and prejudice we saw in 1990 gives us room for pause. Without formal training in business school or at work, many managers are still likely to harbor such ignorance and fear.

The *Harvard Business Review*

The *Harvard Business Review* first tackled AIDS in its May–June 1989 issue, featuring a case on PacBell. In its November–December 1991 issue it carried an article on AIDS and hiring. In its July–August issue, the *Harvard Business Review* published another case on how to manage an employee who has AIDS. The case facts showed a man who got progressively more ill due to HIV infection but refused to accept that he was as sick as he was. Despite his persistent claims that he was getting better and he would work harder to perform to his previous level, his performance continued to slide. As is its practice, the *HBR* asked various business managers and human resource experts to give their opinions. All six who presented their opinions in the article supported sitting down with the man and together working through a mutual plan to retain the employee but allow the manager to reassign much of the work. They pointed out that such a mutual plan would allow the employee to maintain dignity and purpose, while the manager could ensure that work was being handled. As with the gay coming-out case published in 1993, these AIDS cases generated much discussion in business and business-school circles.

• • •

While there is much talk of a "second wave" of HIV infection among gay men, it is less likely to decimate the managerial ranks as the first wave did. Nonetheless, with no end in sight, AIDS will continue to surface as a management issue. While some companies are doing a tremendous job dealing with those who are HIV-positive, many managers continue to be unprepared. No educated person should any longer have fear or ignorance about AIDS. Yet even the most educated and best-meaning managers can face thorny problems with terminally ill employees.

The sad reality today is that the number of HIV-infected individuals is not diminishing. The gay community deserves the credit for starting AIDS organizations, supporting them, and bringing the visibility of AIDS to the general public. But homophobia and AIDS phobia continue to pose barriers to greater awareness, greater understanding, and prevention. As Shawn said, "God didn't send AIDS to punish those who are afflicted. God sent AIDS as a challenge to humanity—to deal with its devastation with compassion and intelligence. Some people are doing just fine, and others need to do quite a bit more work."

We know the lives that have already been lost will not be forgotten. Their memories live on in every gay professional who is inspired by them.

Conclusion

As we have documented throughout this book, the implications of gay people's sexual orientation for their career are numerous. Surprisingly, those who try to be closeted suffer the most disadvantages, while those who are completely open report little or no career difficulties and much personal happiness as a result. Additionally, those who come out in their workplaces have an enormous impact on the business world. In this section, we will highlight our conclusions from the themes we discuss throughout the book and predict what the future holds for gay people in business.

HBS

Business schools are the boot camps of the business world. Watching the trends that develop on their campuses is a good measure of what's to come in the future. Today, the trend is managing diversity, and gay people expect to be included. The current students really are a new generation. While business school is still the first place where some encounter other gay people like themselves and become comfortable with their gay identity, increasing numbers have been openly gay in the business world prior to attending HBS. Today many are completely open on campus and have no intention of hiding their sexual orientation in the closet after graduation. They say, "Closets are for clothes, not people."

As gay MBAs who today are in their twenties and early thirties enter the business world at management level and continue to rise within the ranks, they and their heterosexual peers will create tremendous change in the status of gay people in the workplace. And because American business schools educate so many foreign students and produce so many graduates who work overseas, the gay students who come out at HBS and other business school across the United States will have far-reaching, worldwide effects.

Discrimination

As more gay people come out, there will undoubtedly be some signs of a backlash. As the expectations of gay people working in business continue to rise, some companies will not change as quickly as they should, with resulting discrimination against openly gay professionals—and lawsuits. While some companies cling to their discriminatory conventions until they are forced to change, the publicity surrounding such cases will serve to heighten awareness throughout business and society, fueling broader changes.

As with improved awareness of the business cost of discrimination based on gender, race, religion, or other kinds of identity, there will not be an overnight change that will eradicate discrimination based on sexual orientation. Rather there will be gradual but steady change as gay people in business come out and seek full equality. Given the number of companies that have already enacted nondiscrimination policies protecting gay employees and those that have implemented or are considering domestic partner benefits, we believe the magnitude of change in many industries and locations will be quite far reaching—and quite rapid.

While some will cite religious conviction or other moral arguments against homosexuality, others will turn to their faith to support pluralism and respect for others. As with employees who disagree about the acceptability of single motherhood, interracial or interfaith dating, abortion, or matters of religious faith, companies will find that people who disagree can still be expected to work productively together. And just as white people have learned to work with minorities, men with women, and so on, heterosexuals will learn to work with gay people. As profit making, not morality or politics, is the name of the game of business, we expect management to establish and regulate these new norms. Yet ultimately the responsibility for change will fall on individuals—both heterosexual and gay—and we expect that most will come to see that a gay identity, like a racial, ethnic, or religious one, is not legitimate grounds for discrimination.

There may also be an increase in claims of reverse discrimination by heterosexuals. In the course of writing this book, we found ourselves unable to interview a lesbian professional who was part of such a suit. A heterosexual colleague claimed to be denied a promotion because a lesbian boss favored promoting a lesbian. Like the fear of demands for gay quotas or affirmative-action targets, such assertions, we expect, will be seen as spurious.

Being Closeted and Coming Out

Today, increasingly fewer gay people want to keep their closets intact. Currently most gay professionals envy and admire those who are out at work. As they recognize that the benefits of coming out far exceed the costs of being closeted, more will decide that "keeping their private life private" is no more desirable for them than for heterosexuals.

The effect of gay professionals coming out will be profound. Those who are currently in their twenties and thirties are not satisfied to come out and never discuss the subject again; they expect to continue being themselves in daily conversation, just as their heterosexual peers are. As they rise through the pipeline to the top levels, they expect that being openly gay will be mainly a nonissue in their continued ascent. By coming out and being out long before they reach the top, they and their heterosexual colleagues will have plenty of experience being comfortable working together. Eventually, being gay will be as noneventful—and as beneficial—in the workplace as being female, Black, Hispanic, Asian, Jewish, Catholic, or Mormon. This status will also make equal treatment with respect to employee benefits and corporate socializing seem like a no-brainer to top management.

Meanwhile, more gay professionals in their forties and older will also increasingly stand up to be counted as gay. In particular, gay men—having amassed comfortable nest eggs, having reached their professional goals, and having been affected by younger role models—will increasingly come out, while lesbians will follow at a slightly slower pace. The effect will be far reaching. Longtime colleagues who have watched their friends build their careers will have confirmation of what they suspected all along but were never allowed to discuss. More distant acquaintances will suddenly learn that someone they admire—someone with a proven track record—has succeeded "despite" being gay. As some of these newly out individuals will be part of top management, the changes in the wake of their disclosure will have tremendous impact and be especially far reaching. Also, these newly visible gay professionals will provide much-needed role models and potential mentors for younger gay people in business.

While the trend so far has been for gay people to come out to close work associates, the new trend will be gay people coming out to clients and customers. Currently, gay professionals perceive this as far more risky than coming out to bosses, coworkers, or subordinates, as most did not fear significant career impact by coming out at work. But coming out to clients and customers could mean putting the lifeblood of their business, division, or livelihood on the line. In order to come out in this area, gay people will need to know that their company will stand behind them. In most companies, the customer is king. Before risking coming out outside the company, most gay people want assurances that their employer stands behind them—even in the face of client objections.

Many of those we interviewed are taking active steps toward being more out—whether building up their network of allies at their current workplace, changing jobs, or going into business for themselves. As more gay people work for themselves, and as the information age makes it possible for more to work for others out of their own homes, many will have less interaction with coworkers and more interaction with clients. Additionally, as corporations become more flat, with fewer middle managers, more gay people will find themselves having more responsibility and direct relationships with clients and customers. As relationships build, gay people will come out to their clients and customers, thus establishing a clear precedent for those enmeshed in corporate life to do the same.

Parents

Parents of gay people will continue to be agents of change. With the increasing visibility of a diverse group of gay men and lesbians, they are having an easier time accepting their gay children. Instead of being familiar only with the negative stereotypes about gay lives, they are finding it easier to learn about gay people of all kinds.

The most important result of parents' accepting, understanding, and loving their gay children will be a strengthening of the American family. Real family values of love, acceptance, learning, and togetherness will finally be achieved in families that are now splintered because of religious or moral doctrines opposing homosexuality. Organizations like Parents and Friends of Lesbians and Gays (P-FLAG) will continue to provide role models and support for other families. Love is infectious, and organizations that build on doctrines of improving the world will have lasting effects.

Parents who accept their gay children are unique disseminators of goodwill for gay people. Moms and dads telling their lifelong friends that their child, whom they are so proud of, is gay will have increasingly profound effect on the workplace, as a broad cross section of society in all economic stratas and geographic areas learn that gay people deserve love and respect.

Additionally, parents who are religious and accustomed to turning to their religious leaders for support will continue to have an effect on religion; more religious leaders will preach welcoming, not rejecting, gay people in their congregations and in the lives of their congregants.

Partners

Although we suspected that having a stable long-term relationship was beneficial, we initially underestimated the importance of such a relationship on one's career. Partners provide support, create stability, provide economic cushioning, and provide conversation material in coming out and being out at work. Having a partner also provides a commonality with coworkers who are also in long-term relationships.

For gay men, having a partner breaks down the most negative stereotype working against them—that being a gay man is solely about sex. People who believe that the defining principle of gay male lives takes place in parks, public toilets, or bedrooms learn from coupled gay men that falling in love and nurturing it is an important component of gay male identity. While public affection between men continues to be the major taboo in American life, gay male couples who have earned their colleagues' professional and personal respect are in a good position to challenge this phobia as well.

In the 1980s, with the onslaught of AIDS, many gay men settled down, changed their sexual behaviors, and sought long-term relationships. Some speculated that after gay men became confident that safer sex worked, they would return to previous norms that prioritized sex over romance. However, AIDS phobia did not seem to be a major component of the relationship orientation of the gay men we interviewed. Rather, we anticipate, many will seek relationships because of the satisfaction they bring, as well as the benefits to their careers. While some of these relationships will be monogamous, others will not be, posing challenges to corporate social etiquette.

In this respect, partnered lesbians have an advantage—because their lives resemble the heterosexual mainstream's in many ways. Thus, those who are open may find it especially easy to socialize with other coupled colleagues, rather than inappropriately forming secret liaisons with other women at work. The social bonds they form with other couples from work serve to strengthen their professional ties as well as establish them as stable and sociable individuals.

Increasingly, gay people will expect equal benefits for their partners, just as they will expect colleagues to become comfortable socializing with a gay couple. As the business logic for such changes continues to be more evident, the business world will respond, helping to fully integrate gay businesspeople into the American mainstream.

Children

Certainly if all the lesbians we interviewed who intend to have children go ahead with their plans, there is no end in sight to the lesbian baby boom. In the near future, lesbian parents will be joined by increasing numbers of gay men having children. Although the logistics of becoming parents are more difficult for gay men, their higher earning power will make raising children easier for them in many ways. However, gay men face more discouragement for being parents from both the society at large and the gay male communities.

One notable effect of the trend toward gay parenthood will be the increasing attractiveness of suburban life for gay people. Attention, suburbanites! Gay parents, their children, and their gay friends are heading your way! Increasingly, play groups, school boards, and suburban religious institutions will face involvement by gay parents and their children on the playground, in the classrooms, and in the sanctuary.

As a result, gay children of heterosexual parents will grow up knowing older gay role models; this will help them come out earlier. Gay parents will also increasingly challenge heterosexism in the schools and at work. Having children will play an important role in motivating gay people in business to seek protections and benefits for them and their families.

Religious institutions will also be impacted. As Shari and Cindy or Bob and Rob take little Josh or Susie to synagogue or church, they will be challenging the assumption that families should consist of Mom, Dad, and child. Although some religions set the rules at the top and will be difficult to change, in most religious traditions, leadership responds to the changing needs of its adherents. In increasing numbers of religious classrooms, the Sunday-school teacher will tell Billy that it's OK for Susie to have two dads instead of a mom and a dad—and that Josh's interpretation of the story of Jonathan and David or Ruth and Naomi, which he learned from his two moms, is quite plausible.

We also learned from gay people who have children that their extended families grew closer as a result of the kids. Thus—even if parents have a hard time getting used to the idea that their child is gay—when little ones come along, resistance tends to melt as they find their grandchildren irresistible.

Networking

While gay men are pros at networking, lesbians will quickly catch up. In cities around the country, lesbians are recognizing the benefits of networking with one another, gay men, and heterosexual colleagues. While cities like Atlanta, San Diego, Los Angeles, and San Francisco have long had organizations linking lesbian business professionals, a similar organization was formed in New York City only recently. Other cities will continue to create similar groups to help lesbians in their careers. Additionally, lesbians will increasingly see the benefit of participating in mixed gay organizations; this will create a critical mass of lesbians that will attract other lesbian members.

As more people come out of the closet in the business world, the substance of gay networking will become more substantial. Gay people will help one another find jobs, get promotions, and do business, just as heterosexuals have done for years. Additionally, more gay people will be available to speak publicly about being gay at work, thus sharing a wealth of experience that until recently has been closeted.

Within their companies, the greater openness of gay people means more networking opportunities. The fears that now keep people in the closet are also keeping them from networking with one another and with heterosexuals. By avoiding conversations that could lead to questions about their personal lives, many avoid opportunities for networking and developing mentors. As gay people come out, they become more comfortable with themselves, and as a result they are able to let their personalities shine through. As whole individuals they will bond more closely with their colleagues and have deeper relationships as a result.

Additionally, gay employee groups will continue to gain strength and numbers as they network with each other, resulting in increased benefits at many companies.

Success and Mentors

Gay people will continue to be successful in their chosen careers. The difference in the future will be that they are successful and visible as gay men and lesbians. While the number of openly gay professionals pursuing entrepreneurial opportunities in order to avoid the lavender ceiling will undoubtedly continue, the emerging trend is the belief that openly gay people can achieve success in the mainstream.

Both gay people in their twenties and thirties who are openly gay from the beginning and older gay people who are now coming out will test this belief in the years to come. While some will face obstacles, others will achieve a level of success that openly gay people have never achieved before.

With fewer potential mentors hidden in the closet, more gay people will be available as mentors and role models for less-senior gay people. Additionally, more heterosexuals will become mentors for people they know are gay, further erasing the myth that coming out means career suicide. As gay people become more visible, corporations will realize that some of their best talent is gay and will help employees become more comfortable in working with gay coworkers. As a result, barriers will fade, and gay people will increasingly be promoted to supervisory managerial positions in addition to task-oriented executive ones.

Gender

The most significant trend among lesbians in business is the trend toward greater visibility. Professionally, lesbians will continue to challenge both the glass and lavender ceilings. As lesbians' financial security and expectations rise, they will seek to become more informed about gay issues and politics and more connected to other lesbians and to gay men. As more lesbians pursue business careers, this will also fuel increased interaction with gay men, who will likewise find personal and career benefits in their association with these lesbians. Also, as gay men have children they will also find more common ground with lesbians. As a result, the goals of mixed gay organizations will increasingly reflect the overlapping needs of both genders.

As women earn more money, more venues will emerge to cater to them. There will be more lesbian cafés, bars, coffeehouses, resorts, and entertainment, including movies, plays, and music. The increase in venues will result in greater visibility of lesbians throughout society. As a result of the increased visibility of a diversity of lesbian lives, more lesbians will come out at work about being gay and come out among lesbians about being in business. Ultimately, having more money, having more lesbian establishments, and being more visible will result in more lesbian clout and power—both in the mainstream and in relation to gay men.

Race

Minority gay people can leverage being different to their advantage in coming out at work by exercising their freedom to behave in ways that are different from the norm. As a result, minority gay people are in a particularly strong position to come out at work, and we expect that an increasing number will do so. In addition, various gay and minority communities will increasingly open their doors to minority people who are openly gay. In particular, as gay minorities gain more money and power, more attention will be given to minority issues in the gay community, and there will be more social integration between gay people of different races. The increased openness of minority gay people and their social ties with white gay people will also have an important result in the workplace, helping minority gay people benefit from increased ties to gay people of all races throughout the corporate hierarchy.

International

U.S. cultural norms have tremendous impact worldwide. Media and entertainment have long been the pipelines for spreading American culture. The increased interaction of American businesses and companies with others throughout the world means that American business is having a profound effect on international culture as well. As American companies put policies in place protecting gay employees from discrimination and treating them equally in benefits plans, their global operations will ultimately be affected. At the same time, gay people around the world are wrestling with and winning on many of the same issues American gay people face.

There is much talk today about the shrinking of the world due to improved communications, and in many ways, international networking is becoming a fact of life for the relatively affluent. With millions of people around the world having access to the Internet, consider how many people now have access to information about gay men and lesbians! In countries where gay literature is banned or gay culture does not flourish, gay people have alternative means of getting information and making contacts. Thus gay people are learning and educating themselves about gay life around the world from the comfort of their own homes.

AIDS

On the night we wrote this conclusion we learned that Bart Rubenstein, whom you met in numerous chapters, had died. When we interviewed him nine months earlier, he told us that he was fortunate that he hadn't had any symptoms yet and was hoping to enjoy his early retirement by traveling with his partner. His death and the loss of so many other gay people as well will be strongly felt by the business world.

Many predict that there will be a second wave of people dying of AIDS. Those we interviewed agreed that there are gay men who believe they are immune or were willing to risk not taking precautions, particularly among the young. But they assured us that they and their friends were playing safe. The older gay men who have lost most of the entries in their Rolodex are also acutely aware of the need to practice safer sex. Meanwhile, lesbians are attempting to educate lesbians about safer sex as well. Although there may well be a second wave of AIDS infection among gay men, it is far less likely to decimate the managerial ranks than the first one.

Yet companies and managers will continue to face decisions when employees become ill and are no longer able to fulfill the responsibilities of their jobs. There are many senior gay male professionals who were infected years ago and are still in good health. Also, although the second

HIV-positive wave is likely to affect mostly younger and hourly employees, the numbers may be large. The good news is that many companies have already established a track record of handling employees with AIDS with respect and dignity. As HIV-positive employees increasingly trust companies to do right by them, they will be willing to play a more active role in working together with their managers in developing a plan for their eventual need for a reduced workload.

The Bottom Line

On a balance sheet, the bottom line is what is left after you subtract the liabilities from the assets. On an income statement, the bottom line is the revenues less the expenses. In a case analysis at Harvard Business School, the bottom line is a statement that you put forward for your classmates to agree with, negate, debate, critique, build upon, and contemplate.

In business schools, when the professors ask, "What's the bottom line?" they are looking for the one conclusion that sums up all the points. It should take into consideration all of the pros and cons, all of the issues, everyone's point of view and opinions, all of the contradictions and supporting evidence. The bottom line of *Straight Jobs, Gay Lives* for gay people is this: Align yourself with allies and come out of the closet.

Whether or not you choose to come out, seeking allies is the single best thing you can do for your career. Every gay person needs to find both gay and heterosexual people who will support their career aspirations, their chosen family configuration, and their rightful place in their family of origin. Allies can be your parents, partner, friends, coworkers, mentors, bosses, children, or subordinates. You can be your own best friend, but just as "No man is an island," you can't live a healthy life in a vacuum. Rather, you need a diverse group of people in your life who inherently respect you as a person and support you in taking on new challenges.

While no one can promise that coming out is completely safe, our evidence strongly supports coming out as a more successful career strategy for gay professionals than trying to stay closeted. Being out, you are a whole person who is devoting 100 percent of your energies to your job performance, rather than maneuvering to deny or hide your sexual orientation. Being out, you can draw on all of your creative energy and experiences to perform your job. Being out, you have no hidden vulnerabilities that others can take advantage of.

The bottom line for heterosexuals is: You can be proactive in eliminating homophobia and heterosexism in your working environment—whether or not there are openly gay people where you work. Do whatever you can to let people you think might be gay feel you are an ally and that it is safe for them to come out to you—and support those you know are gay by treating them the way you would want to be treated if you were gay.

We hope that this book inspires both gay and heterosexual people to find new ways to support gay people in their careers and in society. We also hope that our work inspires others to do further study about gay men and lesbians in the workplace. Finally, we hope our work encourages gay men and lesbians to achieve ever-increasing success in their business endeavors.

RESOURCE SECTION

Gay Workplace Resource Guide

Online Resources

America Online: Lifestyles & Interests/Gay & Lesbian Community Forum/Message Boards/At Work

Customizable Electronic Newsfinder
San Jose Mercury News Newshound
Newshound@sjmercury.com
(800) 818-NEWS
(available as a premium feature on America Online)

Digital Queers
DIGIQUEERS@aol.com Web page: http://www.dq.org/dq/
Finding the Gay and Lesbian Community Forum on America Online" (information on using AOL and the internet for gay information, 5 pp., and list of local gay BBS).

Larry Stratton
larry@bradley.bradley.edu
(List of companies with nondiscrimination policies)

Scott Safier's e-mail list on domestic partner benefits
send message containing the words "info domestic" to majordomo-domestic@cs.cmu.edu

Scott Safier's Web Page
http://www.cs.cmu.edu:8001/afs/cs/user/scotts/domestic-partners mainpage

Queer Resource Directory Web page
http:/abacus.oxy.edu/QRD/www
(for other access methods send e-mail to info@qrd.org)

Online Newsgroups
alt.homosexual
alt.politics.homosexuality
bit.listserv.gaynet
clari.news.gay
GLB-News Mailing List (available in newsgroup form from some servers)
soc.motss

Organizations Focusing Extensively on Gay Business, Investment, and Employment Issues

NONPROFIT ORGANIZATIONS

ACLU National Gay & Lesbian Rights Project
1663 Mission St. #460, San Francisco, CA 94103, (415) 621-2488

"Domestic Partnership Information Packet," 1992, 16 pp. Also available through NCLR.

Committee for Equal Opportunity (CEO)
c/o Joe McCormack, McCormack & Associates, 201 N. Figueroa St. #700, Los Angeles, CA 90012, (213) 975-1585

Loose affiliation of people working on gay workplace issues.

Gay & Lesbian Association of the U.S. Small Business Association
Don Kraft, Washington, DC, (202) 205-6942

Information and assistance to gay small-business owners; information on gay business and professional organizations.

Hollywood Supports
Richard Jennings, 8455 Beverly Blvd. #305, Los Angeles, CA 90048, (213) 655-7705. HSupports@aol.com Web page: http://www.datalounge.com/hssupports

Entertainment-industry project working with companies on nondiscrimination regarding gay and HIV issues. Instrumental in obtaining domestic partner benefits in many entertainment companies.

"Group Health Coverage for Employees' Same-Sex Partners: Issues for Entertainment Industry Employers," 1994, 3 pp.; "Guide to Starting an Employee Support Group," 2 pp.; "Model Documents for Extending Group Health Coverage to Employees' Domestic Partners," 1994, 17 pp.; "List of Employers with Domestic Partner Benefits," 1994.

Interfaith Center on Corporate Responsibility
475 Riverside Dr. #566, New York, NY 10015, (212) 870-2296

Lambda Legal Defense & Education Fund
666 Broadway, 12th fl., New York, NY 10012, (212) 995-8585
17 E. Monroe #212, Chicago, IL 60603, (312) 759-8110
6030 Wilshire Blvd. #200, Los Angeles, CA 90036, (213) 937-2728

"Negotiating for Equal Employment Benefits: A Resource Packet," 1994; "Jurisdictions and Companies with DP Registration and/or Benefits," 1994; "Domestic Partnership Issues and Legislation," 1992; "Life Planning: Legal Documents and Protections for Lesbians & Gay Men," 1992; copies of miscellaneous nondiscrimination ordinances.

Lesbian & Gay Employee Rights Unit
1G Leroy House, 436 Essex Rd., London N1 3QP, England, lesbians 071-704-8066, gay men 071-704-6066, fax 071-704-6067

Lesbian & Gay Labor Alliance
763 14 St., San Francisco, CA 94114, (415) 861-0318

Information on collective bargaining for domestic partner benefits.

Lesbian and Gay Labor Network of N.Y.
PO Box 1159, Peter Stuyvesant Station, New York, NY 10009

"Pride At Work: Organization for Lesbian & Gay Rights in Unions," by Miriam Frank and Desma Holcomb, 1990. Also available through NGLTF or NCLR.

Lesbians & Gay Men at Time Warner
Rich Mayora, c/o Home Box Office, 1100 Ave. of the Americas rm. 515, New York, NY 10036, (212) 512-5909

"Organizing and Sustaining an Employee Support Group," 2 pp. Also maintains a list of New York–area gay employee contacts.

National Center for Lesbian Rights (NCLR)
870 Market St. #570, San Francisco, CA 94102, (415) 392-6257

"Recognizing Lesbian and Gay Families: Strategies for Obtaining DP Benefits," 2nd ed., 1992; "Lesbians, Gay Men, and Employment Discrimination: An Annotated Bibliography of Cases and Law Review Articles"; "Preserving and Protecting the Families of Gay Men and Lesbians," 2nd ed., 1990; "Lesbians Choosing Motherhood: Legal Implications," 2nd ed., 1991; miscellaneous domestic partner ordinances.

National Gay & Lesbian Journalists Association (NGLJA)
PO Box 423048, San Francisco, CA 94142-3048, (415) 905-4690. NGLJANews@aol.com Sherry Boschert, Chair, Workplace Benefits, Shaalu@aol.com

National conference, "News Executive's Guide to DP Benefits," including breakdown of media companies' enrollments, Spring 1994, 8 pp. Copies of various corporate policies; list of employers offering domestic partner benefits; studies, surveys and reports, including policies and announcements from Apple Computer, the *Boston Globe,* International Data Group, Levi Strauss, Minnesota Communications Group, Montefiore Medical Center, National Public Radio, the *Seattle Times,* Silicon Graphics, Stanford University, Yale University.

National Gay & Lesbian Task Force (NGLTF)
2320 Seventeenth St. NW, Washington, DC 20009, (202) 332-6483. megngltf@aol.com

Workplace project, "Lesbian, Gay, and Bisexual Civil Rights in the U.S.: A Chart of States, Cities, Counties, and Federal Agencies That Bar Discrimination Based on Sexual Orientation," June 1994; "Gay, Lesbian, Bisexual Employee

Groups," July 1994; "Organizing a GLB Employee Group," June 1994; "Private Companies with EEO Protection," June 1994; "DP Benefits List," June 1994; "Pervasive Patterns of Discrimination," 1992; "DP Organizing Manual," 1992; "1993 *Fortune* 1000 Survey," October 1993; "Who Supports the Gay Rights Movement?" 1990; annual fall workplace conference.

National Gay Task Force Historical publications available from NGLTF: "Employment Discrimination in N.Y.C.: A Survey of Gay Men and Women," 1981; "The NGTF Corporate Survey," 1981; "You and Your Job: A Gay Employee's Guide to Discrimination," 1981; "Are There Gay People Working in My Business?: Answers to Employer's Questions," 1981.

Out at Work (or Not)
Jason Cohen, PO Box 359, Chicago, IL 60690-0359, (312) 794-5218

Articles, reports, and resources on diversity management and domestic partner benefits. "Lesbigay Workplace Issues Resource Directory," 1994, 15 pp.; "How to Start a Gay Employee Group," 1993, 2 pp. Policies and announcements, including *Minneapolis Star Tribune,* University of Minnesota, IDS, Lotus, West Hollywood, University of Chicago, Levi Strauss, Polaroid, NeXT Computers, Fannie Mae, Microsoft.

Spectrum Institute
Thomas Coleman, Executive Director, PO Box 65756, Los Angeles, CA 90065, (213) 258-8955

"Domestic Partners: Couples Are Gaining Recognition from Government and Equal Benefits at Work," October 1993, 12 pp. Also available from NCLR.

The Wall Street Project
Nick Curto, 82 Wall St. #1105, New York, NY 10005-3601, (212) 289-1741

"1993 Census of Sexual Orientation Policies of the Fortune 500 Service and Industrial Corporations."

FOR-PROFIT ORGANIZATIONS

Alexander & Alexander Consulting Group
Mary McMann, Senior Consultant, San Francisco, CA, (415) 222-7200

"Group Letter to the Northern California Newspaper Guild on DP Benefits," 1993, 10 pp.

Arthur Anderson & Co.
Glen Carlson, Tax Partner, Los Angeles, CA, (213) 614-6690

Tax and regulatory benefits issues, executive compensation. Instrumental in getting MCA to adopt domestic partner benefits.

Christopher St. Financial
(212) 269-0110

First gay-owned investment company.

Gales Investment Letter
Wesley Hicks, PO Box 493, Hawkinsville, GA 31036, (912) 892-2303

Investment advisory firm focusing on gay-friendly growth companies.

George Simons International
Amy Zuckerman and George Simons, 740 Front St., #335, Santa Cruz, CA 95060 (408) 426-9608

"Sexual Orientation and the Workplace" workbook for diversity training.

Hewitt Associates
Loralie Van Sluys, 100 Half Day Road, Lincolnshire, IL 60069-1991, (708) 295-5000

Executive compensation and employee benefits. "Domestic Partner Employee Benefits," 1994, 39 pp. Tax implications, finding an insurer, case studies, list of employers offering benefits.

McCormack & Associates
Joseph McCormack, 201 N. Figueroa St. #700, Los Angeles, CA 90012, (213) 975-1585

Executive search firm specializing in placing gay executives.

Progressive Asset Management
Howard Chip Tharsing, 1814 Franklin St. #710, Oakland, CA 94612, (510) 834-3722

Lavender screen for investments on six hundred companies. Looks at nondiscrimination clause, human resources training on gay/HIV issues, domestic partner benefits, gay employee groups.

Sedgwick Consulting Group
Terri DeVito, Certified Employee Benefits Specialist (CEBS), (415) 983-5774
Tony Casabat, 600 Montgomery St., San Francisco, CA 94111, (415) 983-5600

Employee benefits consulting. Instrumental in getting benefits at Supermac Technology, Children's Hospital of Oakland, Gupta Corporation.

The Segal Company
Andrew Sherman, Vice President, Boston, MA 02116-5712, (617) 424-7337

Benefits, compensation, and actuarial consultants. Instrumental in getting Lotus to adopt domestic partner benefits. "Executive Letter," vol. 17, nos. 1 & 2 (1993), on domestic partner benefits, 8 pp. Also available through NCLR.

William Mercer, Inc.
3200 One Union Square, Seattle, WA 98101, (206) 292-7365

"Bulletin 212: Coverage of Domestic Partners Under an Employee Benefit Program," 1993, 2 pp.

Organizational Sources for General Information, Publications, and Networking

Gay Games

Held every four years (1994, 1998, etc.); location varies throughout the world. Information and literature on corporate sponsors of gay events. ilga@gn.apc.org

Gay & Lesbian Alliance Against Defamation (GLAAD)
8455 Beverly Blvd. #305, Los Angeles, CA 90048, (213) 658-6775
150 W. 26 St., New York, NY 10001, (212) 807-1700
Chapters: Atlanta, (404) 876-1398; Chicago, (312) 871-7633; Dallas,

(214) 521-5342; Denver, (303) 331-2773; Kansas City, (816) 374-5927; DC, (202) 429-9500; San Diego, (619) 688-0094; San Francisco, (415) 861-2244. Also on AOL, the Internet, and by BBS.

Newsletter focuses on corporate treatment of gay people in the media, including advertising. Also includes information on domestic partner benefits at media companies.

Gay & Lesbian Parents Coalition International (GLPCI)
PO Box 50360, Washington, DC 20091, (202) 583-8029
GLPCI@aol.com

Eighty-five chapters around the world; annual conference.

Gay & Lesbian Victory Fund
1012 14th St. NW #707, Washington, DC 20005, (202) 842-8679.
VictoryF@aol.com

Helps elect gay and lesbian political officials.

Human Rights Campaign Fund (HRCF)
1101 14th St. NW, Suite 200, Washington, DC 20005, (202) 628-4160. Elizabeth Birch, Executive Director.

Political lobbying regarding workplace issues.

International Gay & Lesbian Human Rights Commission
1360 Mission St. #200, San Francisco, CA 94103, (415) 255-8680.
iglhrc@igc.apc.org

Military Law Task Force
1168 Union St. #201, San Diego, CA, (619) 233-1701

NetGALA (gay alumni groups)
PO Box 53188, Washington, DC 20009

Parents and Friends of Gays & Lesbians (P-FLAG)
1101 Fourteenth Ave. NW #1030, Washington, DC 20005, (202) 638-4200. PFLAGNTL@aol.com

Three hundred fifty chapters in the U.S. and eleven in other countries; various publications.

Servicemembers Legal Defense Network
PO Box 53013, Washington, DC 20009, (202) 328-3244

United Fellowship of Metropolitan Community Churches
5300 Santa Monica Blvd. #304, Los Angeles, CA 90029, (213) 464-5100.
UFMCCKit@aol.com

Three hundred churches in sixteen countries.

World Congress of Gay and Lesbian Jews
PO Box 3345, New York, NY 10008-3345. E-Mail: Beth5051@aol.com

Over sixty gay Jewish organizations worldwide.

Publications That Often Cover Gay Workplace Issues

The *Advocate:* Workline column

Every other issue, Q & A and news about gay workplace issues.

The Family Next Door: For Lesbian and Gay Parents and Their Friends
PO Box 21580, Oakland, CA 94620, (510) 597-1304

Vol. 2, nos. 1–3, 1994, on domestic partner benefits; other coverage of workplace issues.

The Gay/Lesbian/Bisexual Corporate Letter
Arthur C. Bain, PO Box 602, Murray Hill Station, New York, NY 10156-0601

Not published recently. Vol. 2, issue 1, p.2 has information on E-mail lists.

Lesbian and Gay Law Notes
Lesbian and Gay Law Association of Greater New York, 799 Broadway rm. 340, New York, NY 10003, (212) 353-9118.

Monthly newsletter; back issues to January 1988. Contact Audrey Hartman for subscriptions. Information on employment discrimination, domestic partner benefits, gay parenting, and more.

Next News: A Monthly Resource for Gay, Lesbian & Generation X Marketing
George Sanscoucy, 227 East 56th St. floor 4, New York, NY 10022, (212) 750-5687.

Out & About
8 W. 19 St. #401, New York, NY 10011, 800-929-2268, OUTANDABOUT@aol.com

"Fly Free, Girlfriend: Ranking the Frequent Flyer Programs," vol. 3, no. 7, September 1994, pp. 106–107. Occasional information on gay workplace issues, especially those related to the travel industry.

Partners Task Force
Steve Byrant and Demian, PO Box 9685, Seattle, WA 98109-0685 demian@eskimo.com Web page: http://www.eskimo.com/~demian/partners.html

Not published recently. Back issues available. Spring 1992 issue on domestic partner benefits, including case studies and bibliography. Also available: list of companies with domestic partner benefits through July 1994 and publication "How to Negotiate Job Benefits," 2 pp.

Quotient: The Newsletter of Marketing to Gay Men & Lesbians
Daniel B. Baker, Sean O'Brien Strub, and William Henning, 349 W. 12 St., New York, NY 10014

Victory Magazine
2261 Market St. #296, San Francisco CA 94114, (510) 215-7780

For gay business owners and entrepreneurs.

Working It Out: The Newsletter for GLB Employment Issues
Ed Minkins, PO Box 2079, New York, NY 10108, (212) 769-2384

Not published recently.

Video

Gay Issues in the Workplace: Gay, Lesbian and Bisexual Employees Speak for Themselves
Brian McNaught, 1993
Motivation Media, 8430 Santa Monica Blvd., Los Angeles, CA 90069

Selected Reading Guide

Gay Professionals and Workplace Issues

BOOKS

Baker, Daniel B., Sean O'Brien Strub, and William Henning. *Cracking the Corporate Closet.* HarperCollins, New York, NY, 1995.

Diamant, Louis, ed. *Homosexual Issues in the Workplace.* Series in Clinical and Community Psychology. Chapter 2, "Corporate Outlook." Taylor & Francis, Washington, DC, 1993.

Escoffier, Jeffrey. *John Maynard Keynes.* Lives of Notable Gay Men and Lesbians Series. Chelsea House Publishers, New York, NY, 1995.

Gaines, Steven, and Sharon Churcher. *Obsession: The Lives and Times of Calvin Klein.* Carol Publishing Group, New York, NY, 1994.

Lukenbill, Grant. *Untold Millions,* HarperCollins, New York, NY, 1995 (forthcoming).

McNaught, Brian. *Gay Issues in the Workplace.* St. Martin's Press, New York, NY, 1993.

Minkens, Ed. *100 Best Companies for Gay Men and Lesbians: Plus Options and Opportunities No Matter Where You Work.* Pocket Books, New York, NY, 1994.

Out in the Workplace, Alyson Press, Boston, MA, 1995 (forthcoming).

Simons, George, and Amy Zuckerman. *Sexual Orientation in the Workplace* [workbook]. Available through George Simons International, the Galleria Office Park, 740 Front St., #335, Santa Cruz, CA 95060 or GSIINTISCCA@aol.com.

Smith, Tom. *Half Straight: My Secret Bisexual Life.* Prometheus Books, Buffalo, NY, 1992. Autobiography of a corporate executive.

Winans, Christopher. *Malcolm Forbes: The Man Who Had Everything.* St. Martin's Press, New York, NY, 1990.

Winans, R. Foster. *Trading Secrets: Seduction and Scandal at The Wall Street Journal.* St. Martin's Press, New York, NY, 1984. Autobiography of former "Heard on the Street" columnist.

Winfeld, Liz, and Susan Spielman. *Out in the Open: Lesbians and Gay Men at Work,* American Management Association, New York, NY 1995 (forthcoming).

Woods, James D., with Jay H. Lucas. *The Corporate Closet: The Professional Lives of Gay Men in America.* Free Press, New York, NY, 1993.

MASTER'S THESES

Ordering information: University Microfilms International, PO Box 1346, Ann Arbor, MI 48106-1346 or call (800) 521-3042.

Banzhaf, Jane. "Role Model Choice of Gay Students: A Study of Gay White Males Attending College During the 1960s, 70s, and 80s." University of Rochester, 1990, published August 1990, 248 pp. Many said they might have made different career choices if there had been more readily identifiable gay role models.

Eldridge, Natalie Suzanne. "Correlates of Relationship Satisfaction and Role Conflict in Dual-Career Lesbian Couples." The University of Texas at Austin, 1987, published April 1988, 214 pp.

Fogarty, Elizabeth Lee. "Passing as Straight: A Phenomenological Analysis of the Experience of the Lesbian Who Is Professionally Employed." University of Pittsburgh, 1980, published December 1980, 182 pp.

Greer, Ruth Berman. "Predictions of Self-Disclosure of Sexual Orientation in the Workplace Among Gay Males." Columbia University, 1992, published February 1993, 115 pp.

Hall, Marny. "Gays in Corporations: The Invisible Minority." The Union for Experimenting Colleges and Universities, 1981, published March 1982, 161 pp.

Harvey, James Joseph. "A Study of Employment Discrimination and Re-Education of a Selected Group of Homosexuals." East Texas State University, 1978, published May 1979, 185 pp.

Haselkorn, Harry. "The Vocational Interests of a Group of Homosexuals." New York University, 1953, published 1962, 119 pp.

Hodnett, James Hoyce. "Correlates of Relationship Satisfaction in Dual-Career Gay Male Couples." The University of Texas at Austin, 1991, published October 1992, 209 pp.

Jackson, Katrice Jewelean. "The Relationship Between Black Lesbians' Coming Out in the Straight Black Community and Isolation." California State University, 1993, published summer 1994, 62 pp.

Logiudice, Angelo James. "Effects of Sex, Sexual Preference, and Worksetting Based Upon Administrators' Beliefs Toward Gay People." Northeastern University, 1990, published February 1991, 442 pp.

Miller, Gerald Vincent. "From Disempowerment to Empowerment: The Gay Male's Odyssey in the Corporate World." The Union for Experimenting Colleges and Universities, 1987, published December 1988, 110 pp.

Schneider, Beth Elise. "Sexualization of the Workplace." University of Massachusetts, 1981, published February 1982, 403 pp. Finds that lesbians are more likely than heterosexual women to form a committed sexual relationship with someone from work.

Shallenberger, David Bruce. "The Gay Male Professional Who Has Come Out at Work: A Naturalistic Study of His Experience." The Fielding Institute, 1987, published January 1988, 315 pp. Study includes two Stanford MBAs.

Woods, James Desmond. "The Corporate Closet: Managing Identity on the Job." University of Pennsylvania, 1992, published November 1992, 379 pp.

BOOK EXCERPTS AND ARTICLES

Brown, Howard. *Familiar Faces, Hidden Lives: The Story of Homosexual Men in America Today.* Harcourt Brace Jovanovich, New York, NY, 1976.

Davison, Marilyn J., and Jill Wiley, eds. *Vulnerable Workers: Psychosocial and Legal Issues.* John Wiley & Sons, Chichester, England, 1991. Chapter 10: "Lesbians and Gay Men in the Workplace: Psychosocial Issues," Celia Kitzinger; chapter 11: "Homosexuals and Transsexuals at Work: Legal Issues," Jill Earnshaw and Peter Pace.

Ebert, Alan. "Frits Sonnegard, Corporate Executive," in *The Homosexuals: The First Book in Which Homosexuals Speak for and about Themselves.* Macmillan, New York, NY, 1977, pp. 21–47.

Elliott, John E. "Career Development with Lesbian and Gay Clients," *Career Development Quarterly,* March 1993, vol 41(3).

Escoffier, Jeffrey. "Stigmas, Work Environment, and Economic Discrimination Against Homosexuals." *Homosexual*

Counseling Journal, Jan 1975, vol 2(1), pp. 8–17.

Etringer, Bruce D., E. Hillerbrand, and C. Hetherington. "The Influence of Sexual Orientation on Career Decision-Making." *Journal of Homosexuality,* 1964), pp. 103–111.

Fefer, Mark D. "Gay in Corporate America: What It's Like and How Business Attitudes are Changing," *Fortune,* December 16, 1991.

Folbre, Nancy. "Sexual Orientation Showing Up in Paychecks." *Working Woman,* January 1995, p. 15.

Garnets, Linda D., and Douglas C. Kimmel, eds. *Between Women, Between Men: Lesbian and Gay Studies.* Columbia University Press, New York, NY, 1993, pp. 227–286, "Lesbian Career Development, Work Behavior, and Vocational Counseling," Kris S. Morgan and Laura S. Brown.

Hall, Marny. "The Lesbian Corporate Experience," *Journal of Homosexuality,* vol. 12, nos. 3/4 (1986), pp. 59–75.

Hollingsworth, Gaines. "Corporate Gay Bashing," the *Advocate,* September 11, 1990, pp. 28–33.

Jacobs, Bruce A. "Homosexuals in Management," *Industry Week,* July 23, 1979, pp. 52–59.

Jay, Karla, and Allen Young. *The Gay Report: Lesbians and Gay Men Speak Out about Sexual Experiences and Lifestyles.* Summit Books, New York, NY, 1977. Includes responses from 465 gay male and 31 lesbian managers among 5,000 respondents.

Jefferson, David J. "Gay Employees Win Benefits for Partners at More Companies," *Wall Street Journal,* March 18, 1994, pp. 1, 6.

Katchadourian, Herant, and John Boli. "Gay Partnerships," *Cream of the Crop: The Impact of an Elite Education in the Decade After College.* Basic Books, New York, NY, 1994, pp. 191–194. Eight percent of the men and none of the women in this study of Stanford University alumni identify as gay.

Kimmel, Michael S., and Michael A. Messner, eds. *Men's Lives.* Macmillan, New York, NY, 1992. Chapter 4: "The Status of Gay Men in the Workplace," Martin P. Levine.

Kronenberger, G. K. "Out of the Closet," *Personnel Journal,* vol. 70 (1991), pp. 40–44.

Labbs, Jennifer L. "Unmarried . . . with Benefits," *Personnel Journal,* December 1991, pp. 62–70.

Levine, Martin P., and Robin Leonard. "Discrimination Against Lesbians in the Work Force." *Signs: Journal of Women in Culture & Society,* vol. 9:4 (1984), pp. 700–710.

Lynch, Frederick R. "Nonghetto Gays: An Ethnography of Suburban Homosexuals," in Gilbert Herdt, ed., *Gay Culture in America: Essays from the Field.* Beacon Press, Boston, MA, 1992.

Magee, Bryan. "Lesbians at Work," in *One in Twenty: A Study of Homosexuality in Men and Women.* Stein & Day, New York, NY, 1966.

Miller, Merle. "What It Means to Be a Homosexual," parts one and two, *New York Times Magazine,* January 17, 1971 (part one) and October 10, 1971 (part two). (Reprinted as *On Being Different: What It Means to Be a Homosexual,* Popular Library, New York, NY 1971.) The first gay professional to come out in the mainstream press.

Miller, Neil. *In Search of Gay America: Women and Men in a Time of Change.* Perennial Library, New York, NY, 1990 (originally published by Atlantic Monthly Press, 1989). HBS graduate Nick Wilkerson is interviewed on pp. 233–237.

Morgan, Kris S., and Laura S. Brown. "Lesbian Career Development, Work Behavior, and Vocational Counseling," *Counseling Psychologist,* April 1991, vol. 19(2).

Noble, Barbara Presley. "A Quiet Liberation for Gay and Lesbian Employees," *New York Times,* June 13, 1993.

Rubenstein, Willliam B., ed. *Lesbians, Gay Men and the Law.* Law in Context Series Reader. New Press, New York, NY, 1993, chapter 4, "Lesbians and Gay Men in the Workplace," A selection in that chapter called "Work and Career: The Results" is of special interest. It is a summation of the response to a survey that appeared in *Out/Look: A National Lesbian and Gay Quarterly* in the Fall 1988 issue (the last issue published of that magazine).

Singer, Bennett, and David Deschamps, eds. *Gay & Lesbian Stats.* The New Press, New York, NY, 1994, pp. 72–75.

Traub, Marvin, and Tom Teicholz. *Like No Other Store: The Bloomingdale's Legend and the Revolution in American Marketing.* Times Books, New York, NY, 1993, pp. 402–403. Autobiography of an executive with a lesbian daughter who works with him at Bloomingdale's and Conran's.

Weinberg, Martin S., and Colin J. Williams. "Occupation," in *Male Homosexuals: Their Problems and Adaptations.* Oxford University Press, London, England, 1974.

Zoglin, R. "What It's Like to Be Gay in a Pinstriped World," in M. P. Levine, ed., *Gay Men: The Sociology of Male Homosexuality.* Harper & Row, New York, NY, 1979.

Resource Books for Gay Professionals

Clifford, Denis, and Robin Leonard. *A Legal Guide for Lesbian and Gay Couples,* 8th ed. Nolo Press, Berkeley, CA.

Dotson, Edisol W., ed, *Putting Out: The Essential Publishing Resource for Lesbian and Gay Writers,* 3rd ed. Cleis Press, San Francisco, CA, 1994. Pp. 59–102 lists gay magazines and journals. Pp. 103-122 lists gay newspapers and newsletters.

Elkin, Larry M., CPA. *First Comes Love, Then Comes Money: How Unmarried Couples Can Use Investments, Tax Planning, Insurance and Wills to Gain Financial Protection Denied by Law.* Doubleday Currency, New York, NY, 1994.

Gayellow Pages: The National Edition. Renaissance House, New York, NY, 1994. National guidebook.

Hendriks, Aart, Rob Tielman, and Evert van der Veen, eds. *The Third Pink Book: A Global View of Lesbian Liberation and Oppression.* Prometheus Books, Buffalo, NY, 1993. International guidebook.

Hunter, Nan, Sherryl Michaelson, and Thomas B. Stoddard. *The Rights of Lesbians and Gay Men,* 3rd ed. Southern Illinois University Press, Carbondale, IL, 1992.

Petersen, Randy. *The Official Frequent Flyer Guidebook,* 2nd ed. Air Press, Colorado Springs, CO, 1993.

Sherrill, Jan-Mitchell, and Craig A. Hardesty. *The Gay, Lesbian and Bisexual Students' Guide to Colleges, Universities, and Graduate Schools.* New York University Press, New York, NY, 1994.

Gay Professionals in Fiction

Aldridge, Sarah. *Keep to Me Stranger.* Naiad Press, Tallahassee, FL, 1989.

Greene, Harlan. *Why We Never Danced the Charleston.* St. Martin's/ Marek, New York, NY, 1984.

Hall, Richard. *Family Fictions.* Viking Penguin, New York, NY, 1991.

Harris, E. Lynn. *Invisible Life.* Anchor Books, New York, NY, 1994 (originally published by Consortium Press, 1991).

———. *Just As I Am.* Doubleday, New York, NY, 1994.

Holleran, Andrew. *Dancer from the Dance.* William Morrow, New York, NY, 1978.

Kramer, Larry. *Faggots.* Random House, New York, NY, 1978.

Reinhart, Robert. *A History of the Shadows.* Avon, New York, NY, 1982.

Rodi, Robert. *Closet Case.* Dutton, New York, NY, 1993.

Gay and Lesbian History

Berube, Allan. *Coming Out Under Fire: The History of Gay Men and Women in World War Two.* Free Press, New York, NY, 1990.

Chauncey, George. *Gay New York: Gender, Urban Culture, and the Making of the Gay Male World 1890–1940.* Basic Books, New York, NY, 1994. Pp. 349–351, "Professional Men and Businessman's Bars."

D'Emilio, John. *Sexual Politics, Sexual Communities: The Making of a Homosexual Minority in the United States 1940–1970.* University of Chicago Press, Chicago, IL, 1983.

D'Emilio, John, and Estelle Freedman. *Intimate Matters: A*

History of Sexuality in America. Harper & Row, New York, NY, 1988.

Duberman, Martin, Martha Vicinus, and George Chauncey. *Hidden from History: Reclaiming the Gay and Lesbian Past.* New American Library, New York, NY, 1989.

Faderman, Lillian. *Odd Girls and Twilight Lovers: A History of Lesbian Life in Twentieth-Century America.* Penguin, 1992 (originally published by Columbia University Press, 1991). Pp. 175–187, " 'Kiki' " Lesbians: The Upper and Middle Classes and Subculture Clashes in the 1950s and 1960s." Pp. 274–278, "The Shift to Moderation in the 1980s."

Kennedy, Elizabeth Lapovsky, and Madeline D. Davis. *Boots of Leather, Slippers of Gold: The History of a Lesbian Community.* Penguin Books, New York, NY 1994 (originally published by Routledge, 1993). A 1930s to 1950s lesbian community.

Katz, Jonathan. *Gay American History: Lesbians and Gay Men in the U.S.A.* Harper & Row, New York, NY, 1986.

Newton, Esther. *Cherry Grove, Fire Island: Sixty Years in American's First Gay and Lesbian Town.* Beacon Press, Boston, MA, 1993. Covers the 1930s to the 1980s.

Shilts, Randy. *And the Band Played On: Politics, People and the AIDS Epidemic.* St. Martins, New York, NY, 1987; revised ed., Penguin Books, 1988.

Thompson, Mark, ed. *Long Road to Freedom: The Advocate History of the Gay and Lesbian Movement.* St. Martin's Press, New York, NY, 1994.

Gay Lives and Political Theory

Barrett, Martha Barron. *Invisible Lives: The Truth About Millions of Women Loving Women.* William Morrow & Co., New York, NY, 1989.

Bawer, Bruce. *A Place at the Table: The Gay individual in American Society.* Poseidon Press, New York, NY, 1993.

Bell, A., and M. Weinberg. *Homosexualities: A Study of Diversity Among Men and Women.* Simon & Schuster, New York, NY, 1978.

Benkov, Laura, Ph.D. *Reinventing the Family: The Emerging Story of Lesbian and Gay Parents.* Crown, New York, NY, 1994.

Berzon, Betty. *Permanent Partners.* Dutton, New York, NY, 1988.

Blumstein, Philip, Ph.D., and Pepper Schwartz, Ph.D. *American Couples: Money, Work, Sex.* Pocket Books, New York, NY, 1985 (originally published by William Morrow, 1983). Includes significant information on gay male and lesbian couples throughout.

Browning, Frank. *Culture of Desire: Paradox and Perversity in Gay Lives Today.* Vintage Books, New York, NY, 1994 (originally published by Crown, 1993).

Clunis, D. Merilee, and G. Dorsey Green. *Lesbian Couples.* Seal Press, Seattle, WA, 1988.

Eichberg, Rob, Ph.D. *Coming Out: An Act of Love.* Dutton, New York, NY, 1990. Pp. 170–171 on coming out at work.

Griffen, Carolyn Welch, Marian J. Wirth, and Arthur G. Welch. *Beyond Acceptance: Parents of Lesbians and Gays Talk About Their Experiences.* Prentice-Hall, Englewood Cliffs, NJ, 1986.

Helminiak, Daniel A., Ph.D. *What the Bible Really Says About Homosexuality.* Alamo Square Press, San Francisco, CA, 1994.

Johnson, Susan E. *Staying Power: Long-Term Lesbian Couples.* Naiad Press, Tallahassee, FL, 1990.

Kirk, Marshall, and Hunter Madsen. *After the Ball.* Doubleday, New York, NY, 1989.

Lewis, Sasha G. *Sunday's Women: Lesbian Life Today.* Beacon Press, Boston, MA, 1979.

Marcus, Eric. *Is It a Choice? Answers to 300 of the Most Frequently Asked Questions About Gays and Lesbians.* HarperCollins, New York, NY, 1993.

Martin, April, Ph.D. *The Lesbian and Gay Parenting Handbook: Creating and Raising Our Families.* Harper Perennial, New York, NY, 1993.

McWhirter, David P., and Andrew M. Mattison. *The Male Couple.* Prentice-Hall, Englewood Cliffs, NJ, 1984.

Mendola, Mary. *The Mendola Report: A New Look at Gay Couples.* Crown, New York, NY, 1980. Chapter 5 covers mainstream aspects of gay couples' lives.

Michael, Robert T., John H. Gagnon, Edward O. Lauman, and Gina Kolata. *Sex in America: A Definitive Survey.* Little Brown & Co., Boston, MA, 1994. Chapter 9, "Homosexual Partners."

Muller, Ann. *Parents Matter: Parents' Relationship with Lesbian Daughters and Gay Sons.* Naiad Press, Tallahassee, FL, 1987.

Mohr, Richard D. *A More Perfect Union: Why Straight America Must Stand Up For Gay Rights.* Beacon Press, Boston, MA, 1994.

Nava, Michael, and Robert Dawidoff. *Created Equal: Why Gay Rights Matter to America.* St. Martin's Press, New York, NY, 1994.

Orleans, Ellen. *Who Cares If It's a Choice? Snappy Answers to 101 Nosy, Intrusive and Highly Personal Questions About Lesbians and Gay Men.* Laugh Lines Press, Bala Cynwyd, PA, 1994.

Rhoads, Robert A. *Coming Out in College: The Struggle for a Queer Identity.* Bergin & Garvey, Westport, CT, 1994.

Siegal, Stanley, and Ed Lowe Jr. *Uncharted Lives: Understanding the Life Passages of Gay Men.* Penguin Books, New York, NY, 1994.

Signorile, Michelangelo. *Queer in America.* Random House, New York, NY, 1993.

Silverstein, Dr. Charles. *Man to Man: Gay Couples in America.* Morrow, New York, NY, 1981.

Wolf, Deborah Goleman. *The Lesbian Community.* University of California Press, Berkeley, CA, 1979. Pp. 101–102, "Working patterns."

Diversity in Corporations

Cose, Ellis. *The Rage of a Privileged Class: Why Are Middle-Class Blacks Angry? Why Should America Care?* HarperCollins, New York, NY, 1993.

Feagin, Joe R., and Melvin P. Sikes. *Living with Racism: The Black Middle-Class Experience.* Beacon Press, Boston, MA, 1994.

Goffman, Erving. *The Presentation of Self in Everyday Life.* Doubleday, Garden City, NY, 1959.

———. *Stigma: Notes on the Management of Spoiled Identity.* Prentice-Hall, Englewood Cliffs, NJ, 1963.

Hirschman, Albert O. *Exit, Voice and Loyalty: Responses to Decline in Firms, Organizations and States.* Harvard University Press, Cambridge, MA, 1970.

Kanter, Rosabeth Moss, and B. A. Stein. *A Tale of 'O': On Being Different in an Organization.* Harper & Row, New York, NY, 1980.

Kanter, Rosabeth Moss. *Men and Women of the Corporation.* Basic Books, New York, NY, 1977; revised ed., 1993.

Korman, Abraham K. *The Outsiders: Jews and Corporate America.* Lexington Books, Lexington, MA, 1988.

Lester, Joan Steinau. *The Future of White Men & Other Diversity Dilemmas.* Conari Press, Berkeley, CA, 1994.

Financial Reports and Studies

"Beyond Biased Samples—Challenging Economic Myths About Lesbians and Gay Men," 1994, National Organization of Gay and Lesbian Scientists and Technical Professionals, PO Box 91803, Pasadena, CA 91109.

"Carnegie-Mellon University Faculty Senate Report on Domestic Partner Benefits," May 7, 1994.

"Domestic Partner Coverage Survey of Insurance Companies," Charles C. DeWeese, 1992, 5 pp. Available from NGLJA.

Insurers that have provided same-sex domestic partner benefits in some areas or indicated a willingness to do so, including Aetna, Blue Cross, Bridgeway, Cigna, Consumers United, Fireman's Insurance Co., Foundation Health Plan, George Washington University HMO, Great West Life, Group Health Cooperative of Puget Sound, Group Health Cooperative of N.Y., Harvard Community Health Plan, Kaiser Permanente, Liberty Mutual, Mass

Mutual, Pacific Care, Pacific Health, Prudential, Qualmed, Vision Service Plan.

"Funders of Lesbian, Gay and Bisexual Programs: A Directory of Grant Seekers," 1994, Working Group on Funding Lesbian and Gay Issues, 666 Broadway #520, New York, NY 10012. (Lists over 100 foundations and corporations that have supported gay programs.)

"Harvard University Domestic Partner Faculty and Staff Benefits Study," March 12, 1993, 21 pp. Harvard University, Cambridge, MA.

"Hearing of the Committee on Labor and Human Resources," Session on S. 2238, Senate, 103rd Congress, July 29, 1994. U.S. Government Printing Office, Washington, DC.

"Los Angeles County Bar Association Report on Sexual Orientation Bias," June 1994, PO Box 55020, Los Angeles, CA 90055. Survey of gay and heterosexual attorneys.

"Newsweek Poll," June 9–15, 1994, Princeton Survey Research Associates, P.O. Box 1450, Princeton, NJ 08542. Includes income data for names on the Strubco mailing list, which is based on lists of contributors to gay organizations or purchasers of products that are marketed to gay people.

"Overlooked Opinions Study," November 1990, 3162 Broadway, Chicago, IL 60613. Includes income data from readers of gay newspapers and participants in Gay Pride celebrations.

"Presentation on Domestic Partners Benefits at AT&T," 11 pp.

"Questions and Answers for Domestic Partners," 1993, University of Chicago, Office of Staff Benefits.

"Report of the CUNY Study Group on Domestic Partners," 1993, City University of New York, New York, NY.

"Sexual Orientation: An Issue of Workforce Diversity. A Report by the Ad-Hoc Committee of the Pacific Southwest Region Civil Rights Committee," prepared for the Regional Forester, U.S. Dept. of Agriculture Forest Service," September 1992, 56 pp. 630 Sansome St., San Francisco, CA 94111. [Nondiscrimination policy.]

"Simmons Newspaper Survey," 1988, available from the *Advocate,* 48 West 21st St. New York, NY 10010. Includes income data for readers of leading gay newspapers.

"Stanford University Report of the Subcommittee on Domestic Partners' Benefits, Stanford University Committee on Faculty and Staff Benefits," 1992, 70 pp. CUPA News Publisher, (202) 429-0311 x395, (415) 752-6841.

"Understanding the Domestic Partnership Dilemma: Perspectives of Employer and Insurer," Elizabeth Murphy, for the City of West Hollywood, 1993 (2nd ed.). 8611 Santa Monica Blvd., West Hollywood, CA 90069, (310) 854-7400.

University of Iowa Domestic Partner Coverage Study."

"University of Minnesota Report of the Select Committee on Lesbian, Gay & Bi Concerns," 1993, University of Minnesota, Minneapolis, MN, (612) 624-2855.

"University of Pennsylvania Recommendations of the Task Force on Benefits for Domestic Partners," December 10, 1993.

"The Wage Effects of Sexual Orientation Discrimination," M. V. Leigh Badgett, University of Maryland, 1994, *Industrial and Labor Relations Review* (in press, 1995). Income data analysis of a randomly selected group of individuals reporting same-gender sexual behavior in the General Social Study of the National Opinions Research Center in Chicago.

"Yankelovich Partners Study," 1993. 101 Merrit, 7 Corporate Park, Norwalk, CT 06851. Includes income data from a randomly selected group of individuals who identify themselves as gay.

Harvard and MBA-Related Resources

HBS, MBA, and Harvard University

HBS AND HARVARD GAY ALUMNI

Harvard Business School Gay & Lesbian Alumni Association
PO Box 1038, Planetarium Station, New York, NY 10024.

Newsletter and annual party. HBS graduates can also find other gay HBS alumni on America Online: HBS Alumni Forum/Special Interests Board/Gay & Lesbian Alumni folder

The Harvard Gay & Lesbian Caucus
Harvard Gay and Lesbian Review, PO Box 381809, Cambridge, MA 02238-1809. Robert Mack, co-chair, 617-259-71600. 71660.3630@compuserve.com, Web page: http://www.actwin.com/hglc

HARVARD LAW STUDENT PUBLICATIONS

Harvard Law Review, "Sexual Orientation and the Law" pp. 1508-1593, 1989.

Harvard Law Review, "Sexual Orientation and the Law" (Chapter III, "Employment Law Issues Affecting Gay Men and Lesbians"), 1990.

HBS HARBUS ARTICLES

February 1, 1978, p. 9. Classified: "Gays At HBS?" (PO Box listed).

February 27, 1978, p. 2. Letter: "Gays at HBS?" author's name withheld.

April 17, 1978, p. 2. *Harbus* Editorial: "The Invisible Minority at HBS."

April 17, 1978, p. 2. Letter: "An Open Letter to Section A," by the Gay Men and Women of Section A.

May 1, 1978, p. 2. Letter: "Section A Lambasts Publicity on Gays."

May 18, 1978, p. 3. News: "Gay Group Entering Third Year."

November 24, 1979, p. 3. News: "Gays Extend Invitation."

April 7, 1980, p. 3. First Person: "Coming Out at HBS: AEL [Alternative Executive Lifestyles]." Author's name withheld.

September 29, 1980, p. 3. Events: "GSA" by the Gay Students Association (phone number is given).

October 27, 1980, p. 6. Feature: "OB Tries Being Different," by Bob Chalfant, Max Donner, Melissa Weiksnar, Bill Arnold (regarding Section I's caselet on homosexual [sic] manager).

January 19, 1981, p. 7. Feature: "The Gay Minority at HBS," by the Copresident of the Gay Students Association.

September 28, 1981. Feature: "GSA Programs," by the Gay Students Association.

October 15, 1985, p. 2. Opinion: "Gay Students At HBS," by anonymous Second-Year student and president of the Gay Students Association.

February 10, 1986, p. 12. First Person: "Friends, Not Statistics Die of AIDS," by Bonnie Kintzer.

October 17, 1988, p. 3. Letter: "An Open Letter to HBS," author(s)' name(s) withheld (on National Coming Out Day and HBS).

September 25, 1989, p. 4. First Person: "Being Gay At HBS: Back to the Closet?" author's name withheld.

October 2, 1989, p. 3. First Person: "Being Gay at HBS," by the Invisible Booze Cruiser.

October 2, 1989, pp. 2–4. Dialogue: "The Right to Privacy vs. The Right to Know—How Far Inside You Can Interviewing Companies Reach?" ed. Brian Offutt and Mike Russell (one letter raises the issue of gay classmates).

October 2, 1989, pp. 3–5. Letter to the Editor: "Unsigned Letter Hurts Other Gay Students," by Paul Myers.

October 9, 1989, pp. 4–5. Opinion: "Gay At HBS," author's name withheld.

October 9, 1989, p. 2. The *Harbus* News Editorial: "Should Unsigned Letters Be Printed?"

November 13, 1989, p. 3. Opinion: "Gay Marriage Is About Love Too," author's name withheld.

November 20, 1989. Letter: "Unsigned Editorials Are Infuriating," by Kevin Sheehan.

December 4, 1989, p. 3. Opinion: "Will Gay Rights Bill Affect HBS Life?" by Stephen Robbins.

December 11, 1989, p. 3. First Person: "Gay at HBS: A Closet Makes a Lonely Home," by Stephen Robbins (first unambiguous coming out in print by HBS student).

December 11, 1989, p. 15. Book Review: "The Aerodynamics of Pork," by Kumar Harpal.

December 11, 1989, p. 22. Opinion: "Editorials Are Unsigned for a Reason," by Annette Friskopp.

January 16, 1990, p. 11. News: "Non-Discrimination Clause Omitted from 1990 Recruiter's Guide," by Heather Simmons.

February 12, 1990, p. 7. Feature: "A Partner's View Too," by Paul H. Ryder (on domestic partner benefits).

October 1, 1990, p. 2. First Person: "Gay at HBS: The Morning After," by Stephen Robbins.

October 9, 1990, p. 2. Letter to the Editor: "GLSA Ad Misleading," by Andrew Lawrisuk.

October 15, 1990, p. 2. Letter to the Editor: "GLSA Aims for Broader Audience," by Stephen Robbins, president of the GLSA (response to October 9, 1990, letter).

November 5, 1990. Opinion: "Organizational Behavior Week Fears Homophobia," by the directors of the GLSA.

December 3, 1990, p. 1, 5. News: "Law School Suit Prompts Introspection at HBS," by Tad Smith (includes a look at gay issues).

January 22, 1991, p. 1. News: "HBS to Mandate AIDS Seminar for First Years," by Alan Miles.

April 15, 1991, p. 12. First Person: "A Look At the HBS Gay Community," author's name withheld.

April 22, 1991, p. 4. Opinion: "Gay Stereotyping Questioned," by Douglas M. Plummer.

April 22, 1991, p. 18. First Person: "Closet Gays Are Selfish," by James H. Sherman.

April 29, 1991, p. 1, 5. News: "AIDS in the Workplace Set for May 15th," by Alan Miles.

April 29, 1991, p. 2. Letter to the Editor: "Gay Lifestyle Questioned," by Brad and Michaela Berkson.

May 6, 1991, p. 7. Letter to the Editor: "Disguised Homophobia," by John O'Connor (response to April 29, 1991 letter).

May 6, 1991, p. 7. Letter to the Editor: "GLSA President Responds to Lifestyles Question," by Douglas M. Plummer (response to April 29, 1991 letter).

May 6, 1991, p. 7. Letter to the Editor: "Response to Gay Lifestyle Questioning," by Jennifer and

Willem van Heeckeren (response to April 29, 1991 letter).

May 13, 1991, p. 11. Feature: "Being Gay at HBS," by Steven Robbins.

May 20, 1991, p. 9. Opinion: "An AIDS Martyr the Media Can Love," by Tom Ehrenfeld (reprinted with permission from the *New York Times*).

September 23, 1991, p. 3. Airtime Student Q & A: "Is Outing Acceptable?" by John Langbert and Loraine Davis.

September 23, 1991, p. 3. Opinion: "Outing: The End Doesn't Justify the Means," by Ian Rowe.

September 23, 1991, p. 2. Opinion: "Outing Is Telling the Truth," by Max Weston.

January 21, 1992, p. 15. "Big Bucks in Gay/Lesbian Marketing," by Douglas M. Plummer.

April 13, 1992, p. 3. Column: "In The Loop" by Nevada Powe (calls Harvard College Reverend Gomes' coming out a scandal).

April 20, 1992, p. 3. Letter to the Editor: "In The Loop Perpetuates Sexism," by Alistair D. Williamson (response to April 13, 1992, column).

April 20, 1992, p. 3. Letter to the Editor: "In The Loop Perpetuates Bigotry," by Jonathan Rottenberg (response to April 13, 1992, column).

April 27, 1992, p. 3. Letter to the Editor: "GLSA Ads Expose Hypocrisy," by Ian Rowe.

May 4, 1992, p. 5. Letter to the Editor: "Rowe Creates Row About GLSA," by Douglas M. Plummer (response to April 27, 1992 letter).

May 4, 1992, p. 5. Letter to the Editor: "Rowe Creates Row About GLSA," by Jonathan Rottenberg (response to April 27, 1992 letter).

May 4, 1992, p. 5. Letter to the Editor: "Rowe Creates Row About GLSA," by Alistair Williamson (response to April 27, 1992 letter).

October 26, 1992, p. 9. News: "Policing Partners at Shad," by Andrew Hecker (domestic partner benefits policy at HBS).

February 1, 1993, pp. 6–7. Opinion: "I Need You? Hmmmm . . . A Discussion About Gays in the Military," by David Kim (against).

February 1, 1993, p. 8. Opinion: "Gays in the Military? An Inside View," by Hal Barge (against).

February 8, 1993, p. 4. Opinion: "Ten Years Old, Alone in the World, and Without a Rational Basis—America's Ban on Gays in the Military," by Eric Tsuchida.

February 15, 1993, p. 3. Letter to the Editor: "Gays in the Military—Rebuttal," by Hal Barge.

March 22, 1993, p. 5. Opinion: "Gays in the Military—What Kind of Nation

Do We Want To Be?" by Veronica M. Diaz.

May 3, 1993, p. 5. Opinion: "March on Washington Sends Message," by Ann Bilyew.

May 17, 1993, p. 3. Letter to the Editor: "Powell—A Poor Choice," by Jim Ragsdale (on the selection of Gen. Colin Powell as Harvard University commencement speaker).

May 24, 1993, p. 5. Letter to the Editor: "Powell—a Disgraceful Choice," by Eric Tsuchida.

May 24, 1993, p. 5. Letter to the Editor: "Powell—an Excellent Choice," by the African American Student Union.

May 24, 1993, p. 19. News: "Guide to Student Clubs—The Gay and Lesbian Students Association."

October 18, 1993, p. 3. Opinion: "Diversity in the Workplace," by Eric Tsuchida (on HBS course content re gay issues).

November 15, 1993, p. 18. Out & About: "Dismantling the Corporate Closet," by Mel Glapion (book review).

November 22, 1993, pp. 14–15. Feature: "What HBS Students Think," by David Locala (includes students' thoughts on gays in the military).

November 22, 1993, p. 3. Out & About: "Alliances of Gay and Lesbian Professionals Prove Boon to Business," by Ann Bilyew.

December 6, 1993, p. 13. Feature: "Who Is Gay?" by David Geller.

January 24, 1994, p. 2. Out & About: "I Learned a Very Important Lesson Last September," by Veronica M. Diaz (AIDS case taught at HBS; classmates' homophobia).

February 14, 1994, p. 3. Opinion: "The Case for Domestic Partner Benefits," author's name withheld.

February 14, 1994, p. 3. Opinion: "The Closet—Not Just a Gay Thing," by Torrence Boone (reprinted in May 23, 1994 issue.)

March 14, 1994, p. 2. Opinion: "Roseanne and Lesbian Chic," by A Chic First-Year Lesbian.

March 14, 1994, p. 2. Out & About: "Another Perspective . . ." by A Concerned First-Year Partner.

April 11, 1994, p. 3. Letter to the Editor: "Response to 'Roseanne and Lesbian Chic' and 'Another Perspective,' " by Jeffery H. Singer.

April 18, 1994, p. 3. Opinion: "Misdirected Morality," by Leah Modigliani, Torrence Boone, Ann Bilyew, Anna Collins, Mel Glapion, and Chris Hall (response to April 11, 1994, letter).

April 18, 1994, p. 3. Out & About: "Open Minded? NOT!" by Eric Tsuchida (response to April 11, 1994 letter).

May 2, 1994. Opinion: "Religion, Tolerance, and Approval," by John A. Crosy (reprinted in May 23 issue).

September 26, 1994, p. 3. Out & About: "A New Source of Strength," by Torrence Boone (about the GLSA).

September 26, 1994, p. 2. Opinion/ The *HBS Democrat:* "Keep Government Out of the Marriage Decision," by Christopher Herman (on gay marriage).

October 11, 1994, p. 5. Airtime Student Poll: "How Would You React If Someone Came Out to You at HBS?" by Alana Kaplan and Andrew Silbinger.

October 11, 1994, p. 3. First Person: "National Coming Out Day, October 11, 1994—A Very Positive Experience," by a member of GLSA.

October 11, 1994, pp. 3–7. First Person: "Why I've Decided to Be Honest at HBS," by Eric Tsuchida.

October 11, 1994, pp. 1–9. News: "Coming Out at HBS," by John Barabino (on National Coming Out Day at HBS).

October 11, 1994, p. 3. Opinion: "Everyday Ideas For Coming Out," anonymous.

October 19, 1994, p. 3. Opinion: "10% . . . 3% . . . 1% Does It Matter?" by an anonymous GLSA member.

October 31, 1994, p. 6. Opinion: "The Last Bastion of Bigotry" by an anonymous member of Section OH.

November 21, 1994, p. 3. Opinion: "A Worthy Cause" by Mariann Sayer, a Second-Year partner of an OC member (about the Human Rights Campaign Fund dinner).

December 5, 1994, pp. 1, 4. News: "B-School Observes World AIDS Day," by John Barabino.

December 5, 1994, p. 3. Opinion: "Advertising Targets Gays and Lesbians," by an anonymous member of Section OH.

HBS ADMINISTRATION-SUPERVISED PUBLICATIONS

"Academic Standards and Administrative Policies of the HBS MBA Program" (various years), Harvard University Graduate School of Business Administration [nondiscrimination policy].

"Harvard University Domestic Partners Benefits Policy Study," May 12, 1993.

HBS Alumni Directory, Harvard Business School, 1990, 1995 (online).

HBS Bulletin (various issues), Harvard Business School (news reports about classmates).

HBS Class Prospectus (various years), Harvard Business School.

HBS Class Reunion Book (various years), Harvard Business School.

HBS Club of Greater NY Alumni Directory, Harvard Business School Club, New York, NY, 1993.

HBS MBA Application Packet (various years), HBS MBA Admissions Office.

"HBS MBA Program Guide" (various years), HBS MBA Admissions Office [HBS admissions nondiscrimination policy].

HBS Student Association Guide (various years), HBS Student Association [HBS Gay and Lesbian Student Association letter].

Net Present Value (1990–95), official student guide of HBS, HBS Community Board of Publications [chapter on diversity: "A Gay Student's Perspective"].

"There's Something Some of Your Classmates Want You to Know: It's Not Easy Being Gay or Lesbian at Harvard Business School," 1992.

BY AND ABOUT HBS GRADUATES

Butler, Nat. "My Separate Peace," *Men's Style,* March/April 1995, pp. 113–114. Author is an HBS alumnus who discusses his reapproachment with Exeter prep school as an openly gay man.

Eisberg, Jeffrey Leigh. *New York Times* obituary, May 1994. Includes mention of Eisberg as one of the founders of HBS gay student and alumni groups.

Fefer, Mark D. "Gay in Corporate America: What It's Like and How Business Attitudes Are Changing," *Fortune,* December 16, 1991. (Discusses HBS graduates Paul Kowal and Jonathan Rottenberg.)

Gooch, Brad. "The Best Little Boy Grows Up," *Out,* March 1995, pp. 84–87, 114–115 (HBS alumnus Andrew Tobias comes out).

Gross, Larry. *Contested Closets: The Politics and Ethics of Outing.* University of Minnesota Press, Minneapolis, MN, 1993. P. 171 quotes Larry Kramer outing Dick Jenrette in the *Advocate,* December 15, 1992.

Henry, Fran Worden. *Toughing It Out at Harvard: The Making of a Woman MBA.* McGraw-Hill, New York, NY, 1984 (originally published by G. P. Putnam's Sons). Author alludes to her same-sex relationship in the book.

Lyall, Sarah. "Thousands March to Commemorate 20 Years of Gay Pride," *New York Times,* June 26, 1989. Mentions HBS Gay & Lesbian Alumni organization.

McKinley, James C., Jr. "R. A. Campanioni, 34, a Philanthropist, Aiding Gay Projects," *New York Times,* June 1990. First openly gay HBS alumnus to be reported as openly gay in a *New York Times* obituary.

Phillips, Frank. "Two Male Weld Officials Say They Live As a Couple," *Boston Globe,* November 13, 1992, pp. 21, 26. Discusses HBS graduate Mitchell Adams.

Reid, John. *The Best Little Boy in the World.* G. P. Putnam's Sons, New York, NY, 1973. Author is an HBS alumnus.

Rubenstein, Bart. *New York Times* obituary, July 1994. Mentions he was survived by his partner, Greg Campora.

Tobias, Andrew. "Three-Dollar Bills," *Time,* March 23, 1992, p. 47. Discusses HBS graduate Jonathan Rottenberg.

Walker, Blair. "PC-User Pioneer Has 20-Year Plan to Defeat Homophobia," *USA Today,* p. 1. Discusses HBS graduate Jonathan Rottenberg.

Williamson, Paul Bain. *Bay Windows* obituary, May 1994. Mentions he was survived by his partner, Rob Montecalvo.

HARVARD AND MBA-RELATED BOOKS

Abramson, Jill, and Barbara Franklin. *Where They Are Now: The Story of the Women of Harvard Law 1974.* Doubleday & Co., Garden City, NY, 1986.

Cruikshank, Jeffrey L. *A Delicate Experiment: The Harvard Business School 1908–1945.* Harvard Business School Press, Boston, MA, 1987.

Ewig, David W. *Inside the Harvard Business School.* Times Books, New York, NY, 1990.

Gallese, Liz Roman. *Women Like Us: What Is Happening to the Women of the Harvard Business Class of '75.* William Morrow, New York, NY, 1985.

Harrington, Mona. *Women Lawyers: Rewriting the Rules.* Alfred A. Knopf, New York, NY, 1993. Based primarily on interviews with Harvard Law School graduates.

Kelly, Francis J., and Heather Mayfield Kelly. *What They Really Teach You at Harvard Business School.* Warner, New York, NY, 1986.

Lant, Jeffrey L., ed. *Our Harvard: Reflection on College Life by Twenty-Two Distinguished Graduates.* Taplinger Publishing Co., New York, NY, 1982. Includes gay writer Andrew Holleran [pseudonym].

Mark, Paul J. *The Empire Builders: Power, Money and Ethics Inside the Harvard Business School.* Morrow, New York, NY, 1987.

Marotta, Toby. *Sons of Harvard: Gay Men from the Class of 1967.* Quill, New York, NY, 1983. (Originally published by Morrow, 1982.)

Reid, Robert. *Year One: An Intimate Look Inside Harvard Business School.* William Morrow & Co., New York, NY, 1994.

Robinson, Peter. *Snapshots from Hell: The Making of an MBA.* Warner Books, New York, NY, 1994. A Stanford MBA's first year.

Shames, Laurence. *Big Time: 1949—The Harvard Business School's Most Successful Class and How It Shaped America.* Harper & Row, New York, NY, 1986.

Turow, Scott. *One L.* G. P. Putnam & Sons, New York, NY, 1977. Harvard Law.

HARVARD BUSINESS REVIEW CASES

For abstracts or to order call (800) 545-7685 or write Harvard Business School Publishing, Customer Service Department, Box 230-5, Boston, MA 02163, for a current *Harvard Business Review* articles catalog #22022 or gopher:// johnnymac.harvard.edu:70/11/

Banas, Gary E. "Nothing Prepared Me to Manage AIDS," July-August 1992. Reprinted in *Differences That Work.*

Gentile, Mary C., ed. *Differences That Work: Organizational Excellence Through Diversity.* Harvard Business Review Books, Boston, MA, 1944. Includes reprints of various *HBR* articles.

Kirp, David L. "Uncommon Decency: Pacific Bell Responds to AIDS," May-June 1989. Reprinted in *Differences That Work.*

Tedlow, Richard S., and Michele S. Marram. "A Case of AIDS," November-December 1991. Reprinted in *Differences That Work.*

Williamson, Alistair D. "Is This the Right Time to Come Out?" July-August 1993. Reprinted in *Differences That Work.*

HARVARD BUSINESS SCHOOL CASES

For abstracts or to order see information under previous heading. Ask for a current Harvard Business School catalog of teaching materials #23094.

"Ad Council's AIDS Campaign" (A & B cases), by J. Montgomery under the supervision of Prof. V. K. Rangan Originally published 1990, revised 1993; #9-590-105, 19 pp.; #9-590-106, 9 pp.; videotape #9-891-502 and teaching note also available.

"Boston Sobriety Development," by Eller Ratner under the supervision of Prof. Regina E. Herzlinger. 1989. Addiction treatment center includes gay clients in specialized program; #9-190-037, 13 pp.

"Brush with AIDS" (A & B cases), by J. Useem under the supervision of Prof. Joe L. Badaracco Jr. Originally published 1993, revised 1994. Health care products management, #9-394-058, 8 pp., and #9-394-059, 3 pp.; teaching note also available.

"Burroughs Wellcome and ATZ" (A, B, & C cases with background note), by J. O'Regan and M. Brand under the supervision of Prof. Willis Emmons. Originally published 1991, revised 1993; #9-792-004, 21 pp.; #9-793-114, 2 pp.; #9-793-115, 4 pp. Note on pharmaceutical industry regulation, #5-793-022, 24 pp. Two teaching notes also available.

"CBS vs. Andy Rooney," by R. Messins under the supervision of Prof. Joe L. Badaracco Jr. Published 1990. Corporate response to homophobia; #9-390-215, 2 pp.

"Daka International" (A & B cases), by R. J. Robinson, published 1993.

Client seeks firing of food service employee with AIDS; #9-49-051, 8 pp.; #9-494-052; teaching note also available.

"Leeway, Inc." (A & B cases), by E. West under the supervision of Prof. D. G. Dees. Originally published 1990, revised 1991. Nonprofit AIDS care facility; #9-391-085, 27 pp., #9-392-010, 2 pp.

"Levi Strauss & Co. and the AIDS Crisis," by Prof. Richard Tedlow. Originally published 1991, revised 1994; #9-391-198, 31 pp; videotape #9-792-510 is also available.

"Lotus Development Corporation: Spousal Equivalents" (A & B cases), by Mary Gentile. Published 1994; #N394-197, 17 pp.; #N9-394-201, 14 pp.

"Magic Johnson Endorsements 'After' . . . ?" by W. S. Schille under the supervision of Prof. S. A. Greyser. Published 1991; #9-592-057, 2 pp.

"New York Against AIDS: The Saatchi & Saatchi Compton Advertising Campaign" (A & B cases), by S. Karim under the supervision of Prof. V. K. Rangan. Originally published 1990, revised 1992; #9-590-036, 22 pp.; #9-590-037, 4 pp.; videotape #9-891-504 and teaching note also available.

"Paul Cronan and New England Telephone Company" (A, B, C, and D Cases), by Paul S. Myers under the supervision of Prof. Charles C. Heckscher. Originally published 1990, revised 1991. AIDS discrimination by coworkers and management: #9-490-055, 10 pp.; #9-490-056, 8 pp.; #9-490-057, 2 pp.; #9-490-058, 4 pp.; teaching note also available.

"Steven Ross: Self Assessment and Career Development Paper," by Steven Ross under the supervision of Prof. Jeffrey Sonnenfeld, 1984. Gay student's self-assessment for career planning; #9-485-039, out of print, 22 pp.

"Tom Reese," by J. Steele under the supervision of Prof. Joe L. Badaracco Jr. Published 1991. Coming out in the face of homophobia from a client, #9-391-145, 3 pp; teaching note also available.

Top Business School Policies as of February 1995

Business School	Rank	Grade	Total Score (Out of 100)	Nondiscrimination Policy Based on Sexual Orientation	LBG B-School Student Club	LBG Undergraduate Student Club
Harvard	1	A	97.5	Yes	Yes	Yes
Stanford	2	A	95.0	Yes	Yes	Yes
Yale	3	A−	90.0	Yes	Yes	Yes
Michigan	4	B+	87.5	Yes	Yes	Yes
N.Y.U.	4	B+	87.5	Yes	Yes	Yes
U. of Penn.	6	B	85.0	Yes	Yes	Yes
Columbia	7	B−	82.5	Yes	Yes	Yes
Northwestern	7	B−	82.5	Yes	Yes	Yes
U.C.L.A.	7	B−	82.5	Yes	Yes	Yes
U.C. Berkeley	10	B−	80.0	Yes	Yes	Yes
Cornell	11	C	75.0	Yes	(b)	Yes
Dartmouth	11	C	75.0	Yes		Yes
Virginia	11	C	75.0	Yes	Yes	Yes
Chicago	14	C−	72.5	Yes		Yes
Carnegie-Mellon	15	D+	67.5	Yes		Yes
Indiana	15	D+	67.5	Yes	(b)	Yes
M.I.T.	15	D+	67.5	Yes		Yes
Duke	18	D	62.5	Yes		Yes
North Carolina	19	D	60.0	Yes		Yes
Texas at Austin	19	D	60.0	Yes		Yes
U.S.C.	19	D	60.0	Yes		Yes
Purdue	22	F	35.0	(a)		Yes

Note: Duke now offers domestic partner benefits.
Source: Jason Lorber, Stanford Graduate School of Business, Class of 1996; based on schools' published materials, interviews with MBA Directors, Faculty, Administration, Alumni and Students.

Business School	LBG Info. Printed in Admission Brochure	Openly LBG Student in Admission Brochure	Domestic Partner Benefits for Faculty	Students	LBG B-School Alumni Organi-zation	LBG-Specific Job Info. Available	Openly LBG B-School Professors
Harvard	(c, d)		Yes	Yes	Yes	Yes	Yes
Stanford	(c, d)	Yes	Yes	Yes	Yes	Yes	
Yale	(c, d)		Yes	Yes	Yes		
Michigan	(c, d)		Yes	Yes		Yes	
N.Y.U.	(c, d)		Yes			Yes	Yes
U. of Penn.	(c, d)		Yes	Yes			
Columbia	(c, d)		Yes		(b)		
Northwestern	(c, d)	Yes					Yes
U.C.L.A.	(c, d)				(b)		Yes
U.C. Berkeley	(c, d)						Yes
Cornell	(c, d)		Yes				
Dartmouth	(d)		Yes	Yes		Yes	
Virginia	(c, d)						
Chicago	(d)		Yes	Yes			
Carnegie-Mellon	(d)		(e)	(e)			
Indiana	(d)						
M.I.T.	(d)		Yes				
Duke	(d)						
North Carolina							
Texas at Austin							
U.S.C.							
Purdue							

LBG Lesbian, Bisexual, Gay
Yes Criterion met.
☐ Empty box indicates criterion not met.
(a) Prohibits discrimination for "any person . . . for any reason." Nine bases are specified on which discrimination is barred (sex, age, Vietnam veteran, etc.). Sexual orientation is not noted.
(b) Informal network.
(c) LesBiGay B-School student club noted in admissions handbook.
(d) Policy forbidding discrimination based on sexual orientation printed in materials.
(e) Some domestic partner benefits offered, but not health care.

Locations with Nondiscrimination Policies

Nondiscrimination-in-employment policies that apply to all workers. Population residency figures are given. Sources: National Gay & Lesbian Task Force, Lambda Legal, *The Pink Book,* and printed news reports as of April 1995.

Notes: State of California law has very restrictive filing provisions and may invalidate stronger local laws. All Colorado city measures were repealed by statewide voter initiative in November 1992, but the repeal was declared unconstitutional in December 1993. County of Alachua, FL, law was repealed by voters in November 1994. City of Cincinnati, OH, law was repealed by city voters in November 1993, but repeal is stayed by court order. In April 1995 the ordinance was repealed by the city council as well.

As we went to press, the following locations enacted nondiscrimination policies that include sexual orientation: Lawrence, KA, and the State of Rhode Island. In addition, the Supreme Court of Canada ruled that the Charter of Rights prohibits discrimination based on sexual orientation. Meanwhile, Hillsborough County (Tampa) FL, repealed its statute.

CA:	State of California	29,760,021
	County of San Mateo	649,623
	City and County of San Francisco	723,959
	City of Berkeley	102,724
	City of Davis	46,322
	City of Hayward	111,498
	City of Laguna Beach	23,170
	City of Long Beach	423,433
	City of Los Angeles	3,485,398
	City of Oakland	372,272
	City of Sacramento	396,365
	City of San Diego	1,110,549
	City of Santa Cruz	49,711

	City of Santa Monica	86,905
	City of West Hollywood	36,118
CO:	City of Aspen	5,049
	City of Boulder	83,312
	City of Denver	467,610
	City of Telluride	1,309
CT:	State of Connecticut	3,287,116
	City of Hartford	139,739
	City of New Haven	130,474
	City of Stamford	108,056
DC:	City of Washington	606,900
FL:	County of Alachua	181,596
	City of Key West	24,832
	City of Miami Beach	92,639
	City of Tampa	280,015
	City of West Palm Beach	67,643
GA:	City of Atlanta	394,017
HI:	State of Hawaii	1,108,229
IA:	City of Ames	47,198
	City of Iowa City	59,738
IL:	County of Cook	5,105,067
	City of Champagne	63,502
	City of Chicago	2,783,726
	City of Urbana	36,344
IN:	City of Bloomington	60,633
	City of Lafayette	43,764
	City of West Lafayette	23,138
LA:	City of New Orleans	496,938
MA:	State of Massachusetts	6,106,425
	City of Amherst	35,228
	City of Boston	574,283
	City of Cambridge	95,802
	City of Malden	53,884
	City of Worcester	169,759
MD:	County of Howard	187,328
	County of Montgomery	757,027
	City of Baltimore	736,014
	City of Gaithersburg	39,542
	City of Rockville	44,835
ME:	City of Portland	64,358
MI:	City of Ann Arbor	109,392
	City of Detroit	1,027,974
	City of East Lansing	50,677
	City of Flint	140,762
MN:	State of Minnesota	4,375,099
	City of Marshall	12,023

	City of Minneapolis	368,383
	City of St. Paul	272,235
MO:	City of Kansas City	435,146
	City of St. Louis	396,685
NJ:	State of New Jersey	7,730,188
NY:	County of Tompkins	94,097
	City of Albany	101,082
	City of Alfred	4,559
	City of East Hampton	1,402
	City of Ithaca	29,541
	City of New York	7,322,564
	City of Syracuse	163,860
	City of Watertown	29,429
OH:	City of Cincinnati	364,040
	City of Columbus	692,910
	City of Yellow Springs	3,973
OR:	City of Portland	437,319
PA:	City of Harrisburg	52,376
	City of Lancaster	55,551
	City of Philadelphia	1,585,577
	City of Pittsburgh	369,879
	City of York	42,192
TX:	City of Austin	465,622
VA:	City of Alexandria	111,283
VT:	State of Vermont	562,758
	City of Burlington	39,127
WA:	City of Seattle	516,259
WI:	State of Wisconsin	4,891,769
	City of Madison	191,262

Country of Australia: New South Wales, Queensland, Western Australia, and Northern Territory.

Country of Brazil: certain cities.

Country of Canada: provinces of Alberta, British Columbia, Manitoba, New Brunswick, Nova Scotia, Ontario, Quebec, Saskatchewan, Yukon; Vancouver, B.C.; Calgary and Edmonton, Alberta; Toronto, Ontario.

Country of Denmark: since 1987.

Country of France: since 1986.

Country of Germany: Brandenburg area, including Berlin since 1992.

Country of Israel: since 1992.

Country of the Netherlands: since 1994.

Country of New Zealand.

Country of Norway: since 1981.

Country of South Africa: constitutional protection since 1994.

Country of Sweden: since 1988.

Jurisdictions Where Second-Parent Adoptions for Same-Sex Couples Have Been Approved

Source: National Center for Lesbian Rights as of April 1995. An April 1995 New York State Appellate Court ruling has precluded second-parent adoptions in ten jurisdictions: Brooklyn, Queens, Staten Island, Nassau, Suffolk, Westchester, Rockland, Orange, Putnam, and Duchess counties. Legal challenges are forthcoming.

As we went to press, for the first time in Indiana a second-parent adoption was approved.

AL:	Anchorage, Juneau.
CA:	Alameda, Butte, Contra Costa, Fresno, Los Angeles, Marin, San Diego, San Francisco, San Luis Obispo, San Mateo, Santa Clara, Santa Cruz, Sonoma.
DC:	Washington.
MA:	entire state.
MI:	Washtenaw and selected counties.
MN:	Aitkin, Hennepin.
NJ:	Essex, Middlesex.
NY:	Monroe, New York, Rochester, Washington.
OR:	Multnomah, Portland.
PA:	York.
TX:	San Antonio, Tarrant.
VT:	entire state.
WA:	King, Spokane, Thurston.
WI:	Milwaukee (overturned by state Supreme Court).

Employer Policies

The following list of employers is compiled from various sources, including NGLTF; Hollywood Supports; Lambda Legal; the Wall Street Project; *The 100 Best Companies to Work for Gay Men and Lesbians; Cracking the Corporate Closet;* the National Association of Gay & Lesbian Journalists; and various on-line sources listed earlier in the resource section. This list was compiled with the most currently available information as of April 1995.

Company Name = information is for the entire company unless otherwise listed.

Subsidiaries = information listed applies to subsidiaries as well. Parent company information is listed for informational purposes only.

Location = headquarters, unless company name is given as a specific location or division. couples (may also have domestic partner benefits for same-sex couples).

DP = domestic partner

GEG = gay employee group.

Industry = given for informational purposes.

ND = written nondiscrimination policy that includes the words "sexual orientation." It is not our intention to include companies that offer this protection only where required by law but do not offer it in other U.S. locations.

19xx = year adopted.

H = health care benefits for gay (o = officially recognized by company. i = informally recognized by company. no symbol = status unknown.)

[ ] = gay employee group name.

City, county, state, and country health benefits apply only to government employees unless otherwise noted. Many colleges and universities have nondiscrimination policies and gay employee groups. They are on this list only if they offer health care benefits.

ADP, Roseland, NJ: ND

AMR Corp. (subsidiaries: American Airlines, American Eagle, SABRE): ND 1993, GEG [Gay & Lesbian Employees of AMR (GLEAM)]

ARA Services: ND

ASK Computers (parent: Ingeres; subsidiary: Computer Associates), Mountain View, CA: ND

Abbott Laboratories, pharmaceuticals: ND, GEG

Adobe Systems, Mountain View, CA, computer software: ND, H 1994

Advanced Micro Devices, Sunnyvale, CA, electronics/electronic equipment: ND 1991, H

Aetna Life & Casualty, Hartford, CT, insurance: ND, GEGo [Aetna Network of Gay, Lesbian & Bi Employees (ANGLE)]

Air Products & Chemicals, Allentown, PA, chemicals and industrial gas: ND, GEGo [Gay & Lesbian Empowered Employees (GLEE)]

Alamo Rent A Car Inc., Fort Lauderdale, FL: ND 1993, GEG [Gay & Lesbian Employee Alliance (GALEA)]

Albert Einstein College of Medicine, Bronx NY: H 1991

Alberto-Culver consumer products: ND 1993

Aldus Corp., Seattle, WA: ND, GEGi [Aldus Queer Association Network (AQuNet)]

Alexander & Baldwin, transportation: ND

Alias, Toronto, Canada: ND

Allergan, Pharmaceuticals: ND

Allstate, insurance: ND 1992

Amdahl, Sunnyvale, CA, computer hardware: ND, GEGi [Gay & Lesbian Employees of Amdahl (GLEAM)]

America West, transportation: ND 1991

American Airlines, transportation: ND 1993

American Association of Museums: GEG

American Association of University Professors: H

American Civil Liberties Union (ACLU), nonprofit: H 1983

American Cyanamid, pharmaceuticals: ND 1993

American Express, financial services: ND, GEGi

American Friends Service Committee, Philadelphia, PA, nonprofit: ND 1987, H GEGo

American Library Association: H

American Motors: ND

American Psychological Association, Washington, DC, nonprofit: ND, H 1983, GEG

American Red Cross, Minneapolis chapter: H

American Telegraph & Telephone (AT&T), NJ, telecommunications: ND 1975 GEGo [Lesbian, Bi & Gay United Employees (LEAGUE)]
American University, Washington, DC: H 1993
Ameritech, Chicago, IL, telecommunications: ND, GEGo [Gay, Lesbian & Bisexual Employees of Ameritech (GLEAM)]
Ameritech Library Services, Provo, UT: ND
Amgen, pharmaceuticals: ND
Antioch University: H 1995
Apple Computer, Cupertino, CA: ND 1988, H 1993, GEGi [Apple Lambda]
Aptix, San Jose, CA: ND
Arent, Fox, Kinter, law, Washington, DC: H 1995
Arizona Public Service, Phoenix, AZ, utilities: ND 1991
Arthur Anderson & Co., Chicago, IL, worldwide accounting and management consulting: GEGi
Atlantic Pictures, New York, NY: H 1994
Atlantic Records (parent: Time Warner), New York, NY, entertainment: H 1994
Auto-trol, Denver, CO: ND
Autodesk, Sausalito, CA, computer software: ND, H 1994, GEGi
BARRA Inc., Berkeley, CA, computer software: ND, GEGi
Baltimore Gas & Electric, Baltimore, MD, utilities: ND
Banc One Corporation, banking: ND
Bank of America: ND 1978, GEGi
Bank of Boston: ND 1992, GEGo
Bank of California: ND
Bankers Trust: ND 1985
Banyan Systems, Westboro, MA, computer software: ND, H
Barna, Guzy & Steffen, Ltd., Conn Rapids, MN, law: ND
Battelle Corp., Columbus, OH: ND
Baxter Healthcare, McGaw Park, IL, medical: GEGo [Baxter Associates Gay & Lesbian Employees (BAGLE)]
Bay Area Air Quality Management District: H
Bay Area Rapid Transit (BART), San Francisco, CA, transportation: H 1993
Bay View Capital Corp., savings bank: ND 1992
Bear Stearns, investment banking: ND
Bell and Howell: ND
Bell Atlantic: GEG [Gay & Lesbian Organization of Bell Employees (GlOBE)]
Bell Canada (parent Bell Canada Enterprises): DP benefits by court order 1994, GEGo [Gay & Lesbian Organization of Bell Employees (GLOBE)]
Bellcore, Livingston, NJ: ND
Bell-Northern Research, Ontario, Canada, telecommunications: ND, H GEGo
BellSouth Telecommunications: ND, GEG [ANGLE]
Ben & Jerry's Ice Cream, Waterbury, VT, food/beverage: ND, H 1989
Bendix: ND
Berkeley United School District, Berkeley, CA: H 1986
Beth Israel Medical Center, New York, NY, medical: H 1992

Blue Cross/Blue Shield of MA, Boston, MA, insurance: ND, H 1991, GEGi
Blue Cross/Blue Shield of New Hampshire, insurance: H 1994
Blue Cross of CA: ND
Body Shop Inc., Wake Forest, NC, consumer products: ND
Boeing Aircraft, Renton, WA, transportation: GEGi [Boeing Employee Associates of Gays & Lesbians (BEAGLES)]
Bolt, Beranek and Newman, Cambridge, MA: ND
Bonneville Power Administration (parent: U.S. Department of Energy): ND
Booz Allen & Hamilton, New York, NY, worldwide management consulting: ND
Borland International, Scotts Valley, CA, computer software: ND, H 1992
Boston Children's Hospital, Boston, MA, medical: ND, H 1992, GEG [UNITY]
Boston Consulting Group, management consulting: H
Boston Globe, (parent: New York Times Corp.) Boston, MA, media: ND 1987, H 1993
Boston Hotel Workers Union: H
Bowdoin College: H
British Columbia, Canada: H 1991
Brooklyn Law School: H 1995
Brown University, Providence, RI: H 1994
Bureau of National Affairs, Washington, DC, publishing: ND 1989, GEGi
Burroughs Wellcome: ND 1992
CBC (Canadian Broadcasting Company): H by court order
CBS (Central Broadcasting System), media: ND 1978, GEG
CIGNA, Philadelphia, PA, and nationwide, financial services: ND 1990
CMP Publications Inc., Manhasset, NY, computer magazine publisher: ND, H GEGi
CNA Insurance Co., IL: ND
CUNA Mutual Insurance Group, Madison, WI: ND, GEG
Cadence Computer Software: ND, H
California Academy of Science: H
California Edison, Rosemead, CA: ND
California Federal Savings Bank: ND 1990
California Institute of Technology: H 1995
California Pacific Medical Center, San Francisco, CA, medical: H
Cambridge Technology Partners: H 1994
Campbell Soup, food/beverage: ND
Canada Post: H
Canadian Press and Broadcast News, Canada, media: H
Capital Cities/ABC media (subsidiaries: Ft. Worth Star-Telegram, Kansas City Star): ND 1979, H 1994, GEGi [Gay & Lesbian Organized Employees (GLOE)]
Carlton University: H
Carnation: ND
Carnegie Group Inc., Pittsburgh, PA: ND
Carnegie Mellon University: H

Celestial Seasonings, Boulder, CO, food/beverage: ND, H
Central Massachusetts Health Care: H
Charles Schwab & Co., San Francisco, CA, financial services: ND 1989, H 1993
Chase Manhattan Bank, New York, NY: ND
Chevron, San Francisco, CA, oil: ND 1993, GEGi
Children's Television Workshop, entertainment: ND
Chiron Corp., Emeryville, CA, biotechnology: H
Chubb Insurance: ND 1993
Cisco Systems: ND
Citicorp N.A., New York, NY: ND
Citizens Fidelity Bank, KY: ND
City & County of San Francisco, CA: H 1991
City & County of Santa Cruz, CA: H 1986
City of Ann Arbor, MI: H 1992
City of Atlanta, GA: DP invalidated by court order
City of Austin, TX: DP repealed by voters
City of Baltimore, MD: H 1995
City of Berkeley, CA: H 1985
City of Boston, MA: H
City of Brookline, MA: H
City of Burlington, VT: H 1993
City of Cambridge, MA: H 1992
City of Carrboro, NC: ND 1995
City of Chicago, IL: H
City of Delaware, NJ: H
City of East Lansing, MI: H 1992
City of Halifax, Nova Scotia, Canada: H 1994
City of Hartford, CT: H
City of Iowa City, IA: H 1994
City of Ithaca, NY: H 1991
City of Laguna Beach, CA: H 1990
City of Los Angeles, CA: H 1993
City of Madison, WI: H 1988
City of Minneapolis, MN: DP invalidated by court order
City of New Orleans, LA: H
City of New York, NY: H 1993
City of Oak Park, IL: H 1994
City of Oakland, CA: H
City of Olympia, WA: H 1995
City of Portland, ME: H 1994
City of Rochester, NY: H 1994
City of Sacramento, CA: H 1992
City of San Diego, CA: H 1994
City of Santa Cruz, CA: H 1986
City of Seattle, WA: H 1990
City of Takoma Park, MD: H 1988

City of Washington, DC: DP unfunded by Congress
City of West Hollywood, CA: H 1985
City of West Palm Beach, FL: H 1992
City University of New York, NY: H 1993
Claris, Santa Clara, CA: ND
Clark University, Worcester, MA: H
Colby College, Waterville, ME: H
College of William and Mary: H
Colgate-Palmolive, New York, NY, consumer products: ND 1994, GEGi
Columbia University (subsidiaries: Columbia U. Hospital, Press; Lamont-Doherty Observatory) New York, NY: H 1994
Comdisco: ND
Commerce Clearning House, publishing: ND
Committee of Interns & Residents, New York, NY: H
Commonwealth Edison Co., Chicago, IL, utilities: ND 1994, GEGo
Compatible Systems, Boulder, CO: ND
Computer Graphics Inc., computer software: H
Computervision, San Diego, CA: ND
Conoco, oil: ND 1992
Consolidated Electrical Distributors, Thousand Oaks, CA: ND
Consolidated Natural Gas, utilities: ND
Consumers United Insurance Co., Washington, DC: H
Continental Airlines, transportation: ND 1992
Control Data Corp., Minneapolis, MN: ND
Convex Computer Corp., Richardson, TX: ND
Cooley, Godward, Castro, Huddleson & Tatum, San Francisco, CA, law: H
Coopers & Lybrand, New York, NY, nationwide accounting: ND
Coors (Adolph Coors), Golden, CO, alcohol: ND 1978, GEGo [Lesbian and Gay Employee Resource (LAGER)]
CoreStates Bank & Financial Corp., Philadelphia, PA: ND 1990, GEGo [MOSAIC]
Cornell University, Ithaca, NY: H
Country of Canada: DP for government employees in various locations by court order
Country of Denmark: DP applies to all citizens
Country of France: DP applies to workers in some cases
Country of Hungary: DP for citizens through common-law marriage
Country of Israel: DP for government employees in some locations by court order
Country of Norway: DP applies to all citizens, H 1993
Country of Sweden: DP applies to all citizens, H 1995
County of Alameda, CA: H
County of Dane, WI: H
County of Hennepin, MN: H
County of King, WA: H 1993
County of Marin, CA: H

County of Multnomah, OR: H 1993
County of San Mateo, CA: H 1986
County of Wayne, MI: H
Covington & Burling, law, Washington, DC: H 1994
Crawford & Co., Atlanta, GA: ND
Cray Computer Corp., Colorado Springs, CO: ND
Cray Research, Eagan, MN: ND 1981
Crum and Forster Insurance Co.: H
DEC-Belgium, Computers: H
Dana Farber Cancer Institute: H 1995
Dartmouth College, NH: H 1994
Datalogics (parent: Frame Technology), Chicago, IL: ND
Dayton Hudson (subsidiaries: Dayton's, Dayton Hudson, Marshall Field, Mervyn's, Target), Minneapolis, MN, retail: ND, GEG
DeAnza Community College: H
Debevoise & Plimpton: H
Del Monte Foods, food/beverage: ND
Dell Computers, Round Rock, TX: ND
Deloitte & Touche, consulting/accounting: GEG
Delta Airlines, transportation: ND 1994
Digital Equipment Corp. (DEC), Maynard, MA, computer hardware: ND 1986, GEGo [People Like Us (PLUS)]
Disney (Walt Disney Co.), Burbank, CA, entertainment: ND 1992, GEG [LEAGUE]
Dow Chemical, Midland, MI, chemicals: ND 1992
Dow Jones, financial services (subsidiary: the Wall Street Journal): ND
Dow, Lohnes & Albertson, law, Washington, DC: H 1995
Duke University: H 1995
DuPont (E. I. DuPont de Nemours) (subsidiaries: Conoco, oil, DuPont-Merck, pharmaceuticals), Wilmington, DE: ND 1992, GEGi
Dun & Bradstreet, financial services: ND 1988
ESL Inc. (parent: TRW), Sunnyvale, CA: ND
Eastern Mountain Sports, Peterborough, NH, retail: ND 1991
Eastman Kodak, Rochester, NY, scientific and photo equipment: ND 1986, GEGo [Lambda Network]
Electronic Arts, San Mateo, CA: ND
Eli Lily: ND
Entertainment Radio Network: H
Episcopal Diocese of Newark, NJ, nonprofit: H 1992
Equitable Life Assurance, insurance: ND
Ernst & Young, management consulting/accounting: ND 1989
Federal National Mortgage Association (Fannie Mae): Washington, DC, financial services: ND 1992, H 1993, GEGo [Fannie Mae Lesbian & Gay (FLAG)]
Farallon Computing Company, Alameda, CA: ND, GEGi [Out There at Farallon]
Fidelity Federal Bank of Glendale, CA: ND

Field Museum of Natural History, Chicago, IL: H
Finnegan, Henderson, Farabow, law, Washington, DC: H 1995
Fireman's Insurance, Washington, DC: ND
First Bank System: ND 1991, GEGo
First Chicago Corp., banking: ND 1992
First Virginia Bank, VA: ND
First Virginia Insurance Services, VA: ND
Flood Group, Torrance, CA: ND
Florida International University: H
Fluor: ND
Fort Howard Corp.: ND
Fox Inc., entertainment/media: ND
Frame Technology Corp. (subsidiary: Datalogics), San Jose, CA, computer software: ND, H
Fred Hutchinson Cancer Research Center, Seattle, WA, medical: H
Freddie Mac: GEG [Gay, Lesbian, or Bi Employees (GLOBE)]
Fried, Frank, Harris, Shriver & Jacobson, New York, NY, law: H
Fujitsu America, San Jose, CA: ND
GEICO, insurance: ND
Gannett (subsidiaries: USA Today, various newspapers and TV stations), media: ND 1992, GEGo
Gardener's Supply Co., Burlington, VT, consumer products: ND 1990, H 1991
Gateway 2000, computers, North Sioux City, SD: ND
Genentech, South San Francisco, CA, biotechnology: ND 1991, H 1994, GEGo
General Electric, utilities: ND 1992
General Motors, Detroit, MI, motor vehicles: ND 1990, GEGi
Genesys Software Systems, Methuen, MA: ND
Georgia State University: H
Giant Food, retail: ND
Girl Scouts Council, VT, nonprofit: ND H
Globe and Mail, media, Canada: H 1995
Goldman Sachs, investment banking: ND
Golston and Storrs Law Offices, Boston, MA: H
Great Western Bank: GEG
Greenpeace International, Washington, DC, nonprofit: ND 1993, H 1989
Greyhound Lines, transportation: ND
Grinnell College: H
Group Health Co-op of Puget Sound, Seattle, WA, medical: H 1994
Group Health Inc.: H 1993
Gupta Corp (parent: Radius Co.), computer software: H
H&R Block, financial services: ND 1993
H. B. Fuller, consumer products: ND
H. F. Ahmanson & Co. ND
Hamilton College: H 1995
Harley-Davidson, Milwaukee, WI, motor vehicles: ND 1990
Harris Trust: ND 1989

Harvard Community Health Plans, medical: H
Harvard University, Cambridge, MA: H 1994
Health Partners, Minneapolis, MN: GEGo
Herman Miller, Zeeland, MI, manufacturing/furniture: ND 1990
Hewlett-Packard, Palo Alto, CA, computer hardware: ND 1992, GEGo [Gay, Lesbian & Bi Employee Network (GLEN)]
Hibernia: ND
Hoechst-Celanese: ND 1994, GEGo
Home Box Office (HBO) (parent: Time Warner), New York, NY, entertainment: ND 1993, H, GEGo
Homestake Mining: ND
Honeywell, Minneapolis, MN, scientific/control equipment: ND 1993, GEGo [Honeywell Pride Council]
Howard, Rice, Nemerovski, Canady, San Francisco, CA, law: H 1993
Howrey & Simon, law, Washington, DC: H 1995
Human Rights Campaign Fund, Washington, DC, nonprofit: ND, H 1987
IBM, Armonk, NY, computer hardware: ND 1974, GEGi
IDG: H
IDS Financial Services (parent: American Express), Minneapolis, MN: ND, GEG [Gay & Lesbian Employee Network (GLEN)]
ITT Rayonier: ND
Illinois Tool Works, metal products: ND
Indiana University: H
Informix Software, Menlo Park, CA, computer: ND, H, GEGi
Ingres (parent: ASK Computers), Alameda, CA: ND
Intel, Santa Clara, CA, computer: ND 1991, GEGo [Gay, Lesbian, or Bi Employee Network (GLOBE)]
Intercontinental Hotels, New York, NY: ND
Intergraph, Hunstville, AL, computers/office equipment: ND
Interleaf, Boston, MA, computer software: ND, H 1993
Intermedia Partners, media: H
International Data Group, Framingham, MA, publishing for computer industry: ND, H 1993
Irell & Manella, Los Angeles, CA, entertainment law: H
J. P. Morgan & Co., New York, NY, investment banking: ND
JC Penney, retail: ND
Jet Propulsion Lab (parent: CA Institute of Technology), Pasadena, CA, aerospace: ND, H 1995, GEGo
Jewish Board of Family and Children Services, New York, NY: H
Johnson & Higgins Insurance: ND
Johnson & Johnson, Raritan, NJ, consumer products: ND
Jostens Learning Corp., San Diego, CA: ND
KPMG Peat Marwick, management consulting and accounting: ND
KQED Radio, San Francisco, CA, media: H 1994
Kaiser-Permanente Insurance: ND and H 1995 for all divisions in northern California division, GEGo for northern and southern California divisions

Kellogg, food/beverage: ND
Kentucky Fried Chicken (parent PepsiCo): ND 1986
Keyport Life Insurance: ND
Knight-Ridder, media: ND, GEG
Kodak (Eastman Kodak), Rochester, NY, scientific and photo equipment: ND 1985, GEG [Lambda Network]
KPMG Peat Marwick, accounting: ND
Krum and Foster Insurance: H
Kubota Pacific Computer, Santa Clara, CA: ND
LSI Logic, Milipitas, CA, electronics/electric equipment: ND 1990
Lambda Legal Defense & Education Fund, New York, NY, nonprofit: H 1988
Lawrence Berkeley Lab, Berkeley, CA: ND
Legal Aid Society: H
Levi Strauss & Co., San Francisco, CA, apparel: ND 1975, H 1992, GEGo
Lexis-Nexis, Dayton, OH: ND
Lilienthal & Fowler, San Francisco, CA, law: H 1988
Lillian Vernon: ND 1995
Lincoln National Life Insurance: ND 1991
Little Brown, New York, NY (parent: Time Warner), publishing: ND
Lockheed Missiles and Space (parent: Lockheed Corp./Lockheed Martin Corp.) Sunnyvale, CA, aerospace: ND, GEGo. [Gay, Lesbian, or Bisexual at Lockheed (GLOBAL)]
Long Island Lighting Co., utilities: ND
Los Alamos National Laboratory, Los Alamos, NM: ND
Los Angeles Philharmonic, CA, nonprofit: H
Los Angeles Times, CA, media: ND 1990, GEG
Lotus Development Corp., Cambridge, MA, computer software: ND 1985, H 1991, GEGi [LAMBDA]
Lucas Films, entertainment: H 1995
MBIA: ND
MCA/Universal, Universal City, CA, entertainment: ND 1993, H 1992, GEGi [Employee Association of Gays & Lesbians (EAGLE)]
MCI, telecommunications: ND 1988
MCNC, Research Triangle Park, NC: ND
MONY, insurance: ND
Marriott, hospitality: ND
Mary Washington College: H
Massachusetts Institute of Technology (MIT), Cambridge, MA: ND 1988, H, GEG
Mass Mutual Life Insurance, Springfield, MA: ND 1991, GEGi [GALA]
Maxtor Corp., San Jose, CA, computers/office equipment: ND 1990
McCaw Cellular Communication, telecommunications: ND 1989
McDonnell Douglas Aerospace Division: ND
McGill University: H
McGraw Hill, publishing: ND
Mead Data Central, Dayton, OH: ND

Medtronic, Fridley, MN, scient/photo/control equip.: ND, GEG [GEM]
Mellon Bank Corp: ND
Mentor Graphics, Wilsonville, OR: ND, GEGi
Merck pharmaceuticals: ND
Merrill Lynch & Co., investment banking: ND
Methodist Hospital of Indianapolis, IN, medical: ND 1980
Metropolitan Life Insurance: ND
Microsoft, Redmond, WA, computer software: ND 1990, H 1993, GEGo [Gay, Lesbian & Bi Employees at Microsoft (GLEAM)]
Middlebury College, Middlebury, VT: H
Midlantic Corporation, banking: ND 1992
Milbank, Tweed, Hadley & McCloy, New York, NY, law: ND 1990, H 1993, GEGi
Millennium Global Inc.: H
Minnesota Communications Group (MCG) (subsidiary: Minnesota Public Radio, American Public Radio), St. Paul, MN: ND 1989, H 1993, GEGi
Minnesota Mining & Manufacturing (3M), St. Paul, MN, scientific/control equipment: ND 1992, GEGo
Minnesota Public Radio: ND
Minnesota Star-Tribune, Minneapolis, MN, media: H 1995, GEGo [PAPER EAGLES]
Mintz, Levin, Ferris Law Offices, Boston, MA, law: H
Mips Technologies (parent: Silicon Graphics), Mountain View, CA: ND
Mission College: H
Mobil Oil: ND
Monitor Co., management consulting: ND, H
Montefiore Medical Center (parent: Albert Einstein College), Bronx, NY: H 1991
Morrison & Foerster, San Francisco, CA, law: ND 1978, H 1993, GEGi
Motorola LMPS division: GEGo
Mt. Sinai Hospital Nurses: H
Mt. Xinu, Berkeley, CA: ND
Museum of Modern Art, New York, NY, nonprofit: H
Mutual of N.Y. Insurance: ND
NOTIS Systems (parent: Ameritech), Evanston, IL: ND
NSP, Minneapolis, MN: H
N.Y. United University Professions: H
NYNEX, telecommunications: ND 1987, GEGo [Gays & Lesbians for Corporate Diversity]
National Broadcasting Company (NBC), entertainment/media: ND, GEGi
National Computer Systems, San Jose, CA: ND
National Center for Lesbian Rights: H
National Gay & Lesbian Task Force, Washington, DC, nonprofit: H 1992
National Organization of Women (NOW), Washington, DC, nonprofit: ND 1970, H
National Public Radio (NPR), Washington, DC, media: ND, H 1993, GEG

National Safe Depositories, San Jose, CA: ND
National Writers Guild: H 1994
Nestle Beverage Co., San Francisco, CA, food/beverage: ND 1991, GEGi
New England Medical Center: H
New England Mutual Life Insurance: ND
New York Life & Annuity Insurance: ND
New York Times Company (subsidiaries: the New York Times, the Boston Globe), New York, NY, media: ND 1993, H 1994, GEGo
New York University, NY: H 1994
NeXT Computers, Redwood City, CA, computer software: ND 1985, H, GEGo [LAMBDA]
Nordstrom, retail: ND
North Dakota University: H
Northeastern University: H 1994
Northern States Power, Minneapolis, MN: H
Northern Telecom Ltd. (parent: Bell Canada Enterprises), Canada, telecommunications: ND, H 1994
Northern Trust Corp., banking: ND
Northwest Airlines, transportation: ND
Norton Simon: ND
Novell: H 1992
Oakland Children's Hospital, Oakland, CA: H 1995
Oberlin College: H
Objectivity Inc., Menlo Park, CA: ND
Ogden: ND
Olin, chemicals: ND
Open Software Foundation, Cambridge, MA, computer software: ND
Oracle Corporation, Redwood City, CA, computer software: ND 1986, H 1993, GEGo [Lambda]
Oregon State University: H
Orrick, Herrington & Sutcliffe, San Francisco, CA, law: ND, H 1993
Pacific Gas & Electric (PG&E), San Francisco, CA, utilites: ND 1982, GEGo
Pacific Mutual Life Insurance: ND
Pacific Telesis Group (subsidiary: Pacific Bell), San Francisco, CA, telecommunications: ND 1980, GEGo [GALEMAS]
Paramax Systems (parent: Unisys): ND
Paramount Pictures, entertainment: ND 1992, H 1995
Para Transit, Sacramento, CA, transportation: H
ParcPlace Systems, Sunnyvale, CA: ND
Park Nicollet Medical Center, Minneapolis, MN: H
Penn Mutual Life Insurance: ND 1989
People's Bank: ND 1994
PepsiCo, food and beverage: ND
Perkin-Elmer, scientific/control equipment: ND
Petro Canada: H
Pfizer, pharmaceuticals: ND

Pharmaco-LSR: GEG
Philadelphia Electric, utilities: ND
Phillip Morris, tobacco: ND
PictureTel Corporation, Danvers, MA: ND
Pillsbury, Madison & Sutro, San Francisco, law: H
Pillsbury, Minneapolis, MN: GEG [Friends of Pride]
Pinnacle West Capital: ND 1988
Piper Jaffray, financial services: ND 1991
Pitney Bowes, scientific/control equipment: ND 1991
Pitzer College, Claremont, CA: H
Planned Parenthood, nonprofit: ND, H 1993, GEG
Polaroid, Cambridge, MA, scientific/photographic equipment: ND 1990, GEGo
Pomona College, CA: H
Portland Cable Access, Portland, OR, nonprofit: ND 1983, H
Primerica, financial services: ND
Princeton University, Princeton, NJ: H
Principal Financial Group, Des Moines, IA, financial services: ND 1989, H GEGi
Principal Mutual Life Insurance: ND, H GEG
Procter & Gamble, Cincinnati, OH, consumer products: ND 1992
Progressive Insurance, Cleveland, OH: ND
Proskauer, Rose, Goetz & Mendelsohn, law: H
Prudential Insurance Co.: ND 1991, GEGo [Employee Association of Gays & Lesbians (EAGLES)]
Public Broadcasting System (PBS), Washington, DC, nonprofit: ND, H
Public Service Electric & Gas, utilities: ND
Public Service Enterprise Group, utilities: ND
Pyramid Technology, San Jose, CA: ND
Quaker Oats, Chicago, IL, food: ND 1994, GEG [A Safe Place]
Qualcomm, communications, San Diego, CA: ND 1995, GEGi
Quark, Boulder, CO, computer software: ND 1983, H, GEGo
RECOM Technologies, San Jose, CA: ND
RJ Reynolds: ND
RJR Nabisco (subsidiaries: Nabisco Foods, RJ Reynolds Tobacco), food/tobacco: ND 1988, GEGo
Ralston Purina, consumer products: ND
Recreational Equipment Inc. (REI), Kent, WA, athletic: ND 1979, GEGi
Relational Technology Inc.: ND
Republic of N.Y. Corp., banking: ND
Research Triangle Park, NC: H
Riggs National Corp., banking: ND
Rockefeller University: H
Rockwell: ND
Rolm Systems Inc. (parent: Siemens), Santa Clara, CA: ND
Ryder Systems: ND 1993

SAS Institute, Cary, NC: ND
SCM Corp.: ND
SPSS Inc., Chicago, IL: ND
Saatchi & Saatchi, advertising: GEGo
Sacramento Para Transit: H
Salomon Bros., New York, NY, investment banking: ND
San Francisco Chronicle, San Francisco, CA, media: H 1994, GEG
San Francisco Examiner, San Francisco, CA, media: H 1994
San Francisco Federal: ND 1980
San Francisco Giants, CA, athletic: H
San Jose School District, San Jose, CA: H
Santa Cruz Metropolitan Transit District, Santa Cruz, CA, transportation: H 1985
Santa Cruz Operations, Santa Cruz, CA: ND, H 1992
Sarnoff: H 1994
Schiff, Hardin & Waite, Chicago, IL, law: ND, H 1993
Scholastic Inc., New York, NY, education: ND, GEG
Science Applications International, San Diego, CA: ND
Scientific & Engineering Software, Austin, TX, computer software: ND
Scott Paper, forestry/paper products: ND
Seagram (Joseph E. Seagram & Sons), alcohol/tobacco: ND 1988
Sears Roebuck, Chicago, IL, retail: ND
Seattle City Light Co., Seattle, WA, utilities: ND 1979, H, GEG
Seattle Mental Health Institute, Seattle, WA, medical: H
Seattle Public Library, Seattle, WA: H
Seattle Symphony Orchestra: H
Seattle Times, Seattle, WA, media: ND, H 1994, GEG
Segal Company, Boston, MA, benefits consulting: H
Sequent Computer Systems, Beaverton, OR: ND
Shaw, Pittman, Potts, Washington, DC, law: H 1995
Sherman & Sterling: H
Shiff, Harden, & Waite, Chicago, IL, law: H
Showtime Entertainment (parent: Viacom), New York, NY, entertainment: ND, H
Silicon Graphics (subsidiary: Mips Technologies), Mountain View, CA, computer software: ND, H 1992, GEGo [Lavender Vision]
Simmons College, Boston, MA: H
Smith & Hawken, Strawberry, CA: H
Smith College, Northampton, MA: H
Software Transformation, Cupertino, CA, computer software: ND
Solburnce Computer, Longmont, CO: ND
Sony Pictures Entertainment (parent: Sony; subsidiaries: Columbia, TriStar): ND, H 1994
Southern California Edison, utilities: ND 1993
Southwestern Bell, telecommunications: ND
Springfield College: H 1995

Sprint: ND 1990, GEGi
St. Paul Companies, MN, insurance: ND 1991, H 1994, GEG
Standard Oil: ND
Stanford University, Stanford, CA: H 1993
Stanley Works, metal products: ND
Starbucks Coffee, Seattle, WA, food/beverage: ND 1991, H 1993
State of Delaware: H
State of New York: H 1995
State of Vermont: H 1994
State Universities of New York, NY: H
Stentor Resource Center (parent: Bell Canada Enterprises), Canada: H
Steptoe & Johnson, Washington, DC, law: H 1995
Storage Technology, computers/office equip: ND
Stratus Computer, Marlboro, MA: ND
Sun Microsystems, Mountain View, CA, computer software: ND 1989, H 1993, GEGo [GLAF]
Suntrust Banks: ND
SuperMac Technologies (parent: Radius), Sunnyvale, CA, computer software: ND, H
Supermarket General Corp., retail: ND 1984
Swarthmore College, Swarthmore, PA: H
Swope Parkway Medical Center, Kansas City, MO: H
Sybase Inc., Berkeley, CA, computer software: ND, H 1993
Synopsys, Mountain View, CA: ND
TGI Fridays, Dallas, TX, food/restaurant: ND
TIAA-CREF, financial services: ND 1991
TRW Inc., Cleveland, OH, aerospace/credit: ND
Tambrands, consumer products: ND
Tandem Computers, Cupertino, CA: ND 1989
Tandy, Dallas, TX, retail: ND
Teach for America, New York, NY: ND
Teachers College: H
Teachers Insurance & Annuity (TIAA): ND 1991
Tech Resources Group, Raleigh, NC: ND
Tektronix, Inc. Wilsonville, OR: ND
Thinking Machines, Cambridge, MA, computer software: H
Thomas Jefferson University & Hospital, Philadelphia, PA: H 1995
Ticketmaster: H
Time Inc. (parent: Time Warner), New York, NY, media: H 1994
Time Warner Co. (subsidiaries: HBO, Warner Brothers Pictures, Atlantic Pictures), New York, NY: ND, H, GEGo
Toronto Dominion Bank: H 1994 (for Canadian employees only)
TransAmerica Occidental Life Insurance: ND
Trek Bicycle, athletic: ND
Tufts University: H
UJB Financial: ND 1992

UNUM Life Insurance, Portland, ME: ND 1990
US BanCorp, banking: ND
U.S. Coast Guard civilian employees: ND
U.S. Customs Service: ND
U.S. Dept. of Agriculture: ND
U.S. Dept. of Commerce: ND 1994, GEG [Gay, Lesbian, or Bi Employees (GLOBE)]
U.S. Dept. of Energy: ND
U.S. Dept. of Health & Human Services: ND
U.S. Dept. of Housing & Urban Development: ND
U.S. Dept. of the Interior: ND 1994
U.S. Dept. of Labor: GEG [GLOBAL]
U.S. Dept. of State: ND
U.S. Dept. of Transportation: ND, GEGo [Gay, Lesbian, or Bi Employees (GLOBE)]
U.S. Dept. of Veterans Affairs: GEGi
U.S. Environmental Protection Agency: ND 1994
U.S. Executive Office of the President, The White House: ND
U.S. Federal Aviation Administration: GEG
U.S. Federal Bureau of Investigation: ND
U.S. Federal Employees: GEG [Gay, Lesbian, or Bi Employees (GLOBE)]
U.S. Foreign Affairs Agencies: GEGi
U.S. Forest Services: GEGi
U.S. General Accounting Office: GEGi
U.S. Information Agency: ND
U.S. Internal Revenue Service: GEGi
U.S. Justice Dept (subsidiary: Federal Bureau of Investigation): ND
U.S. Library of Congress: GEG [Gay, Lesbian, or Bi Employees (GLOBE)]
U.S. National Institutes of Health: GEG
U.S. Naval civilian employees: ND, GEG [Gay, Lesbian or Bi Employees (GLOBE)]
U.S. Office of Personnel Management: ND
U.S. Postal Service: GEG
U.S. Small Business Administration: GEG
U.S. State Department (subsidiary: U.S. Foreign Service): ND 1993, GEG [Gays & Lesbians in Foreign Affairs (GLIFFA)]
U.S. West, transportation: ND 1988, GEGo [Employee Association for Gays & Lesbians (EAGLE)]
UUNET Technologies Inc., Falls Church, VA: ND
Ungerman-Bass, Santa Clara, CA: ND
Union Bank: ND
Union Carbide, chemicals: ND
Union of American Hebrew Congregations, religious: ND, H
Union Theological Seminary: H
Unions:
  AFSCME Council 57: H

AFSCME Council 82: H
AFSCME Local 829: H
Greater Boston Hotel Employees Local 26: H
Los Angeles International Brotherhood of Electrical Workers Local 2: H
Oil Chemical and Atomic Workers Union Local 8-149, Rahway, NJ: H
San Francisco Hotel & Restaurants Union Local 2: H 1994
United Auto Workers, Detroit, MI: ND

Unisys (subsidiary: Paramax Systems), Reston, VA, computer hardware and software: ND 1991
Unitarian Universalist Church Association of Congregations, Boston, MA: ND
United Airlines, San Francisco, CA, transportation: ND 1993, GEGi [Gay & Lesbian United Employees (GLUE)]
United Church Board for Homeland Ministries: H
United Technologies, aerospace/manufacturing: ND
United University Professors: H
United Way, nonprofit: H
University of Alaska, Fairbanks, AK: H 1995 by court order
University of British Columbia, Vancouver, B.C., Canada: H
University of California, Los Angeles: H
University of Chicago, IL: H 1993
University of Colorado, Boulder, CO: H
University of Iowa, Iowa City, IA: H 1993
University of Lethbridge, Canada: H 1995 by court order.
University of Michigan, MI: H 1994
University of Minnesota, St. Paul, MN: H 1993
University of New Brunswick, Canada: H
University of New Mexico: H
University of Pennsylvania, Philadelphia, PA: H 1994
University of Pennsylvania Health Systems, Philadelphia, PA: H 1994
University of Tampa, FL: H
University of Toronto, Canada: H
University of Vermont, Burlington, VT: H
University of Waterloo, Ontario, Canada: H
University of Windsor, Ontario, Canada: H
University of Wisconsin, Madison, WI: H
University Students Cooperative, Berkeley, CA: H
Varian Associates, Palo Alto, CA, scientific/control equipment: ND
Veritas Software, Santa Clara, CA, computer software: ND
Verity Inc., Mountain View, CA: ND
Vermont Girl Scouts Council: H
Viacom International (subsidiaries: Showtime, MTV, Paramount Studios): ND, H 1993, GEG
Videomaker Magazine, Chico, CA, entertainment/publishing: ND
Village Voice, New York, NY, media: ND 1977, H 1982, GEG
WGBH Public Television, Boston, MA, nonprofit: ND 1983, H 1993, GEG
WQED Radio, Pittsburgh, PA, nonprofit: ND 1988, H

Wachovia Corporation: ND
Walker Art Center: H
Wall Street Journal, New York, NY, media: ND
Walt Disney, Burbank, CA, entertainment: ND, 1992, GEGo [Lesbian & Gay United Employees (LEAGUE)]
Warner Brothers Pictures (parent: Time Warner), entertainment: H 1993
Warner Lambert, pharmaceuticals: ND
Washington Mutual Life Insurance: ND 1989
Washington Post, media: ND
Washington State University, Pullman, WA: H
Wayne State University, Detroit, MI: H
Wellesley College, Wellesley, MA: H 1994
Wells Fargo & Co., San Francisco, CA, banking: ND 1988, GEGi
Wesleyan University, Middletown, CT: H
Weyerhaeuser Paper Co., forestry/paper products: ND
Wilder Foundation, Minneapolis, MN: H
Wiley, Rein & Fielding, Washington, DC, law: H 1995
Wilfrid Laurier University, Waterloo, Ontario, Canada: H
Williams College, Williamstown, MA: H
Wm. Wrigley Jr., consumer products: ND
Word Perfect Co., Orem, UT, computer software: ND
Working Assets Funding Service, San Francisco, CA, financial services/telecommunications: ND 1986, H
Wright State University: H
Wyatt Company: H
Xerox, Rochester NY, scientific/control equipment: ND 1991, H 1995 GEGo [GALAXE]
YMCA of Greater Milwaukee, WI, nonprofit: ND
Yale University, New Haven, CT: H 1994
York University, Toronto, Ontario, Canada: H
Young & Rubicam, advertising: ND 1991
Zenith Data Systems, St. Joseph, MI, computer hardware: ND
Zenith Electronics, Glenview, IL, electronics/electronic equipment: ND, GEGo
Ziff Communications: H
Ziff-Davis Publishing, New York, NY, publishing: ND 1989, H 1993

Gay Employee Groups

Source: independently verified by the authors as of April 1995. Nonetheless, please do not use the words "gay" or "lesbian" on the envelope or in the subject header of E-mail when writing these individuals for information. You may assume that recorded phone messages are private, but please do not leave a message using the words "gay" or "lesbian" with someone other than the person listed. (This message is at the request of some of those on this list.)

GEGo = officially recognized by company
GEGi = informal group

Local Umbrella Organizations

Chicago Out at Work (or Not)
Jason Cohen, PO Box 359, Chicago, IL 60690-0359, (312) 794-5218

Over 25 Chicago-area companies; newsletter and publications; quarterly meetings.

A Group of Groups
P. James, PO Box 14513, San Francisco, CA 94114, (415) 627-7533

Forty-five Bay Area companies.

Minnesota Workplace Alliance
Scott Fearing, c/o Gay & Lesbian Community Action Council, 310 E. 38th St. #204, Minneapolis, MN 55409-1364, (800) 800-0350

Forty-seven Minneapolis-area companies.

Northwest Gay & Lesbian Employee Networks
Jeff Howard, 1202 E. Pike St. #1022, Seattle, WA 98122-3934, (206) 328-9406

Company-Based Groups

Aetna Network of Gay and Lesbian Employees
Carol Walter, 1000 Middle St., Convey MA-22, Middletown, CT 06457 (203) 636-2824, or Rick Balmer (203) 636-4691
GEGo

Air Products & Chemicals
Gay & Lesbian Empowered Employees (GLEE)
Dale Miller, 7201 Hamilton Blvd., Allentown, PA 18195, (610) 481-8212
GEGo

Alamo Rent A Car
Gay & Lesbian Alliance [GALEA]
Brad Behnke, 455 NE 16 Ave. #3, Fort Lauderdale, FL 33301-1379, (305) 760-7890

Amdahl
Gay and Lesbian Employees at Amdahl (GLEAM)
Lisa Malachowsky, 1250 E. Arques Ave. Mail Stop S 342, Sunnyvale, CA 94086, (408) 944-3681
GEGi

American Telegraph & Telephone (AT&T)
Lesbian and Gay United Employees at AT&T (LEAGUE)
jklenert@ATTMAIL.COM
John Klenert, 8403 Colesville Rd., Silver Springs, MD 20910, (301) 608-4594
GEGo

Ameritech
Gay, Lesbian and Bisexual Employees of Ameritech (GLEAM)
KaseyR@aol.com
Kasey Reese, PO Box 14308, Chicago, IL 60614, (708) 248-6403
GEGo

Apple Computer
Apple Lambda
Jenifa Johnson and Brad Zaller, 20525 Mariani Ave., Cupertino, CA 95014, Johnson (408) 974-3585; Zaller (408) 974-5416
GEGo

Arthur Anderson & Co.
Anderson Gay and Lesbian Employees (ANGLES)
DianeM.Scholten@AC.com
Diane Scholten, PO Box 359, Chicago, IL 60659-0359, (312) 507-4127
GEGi

Autodesk
Gays/Lesbians/Independents/Bisexuals at Autodesk (GLIB)
glib@autodesk.com
Pat Keany, 111 McInnis Parkway, San Rafael, CA 94903, (415) 507-8506
GEGi

BARRA Inc.
Lesbian & Gay Employees of BARRA
joshm@barra.com
Joshua Margolis, 1995 University Ave., Berkeley, CA 94704, (510) 649-4594
GEGi

Bank of America
The Luncheon Group
Daniel Ray-Carothers, 1655 Grant St. bldg. A floor 7, Concord, CA 94520, (510) 675-1621
GEGi

Bank of Boston
Gay and Lesbian Resource Group
Chris Palmer, 100 Federal St.,
Boston, MA 02110, (617) 434-1857
GEGo

Baxter Healthcare
Baxter Association of Gay & Lesbian Employees (BAGLE)
John Hnilicka, Mail Stop #MPA-1A, 1430 Waukegan Rd., McGaw Park, IL 60085, (708) 578-6682
GEGo

Bell Canada Enterprises
(Bell Canada, Stentor Resource Centre Inc., Northern Telecom, Bell Sygma)
Gay and Lesbian Organization of Bell Enterprises (GLOBE)
BrownCA@Stentor
Carrie Brown (416) 353-2504,
Sandra Peden (416) 353-8907, P.O. Box 100, 552 Church Street,
Toronto, Ontario, Canada M4Y 2E3
GEGo

Blue Cross/Blue Shield of MA
Blue Pride
bluepride@aol.com
Nikki Woelk, MS 01-05, 100 Summer St., Boston, MA 02110

Bell Northern
Gay, Lesbian & Bisexual Association
Jonathan File, PO Box 3511, Station C, Ottawa, Ontario, Canada K1Y 4H7, (613) 765-2861

Boeing Aircraft
Boeing Employees Association of Gays & Lesbians (BEAGLES)
Resource Coordinator Ed Gentzler, PO Box 1733, Renton, WA 98057, (206) 781-3587
GEGi

Boston Children's Hospital
UNITDRUMMD@AI.TCH.HARVARD.EDU
Debra Drumm, 300 Longwood Ave., Boston, MA 02115, (617) 735-6000 x4759

Capital Cities/ABC
Gay & Lesbian Organization of Employees (GLOE)
Sherry Boscher, Shaalu@aol.com
GEGi

Chevron
Chevron Gay & Lesbian Employees Association
Kirk Nass, tkana@chevron.com
100 Chevron Way Rm 10-1308,
Richmond, CA 94802, (510) 242-3932
GEGi

Commonwealth Edison Co.
Commonwealth Edison Employees Gay & Lesbian Organization (CEEGLO)
CEEGLO@aol.com
Tim Hickernell, 3266 N. Clark #2H,
Chicago, IL 60657, (312) 394-8391
GEGo

Coors (Adolph Coors)
Lesbian & Gay Employee Resource (LAGER)
Leslie Wright, PO Box 643, Golden, CO 80403, (303) 277-2554
GEGo

CoreStates Financial Corp.
MOSAIC
Pat Quigley, 1500 Market St. F.C. 1-13-12-6, Philadelphia, PA 19102, (215) 973-7762
GEGo

Dayton's
c/o Nancy Landis, Central H.R. Director, PO Box 859, Minneapolis, MN 55402, (612) 375-3087

Digital Equipment Corp. (DEC)
Corporate Policy Action Committee (DECPAC)
Martha Comfort, 129 Parker St., Marlboro, MA 01754, (508) 493-3135
GEGo

DuPont (E.I. DuPont de Nemours)
Bis, Gays, Lesbians and Allies at DuPont (BGLAD)
Robert Hill, PO Box 2192, Wilmington, DE 19898-2192, (302) 571-2192
GEGi

Eastman Kodak
Lambda Network
Steering Committee/David Kosel, PO Box 14067, Rochester, NY 14614-0067, (716) 234-4388
GEGo

Fannie Mae
Fannie Mae Lesbians and Gays (FLAG)
Herb Moses, 3900 Wisconsin Ave. NW, Mail Stop #3H-3N, Washington, DC 20016, (202) 752-6011
GEGo

Farallon Computing Company
Out There at Farallon
lezliel@farallon.com
Lezlie Lee, 2470 Mariner Square Loop, Alameda, CA 94501, (510) 814-5288
GEGi

First Chicago
Barbara Daly, (312) 407-4928; Ivan Noah Uldall, (312) 407-3551; One First National Plaza #0069, Chicago, IL 60670-0069
GEGi

Genentech
Genentech Gays, Lesbians, Bis & Friends (GGLBF)
Lisa Kenney, 460 Point San Bruno Blvd., So. San Francisco, CA 94080, (415) 225-6260
GEGo

General Mills
Betty's Family
Daniel Duty, 4900 Park Avenue So. Minneapolis, MN 55417, (612) 540-3227
GEGi

Hewlett-Packard
Gay, Lesbian & Bi Employee Network (GLEN)
Kim Harris, (415) 857-7771; Greg Gloss, (408) 447-6123; PO Box 70054, San Jose, CA 95170
GEGo

Honeywell
Honeywell Pride Council
Dan Lyden, 2701 Fourth Ave. So. MS 26-4138, Minneapolis, MN 55408, (612) 951-3163
GEGo

IBM
HIKEYOS@VNET.IBM.COM
Ed McCanless, 5600 Cottle Rd. MS 802/032 GTWY, San Jose, CA 95193
GEGi

Intel
Gay, Lesbian or Bi Employees (GLOBE)
LParrish@Gomez.sc.intel.com
Andy Rice, (408) 765-6134; Liz Parish (408), 765-4199; PO Box 58119, Santa Clara, CA 95052-8119
GEGo

Jet Propulsion Lab
Gay, Lesbian, Bi Support Group
rgh@rodan.jpl.nasa.gov
Randy Herrera, 4800 Oak Grove Dr., Mail Stop 246-325, Pasadena, CA 91109-8099, (818) 393-0664
GEGo

Kaiser Permanente
LEAGUE
chris.rich@ncal.kaiperm.org
Sarah Fairchild, Randy DeBoer, PO Box 31651, Oakland, CA 94604, (510) 987-4148
GEGi

Levi Strauss & Co.
Lesbian & Gay Employee Association
Michele Dryden, 1155 Battery St., PO Box 7215, San Francisco, CA 94120-6906, (415) 544-7103

Lockheed Missiles and Space
Gay, Lesbian or Bi at Lockheed (GLOBAL)
Patrick Miller, (408) 369-1713; Frederick Parsons, FParsons@aol.com
Dept. 27-62, bldg. 599, P.O. Box 3504, Sunnyvale, CA 94088-3504, (408) 369-1713
GEGo

Los Angeles Times
Joe Hanania, 500 California Ave. #14, Burbank, CA 91502

Lotus Development Corp.
Lotus LAMBDA
Polly Laurelchild-Hertig, Kay Wilkins, Helene Newberg, 55 Cambridge Parkway, Cambridge, MA 02142, Polly: (617) 693-1737
GEGi

MCA/Universal
Employee Association of Gay & Lesbian Employees (EAGLE)
DIONDION@aol.com
Dion McFall, 100 Universal Plaza Bldg. SC79/4, Universal City, CA 91608, (818) 622-9506
GEGi

Mass Mutual Life
GALA
BILLC18925@aol.com
William Conley, 1295 State St., Springfield, MA 01111, (413) 744-4927
GEGi

Medtronic
c/o Carolyn Pitre, Workforce Diversity Project, 700 Central Ave. NE #240, Fridley, MN 55432, (612) 574-3600

Mentor Graphics
Gay & Lesbian Employees
glbfmrequest@warren.mentor.org
Chris McCabe, 8005 SW Boeckman Rd. Building D, Wilsonville, OR 97070-7777, (503) 685-7000
GEGi

Microsoft
Gay, Lesbian & Bi Employees at Microsoft (GLEAM)
jeffh@microsoft.com
Jeff Howard, One Microsoft Way, Redmond, WA 98052-6399, (206) 936-5581
GEGo

Minneapolis Star Tribune
PAPER EAGLES
lackasa@startribune.com
Jill Schons, 425 Portland Ave., Minneapolis, MN 55488, (612) 673-1757
GEGo

Minnesota Mining & Manufacturing (3M)
People Like Us (3M PLUS)
Janice Ross, Mail Stop #224-6N-03, St. Paul, MN 55144-1000, (612) 736-9706
GEGo

Motorola (LMPS division)
LMPS Bi, Gay, Lesbian Employee Network
Jill Olkoski-ECPD@email.mot.com
Jill Olkoski, 8000 Sunrise Blvd. rm. 1381, Plantation, FL 33304, (413) 744-4927
GEGo

NBC News
Gay & Lesbian Employees
Mike Schreiberman, 30 Rockefeller Plaza, Rm. 901-E, New York, NY 10112, (212) 664-4300
GEGo

NYNEX
Gays & Lesbians for Cultural Diversity
GLCD9X@aol.com
Mike Snow, PO Box 116, Boston, MA 02101, (508) 762-2350
GEGo

Nestle Beverage Co.
Gay & Lesbian Association of Nestle
Jim Ahlers, 345 Spear St., PO Box 7449, San Francisco, CA 94105, (415) 546-4840
GEGi

New York Times
Gay & Lesbian Caucus
David Dunlap, 229 W. 43rd St., New York, NY 10036, (212) 556-7082
GEGo

NeXT Computers
Next Lambda
RON@NEXT.COM
Ron Hayden, 900 Chesapeake Dr., Redwood City, CA 94063, (415) 780-4603
GEGo

Northern States Power
Supportive Association of Gay, Lesbian & Bisexual Employees (SAGE)
Tom Schuster, PO Box 13008, Roseville, MN, 55113, (612) 330-5522

Norwest Corp.
Gregory Pleimling, 3601 Minnesota Dr. #200, Bloomington, MN 55435, (612) 844-2310
GEGo

Oracle Corporation
Oracle Lambda
Kmallory@us.oracle.com
Kevin Mallory, 500 Oracle Parkway, Box 659412, Redwood Shores, CA 94065, (415) 506-6168
GEGo

Pacific Gas & Electric (PG&E)
Lesbian & Gay Employees Assoc.
cacb%geospl%ggrsfo@bangate.pge.com
Cindi Collins, PO Box 19131, San Francisco, CA 94119-1311, (415) 695-3557
GEGo

Pacific Telesis Group
GALEEMAS
GMHEIL@PACBELL.COM
Gary Heil, PO Box 2711, San Ramon, CA 94583-2711, (510) 567-5407
GEGo

Polaroid
Gay, Lesbian, Bi Employee Association
Richard Williams, Ph.D., 565 Technology Sq. #7, Cambridge, MA 02139, (617) 386-3879
GEGo

Prudential Insurance Co.
EAGLES
USPRUTM2@IBMMAIL.COM
Alan Serio, 213 Washington St., Newark, NJ 07102-2992, (201) 802-2695
GEGo

Quaker Oats Company
A Safe Place
Bob Singer, PO Box 9001 LOC 12-1, Chicago, IL 80804, (312) 222-8750
GEGo

Seattle Times
Gay and Lesbian Association (GALA Times)
Tom Gangewer, PO Box 70, Seattle, WA 98111, (206) 464-2721

Sequent Computer Systems
scooter@sequent.com
Scott Guthridge, M/S DES 2-745, 15450 S.W. Koll Parkway, Beaverton, OR 97006, (503) 578-5236

Silicon Graphics
Lavender Vision
dauber@sgi.com
Jeff Dauber, 2011 N. Shoreline Blvd., Mountain View, CA 94039-7311, (415) 390-4511

St. Paul Companies
Gay/Lesbian & Friends Network
USSPCZDB@IBMMAIL.COM
Monica Bryand, 122 West Winifred, St. Paul, MN 55107, (612) 223-2164
GEGo

Sun Microsystems
Gays, Lesbians & Friends at SUN (GLAF)
GLAF@sun.com
Mark Stein, 2550 Garcia Ave., Atten. SDI, Mountain View, CA 94043, (415) 336-2435
GEGo

Time Warner
Lesbians & Gay Men at Time Warner
Bill Hooper: (212) 522-1063, Richard Mayora: (212) 512-5909, 1100 Sixth Avenue, Rm 515, New York, NY 10036
GEGo

U.S. Federal Employees
Gay, Lesbian or Bisexual Employees (GLOBE)
sachstom@aol.com
PO Box 45237, Washington, DC 20026-5237, (202) 986-1101
Includes: Dept. of Agriculture [GLOBE], Dept. of Commerce [GLOBE], Federal Aviation Association [GLOBE], Foreign Affairs Agencies [GLIFFA], Navy [GLOBE], Dept. of Education [GLOBE], Dept. of Energy [GLOBE], Dept. of Health and Human Services/Food and Drug Administration [GLOBE], Dept. of the Interior [GLOBE], Dept. of Justice [PRIDE], Dept. of Labor [GLOBAL], Library of Congress [GLOBE], Dept. of the Treasury [GLOBE], Veterans Administration [GLOBE], Environmental Protection

Agency [GLOBE], General Services Administration [GLOBE], National Science Foundation [GLOBE], Office of Personnel Management [GLOBE], Small Business Administration [GLOBE], Smithsonian Institution [Lesbian and Gay Issues Committee], National Institutes of Health [GLOBE], Bonneville Power Administration [Gay Resource Group]

U.S. Postal Service
Gay & Lesbian Postal Employees Network (G/L PEN)
KayJay2306@aol.com
PO Box 580397, Minneapolis, MN 55458-0397, (612) 866-9609
GEG

US West
Employee Association for Gays & Lesbians (EAGLE)
Dawn Tubbs, 1600 7 Ave. #203, Seattle, WA 98191, (206) 346-7483
GEGo

United Airlines
Gay & Lesbian United Employees (GLUE)
76250.1330@compuserv.com
Tom Cross, 108 Delores St., San Francisco, CA 94103, (415) 863-3488
GEGi

Village Voice
Lesbian & Gay Caucus
Richard Goldstein, 36 Cooper Sq., New York, NY 10003, (212) 475-3300

Walt Disney
Lesbian and Gay United Employees (LEAGUE)
Garrett Hicks, (818) 544-3363; Tina Shafer, (818) 544-3528; 500 S. Buena Vista St., Burbank, CA 91521-5209
GEGo

Wells Fargo & Co.
Gay & Lesbian Employee Group
Barbara.Zoloth@WellsFargo.com
Barbara Zoloth, (415) 396-2767; Randy Diaz, (415) 396-3020; 111 Sutter St., 13 fl., San Francisco, CA 94104
GEGi

Xerox
Gays and Lesbians at Xerox (GALAXE)
GALAXE@aol.com
David Frishkorn, (716) 422-1250; Jane Moyer, (716) 383-7809; PO Box 25382, Rochester, NY 14625
GEGo

Zenith Electronics
LEAGUE
Al Lewis, (203) 968-3572
GEGo

Gay Professional Organizations

Source: independently verified by the authors as of April 1995.

All organizations are coed unless "woman," "lesbian," or "man" is in their name. Information on these groups, especially meeting times and locations, changes occasionally; it's best to call or write before showing up somewhere. Good sources for the most up-to-date addresses and phone numbers of member groups are Golden Gate Business Association (for Western-region groups), (415) 441-3651, and Gay and Lesbian Organizations Bridging Across the Lands (GLOBAL) at MikeMS2@aol.com or PO Box 40567, Cincinnati, OH 45240-0567.

National Scope

Association Executives Human Rights Caucus
(Association Management Industry)
AEHRC@aol.com
PO Box 60001, Chicago, IL 60660-0001, (312) 743-6554

Digital Queers
Diqueers@aol.com
584 Castro St. #150,
San Francisco, CA 94114,
(415) 252-6282

San Francisco and other chapters; various parties, including at the annual MacWorld conference.

National Lesbian & Gay Journalists Association (NLGJA)
PO Box 423048, San Francisco, CA 94142-3048, (415) 905-4690
Annual conference.

National Organization of Gay & Lesbian Scientists & Technical Professionals (NOGLSTP)
diamond@cco.caltech.edu
PO Box 91803, Pasadena, CA 91109-9813, (818) 791-7689
Caucuses for actuaries, statisticians, scientists, and others.

By State

ALABAMA

Alabama Gay & Lesbian Organization of Professionals
PO Box 914, Huntsville AL, 35804-0914, (205) 517-6127
Fourth Tuesday, 7 P.M., at Rainbow Bookstore, 4123 University #400B.

ARIZONA

Camelback Business & Professional Association
PO Box 2097, Phoenix, AZ 85001-2097, (602) 225-8444
Second Wednesday mixers; dinner once a month.

Old Pueblo Business & Professional Association
PO Box 2097, Tucson, AZ 85011-2097, (602) 225-8444
Second Wednesday and third Thursday.

Valley Career Women
PO Box 33393, Phoenix, AZ 85067, (602) 491-3980

NORTHERN CALIFORNIA

Bay Area Career Women
55 Montgomery St. #606, San Francisco, CA 94105, (415) 495-5393
Varies by chapter: East Bay, Marin, Mid-Peninsula, Santa Cruz, South Bay, Sonoma, Central Valley, San Francisco.

East Bay Business & Professional Alliance
PO Box 20980, Oakland, CA 94620-0980, (510) 287-2571
Monthly in three locations: South Alameda, Contra Costa, Berkeley-Oakland.

Golden Gate Business Association
1550 California St. #5L, San Francisco, CA 94109-4708, (415) 441-3651

High Tech Gays
info@htg.org
PO Box 6777, San Jose, CA 95150, (408) 289-1484
Second Sunday women's caucus, 6 P.M.; potluck, 6:30 P.M.; general, 7:30 P.M., at San Jose Lesbian and Gay Community Center, 175 Stockton Ave.

Men's Associated Exchange (MAX)
2261 Market St. #433, San Francisco, CA 94114, (415) 442-1994
First and third Fridays 6 P.M.–9 P.M., 155 Sansome St., Fl. 10.

Sacramento Gay & Lesbian Business Alliance
1500 West El Camino #324, Sacramento, CA 95833, (916) 863-9733
Third Wednesday 7–9 P.M., Carrow Restaurant, 28th St. & J St.

Silicon Valley Business Association
265 Meridian Ave. Suite 6-509, San Jose, CA 95126, (408) 999-8804

CENTRAL CALIFORNIA

Central Coast Business & Professional Association
PO Box 14433, San Luis Obispo, CA 93406, (805) 546-9394
Second Wednesdays.

Gold Coast Business & Professional Alliance
PO Box 7336, Ventura, CA 93066, (805) 388-1545

Greater Santa Barbara Community Association
PO Box 90907, Santa Barbara, CA 93190, (805) 568-3995
Fourth Tuesday, 7:30 P.M., Westside Community Center, 423 West Victoria St.

SOUTHERN CALIFORNIA

Desert Business Association
PO Box 773, Palm Springs, CA 92263, (619) 324-0178
First Tuesday, 6–8 P.M., Prudential California Realty Offices, 980 East Tahquitz Canyon Way.

Gay PR Network
Los Angeles, CA, (310) 659-2340
Bimonthly meeting, 6:30–8:30 P.M.

Greater San Diego Business Association
PO Box 33848, San Diego, CA 92163-3848, (619) 296-4543
Monthly mixer, monthly dinner, monthly lesbian breakfast.

L.A. Business & Professional Association
PO Box 69982, West Hollywood, CA 90069, (213) 896-1444
Monthly meetings.

L.A. Professional Women's Network
8033 Sunset Blvd. #146, West Hollywood, CA 90046, (310) 285-8504

L.A. Women's Professional & Business Alliance
c/o L.A. GLCC Services Center, 1625 Shrader Blvd., Los Angeles, CA 90028, (213) 993-7430
Meetings held every third Monday at Hyatt Hotel, 8401 Sunset Blvd., West Hollywood; networking at 6:30 P.M., program at 7:30 P.M.

Lesbians in Film & Television (LIFT) LA
Los Angeles, CA (contact New York City group for more information.)

San Diego Career Women
PO Box 880384, San Diego, CA 92168, (619) 688-8002
First Friday, 5:30–7:30 P.M., Quality Resort, 875 Hotel Circle So.

So Cal Community Business Networkers
PO Box 486, Anaheim, CA 92815-0486; for L.A. and Long Beach, (800) 404-4226; for Orange County, Pomona, Inland Empire, (800) 404-4226
Monthly meetings.

Southern California Women for Understanding
7985 Santa Monica Blvd. #207, Los Angeles, CA 90046
Many chapters all over California.

Valley Business Alliance
PO Box 57555, Sherman Oaks, CA 91413, (818) 982-2650
Second Monday, 6:30 P.M., Beverly Garland's Holiday Inn, 4222 Vineland Ave., Studio City.

COLORADO

Colorado Business Council
PO Box 480794, Denver, CO 80248-0794, (303) 595-8042
Monthly luncheon, monthly mixer. Also leads club first and third Tuesday, 8 A.M., Racine's, 850 Bannock St.

Rocky Mountain Career Women Association
PO Box 18156, Denver, CO 80218

CONNECTICUT

Connecticut Business Guild
PO Box 1597, New Britain, CT 06050, (203) 278-6666 x104
Last Monday. Metroline offices, 1841 Broad St., and various.

The Hartford Gay Men's Professional Network
Hartford, CT, (203) 645-3011
Second Monday unless a major holiday; 6:30, social; 7:30, dinner; 8:30, program.

DISTRICT OF COLUMBIA

Mercury (Marketing & PR)
1760 U St. NW, Washington, DC 20009-1712, (202) 265-4264
March, June, September, November

Potomac Executive Network
PO Box 27085, Washington, DC 20038-7085, (202) 638-3311
Second Thursday, 6–8 P.M.

FLORIDA

Broward Women in Network
PO Box 9744, Fort Lauderdale, FL 33310, (305) 537-0866
First Wednesday, Unitarian Church, 3970 NW 21 Ave.

Key West Business Guild
PO Box 1208, Key West, FL 33041, (800) 535-7797
First Monday lunch; second Wednesday evening mixer.

Miami Women in Network
7463 SW 64 St., Miami, FL 33143

Orlando Area Metropolitan Business Association
PO Box 150364, Altamonte Springs, FL 32715-0364, (407) 420-2182
First Thursday, 6:30–7:30, social; 7:30–9:00, program. Radisson Hotel at Lake Ivanhoe in Orlando.

Tampa Bay Business Guild
1222 South Dale Mabry #656, Tampa, FL 33629, (813) 237-3751

GEORGIA

Atlanta Executive Network
PO Box 77267, Atlanta, GA 30357-1267, (404) 814-1418
Meetings on third Thursday, 6–8 P.M.

Atlanta Voices Out Front: Gay & Lesbian Media Association
2103 N. Decatur Rd. #185, Atlanta, GA 30033, (404) 734-2473
Monthly.

Fourth Tuesday Lesbians
PO Box 7817, Atlanta, GA 30357-0817, (404) 662-4353
Fourth Tuesday.

Greater Atlanta Business Coalition
2103 North Decatur Rd. #190, Atlanta, GA 30033, (404) 377-4258
Second Wednesday, Sheridan Colony Square Hotel.

ILLINOIS

Chicago Professional Networking Association
990 W. Fullerton Ave., PO Box 146368, Chicago, IL 60614, (312) 296-2762
Third Wednesday, Ann Sather's Restaurant, 929 W. Belmont.

INDIANA

Indiana Business Outreach Association
PO Box 501915, Indianapolis, IN 46250-1915, (317) 726-9746
Third Tuesday, 6 P.M., social; 7 P.M., dinner and speaker. Tarkington Tower, 4000 N. Meridian.

KANSAS

Kansas Alternate Professionals Together
4318 Rainbow Blvd. #348, Overland Park, KS 66103, (816) 464-1714
First Thursday, 5:30–7:30 P.M.

Wichita Business and Professional League
PO Box 698, Wichita, KS 67201

KENTUCKY

Kentuckia Business & Professional Alliance
PO Box 7413, Louisville, KY 40257-0413, (502) 329-1271

LOUISIANA

Third Thursday
816 Aline St., New Orleans, LA 70115, (504) 891-4758
Meetings on third Thursday.

MASSACHUSETTS

Boston Professional Alliance
398 Columbus Ave. #262, Boston, MA 02116, (617) 499-8669
Includes Rt. 128 lunch club.

Greater Boston Business Council
PO Box 1059, Boston, MA 02117-1059, (617) 236-4222

Northampton Area Lesbian & Gay Business Guild
PO Box 593, Northampton, MA 01061-0593, (413) 585-0683

Provincetown Business Guild
PO Box 421, Provincetown, MA 02657, (508) 487-2313

MARYLAND

Baltimore Professionals Like Us
PO Box 6767, Baltimore, MD 21285-6767, (410) 418-8526
Third Monday, 5:30–7:30 P.M.

MISSOURI

St. Louis Business Guild
PO Box 23037, St. Louis, MO 63156-3037, (314) 993-7533
First Sunday, 4:30 P.M., Top of the Sevens Restaurant, 7777 Bonhomme.

NORTH CAROLINA

Charlotte Business Guild
PO Box 35445, Charlotte, NC 28235, (704) 565-5075

Triad Business & Professional Guild
PO Box 2038, Greensboro, NC 27402, (910) 274-2100

Triangle Business & Professional Guild
1630 White Forest Rd., Raleigh, NC 27604, (919) 836-8609

NEW JERSEY

Lesbians & Gays in Telecommunications
PO Box 8143, Red Bank, NJ 07701
Twice monthly in central N.J.

New Jersey Gay & Lesbian Professionals
PO Box 137, Convent Station, NJ 07961

NEW MEXICO

Duke City Business & Professional Association
PO Box 27207, Albuquerque, NM 87125, (505) 897-1443
Third Wednesday 11:30 A.M.–1 P.M., Grandma's Restaurant. First Wednesday 5:30–8 P.M., dinner at ABQ Petroleum Club at the top of 500 Marquette.

NEVADA

Lambda Business Association of Las Vegas
1350 East Flamingo Rd. #370, Las Vegas, NV 89119, (702) 593-2875

Las Vegas Professional Men's Club
PO Box 60631, Las Vegas, NV 89160-0631, (702) 593-1173

NEW YORK

Business Owners Strategy Sessions
350 Third Ave. #3C, New York, NY 10010-2310, (212) 228-8683
Third Thursday, 6–8 P.M., 208 W. 13 St.

Lesbians in Film & Television (LIFT) NY
230 Riverside Dr. #15F, New York, NY 10025, (212) 865-5449

N.Y. Advertising & Communications Network
332 Bleecker St. #149, New York, NY 10014-2980, (212) 517-0380
Third Wednesday, 6:30–9:30 and many other events at NYLGCC, 208 W. 13 St. floor 3.

N.Y. Bankers Group (for all financial professionals)
PO Box 867, Bowling Green Station, New York, NY 10274-0867, (212) 807-9584 x24
E-mail: NYBG INC@aol.com

N.Y. Network of Business & Professional Organizations
332 Bleecker St. Box G32, New York, NY 10014-2980, (212) 517-0771
Annual winter and spring parties; miscellaneous meetings.

NYC Stonewall Business Association
PO Box 613, FDR Station, New York, NY 10150-0613, (212) 629-1764
Second Monday, 6:30, networking; 7:30, meeting; at NYLGCC, 308 W. 13 St.

Professionals in Film/Video
336 Canal St. 8th floor, New York, NY 10013, (212) 387-2022

Publishing Triangle
PO Box 114, Prince St. Station, New York, NY 10012, (212) 572-6142

Second Thursday Networking Women
245 Eighth Ave., New York, NY 10011, (212) 517-0180

Second Thursday, 6, networking; 7, program; 8, networking; Holiday Inn Crowne Plaza, 49 St. and Broadway.

Westchester Gay & Lesbian Business & Professionals Guild
PO Box 8392, White Plains, NY 10602-8392, (914) 663-3472

Third Thursday, 6:30 P.M. ARCS building #1, 2269 Saw Mill River Rd., in Elmsford.

OHIO

Cleveland Lesbian Business Network
PO Box 5614, Cleveland, OH 44101, (216) 962-3662

Columbus Lesbian Business Association
PO Box 02086, Columbus, OH 43202, (614) 267-3953

First Monday, 7:30–9:30 (except legal holidays), Whetstone Library, 3909 No. High St.

Queen City Careers Association
PO Box 3663, Cincinnati, OH 45201-3663, (513) 230-6006

Second Monday, Omni Netherland Hotel 4th floor.

OREGON

Portland Area Business Association
PO Box 6344, Portland, OR 97208-4724, (503) 241-2222

Second Monday lunch, 11:30 A.M. to 1:30 P.M., Marriott Hotel, 1401 SW Front Ave.

PENNSYLVANIA

Greater Philadelphia Professional Association
PO Box 42366, Philadelphia, PA 19101-2366, (215) 336-9676

Greater Pittsburgh Professional Men's Society
312 Lamplighter Circle, Pittsburgh, PA 15212

Greater Roundtable of Women Professionals
PO Box 35010, Philadelphia, PA 19128, (610) 789-4938

SOUTH CAROLINA

South Carolina Gay & Lesbian Business Guild
PO Box 7913, Columbia, SC 29202-7913, (803) 771-7713

TEXAS

Austin Stonewall Business Society
PO Box 49976, Austin, TX 78765, (512) 707-3794

Second Monday, 6:00, networking; 6:30, program.

Dallas Stonewall Business Society
PO Box 191343, Dallas, TX 75219, (214) 526-6216
Third Friday lunch; 11:25, network; 12, program. First Friday mixer, 6–8 P.M., Southland Center Hotel, 400 N. Olive, 2nd floor.

Houston Lesbians in Business (LIB)
PO Box 66748, Houston, TX 77266-6748, (713) 529-0077
Third Friday, Innova Building, Greenway Plaza.

Houston Professionals
PO Box 3840, Humble, TX 77347-3840, (713) 821-7126

UTAH

Utah Gay & Lesbian Professional Alliance
476 E. South Temple #223, Salt Lake City, UT 84111, (801) 484-4547
Second Tuesday

VIRGINIA

Lesbians & Gays United for Enterprise
Hot Rapids, VA (804) 490-0707

WASHINGTON

Greater Seattle Business Association
2033 Sixth Ave. #804, Seattle, WA 98121-2526, (206) 443-4722
Monthly luncheon and social/networking evening, Kayak Grill, 1200 Westlake Ave. No.

Canada

Calgarian Networking Club
PO Box 561 Stn M, Calgary, Alberta T2P 2J2, (403) 293-6541
First Tuesday except July and August, The Boxxe Cafe, 1509 Centre St. SW.

Gazebo Connection
382-810 West Broadway, Vancouver, British Columbia V5Z 4C9, (604) 438-5442

Greater Vancouver Business Association
204-1810 Alberni St., Vancouver, British Columbia V6G 1B3, (604) 689-5107
First Fridays, 11:30 social; 12 lunch, Raintree Restaurant, 1630 Alberni St.

Lambda Business & Professional Club of Winnipeg
118 Winston Road, Winnipeg, Manitoba R3J 1M9, (204) 832-5622
Bimonthly.

Lambda Ottawa
PO Box 1445 Stn B, Ottawa, Ontario K1P 5P6, (613) 233-8212
Third Tuesday 6:30 P.M. social/7.30 P.M. dinner.

The Fraternity for Gay Men
552 Church St. Box 500-29, Toronto, Ontario M4Y 2E3, (416) 925-9872 x2930.

Toronto Women for Recreation and Business
552 Church St Box 34, Toronto, Ontario M4Y 2E3, (416) 925-9872 x2083

Second Tuesday, Primrose Hotel.

England

Gay Business Association (GBA)
225 Valley Rd., Streatham, London SW16 2 AF, (0181) 677-0020

Gay and Lesbian Group of the Banking, Insurance and Finance Union
Christine or Hugh (0222) 224-483

Gay London Professionals (GLP)
Mondays and Fridays 6–11 P.M., Club Circa at 59 Berkeley Sq., W1

Women Mean Business
London (0171) 837-7324

For updates and corrections to the resource section, please contact the authors.

Via E-mail:
SJGL@aol.com

For U.S. mail correspondence:
Straight Jobs, Gay Lives
3525 Del Mar Heights Rd. Box 384
San Diego, CA 92130

The Straight Jobs, Gay Lives web page can be found at: http://www.nyu.edu/pages/sls/sjgl/